UNDERSTANDING PRODUCTS LIABILITY LAW

UNDERSTANDING PRODUCTS LIABILITY LAW

Second Edition

Bruce L. Ottley
Professor of Law
DePaul University College of Law

Rogelio A. Lasso
Professor of Law
The John Marshall Law School

Terrence F. Kiely
Late Professor of Law
DePaul University College of Law

ISBN: 978–0–7698–6375–7 (print)
ISBN: 978–0–3271–8526–0 (eBook)

Library of Congress Cataloging-in-Publication Data

Kiely, Terrence F.
   Understanding products liability law / Bruce L. Ottley, Professor of Law, DePaul University College of Law; Rogelio A. Lasso , Professor of Law, The John Marshall Law School; Terrence F. Kiely, Late Professor of Law, DePaul University College of Law. -- Second edition.
     pages cm
   Includes index.
   ISBN 978-0-7698-6375-7
1. Products liability--United States. I. Ottley, Bruce L. II. Lasso, Rogelio A. III. Title.
   KF1296.K54 2013
   346.7303'8--dc23
2013005961

This publication is designed to provide authoritative information in regard to the subject matter covered. It is sold with the understanding that the publisher is not engaged in rendering legal, accounting, or other professional services. If legal advice or other expert assistance is required, the services of a competent professional should be sought.

LexisNexis and the Knowledge Burst logo are registered trademarks of Reed Elsevier Properties Inc., used under license. Matthew Bender and the Matthew Bender Flame Design are registered trademarks of Matthew Bender Properties Inc.

NOTE TO USERS

To ensure that you are using the latest materials available in this area, please be sure to periodically check the LexisNexis Law School web site for downloadable updates and supplements at www.lexisnexis.com/lawschool.

Editorial Offices
121 Chanlon Rd., New Providence, NJ 07974 (908) 464-6800
201 Mission St., San Francisco, CA 94105-1831 (415) 908-3200
www.lexisnexis.com

MATTHEW◊BENDER

Dedication

To
Younghee Jin Ottley and Marianne Deagle

Introduction

The seven years that have passed since the completion of the First Edition of this book in October 2005 have not seen any let-up in products liability litigation or in the development of products liability law. Suits continue to be filed in federal and state courts alleging the traditional grounds of warranty, misrepresentation, and negligence. While the basic structure of strict liability law has been shaped by § 402A of the Restatement (Second) of Torts, it is impossible to overstate the growing influence of the approach to products liability taken in the 21 sections of the Restatement (Third) of Torts: Products Liability. While some courts have rejected individual sections of the Restatement (Third), more and more courts are citing and adopting specific sections of it.

The continuing debate over "tort reform" also has not diminished the number of products liability suits filed during the past seven years. These suits, many of which are brought as class actions, involve a full range of products: automobiles, chemicals, consumer electronics, food, medical devices, pharmaceuticals, and toys. As government agencies such as the Consumer Products Safety Commission (CPSC), Food and Drug Administration (FDA), and National Highway Traffic Safety Commission (NHTSC) have adopted regulations over many of these products, courts have been called upon to decide, with increasing frequency, whether statutes and agency regulations preempt individuals from bringing products liability lawsuits against the manufacturers of the products.

In order to provide an *understanding* of the products liability law that is the basis of litigation and the focus of debate, this book preserves the structure of the First Edition. First, Part I (Chapters 1–10) provides an overview of the complex body of products liability case law and statutory law. The chapters follow a functional approach and begin with the four theories that are the foundation of products liability law: warranty, misrepresentation, negligence, and strict liability. Separate chapters in Part I then examine the principle types of product defects (design, manufacturing, and failure to warn) and some of the problems involved with proving that the product was defective and that the defect was the cause of the injury. The last two chapters in Part I focus on the defenses available in a products liability action and the types of damages that a plaintiff may seek. These chapters contain references to recent statutes and cases as well as major revisions of the sections on federal preemption and punitive damages.

An *understanding* of products liability law also requires an examination of the issues involved in the prosecution or defense of a products liability case. Part II (Chapters 11–19) addresses a range of those issues, including: researching the case; drafting the complaint; interrogatories and requests to admit facts; requests for the production of documents; discovery and evidence depositions; protective orders; and discovery enforcement. These chapters also have been updated to reflect recent developments. It is hoped that this combination of the theory and the practice of products liability law will make the book useful not only to law students and law professors but also to those who are or may become involved in products liability cases, whether as judges, corporate counsel, plaintiffs' or defendants' counsel, or expert witnesses.

Unfortunately, the legal profession suffered a major loss since the publication of the First Edition. Professor Terrence F. Kiely, who coauthored the First Edition, died in July 2012. Fortunately, Professor Rogelio Lasso of The John Marshall Law School in Chicago

Introduction

has stepped in and revised the chapters originally written by Professor Kiely; however, the authors greatly miss Professor Kiely, and the Second Edition will not be the same without his hard work, insights, and wisdom from his many years teaching and litigating products liability cases.

As with any project of this size, this book is the product of the efforts of more than the coauthors. In particular, the authors want to acknowledge the excellent research of a number of DePaul University College of Law students in the preparation of the Second Edition: Jade Alston, Else Buss, Andrew Cunniff, Daniel Ember, Jennifer Fese, Thomas Flowers, Zeke Hacker, Robert Hunger, Stephen Jarvis, Mary Kane, Julie Kim, Jordan Klein, Nicholas Liadis, Greg Markwell, Kevin Mesteis, Joanne Moon, Kevin Pacini, Andrew Resor, Nicholas Rubino, Rachel Simcox, Z. Stein, Dan Sylvester, Jordan Treshansky, and Desalina Williams.

Table of Contents

Chapter 1   **THE DEVELOPMENT OF PRODUCTS LIABILITY LAW** 1

§ 1.01 INTRODUCTION 1
§ 1.02 THE INFLUENCE OF CONTRACT LAW 2
  [A]   *Caveat Emptor* 2
  [B]   The Privity Rule 4
  [C]   Exceptions to the Privity Rule 6
§ 1.03 THE RISE OF NEGLIGENCE 9
  [A]   The Fall of Privity 10
  [B]   The Adoption of Negligence 11
  [C]   *Res Ipsa Loquitur* 12
§ 1.04 FROM NEGLIGENCE TO STRICT LIABILITY 13
  [A]   The Theory Behind Strict Liability 14
  [B]   "The Fall of the Citadel of Privity" 15
  [C]   The Triumph of Strict Liability in Tort 17
§ 1.05 THE RESTATEMENTS 19
§ 1.06 THE CHOICE OF THEORIES IN A PRODUCTS LIABILITY CASE . . . 22

Chapter 2   **WARRANTY** 25

§ 2.01 THE ROLE OF WARRANTY IN PRODUCTS LIABILITY LITIGATION 26
§ 2.02 EXPRESS WARRANTIES 27
  [A]   Introduction 27
  [B]   Statement of Fact v. Opinion 29
  [C]   Basis of the Bargain 32
§ 2.03 IMPLIED WARRANTY OF MERCHANTABILITY 34
  [A]   Introduction 34
  [B]   The Seller as Merchant of the Goods 35
  [C]   Merchantability 36
  [D]   Unforeseeable Use of the Goods 39
§ 2.04 IMPLIED WARRANTY OF FITNESS FOR A PARTICULAR PURPOSE 39
  [A]   Introduction 39
  [B]   The "Particular Purpose" 41
  [C]   Reliance 42
§ 2.05 THE SCOPE OF WARRANTIES 44
  [A]   Introduction 44
  [B]   Horizontal Privity 45

Table of Contents

[C]   Vertical Privity 47

§ 2.06   NOTICE 48

[A]   Introduction 48

[B]   "Buyer" and "Seller" 49

[C]   Adequate Notice 50

[D]   "Reasonable Time" 50

§ 2.07   DISCLAIMERS AND LIMITATIONS OF WARRANTIES 51

[A]   Exclusion or Modification of Warranties 51

[1]   Express Warranties 51

[2]   Implied Warranties of Merchantability 52

[3]   Implied Warranties of Fitness for Particular Purpose 53

[4]   "As Is" Disclaimers 53

[B]   Limitations on Warranties 54

§ 2.08   DAMAGES FOR BREACH OF WARRANTY 55

§ 2.09   THE MAGNUSON-MOSS ACT 57

Chapter 3   **MISREPRESENTATION** **61**

§ 3.01   INTRODUCTION 62

§ 3.02   FRAUDULENT MISREPRESENTATION 62

[A]   Introduction 62

[B]   A False Statement of a Material Fact 64

[C]   *Scienter* 65

[D]   Intent to Induce Reliance on the Misrepresentation 66

[E]   Justifiable Reliance 66

[F]   Damages 67

§ 3.03   NEGLIGENT MISREPRESENTATION 68

[A]   Elements of an Action 68

[B]   Damages 70

§ 3.04   INNOCENT (STRICT LIABILITY) MISREPRESENTATION 71

[A]   Restatement (Second) of Torts, Section 402B 71

[B]   "Engaged in the Business of Selling Chattels" 72

[C]   "Material Fact" Concerning "the Character or Quality of the Chattel" . . 73

[D]   Advertising 74

[E]   "Justifiable Reliance" 75

[F]   Damages 76

§ 3.05   RESTATEMENT (THIRD) OF TORTS: PRODUCTS LIABILITY 76

§ 3.06   DECEPTIVE TRADE PRACTICES STATUTES 77

[A]   Introduction 77

[B]   The Food Industry and Deceptive Trade Practices Statutes 78

[C]   Helmets and Deceptive Advertising 80

Table of Contents

Chapter 4	NEGLIGENCE AND STRICT LIABILITY: POLICIES, PARTIES, AND PRODUCTS	83

§ 4.01	INTRODUCTION	84
§ 4.02	AN OVERVIEW OF NEGLIGENCE AND STRICT LIABILITY	84
[A]	Negligence	84
[B]	Strict Liability	87
[C]	Policy Reasons Underlying Strict Liability	89
§ 4.03	POTENTIAL PLAINTIFFS	92
[A]	The Duty Issue in Negligence	92
[B]	The "User or Consumer" in Strict Liability	94
[C]	Bystanders	95
[D]	Unintended Users and Uses of Products	97
§ 4.04	POTENTIAL DEFENDANTS	98
[A]	Persons "Engaged in the Business of Selling"	98
[B]	Special Categories of Sellers	101
[1]	Component Part Manufacturers	101
[2]	Sellers of Used Products	103
[3]	Successor Corporations	105
[C]	Persons Not Covered by Strict Liability	107
[D]	Distributor Statutes	109
§ 4.05	WHAT IS A PRODUCT?	111
[A]	Introduction	111
[B]	Animals	112
[C]	Blood and Human Tissue	114
[D]	Electricity	115
[E]	Information	116
[F]	Raw Materials	118
[G]	Real Estate	118

Chapter 5	DESIGN DEFECTS	121

§ 5.01	PRODUCT DEFECTS	122
§ 5.02	DESIGN DEFECT	124
[A]	Characteristics of a Design Defect	124
[B]	Negligence, Strict Liability, and Product Designs	125
[1]	Introduction	125
[2]	Negligent Design	125
[3]	Strict Liability	127
[C]	Crashworthiness Doctrine	128
§ 5.03	TESTS FOR DETERMINING A DESIGN DEFECT	130
[A]	Introduction	130
[B]	Consumer Expectation Test	132

Table of Contents

[1]	Introduction		132
[2]	Who is an Ordinary Consumer?		134
[3]	What Does an Ordinary Consumer Expect of a Product?		134
[4]	When Does the Consumer Expectations Test Apply?		136
[C]	Risk-Utility Analysis		138
[1]	Introduction		138
[2]	Factors Used in Risk-Utility Analysis		141
[3]	Reasonable Alternative Design		144
[4]	Burden of Proof		147
[D]	Alternative Tests		148
§ 5.04	OPEN AND OBVIOUS DANGERS		151
§ 5.05	STATE-OF-THE-ART		152

Chapter 6   MANUFACTURING DEFECTS 157

§ 6.01	MANUFACTURING DEFECTS		157
[A]	Deviation from the Design		157
[B]	Manufacturing Defects and Design Defects		159
§ 6.02	THE DIVERSITY OF MANUFACTURING DEFECTS		161
[A]	Types of Manufacturing Defects		161
[B]	Testing and Inspection		162
[C]	Labeling and Packaging		163
§ 6.03	NEGLIGENT AND STRICT LIABILITY MANUFACTURE		164
[A]	Negligence		164
[B]	Strict Liability		165
§ 6.04	TESTS FOR DETERMINING A MANUFACTURING DEFECT		165
[A]	Consumer Expectations Test		165
[B]	Rejection of the Risk-Utility Analysis		167
§ 6.05	FOOD AND DRINK CASES		168
[A]	Foreign-Natural Test		168
[B]	Consumer Expectations Test		170
[C]	Hybrid Test		172
[D]	Proof of a Food Defect		172

Chapter 7   WARNING DEFECTS 175

§ 7.01	CHARACTERISTICS OF A WARNING DEFECT		176
[A]	Warnings and Instructions		176
[B]	Persons Who Have a Duty to Warn		177
[C]	Negligence and Strict Liability		178
[D]	Design Defects and the Failure to Warn		180
§ 7.02	WHEN A WARNING MUST BE GIVEN		182
[A]	Introduction		182

Table of Contents

[B]	Unavoidably Unsafe Products		184
[C]	Open and Obvious Dangers		186
§ 7.03	PERSONS WHO MUST BE WARNED		190
[A]	Users, Consumers, and Bystanders		190
[B]	Persons with Allergic Reactions		191
[C]	Bulk Supplier/Sophisticated User/Sophisticated Supplier Doctrine		192
§ 7.04	ADEQUACY OF THE WARNING		194
[A]	Criteria for Determining the Scope and Adequacy of a Warning		194
[B]	Form of the Warning		195
[C]	Content of the Warning		197
§ 7.05	POST-SALE DUTY TO WARN OR RECALL		200
[A]	Post-Sale Duty to Warn		200
[B]	Product Recalls		202
[1]	Judicially Mandated Product Recalls		202
[2]	Legislative Product Recalls		204
§ 7.06	THE LEARNED INTERMEDIARY DOCTRINE		206
[A]	Origin and Scope of the Learned Intermediary Doctrine		206
[B]	When a Warning Must Be Given to Physicians		209
[C]	Adequacy of the Warning		210
[D]	Causation		211
[E]	Exceptions to the Learned Intermediary Doctrine		212
[1]	Mass Immunization		212
[2]	Oral Contraceptives and Contraceptive Devices		213
[3]	FDA Mandate		214
[4]	Direct-to-Consumer Advertising		215

Chapter 8   **PROBLEMS OF PROOF: DEFECT AND CAUSATION . 217**

§ 8.01	INTRODUCTION		218
§ 8.02	PROOF OF A DEFECT		218
[A]	Direct and Circumstantial Evidence		218
[B]	*Res Ipsa Loquitur* and "An Inference of a Product Defect"		222
[C]	Product Testing and Spoliation of Evidence		225
[1]	Product Testing		225
[2]	Spoliation of Evidence		227
§ 8.03	EXPERT WITNESSES		230
[A]	Introduction		230
[B]	The Standards for the Admissibility of Expert Testimony		231
[1]	The *Frye* Test		231
[2]	The *Daubert* Test		232
[3]	*Daubert* and Opinion Testimony		233
[4]	The Scope of *Daubert*		234

Table of Contents

[5]   The District Court Judge as "Gatekeeper" 235

  [a]   Reliability 236

  [b]   Relevance 237

[6]   Review of the District Court Decision 238

[C]   The Qualifications for an Expert 239

[D]   The Permissible Scope of Expert Testimony 240

§ 8.04   CAUSE-IN-FACT 241

[A]   Introduction 241

[B]   "But For" and "Substantial Factor" Tests 242

[C]   Establishing the Identity of the Manufacturer 244

[D]   Exposure to Risk of Future Injury 247

§ 8.05   PROXIMATE CAUSE 249

[A]   Introduction 249

[B]   Foreseeability 250

[C]   Natural and Probable Consequences 253

[D]   Condition v. Cause 255

Chapter 9   **DEFENSES** **257**

§ 9.01   INTRODUCTION 258

§ 9.02   CONDUCT-BASED DEFENSES 259

[A]   Introduction 259

[B]   Contributory Negligence 259

[C]   Assumption of Risk 262

[D]   Alteration of a Product 265

[E]   Misuse of the Product 267

[F]   Comparative Fault 270

§ 9.03   STATUS-BASED DEFENSES 273

[A]   Employer Immunity 273

  [1]   Employer Liability to Employees 273

  [2]   Employer Liability to Third Parties 275

[B]   Government Contractor Defense 275

  [1]   Framework for the Defense 275

  [2]   The Three Prongs of the Defense 276

  [3]   Expansion of the Defense 279

§ 9.04   TIMES-BASED DEFENSES 280

[A]   Statute of Limitations 280

[B]   Statute of Repose 281

[C]   Useful Shelf-Life 283

§ 9.05   GOVERNMENT AND INDUSTRY STANDARDS 284

[A]   Government Standards 284

[B]   Government Standards and the Pharmaceutical Industry 287

Table of Contents

[C]   Industry Standards 288

§ 9.06   PREEMPTION 289

[A]   Introduction 289

[B]   Express Preemption 291

[C]   Field Preemption 294

[D]   Conflict Preemption 296

Chapter 10   **DAMAGES** **301**

§ 10.01   INTRODUCTION 301

§ 10.02   COMPENSATORY DAMAGES 302

[A]   Damages for Personal Injury 302

[1]   General Damages and Special Damages 302

[2]   Present Cash Value 305

[3]   Collateral Source Rule 305

[4]   Loss of Consortium 306

[B]   Damages for Pain and Suffering 307

[C]   Damages for Emotional Distress 309

[1]   The Impact Rule 309

[2]   Medical Monitoring 310

[3]   Bystanders 312

[D]   Limitations on Noneconomic Damages 314

[E]   Wrongful Death and Survival Actions 315

[F]   Damage to Property 317

§ 10.03   ECONOMIC LOSS DOCTRINE 317

§ 10.04   PUNITIVE DAMAGES 322

[A]   Introduction 322

[B]   Conduct and Standard of Proof Required for Punitive Damages 323

[C]   Statutory Controls on Punitive Damage Awards 325

[D]   The Constitutionality of Punitive Damages 327

§ 10.05   PRE-JUDGMENT AND POST-JUDGMENT INTEREST 332

§ 10.06   JOINT AND SEVERAL LIABILITY 333

Chapter 11   **RESEARCH AND PRACTICE IMPLICATIONS OF CHOICE OF THEORY** **335**

§ 11.01   INTRODUCTION 335

§ 11.02   PRE-FILING QUESTIONS IN PRODUCTS LIABILITY LITIGATION 337

§ 11.03   THE MAJOR RESEARCH TASKS IN PRODUCTS LIABILITY LITIGATION 340

§ 11.04   RESEARCH TIME FRAMES 341

§ 11.05   CRITERIA FOR SELECTION OF TIME FRAMES 345

Table of Contents

Chapter 12 **RESEARCHING THE PRODUCTS CASE** **347**

§ 12.01 INTRODUCTION 348

§ 12.02 THE RANGE OF WORK AREAS IN PRODUCTS LIABILITY
LITIGATION 350

§ 12.03 DUAL ASPECTS OF RESEARCH DATA 351

§ 12.04 RESEARCH POINTS OF REFERENCE 352

§ 12.05 IDENTIFICATION OF THE THEORETICAL DEFECT TYPE 352

§ 12.06 IDENTIFYING THE PRODUCT'S INJURY-PRODUCING ASPECT . . 353

§ 12.07 THE EXTENT OF THE ALLEGED INJURIES TO CONSUMERS 354

§ 12.08 THE SERIOUSNESS OF THE ALLEGED INJURIES TO
CONSUMERS 354

§ 12.09 STATE-OF-THE-ART COMMENTARY ON THE ALLEGED DEFECTS
AND INJURIES 355

§ 12.10 GOVERNMENT REGULATION OF THE DEFENDANT'S
INDUSTRY 356

§ 12.11 THE HISTORY OF THE INDUSTRY REACTION TO THE SCIENTIFIC
PROBLEM 358

§ 12.12 STUDY OF DEFENDANT CORPORATION'S ORGANIZATION AND
MANUFACTURING PROCESSES 359

§ 12.13 THE DEVELOPMENT OF THE CORPORATE DEFENDANT'S
REACTION TO THE ALLEGED SCIENTIFIC DEFECT 360

§ 12.14 PRIOR LITIGATION, SETTLEMENTS, OR CASE FILINGS 361

§ 12.15 MATERIALS SUPPLIERS AND COMPONENT PART
MANUFACTURERS INFORMATION SOURCE CATEGORIES 362

§ 12.16 LIBRARY COLLECTIONS 362

§ 12.17 GOVERNMENT DATABASES 362

§ 12.18 BOOKS AND PERIODICALS 364

§ 12.19 DIALOG INFORMATION SERVICES 364

§ 12.20 POPULAR PUBLICATIONS 365

§ 12.21 ACADEMIC AND PROFESSIONAL JOURNALS 366

§ 12.22 ACADEMIC AND PROFESSIONAL ANNUAL MEETINGS AND
SPECIAL CONFERENCES 367

§ 12.23 RESEARCH IN PROGRESS AND GRANTS 367

§ 12.24 STATISTICAL PUBLICATIONS AND DATA BANKS 368

§ 12.25 MATERIALS, DESIGN, AND PERFORMANCE STANDARDS 369

§ 12.26 CONSUMER INTEREST GROUPS AND ASSOCIATED
PUBLICATIONS 370

§ 12.27 PROFESSIONAL AND TRADE ASSOCIATIONS AND
ORGANIZATIONS 371

§ 12.28 TRADE ASSOCIATIONS 372

§ 12.29 PATENTS 373

§ 12.30 COMPANY RESEARCH 373

§ 12.31 ANNUAL REPORTS 374

Table of Contents

§ 12.32   DIRECTORY OF CORPORATE AFFILIATIONS   374

§ 12.33   THOMAS REGISTER OF AMERICAN MANUFACTURERS   375

§ 12.34   FOREIGN CORPORATIONS   375

§ 12.35   SUMMARY   375

§ 12.36   APPENDIX: PRODUCTS LIABILITY INTERNET RESEARCH
          SITES   376

Chapter 13   THE EXPERT WITNESS   385

§ 13.01   EXPERT WITNESSES: PRE-TRIAL CONSIDERATIONS   385

  [A]   Analyzing Expert Witness Needs   386

  [1]   Determining Expert Witness Needs   386

  [2]   Categorizing Expert Witness Needs   386

  [B]   Choosing the Expert Witness   387

  [1]   Expert Witness Research Sites   387

  [2]   Expert Witness Clearing Houses   387

  [3]   ATLA Exchange and DRI   387

  [4]   Lexis and Westlaw Listings   388

  [C]   Organizational Factors   388

  [D]   Categories of Experts   389

§ 13.02   PLAINTIFF REQUIRED TO PRESENT EXPERT TESTIMONY   390

§ 13.03   THE LEGAL REQUIREMENTS OF EXPERT TESTIMONY   390

§ 13.04   EXPERT TESTIMONY NOT SUPPORTED BY RELIABLE
          SCIENCE   392

§ 13.05   TESTING ALTERNATIVES IN UNIT DEFECT CASES   395

§ 13.06   TESTING ALTERNATIVES IN DESIGN DEFECT CASES   396

§ 13.07   QUALIFICATIONS TO TESTIFY AT TRIAL   400

§ 13.08   SOURCES REASONABLY RELIED UPON BY EXPERTS IN THE
          FIELD   407

**Chapter 14   DRAFTING THE COMPLAINT AND DISCOVERY
                      FOCUS 411**

§ 14.01   INTRODUCTION   411

§ 14.02   STANDARD ALLEGATIONS IN THE PRODUCTS CASE   412

§ 14.03   SAMPLE COMPLAINT: PRESSURIZED BEVERAGE CANISTER . . .   413

§ 14.04   DISTRIBUTIVE CHAIN   414

§ 14.05   ABSENCE OF ALTERATION OR MODIFICATION   414

§ 14.06   DEFENDANT'S DUTY OR OBLIGATION   415

§ 14.07   INTENDED USE   416

§ 14.08   INJURY-PRODUCING EVENT   416

§ 14.09   BREACH OF DUTY OR OBLIGATION: SETTING OUT THE DEFECT
          MODES   416

Table of Contents

§ 14.10   PROXIMATE CAUSE 419

§ 14.11   PUNITIVE DAMAGES 419

§ 14.12   SAMPLE COMPLAINT: STANDUP FORKLIFT TRUCK 420

Chapter 15   PRODUCTS LIABILITY AND DISCOVERY 425

§ 15.01   INTRODUCTION 425

§ 15.02   THE PURPOSES AND REACH OF DISCOVERY 429

[A]   Illinois Supreme Court Rule 201. General Discovery Provisions 429

[B]   FRCP 26. General Provisions Governing Discovery; Duty of
            Disclosure 430

§ 15.03   THE DISCOVERY TOOLS 430

§ 15.04   INTERROGATORIES 431

§ 15.05   REQUESTS TO PRODUCE DOCUMENTS 432

§ 15.06   REQUESTS TO ADMIT FACTS OR THE GENUINENESS OF
            DOCUMENTS 433

§ 15.07   DEPOSITIONS 434

§ 15.08   RELEVANCY IN THE DISCOVERY PROCESS 439

§ 15.09   SETTING THE DISCOVERY TIME FRAME 442

§ 15.10   DEFECT CATEGORY AND TIME FRAMES 444

§ 15.11   TIME FRAMES IN UNIT DEFECT CASES 444

§ 15.12   TIME FRAMES IN DESIGN DEFECT CASES 445

§ 15.13   TIME FRAMES IN FAILURE TO INSTRUCT OR WARN CASES ... 446

§ 15.14   TIME FRAMES IN MISREPRESENTATION CASES 447

§ 15.15   ORGANIZATION AND DRAFTING OF DISCOVERY REQUESTS .. 447

§ 15.16   INADVERTENT DISCLOSURE IN DISCOVERY 448

§ 15.17   ELECTRONIC DISCOVERY 449

§ 15.18   SUMMARY 454

**Chapter 16   INTERROGATORIES AND REQUESTS TO ADMIT
                      FACTS 455**

§ 16.01   INTRODUCTION 455

§ 16.02   INTERROGATORIES: STATUTORY DEFINITIONS — FEDERAL .. 455

§ 16.03   INTERROGATORIES: STATUTORY DEFINITIONS — STATE 457

§ 16.04   INTERROGATORIES: LIMITATIONS ON NUMBER 459

§ 16.05   ORGANIZING AND DRAFTING THE INTERROGATORIES 462

§ 16.06   SAMPLE INTERROGATORIES 462

§ 16.07   SAMPLE INTERROGATORIES: FOURWHEEL CORPORATION ... 463

§ 16.08   PLAINTIFF'S FIRST SET OF INTERROGATORIES TO DEFENDANT
            ROLLBAR CORPORATION 469

§ 16.09   SAMPLE INTERROGATORIES: PRESSURIZED STAINLESS STEEL
            BEVERAGE CANISTER 475

Table of Contents

§ 16.10   SAMPLE INTERROGATORIES: STANDUP FORKLIFT TRUCK 480

§ 16.11   OBSERVATIONS ON SAMPLE INTERROGATORIES 488

§ 16.12   REQUESTS TO ADMIT FACT OR THE GENUINENESS OF
DOCUMENTS 488

Chapter 17   REQUESTS TO PRODUCE DOCUMENTS 491

§ 17.01   INTRODUCTION 491

§ 17.02   THE DISCOVERY RULES — DOCUMENT PRODUCTION 492

§ 17.03   PLANNING DOCUMENT REQUESTS 495

§ 17.04   THE GENERATION OF CORPORATE DOCUMENTS 495

§ 17.05   STAGES OF DOCUMENT GENERATION 496

§ 17.06   SAMPLE: AUTOMOBILE MANUFACTURING PROCESSES 496

[A]   OVERALL PRODUCT PLANNING 497

[B]   PRODUCT DESIGN TESTING 497

[C]   PRODUCT PRODUCTION RUNS 497

[D]   PRODUCT MARKETING 497

[E]   PRODUCT POST-MARKETING 497

§ 17.07   OVERLAP IN DOCUMENT GENERATION 498

§ 17.08   DRAFTING REQUESTS FOR DOCUMENTS 498

§ 17.09   SAMPLE REQUEST FOR DOCUMENTS: PRESSURIZED STAINLESS
STEEL BEVERAGE CANISTERS 499

§ 17.10   SAMPLE REQUEST FOR DOCUMENTS: JEEP-TYPE VEHICLE
ROLLOVER 502

§ 17.11   SAMPLE REQUEST FOR DOCUMENTS: STAND-ALONE FORKLIFT
TRUCK 505

§ 17.12   SUPPLEMENTAL DISCOVERY 511

§ 17.13   SUMMARY 512

Chapter 18   DISCOVERY AND EVIDENCE DEPOSITIONS 513

§ 18.01   INTRODUCTION 513

§ 18.02   THE DEPOSITION RULES 515

§ 18.03   RELEVANCY AND DEPOSITIONS 520

§ 18.04   OBJECTIONS IN DEPOSITIONS 523

§ 18.05   DEPOSITION PLANNING 526

§ 18.06   DOCUMENT ORGANIZATION AND DEPOSITION
PREPARATION 527

§ 18.07   DEPOSING DEFENSE EXPERTS 529

Table of Contents

Chapter 19   **PROTECTIVE ORDERS AND DISCOVERY
                      ENFORCEMENT** **531**

§ 19.01   INTRODUCTION 531
§ 19.02   PROTECTIVE ORDERS: THE RULES 532
§ 19.03   PROTECTIVE ORDERS IN PRODUCTS LITIGATION 533
§ 19.04   REQUIREMENT OF SPECIFIC SUPPORTIVE FACTS 534
§ 19.05   INFORMATION SHARING 535
§ 19.06   PROTECTION AGAINST FRAUD 537
§ 19.07   ANNOYANCE, EMBARRASSMENT, OPPRESSION 538
§ 19.08   TRADE SECRETS AND CONFIDENTIAL COMMERCIAL
           INFORMATION 538
§ 19.09   FACTUAL COMPONENTS OF THE ARGUMENT IN
           OPPOSITION 540
§ 19.10   MEETING THE ARGUMENTS FOR EACH DOCUMENT 541
§ 19.11   DISCOVERY ENFORCEMENT 541
§ 19.12   SAMPLE DISCOVERY ENFORCEMENT MEMORANDUM —
           STAINLESS STEEL PRESSURIZED BEVERAGE CANISTER
           LITIGATION 543
§ 19.13   THE DENTON v. FREMANTLE DISCOVERY ENFORCEMENT
           SUPPORT MEMORANDUM 544
§ 19.14   CONCLUSION 559

Table of Cases **TC-1**

Index **I-1**

Chapter 1

THE DEVELOPMENT OF PRODUCTS LIABILITY LAW

SYNOPSIS

§ 1.01   INTRODUCTION

§ 1.02   THE INFLUENCE OF CONTRACT LAW

   [A]   *Caveat Emptor*

   [B]   The Privity Rule

   [C]   Exceptions to the Privity Rule

§ 1.03   THE RISE OF NEGLIGENCE

   [A]   The Fall of Privity

   [B]   The Adoption of Negligence

   [C]   *Res Ipsa Loquitur*

§ 1.04   FROM NEGLIGENCE TO STRICT LIABILITY

   [A]   The Theory Behind Strict Liability

   [B]   "The Fall of the Citadel of Privity"

   [C]   The Triumph of Strict Liability in Tort

§ 1.05   THE RESTATEMENTS

§ 1.06   THE CHOICE OF THEORIES IN A PRODUCTS LIABILITY CASE

§ 1.01   INTRODUCTION

More than most areas of the law, an understanding of the theory and practice of products liability law requires an understanding of its history and development. In part, this is because the laws governing the liability of those who manufacture and sell products that cause injury or death have undergone fundamental changes since the middle of the nineteenth century. While the recovery of damages resulting from defective products originally was governed (and limited) by principles of contract law, the theories of liability gradually expanded to include negligence, beginning in the second decade of the twentieth century, and strict liability, starting in the mid-1960s. As a result of those developments, lawsuits against product manufacturers and sellers are not limited to a single theory of liability. Instead, a products liability claim may be based upon one or more of a number of complex theories: express warranty; implied warranty; misrepresentation; negligence; strict liability. In addition, a number of individuals and government entities have filed suits against the manufacturers and sellers of products such as lead paint, pesticides found in contaminated groundwater, firearms, and alcohol using nuisance theory or including a nuisance count along with the traditional products liability theories.[1] However, most of the nuisance claims have not been successful.[2] The publication of the American Law Institute (ALI) in 1998 of the Restatement (Third) of Torts: Products Liability has led to further changes in the approaches to recovery for products that cause harm. Because the different causes of action in products liability actions, along with their elements, defenses, and damages, are the result of a constantly evolving process, it is necessary to begin by putting them into perspective and explaining how and why products liability law has developed.

§ 1.02   THE INFLUENCE OF CONTRACT LAW

Products liability law has its origins in early nineteenth century cases where a defect in a product meant that it did not meet the buyer's expectations. However, during the second quarter of the nineteenth century, buyers who suffered bodily injuries as a result of product defects began to bring claims alleging negligence in the manufacturing of the goods.[3] Because negligence was a developing area of the law at that time, courts looked to contract law to define the scope of the duty owed by manufacturers and sellers. As a result, persons seeking compensation for bodily injuries caused by defective products faced the two principal limitations of contract law: *caveat emptor* and privity. Although these doctrines have been rejected or severely limited over the years, they have exerted an extremely important influence on the development of products liability law.

[A]   *Caveat Emptor*

Until the early nineteenth century, people bought most of the goods they needed for their personal and commercial use directly from the makers of those goods. The complexity of products and the layers of distribution that arose during the industrial revolution did not yet exist. As a result, buyers usually knew the manufacturers and had an opportunity to inspect their products before they purchased them. Because buyers and sellers bargained with each other for the goods they bought and sold, the right to recover for any defects in the products was governed by the contract of sale. However, with coming of the industrial revolution, manufacturers became insulated from the buyers of their products due to the increase of middlemen, such as wholesalers and retailers. This also meant that buyers no longer were able to bargain with the manufacturers of the items they purchased. In addition, the rise of large factories and the complexity of many

---

[1] In re Methyl Tertiary Butyl Ether (MTBE) Products, 457 F. Supp. 2d 455 (S.D.N.Y. 2006) (applying California law); City of Milwaukee v. NL Indus., 762 N.W.2d 757 (Wis. 2008); County of Santa Clara v. Atlantic Richfield Co., 40 Cal. Rptr. 3d 313 (Ct. App. 2006).

[2] Examples of unsuccessful suits include City of Philadelphia v. Beretta U.S.A. Corp., 277 F.3d 415 (3d Cir. 2002) (applying Pennsylvania law); In re Lead Paint Litigation, 924 A.2d 484 (N.J. 2007); State of Rhode Island v. Lead Indus. Ass'n. Inc, 951 A.2d 428 (R.I. 2008); City of Chicago v. American Cyanamid Co., 823 N.E.2d 126 (Ill. App. Ct. 2005); City of Modesto Redevelopment Agency v. Superior Court, 13 Cal. Rptr. 3d 865 (Ct. App. 2004); People *ex rel.* Spitzer v. Sturm, Ruger & Co., Inc., 761 N.Y.S.2d 192 (App. Div. 2003).

[3] Dixon v. Bell, 5 Maule & Selwyn 198 (1816).

of the new mass-produced goods meant that buyers were unable to inspect them before purchase or to understand how they operated. Because the lawsuits seeking compensation for the bodily injuries caused by defects in these new products threatened their industries, manufacturers sought protection from liability in the traditional requirements of contract law. As a result, courts continued to apply the earlier common law rule of *caveat emptor* (let the buyer beware).[4] A defense of this rule was offered by the Supreme Court in its 1871 decision in *Barnard v. Kellogg*:[5]

> No principle of the common law has been better established, or more often affirmed, both in this country and in England than that in sales of personal property, in the absence of express warranty, where the buyer has an opportunity to inspect the commodity, and the seller is guilty of no fraud . . . the maxim of caveat emptor applies. . . . And there is no hardship in it, because if the purchaser distrusts his judgment he can require of the seller a warranty that the quality or condition of the goods he desires to buy corresponds with the sample exhibited. If he is satisfied without a warranty and can inspect and declines to do so, he takes upon himself the risk that the article is merchantable. And he cannot relieve himself and charge the seller on the ground that the examination will occupy time, and is attended with labor and inconvenience. . . . Of such universal acceptance is the doctrine of caveat emptor in this country, that the courts of all the States in the Union where the common law prevails, with one exception (South Carolina), sanction it.[6]

Demands by businesses during the late nineteenth century that government leave the regulation of commerce to the laws of the marketplace led to a philosophy of *laissez-faire.*[7] Ideas of the freedom and sanctity of contract resulted, among other things, in the rejection of any idea that a general implied warranty accompanied the sale of goods. At the same time, however, courts recognized the need to create exceptions to the rule of *caveat emptor* to protect buyers from harm in specific situations. This led courts to hold that, even in the absence of fraud or an express warranty, an "implied warranty of merchantability" or an "implied warranty of fitness for a particular purpose" accompanied the sale of some products. These implied warranties began the movement (that culminated with the adoption of strict liability in the 1960s) toward focusing on the dangerous condition of products themselves rather than on any fault in the process of manufacturing or selling them. Thus, as early as 1815, a New York court held that there was an implied warranty of fitness in the sale of food.[8] According to the Illinois Supreme Court, the imposition of such a warranty was based upon public policy:

---

[4] National Oil Co. v. Rankin, 75 P. 1013 (Kan. 1904); Sexias Woods, 2 Am. Dec. 215 (N.Y. Sup. Ct. 1804). For a detailed study of the doctrine, see Walton H. Hamilton, *The Ancient Maxim Caveat Emptor*, 40 YALE L.J. 1133 (1931).

[5] 77 U.S. (10 Wall.) 383 (1871).

[6] *Id.* at 388–89. *See also* Slaughter's Administrator v. Gerson, 80 U.S. 379 (1872).

[7] *See* John W. Metzger, *The Social Revolution in Products Liability*, 49 ILL. B.J. 710 (1961).

[8] Van Bracklin v. Fonda, 7 Am. Dec. 339 (N.Y. Sup. Ct. 1815). *See* Jacob E. Decker & Sons v. Capps, 139 Tex. 609, 164 S.W.2d 828 (Tex. 1942); Ward v. Morehead City Sea Food Co., 87 S.E. 958 (N.C. 1916).

Where . . . articles of food are purchased from a retail dealer for immediate consumption, the consequences resulting from the purchase of an unsound article may be so serious and may prove so disastrous to the health and life of the consumer that public safety demands that there should be an implied warranty on the part of the vendor that the article sold is sound and fit for the use for which it was purchased.[9]

Similarly, where a person sold drugs, medicines or other chemicals, the rule of *caveat emptor* did not apply if the buyer was not an expert and relied on the knowledge and skill of the seller. In such a case, there was an implied warranty of fitness for the use to which the product usually was put or was recommended by the seller.[10] According to Kentucky's highest court: "As applicable to the owners of drugs stores, or persons engaged in vending drugs and medicines by retail, the legal maxim should be reversed. Instead of caveat emptor, it should be caveat vendor."[11] Finally, courts came to hold that the rule of *caveat emptor* did not apply if the seller undertook to furnish goods for a particular purpose specified by the buyer.[12]

Despite the exceptions to the rule of *caveat emptor*, the concept of general implied warranties of merchantability and fitness did not begin to gain acceptance until the early twentieth century. Changing views about how the marketplace actually operated made the idea that consumers were able to bargain with sellers from a position of equal knowledge and strength a fiction. In addition, the injuries and deaths that resulted from a general lack of any government regulation of contracts led to pressure for the protection of workers and consumers. Among the many reforms of the progressive era were the implied warranty provisions adopted by the Uniform Sales Act (USA) in 1906[13] that created the basis for the current implied warranty provisions in Article 2 of the Uniform Commercial Code (UCC).[14]

[B] The Privity Rule

Although exceptions to the rule of *caveat emptor* developed during the nineteenth century, they extended the right to recover no further than the immediate buyer of the defective product. That was in keeping with the general requirement that, ordinarily, a contract created no duties except to the parties to it and to their privies.[15] Although originally a requirement of contract law, privity of contract between the plaintiff and defendant became an essential element in negligence actions as well. Thus, at common law, a person injured by a product had no cause of action against the manufacturer of the product unless that person was in privity of contract with the manufacturer. However, as with the rule of *caveat*

---

[9] Wiedeman v. Keller, 49 N.E. 210, 211 (Ill. 1897).

[10] Thomas v. Winchester, 6 N.Y. 397 (1852); Salmon v. Libby, McNeil & Libby, 114 Ill. App. 258 (1904).

[11] Fleet and Semple v. Hollenkemp, 52 Ky. (1 B. Mon.) 219 (1852).

[12] Shoenberger v. Mcewen, 15 Ill. App. 496 (1884).

[13] *See* Uniform Sales Act § 15(2) (implied warranty of merchantability) and §§ 15(1), 15(4), and 15(5) (implied warranty of fitness for a particular purpose).

[14] *See* UCC § 2-314 (implied warranty of merchantability) and § 2-315 (implied warranty of fitness for a particular purpose).

[15] 2 EDWIN A. JAGGARD, HANDBOOK OF THE LAW OF TORTS, § 260 (1895).

emptor, the privity rule became subject to a number of judicially created exceptions.

The origin of the privity rule in products liability cases was the 1842 English decision in *Winterbottom v. Wright,*[16] in which Winterbottom, a coachman, suffered permanent injuries when the mail-coach he was driving collapsed. The coach had been built by Wright, who had contracted with the Postmaster-General to supply coaches for the delivery of mail and to keep those coaches in good repair. The Postmaster-General then contracted with Atkinson to supply horses and drivers for the coaches to deliver the mail. Winterbottom was, in turn, one of the coachmen hired by Atkinson under that contract. Although not a party to the contract between Wright and the Postmaster-General, Winterbottom's declaration stated that, "by virtue of the said contract," Wright undertook a duty "to keep the carriage in a safe condition."[17] Winterbottom alleged that his right to recover was based upon his knowledge of, and reliance upon, the contract and that Wright's "omission" resulted in his injuries.

In what one of the judges, Lord Abinger, termed "an action of first impression,"[18] the Court of Exchequer dismissed Winterbottom's suit against Wright because there was no privity of contract between the parties. Although Wright breached the duty that he undertook to keep the coaches in a state of good repair, another of the judges, Baron Rolff, explained that the duty arose solely out of the contract between Wright and the Postmaster-General. Since Winterbottom was not a party to that contract, Wright owed him no duty of care.[19] The emphasis by the judges on the privity rule was prompted by their fear that, if Winterbottom was permitted to recover, "every passenger, or even any person passing along the road, who was injured by the upsetting of the coach, might bring a similar action."[20] Since Lord Abinger felt that, unless liability was limited to those who had entered into the contract, "the most absurd and outrageous consequences, to which I see no limit, would ensue,"[21] the third judge in the case, Baron Alderson, concluded:

> The only safe rule is to confine the right to recover to those who enter into the contract; if we go one step beyond that, there is no reason why we should not go fifty. The only real argument in favour of the action is that this is a case of hardship; but that might have been obviated, if the plaintiff had made himself a party to the contract.[22]

Although Winterbottom based his action on Wright's "omission" in the performance of his contract with the Postmaster-General and not on tort, the *dicta* of Lord Abinger and Baron Alderson was interpreted by courts in England and in the

---

[16] 152 Eng. Rep. 402 (Ex. 1842).

[17] *Id.* at 405.

[18] *Id.* at 404.

[19] *Id.* at 405. Although Baron Rolff did not use the word "negligence" or "tort" in his opinion, Lord Abinger referred to the case as an "action of tort" at the end of his opinion. *Id.* at 405.

[20] *Id.*

[21] *Id.*

[22] *Id.*

United States to mean that a manufacturer or seller of a defective product was not liable, either in contract or in negligence, to a buyer in the absence of a contractual relationship between them.[23] As a result, the duty in negligence actions against manufacturers and sellers for defective products was defined as arising solely out of the contract of sale. Since the contract of sale applied only to the parties who entered into that contract, the privity rule prevented a consumer or user from recovering damages from the manufacturers or seller of the product for their injuries unless the purchase had been made directly from the manufacturer.[24]

American courts expressed similar fears as those stated in *Winterbottom* about the "far-reaching consequences" to the "general prosecution of mercantile business" of extending liability in negligence actions to persons who were not in privity of contract with the manufacturer or seller of a product.[25] One reason for this fear was that manufacturers and sellers did not know who would use their products or where or how they would be used. That was the concern expressed by the Pennsylvania Supreme Court in *Curtin v. Somerset*,[26] in which a hotel guest was injured when a porch collapsed. The court denied recovery for negligence in an action based upon the construction of the porch, declaring:

> The consequences of holding the opposite doctrine would be far reaching. If . . . a manufacturer who constructs a boiler, piece of machinery, or a steamship, owes a duty to the whole world, that his work or his machine or his steamship shall contain no hidden defect, it is difficult to measure the extent of his responsibility, and no prudent man would engage in such occupations upon such conditions. It is safer and wiser to confine such liabilities to the parties immediately concerned.[27]

Courts restricted the scope of a manufacturer's liability by using one of the essential elements of negligence: causation. They took the position that injuries to persons other than the immediate buyer of the product were not "the natural or probable effect of negligence" in the manufacture of products. That was because such injuries were not foreseeable and the act of the purchaser "insulated" the negligence of the manufacturer from the buyer.[28]

[C] Exceptions to the Privity Rule

Although it became a general rule of common law that a manufacturer or seller of a product was not liable, regardless of its negligence, to third persons with whom it had no contractual relations, courts developed a number of exceptions to the

---

[23] Goodlander Mill Co. v. Standard Oil Co., 63 F. 400 (7th Cir. 1894); Bragdon v. Perkins-Campbell Co., 87 F. 109 (3d Cir. 1898); Davidson v. Montgomery Ward, 171 Ill. App. 355 (1912). For a discussion of Winterbottom v. Wright in the United States, see Francis H. Bohlen, *The Basis of Affirmative Obligations in the Law of Tort*, 44 Am. L. Reg. (N.S.) 209 (1905).

[24] Huset v. J. I. Case Threshing Machine Co., 120 F. 865 (8th Cir. 1903); Losee v. Clute, 10 Am. Rep. 638 (N.Y. 1873); Loop v. Litchfield, 42 N.Y. 351 (1870).

[25] Lebourdais v. Vitrified Wheel Co., 80 N.E. 482, 483 (Mass. 1907).

[26] 21 A. 244 (Pa. 1891).

[27] *Id.* at 245.

[28] Huset v. J.I. Case Threshing Machine Co., 120 F. 865 (8th Cir. 1903).

privity requirement.[29] These exceptions, which led to the development of the modern rules of negligence, strict liability, and misrepresentation, fell into four broad categories. First, privity did not protect a manufacturer or seller's negligence where the product was "imminently' or "inherently" dangerous to human life or health.[30] As with implied warranties (and later strict liability), this exception was based on the condition of the product itself rather than any conduct by the manufacturer or seller. The classic example of this is *Thomas v. Winchester*,[31] a case decided in 1852, just 10 years after *Winterbottom v. Wright.* In *Thomas*, a chemist negligently labeled a bottle of poison as harmless medicine and sold it to a retail druggist who, in turn, sold it to a man who purchased it for his wife. As in *Winterbottom*, there was no privity of contract between the chemist and the woman who took the poison. However, despite the absence of privity of contract, the New York Court of Appeals distinguished *Winterbottom*, saying that negligent mislabeling "put human life in imminent danger" and was much more likely to affect a remote purchaser than the druggist to whom the chemist sold it.[32] Because the extent of the danger posed by the mislabeled poison could be foreseen, the "duty" owed by the chemist did not arise out of the contract of sale but in selling a dangerous product which the chemist knew would be put into the stream of commerce. Thus, the chemist owed a duty of care to anyone who foreseeably could take the poison, not just to the immediate purchaser.[33] The "inherently dangerous" exception to the privity requirement later was extended from drugs to the manufacturer of household item, a coffee urn.[34]

The second exception to the privity rule arose when a property owner's negligence injured a person who was invited by the property owner to use his defective product on his property.[35] The application of this exception was far more limited than the first one. The leading example is *Devlin v. Smith*,[36] in which a painter hired a scaffold builder to construct a scaffold for the specific purpose of enabling his workers to stand on it to paint the 90-foot dome of a court-house. The scaffold was constructed negligently and, while one of the workers was using it, it gave way, resulting in the death of the worker. Since the builder undertook to construct a scaffold for workers to use while painting, any negligence in the construction of the scaffold would result in the workers falling from a significant height. As in *Thomas v. Winchester*, injury to persons who were not party to the contract "would be a natural and necessary consequence of the builder's

---

[29] *See* Francis H. Bohlen, Studies in the Law of Torts 109–55 (1926); Thomas M. Cooley & Archibald H. Throckmorton, A Treatise on the Law of torts, § 345 (1930).

[30] For a list of cases dealing with this exception, see Huset v. J. I. Case Threshing Machine Co., 120 F. 865, 870 (8th Cir. 1903). *See also* Edward Levi, *An Introduction to Legal Reasoning*, 15 U. Chi. L. Rev. 501, 506–19 (1948).

[31] 6 N.Y. 397 (1852).

[32] *Id.* at 409.

[33] *Id.* at 409–10.

[34] Statler v. George A. Ray Manufacturing Co., 88 N.E. 1063 (N.Y. 1909).

[35] For a list of cases dealing with this exception, see Huset v. J. I. Case Threshing Machine Co., 120 F. 865, 870–71 (8th Cir. 1903). *See also* Coughtry v. Globe Woolen Co., 56 N.Y. 124 (1874).

[36] 89 N.Y. 470 (1882).

negligence."[37] Since the builder's duty of care extended to the workers who used his scaffold, the New York Court of Appeals held that a jury should decide whether the death of the worker was caused by the builder's breach of that duty in the construction of the scaffold.[38]

The third exception to the privity rule involved persons who sold products which they knew were imminently dangerous to life or health but concealed the dangers from the buyers.[39] Under this exception, both the condition of the product and the manufacturer's knowledge and concealment of the danger posed by it were essential. In *Huset v. J. I. Case Threshing Machine Co.*,[40] the defendant, manufactured a threshing machine, that it sold to the employer of the plaintiff. The machine had an iron covering over the top of the cylinder which employees walked on while operating the machine. However, due to a defect in the construction, the covering was unable to hold the weight that was placed upon it. As a result, it collapsed and the plaintiff's leg was crushed. Although manufacturer knew that the machine was dangerous when it shipped it to the plaintiff's employer, it concealed the defective and dangerous condition so that it could not be discovered by persons using the machine. The Court of Appeals held the manufacturer liable since it negligently produced a product "imminently dangerous to the lives and limbs of those who should use the machine" and knowingly concealed the dangerous condition of the product when it shipped it to the retailer.[41] Similarly in *Kuelling v. Roderick Lean Manufacturing Co.*,[42] a farmer injured by a road roller alleged that the manufacturer "intentionally, willfully, maliciously, negligently, and fraudulently" constructed a machine that was unfit for its use and concealed the dangers so they could not be seen on inspection.[43] The New York Court of Appeals found not only "fraudulent deceit and concealment" of the dangers in the product but also what amounted to "an affirmative representation" that the product was fit for its intended use.[44] In such a situation, the manufacturer was liable to any person, including those not in privity of contract, who was injured because of the fraudulent deceit and concealment.[45]

The final exception to the requirement of privity arose in cases where the seller was guilty of fraud. In an English case, *Langridge v. Levy*,[46] the son of the buyer of a gun was severely injured when the gun exploded while he was using it. The seller had told his father that the gun had been manufactured by a well-known gun-

---

[37] *Id.* at 478.

[38] *Id.* at 479.

[39] The earliest example of this exception is an English decision, Langridge v. Levy, 150 Eng. Rep. 863 (Ex. 1837). For a list of American cases dealing with this exception, see Huset v. J. I. Case Threshing Machine Co., 120 F. 865, 871 (8th Cir. 1903).

[40] 120 F. 865 (8th Cir. 1903).

[41] *Id.* at 872–73.

[42] 75 N.E. 1098 (N.Y. 1905).

[43] *Id.* at 1099.

[44] *Id.* at 1101.

[45] *Id.* at 1102.

[46] 150 Eng. Rep. 863 (Ex. 1837).

maker and was a "good, safe and secure gun."[47] In fact, the seller knew that the gun had been made by a different gun-maker and was "a very bad, unsafe, ill-manufactured, and dangerous gun, wholly unsound and of very inferior materials."[48] Since the son had not been a party to the contract for the sale of the gun and since the gun was not inherently dangerous, the Court of Exchequer rejected liability based on the warranty as a contract. The court feared, as had the court in *Winterbottom v. Wright*, that permitting anyone to recover whenever a duty was imposed by contract would lead to an "indefinite extent of liability."[49] Instead, the court based its finding of the seller's liability for the son's injuries on fraud: the seller knowingly made a false statement that a product was safe in order to induce a sale; the person to whom the false statement was made relied upon it in purchasing and using the product; and the person injured was the person to whom the false statement was made or a person within the seller's contemplation at the time of the sale.[50] These elements later became the basis for the independent theory of fraudulent misrepresentation.

§ 1.03 THE RISE OF NEGLIGENCE

Just as changing views about the nature of the market place led to the decline of the doctrine of *caveat emptor*, social and economic changes in the United States during the first half of the twentieth century resulted in the rejection of the privity limitations in negligence cases and led, ultimately, to the creation of a new theory of strict liability in products liability cases. Scholars have posited a number of forces that were responsible for these changes: increasing governmental control and responsibility for the welfare of the individual; increasing mechanization and the growing complexity of product design; the rise of the welfare state; increasing urbanization; a policy of "internalizing" costs to achieve an efficient level of manufacturing operations; the gradual evolution of the fault system; and the rise of the theory of enterprise liability.[51] The first tangible effect these changing views had on products liability law came in 1916 when Judge Benjamin Cardozo, writing for the New York Court of Appeals in *MacPherson v. Buick Motor Co.*,[52] rejected the privity rule in negligence cases.

---

[47] *Id.*

[48] *Id.*

[49] *Id.* at 530.

[50] *Id.* at 531–32.

[51] For a discussion of these factors, see George L. Priest, *The Invention of Enterprise Liability: A Critical History of the Intellectual Foundations of Modern Tort Law*, 14 J. LEGAL STUD. 461 (1985). Priest takes the position that modern product liability law is the result of the enterprise theory which provides that "business enterprises ought to be responsible for losses resulting from products they introduce into commerce." *Id.* at 463.

[52] 111 N.E. 1050 (N.Y. 1916). For a discussion of the case, see James Henderson, MacPherson v. Buick Motor Co.: *Simplifying the Facts While Reshaping the Law*, in ROBERT L. RABIN & STEPHEN D. SUGARMAN (EDS.), TORT STORIES 41 (2003).

[A] The Fall of Privity

In *MacPherson*, the defendant, an automobile manufacturer, sold an automobile to a retail dealer who resold it to the plaintiff. One of the wheels on the automobile was made of defective wood and, when its spokes suddenly collapsed while the plaintiff was driving the automobile, he was injured. The wheel had been manufactured by another company and purchased by the defendant for incorporation into the automobile. In a negligence action brought by the plaintiff, the question for the court was whether the automobile manufacturer owed a duty of care to anyone except the immediate purchaser (the retail dealer) of the automobile. Since the manufacturer did not know of the defect in the wheel and conceal it, and since there was no evidence that the defect could have been discovered by ordinary inspection, the case did not fall into the exceptions to the privity rule of *Huset v. J. I. Case Threshing Machine Co.* and *Kuelling v. Roderick Lean Manufacturing Co.*

The manufacturer in *MacPherson* argued that, since an automobile is not an "inherently" dangerous product, it was not liable to a third party in "simple negligence."[53] In deciding whether the manufacturer owed a duty of care to anyone except the immediate purchaser, Judge Cardozo began by analyzing the exceptions to the privity rule set out in *Thomas v. Winchester.* However, rather than simply adding automobiles to the growing list of exceptions to the privity rule based on "inherently" dangerous products, Judge Cardozo "buried the general rule under the exception."[54] Judge Cardozo concluded:

> We hold . . . that the principle of Thomas v. Winchester is not limited to poisons, explosives, and things of like nature, to things which in their normal operation are implements of destruction. If the nature of a thing is such that it is reasonably certain to place life and limb in period when negligently made, it is then a thing of danger. Its nature gives warning of the consequences to be expected. If to the element of danger there is added knowledge that the thing will be used by persons other than the purchaser, and used without new tests, then, irrespective of contract, the manufacturer of this thing of danger is under a duty to make it carefully.[55]

In his opinion, Judge Cardozo emphasized that the case dealt with the liability of a manufacturer of a finished product who puts it on the market knowing that it will be used without inspection by its customers. For Judge Cardozo, a manufacturer's duty to third parties in such a situation required a showing of the foreseeability of harm. That meant that the manufacturer had to have knowledge of a danger posed by the product and had to know that the danger was probable, not merely possible. Foreseeability also required that the manufacturer must know that, in the usual course of things, the danger would not be limited to the immediate buyer of the product. In keeping with proximate cause as a limit on liability in negligence cases, Judge Cardozo held that the proximity or remoteness of the relationship between

---

[53] *Id.* at 383.

[54] William L. Prosser, *The Assault Upon the Citadel (Strict Liability to the Consumer)*, 69 YALE L.J. 1099, 1100 (1960).

[55] MacPherson v. Buick Motor Co., 111 N.E. 1050, 1053 (N.Y. 1916).

the manufacturer and the person injured by the product was a factor for the jury's consideration.[56]

The discussion of foreseeability and proximate cause was not simply part of a redefinition of what constituted "a thing of danger" for purposes of broadening *Thomas v. Winchester.* Judge Cardozo concluded his opinion by stating that he had severed the tie of negligence to contract law in products liability cases. "We have put aside the notion that the duty to safeguard life and limb, whenever consequences of negligence may be foreseen, grows out of contract and nothing else. We have put the source of obligation where it ought to be. We have put its source in the law."[57]

Applying his negligence analysis to the facts in *MacPherson*, Judge Cardozo held that the nature of automobiles is such that probable danger is foreseeable if they are constructed defectively. Since the automobile in the case "was designed to go fifty miles an hour," injury was almost certain to happen if the wheels were defective. The manufacturer knew of that danger and also knew that the automobile would be used by persons other than the immediate buyer, an automobile dealer who bought it for resale. Proximate cause did not limit the manufacturer's liability since, according to Judge Cardozo, the dealer was the person least likely to use the automobile.[58] Finally, Judge Cardozo refused to hold that the automobile manufacturer was not liable because it had purchased the wheels from a reputable component-part manufacturer. Since the defendant was a manufacturer of automobiles, it was responsible for the finished product and had a duty to subject the component parts to ordinary testing.[59]

[B]　The Adoption of Negligence

MacPherson did not mean the immediate end to the privity requirement in negligence cases. Although in 1946 the Massachusetts Supreme Judicial Court stated that "[t]he doctrine of the *MacPherson* case is now generally accepted,"[60] some state courts did not eliminate entirely the privity requirement in negligence actions until later.[61] However, *MacPherson* began the development of what now is the modern law of negligence in products liability cases.[62] Beginning in the 1920s, the theory of negligence expanded to apply to manufacturers of component parts[63] to include property damage,[64] and to give a right of action to bystanders[65] and

---

[56] *Id.*

[57] *Id.*

[58] *Id.*

[59] *Id.* at 1055.

[60] Carter v. Yardley & Co., 64 N.E.2d 693, 700 (Mass. 1946).

[61] The Illinois Supreme Court, for example, waited until 1965 to abolish privity entirely in negligence suits. *See* Suvada v. White Motor Co., 210 N.E.2d 182 (Ill. 1965). Maine did not abolish privity in products liability cases until 1982. *See* Adams v. Buffalo Forge Co., 443 A.2d 932 (Me. 1982).

[62] *See* FOWLER V. HARPER, A TREATISE ON THE LAW OF TORTS, § 106 (1933).

[63] Smith v. Peerless Glass Co., 181 N.E. 576 (N.Y. 1932).

[64] Marsh Wood Products Co. v. Babcock & Wilcox Co., 240 N.W. 392 (Wis. 1932).

[65] McLeod v. Linde Air Products Co., 1 S.W.2d 122 (Mo. 1927).

other non-purchasers.[66]

The influence of *MacPherson* also can be seen in the Restatement of the Law of Torts, adopted by the American Law Institute in 1934. Chapter 14 of the Restatement was devoted to the "Liability of Persons Supplying Chattels for the Use of Others." Section 388, which was entitled "Chattel Known to be Dangerous for Intended Use," drew upon the language of *MacPherson* and applied negligence to "one who supplies directly or through a third person a chattel for another to use." Such suppliers were liable for bodily harm if they knew or should have known that the chattel was likely to be "dangerous for the use for which it was supplied;" did not have any reason to believe that the user of the product would realize the dangerous condition; and failed to use "reasonable care" to inform the user of the dangerous condition. Other sections dealt specifically with manufacturers and held them liable for a "Chattel Known to be Dangerous"[67] and for the "Negligent Manufacture of Chattel; Dangerous Unless Carefully Made."[68] Although liability was limited to products that posed "an unreasonable risk of causing substantial bodily harm," in those situations liability was not limited by privity and extended liability to "those who lawfully use [the product] for a purpose for which it is manufactured and to those whom the supplier should expect to be in the vicinity of its probable use."[69] Retailers also had a duty to take reasonable steps to prevent injury from a known danger in the products they sold when they should know that the danger was likely to pass unnoticed to the buyer or others likely to use the product.[70] By the late 1950s, the influence of the Restatement sections was such that the "Liability of Suppliers of Chattels" based on negligence had become an all but universal part of tort law.[71] The acceptance of negligence as a theory of recovery in products liability and the influence of the sections of Chapter 14 is reflected in the fact that they were retained in the Restatement (Second) of Torts, adopted by the American Law Institute in 1964.

[C] *Res Ipsa Loquitur*

With the elimination of the privity requirement in products liability actions based upon negligence, a plaintiff had to show that the manufacturer or seller owed a duty of reasonable care in connection with the manufacture or sale product, that the manufacturer or seller breached that duty, and that the injuries that resulted were caused by the breach of the duty. The principal difficulty with a negligence action, however, is that the plaintiff has the burden of pleading and proving how the manufacturer or seller breached the duty. The plaintiff must show both that the product was defective and that the manufacturer or seller failed to exercise reasonable care in its manufacture or sale. In some cases, the defect may not be

---

[66] Reed & Barton Corp. v. Maas, 73 F.2d 359 (1st Cir. 1934) (applying Wisconsin law).

[67] RESTATEMENT OF THE LAW OF TORTS, § 394 (1934).

[68] *Id.* at § 395.

[69] *Id.*

[70] *Id.* at § 399.

[71] *See* 2 FOWLER V. HARPER & FLEMING JAMES, JR., THE LAW OF TORTS, §§ 28.1–28.14 (1956); WILLIAM L. PROSSER, HANDBOOK OF THE LAW OF TORTS, § 84 (2d ed. 1955).

the result of any negligence. In other cases, the plaintiff may not know the specific circumstances that led to the injury or who was responsible for the defect.

In order to overcome the hurdle of establishing a *prima facie* case in such situations, some courts turned to the evidentiary rule of *res ipsa loquitur.* In *Escola v. Coca Cola Bottling Co.*,[72] a waitress suffered severe injuries when a soft drink bottle broke in her hand while she was restocking the restaurant's refrigerator. In her suit against the company that bottled and delivered the defective bottle to her employer, she claimed that the company had been negligent in selling "bottles containing said beverage which on account of excessive pressure of gas or by reason of some defect in the bottle was dangerous . . . and likely to explode."[73] However, since the waitress could not prove any specific acts of negligence on the part of the bottling company, she relied on the rule of *res ipsa loquitur.* The company alleged that the rule did not apply, since exclusive control of the item causing the injury is an essential element of *res ipsa loquitur* and, in this case, the bottle had been out of its control for some time.[74] The California Supreme Court, however, held that it was not necessary for the plaintiff to eliminate every remote possibility of injury after the bottle left the defendant's control. It was sufficient if there was evidence "permitting a reasonable inference that it was not accessible to extraneous forces and that it was carefully handled by plaintiff or any third person who may have touched it."[75] In *Escola*, the court held that the record supported an inference that the bottle had not been damaged by any extraneous force after the defendant had delivered it to the restaurant. Thus, the bottle had to have been defective at the time it left the defendant's control.

§ 1.04   FROM NEGLIGENCE TO STRICT LIABILITY

With the growing acceptance of negligence as a basis of products liability actions, the first arguments were made during the 1940s and 1950s for a new theory of liability that would go beyond negligence and based liability not on the conduct of the manufacturer but on the condition of the product.[76] While warranties already provided such a basis of liability in contract law, warranties still were limited by the privity requirement.[77] In the 20 years preceding the American Law Institute's adoption in 1965 of § 402A of the Restatement (Second) of Torts, a series of decisions and law review articles laid the ground work for strict liability by proposing new bases for liability and modifying existing ones.[78]

---

[72] 150 P.2d 436 (Cal. 1944). For a discussion of the case, see Mark Geistfeld, Escola v. Coca Bottling Co.: *Strict Products Liability Unbound*, in Robert & Stephen D. Sugarman (Eds.), Torts Stories 229 (2003).

[73] 150 P.2d at 437.

[74] *Id.* at 438.

[75] *Id.* at 439.

[76] For articles by Fleming James, Leon Green, Marcus Plant, and Noel Dix dealing, from differing points of view, with the question whether manufacturers should be held strictly liable, see 24 Tenn. L. Rev. 923, 923–18 (1957).

[77] *See* Fleming James, *Products Liability*, 34 Tex. L. Rev. 192 (1955).

[78] For a discussion of the evolution of strict liability theory from the 1930s to the 1960s, see George

[A] The Theory Behind Strict Liability

The first articulation of a rationale for a tort theory of strict liability in products liability cases came in 1944 in *Escola v. Coca Cola Bottling Co.*[79] The real significance of that decision is not its extension of *res ipsa loquitur* to situations in which the plaintiff was able to negate the possibility that the injury might have been caused by the negligence of some intervening party. Instead, its importance lies in Justice Roger Traynor's concurring opinion. He took a position that was not argued by any of the parties: liability should be grounded in absolute liability. According to Justice Traynor: "In my opinion it should now be recognized that a manufacturer incurs an absolute liability when an article that he has placed on the market, knowing that it is to be used without inspection, proves to have a defect that causes injury to human beings."[80] Justice Traynor based his support for absolute liability not on "inherent dangers" or the consumer expectations that had marked the decline of *caveat emptor* and privity but on enterprise liability, the idea that business should be liable for the inevitable injuries that resulted from its activities. More specifically, Justice Traynor offered three rationales for absolute liability. First, he stated that it would provide an incentive for manufacturers to produce safer products and minimize the losses to society from those products.

> Even if there is no negligence, . . . public policy demands that responsibility be fixed wherever it will most effectively reduce the hazards to life and health inherent in defective products that reach the market. It is evident that the manufacturer can anticipate some hazards and guard against the recurrence of others, as the public cannot.[81] Secondly, Justice Traynor felt that the manufacturer was better able than the consumer to absorb or pass on the costs from the inevitable losses that result from defective products. Those who suffer injury from defective products are unprepared to meet its consequences. The cost of an injury or loss of time or health may be an overwhelming misfortune to the person injured, and a needless one, for the risk of injury can be insured by the manufacturer and distributed among the public as a cost of doing business. It is to the public interest to discourage the marketing of products having defects that are a menace to the public.[82]

Finally, Justice Traynor saw absolute liability as a means to eliminate the problems of proof that confronted plaintiffs in negligence actions. "An injured person . . . is not ordinarily in a position to refuse [a showing of proper care] or identify the cause of the defect, for he can hardly be familiar with the manufacturing process as the manufacturer himself is."[83]

L. Priest, *The Invention of Enterprise Liability: A Critical History of the Intellectual Foundations of Modern Tort Law*, 14 J. LEGAL STUD. 461 (1985).

[79] 150 P.2d 436 (Cal. 1944).

[80] *Id.* at 440.

[81] *Id.* at 440–41.

[82] *Id.* at 441.

[83] *Id.*

Although Justice Traynor's concurring opinion later would provide a major rationale for the adoption of strict liability in products liability cases, it received little attention at the time and he had to wait almost 20 years for his position to be accepted. However, the 1950s and early 1960s saw an increased interest in strict liability in general and products liability in particular. The two most prolific advocates of strict liability during those decades were Professors Fleming James and William Prosser. However, they took different views as to what the basis of strict liability should be. Professor James advocated a system of "strict enterprise liability" that would help reduce the number of accidents resulting from defective products and administer the losses from such accidents in a way that would minimize their individual and social costs.[84] While Professor James felt that traditional negligence and warranty were not equipped to meet the modern challenges presented by accidents from defective products and should be abandoned, he took the position that courts could develop a new warranty theory for products liability cases "which is tailored to meet modern needs in that field."[85] In contrast, Professor Prosser, in his two influential articles, *The Assault Upon the Citadel*[86] in 1960 and *The Fall of the Citadel*[87] in 1966, analyzed the entire area of products liability law and urged: "If there is going to be strict liability in tort, let there be strict liability in tort, declared outright, without an illusory contract mask."[88] Although Professor James' warranty theory, "tailored to meet modern needs," initially was the victor in the competition for a new approach to products liability, the ultimate winner was the tort strict liability theory of Professor Prosser.

[B] "The Fall of the Citadel of Privity"

Despite the abolition of the privity requirement for products liability actions brought in negligence, courts continued to hold that actions for breach of warranty were contract actions and thus could be brought only by the party to the contract.[89] As with the earlier privity requirement in negligence, there was an exception in food cases. Parties who were not in privity to the manufacturer could bring an action against the manufacturer on the ground that the implied warranty ran with the sale of the food.[90] According to the Texas Supreme Court, the reason

---

[84] Fleming James, *General Products — Should Manufacturers Be Liable Without Negligence?* 24 Tenn. L. Rev. 923 (1957).

[85] Fleming James, *Products Liability*, 34 Tex. L. Rev. 192, 228 (1955).

[86] William Prosser, *The Assault Upon the Citadel (Strict Liability to the Consumer)*, 69 Yale L.J. 1099 (1960).

[87] William Prosser, *The Fall of the Citadel (Strict Liability to the Consumer)*, 50 Minn. L. Rev. 791 (1966).

[88] William Prosser, *The Assault Upon the Citadel (Strict Liability to the Consumer)*, 69 Yale L.J. 1099, 1134 (1960).

[89] Paul Harris Furniture Co. v. Morse, 139 N.E.2d 275 (Ill. 1956). *See* Fowler Harper & Fleming James, The Law of Torts, § 28.16 (1956).

[90] In Ward v. Morehead City Sea Food Co., 87 S.E. 958 (N.C. 1916), the North Carolina supreme court held that a packer was liable in negligence in packing fish it knew were unfit for human consumption. The court based its finding of negligence on a violation of state statutes making it a crime to sell adulterated food. *See* Mazetti v. Armour & Co., 135 P. 633 (Wash. 1913) and William Prosser, *The Assault Upon the Citadel*, 69 Yale L.J. 1099 (1960).

for that was that "the liability of the manufacturer and vendor [of food] is imposed by operation of law as a matter of public policy for the protection of the public, and is not dependent on any provision of the contract, either expressed or implied."[91]

Just as *MacPherson v. Buick Motor Co.* eliminated privity in negligence cases, "[t]he fall of the citadel of privity"[92] in warranty actions came in 1960 when the New Jersey Supreme Court decided *Henningsen v. Bloomfield Motors*.[93] Based upon an implied warranty of fitness, the court extended protection of that warranty to the "ultimate purchaser" and to other foreseeable users of the product. In *Henningsen*, a husband purchased a new automobile manufactured by Chrysler and sold by Bloomfield Motors, an automobile dealership. The husband gave the automobile to his wife as a gift and, while driving it, she was injured when a defect in the steering mechanism caused the automobile to crash into a wall. The husband and wife brought suit against the manufacturer and dealer of the automobile. Their complaint was based upon breach of express and implied warranties and upon negligence. At the trial, the judge dismissed the negligence counts and the case was submitted to the jury solely on the issue of breach of implied warranty of merchantability. The jury returned a verdict for the plaintiffs against both defendants.

The problem for the plaintiffs was the sales contract for the automobile signed by the husband. It contained, in eight-and-a-half inches of fine print on the back of the contract, a "warranty" provision that limited the manufacturer's liability to replacing defective parts within 90 days of the sale or until the car had been driven 4000 miles, whichever came first, if the part was shipped, at the buyer's expense, to the manufacturer's factory and an examination revealed that the part was defective. The provision also stated that the repair warranty was "expressly in lieu of all other warranties expressed or implied, and all other obligations or liabilities" on the part of the manufacturer. That language not only disclaimed all implied warranties, it barred all claims for consequential damages for personal injury resulting from a defect in the automobile.[94]

Writing for a unanimous New Jersey Supreme Court, Judge Francis reviewed the history and rationale for warranties and the privity doctrine and the limited exceptions to the privity requirement, beginning with food.[95] However, he then stated that there was "no rational doctrinal basis" for distinguishing between a defective bottle of a beverage and a defective automobile.[96] While a defective beverage could make a person sick, a defective automobile had an even greater potential to cause harm. Under modern methods of manufacturing and marketing, the ordinary purchaser has no opportunity or ability to inspect an automobile to determine its fitness. Thus, the court felt that the remedies in such a situation

---

[91] Decker & Sons v. Capps, 164 S.W.2d 828, 831–32 (Tex. 1942).

[92] William Prosser, *The Fall of the Citadel (Strict Liability to the Consumer)*, 50 MINN. L. REV. 791 (1966).

[93] 161 A.2d 69 (1960).

[94] *Id.* at 74.

[95] *Id.* at 80–81.

[96] *Id.* at 83.

should not depend "upon the intricacies of the law of sales" or be based solely on privity of contract. Instead, they should rest on "the demands of social justice."[97] The court then held that, "under modern marketing conditions, when a manufacturer puts a new automobile in the stream of trade and promotes its purchase by the public, an implied warranty that it is reasonably suitable for use as such accompanies it into the hands of the ultimate purchaser."[98] The court concluded by taking one more giant step when it stated the implied warranty of merchantability extended not only to the "ultimate purchaser" of the automobile but also to members of his family, and to other persons occupying or using it with his consent. It would be wholly opposed to reality to say that use by such persons is not within the anticipation of the parties to such a warranty of reasonable suitability of an automobile for ordinary highway operation. Those persons must be considered within the distributive chain.[99]

Although *Henningsen* involved a defective automobile, personal injury, and what the New Jersey Supreme Court considered an extremely unfair standard form sales contract, the effect of the decision was not limited to its facts. By invalidating the disclaimer of liability for injuries in the standard form sales contract provided by the manufacturer, the court eliminated the ability of manufacturers to use the most important limitations of contract law — disclaimers and privity — to restrict their liability for personal injuries. In addition, since recovery did not depend upon proof of negligence or knowledge of any defect, courts were well on their way toward strict liability. Although *Henningsen* did not use the term "absolute liability" or "strict liability," it articulated the rationale upon which the transition from warranty to strict liability ultimately would be made.

[C] The Triumph of Strict Liability in Tort

The final steps toward the development of a tort theory of strict liability in products liability cases began in 1963 in the California Supreme Court decision of *Greenman v. Yuba Power Products.*[100] In *Greenman,* a woman purchased a combination power tool that could be used as a saw, drill, and lathe and gave it to her husband for Christmas as a present for his home workshop. Two years later, he bought an attachment to use the machine as a lathe. While using it as a lathe, a piece of wood flew out of it and struck the husband on the forehead, causing serious injury. About 10-and-a-half months later, he gave the retailer and manufacturer written notice of a claim for breach of warranty and filed a suit for breach of warranty and negligence.

The plaintiff introduced evidence that the saw had been defectively designed and manufactured by the defendant. The jury returned a verdict for the plaintiff after it concluded that the manufacturer was negligent and that the statements in the manufacturer's brochure constituted an express warranty. On appeal, the

---

[97] *Id.*

[98] *Id.* at 84.

[99] *Id.* at 100.

[100] 377 P.2d 897 (Cal. 1963). For an analysis of Justice Roger Traynor's opinion, see RICHARD A. EPSTEIN, MODERN PRODUCTS LIABILITY LAW 36–48 (1980).

manufacturer argued that the plaintiff did not give notice of the breach of warranty within a reasonable time and that the claim was barred by the Civil Code. However, Justice Roger Traynor, writing for a unanimous court, rejected the "timely notice" argument, stating that the notice provision was not "an appropriate one for the court to adopt in actions by injured consumers against manufacturers with whom they have not dealt."[101]

As in his concurring opinion in *Escola* 19 years earlier, Justice Traynor did not limit his analysis to the theories put forth by the plaintiff. Instead, he used the case as the opportunity to impose liability based on strict liability. According to Justice Traynor: "A manufacturer is strictly liable in tort when an article he places on the market, knowing that it is to be used without inspection for defects, proves to have a defect that causes injury to a human being."[102] After listing a variety of situations, beginning with food, in which strict liability long had been applied by the courts because of the hazard posed by the product if it was defective, Justice Traynor stated:

> Although in these cases strict liability usually has been based on the theory of an express or implied warranty running from the manufacturer to the plaintiff, the abandonment of the requirement of a contract between them, the recognition that the liability is not assumed by agreement but imposed by law . . . , and the refusal to permit the manufacturer to define the scope of its own responsibility for defective products . . . makes clear that the liability is not one governed by the law of contract warranties but by the law of strict liability in tort. Accordingly, the rules defining and governing warranties that were developed to meet the needs of commercial transactions cannot properly be invoked to govern the manufacturer's liability to those injured by its defective products unless those rules also serve the purposes for which such liability is imposed.[103]

Although Justice Traynor referred to Harper and James' treatise on torts, Prosser's law review articles, and to his own concurring opinion in *Escola* to provide support for his reasons for imposing strict liability, his opinion was a triumph of the enterprise liability theory. According to Justice Traynor, the purpose of strict liability is "to insure that the costs of injuries resulting from defective products are borne by the manufacturers that put such products on the market rather than by the injured persons who are powerless to protect themselves."[104] Since strict liability based upon "the intricacies of the law of sales" did not fully achieve that goal, it was necessary to develop a new theory based upon strict liability in tort. Under that new theory, it was sufficient for the plaintiff to prove that "he was injured while using the [power tool] in a way it was intended to be used as a result of a defect in design and manufacture of which plaintiff was not aware that made the [power tool] unsafe for its intended use."[105]

---

[101] *Id.* at 900.

[102] *Id.*

[103] *Id.* at 901.

[104] *Id.*

[105] *Id.*

The year after it held manufacturers strictly liable in *Greenman*, the California Supreme Court, in an opinion written by Justice Traynor, applied strict liability to retailers in *Vandermark v. Ford Motor Co.*[106] The court justified its extension of strict liability to include retailers on a number of business, safety, and economic grounds:

> Retailers like manufacturers are engaged in the business of distributing goods to the public. They are an integral part of the overall producing and marketing enterprise that should bear the cost of injuries resulting from defective products. . . . In some cases the retailer may be the only member of the enterprise reasonably available to the injured plaintiff. In other cases the retailer himself may play a substantial part in insuring that the product is safe or may be in a position to exert pressure on the manufacturer to that end; the retailer's strict liability thus serves as an added incentive to safety. Strict liability on the manufacturer and retailer alike affords maximum protection to the injured plaintiff and works no injustice to the defendants, for they can adjust the costs of such protection between them in the course of their continuing relationship.[107]

§ 1.05 THE RESTATEMENTS

The decision in *Greenman* was followed two years later (1965) by the ALI's statement of a general principle of strict liability in § 402A of the Restatement (Second) of Torts. That section, which was the work of Professor William Prosser who served as the Reporter for the entire Restatement (Second) of Torts, provides:

(1) One who sells any product in a defective condition unreasonably dangerous to the user or consumer or to his property is subject to liability for physical harm thereby caused to the ultimate user or consumer, or to his property, if

    (a) the seller is engaged in the business of selling such a product, and

    (b) it is expected to and does reach the user or consumer without substantial change in the condition in which it is sold.

Liability under § 402A does not require any showing of fault on the part of the manufacturer or seller, nor does it require any contractual or privity relationship between the consumer and the seller. Instead, liability is "strict" — the seller is liable even though it used reasonable care in the preparation and sale of the product to prevent harm.

Although § 402A makes a significant break with negligence, the drafters were unable to reach agreement on three questions: (1) Whether strict liability applies to persons other than users or consumers (i.e. bystanders); (2) whether it applies to a product, such as raw materials, that the seller expected to change substantially before it reaches the consumer; and (3) whether component part manufacturers are strictly liable. These questions would have to be answered by the courts.

---

[106] 391 P.2d 168 (Cal. 1964).

[107] *Id.* at 262–63.

Although § 402A is part of the "restatement" of torts, only California had adopted strict tort liability for defective products at the time the section was approved by the ALI. Thus, rather than a "restatement" of existing law, the section was a statement of what Professor Prosser felt the law should be in the hope that courts would move in that direction. Strict liability under § 402A differs from a negligence or warranty in that it does not require any fault by the manufacturer of the product (*see* § 402A(2)(a)), any representation about the product by the seller, or any reliance by the buyer on the skill or judgment of the seller (§ 402A(2)(b)). Since § 402A does not depend upon a contract, it is not affected by the specific requirements of a warranty, such as notice or disclaimers of privity. However, § 402A does not make the seller an insurer of the consumer's safety. Instead of absolute liability, it adopts a system of liability that does not require negligence or a warranty.

In the decades following the publication of § 402A by the ALI, almost every state adopted strict liability in tort, either in the form of § 402A or some judicial or legislative variation of it. At the present time (2012), only five states — Delaware, Massachusetts, Michigan, North Carolina, and Virginia — do not have strict tort liability in products liability cases.[108] However, § 402A is a product of the 1960s and, like many other innovations of that decade, its effects continue to be felt in American society after almost 50 years. As the twentieth century drew to an end, the ALI attempted to move products liability law in a new direction by replacing § 402A with the Restatement (Third) of Torts: Products Liability (the "Restatement (Third)"). However, unlike § 402A, which covers strict liability in a single section, the Restatement (Third) consists of 21 sections. These sections are both a traditional "restatement" of what courts have done since the adoption of § 402A and a change in some areas of strict liability in the law. Unlike § 402A, the sections of the Restatement (Third) address almost every aspect of products liability law:

- the liability of a commercial seller or distributor for harm caused by defective products (§ 1);

- the categories of product defects (§ 2);

- circumstantial evidence supporting an inference of a product defect (§ 3);

- noncompliance and compliance with product safety statutes and regulations (§ 4);

- the liability of a commercial seller or distributor of product components for harm caused by products into which the components are integrated (§ 5);

- the liability of a commercial seller or distributor for harm caused by defective prescription drugs and medical devices (§ 6);

- the liability of a commercial seller or distributor for harm caused by defective food products (§ 7);

---

[108] However, the Massachusetts Supreme Judicial Court has held that its state legislature has decided that implied warranty "should establish liability as comprehensive as that to be found in other jurisdictions that have adopted the tort of strict product liability." Commonwealth v. Johnson Insulation, 425 Mass. 650, 653, 682 N.E.2d 1323, 1326 (Mass. 1997). *See* Hatch v. Trail King Indus., Inc., 656 F.3d 59 (1st Cir. 2011) (applying Massachusetts law).

- the liability of a commercial seller or distributor for defective used products (§ 8);

- the liability of a commercial product seller or distributor for harm caused by misrepresentation (§ 9);

- the liability of a commercial product seller or distributor for harm caused by a post-sale failure to warn (§ 10);

- the liability of a commercial product seller or distributor for harm caused by a post-sale failure to recall a product (§ 11);

- the liability of successor for harm caused by defective products sold commercially by a predecessor (§ 12);

- the liability of a successor for harm caused by the successor's own post-sale failure to warn (§ 13);

- selling or distributing as one's own a product manufactured by another (§ 14);

- general rule governing the causal connection between a product defect and harm (§ 15);

- increased harm due to a product defect (§ 16);

- apportionment of responsibility between or among the plaintiff, sellers, and distributors of defective products, and others (§ 17);

- disclaimers, limitations, waivers, and other contractual exculpations as defenses to products liability claims for harm to persons (§ 18);

- the definition of a "product" (§ 19);

- the definition of "one who sells or otherwise distributes" (§ 20);

- the definition of "harm to persons or property": recovery for economic loss (§ 21).

Since its publication by the ALI in 1998, the Restatement (Third) has generated widespread discussion in the literature and by courts.[109] Sections of the Restatement (Third) have been cited or quoted by state and federal courts in more than 35 states,[110] the District of Columbia,[111] and by the United States Supreme Court.[112] However, because the Restatement (Third) is much more complex than § 402A, no

---

[109] The articles discussing whether states should adopt the RESTATEMENT (THIRD) include *Who's Afraid of the Restatement (Third) of Torts?* WIS. L.J. Sept. 17, 2010, *available at* wislawjournal.com/2010/09/17/whos-afraid-of-the-restatement-third-of-torts/; Erin L. Ginsberg, *Revisiting Restatement Second or Third? The Uncertain Status of Product Liability Law in Pennsylvania,* PA. BAR ASSOC. Q./Oct. 2010, 139; Robert S. Stevens, *The Restatement (Third) of Products Liability: Is It a Reasonable Alternative Design to Tennessee's Products Liability Statute?* 39 U. MEM. L. REV. 463 (2009); Matthew R. Sorenson, *A Reasonable Alternative? Should Wyoming Adopt the Restatement (Third) of Torts: Products Liability?* 3 WYO. L. REV. 257 (2002); Robert D. Klein, *A Comparison of the Restatement (Third) of Torts: Products Liability and the Maryland Law of Products Liability,* 30 U. BALT. L. REV. 273 (2001); Thomas V. Van Flein, *Prospective Application of the Restatement (Third) of Torts: Products Liability in Alaska,* 17 ALASKA L. REV. 1 (2000).

[110] For examples, *see* Ex parte Chevron Chemical Co., 720 So. 2d 922, 928 (Ala. 1998); Bell v.

court has adopted or rejected it entirely. Instead, some state supreme courts have adopted one or more sections of the Restatement (Third),[113] while some of those same states and other states have rejected other sections of the Restatement.[114]

§ 1.06 THE CHOICE OF THEORIES IN A PRODUCTS LIABILITY CASE

In most states, plaintiffs can choose from a number of different theories in framing their products liability claims: express and implied warranty; intentional, negligent, or innocent misrepresentation; negligence; and strict liability.[115] Which theory or theories a plaintiff chooses depends upon the facts of each case, including any statements made by the seller, the difficulty and expense of proof, the relationship between the injured party and the manufacturer or seller, the type of damages sought, anticipated defenses, and the statute of limitations and repose. The choice also is determined by the differences among the states in the requirements for the particular theories, by who bears the burden of proof on particular issues, and by the tests for determining whether the product was defective.

Mention also must be made of the approach taken by 10 states — Alabama,[116] Colorado,[117] Connecticut,[118] Indiana,[119] Kansas,[120] Louisiana,[121] Mississippi,[122]

Precision Airmotive Corp., 42 P.3d 1071 (Alaska 2002); Freeman v. Hoffman-La Roche, Inc., 618 N.W.2d 827, 843 (Neb. 2000).

[111] Weakley v. Burnham Corp., 871 A.2d 1167, 1177 (D.C. 2005).

[112] Geier v. American Honda Motor Co., 529 U.S. 861 (2000).

[113] See Wright v. Brooke Group, Ltd., 652 N.W.2d 159 (Iowa 2002), in which the Iowa Supreme Court adopted §§ 1 and 2 of the RESTATEMENT (THIRD).

[114] See Mikolajczyk v. Ford Motor Co., 231 Ill. 2d 516, 901 N.E.2d 329 (Ill. 2008), in which the Illinois Supreme Court refused to adopt § 2(b) of the RESTATEMENT (THIRD).

[115] See Carpenter v. Victoria's Secret Stores, LLC, 2012 U.S. Dist. LEXIS 45314 (W.D. Tenn. Mar. 31, 2012) (applying Mississippi law) (plaintiff brought suit in strict liability, negligence, breach of express and implied warranties, and negligent misrepresentation); Miles v. Desa Heating LLC, 2012 U.S. Dist. LEXIS 45433 (D.S.C. Mar. 27, 2012) (plaintiff brought suit in negligence, strict liability, and for breach of express and implied warranties).

[116] Alabama Extended Manufacturer's Liability Doctrine (AEMLD), ALA. CODE § 6-5-500 et seq. See Casrell v. Altec Indus., Inc., 335 So. 2d 128 (Ala. 1976); Atkins v. American Motors Corp., 335 So. 2d 134 (Ala. 1976).

[117] Colorado Product Liability Act, COLO. REV. STAT. § 13-21-401 et seq.

[118] Connecticut Products Liability Act, CONN. GEN. STAT. §§ 52-240a, 52-240b, 52-572m-52-572q, 52-577a. For an analysis of the Act, see JAMES H. ROTONDO & PAUL D. WILLIAMS, CONNECTICUT PRODUCT LIABILITY LAW (1998).

[119] Indiana Product Liability Act, IND. CODE ANN. § 34-20-1-1 et seq.

[120] Kansas Product Liability Act, KAN. STAT. ANN. § 60-3301 et seq. For a discussion of the policy rationales underlying the Act, see Gaumer v. Rossville Truck and Tractor Co., Inc., 257 P.3d 292, 303–05 (Kan. 2011).

[121] Louisiana Products Liability Act, LA. REV. STAT. ANN. § 9:2800.51 et seq. See Matthews v. Remington Arms Co., 641 F.3d 635 (5th Cir. 2011) (applying Louisiana law); Hutto v. McNeil-PPC, Inc., 79 So. 3d 1199 (La. Ct. App. 2011).

[122] Mississippi Product Liability Act, MISS. CODE ANN. § 11-1-63. See Williams v. Bennett, 921 So. 2d

New Jersey,[123] Ohio,[124] Tennessee,[125] Utah,[126] and Washington[127] — that have enacted product liability acts. Many of these statutes provide the exclusive remedy for claims based on warranty, negligence, and strict liability and preclude common law claims for harm caused by a defective product.[128] An example of these statutes is the Kansas Product Liability Act ("KPLA"),[129] which is based on the Model Uniform Product Liability Act ("Model Act").[130] The purpose both of the Model Act and the KPLA is "to consolidate all products liability actions, regardless of theory into one theory of legal liability."[131] In order to achieve this goal, the KPLA covers both "product sellers" and "manufacturers."[132] It defines a "product liability claim" as "any claim or action brought for harm caused by the manufacture, production, making, construction, fabrication, design, formula, preparation, assembly, installation, testing, warnings, instructions, marketing, packaging, storage or labeling of the relevant product."[133] The KPLA applies to every "product liability claim" regardless of the substantive theory of recovery. This includes, but is not limited to "any action based on strict liability in tort, negligence, breach of express or implied warranty, breach of, or failure to, discharge a duty to warn or instruct, whether negligent or innocent, misrepresentation, concealment or nondisclosure, whether negligent or innocent, or under any other substantive legal theory."[134] The comprehensiveness of the KPLA is illustrated further by the fact that it applies to every "product seller," a term that is defined as "any person or entity that is engaged in the business of selling products, whether the sale is for resale, or for use or consumption. The term includes a manufacturer, wholesaler, distributor or retailer of the relevant product."[135] Finally, the KPLA defines "harm" to include

---

1269 (Miss. 2006), for a discussion of the history of the statute, the basic framework for claims, and proof requirements.

[123] Products Liability Act, N.J. Stat. Ann. § 2A:58C-1 *et seq.* *See* Worrell v. Elliott & Frantz, 799 F. Supp. 2d 343 (D.N.J. 2011) (applying New Jersey law).

[124] Ohio Product Liability Act, Ohio Rev. Code Ann. § 2307.71 *et seq.*

[125] Tennessee Products Liability Act, Tenn. Code Ann. § 29-28-101 *et seq.* *See* Maness v. Boston Scientific, 751 F. Supp. 2d 962 (E.D. Tenn. 2010) (applying Tennessee law); Brown v. Crown Equipment Co., 181 S.W.3d 268 (Tenn. 2005).

[126] Utah Products Liability Act, Utah Code Ann. § 78B-6-701 *et seq.* *See* Niemela v. Imperial Mfg. Co., 263 P.3d 1191 (Utah Ct. App. 2011).

[127] Washington Product Liability Act, Wash. Rev. Code § 7.72.010 *et seq.*

[128] Gerrity v. R.J. Reynolds Tobacco Co., 818 A.2d 769 (Conn. 2003); Savina v. Sterling Drug, Inc., 795 P.2d 915 (Kan. 1990).

[129] Kan. Stat. Ann. § 60-3301 *et seq.* For a discussion of the history and structure of the KPLA, see Gaumer v. Rossville Truck and Tractor Co., Inc., 292 Kan. 749, 257 P.3d 292 (Kan. 2011).

[130] 44 Fed. Reg. 62,714 *et seq.* (1979). In 1967, Department of Commerce promulgated a Model Uniform Products Liability Act for adoption by the states. Although no state has adopted the Model Act, it has influenced some state products liability statutes such as the one in Kansas. In addition, sections of the Act have been adopted by some states.

[131] David v. Hett, 293 Kan. 679, 685 (Kan. 2011).

[132] Kan. Stat. Ann. § 60-3302(a), (b). *See* Golden v. Den-Mat Corp., 276 P.3d 773, 802–03 (Kan. Ct. App. 2012).

[133] Kan. Stat. Ann. § 60-3302(c).

[134] *Id.* *See* Savina v. Sterling Drug, Inc., 795 P.2d 915 (Kan. 1990).

[135] Kan. Stat. Ann. § 60-3302(a).

"(1) damage to property; (2) personal physical injuries, illness and death; (3) mental anguish or emotional harm attendant to such personal physical injuries or death." However, "harm" does not include direct or consequential economic loss.[136] Although the KPLA does not define "direct or consequential economic loss," case law indicates that such loss includes damages for inadequate value, costs or repair, replacement costs, and loss of use of the defective product.[137]

The elements of a "product liability claim" are not set out in the KPLA. However, Kansas courts have stated that, to establish a *prima facie* case based either on negligence or strict liability under the KPLA, the plaintiff must prove three elements: (1) the "harm" resulted from a condition in the product; (2) the condition of the product was an unreasonably dangerous one; and (3) the unreasonably dangerous condition of the product existed at the time it left the manufacturer's control.[138] Thus, regardless of the theory of recovery in Kansas, proof that a product defect caused the plaintiff's injury is a prerequisite to recovery under the KPLA and the condition that caused the injury — whether it is a design defect, a manufacturing defect, or a failure to warn — must have existed at the time the product left the defendant's control.[139]

---

[136] *Id.* at § 60-3302(d).

[137] Koss Construction v. Caterpillar, 960 P.2d 255 (Kan. Ct. App. 1998).

[138] Stadtherr v. Elite Logistics, Inc., 2002 U.S. Dist. LEXIS 9701 (D. Kan. May 7, 2002) (applying Kansas law).

[139] Messer v. Amway Corp., 210 F. Supp. 2d 1217 (D. Kan. 2002) (applying Kansas law).

Chapter 2

WARRANTY

SYNOPSIS

§ 2.01   THE ROLE OF WARRANTY IN PRODUCTS LIABILITY
LITIGATION

§ 2.02   EXPRESS WARRANTIES

[A]   Introduction

[B]   Statement of Fact v. Opinion

[C]   Basis of the Bargain

§ 2.03   IMPLIED WARRANTY OF MERCHANTABILITY

[A]   Introduction

[B]   The Seller as Merchant of the Goods

[C]   Merchantability

[D]   Unforeseeable Use of the Goods

§ 2.04   IMPLIED WARRANTY OF FITNESS FOR A PARTICULAR
PURPOSE

[A]   Introduction

[B]   The "Particular Purpose"

[C]   Reliance

§ 2.05   THE SCOPE OF WARRANTIES

[A]   Introduction

[B]   Horizontal Privity

[C]   Vertical Privity

§ 2.06   NOTICE

[A]   Introduction

[B]   "Buyer" and "Seller"

[C]   Adequate Notice

[D]   "Reasonable Time"

§ 2.07   DISCLAIMERS AND LIMITATIONS OF WARRANTIES

[A]   Exclusion or Modification of Warranties

[1]   Express Warranties

[2]   Implied Warranties of Merchantability

[3]   Implied Warranties of Fitness for Particular Purpose

[4]   "As Is" Disclaimers

[B]   Limitations on Warranties

§ 2.08   DAMAGES FOR BREACH OF WARRANTY

§ 2.09   THE MAGNUSON-MOSS ACT

§ 2.01   THE ROLE OF WARRANTY IN PRODUCTS LIABILITY LITIGATION

Most of the attention in products liability law focuses on tort law and its theories of negligence and strict liability. However, warranty law also plays a very important role in products liability litigation. Actions for breach of warranty are governed by Article 2 of the Uniform Commercial Code (UCC) which has been adopted in every state except Louisiana.[1] In 2003, the American Law Institute (ALI) and National Conference of Commissioners on Uniform State Laws (NCCUSL) published for adoption by the states a Revised Article 2 that includes a revision of the sections dealing with warranties. However, because none of the states enacted the amendments, the ALI and NCCUSL withdrew them in 2011. Thus, this chapter focuses exclusively on actions for breach of express and implied warranties under Article 2 of the UCC as it was prior to 2003. This chapter also examines actions under the Magnuson-Moss Warranty Act,[2] the federal statute that provides warranty protection for the sale of consumer products to the public.

As with negligence and strict liability in tort, there are advantages and disadvantages of bringing a products liability action based on breach of warranty. One reason why "buyers"[3] often allege breach of warranty is that the proof may be simpler than with a tort. The focus of a warranty claim is on the condition of the goods — whether they complied with the express representations made by the seller or with the "merchantability" implied by law — rather than on any "fault" on the part of the seller in the failure of the goods to possess the required quality.[4] In addition, although persons who suffer personal injury or damage to property other than the product frequently include breach of warranty counts in their complaints along with counts for negligence and strict liability,[5] persons who claim only loss of the product or economic damages are limited to actions for breach of warranty. This

---

[1] Louisiana's sales law is similar to, but is not based on, the UCC.

[2] 15 U.S.C. § 2301 *et seq.* The act is discussed *infra* at § 2.09.

[3] The UCC uses the word "buyer" in its sections dealing with warranties. However, UCC § 2-318 has expanded horizontal privity to include persons who are not the actual "buyer" of the goods. *See infra* at § 2.05.

[4] Vlases v. Montgomery Ward & Co, Inc., 377 F.2d 846 (3d Cir. 1967) (applying Pennsylvania law).

[5] *See* Denny v. Ford Motor Co., 662 N.E.2d 730, 739 (N.Y. 1995) ("[T]he causes of action for strict products liability and breach of implied warranty of merchantability are not identical in New York and . . . the latter is not necessarily subsumed by the former. It follows that, under the circumstances presented, a verdict such as the one occurring here — in which the manufacturer was found liable under an implied warranty cause of action and not liable under a strict products cause of action — is theoretically reconcilable under New York law."). *See also* Stones v. Sears, Roebuck & Co., 558 N.W.2d 540 (Neb. 1997); McLaughlin v. Michelin Tire Corp., 778 P.2d 59 (Wyo. 1989); Realmuto v. Straub Motors, Inc., 322 A.2d 440 (N.J. 1974).

is because the economic loss doctrine bars recovery for such damages in actions based on negligence or strict liability.[6] A third advantage of breach of warranty theories is that the statute of limitations usually is longer than for negligence or strict liability.[7] As a result, plaintiffs who otherwise would bring claims for personal injury or property damage in negligence or strict liability use breach of warranty if the statute of limitations under those theories has run. Finally, alleging breach of warranty in the complaint may enable the buyer, during the discovery process, to obtain information about the seller's operations that would not be relevant in a negligence or strict liability action.

At the same time, however, there are important limitations that buyers must consider before using breach of warranty theories in products liability actions. Although the requirement of horizontal privity has been liberalized by the UCC,[8] the contract basis of warranty means that vertical privity still is more restrictive than in negligence and strict liability. Another hurdle for buyers in breach of warranty actions is that they are required, as a prelude to filing their suits, to notify the seller of the breach within a "reasonable time" after discovering it.[9] Failure to do so may bar their warranty action. Finally, and most importantly, the UCC permits a seller, in some situations, to disclaim express and implied warranties entirely or to limit the buyer's remedy to "repair or replacement."[10]

§ 2.02   EXPRESS WARRANTIES

[A]   Introduction

All of the new Ford cars have a Triplex shatter-proof glass windshield — so made that it will not fly or shatter under the hardest impact. This is an important safety factor because it eliminates the dangers of flying glass — the cause of most of the injuries in automobile accidents. In these days of crowded, heavy traffic, the use of this Triplex glass is an absolute necessity.[11]

The above statement, included in printed materials furnished by an automobile manufacturer to potential purchasers of its cars in the 1932 case *Baxter v. Ford Motor Company*,[12] is a classic example of an express warranty.[13] It is a represen-

---

[6] Purina Mills, Inc. v. Odell, 948 S.W.2d 927 (Tex. App. 1997). Economic loss includes the loss of the benefit of the bargain resulting from the diminished value from defective goods as well as consequential damages such as the cost of repair or replacement of the defective goods and lost profits resulting from a loss of use of the goods. The economic loss doctrine is discussed in detail in Chapter 10.

[7] UCC § 2-725. *See* Cleveland v. Square-D Co., 613 S.W.2d 790 (Tex. Civ. App. 1981). The statute begins to run on the date of sale of the goods (Pitts v. Northern Telecom, Inc., 24 F. Supp. 2d 437 (E.D. Pa. 1998) (applying Pennsylvania law)). For a discussion of the statute of limitations in warranty actions, see Chapter 9.

[8] *See* UCC § 2-318.

[9] UCC § 2-607(3). The notice requirement is discussed *infra* at § 2.06.

[10] *See* UCC § 2-719. These limitations are discussed *infra* at § 2.07.

[11] Baxter v. Ford Motor Co., 12 P.2d 409, 410 (Wash. 1932).

[12] 12 P.2d 409 (Wash. 1932).

tation of fact made by the seller of a product to a potential buyer that the product has a particular quality and will perform in a specific manner (i.e., the windshield "will not fly or shatter under the hardest impact"). In *Baxter*, a pebble from a passing vehicle struck the windshield of one of the manufacturer's cars, causing small pieces of glass to fly into the eyes of the purchaser of that car, resulting in injuries. The Washington Supreme Court held that the purchaser could proceed with an action for breach of express warranty against the manufacturer.[14]

With the adoption of § 2-313(1) of the Uniform Commercial Code (UCC), an express warranty now is created in one of three ways:

(a) Any affirmation of fact or promise made by the seller to the buyer which relates to the goods and becomes part of the basis of the bargain creates an express warranty that the goods shall conform to the affirmation or promise.

(b) Any description of the goods which is made part of the basis of the bargain creates an express warranty that the goods shall conform to the description.

(c) Any sample or model which is made part of the basis of the bargain creates an express warranty that the whole of the goods shall conform to the sample or model.

Why the windshield shattered was not an issue in *Baxter.* That was in keeping with the view, still followed in most states after adoption of the UCC, that an action based on breach of express warranty does not require the buyer to prove that there was an identifiable defect in the goods.[15] Instead, it is sufficient for the buyer to show that the product did not perform as expressly warranted. However, an action based on UCC § 2-313 does require the buyer to establish a number of elements.[16] First, an express warranty must guarantee that "goods" are of a specific quality. A promise to repair defects in goods is not a warranty about their quality.[17] Second, the defendant must have been a "seller" of the goods. UCC § 2-103(1)(d) defines a "seller" as "a person who sells or contracts to sell goods." The term includes both manufacturers and retailers of goods.[18] Third, the "seller" must have made an

---

[13] For a brief review of the historical development of express warranties, see Southwest Bell Telephone Co. v. FDP Corp., 811 S.W.2d 572, 574–575 (Tex. 1991).

[14] 12 P.2d at 413. At the second trial the jury found for the plaintiff and the Washington Supreme Court affirmed. *See* Baxter v. Ford Motor Co., 35 P.2d 1090 (Wash. 1934).

[15] Collins v. Uniroyal, Inc., 315 A.2d 16 (N.J. 1974) ("A cause of action for breach of express warranty . . . does not depend upon a defect in the goods. Indeed, the affirmative establishment by the defendant of freedom from defect would be irrelevant to such an action." *Id.* at 17.). *See* Caboni v. General Motors Corp., 398 F.3d 357 (5th Cir. 2005) (applying Louisiana law); Harte v. Stuttgart Autohaus, Inc., 706 P.2d 394 (Ariz. Ct. App. 1985). However, in few states, proof of a defect in the goods is essential to establish a breach of an express warranty. *See* McLaughlin v. Michelin Tire Corp., 778 P.2d 59 (Wyo. 1989).

[16] In about 10 states, claims for breach of express warranty not governed exclusively by the UCC. For a discussion of state products liability statutes and express warranty, see Louis R. Frumer & Melvin I. Friedman, Products Liability § 9.02[1][b] (2007).

[17] In Mydlach v. DaimlerChrysler Corp., 875 N.E.2d 1047, 1060 (Ill. 2007), the Illinois Supreme Court stated that a repair warranty is not a UCC express warranty.

[18] In Hughes v. The Tobacco Institute, Inc., 278 F.3d 417 (5th Cir. 2001) (applying Texas law), one of

"affirmation of fact or promise," given a "description," or provided a "sample or model" of its goods. Fourth, the affirmation, description, sample or model must have formed "part of the basis of the bargain" between the seller and the buyer. Fifth, the buyer must establish that the express warranty was breached because the goods did not conform to the seller's statements about their quality or performance. Finally, the breach of the warranty must have been the cause of the injury to the buyer.[19] However, despite these elements, most products liability cases involving express warranties center on only two questions: (1) Did the seller make an "affirmation of fact or promise" or gave a "description" of the goods? and (2) Was that statement or description "part of the basis of the bargain" between the seller and the buyer?

[B]   Statement of Fact v. Opinion

In any action for breach of express warranty, the buyer must prove that, in the contract of sale, the seller made an "affirmation of fact or promise" or provided a "description of the goods." An affirmation of fact or description of goods can take a number of different forms. Among these are written statements or pictures in advertising brochures,[20] instructions manuals,[21] or product literature;[22] oral statements by salespersons;[23] and samples or models of the goods.[24] Past deliveries of the goods also may set the description of quality warranted.[25] However, in all of these situations, the buyer must plead and prove the exact

---

the few cases in which the meaning of a "seller" under § 2-313 was at issue, the court held that a trade association was not a "seller" and was not liable for breach of express warranties made by its members.

[19] Scott v. Dorel Juvenile Group, Inc., 2012 U.S. App. LEXIS 155 (5th Cir. Jan. 4, 2012) (applying Texas law); Rodarte v. Philip Morris, Inc., 2003 U.S. Dist. LEXIS 25067 (C.D. Cal. June 23, 2003) (applying California law). In Goodman v. PPG Industries, Inc., 849 A.2d 1239, 1245–1246 (2004), the Pennsylvania Superior Court stated: "[G]iven that express warranties are based on the notion of offer and acceptance, it would appear incongruous to allow third parties the benefit of an express warranty when no evidence exists that they were aware of the terms of the warranty or the identity of the party issuing the warranty. Thus, in order to preserve the unique character of express warranties, we hold that third parties may enforce express warranties only under circumstances where an objective fact-finder could reasonably conclude that (1) the party issuing the warranty intends to extend the specific terms of the warranty to the third party (either directly, or through an intermediary); and (2) the third party is aware of the specific terms of the warranty, and the identity of the party issuing the warranty." The court stated, however, that the opinion "should be construed as resurrecting a privity requirement." *Id. See* Hoffman v. Paper Converting Machine Co., 694 F. Supp. 2d 359 (E.D. Pa. 2010) (applying Pennsylvania law); Golden v. Den-Mat Corp., 276 P.3d 773, 795–796 (Kan. Ct. App. 2012) (a brief overview of express warranties under Kansas law).

[20] Neville Construction Co. v. Cook Paint & Varnish Co., 671 F.2d 1107 (8th Cir. 1982) (applying Nebraska law); Touchet Valley Grain Growers, Inc., v. Opp & Seibold General Construction, Inc., 831 P.2d 724 (Wash. 1992).

[21] Kinlaw v. Long Manufacturing N.C., Inc., 259 S.E.2d 552 (N.C. 1979). See, however, Corral v. Rollins Protective Services Co., 732 P.2d 1260 (Kan. 1987), in which the court held that the statements in a manual for a fire alarm were instructional and not an express warranty.

[22] Beyette v. Ortho Pharmaceuticals Corp., 823 F.2d 990 (6th Cir. 1987) (applying Michigan law).

[23] Crothers v. Cohen, 384 N.W.2d 562 (Minn. Ct. App. 1986).

[24] UCC § 2-313(1)(c). *See* Jones v. Davenport, 2001 Ohio App. LEXIS 226 (Jan. 26, 2001).

[25] UCC § 2-313, cmt. 5. *See* The Shutter Shop, Inc v. Amersham Corp., 114 F. Supp. 2d 1218 (M.D. Ala. 2000) (applying Alabama law).

representation or the specific advertisement used by the seller.[26] Although comment 5 to UCC § 2-313 states that "all descriptions by merchants must be read against the applicable trade usages with the general rules as to merchantability resolving any doubts," many states treat the issue of whether a particular affirmation or description amounts to a warranty as a question for the trier of fact to decide.[27]

The most difficult issue in express warranty cases is determining whether the seller's representation of the goods was a statement of fact or simply an expression of opinion. According to UCC § 2-313(2), it is not necessary for the creation of an express warranty that the seller use formal words such as "warranty" or "guarantee" or even have the specific intention to make a warranty.[28] However, both the UCC and the cases make it clear that "representations which merely express the seller's opinion, belief, judgment, or estimate do not constitute a warranty."[29] Although courts state that they use a reasonable person standard to determine whether language is an affirmation of fact or a statement of opinion,[30] it often is difficult to draw a distinction between the two. For example, an Illinois court interpreted assurances by the seller of a 10-year-old used car that the car was "mechanically sound," "in good condition," and had "no problems" to be "affirmations of fact and descriptions of the car that created an express warranty."[31] In contrast, an Alabama court held that statements that a vehicle was "a good car" and "in good shape" were not representations of material fact but statements of opinion, "sales talk," and "puffery."[32] Similarly, a statement by a company that its copying machines and their component parts were of "high quality" was held to be a statement of the seller's opinion, "the kind of puffing to be expected in any sales transaction, rather than a positive averment of the fact describing a product's capabilities to which an express warranty could attach."[33]

Because of the wide variety of statements made about goods by sellers, there is no clear test for distinguishing between a statement of fact and an expression of opinion. The determination depends upon the circumstances surrounding each

---

[26] Rodarte v. Philip Morris, Inc., 2003 U.S. Dist. LEXIS 25067 (C.D. Cal. June 23, 2003) (applying California law).

[27] Moore v. Mack Trucks, Inc., 40 S.W.3d 888 (Ky. Ct. App. 2001). In Kolarik v. Cory International Corp., 721 N.W.2d 159 (Iowa 2006), the Iowa Supreme Court held that, in light of how large quantities of olives are pitted and stuffed, the words "minced pimento stuffed" were not an express warranty that olives in a jar were entirely free of pits or pit fragments.

[28] Rite Aid Corp. v. Levy-Gray, 894 A.2d 563 (Md. 2006); Kelleher v. Marvin Lumber and Cedar Co., 891 A.2d 477 (N.H. 2005); James River Equipment Co. v. Beadle County Equipment, Inc., 646 N.W.2d 265 (S.D. 2002).

[29] UCC § 2-313(2). *See* Beyette v. Ortho Pharmaceutical Corp., 823 F.2d 990 (6th Cir. 1987) (applying Michigan law); McLaughlin v. Michelin Tire Corp., 778 P.2d 59 (Wyo. 1989).

[30] Rawson v. Conover, 20 P.3d 876 (Utah 2001).

[31] Weng v. Allison, 678 N.E.2d 1254, 1256 (Ill. App. Ct. 1997).

[32] Scoggin v. Listerhill Employees Credit Union, 658 So. 2d 376 (Ala. 1995). *See also* Oak Point Associates v. Southern States Screening, Inc., 1994 U.S. Dist. LEXIS 6912 (S.D.N.Y. May 4, 1994) (applying New York law); Web Press Service Corp. v. New London Motors, Inc., 525 A.2d 57 (Conn. 1987).

[33] Royal Business Machines, Inc. v. Litton Business Systems, Inc., 633 F.2d 34, 42 (7th Cir. 1980) (applying Indiana law).

particular case. Among the factors courts consider is the specificity of the representation. The more specific the statement about the characteristics of goods, the more likely a court will hold that it constitutes a warranty.[34] Thus, the Oklahoma Supreme Court held that a jury was entitled to find that a statement that a new automobile engine "would be guaranteed for six thousand miles or six months" was an express warranty.[35] According to the court, the statement was not an expression of opinion but a "definite and unqualified statement that the engine was 'guaranteed' for the specific time or distance."[36] However, a statement in a sales brochure that a particular model fishing boat "delivers the kind of performance you need to get to the prime offshore fishing grounds" was held to be merely a commendation of the boat's performance and not a description of a specific characteristic of the boat.[37]

Closely related to the specificity of the statement is whether the representation was objective in nature, that is, whether it was capable of being proven true or false. Thus, statements that a pressing machine was "one year old" (when it was at least five years old) and was "in perfect condition" were specific and objective enough to create an express warranty.[38] However, advertising language that bungee cords were "Premium Quality" was held to be puffery as "generalized statements of salesmanship" and not "descriptions of particular characteristics of the goods."[39] Similarly, assertions in a brochure that a yacht offered the "best performance" and "superb handling" were held to be "characteristic of an opinion" since they relied on "inherently subjective words."[40]

Courts also compare the knowledge and sophistication of the buyer and the seller about the goods. They ask whether the seller made a representation of fact about the goods that the buyer would not be expected to know or expressed an opinion about an aspect on which they each would have an opinion.[41] Thus, courts often hold that statements made by cigarette companies about their products are not express warranties because it long has been common knowledge that smoking is addictive and a health risk.[42] Finally, courts look to see whether the representation concerned the present condition of goods or was a specific reference to the future. A representation about the present quality or performance of goods

---

[34] Downie v. Abex Corp., 741 F.2d 1235 (10th Cir. 1984) (applying Utah law).

[35] Scovil v. Chilcoat, 424 P.2d 87, 92 (Okla. 1967).

[36] *Id.*

[37] Bayliner Marine Corp. v. Crow, 509 S.E.2d 499 (Va. 1999). *See also* Royal Business Machines, Inc. v. Litton Business Systems, Inc., 633 F.2d 34 (7th Cir. 1980) (applying Indiana law) (a statement by company representatives that experience and testing had shown that the frequency of repair of their copying machines was "very low" and would remain so lacked the specificity of an affirmation of fact).

[38] Kates Millinery, Ltd. v. Benay-Albee Corp., 450 N.Y.S.2d 975 (Civ. Ct. 1982).

[39] Anderson v. Bungee International Manufacturing Corp., 44 F. Supp. 2d 534, 541 (S.D.N.Y. 1999) (applying New York law).

[40] Boud v. SDNCO, Inc., 54 P.3d 1131 (Utah 2002).

[41] Liberty Lincoln-Mercury, Inc. v. Ford Motor Co., 171 F.3d 818 (3d Cir. 1999) (applying New Jersey law); Peterson v. North American Plant, 354 N.W.2d 625 (Neb. 1984).

[42] White v. R. J. Reynolds Tobacco Co., 2000 U.S. Dist. LEXIS 16172 (S.D. Tex. Sept. 26, 2000) (applying Texas law).

without a specific reference to the future is not an express warranty of their future performance, even if the representation implies that the goods will perform a certain way in the future.[43]

[C]   Basis of the Bargain

Under UCC § 2-313(1) a buyer must show that the "affirmation of fact," "description," or "sample or model" was "made part of the basis of the bargain." Since the term "basis of the bargain" is not defined by the UCC,[44] courts are divided as to whether the phrase means that the buyer must have relied specifically upon the language of the express warranty in deciding whether to purchase the goods.[45] This is important because, in many cases, buyers do not become aware of the sellers' specific representations about the goods until after they purchase them, take them home, and read the literature contained in the boxes.

Under the old Uniform Sales Act (USA), reliance was a key element of an action for breach of an express warranty.[46] With the adoption of the UCC, several states interpret "part of the basis of the bargain" to be a continuation of the USA requirement that the buyer must show some type of reliance upon the affirmation of fact or description in deciding to purchase the goods.[47] Under this view, the "basis of the bargain" is part of the determination of whether the language of the representation constituted an express warranty since statements of fact and descriptions tend to become part of the basis of the bargain.[48] However, in states that take this view, a buyer who establish that the seller's representation was a statement of fact often fails to show the necessary reliance on the statement. This has been a particular problem for smokers in their suits against tobacco companies. Courts have held that reliance on the manufacturers' representations about their products is not established simply from the fact that buyers purchased particular brands of cigarettes. Buyers must show that they saw the companies' advertisements making claims about their cigarettes or disputing the link between smoking and health problems and that they relied on those advertisements in their decisions to begin smoking or to switch from one brand to another.[49]

The majority of states take the view that the phrase "basis of the bargain" in UCC § 2-313 means that it is no longer necessary for buyers to show reliance on an

---

[43] Employers Mutual Casualty Co. v. Collins & Aikman Floor Coverings, Inc., 2004 U.S. Dist. LEXIS 7192 (S.D. Iowa Feb. 13, 2004) (applying Iowa law).

[44] According to one court, the term describes "the commercial relationship between the parties as to the product." *See* Autzen v. John C. Taylor Lumber Sales, Inc., 572 P.2d 1322, 1325 (Or. 1977).

[45] Compaq Computer Corp. v. Lapray, 135 S.W.3d 657 (Tex. 2004). *See* Enpro Systems, Ltd. v. Namasco Corp., 382 F. Supp. 2d 874 (S.D. Tex. 2005) (applying Texas law).

[46] Uniform Sales Act, § 12.

[47] McManus v. Fleetwood Enterprises, Inc., 320 F.3d 545 (5th Cir. 2003) (applying Texas law); Freeman v. Hoffman-La Roche, Inc., 618 N.W.2d 827 (Neb. 2000); Smith v. Anheuser-Busch, Inc., 599 A.2d 320 (R.I. 1991).

[48] Stang v. Hertz Corp., 490 P.2d 475 (N.M. Ct. App. 1971).

[49] *See* Hughes v. The Tobacco Institute, Inc., 278 F.3d 417 (5th Cir. 2001) (applying Texas law).

affirmation or promise before statements by sellers can be an express warranty.[50] This view is based upon comment 3 to UCC § 2-313 which states that "no particular reliance on [the affirmations of fact made by the seller] need be shown to weave them into the fabric of the agreement." An example of a case where reliance was inferred is *Bernick v. Jurden*,[51] in which the plaintiff brought an action against the manufacturer of a mouth guard for injuries he suffered while playing ice hockey. Although neither the plaintiff nor his mother (who purchased the mouth guard) actually read the advertising label, the North Carolina Supreme Court held that the reliance of the plaintiff could be inferred from allegations of the purchase or use of the product if the natural tendency of the seller's representations is to induce purchase or use. Since the manufacturer promoted the product in hockey catalogue advertisements and in parent guides, the court concluded that the natural tendency of a representation that the mouth guard provided "maximum protection to the lips and teeth" was to induce the purchase of the product.

Although most representations about products are made before their sale, comment 7 to UCC § 2-313 states that "[t]he precise time when words of description or affirmation are made or samples are shown is not material." Instead:

> The sole question is whether the language or samples or models are fairly to be regarded as part of the contract. If language is used after the closing of the deal (as when the buyer taking delivery asks and receives an additional assurance), the warranty becomes a modification, and need not be supported by consideration if it is otherwise reasonable and in order.[52]

An example of a post-sale statement that became "part of the basis of the bargain" is *Bigelow v. Agway, Inc.*,[53] in which a farmer sued the manufacturer and distributor of a chemical used to treat hay before baling. The farmer was told that the chemical would permit him to bale hay at a higher moisture level than normal. Two months after the sale and use of the chemical, the defendant's salesman guaranteed that hay treated with the chemical was safe to bale even though the hay contained a moisture level well above normal. The farmer baled the hay and the level of moisture resulted in a fire that destroyed his entire crop. The Court of Appeals held that the salesman's representation was a basis of the bargain, even though it was made two months after the sale. According to the court, "it is undisputed that the [salesman's] visit [after the delivery of the chemical] . . . was to promote the sale of the product. Thus, [his representations] might constitute an actionable modification of the warranty."[54]

---

[50] Lutz Farms v. Asgrow Seed Co., 948 F.2d 638, 645 (10th Cir. 1991) (applying Colorado law); Massey-Ferguson, Inc. v. Laird, 432 So. 2d 1259 (Ala. 1983).

[51] 293 S.E.2d 405 (N.C. 1982). See Kelleher v. Marvin Lumber and Cedar Co., 891 A.2d 477 (N.H. 2005), in which the New Hampshire Supreme Court adopted an "intermediate approach" when deciding whether representations in a catalog or brochure constitute part of the basis of the bargain in an express warranty claim.

[52] *See* Rite Aid Corp. v. Levy-Gray, 894 A.2d 563 (Md. 2006).

[53] 506 F.2d 551 (2d Cir. 1974) (applying Vermont law).

[54] *Id.* at 555, n.6.

§ 2.03 IMPLIED WARRANTY OF MERCHANTABILITY

[A] Introduction

In addition to express warranties, the Uniform Commercial Code creates two types of implied warranties: an implied warranty of merchantability[55] and an implied warranty of fitness for a particular purpose.[56] Often, buyers include counts alleging a breach of each type of these warranties in their complaints.[57]

The oldest and most common implied warranty is the implied warranty of merchantability.[58] Unlike an express warranty and an implied warranty of fitness for a particular purpose that are created by representations made by the seller, an implied warranty of merchantability arises by law from a contract for the sale of most goods if "the seller is a merchant with respect to goods of that kind."[59] The seller does not have to make any statement about the goods in order to create an implied warranty of merchantability. The warranty is a representation about the quality (i.e., "merchantability") of goods that the law implies in the sales contract based upon the facts and circumstances of the transaction, the nature of the goods, trade usages, and the knowledge common to the community about the goods.[60] An example of this is the implied warranty of merchantability that accompanies the sale of a new automobile by an automobile dealer. The warranty is a promise that the automobile is in the proper condition for the ordinary functions for which an automobile is intended. However, it is not a guarantee that nothing ever will go wrong with the automobile. There is a breach of this warranty only if a defect existed in the automobile at the time of sale. However, it is not necessary that a defect become evident immediately after the sale of the automobile. Instead:

> [E]vidence of reasonable and proper handling of a product between the time it left the possession and control of the defendant manufacturer or seller and the time of the occurrence of the injury is an indication that the defect alleged to have existed at the time of the injury did not come into being in the interim, but existed prior thereto.[61]

As with an express warranty, there are a number of elements that a buyer must establish in order to recover damages for a breach of an implied warranty of merchantability under UCC § 2-314: (1) the "seller" must have been a "merchant with respect to goods" of the kind in question; (2) the goods must not have been "merchantable" at the time of the sale; (3) the buyer must have suffered injury or

---

[55] UCC § 2-314. *See* Golden v. Den-Mat Corp., 276 P.3d 773, 796–799 (Kan. Ct. App. 2012).

[56] UCC § 2-315.

[57] Dickerson v. Mountain View Equipment, 710 P.2d 621 (Idaho Ct. App. 1985).

[58] As early as 1815, courts recognized an implied warranty in the sale of food. *See* Van Bracklin v. Fonda, 12 Johns. 468 (N.Y. 1815). For a proposed modern use of this warranty, see Franklin E. Crawford, *Fit for Its Ordinary Purpose? Tobacco, Fast Food and the Implied Warranty of Merchantability*, 63 OHIO ST. L.J. 1165 (2002/2003).

[59] UCC § 2-314(1). *See* Mocek v. Alfa Leisure, Inc., 7 Cal. Rptr. 3d 546 (Ct. App. 2003).

[60] Hodges v. Johnson, 199 P.3d 1251, 1257–1258 (Kan. 2009).

[61] Alvarez v. American Isuzu Motors, 749 N.E.2d 16, 24 (Ill. App. Ct. 2001) (quoting Fullreide v. Midstates Beverage Co., 388 N.E.2d 1070, 1073 (Ill. App. Ct. 1979).

damage to his or her property; (4) the injury or damage must have been caused, in fact and caused, by the defective nature of the goods; and (5) the buyer must have given the required notice of the injury to the seller.[62] An implied warranty of merchantability can be excluded or modified only in a manner that complies with UCC § 2-316.

[B] The Seller as Merchant of the Goods

Unlike an express warranty and an implied warranty of fitness for a particular purpose, which apply to any "seller," an implied warranty of merchantability requires that the "seller" be a "merchant with respect to goods of that kind."[63] The UCC defines a "merchant" as

[A] person who deals in goods of the kind or otherwise by his occupation holds himself out as having knowledge or skill peculiar to the practices or goods involved in the transaction or to whom such knowledge or skill may be attributed by his employment or an agent or broker or other intermediary who by his occupation holds himself out as having such knowledge or skill.[64]

Using this definition, courts have held that an implied warranty applies to merchants who sell both new goods and used goods.[65] However, an implied warranty of merchantability does not extend to the causal sale by an individual of personal goods[66] or to a single isolated transaction by a merchant of goods with which it otherwise does not deal.[67] Such a warranty also does not extend to a claim by an ultimate purchaser for economic loss against a manufacturer of a component part.[68] In addition, while the definition of a "merchant" includes a commercial

---

[62] James J. White & Robert S. Summers, Uniform Commercial Code 480–489 (6th ed. 2010). As with negligence, causation is an essential element of a breach of warranty claim. Coons v. A.F. Chapman Corp., 460 F. Supp. 2d 209 (D. Mass. 2006) (applying Massachusetts law). Iowa courts have held that § 2-314 requires proof of a product defect as defined in the Restatement (Third) of Torts: Products Liability § 2. Since a manufacturing defect claim and an implied warranty of merchantability claim rest of on the factual basis, the two claims cannot be pursued together in the same case. Depositors Insurance Co. v. Wal-Mart Stores, Inc., 506 F.3d 1092 (8th Cir. 2007) (applying Iowa law).

[63] Lish v. Compton, 547 P.2d 223 (Utah 1976).

[64] UCC § 2-104(1). See Siemen v. Alden, 341 N.E.2d 713 (Ill. App. Ct. 1975).

[65] Hodges v. Johnson, 199 P.3d 1251 (Kan. 2009); Whittle v. Timesavers, Inc., 614 F. Supp. 115 (W.D. Va. 1985) (applying Virginia law); Dickerson v. Mountain View Equipment Co., 710 P.2d 621 (Idaho 1985). For the quality expected of used goods, see UCC § 2-314 cmt. 3.

[66] UCC § 2-314 cmt. 3. See Smith v. Stewart, 667 P.2d 358 (Kan. 1983); Ballou v. Trahan, 334 A.2d 409 (Vt. 1975).

[67] Mozee v. Kuplen, 1990 U.S. Dist. LEXIS 11974 (D. Kan. July 16, 1990) (applying Kansas law); Donald v. City National Bank, 329 So. 2d 92 (Ala. 1976); Foley v. Dayton Bank & Trust, 696 S.W.2d 356 (Tenn. Ct. App. 1985).

[68] In Hininger v. Case Corp., 23 F.3d 124 (5th Cir. 1994), the Fifth Circuit felt that the Texas Supreme Court would distinguish between the manufacturer of a finished product and a component part manufacturer because of the component supplier's inability to disclaim effectively its warranty liability. That distinction, along with the purchasers' lack of any expectation that the component part manufacturer would respond to defects in the finished product, led the court to hold that the purchaser had no implied warranty action.

restaurateur, a court held that it did not apply to a voluntary association of mothers of high school band students who sold food to raise money.[69] Finally, since UCC Article 2 applies to "transactions in goods," if the defective goods were provided as part of a transaction that was primarily one for services rather than for goods, no implied warranty of merchantability applies.[70]

The UCC defines "goods" to include "all things (including specifically manufactured goods) which are moveable at the time of identification to the contract of sale."[71] However, goods need not be "manufactured" to be covered by an implied warranty of merchantability. For example, granite blocks sold to a headstone manufacturer were held to be "goods" covered by an implied warranty when monuments made from the stone discolored.[72] Also included within the definition of "goods" under the UCC are "the unborn young of animals and growing crops and other identified things attached to realty." Thus, cattle have been held to be "goods" under the section even though they are not manufactured.[73]

[C] Merchantability

Key to recovery for a breach of an implied warranty of merchantability is a showing that the goods were not "merchantable" at the time of the sale. Although the UCC does not define that term, some basis for determining the merchantability of goods is provided by UCC § 2-314(2), which requires that the goods meet "at least" six standards:

(a)   pass without objection in trade under the contract description; and

(b)   in the case of fungible goods, are of fair average quality within the description; and

(c)   are fit for the ordinary purposes for which such goods are used; and

(d)   run, within the variations permitted by the agreement, of even kind, quality and quantity within each unit and among all units involved; and

(e)   are adequately contained, packaged, and labeled as the agreement may require; and

(f)   conform to the promises or affirmations made on the container or label if any.

Unless excluded or modified according to UCC § 2-316, other implied warranties may arise from the course of dealings between the parties or from the usage of trade.[74] In all situations, whether the goods were "merchantable" is a question for

---

[69] Samson v. Riesing, 215 N.W.2d 662 (Wis. 1974).

[70] Brandt v. Boston Scientific Corp., 792 N.E.2d 296 (Ill. 2003); Golden v. Den-Mat Corp., 276 P.3d 773 (Kan. Ct. App. 2012).

[71] UCC § 2-105(1). A prescription drug meets the definition of "goods." Rite Aid Corp. v. Levy-Gray, 894 A.2d 563 (Md. 2006).

[72] Willis Mining, Inc. v. Noggle, 509 S.E.2d 731 (Ga. Ct. App. 1998).

[73] Vince v. Broome, 443 So. 2d 23 (Miss. 1983).

[74] *See* UCC § 2-314(3) and cmt. 11.

the trier of fact.[75]

An action for implied warranty of merchantability is similar to one in express warranty or strict liability in that it is not necessary for the buyer to prove any fault by the seller.[76] In addition, the inquiry in such an action is not whether the goods were the best or whether they met the buyer's every expectation. Instead, courts focus on UCC § 2-314(2)(c) and ask whether the goods were "fit for the ordinary purposes for which such goods are used"[77] that is, whether the goods were of an average quality when compared to that generally acceptable in the trade for goods of the kind.[78] This requirement is illustrated by *Birdsong v. Apple, Inc.*,[79] in which the plaintiff alleged a breach of warranty of merchantability and fitness for a particular purpose resulting from his purchase of an Apple iPod. The plaintiff alleged that listening to music through the "earbud" headphones that accompanied the iPod posed an unreasonable risk of noise-induced hearing loss to users because (1) the iPod is *capable* of playing 115 decibels of sound; (2) consumers *may* listen at unsafe levels; and (3) iPod batteries can last 12 to 14 hours and are rechargeable, giving users the *opportunity* to listen for long periods of time. Apple included a warning with each iPod that advised users of the risk of hearing loss if the earphones were set at high volume. It advised users to set the volume at a safe level and to discontinue using the iPod if they experienced ringing in their ears.[80] The district court dismissed the complaint and the Court of Appeals affirmed. According to the court, the plaintiff's allegations suggested only that users had the option of using an iPod in a risky manner, not that the product lacked any minimum level of quality. He made no allegations of any history of malfunction and only suggested possible changes to the iPod which he believe would make it safe. The plaintiff also failed to allege how the absence of the suggested changes caused any user an injury. Thus, the plaintiff did not allege that the iPods failed to do anything they were designed to do or that he, or anyone else suffered or are substantially certain to suffer inevitable hearing loss or other injury from iPod use.[81]

A few courts hold that a cause of action for breach of an implied warranty requires only a showing that the goods did not meet the standards of UCC § 2-314(2), regardless of whether they were defective.[82] However, most courts speak of an implied warranty as a guarantee that the goods will perform in the ordinary

---

[75] Criscuolo v. Mauro Motors, Inc., 754 A.2d 810 (Conn. App. Ct. 2000).

[76] Delta Marine, Inc. v. Whaley, 813 F. Supp. 414 (E.D.N.C. 1993) (applying North Carolina law).

[77] *See* Phillips v. Cricket Lighters, 883 A.2d 439 (Pa. 2005) (since the ordinary purpose of a lighter is for adult use and not a plaything for a child, a lighter without a safety catch was fit for its ordinary purpose and was merchantable).

[78] Castro v. QVC Network, 139 F.3d 114 (2d Cir. 1998) (applying New York law); Golden v. Den-Mat Corp., 276 P.3d 773 (Kan. Ct. App. 2012).

[79] 590 F.3d 955 (9th Cir. 2009) (applying California law).

[80] *Id.* at 957–958.

[81] *Id.* at 958–959.

[82] Hyundai Motor Co. v. Rodriguez, 995 S.W.2d 661 (Tex. 1999); Maldonado v. Creative Woodworking Concepts, Inc., 796 N.E.2d 662, 666 (Ill. App. Ct. 2003).

way that goods of that kind should perform.[83] For these courts, a showing that the product was defective is an essential element under all theories of recovery in products liability: negligence, strict liability, and breach of an implied warranty.[84] However, states differ over whether the requirements for a defect are the same for implied warranty of merchantability as for strict liability. In *Larsen v. Pacesetter Systems, Inc.*,[85] for example, the Hawaii Supreme Court held that, in order to bring an action in implied warranty for personal injury, a buyer must show product unmerchantability sufficient to avoid summary judgment on the issue of defectiveness in a tort strict liability action. This requires applying the balancing factors in the risk/benefit analysis or the consumer expectation test to implied warranty as well as strict liability actions.[86]

For some other states, the implied warranty of merchantability is breached when the goods are defective to a normal buyer who makes ordinary use of them.[87] This requires the buyer to prove only that something went wrong with the goods consistent with the existence of a defect.[88] While most buyers attempt to establish the specific condition in the goods that made them not of an acceptable quality, in some cases that may not be possible. In those cases, the buyer will attempt to draw an inference of a defect from circumstantial evidence that he or she used the goods in an ordinary manner and that they did not function as they should have.[89] This does not require use of the risk/benefit analysis. How circumstantial evidence can provide a sufficient basis for a finding of a defect is illustrated by *Dewitt v. Eveready Batteries, Inc.*,[90] in which a buyer was injured when batteries he purchased for a lantern leaked. In a suit against the manufacturer of the batteries, for breach of the implied warranty of merchantability, the North Carolina Supreme Court held that the buyer did not have to prove a specific defect in order to meet his burden of proof. The court held that the buyer raised a genuine issue of material fact by producing circumstantial evidence of a defect in the batteries by showing: (1) the malfunction of the batteries; (2) expert testimony as to a variety of possible causes that were due to defects in the batteries; (3) use of the batteries in their ordinary manner when the buyer was injured; (4) the possibility of similar

---

[83] Employers Mutual Casualty Co. v. Collins & Aikman Floor Coverings, Inc., 2004 U.S. Dist. LEXIS 7192 (S.D. Iowa Feb. 13, 2004).

[84] McLaughlin v. Michelin Tire Corp., 778 P.2d 59 (Wyo. 1989); Lariviere v. Dayton Safety Ladder Co., 525 A.2d 892 (R.I. 1987).

[85] 837 P.2d 1273 (Haw. 1992).

[86] Cigna Insurance Co. v. OY Saunatec, Ltd., 241 F.3d 1 (1st Cir. 2001) (applying Massachusetts law). See Hollister v. Dayton-Hudson Corp., 201 F.3d 731 (6th Cir. 2000), in which the Sixth Circuit, applying Michigan law, stated that a claim for a breach of an implied warranty required a showing that the product sold was in a defective condition. In *Hollister*, the plaintiff claimed that the product was defective because of a design defect and the failure to warn of the dangers.

[87] *See* Landree v. University Medical Products, USA, Inc., 2004 U.S. Dist. LEXIS 3165 (D. Minn. Mar. 1, 2004) (applying Minnesota law).

[88] Fleck v. Titan Tire Corp., 177 F. Supp. 2d 605 (E.D. Mich. 2001) (applying Michigan law).

[89] Alvarez v. American Isuzu Motors, 749 N.E.2d 16 (Ill. App. Ct. 2001).

[90] 565 S.E.2d 140 (N.C. 2002). For a discussion of the six factors that *DeWitt* said were relevant in determining whether a plaintiff adequately has established the existence of a defect through circumstantial evidence, see Manley v. Doe, 849 F. Supp. 2d 594 (E.D.N.C. 2012) (applying North Carolina law).

accidents to that involving the buyer; (5) the elimination of possible causes of the accident unrelated to the manufacturer; and (6) proof that such an accident ordinarily does not occur in the absence of a manufacturing defect.[91]

[D] Unforeseeable Use of the Goods

An implied warranty of merchantability is based on the idea that the goods are fit for the ordinary purposes for which they are used. As in negligence cases, "ordinary purposes" include all of the foreseeable uses of the goods, even if they are not intended specifically by the seller. According to one court: "[A] manufacturer must anticipate the environment in which its product will be used, and it must design against the reasonably foreseeable risks attending the product's use in that setting."[92] Thus, the basis of the analysis is the foreseeability of the use of a product. The manufacturer must anticipate the intended as well as the reasonably foreseeable misuses of its products.[93] However, buyers in such actions must prove that, at the time of the injury or damage, they were using the goods in a reasonable manner, that is, a manner that the seller reasonably could have foreseen.[94]

§ 2.04 IMPLIED WARRANTY OF FITNESS FOR A PARTICULAR PURPOSE

[A] Introduction

UCC § 2-315 sets out the requirements for an implied warranty of fitness for a particular purpose:

> Where the seller at the time of contracting has reason to know any particular purpose for which the goods are required and that the buyer is relying on the seller's skill or judgment to select or furnish suitable goods, there is unless excluded or modified under the next section an implied warranty that the goods shall be fit for such purpose.

Based upon this section, courts have stated that a plaintiff must establish four elements to prove a breach of an implied warranty of fitness for a particular purpose: (1) a sale of goods; (2) that the seller had reason to know any particular purpose for which the goods were required; (3) that the plaintiff, as the buyer of the goods, relied upon the seller's skill or judgment to select suitable goods; and (4) that the goods were not fit for the particular purpose for which they were used.[95]

---

[91] *Id.* at 151–154.

[92] Venturelli v. Cincinnati, Inc., 850 F.2d 825, 827 (1st Cir. 1988) (applying Massachusetts law).

[93] Cigna Insurance Co. v. OY Saunatec, Ltd., 241 F.3d 1 (1st Cir. 2001) (applying Massachusetts law).

[94] Venturelli v. Cincinnati, Inc., 850 F.2d 825 (1st Cir. 1988) (applying Massachusetts law).

[95] *See* Malawy v. Richards Manufacturing Co., 501 N.E.2d 376, 382 (Ill. App. Ct. 1986). *See* Hoffman v. Paper Converting Machine Co., 694 F. Supp. 2d 359, 373 (E.D. Pa. 2010) (applying Pennsylvania law); Golden v. Den-Mat Corp., 276 P.3d 773 (Kan. Ct. App. 2012).

An example of an implied warranty of fitness is *Klein v. Sear Roebuck and Co.*,[96] in which plaintiff's parents decided to purchase a riding lawn mower as a gift for him. They visited a local Sears store where they consulted a salesman about the intended purchase. They told the salesman that they had no experience with lawnmowers and that the property on which the mower would be used contained numerous hills. The salesman recommended a particular brand and model of mower but conditioned the sale on his inspection of the property. When the mower was delivered a few days later, the salesman inspected the property and stated that it was suitable for the property but that it should be driven vertically up and down the hills. The plaintiff used the mower without incident for a year but then, while mowing vertically up a 19 degree hill, the mower tipped over, severely injuring his hand. In an action against Sears for breach of an implied warranty of fitness for a particular purpose, the jury awarded the plaintiff damages and the Fourth Circuit affirmed.

In *Klein*, all three elements necessary for the creation of an implied warranty of fitness for a particular purpose under UCC § 2-315 were present. First, at the time of the sale, the salesman knew the "particular purpose" for which the lawnmower was required (mowing a large lot with numerous hills). Second, the salesman also knew that the buyers were relying on his skill and judgment to select a suitable mower, since they told him they had no experience with lawnmowers. Finally, the buyers in fact relied upon the salesman's skill to select the particular brand and model of lawnmower.[97]

Unlike an implied warranty of merchantability, the implied warranty of fitness in *Klein* did not arise from the sale itself. Instead, like an express warranty, it arose from the recommendation of a particular brand and model and representation that the lawn mower was suitable for the plaintiff's property made by the salesman and relied upon by the buyers. *Klein* also illustrates the concept of a defect in an implied warranty of fitness case. The lawnmower tipped over while it was being used in the manner intended by the buyers (to mow a property with hills) and that intended use was known to the salesman. The failure of the lawnmower to function in the way represented by the salesman, coupled with the other requirements of UCC § 2-315, resulted in the product being sufficiently defective for the plaintiff to recover. The defect was not in the lawnmower itself but in the conduct of the salesman in furnishing one that was not fit for the buyers' particular purpose.[98]

Four other general comments must be made about implied warranties of fitness. First, although the implied warranty of merchantability was not an issue in *Klein*, implied warranties of merchantability and fitness for a particular purpose are not mutually exclusive. Both warranties can exist for a single product and a buyer may bring an action alleging breaches of both implied warranties.[99] Similarly, an implied warranty of fitness also may overlap with express warranties. In *Filler v. Rayex*

---

[96] 773 F.2d 1421 (4th Cir. 1985) (applying Maryland law).

[97] *See also* Daniell v. Ford Motor Co., 581 F. Supp. 728 (D.N.M. 1984) (applying New Mexico law); Stones v. Sears, Roebuck & Co., 558 N.W.2d 540 (Neb. 1997).

[98] *See* McLaughlin v. Michelin Tire Corp., 778 P.2d 59 (Wyo. 1989).

[99] Lariviere v. Dayton Safety Ladder Co., 525 A.2d 892 (R.I. 1987).

Corp.,[100] the seller sold sunglasses that were advertised as "baseball sunglasses." Based on this advertising, the buyer purchased the sunglasses and wore them while playing baseball. The sunglasses splintered when hit by a baseball and injured the buyer. The court found that seller breached both an express warranty and an implied warranty of fitness because the sunglasses were advertised as being fit for the particular purpose being worn while playing baseball. Second, although the seller in *Klein* was a "merchant," implied warranties of fitness are not limited to merchants as are implied warranties of merchantability.[101] It is sufficient that the defendant is a "seller" within the meaning of the UCC. Third, while *Klein* involved simply the sale of a product, an implied warranty of fitness for a particular purpose also may arise where goods are provided as part of a service. Thus, when a beauty parlor operator used a waving solution on a customer in connection with administering a permanent wave, the service carried with it the implied warranty that the product used on the customer was reasonably fit for the purpose for which it was to be used.[102] Finally, although *Klein* involved the sale of a new lawnmower, implied warranties of fitness for a particular purpose apply to the sale both of new and used goods.[103]

[B]   The "Particular Purpose"

While an implied warranty of merchantability is meant to guarantee that the goods are fit for the ordinary purposes for which such goods are used, an implied warranty of fitness provides that goods are fit for the "particular purpose" for which the buyer made known to the seller. UCC § 2-315, comment 2, states:

> A "particular purpose" differs from the ordinary purpose for which the goods are used in that it envisages a specific use by the buyer which is peculiar to the nature of his business whereas the ordinary purposes for which goods are used are those envisaged in the concept of merchantability and go to uses which are customarily made of the goods in question. For example, shoes are generally used for the purpose of walking upon ordinary ground, but a seller may know that a particular pair was selected to be used for climbing mountains.

The "particular purpose" of goods is narrower than the "ordinary purpose" covered by an implied warranty of merchantability. The "particular purpose" envisages a specific use by the buyer that is peculiar to the nature of his or her business, while the "ordinary purpose" goes to uses that customarily are made of the goods.[104] The purchase of a boat as a personal pleasure craft on a lake is within the "ordinary purpose" of a boat. If the buyer did not intend to use the boat for any

---

[100] 435 F.2d 336 (7th Cir. 1970) (applying Indiana law).

[101] International Petroleum Services, Inc. v. S & N Well Service, Inc., 639 P.2d 29 (Kan. 1982).

[102] Newmark v. Gimbel's Inc., 246 A.2d 11 (N.J. Super. Ct. 1968). For a discussion of the different state positions concerning a transaction for the sale of goods and one for the provision of services, see Stephenson v. Greenberg, 617 A.2d 364 (Pa. Super. Ct. 1992).

[103] International Petroleum Services, Inc. v. S & N Well Service, Inc., 639 P.2d 29 (Kan. 1982).

[104] *See* UCC § 2-315 cmt. 2.

purpose other than its ordinary purpose, there is no implied warranty of fitness.[105] Thus, in *Klein*, the buyers sought to purchase a lawnmower that would be suitable for a specific use: a large lot with numerous hills. Most courts now take the position that UCC § 2-315 applies only when "goods do not fulfill the specific need for which they were purchased."[106] If the seller was not aware of the "particular purpose" for which the goods were to be used, there is no implied warranty of fitness.[107] An example of this is *Moss v. Batesville Casket Co.*,[108] in which the plaintiffs purchased a wooden casket for use in a concrete vault when their mother died. Two-and-a-half years later, her remains were exhumed for an autopsy as part of a medical malpractice lawsuit. At that time, the plaintiffs observed visible cracks and separation in the casket and, as it was removed, it began to come apart. However, there was no evidence showing any damage to the body from the separation of the casket. In affirming a grant of summary judgment in a suit that included a count for implied warranty of fitness for a particular purpose, the Mississippi Supreme Court found nothing in the record to show that the plaintiffs indicated any particular purpose to the defendants when they selected the casket and that the defendants made no representations about the casket. Instead, evidence obtained during discovery showed that the plaintiffs chose the casket for its esthetic value since their mother "just liked cherry wood furniture."[109] According to the court, the *fitness* purpose was served during the time the mother's body was placed in the casket and viewed by family members and friends.[110]

[C] Reliance

In determining whether or not goods are covered by an implied warranty of fitness, the trier of fact must decide whether the buyer relied on "the seller's skill or judgment to select or furnish suitable goods." In *Klein*, the buyers specifically told the salesman that they had no experience with lawn mowers and told him they wanted him to recommend a mower that would be suitable to their son's property. However, in most cases such direct statements are absent. While it is not necessary that the buyer have told the seller of the particular purpose in purchasing the goods, it is necessary that the seller had reason to know of the buyer's particular purpose and that the buyer was relying on the seller's skill or judgment to furnish the appropriate goods.[111]

---

[105] Smith v. Stewart, 667 P.2d 358 (Kan. 1983). See Doe v. Miles, Inc., 2000 Mo. App. LEXIS 770 (May 23, 2000), for a discussion of the different state views as to whether there must be a showing of a purpose distinct from the product's ordinary purpose to establish a claim for breach of implied warranty of fitness for a particular purpose.

[106] Matos v. Nextran, Inc., 2009 U.S. Dist. LEXIS 71041 (D.V.I. Aug. 10, 2009) (applying Virgin Islands law); Stones v. Sears, Roebuck & Co., 558 N.W.2d 540, 547 (Neb. 1997).

[107] Ambassador Steel Co. v. Ewald Steel Co., 190 N.W.2d 275 (Mich. Ct. App. 1971).

[108] 935 So. 2d 393 (Miss. 2006).

[109] *Id.* at 400.

[110] *Id.* See Adsit Company, Inc. v. Gustin, 874 N.E.2d 1018 (Ind. Ct. App. 2007), in which the court found no breach of any implied warranty of fitness for a particular purpose since there was no evidence that a retailer was aware that customers, who purchased seat covers over the Internet, intended to use them in the restoration of an automobile.

[111] Bergquist v. MacKay Engines, Inc., 538 N.W.2d 655 (Iowa Ct. App. 1995). *See* Smith v. Pfizer, Inc.,

Whether the statements of the parties or the circumstances surrounding the transaction support a finding that the buyer relied on the seller's skill or judgment is an issue for the trier of fact.[112] Among the factors that influence a court's determination of this issue is the relative expertise of the parties with the goods sought for purchase.[113] In *Barb v. Wallace*,[114] the buyer purchased a gasoline-powered engine for use in a go-cart. When he attempted to start the engine, it exploded, severely injuring him. The buyer alleged that he told the seller that he intended to use the engine in a go-cart and that the seller told him that the engine "ran real good" and that it could be used in a go-cart "cause the shaft was out of the side of the engine."[115] The seller, however, argued that the buyer's judgment and skill was just as good as his since, at the time of the purchase, the buyer was taking a course in auto mechanics and had worked on small engines. The Maryland appellate court felt that this presented a factual dispute for the jury. However, the court said that the fact that the buyer may have had some experience with the goods did not necessarily preclude the possibility that he relied on the seller's knowledge of the capabilities of the particular engine.[116]

Another factor that courts consider when determining the existence of an implied warranty of fitness is whether or not the buyer participated in the selection of the goods. Where a buyer inspected the goods before purchase, there is less likelihood of reliance on the seller's skill and judgment. This extends to cases where a buyer had an agent examine the goods before purchase. In *Sessa v. Riegle*,[117] a buyer sent his agent to examine a horse before purchasing it. He purchased the horse after the agent examined it and without any reliance on the seller's judgment. As a result, the Pennsylvania federal court held there was no implied warranty of fitness because the buyer relied on statements from his own agent rather than from the seller. This position is supported by UCC § 2-316(3)(b) which states:

> When the buyer before entering into the contract has examined the goods or the sample or model as fully as he desired or has refused to examine the goods there is no implied warranty with regard to defects which an examination ought in the circumstances to have revealed to him.[118]

A third factor that may influence a court in deciding whether or not there was reliance is whether the goods were manufactured according to specifications provided by the buyer. If they were, an argument for an implied warranty of fitness

---

688 F. Supp. 2d 735 (M.D. Tenn. 2010) (applying Tennessee law).

[112] Norcold, Inc. v. Gateway Supply Co., 798 N.E.2d 618 (Ohio Ct. App. 2003).

[113] Glasstech, Inc. v. Chicago Blower Corp., 675 F. Supp. 2d 752 (N.D. Ohio 2009).

[114] 412 A.2d 1314 (Md. Ct. Spec. App. 1980).

[115] *Id.* at 1315–1316.

[116] *Id.* at 1319. See Driscoll v. Standard Hardware, 785 N.W.2d 805 (Minn. Ct. App. 2010), in which the court concluded that the deceased's extensive use of an industrial drill during the lease period gave him knowledge of it capabilities and precluded any reliance on representations of the drill's slope capabilities.

[117] 427 F. Supp. 760 (E.D. Pa. 1977) (applying Pennsylvania law).

[118] *See* Pilcher v. Suttle Equip. Co., 223 S.W.3d 789 (Ark. 2006).

is weakened since the buyer did not rely on the seller's skill or judgment.[119] The position is supported by UCC § 2-316, comment 9, which states:

> The situation in which the buyer gives precise and complete specifications to the seller is not explicitly covered in this section, but this is a frequent circumstance by which the implied warranties may be excluded. The warranty of fitness for a particular purpose would not normally arise since in such a situation there is usually no reliance on the seller by the buyer.

Finally, although purchase of a particular brand of goods does not necessarily mean that the buyer did not rely on the seller's judgment, a buyer's claim of reliance will be weakened if he or she insisted upon purchasing a particular brand. In *Siemen v. Alden*,[120] the buyer heard that a particular brand of "gang-rip saw" was of good quality and decided to purchase one. When he went to the dealer, there was a six-month delay for the brand he wanted. The buyer purchased a used saw of the same brand thinking that it would be of the same high quality. The Illinois appellate court held that the buyer acted on his own opinion of the brand rather than on any judgment by the seller. As a result, no implied warranty of fitness attached to the sale of the used saw. The position is supported by UCC § 2-315, comment 5, which states, in part, that "[i]f the buyer himself is insisting on a particular brand he is not relying on the seller's skill and judgment and so no warranty results."

§ 2.05 THE SCOPE OF WARRANTIES

[A] Introduction

The common law required privity of contract between the seller and the buyer of goods in all actions based upon a breach of an express or implied warranty.[121] A buyer or user of goods was barred from recovering against those in the chain of distribution with whom he or she did not have a direct contractual relationship. The effect of this was to prevent consumers from bringing suits for breach of warranty against manufacturers, manufacturers of component parts, and wholesalers, and to limit their suits to their immediate retail seller. Although "the citadel of privity" began to decline in the early part of the twentieth century, first in cases involving the sale of food[122] and then in negligence cases,[123] the New Jersey Supreme Court was the first court to abolish privity as a defense in actions based on breach of implied warranties.[124] Although a number of states have followed New Jersey's lead, privity has not disappeared in warranty actions.

---

[119] Smith v. Pfizer Inc., 688 F. Supp. 2d 735 (M.D. Tenn. 2010) (applying Tennessee law); Controltek, Inc. v. Kwikee Enterprises, Inc., 585 P.2d 670 (Or. 1978); Layne Atlantic Co. v. Koppers Co., Inc., 201 S.E.2d 609 (Va. 1974).

[120] 341 N.E.2d 713 (Ill. App. Ct. 1975).

[121] Wood v. Advanced Rumely Thresher Co., 234 N.W. 517 (N.D. 1931).

[122] Mazetti v. Armour & Co., 135 P. 633 (Wash. 1913).

[123] MacPherson v. Buick Motor Co., 111 N.E. 1050 (N.Y. 1916).

[124] Henningsen v. Bloomfield Motors, Inc., 161 A.2d 69 (N.J. 1960).

Fundamental to the role of privity in breach of warranty actions is the classification of *vertical* and *horizontal* privity. *Vertical privity* deals with who the buyer can sue. Cases in which vertical privity is an issue involve buyers who did not purchase the goods directly from the named defendant.[125] An example of this is the buyer who purchases defective goods from a retail store and then brings an action against the manufacturer of those goods. Although the buyer is in the chain of distribution from the manufacturer, the buyer's contractual relationship (i.e., privity) extends no further than to the retailer. In contrast, *horizontal privity* deals with who can sue. Cases in which horizontal privity is an issue involve users of defective goods who were not the purchasers of the goods and thus are outside the direct chain of distribution. An example of the problem of horizontal privity is *Henningsen v. Bloomfield Motors, Inc.*,[126] in which a woman was injured while driving an automobile that had been purchased and given to her as a present by her husband. Since she was not the purchaser of the automobile, Mrs. Henningsen was not in the chain of distribution. She was able to recover only because the New Jersey court struck down the privity requirement.

The role privity plays in breach of warranty actions has become more complicated in recent years. Although the UCC governs horizontal privity cases, vertical privity has been left to the individual states. As a result, who can be sued for breach of warranty often depends upon whether the buyer is seeking damages for personal injury, property damage, economic loss, or consequential damages. In addition some states take different approaches to privity in cases of express and implied warranties. They permit recovery for breach of implied warranty in situations where it is restricted for breach of express warranty.[127] One reason for this is that implied warranties arise by operation of law without specific adoption by the seller.[128]

[B] Horizontal Privity

UCC § 2-318 offers the states three alternative versions of the scope of a seller's liability for an express or implied warranty:[129]

Alternative A

A seller's warranty whether express or implied extends to any natural person who is in the family or household of his buyer or who is a guest in his home if it is reasonable to expect that such person may use, consume, or be affected by the goods and who is injured in person by breach of the warranty. A seller may not exclude or limit the operation of this section.

---

[125] Rheem Manufacturing Co. v. Phelps Heating & Air, 714 N.E.2d 1218 (Ind. Ct. App. 1999).

[126] 161 A.2d 69 (N.J. 1960). In Johansson v. Central Garden & Pet Co., 804 F. Supp. 2d 257 (D.N.J. 2011) (applying California law), the court held that the privity exception for pesticides did not apply when the plaintiffs' pets, rather than the plaintiffs themselves, were injured by a flea and tick treatment.

[127] Nobility Homes of Texas, Inc. v. Shivers, 557 S.W.2d 77 (Tex. 1977); Reichhold Chemical, Inc. v. Haas, 1989 Ohio App. LEXIS 4129 (Nov. 3, 1989).

[128] *See* Tex Enterprises, Inc. v. Brockway Standard, Inc., 66 P.3d 625 (Wash. 2003).

[129] The three alternatives offered by UCC § 2-318 are not exhaustive. A number of states have adopted variations on the alternatives.

Alternative B

A seller's warranty whether express or implied extends to any natural person who may reasonably be expected to use, consume or be affected by the goods and who is injured in person by breach of the warranty. A seller may not exclude or limit the operation of this section.

Alternative C

A seller's warranty whether express or implied extends to any person who may reasonably be expected to use, consume or be affected by the goods and who is injured by breach of the warranty. A seller may not exclude or limit the operation of this section with respect to injury to the person of an individual to whom the warranty extends.

Alternative A, which has been adopted by the largest number of states, is, by its wording, the most restrictive of the three approaches to privity. It extends the protection of an express or implied warranty to "any natural person who is in the family or household of his buyer or a guest in his home if it is reasonable to expect that such person may use, consume or be affected by the goods."[130] However, there is no "third-party exception" and if the plaintiff is not within the group set out in Alternative A, the warranty extends only to the first buyer or user of the product.[131] In addition, it limits recovery to injuries "in person" from the breach of the warranty. This excludes property damage and economic loss.

Although the extent of the protection of a warranty under Alternative A appears to be limited, some states have held that its list of potential plaintiffs is not necessarily exhaustive. For example, Illinois courts have expanded the class to include employees of the ultimate purchaser who suffer personal injury.[132] In *Reed v. City of Chicago*,[133] an Illinois federal district court further expanded the category of plaintiffs who can recover for personal injury by holding that the estate of a man who hanged himself while in jail could bring a suit for breach of express and implied warranties against the manufacturer of the paper gown that the man used to kill himself. According to the court, the beneficiary of any warranty made by the manufacturer of the gown included potentially suicidal detainees. In designing and manufacturing the gown, the manufacturer knew that its users would be jail detainees. Since the safety of those detainees was explicitly or implicitly part of the bargain between the manufacturer and the city (which bought the gowns), a person detained by the city should be able to enforce the protections of any warranties.[134]

Alternative B to UCC § 2-318 is broader. Although it also applies to a "natural person," it omits the requirement that the third party be in the family, household,

---

[130] Smith v. Mitlof, 198 F. Supp. 2d 492 (S.D.N.Y. 2002) (applying New York law). Some states have abolished the distinction between "natural" and "legal persons." JKT Co., Inc. v. Hardwick, 265 S.E.2d 510 (S.C. 1980).

[131] Barnett v. Royal Cup, Inc., 968 F. Supp. 690 (N.D. Ga. 1997) (applying Georgia law).

[132] Thomas v. Bombardier-Rotax Motorenfabrik, 869 F. Supp. 551 (N.D. Ill. 1994) (applying Illinois law).

[133] 263 F. Supp. 2d 1123 (N.D. Ill. 2003) (applying Illinois law).

[134] *Id.* at 1126.

or guest of the buyer. Instead, it extends protection of the warranty to anyone who "may reasonably be expected to use, consume or be affected by the goods." However, it still limits recovery to personal injuries. Thus, a buyer who claimed injury to his boat was unable to recover under a warranty claim because he suffered property damage.[135]

The most expansive (but least adopted) alternative is Alternative C. It permits "any person who may reasonably be expected to use, consume or be affected by the goods" to bring an action for breach of warranty. Since this alternative is not limited to "natural" persons, it also includes corporations. In addition, it does not limit recovery to personal injury. Instead, anyone who is "injured by breach of the warranty" may bring an action.[136]

[C] Vertical Privity

The more difficult question in breach of warranty cases has been vertical privity. This is because whether privity is required to recover against a remote seller (i.e., the manufacturer of goods sold by a retailer) is not covered explicitly by UCC. Comment 3 to UCC § 2-318 states that the section "is not intended to enlarge or restrict the developing case law on whether the seller's warranties, given to his buyer who resells, extends to other persons in the distributive chain." Thus, the drafters of the UCC left it to the courts to determine whether vertical privity is required in a warranty action between a buyer and a remote seller. As a result, there are a number of different approaches to vertical privity.

The majority of states have abandoned the vertical privity requirement, in all or certain situations, either by statute or by judicial decision.[137] The New Jersey Supreme Court, for example, held that, in a case involving economic and consequential damages, the absence of privity between the ultimate purchaser of a truck and a remote supplier did not prevent the extension to the purchaser of the warranties the supplier gave to the manufacturer.[138] Other states have abolished the requirement of vertical privity only in cases where the buyer seeks personal injury or property damages.[139] According to one court, the reason for the privity requirement is to prevent "a manufacturer from being held liable for damages of unknown and unlimited scope."[140] Although a number of states still require privity in order to recover economic and consequential damages,[141] a growing number

---

[135] Hedges v. U.S., 2003 U.S. Dist. LEXIS 23383 (D.V.I. June 30, 2003) (applying Virgin Islands law).

[136] Stoney v. Franklin, 54 Va. Cir. 591 (2001).

[137] Pack v. Damon, 434 F.3d 810 (6th Cir. 2006) (applying Michigan law); Hyundai Motor America, Inc. v. Goodin, 822 N.E.2d 947 (Ind. 2005).

[138] Spring Motors Distributors, Inc. v. Ford Motor Co., 489 A.2d 660 (N.J. 1985).

[139] Szajna v. General Motors Corp., 503 N.E.2d 760 (Ill. 1986). Although the purchasers of automobiles in *Szajna* could not bring an action based on implied warranty against the manufacturers because of the lack of privity, the court stated that the UCC creates implied warranties "running from the dealer to the purchaser." *Id.* at 767.

[140] *Id.* at 767.

[141] Hyundai Motor America, Inc. v. Goodin, 822 N.E.2d 947 (Ind. 2005); Tex Enterprises, Inc. v.

permit non-privity plaintiffs to recover such losses.[142] Finally, even states that take a strict approach to vertical privity recognize two exceptions to the rule: where the immediate seller of the product was an agent of the manufacturer and where the manufacturer participated significantly in the sale of the product.[143]

Some states still require vertical privity between the buyer and the defendant regardless of the type of damage.[144] In *Keaton v. A.B.C. Drug Co.*,[145] a woman taking a bottle of bleach from a shelf in a store was injured when bleach splashed on her face due to an unseen loose cap on the bottle. In her suit against the store for breach of an implied warranty of merchantability because it displayed the bleach at a dangerous height with a loose cap, the Georgia Supreme Court stated that, in order to recover, she had to have privity with the store. However, the court held that, by taking possession of bottle with intent to purchase it, the woman established the required privity.

§ 2.06   NOTICE

[A]   Introduction

One aspect of an action for breach of warranty that sets it apart from negligence and strict liability is the requirement that the buyer give the seller notice of the breach of warranty before filing suit.[146] Under UCC § 2-607(3), "[w]here tender has been accepted, the buyer must within a reasonable time after he discovers or should have discovered any breach notify the seller of the breach or be barred from any remedy."[147] The term "within a reasonable time" is determined on a case-by-case basis, and in light of the nature, purpose, and circumstances of the case. Courts have given a number of reasons for making notice a prerequisite for recovering damages. Notice provides the seller with an opportunity to correct any defect in the goods. Notice also makes it possible for the parties to resolve any problems with the goods through negotiations. Finally, and perhaps most important, notice minimizes the possibility of prejudice to the seller by giving it the opportunity to investigate the claim and take whatever steps may be required to defend itself or to minimize its damages while the facts still are fresh in the minds of the parties.[148] Because of the importance of the notice requirement, it is excused only in two situations: where the seller already had actual knowledge of the defect

---

Brockway Standard, Inc., 66 P.3d 625 (Wash. 2003); Mekertichian v. Mercedes-Benz U.S.A., 807 N.E.2d 1165 (Ill. App. Ct. 2004).

[142] AgGrow Oils LLC v. National Union Fire Ins. Co. of Pittsburgh, 276 F. Supp. 2d 999 (D.N.D. 2003) (applying North Dakota law).

[143] Hyundai Motors America, Inc. v. Goodin, 804 N.E.2d 775, 787 (Ind. Ct. App. 2004).

[144] *See* Complex Int'l Co. v. Taylor, 209 S.W.3d 462 (Ky. 2006).

[145] 467 S.E.2d 558 (Ga. 1996). *See* Lee v. Mylan, 806 F. Supp. 2d 1320 (M.D. Ga. 2011) (applying Georgia law) for a discussion of vertical privity under Georgia law.

[146] For a detailed examination of the notice requirement in one state, see Lisa Macrito, *A Buyer's Obligation to Give Notice of a Defective Product in Illinois*, 89 ILL. BAR. J. 34 (2001).

[147] Smith v. Pfizer Inc., 688 F. Supp. 2d 735 (M.D. Tenn. 2010) (applying Tennessee law).

[148] Palmer v. A.H. Robins Co., 684 P.2d 187 (Colo. 1984); Maybank v. S. S. Kresge Co., 273 S.E.2d 681 (N.C. 1981); Wal-Mart Stores, Inc. v. Wheeler, 586 S.E.2d 83 (Ga. Ct. App. 2003).

of the particular product, or where the buyer or consumer suffers personal injury. In the second situation, the notice requirement is satisfied by filing a lawsuit against the seller.[149]

[B] "Buyer" and "Seller"

Since UCC § 2-607 requires the "buyer" to notify the "seller" of any breach of warranty, the first question is who qualifies as a "buyer" and a "seller." The issue of who is a "buyer" has arisen when the potential plaintiff either did not purchase the goods (i.e., was a third-party beneficiary) or purchased the goods from a retailer rather than the manufacturer whom they are suing (i.e., was a subpurchaser). Although comment 5 to UCC § 2-607(3)(a) states that the section extends to requiring the third-party beneficiary to notify the seller that an injury has occurred, most courts have looked, instead, to the language of the UCC. UCC § 2-103(1)(d) defines a "buyer" as "a person who buys or contracts to buy goods." Using this definition and interpreting UCC § 2-607(3)(a) literally, courts have held that notice of a breach of warranty is required only from actual buyers[150] and subpurchasers[151] of the goods. Nonbuyer beneficiaries of goods have no obligation to provide notice.[152] Thus, in *Tomczuk v. Town of Cheshire*,[153] a young girl was visiting the home of her friend and while there was injured due to a defect in a bicycle owned by her friend. The Connecticut court held that, since the young girl was a third-party beneficiary and not the "buyer" of the bicycle, she was not required to give notice to the manufacturer.

Closely related to the issue of who is a "buyer" is that of who the buyer must notify (i.e., who is a "seller"). For example, if a buyer wishes to bring a breach of warranty action against an automobile manufacturer, must the buyer notify the manufacturer or is it sufficient for the buyer to notify the dealer who sold the automobile? The majority of courts that have considered the question have held that buyers need only notify the immediate seller of the goods, not remote sellers such as the manufacturer.[154] The reason for this is that, for purposes of UCC § 2-607, courts view each transaction in the marketing chain as separate.[155] However,

---

[149] Allstate Insurance Co. v. Daimler Chrysler, 2004 U.S. Dist LEXIS 3811 (N.D. Ill. Mar. 9, 2004) (applying Illinois law).

[150] Phipps v. General Motors Corp., 363 A.2d 955 (Md. Ct. App. 1976).

[151] Snell v. G.D. Searle & Co., 595 F. Supp. 654 (N.D. Ala. 1984) (applying Alabama law); Goldstein v. G. D. Searle & Co., 378 N.E.2d 1083 (Ill. App. Ct. 1978).

[152] Matos v. Nextran, Inc., 2009 U.S. Dist. LEXIS 71041 (D.V.I. Aug. 10, 2009) (applying Virgin Islands law); Ayala v. Joy Manufacturing Co., 1983 U.S. Dist. LEXIS 18967 (D. Colo. Feb. 25, 1983) (applying Colorado law). See, however, Ratkovich v. SmithKline and French Lab., 711 F. Supp. 436 (N.D. Ill. 1989) (applying Illinois law), in which the court held that the UCC intended the notice provision to extend to third-party beneficiaries.

[153] 217 A.2d 71 (Conn. Super. Ct. 1965). *Tomczuk* was followed by Gerrity v. R.J. Reynolds Tobacco Co., 399 F. Supp. 2d 87 (D. Conn. 2005) (applying Connecticut law).

[154] Hubbard v. General Motors Corp., 1996 U.S. Dist. LEXIS 6974 (S.D.N.Y. May 22, 1996) (applying New York law); Sullivan v. Young Brothers & Co., Inc., 893 F. Supp. 1148 (D. Me. 1995) (applying Maine law).

[155] Firestone Tire and Rubber Co. v. Cannon, 452 A.2d 192 (Md. Ct. Spec. App. 1982).

courts in a few states have required the buyer to notify the remote manufacturer directly.[156]

[C] Adequate Notice

Another problem with the notice requirement of § 2-607 is determining what constitutes adequate notice. Comment 4 to the section states that "[t]he content of the notification need merely be sufficient to let the seller know that the transaction is still troublesome and must be watched." Notification does not have to include a statement of all of the objections that the buyer has with the goods or be a claim for damages. In interpreting UCC § 2-607, courts have been liberal in interpreting what constitutes sufficient notice. Oral notice to the seller is acceptable as is returning the goods to the seller for repair.[157] A letter from a buyer's attorney to the manufacturer of a ladder stating that the attorney had been retained by the buyer to represent him in his claim for personal injuries resulting from the seller's faulty equipment also was held to be sufficient notice even though it did not identify the equipment or indicate that the buyer was injured when he fell from a ladder.[158] Finally a buyer's calling his dissatisfaction with the goods to the attention of the manufacturer's repairman was held to be adequate notice.[159]

[D] "Reasonable Time"

A third issue in interpreting UCC § 2-607 is what constitutes "a reasonable time" within which to give the seller notice. This depends upon the nature, the purpose, and the circumstances of the particular case. Comment 4 to UCC § 2-607 states that what constitutes a reasonable time where the buyer is a retail consumer is judged differently from a reasonable time when the buyer is a merchant. The comment goes on to state that "the rule of requiring notification is designed to defeat commercial bad faith, not to deprive a good faith consumer of his remedy." Thus, in cases involving retail consumers, many courts hold that delay alone is not sufficient to prevent recovery.[160] Instead, the seller must show that the delay in giving notice prejudiced it by increasing the claim for damages, hindering the discovery of evidence, or resulting in the loss of evidence that might have helped the seller defend against the claim.[161] The burden is on the seller to show that the delay resulted in prejudice. However, other courts hold that a showing of prejudice

---

[156] Compaq Computer Corp. v. Lapray, 135 S.W.3d 657 (Tex. 2004); Berry v. G.D. Searle & Co., 309 N.E.2d 550 (Ill. 1974).

[157] Tufano Motorcar, Inc. v. Equipment and Resources International, Ltd., 1992 Conn. Super. LEXIS 2777 (Sept. 18, 1992).

[158] Lariviere v. Dayton Safety Ladder Company, 525 A.2d 892 (R.I. 1987).

[159] Vintage Homes, Inc. v. Coldiron, 585 S.W.2d 886 (Tex. Civ. App. 1979).

[160] Maybank v. S. S. Kresge Co., 273 S.E.2d 681 (N.C. 1981) (a delay of three years was not unreasonable as a matter of law under the facts of the case); Golden v. Den-Mat Corp., 276 P.3d 773 (Kan. Ct. App. 2012).

[161] Smith v. Robertshaw Controls Co., 2003 U.S. Dist. LEXIS 23639 (D. Mass. Dec. 31, 2003) (applying Massachusetts law) (a water heater accidently was destroyed after a year of being stored in case an insurance adjuster wanted to inspect it; the failure of the owner to notify the manufacturer of the accident during that year deprived it of the opportunity to inspect it).

is not required.[162] Notification within a reasonable period of time is a condition precedent to recovery and that without proof of notification, a warranty action must fail. These courts look simply to the length of time after the buyer discovered the defect and whether there was an explanation for the delay in providing notice. Thus, an unexplained delay of giving notice for almost four years after an accident was held to be unreasonable.[163]

§ 2.07   DISCLAIMERS AND LIMITATIONS OF WARRANTIES

Although selling goods without a warranty, or with limitations on the buyer's remedy if the goods are defective, may send a message to potential buyers that the seller does not stand behind its product, UCC § 2-316 permits a seller to exclude or modify warranties. In addition, UCC § 2-719 allows a seller to limit the remedies or damages available to a buyer. If a seller follows the procedures set out in these sections, a buyer may be prevented from recovering all or part of the damages caused by the failure of the goods.[164] However, disclaimers and limitations of warranties are not favored by the courts and are construed strictly against a seller.[165]

[A]   Exclusion or Modification of Warranties

[1]   Express Warranties

UCC § 2-316(1) permits a seller to exclude or limit an express warranty but only when it is "reasonable." Since a seller is not required to provide a buyer with an express warranty, a seller may include a provision in the contract stating that none is given. However, if the seller makes a representation that amounts to an express warranty, the UCC makes it difficult to disclaim or modify that warranty if it formed "part of the basis of the bargain." Thus, a seller cannot make an affirmation of fact about goods and then insert a provision in the sales contract excluding "all warranties, express or implied."[166] In order for a disclaimer or modification of an express warranty to be valid, its language must be consistent with the language of the express warranty.[167] In addition, although the UCC does not require that the language of a disclaimer of an express warranty to be "conspicuous," as it does for an implied warranty of merchantability, the New Jersey Supreme Court has stated that "it is inconceivable that such a disclaimer or limitation of an express warranty which is other than clear and conspicuous could be regarded as valid and

---

[162] San Antonio v. Warwick Club Ginger Ale Co., 248 A.2d 778 (R.I. 1968).

[163] Salmon Rivers Sportsman Camps Inc. v. Cessna Aircraft Co., 544 P.2d 306 (Idaho 1975).

[164] *See* Moore v. Mack Trucks, 40 S.W.3d 888 (Ky. Ct. App. 2001). However, where "an exclusive or limited remedy . . . fail[s] of its essential purpose," the buyer is entitled to other remedies. § 2-719(2). *See* Pack v. Damon Corp., 434 F.3d 810 (6th Cir. 2006) (applying Michigan law).

[165] James River Equipment Co. v. Beadle County Equipment, Inc., 646 N.W.2d 265 (S.D. 2002).

[166] UCC § 2-316 cmt. 1.

[167] Boud v. SDNCO, Inc., 54 P.3d 1131 (Utah 2002); Mercedes-Benz of North America, Inc. v. Dickenson, 720 S.W.2d 844 (Tex. App. 1986).

enforceable."[168]

An example of what one court called "the remote case in which a seller has effectively limited an express warranty" is *Jones v. Davenport*,[169] in which the buyer was building a new home and contracted with the seller for the brick work on the outside of the house and interior fireplaces. The buyer selected the brick on his own and verified the color and style on a sample board belonging to the seller. However, the majority of the brick delivered to the site was not the color the buyer ordered and the few that were correct contrasted and diminished the appearance of the house. The Ohio appellate court held that, although the sample board created an express warranty, the board also contained a disclaimer that read: "Samples prepared to show general color and texture. Usual color variations from these samples may be expected."[170] Since the buyer admitted that he read the disclaimer when he viewed the sample board, the court held that anyone would have seen that any warranty was limited by the disclaimer language.

[2] Implied Warranties of Merchantability

UCC § 2-316(2) recognizes a seller's right to exclude or modify an implied warranty of merchantability. However, the section imposes two important requirements on the right and the omission of either of the requirements makes an attempted disclaimer ineffective.[171] First, the language of the disclaimer specifically must mention "merchantability."[172] Second, if the disclaimer is in writing, it must be "conspicuous."[173] UCC § 2-201(10) defines "conspicuous" as a term

> so written, displayed, or presented that a reasonable person against which it is to operate ought to have noticed it. Whether a term is "conspicuous" or not is a decision for the court. Conspicuous terms include the following:
>
> (A) a heading in capitals equal to or greater in size than the surrounding text, or in contrasting type, font, or color to the surrounding text of the same or lesser size; and
>
> (B) language in the body of a record or display in larger type than the surrounding text, or in contrasting type, font, or color to the surrounding text of the same size, or set off from surrounding text of the same size by symbols or other marks that call attention to the language.

Cases dealing with whether a disclaimer of an implied warranty of merchantability was "conspicuous" turn on whether the size of the type and color of the

---

[168] Gladden v. Cadillac Motor Car Division, 416 A.2d 394, 399 (N.J. 1980).

[169] 2001 Ohio App. LEXIS 226 (Jan. 26, 2001).

[170] *Id.* at 18.

[171] Providence & Worcester Railroad Co. v. Sargent & Greenleaf, Inc., 802 F. Supp. 680, 687 (D.R.I. 1992) (applying Rhode Island law).

[172] H&H Laundry v. TheLaundryList.Com, 2010 U.S. Dist. LEXIS 82663 (M.D. Fla. Aug. 6, 2010) (applying Florida law) (discussing the use of the term "as is" in merchantability cases); Jordan v. Carlisle Construction Co., 2001 U.S. Dist. LEXIS 24287 (D. Neb. May 3, 2001) (applying Nebraska law).

[173] Tennessee Carolina Transportation, Inc. v. Strick Corp., 196 S.E.2d 711 (N.C. 1973); Leland Industries, Inc. v. Suntek Industries, Inc., 362 S.E.2d 441 (Ga. Ct. App. 1987).

printed disclaimer distinguished it from other provisions in the contract.[174] A textbook example of what constitutes a conspicuous disclaimer is *Mitsch v. General Motors Corp.*,[175] in which the plaintiffs purchased a used automobile from a General Motors dealership in 2002. Over the next 18 months, the plaintiffs experienced various problems with the vehicle and took it to two General Motors dealerships for repairs. When the repairs proved unsuccessful, the plaintiffs sought to revoke the acceptance of the vehicle, alleging among other things, breach of implied warranty of merchantability against General Motors and the dealership.[176] The defendants asserted that there was no warranty since the purchase agreement stated that the vehicle was sold "as is — no warranty."[177] The Illinois appellate court, however, affirmed the grant of summary judgment to the defendants even though the disclaimer did not use the word "merchantability." According to the court the conspicuousness of the disclaimer outweighed any other concerns.

> [T]he term "as is" appeared prominently at the top of the disclaimer along with notice that plaintiffs would bear the entire expense of repairing or correcting any defects that currently existed in the vehicle or may develop in the future. The disclaimer was in all capital letters, the terms "entire expense" and "without" were underlined, and plaintiff . . . signed his name below that provision. . . . [W]e conclude that "as is" was sufficient to disclaim the implied warranty of merchantability and that the prominent placement and size of the disclaimer in the purchase agreement are fatal to the plaintiff's argument.[178]

[3] Implied Warranties of Fitness for Particular Purpose

UCC § 2-316(2) also provides for the exclusion or modification of an implied warranty of fitness for a particular purpose. Although the disclaimer of such a warranty may be in general language, it must be "by a writing and conspicuous." According to the section, language to exclude all implied warranties of fitness is sufficient if it states: "There are no warranties which extend beyond the description of the face hereof." However, the restrictive attitude of some courts towards the disclaimer of implied warranties is expressed in their view that, even if a disclaimer strictly complies with the language of UCC § 2-316(2), a court still may find it unconscionable as a matter of law and thus unenforceable.[179]

[4] "As Is" Disclaimers

An alternative method of disclaiming implied warranties is provided by UCC § 2-316(3). This section provides that, "unless the circumstances indicate otherwise, all implied warranties are excluded by expressions like 'as is', 'with all faults' or other language which in common understanding calls the buyer's attention to the

---

[174] Koellmer v. Chrysler Motors, Inc., 276 A.2d 807 (Conn. Cir. Ct. 1970).

[175] 359 Ill. App. 3d 99 (2005).

[176] *Id.* at 101–102.

[177] *Id.* at 102.

[178] *Id.* at 105.

[179] Schmaltz v. Nissen, 431 N.W.2d 657, 661–662 (S.D. 1988).

exclusion of warranties and makes plain that there is no implied warranty."[180] According to comment 7 to UCC § 2-316, these are terms of ordinary commercial usage that are understood to mean that the buyer takes the entire risk as to the quality of the particular goods. Since the subsection does not specifically state that the seller must mention the term "merchantability" or require that the language of the disclaimer be "conspicuous," courts are split whether to read those requirements into UCC § 2-316(3).[181] Despite the UCC provision, approximately a dozen states and the District of Columbia do not permit the "as is" sale of consumer products.

Since UCC § 2-316(3) applies only to implied warranties, an "as is" clause cannot exclude an express warranty. An example of this is *Gable v. Boles*,[182] in which a salesman sold a used boat to a buyer, claiming that it was "winterized." The buyer signed a sales contract that stated that the boat was sold "as is." In reality, the boat had not been "winterized" and, as a result, it did not operate properly. The Alabama appellate court held that the salesman's claim that the boat was "winterized" created an express warranty that was not defeated by the subsequent "as is" clause in the contract for sale.

[B] Limitations on Warranties

In many sales situations, sellers will warrant in the sales contract that its goods are free from defects for a limited period of time (i.e., one year) or, in the case of automobiles, for a certain number of miles they are driven. The seller then will limit the extent of its liability if the goods are defective during that time by inserting a limitation of remedy provision in the sales contract. An example of such a provision is one that stated:

> UNDER NO CIRCUMSTANCES WILL SELLER BE LIABLE FOR ANY INCIDENTAL OR CONSEQUENTIAL DAMAGES, OR FOR ANY OTHER LOSS, DAMAGES OR EXPENSE OF ANY KIND, INCLUDING LOSS OF PROFITS ARISING IN CONNECTION WITH THIS CONTRACT OR WITH THE USE OR INABILITY TO USE SELLER'S PRODUCTS FURNISHED UNDER THIS CONTRACT. . . . BUYER'S REMEDY IS LIMITED TO EITHER (i) REPAIR OR REPLACEMENT OF THE DEFECTIVE PART OF PRODUCT, OR AT SELLER'S OPTION, (ii) RETURN OF THE PRODUCT AND REFUND OF THE PURCHASE PRICE, AND SUCH REMEDY SHALL BE BUYER'S ENTIRE AND EXCLUSIVE REMEDY.[183]

Limitation of remedy clauses in contracts are a means of allocating the risks between the seller and the buyer. UCC § 2-719(1) provides that a sales contract may limit the damages that a buyer may recover or limit the remedy to "return of the

---

[180] Rawson v. Conover, 20 P.3d 876 (Utah 2001); Russell v. Wilson, 991 So. 2d 745 (Ala. Civ. App. 2008).

[181] *See* Gaylord v. Lawler Mobile Homes, Inc., 477 So. 2d 382 (Ala. 1985) (holding that the requirements are not required); Gindy Manufacturing Corp. v. Cardinale Trucking Corp., 268 A.2d 345 (N.J. Super. Ct. Law Div. 1970) (the requirements applied to § 2-316(2)).

[182] 718 So. 2d 68 (Ala. Civ. App. 1998).

[183] Kearney & Trecker Corp. v. Master Engraving Co., 527 A.2d 429, 431 (N.J. 1987).

goods and repayment of the price or to repair and replacement" of the defective goods.[184] UCC § 2-791(3) also permits a seller to limit or exclude consequential damages unless the "limitation or exclusion is unconscionable."[185] This section provides that, while consequential damages for breach of warranty may be excluded unless "unconscionable," such a limitation with respect to damages for personal injuries is "prima facie unconscionable." In cases involving consumer goods, the limitation of consequential damages for personal injury is considered prima facie unconscionable.[186] However, where the buyer's loss is commercial, such a limitation is not prima facie unconscionable.[187] In addition, a limitation that is presented as part of a warranty may be so deceptive, confusing, or misleading as to be invalid.[188]

A seller's ability to create an exclusive or limited remedy also becomes ineffective if the remedy fails of its "essential purpose."[189] Thus, if the seller limits the buyer's remedy to repair the defective goods and the seller is unable to correct the defect within a reasonable period of time, the exclusive remedy fails.[190] However, courts are split on the effect of the failure of the exclusive remedy to achieve its essential purpose. A number of courts have adopted the view that the failure of the limited remedy also invalidates the exclusion of consequential damages. Others hold that the exclusion of consequential damages is independent of the limited warranty so that if the repair or replacement remedy fails, the validity of the exclusion of consequential damages depends on the intention of the parties.[191]

§ 2.08   DAMAGES FOR BREACH OF WARRANTY

If goods do not comply with an express or implied warranty, the buyer may suffer one or more of five different types of damages: loss of value of the product; damage to (or loss of) the product; economic loss from the inability to use the product; personal injury; or damage to property other than the product. Courts have stated that the purpose of the UCC is to shift those losses from the individual victims to those responsible for manufacturing or selling the product.[192] Since the UCC does not make any distinction between damages recoverable for the breach of an express warranty and the breach of an implied warranty, damages for both are governed by UCC § 2-714 and § 2-715.

---

[184] For an example of a seller limiting its liability for consequential damages for any breach of warranty, see Moore v. Mack Trucks, Inc., 40 S.W.3d 888 (Ky. Ct. App. 2001).

[185] Schmaltz v. Nissen, 431 N.W.2d 657 (S.D. 1988).

[186] Figueroa v. Boston Scientific Corp., 254 F. Supp. 2d 361 (S.D.N.Y. 2003) (applying New York law); Collins v. Uniroyal, Inc., 315 A.2d 16 (N.J. 1974); Moore v. Coachmen Industries, Inc., 499 S.E.2d 772 (N.C. Ct. App. 1998).

[187] Gladden v. Cadillac Motor Car Division, 416 A.2d 394 (N.J. 1980).

[188] Id.

[189] UCC § 2-719(2).

[190] Ford Motor Co. v. Mayes, 575 S.W.2d 480 (Ky. Ct. App. 1978).

[191] Kearney & Trecker Corp. v. Master Engraving Co., 527 A.2d 429 (N.J. 1987). See Skalski v. Elliot Equipment Co., 2010 U.S. Dist. LEXIS 21836 (D.N.J. Mar. 9, 2010) (applying New Jersey law).

[192] See McDonald v. Mazda Motors of America, 603 S.E.2d 456, 460 (Ga. Ct. App. 2004).

UCC § 2-714 provides that a buyer who accepts goods that turn out not to conform to the express or implied warranty may recover for the decreased value of the goods. This is defined as the difference between the value of the goods accepted and the value they would have had if they had been as warranted, unless special circumstances show proximate damages of a different amount.[193] In order to give the buyer the benefit of the bargain, this may require compensation for: (1) the cost to replace the goods, or (2) the cost to repair the goods.[194] Plaintiffs also may suffer personal injury, property damage, or economic loss as the result of a breach of a warranty. UCC § 2-714(3) provides for recovery of incidental and consequential damages under § 2-715 in proper cases.

Incidental damages are those costs that a buyer incurs in dealing with the breach of a warranty. Although the UCC does not define incidental expenses, UCC § 2-715(1) states that they include "the expenses reasonably incurred in inspection, receipt, transportation and care and custody of goods rightfully rejected, any commercially reasonable charges, expenses, or commissions in connection with effecting cover and any other reasonable expenses incident to the delay or other breach." An example of an award of incidental damages is *Keller v. Inland Metals All Weather Conditioning, Inc.*,[195] in which an Idaho trial court found the defendants breached express and implied warranties that a dehumidifier sold to the plaintiffs for use in their athletic club was fit for its intended purpose. The trial court's held that the plaintiffs were entitled to recover for the decreased value of the dehumidifier as well as incidental or consequential damages. The Idaho Supreme Court affirmed the award for incidental damages, saying that the plaintiffs were entitled to recover expenses reasonably incurred in the inspection, receipt, transportation and care and custody of the dehumidifier, and any reasonable expense incident to the delay or breach. Those incidental expenses were: (1) $1,092 for the time one of the plaintiff's employees spent gathering temperature and humidity data during the period between the installation of the dehumidifier and the filing of this lawsuit; (2) $1,001.00 for the time another employee spent transporting water samples for testing during the same time period; (3) $700 the plaintiffs spent to have additional testing of the water and air in their athletic club. The court found that those expenses reasonably were incurred in inspecting the dehumidifier to determine whether it conformed to the express warranty and that they were caused by defendant's breach.

The UCC also permits recovery of consequential damages that result from a seller's breach of warranty. Consequential damages resulting from seller's breach include injury to person or property proximately resulting from any breach of warranty. UCC § 2-715(2) defines consequential damages as:

(a)   any loss resulting from general or particular requirements and needs of which the seller at the time of contracting had reason to know and which

---

[193] *See* Gill v. Bluebird Body Co., 2005 U.S. Dist. LEXIS 4611 (M.D. Ga. Jan. 21, 2005) (applying Georgia law); Mayberry v. Volkswagen of Am., Inc., 692 N.W.2d 226 (Wis. 2005); Chapman v. Upstate RV & Marine, 610 S.E.2d 852 (S.C. Ct. App. 2005).

[194] *See* Schroeder v. Barth, Inc., 969 F.2d 421, 423–424 (7th Cir. 1992) (applying Indiana law); Davis Industries Sales, Inc. v. Workman Construction Co., 856 S.W.2d 355 (Mo. Ct. App. 1993).

[195] 76 P.3d 977 (Idaho 2003).

could not reasonably be prevented by cover or otherwise; or

(b)   injury to person or property proximately resulting from any breach of warranty.[196]

Consequential damages for lost profits are permitted if they meet the requirements of foreseeability and certainty.[197] This requires the buyer to show (1) the seller to have known, or have had reason to know, at the time of contracting, that if it breached the warranty the buyer would suffer lost profits; (2) the lost profits were readily ascertainable; and (3) the lost profits could not have been reasonably prevented.[198]

A few states permit the award of punitive damages when the breach of warranty is willful or the result of a tort such as fraud.[199] However, punitive damages are not favored and generally are not available in breach of warranty cases.[200]

§ 2.09   THE MAGNUSON-MOSS ACT

In response to the misuse of express warranties and disclaimers by manufacturers and sellers, Congress enacted the Magnuson-Moss Warranty-Federal Trade Commission Improvement Act (the "Act")[201] in 1975. The Act does not create new warranties or preempt the UCC, unless a section is inconsistent with the Act.[202] Instead, the Act regulates the terms of a written warranty and any implied warranty in order to "improve the adequacy of information available to consumers, prevent deception, and improve competition in the marketing of consumer products."[203] In order to accomplish these goals, the Act permits a "consumer"[204] to

---

[196] *See* Federal Insurance Company v. The Village of Westmont, 649 N.E.2d 986 (Ill. App. Ct. 1995) (property damage); Garavalia v. Heat Controller, Inc., 570 N.E.2d 1227 (Ill. App. Ct. 1991) (personal injury).

[197] The foreseeability and certainty requirements for consequential damages arise out of the English case, Hadley v. Baxendale, 156 Eng. Rep. 145 (Ex. 1854).

[198] Lewis v. Mobil Oil Corp., 438 F.2d 500 (8th Cir. 1971) (applying Arkansas law); Parker Tractor & Implement Co. v. Johnson, 819 So. 2d 1234 (Miss. 2002).

[199] RESTATEMENT (SECOND) OF CONTRACTS § 355 (1981) ("Punitive damages are not recoverable for a breach of contract unless the conduct constituting the breach is also a tort for which punitive damages are recoverable."). *See* West v. Jayne, 484 N.W.2d 186 (Iowa 1992); Romero v. Mervyn's, 784 P.2d 992 (N.M. 1989); Gasque v. Mooers Motor Car, Inc., 313 S.E.2d 384 (Va. 1984).

[200] *See* MacKenzie v. Chrysler Corporation, 607 F.2d 1162 (5th Cir. 1979) (applying Mississippi law); Rhodes v. McDonald, 548 S.E.2d 220 (S.C. Ct. App. 2001).

[201] 15. U.S.C. §§ 2301–2312.

[202] The New Hampshire Supreme Court has stated that the Magnuson-Moss Act is most closely analogous to the UCC. Kelleher v. Marvin Lumber and Cedar Co., 891 A.2d 477 (N.H. 2005). *See* Curl v. Volkswagen of Amer., Inc., 871 N.E.2d 1141 (Ohio 2007) (the Act does not establish new implied warranties or modify implied warranties under state law).

[203] 15 U.S.C § 2302(a). The Act is a "remedial statute designed to protect consumers from deceptive warranty practices." Mydlach v. DaimlerChrysler Corp., 875 N.E.2d 1047 (Ill. 2007). It supplements state law with regard to warranty provisions. Laing v. Volkswagen of Amer., Inc., 949 A.2d 26 (Md. Ct. Spec. App. 2008).

[204] "The term 'consumer' means a buyer (other than for purposes of resale) of any consumer product, any person to whom such product is transferred during the duration of an implied or written warranty

bring an action against a "supplier"[205] or "warrantor"[206] of a "consumer product"[207] for the failure to honor a "written warranty"[208] or an "implied warranty."[209] The Act prohibits tie-in sales provisions as a condition for a written or implied warranty.[210]

Although the Act does not require a supplier to provide a written warranty to a consumer, if it does, the warranty must comply with the disclosure requirements of the Act.[211] The terms of the Act go beyond the UCC and specify that the warranty "fully and conspicuously disclose in simple and readily understood language the terms and conditions of such warranty."[212] The Act contains a list of the information that may be required in the warranty.[213] All written warranties must be designated either as a "full warranty" or a "limited warranty."[214] In order to be a full warranty, a number of conditions must be met. The "warrantor" (1) must provide a remedy within a reasonable time and without charge to the consumer for any defect or failure to conform with the warranty; (2) must not impose any limitation on the duration of any implied warranty; (3) must not exclude or limit consequential damages for the breach of any written or implied warranty unless the limitation or exclusion appears conspicuously on the face of the warranty; and (4) must permit the consumer to elect a refund or replacement of the product without charge if, after a reasonable number of attempt, the defect cannot be remedied.[215] A warranty that does not meet all of the standards for a full warranty is a "limited warranty."[216]

(or service contract) applicable to the product, and any other person who is entitled by the terms of such warranty (or service contract) or under applicable State law to enforce against the warrantor (or service contractor) the obligations of the warranty (or service contract)." 15 U.S.C. § 2301(3). States have differed as to whether a "lessee" is a "consumer" for purposes of the Act. The Arizona Supreme Court has held that such a person is not a consumer. Parrot v. DaimlerChrysler Corp., 130 P.3d 530 (Ariz. 2006). New Jersey and Illinois have held that a lessee qualifies as a consumer under the Act. See Ryan v. Amer. Honda Motor Corp., 896 A.2d 454 (N.J. 2006); Mattuck v. DaimlerChrysler Corp., 852 N.E.2d 485 (Ill. App. Ct. 2006).

[205] A "supplier" is "any person engaged in the business of making a consumer product directly or indirectly available to consumers." In keeping with the goals of the Act, it applied to the creation of a "written warranty." Id. at § 2301(4).

[206] A "warrantor" is any supplier or other person who gives or offers to give a written warranty or who is or may be obligated under an implied warranty. Id. at § 2301(5).

[207] A "consumer product" includes tangible personal property distributed in commerce that normally is used for personal, family, or household purposes and may include property attached to or installed on real property. This excludes products purchased for resale and commercial products. Id. at 2301(1).

[208] A "written warranty" is defined as a written promise that the product is free of defects or will meet a specific level of performance over a specified time period.

[209] The Act defines an "implied warranty" as an "an implied warranty arising under state law . . . in connection with the sale by a supplier of a consumer product." Id. at § 2301(7). Thus, an "implied warranty" under the Act is an implied warranty of merchantability under the UCC. See Alvarez v. American Isuzu Motors, 749 N.E.2d 16 (Ill. App. Ct. 2001).

[210] 15 U.S.C. § 2302(c).

[211] Boelens v. Redman Homes, Inc., 748 F.2d 1058, 1061 (5th Cir. 1984).

[212] 15 U.S.C. § 2302(a).

[213] Id.

[214] Id. at § 2303.

[215] Id. at § 2304(a).

[216] Id. at § 2303(a)(2).

In order to protect consumers, the Act prohibits a full warranty from disclaiming or modifying an implied warranty.[217] However, a limited warranty may limit an implied warranty to the duration of the limited written warranty "if such limitation is conscionable and is set forth in clear and unmistakable language and prominently displayed on the face of the warranty."[218]

Remedies available under the Act for failure to honor a warranty include damages and injunctions.[219] The type and amount of damages under the Act depend upon state law.[220] Damages may include recovery of the purchase price, market price of a replacement, or loss in value due of the product. State law determines whether punitive damages are available under the Act.[221] In addition to damages, a consumer also may recover court costs and expenses as well as reasonable attorney fees.[222]

Enforcement of the Act lies with the Attorney General or the Federal Trade Commission (FTC).[223] The Act also provides for a class action[224] or an individual right of action to a consumer who is "damaged by the failure of a supplier, warrantor, or service contractor to comply with any obligation under this chapter, or under a written warranty, implied warranty, or service contract."[225] The consumer may bring the action in federal or state court. Because of the jurisdictional requirements for bringing a claim under the Act in federal court,[226] most suits are brought in state court. However, before bringing a suit, the class or an individual consumer must give the supplier a reasonable opportunity to "cure" the failure to comply with the Act.[227] In addition, the Act allows warrantors to establish informal dispute resolution procedures if they meet stated requirements.[228] If a warrantor establishes a dispute resolution procedure that meets the Act's requirements, a consumer may not file a civil action until he or she has attempted to resolve the dispute through those procedures.[229]

---

[217] *Id.* at § 2308(a).

[218] *Id.* at § 2308(b). For a case in which an automobile deal complied with all of the disclaimer requirements of the UCC the Magnusson-Moss Act and was granted summary judgment in a suit by a buyer, see Tague v. Autobarn Motors, Ltd., 914 N.E.2d 710 (Ill. App. Ct. 2009).

[219] *Id.* at § 2310.

[220] Mitsch v. General Motors Corp., 359 Ill. App. 3d 99 (2005).

[221] Kelly v. Fleetwood Enterprises, Inc., 377 F.3d 1034, 1039 (9th Cir. 2004); Boelens v. Redman Homes, Inc., 748 F.2d 1058, 1069 (5th Cir. 1984); Stoebner Holdings, Inc. v. Automobili Lamborghini S.P.A., 2007 U.S. Dist. LEXIS 88227 (D. Haw. Nov. 30, 2007).

[222] 15 U.S.C. § 2310(d)(2).

[223] *Id.* at § 2310.

[224] *Id.* at § 2310(a).

[225] *Id.* at § 2310(d)(1).

[226] Individual claims under the Act may only be brought in federal court if the amount in controversy reaches is at least $50,000.00. In addition, for class actions, there must be at least 100 named plaintiffs whose individual claims exceed $25 each. *Id.* at § 2310(d).

[227] 15 U.S.C. § 2310(e).

[228] *Id.* at § 2310(a).

[229] *Id.*

Chapter 3

MISREPRESENTATION

SYNOPSIS

§ 3.01 INTRODUCTION

§ 3.02 FRAUDULENT MISREPRESENTATION

    [A] Introduction

    [B] A False Statement of a Material Fact

    [C] *Scienter*

    [D] Intent to Induce Reliance on the Misrepresentation

    [E] Justifiable Reliance

    [F] Damages

§ 3.03 NEGLIGENT MISREPRESENTATION

    [A] Elements of an Action

    [B] Damages

§ 3.04 INNOCENT (STRICT LIABILITY) MISREPRESENTATION

    [A] Restatement (Second) of Torts, Section 402B

    [B] "Engaged in the Business of Selling Chattels"

    [C] "Material Fact" Concerning "the Character or Quality of the Chattel"

    [D] Advertising

    [E] "Justifiable Reliance"

    [F] Damages

§ 3.05 RESTATEMENT (THIRD) OF TORTS: PRODUCTS LIABILITY

§ 3.06 DECEPTIVE TRADE PRACTICES STATUTES

    [A] Introduction

    [B] The Food Industry and Deceptive Trade Practices Statutes

    [C] Helmets and Deceptive Advertising

§ 3.01   INTRODUCTION

Closely related to breach of express warranty and breach of implied warranty of fitness for a particular purpose are products liability actions based upon claims of fraudulent, negligent, or innocent misrepresentations.[1] Although both breach of warranty and misrepresentation claims require a showing that the manufacturer or seller made a false or misleading statement about the qualities of its product, there are significant differences between the two causes of action. First, unlike breach of warranty, which is a contract action, misrepresentation is a tort and does not require any contractual relationship between the parties, even though a misrepresentation usually arises in a contractual setting.[2] Secondly, breach of warranty focuses on the condition of the product and whether it had the qualities attributed to it by the manufacturer or seller. Fault on the part of the person providing the express warranty or implied warranty of fitness is not an element of proof in that determination. While the condition of the product also is important in misrepresentation actions, the focus in such cases is on the state of mind of the person who made the statement about the product and whether the person who acted upon it was justified in doing so. Fraud, recklessness, or negligence may be crucial to this analysis. Thirdly, despite the expansion of potential plaintiffs in breach of warranty actions, the scope of persons who can recover for a misrepresentation is broader. Finally, there are important differences between the damages that can be awarded for breach of warranty and misrepresentation.

In addition to the differences between breach of warranty and misrepresentation, there are significant differences between the three categories of misrepresentation as well. Although the Restatement (Third) deals with all three categories of misrepresentation in § 9, they are distinct causes of action with their own requirements. This makes it necessary to examine each form of misrepresentation separately.

§ 3.02   FRAUDULENT MISREPRESENTATION

[A]   Introduction

The oldest of the theories of misrepresentation is based upon fraud and deceit in a statement made by the manufacturer or seller of a product.[3] In recent years, advertising and mass marketing have given rise to claims of fraudulent and deceptive representations concerning a variety of products including automobiles,[4] IUDs,[5] prescription medicine,[6] silicon breast implants,[7] tobacco,[8] and video

---

[1] "Breach of these warranties provides an independent basis of liability under the Uniform Commercial Code and may be combined in the same case with a claim for misrepresentation" RESTATEMENT (THIRD) OF TORTS: PRODUCTS LIABILITY § 9 cmt. *e* (1998).

[2] Keller v. A.O. Smith Harvestore Products, Inc., 819 P.2d 69 (Colo. 1991).

[3] *See* Langridge v. Levy, 150 Eng. Rep. 863 (1837), *aff'd*, 150 Eng. Rep. 1458 (1838).

[4] *In re* Toyota Motor Corp., 754 F. Supp. 2d 1208 (C.D. Cal. 2010) (applying California law).

[5] Adams v. G.D. Seale & Co., 576 So. 2d 728 (Fla. Dist. Ct. App. 1991).

[6] In re Rezulin Products Liability Litigation, 133 F. Supp. 2d 272 (S.D.N.Y. 2001) (applying

games.[9]

Courts require plaintiffs to prove a number of elements in order to establish a *prima facie* case of fraudulent misrepresentation.[10] Despite differences in language among the states as to the exact formulation of the requirements, six elements are at the heart of recovery for fraud: (1) a misrepresentation; (2) concerning an existing material fact; (3) knowledge of the falsity of the representation, or recklessness based on insufficient information, by the person who made it; (4) an intention to induce the person to whom the misrepresentation was made to rely on it; (5) justifiable reliance on the misrepresentation by the person to whom it was made; and (6) resulting damage. These elements also are reflected in § 310 of the Restatement (Second) of Torts, which states:

> An actor who makes a misrepresentation is subject to liability to another for physical harm which results from an act done by the other or a third person in reliance upon the truth of the representation, if the actor:
>
> (a) intends his statement to induce or should realize that it is likely to induce action by the other, or a third person, which involves an unreasonable risk of physical harm, and
>
> (b) knows
>
> (i) that the statement is false, or
>
> (ii) that he has not the knowledge which he professes.

Unlike claims based on breach of express warranty, the Federal Rules of Civil Procedure, as well as many state codes of civil procedure, require a plaintiff to plead the circumstances constituting a fraudulent misrepresentation "with particularity."[11] Many states also place a heightened burden of proof on a plaintiff in a case of fraudulent misrepresentation, i.e., "clear and convincing evidence," as opposed to a "preponderance of the evidence," the usual standard for recovery in civil cases.[12]

Mississippi law); Freeman v. Hoffman-La Roche, Inc., 618 N.W.2d 827 (Neb. 2000).

[7] Barrow v. Bristol-Myers Squibb Co., 1998 U.S. Dist. LEXIS 23187 (M.D. Fla. 1998) (applying Florida law).

[8] Cipollone v. Liggett Group, Inc., 505 U.S. 504 (1992); Clinton v. Brown & Williamson Holdings, Inc., 498 F. Supp. 2d 639 (S.D.N.Y. 2007) (applying New York law).

[9] Smallwood v. Ncsoft Corp., 730 F. Supp. 2d 1213 (D. Haw. 2010) (applying Hawaiian law).

[10] For examples of the different formulations of the required elements, see Indian Brand Farms, Inc. v. Novartis Crop Protection Inc., 617 F.3d 207 (3d Cir. 2010) (applying New Jersey law); Tuosto v. Philip Morris USA, Inc., 672 F. Supp. 2d 350 (S.D.N.Y. 2009) (applying New York law); Woods v. R. J. Reynolds Tobacco Co., 635 F. Supp. 2d 530 (S.D. Miss. 2009) (applying Mississippi law); Montgomery Rubber and Gasket Co., Inc. v. Belmont Machinery Co., Inc., 308 F. Supp. 2d 1293 (M.D. Ala. 2004) (applying Alabama law); Valente v. Sofamor, 48 F. Supp. 2d 862 (E.D. Wis. 1999) (applying Wisconsin law); Dobbin v. Pacific Coast Coal Co., 170 P.2d 642 (Wash. 1946).

[11] Federal Rules of Civil Procedure, Rule 9(b). *See* Woods v. Maytag Co., 807 F. Supp. 2d 112 (E.D.N.Y. 2011).

[12] Marvin Lumber and Cedar Co. v. PPG Industries, Inc., 223 F.3d 873 (8th Cir. 2000) (applying Minnesota law); Torkie-Tork v. Wyeth, 739 F. Supp. 2d 908 (E.D. Va. 2010) (applying Virginia law).

[B]   A False Statement of a Material Fact

The first requirement for fraudulent misrepresentation is that the defendant made a false statement about a material fact concerning the product. A statement of "fact" has been defined as one that "(1) admits of being adjudged true or false in a way that (2) admits of empirical verification."[13] A "material fact" is one that influences a person's decision whether or not to purchase a product.[14] The requirement that a statement be one of material fact is meant to distinguish it from a nonactionable expression of opinion or sales "puffery" that often is associated with the advertising of products.[15] One court has stated that the reason such statements are not actionable as fraud is that they are "meaningless superlatives that no reasonable person would take seriously."[16] The distinction between "fact" and "opinion" is illustrated by the statements the manufacturer of a roof made to a customer about its product in *Cummings v. HPG International, Inc.*[17] In that case, the manufacturer's statement that the roof would last for 20 years was held to be a statement of "fact," while its statement that the roof "would perform better and last the same or longer than other commercial roof systems on the market" fell into the "opinion category, as normal commercial puffing."[18] The difficulty in distinguishing between the two types of statements is illustrated by the manufacturer's additional statement that the roof was suitable for the variable climate of the particular state. Although that statement was close to the line between the two categories, the Court of Appeals concluded that it was, arguably, more like a statement of "fact" than "opinion."[19]

A misrepresentation usually is contained in advertising, product literature, or an oral statement made by the seller. In addition, it can result from the concealment of a material fact about a product.[20] While silence does not amount to a misrepresentation where the parties are experienced business people, a manufacturer or seller has a duty to disclose information about a product in a number of situations, including where there is a fiduciary relationship[21] or where the manufacturer or seller has superior knowledge about the product and the

---

[13] Presidio Enterprises, Inc. v. Warner Bros. Distributing Corp., 784 F.2d 674, 679 (5th Cir. 1986).

[14] The Shutter Shop, Inc. v. Amersham Corp., 114 F. Supp. 2d 1218 (M.D. Ala. 2000) (applying Alabama law); Trenholm v. Ratcliff, 646 S.W.2d 927 (Tex. 1983).

[15] Oestreicher v. Alienware Corp., 544 F. Supp. 2d 964 (N.D. Cal. 2008) (applying California law) (a computer manufacturer's statements that its computers were of a "suburb, uncompromising quality" and "faster, more powerful, and more innovative than competing machines" was non-actionable puffery). *See In re* Toyota Motor Corp., 754 F. Supp. 2d 1208 (C.D. Cal. 2010) (applying California law).

[16] Hanson-Suminski v. Rohrman Midwest Motors, Inc., 898 N.E.2d 194, 204 (Ill. App. Ct. 2008) (quoting Speakers of Sport, Inc. v. ProServ, Inc., 178 F.3d 862, 866 (7th Cir. 1999) (applying Illinois law).

[17] 244 F.3d 16 (1st Dist. 2001) (applying Massachusetts law).

[18] *Id.* at 21.

[19] *Id.*

[20] Smith v. Pfizer Inc., 688 F. Supp. 2d 735 (M.D. Tenn. 2010) (applying Tennessee law); Grills v. Philip Morris USA, Inc., 645 F. Supp. 2d 1107 (M.D. Fla. 2009) (applying Florida law). For a discussion of fraudulent concealment, see Taylor v. American Chemical Council, 576 F.3d 16, 31–34 (1st Cir. 2009) (applying Massachusetts law); Lloyd v. General Motors Corp., 916 A.2d 257, 274–75 (Md. 2007).

[21] Woods v. R. J. Reynolds Tobacco Co, 635 F. Supp. 2d 530 (S.D. Miss. 2009) (applying Mississippi law).

purchaser lacks expertise with it.[22] A fraudulent misrepresentation also can be created by a statement that is a "half-truth" about a product. An example of this is *St. Joseph Hospital v. Corbetta Construction Co.*,[23] in which the Illinois appellate court upheld a verdict against the manufacturer-supplier of wall paneling installed in a hospital. The manufacturer failed to disclose to the architect and the builder that testing by an independent company had revealed that the paneling had a flame spread 17 times the maximum allowed under the city building code. When the testing company refused to rate the wall-paneling because the flame spread was so high, the manufacturer told the contractor that the paneling "does not carry a flame spread rating of any kind."[24] Although that statement technically was true, the Illinois court held that it was fraudulent since the failure to disclose the dangerously high flame spread was misleading. "In other words, a half-truth is sometimes more misleading than an outright lie."[25]

[C] *Scienter*

The second element of a fraudulent misrepresentation is that the person who made the statement had the requisite degree of knowledge of its falsity (*scienter*). According to the Restatement (Second) of Torts, § 526, a misrepresentation is fraudulent if the person who makes it "(a) knows or believes that the matter is not as he represents it to be, (b) does not have the confidence in the accuracy of his representation that he states or implies, or (c) knows that he does not have the basis for his representation that he states or implies."[26] This element of *scienter* often is the most difficult for a plaintiff to prove. It requires proof of what the manufacturer or seller knew about its product at the time they made the statement. In *Gillham v. Admiral Corp.*,[27] for example, the Sixth Circuit upheld a judgment against a manufacturer for compensatory and punitive damages resulting from a fire ignited by one of its televisions. The evidence showed that the manufacturer used unsafe high voltage transformers in its television sets. The evidence also supported the jury's finding that the manufacturer knew that its transformers were causing fires because of their design and knew that the safety device designed to contain fires was ineffective. However, despite that knowledge, the manufacturer not only failed to inform prospective purchasers of the danger, it told them that the television sets were safe.

Although the evidence in *Gillham* showed that the manufacturer knew of the dangers posed by the product, it is not necessary for the plaintiff to prove that the person making the allegedly fraudulent representation had actual knowledge of its

---

[22] *In re* Bisphenol-A (BPA) Polycarbonate Plastic Products Liability Litigation, 687 F. Supp. 2d 897 (2009) (applying Missouri law). *See* RESTATEMENT (SECOND) OF TORTS § 551.

[23] 316 N.E.2d 51 (Ill. App. Ct. 1974). *See* Whiteley v. Philip Morris Inc., 11 Cal. Rptr. 3d 807 (Ct. App. 2004).

[24] *Id.* at 69.

[25] *Id.* at 71.

[26] *See* Neri v. R. J. Reynolds Tobacco Co. Inc., 2000 U.S. Dist. LEXIS 22223 (N.D.N.Y. 2000) (applying New York law) (a smoker failed to show that a tobacco company knew that its statement included false statements at the time it was published).

[27] 523 F.2d 102 (6th Cir. 1975) (applying Ohio law).

falsity. If a person makes a false statement with reckless disregard of the lack of information as to the truth of the statement, a court will infer the person's knowledge of its falsity.[28]

[D]   Intent to Induce Reliance on the Misrepresentation

The third element of fraudulent misrepresentation is that the manufacturer or seller who made the false statement did so with the intent to induce the user to act or rely on the statement in a way that created a risk of harm.[29] In order to establish this element, the user of the product must show that the manufacturer or seller not only knew that the statement was false but also knew that the user would rely upon it.[30] While the misrepresentation usually will create a risk of harm to the person to whom the statement was made or who read the advertising or product literature, a person who makes a fraudulent misrepresentation may be liable to third persons who are within the class of persons whom they should expect to act based upon their misrepresentation.[31] Thus, privity is not required for fraudulent misrepresentation.

[E]   Justifiable Reliance

The requirement of intent to induce action or reliance is tied to the fourth element of fraudulent misrepresentation: a plaintiff must show not only that he or she relied upon the truth of the representation but also that the reliance was justified.[32] The California Supreme Court has stated that "[r]eliance exists when the misrepresentation or nondisclosure was an immediate cause of the plaintiff's conduct which altered his or her legal relations, and when without such misrepresentation or nondisclosure he or she would not, in all reasonable probability, have entered into the contract or other transaction."[33] The requirement of showing justifiable reliance has been a particular issue in lawsuits against tobacco companies in which smokers allege that they began smoking or continued smoking because of representations in the company advertisements.[34] Suits have been dismissed where the plaintiffs could not show that they actually relied upon the advertisements made by the companies in their decisions to

---

[28] Aaron v. Hampton Motors, Inc., 124 S.E.2d 585 (S.C. 1962); Hurley v. Frontier Ford Motors, Inc., 299 N.E.2d 387 (Ill. App. Ct. 1973).

[29] Roginsky v. Richardson-Merrell, Inc., 378 F.2d 832 (2d Cir. 1967) (applying New York law); *In re* Neurontin Marketing, Sales Practices and Products Liability Litigation, 618 F. Supp. 2d 96 (D. Mass. 2009); Whiteley v. Philip Morris Inc., 11 Cal. Rptr. 3d 807 (Ct. App. 2004).

[30] Reservoir Manor Corp. v. Lumbermens Mutual Casualty Co., 137 N.E.2d 912 (Mass. 1956).

[31] Learjet Corp. v. Spenlinhauer, 901 F.2d 198 (1st Cir. 1990) (purchaser of an airplane relied upon a statement made by the airplane manufacturer for certification to the FAA); Levine v. Wyeth, Inc., 684 F. Supp. 2d 1338 (M.D. Fla. 2010).

[32] Miller v. Pfizer Inc., 196 F. Supp. 2d 1095 (D. Kan. 2002) (applying Kansas law); White v. R. J. Reynolds Tobacco Co., 109 F. Supp. 2d 424 (D. Md. 2000) (applying Maryland law).

[33] Alliance Mortgage Co. v. Rothwell, 900 P.2d 601, 608 (Cal. 1995).

[34] Neri v. R. J. Reynolds Tobacco Co., 2000 U.S. Dist. LEXIS 22223 (N.D.N.Y. 2000) (applying New York law).

smoke.[35] Simply having read newspapers and magazines during the time when the alleged statements were made was not sufficient to establish reliance.[36] However, in *Whiteley v. Philip Morris, Inc.*,[37] the California Court of Appeals found that the evidence showed that the cigarette manufacturers and their agents issued numerous false denials regarding the hazards of smoking and falsely assured the public that they were engaged in research to determine any health risks from smoking. Based on those false assurances and denials, the jury was justified in finding that the plaintiff's decedent was led to believe that smoking was safe and would not cause cancer.[38] The court also held that the plaintiff did not have to prove that his wife saw or heard any specific representations; it was sufficient that the defendants made the statements to the public.[39]

[F] Damages

Reliance upon the misrepresentation leads to the final element the plaintiff must establish for fraudulent misrepresentation: harm resulting from reliance on the statement. Most cases involve claims for "physical harm"[40] resulting from the misrepresentation either to the person to whom the false statement was made or to a third person who acted in reliance on the representation. In addition, one of the advantages of suing for fraudulent misrepresentation is that a plaintiff also may recover punitive damages.[41] While some states hold that the economic loss doctrine bars claims of fraudulent misrepresentation when the only damage is to the product itself, other states hold that the doctrine does not apply to fraudulent misrepresentation.[42]

---

[35] Tompkins v. R. J. Reynolds Tobacco Co., 92 F. Supp. 2d 70 (N.D.N.Y. 2000) (applying New York law).

[36] Allgood v. R. J. Reynolds Tobacco Co., 80 F.3d 168 (5th Cir. 1996) (applying Texas law); Small v. Lorillard Tobacco Co. Inc., 679 N.Y.S.2d 593 (1998).

[37] 11 Cal. Rptr. 3d 807 (Ct. App. 2004).

[38] *Id.* at 844.

[39] *Id.* at 845. *See* Scott v. American Brands Tobacco Co., Inc., 949 So. 2d 1266 (La. Ct. App. 2007).

[40] RESTATEMENT (SECOND) OF TORTS § 310 (1965). The RESTATEMENT (THIRD) § 9 (1998) speaks of "harm to persons or property."

[41] In Robinson Helicopter Co., Inc. v. Dana Construction, 102 P.3d 268 (Cal. 2004), the jury found the defendant liable for fraudulent misrepresentation and awarded compensatory damages of $1.5 million and punitive damages of $6 million. *See also* Gillham v. Admiral Corp., 523 F.2d 102 (6th Cir. 1975) (applying Ohio law); First National Bank of Louisville v. Brooks Farms, 821 S.W.2d 925 (Tenn. 1991).

[42] Robinson Helicopter Co., Inc. v. Dana Construction, 102 P.3d 268 (Cal. 2004); Tietsworth v. Harley-Davidson, 677 N.W.2d 233 (Wis. 2004). *See* R. Joseph Barton, *Note: Drowning in a Sea of Contract: Application of the Economic Loss Rule to Fraud and Negligent Misrepresentation Claims*, 41 WM. & MARY L. REV. 1789 (2000).

§ 3.03 NEGLIGENT MISREPRESENTATION

[A] Elements of an Action

In addition to fraudulent misrepresentation, a manufacturer or seller also may be liable for negligent misrepresentation. As they do with fraudulent misrepresentation, courts define the elements of this tort in a number of ways.[43] One of the most detailed statements of the elements of negligence misrepresentation was provided by a California court which stated that a plaintiff must establish that: (1) the defendant made a representation as to a past or existing material fact; (2) the representation was untrue; (3) regardless of his actual belief, the defendant made the representation without any reasonable ground for believing it was true; (4) the representation was made with the intent to induce the plaintiff to rely upon it; (5) the plaintiff was unaware of the falsity of the representation, acted in reliance upon the truth of the representation and was justified in relying upon the representation; and (6) as a result of the reliance upon the truth of the representation, the plaintiff suffered damage.[44] As with fraudulent misrepresentation, the elements of negligent misrepresentation also are contained in the Restatement (Second) of Torts. Section 311 of the Restatement provides:

(1) One who negligently gives false information to another is subject to liability for physical harm caused by action taken by the other in reasonable reliance upon such information, where such harm results

    (a) to the other, or

    (b) to such third persons as the actor should expect to be put in peril by the action taken.

(2) Such negligence may consist of failure to exercise reasonable care:

    (a) in ascertaining the accuracy of the information, or

    (b) in the manner in which it is communicated.

An action for negligent misrepresentation requires the plaintiff to prove that the defendant made a false statement of a material fact (as opposed to an opinion) about the product and that the plaintiff justifiably relied on the statement to his or her detriment.[45] However, the scope of those who can recover for a negligent misrepresentation is not as broad as for other types of negligence. According to one California court, the "class of persons entitled to rely upon the representations

---

[43] See Jimenez v. Daimler Chrysler Corp., 269 F. 3d 439 (4th Cir. 2001) (applying South Carolina law); Cummings v. HPG International, Inc., 244 F.3d 16 (1st Cir. 2001) (applying Massachusetts law); Wilson v. Dryvit Systems, Inc., 206 F. Supp. 2d 749 (E.D.N.C. 2002) (applying North Carolina law). See also RESTATEMENT (SECOND) OF TORTS § 311 (1965).

[44] Friedman v. Merck & Co., Inc., 131 Cal. Rptr. 2d 885, 900 (Ct. App. 2003). For other statements of the elements, see Lee v. Mylan, Inc., 806 F. Supp.2d 1320 (M.D. Ga. 2011) (applying Georgia law); Fisher v. APP Pharmaceuticals, LLC, 783 F. Supp. 2d 424 (S.D.N.Y. 2011) (applying New York law); Woods v. R. J. Reynolds Tobacco Co., 635 F. Supp. 2d 530 (S.D. Miss. 2009) (applying Mississippi law); Lloyd v. General Motors, 916 A.2d 257 (Md. 2007); The Conveyor Company v. Sunsource Technology Serv. Inc., 398 F. Supp. 2d 992 (N.D. Iowa 2005) (applying Iowa law).

[45] Jimenez v. Daimler Chrysler Corp., 269 F. 3d 439 (4th Cir. 2001) (applying South Carolina law).

is restricted to those to whom or for whom the misrepresentations were made. Even though the defendant should have anticipated that the misinformation might reach others, he is not liable to them."[46]

As with fraudulent misrepresentation, the failure to disclose information also may be the basis for a negligent misrepresentation.[47] However, the crucial difference between the two forms of misrepresentation is the defendant's mental state. Unlike fraudulent misrepresentation, in which the plaintiff must prove that the defendant actually knew that the statement was false, the degree of culpability required to establish negligent misrepresentation is less stringent. In a negligent misrepresentation action, it is sufficient for the plaintiff to prove that the defendant was negligent in making the statement to the plaintiff. This places the focus on the degree of care taken by the person making the statement in discovering the truth or falsity of the statement and requires the plaintiff to prove that an ordinary person who is engaged in the particular business would not have made the false statement to a customer.[48]

Negligent misrepresentations usually result from oral statements, advertising, or product literature provided by the manufacturer or seller of the product. However, most cases of negligent misrepresentation involve sellers rather than manufacturers. These sellers also can include third parties, such as those who endorse products manufactured by someone else.[49] In the classic case of *Hanberry v. Hearst Corp.*,[50] the California court of appeals recognized a cause of action for negligent misrepresentation against a publishing company that advertised, in one of its magazines, that a certain brand of shoes met the "Good Housekeeping's Consumers' Guaranty Seal," that the shoes were a good product and that "the advertising claims made for them in our magazine are truthful."[51] The plaintiff read the advertisement, purchased a pair of the shoes, and was injured when she slipped on a vinyl floor, allegedly because the shoes were defective. In allowing the complaint, the court stated that the plaintiff alleged that the magazine permitted its seal to use in connection with shoes it had not tested or inspected or, if it had inspected and examined the shoes, had done so negligently. According to the court, if either of those allegations was true, the plaintiff's conduct would amount to negligent misrepresentation.

All of the elements required for negligent misrepresentation are illustrated by another frequently cited case, *Pabon v. Hackensack Auto Sales, Inc.*,[52] in which the service manager of an automobile dealership told the plaintiff that the "clicking" and "chopping" sensation in the steering of his automobile was because it was "a

---

[46] Friedman v. Merck & Co., Inc., 131 Cal. Rptr. 2d 885, 901 (Ct. App. 2003).

[47] *Id.*

[48] Cummings v. HPG International, Inc., 244 F.3d 16 (1st Cir. 2001) (applying Massachusetts law); Cunningham v. C. R. Pease House Furnishing Co., 69 A. 120 (N.H. 1908).

[49] *See* Walters v. Seventeen Magazine, 241 Cal. Rptr. 101 (Ct. App. 1987) (defendant did not sponsor or endorse the product by advertising it in its magazine).

[50] 81 Cal. Rptr. 519 (Ct. App. 1969).

[51] *Id.* at 521.

[52] 164 A.2d 773 (N.J. Super. Ct. 1960).

new car. Don't worry about it. It'll wear out."[53] However, the service manager never checked the steering system and the plaintiff was injured in a crash when the steering locked. The New Jersey appellate court held that a jury could find the dealership liable for negligent misrepresentation. According to the court: "Negligence may be inferred not only from Hackensack's failure or refusal to repair or even to examine the reported defect, but also from its representation to [the plaintiff] that the steering deficiency was normal and should cause him no concern."[54]

[B] Damages

Damages for negligent misrepresentation are more limited than those for fraudulent misrepresentation. Because the action is based upon negligence, punitive damages are not available to plaintiffs.[55] Courts also have refused to recognize a cause of action for negligent misrepresentation resulting in emotional distress. A plaintiff may recover for a negligent misrepresentation that involves a risk of harm only if actual physical harm results.[56]

Damages for negligent misrepresentation usually are limited to situations where the defective product caused personal injury or damage to property other than the product itself.[57] This is because most states follow the economic loss doctrine, which bars a person from recovering purely economic losses (i.e., loss of the product itself) in tort actions based upon strict liability and negligence (including negligent and innocent misrepresentations). In such cases, a cause of action lies only in contract for breach of warranty.[58] However, many states recognize an exception to the economic loss doctrine for a negligent misrepresentation where the plaintiff's damages were caused by a negligent misrepresentation by a person in the business of supplying information for the guidance of others in their business transactions. Most of the litigation involving this exception has turned on the question of whether the defendant was in the business of supplying information and whether the information was ancillary to the sale or in connection with the sale of other merchandise.[59]

If a negligent misstatement results in personal injury or property damage, the defendant is liable both to the person to whom it was made and "to such third

---

[53] *Id.* at 784.

[54] *Id.*

[55] Klein v. Sears Roebuck and Co., 773 F.2d 1421 (4th Cir. 1985) (applying Maryland law); Soufflas v. Zimmer, Inc., 474 F. Supp. 2d 737 (E.D. Pa. 2007) (applying Pennsylvania law).

[56] Friedman v. Merck & Co., Inc., 131 Cal. Rptr. 2d 885 (Ct. App. 2003).

[57] However, Maryland has held that personal injury is not required to recover for negligent misrepresentation. Lloyd v. General Motors Corp., 916 A.2d 257 (Md. 2007). *See also* Aig Aviation Insurance v. Avco Corp., 709 F. Supp. 2d 1124 (D.N.M. 2010) (applying New Mexico law).

[58] *See* Giddings & Lewis, Inc. Vv. Industrial Risk Insurers, 348 S.W.3d 729 (Ky. 2011); Moorman v. National Tank Co., 435 N.E.2d 443 (Ill. 1982).

[59] Haimberg v. R & M Aviation, Inc., 2001 U.S. App. LEXIS 4429 (7th Cir. Mar. 13, 2001) (applying Illinois law). *See* R. Joseph Barton, *Note: Drowning in a Sea of Contract: Application of the Economic Loss Rule to Fraud and Negligent Misrepresentation Claims*, 41 Wm. & Mary L. Rev. 1789 (2000).

persons as the actor should expect" to rely on the statement.[60] In *Cunningham v. C. R. Pease House Furnishing Co.*,[61] the defendant retailer sold a stove blackening chemical to a woman. Two days later her daughter was injured while using the product. Although the defendant dealt with the mother and probably did not think about whether she had a daughter who might use the product as well, the New Hampshire Supreme Court permitted the case to go to the jury, stating that it "knew the mother bought it to use on her stove and that other members of the family were likely to use it; consequently the plaintiff can recover, if her mother could have recovered had she been injured instead of the plaintiff."[62]

§ 3.04   INNOCENT (STRICT LIABILITY) MISREPRESENTATION

[A]   Restatement (Second) of Torts, Section 402B

The third category of misrepresentation does not require any showing of fault on the part of the person making the statement. According to § 402B of the Restatement (Second) of Torts, which has been adopted by approximately half of the states:

> One engaged in the business of selling chattels who, by advertising, labels, or otherwise, makes to the public a misrepresentation of a material fact concerning the character or quality of a chattel sold by him is subject to liability for physical harm to a consumer of the chattel caused by justifiable reliance upon the misrepresentation, even though:
>
> (a)   it is not made fraudulently or negligently, and
>
> (b)   the consumer has not bought the chattel from or entered into any contractual relation with the seller.[63]

Section 402B has its origins in a series of cases, beginning in the 1930s, holding manufacturers liable to consumers who relied on their express representations concerning the safety or quality of products.[64] Although those cases were brought in contract under a theory of breach of an express warranty, the decisions of the courts, rejecting contractual privity, were part of the gradual move toward strict liability in tort. In *Baxter v. Ford Motor Co.*,[65] a man was injured when a pebble struck the windshield of a new automobile he was driving, shattering the glass and injuring his eyes. In the sales literature that the automobile manufacturer furnished

---

[60] RESTATEMENT (SECOND) OF TORTS § 311 (1965).

[61] 69 A. 120 (N.H. 1908).

[62] *Id.* at 121.

[63] For a discussion of the evolution of misrepresentation under § 402B, see American Safety Equipment Corp. v. Winkler, 640 P.2d 216, 219–20 (Colo. 1982).

[64] For a discussion of the evolution of the theory of misrepresentation in § 402B, see American Safety Equipment Corp. v. Winkler, 640 P.2d 216, 219–20 (Colo. 1982) and RESTATEMENT (SECOND) OF TORTS § 402B cmt. *c* (1965).

[65] 12 P.2d 409 (Wash. 1932).

to dealers for distribution to potential customers were statements such as: "All of the new Ford cars have a Triplex shatter-proof glass windshield — so made that it will not fly or shatter under the hardest impact."[66] Since ordinary consumers were unable to discover the truth of such a statement, the Washington Supreme Court held the manufacturer liable, even though the plaintiff had purchased the automobile from a third party, a dealership, and was not in privity of contract with the manufacturer. The reason for this, according to the court, was that its decision did not rest on express warranty

> but rather on the principle that the original act of delivering an article is wrong, when, because of the lack of those qualities which the manufacturer represented it as having, the absence of which could not be readily detected by the consumer, the article is not safe for the purposes for which the consumer would ordinarily use it.[67]

The second influence on § 402B were a series of decisions in the 1950s and early 1960s holding manufacturers strictly liable for representations they made to consumers using what the courts termed "modern merchandising practices." In *Rogers v. Toni Home Permanent Co.*,[68] for example, a woman suffered injury to her hair and scalp after using a home permanent advertised by the manufacturer to be "Very Gentle." The Ohio Supreme Court focused on the extensive use of advertising by manufacturers to promote their products directly to consumers in newspapers, magazines, signboards, and on radio and television. The advertising extolled the qualities and benefits of the products in "glowing terms" and consumers relied heavily on those advertisements in making their purchasing decisions. In such situations:

> The warranties made by the manufacturer in his advertisements and by the labels on his products are inducements to the ultimate consumers and the manufacturer ought to be held to strict accountability to any consumer who buys the product in reliance on such representations and later suffers injury because the product proves to be defective or deleterious.[69]

[B]   "Engaged in the Business of Selling Chattels"

Following the approach taken by the courts in cases such as *Baxter* and *Rogers*, liability under § 402B is not based upon whether the product is defective but upon whether the product conforms to the manufacturer's express statements about the product. Although fraud or negligence in making the statements is not required, § 402B does not create absolute liability. Instead, the section has its own distinct requirements that a plaintiff must satisfy in order to establish a *prima facie* case. The first requirement of these is that the defendant was "engaged in the business of selling chattels." In deciding who is a "seller" for purposes of § 402B, courts have adopted the definition of the term used in the context of strict liability under

---

[66]   *Id.* at 411.

[67]   *Id.* at 412.

[68]   147 N.E.2d 612 (Ohio 1958).

[69]   *Id.* at 615–16. *See* Randy Knitwear, Inc. v. American Cyanamid Co., 181 N.E.2d 399 (N.Y. 1962); Hamon v. Digliani, 174 A.2d 294 (Conn. 1961).

§ 402A: "anyone in the business of selling any type of chattel."[70] Those "in the business" of selling include not only manufacturers but also wholesalers, retailers, and distributors.[71] Neither § 402B nor the comments to it define what constitutes a "chattel." As a result, courts have looked both to the ordinary dictionary meaning of the designate with a term and to the way it is used in cases involving § 402A: tangible property.[72] Applying this definition of "chattels" to a claim of misrepresentation under § 402B, one federal court held that it did not to apply to ideas and expressions in a book.[73]

[C]   "Material Fact" Concerning "the Character or Quality of the Chattel"

The second element in an action under § 402B is that the misrepresentation was a statement of a "material fact" concerning "the character or quality of the chattel." As with the other forms of misrepresentation, liability under § 402B arises only from an affirmative, express, and specific misrepresentation of material fact concerning the product.[74] An implied representation of the product's character or quality is not sufficient.[75] In *Crocker v. Winthrop Laboratories*,[76] the plaintiff's husband died as the result of a weakened condition brought on by addiction to a drug. The drug company argued that, because of the state of medical knowledge and the rare susceptibility of the user, the addiction could not have been foreseen. In affirming the judgment of the trial court for the plaintiff, the Texas Supreme Court held that, regardless of those facts, when a drug company "positively and specifically represents its product to be free and safe from all dangers of addiction," the company will be liable for misrepresentation if the treating physician relies on the representation and it proves to be false and results in harm.[77]

In contrast to a statement of a "material fact" concerning the quality of the product are statements of general assurances of good quality, opinion, and sales talk characterized as "puffing."[78] As with the other forms of misrepresentation,

---

[70] Restatement (Second) of Torts § 402B cmt. *e* (1965). *See* Kirby v. B. I. Incorporated, 2003 U.S. Dist. LEXIS 16964 (N.D. Tex. Sept. 26, 2003) (applying Texas law).

[71] Restatement (Second) of Torts § 402B cmt. *e* (1965).

[72] Winter v. G. P. Putnam's Sons, 938 F.2d 1033 (9th Cir. 1991); Pitler v. Michael Reese Hosp., 415 N.E.2d 1255 (Ill. App. Ct. 1980).

[73] Winter v. G. P. Putnam's Sons, 938 F.2d 1033 (9th Cir. 1991).

[74] English v. Suzuki Motor Co., Ltd., 1997 U.S. App. LEXIS 19865 (10th Cir. July 30, 1997) (applying Colorado law); Kirby v. B. I. Incorporated, 2003 U.S. Dist. LEXIS 16964 (N.D. Tex. Sept. 26, 2003) (applying Texas law); Klages v. General Ordinance Equipment Co., 367 A.2d 304 (Pa. Super. Ct. 1976).

[75] Hilbrenner v. Kawasaki Motors Corp., 1988 U.S. Dist. LEXIS 8373 (W.D. Mo. Aug. 2, 1988) (applying Missouri law).

[76] 514 S.W.2d 429 (Tex. 1974).

[77] *Id.* at 433.

[78] Restatement (Second) of Torts § 402B cmt. *g* (1965). *See* Adkins v. Ford Motor Co., 446 F.2d 1105 (6th Cir. 1971) (applying Tennessee law); Hittle v. Scripto-Tokai Corp., 166 F. Supp. 2d 142 (M.D. Pa. 2001) (applying Pennsylvania law); Pappas v. Pella Corp., 844 N.E.2d 995 (Ill. App. Ct. 2006).

§ 402B does not apply to these statements. In *Hauter v. Zogarts*,[79] the defendant manufactured a training device designed to help unskilled golfers improve their game. The labels on the shipping carton and the cover of the instruction booklet urged players to "drive the ball with full power" and stated: "COMPLETELY SAFE BALL WILL NOT HIT PLAYER." The plaintiff was seriously injured by a golf ball while using the product. The California Supreme Court held that the statement fell within the ambit of § 402B, leading the plaintiff to believe that he could use the product with safety. According to the court: "The assertion that the [product] is completely safe, that the ball will not hit the player, does not indicate the seller's subjective opinion about the merits of the product but rather factually describes an important characteristic of the product."[80]

[D] Advertising

Section 402B contains two caveats, in the first of which the drafters took no position on whether the section should apply "where the representation is not made to the public, but to an individual."[81] However, according to comment h, § 402B is limited to "misrepresentations which are made by the seller to the public at large, in order to induce purchase of the chattels sold, or are intended by the seller to, and do, reach the public." These misrepresentations may be made to the public "in newspapers or television, by literature distributed to the public through dealers, by labels on the product sold, or leaflets accompanying it, or in any other manner, whether it be oral or written."[82] In keeping with trends in modern advertising, the posting by a manufacturer or seller of an advertisement on its internet website also has been held to be a "public representation."[83] However, statements made by an automobile salesman to prospective buyers have been held not to be made to the "public at large."[84]

Another issue related to representations made to the public is whether an advertisement must be for the specific model or brand of the product at issue or whether it can include similar types of goods. Although three cases in the 1970s and 1980s were divided on the question,[85] the most recent decision is *Ladd v. Honda Motor Co.*[86] in which the plaintiff alleged that the defendant misrepresented the handling characteristics of all-terrain vehicles by advertising that they were safe enough to be operated by children. The defendant argued that the plaintiff could not recover unless he could prove that it had misrepresented the handling characteristics of the particular model of all-terrain vehicle involved in the

---

[79] 534 P.2d 377 (Cal. 1975).

[80] *Id.* at 381.

[81] Lewis & Lambert Metal Contractors, Inc. v. Jackson, 914 S.W.2d 584 (Tex. App. 1994).

[82] RESTATEMENT (SECOND) OF TORTS § 402B cmt. *h* (1965).

[83] Kirby v. B. I. Incorporated, 2003 U.S. Dist. LEXIS 16964 (N.D. Tex. Sept. 26, 2003) (applying Texas law).

[84] Chandler v. Gene Messer Ford, Inc., 81 S.W.3d 493 (Tex. App. 2002).

[85] *See* Haynes v. American Motors Corp., 691 F.2d 1268 (8th Cir. 1982) (applying Arkansas law); Collins v. Wayne Corp., 621 F.2d 777 (5th Cir. 1980) (applying New Mexico law); Jacobson v. Benson Motors, Inc., 216 N.W.2d 396 (Iowa 1974).

[86] 939 S.W.2d 83 (Tenn. Ct. App. 1996).

case. The plaintiff replied that his claim could rest on proof that the defendant misrepresented the handling characteristics of all-terrain vehicles in general. The Tennessee court felt that manufacturers should not be able to insulate themselves from liability under § 402B by using general advertisements of an entire product line. It held that manufacturers would be liable if their general advertisements of a product line contain representations of the "character or quality" of particular models in the product line.

[E] "Justifiable Reliance"

As with fraudulent and negligent misrepresentation, it is essential to a claim under § 402B that there was "justifiable reliance" on the misrepresentation concerning the product and that physical harm resulted from the reliance.[87] An example of a lack of reliance is *Wolfe v. McNeil-PPC, Inc.*,[88] in which a mother gave her nine-year-old daughter Children's Motrin for her headache. The child's condition became worse and she developed a rash and blisters. The mother took her child to a doctor, whose nursing staff told the mother to continue giving her daughter Motrin. At the time, the warning label on the bottle of Motrin did not warn of the risk of rashes or blisters, although, 10 years later, the FDA recommended that the label include such warnings. However, the mother did not read any of the bottle's warnings the first time she gave her daughter Motrin and only read the label several days later. The federal court applied § 402B and ruled in favor of the drug manufacturer, stating that she was unable to show any reliance on the warning label while purchasing or using the drug.[89]

Although a claim under § 402B requires "justifiable reliance" on representations made about the product, comment j to § 402B states that "[t]he reliance need not necessarily be that of the consumer who is injured. It may be that of the ultimate purchaser of the chattel, who because of such reliance passes it on to the consumer who is in fact injured, but is ignorant of the misrepresentation." Thus, a person who purchases a product in justifiable reliance upon statements about it, and then permits another person to use the product, has provided the element of reliance even though the person using the product never knew of the statements.[90]

It is a factual question in each case whether the representation influenced the purchase or use of the product.[91] According to comment j to § 402B, the rule "does not apply where the misrepresentation is not known, or there is indifference to it, and it does not influence the purchase or subsequent conduct." However, since § 402B applies to "consumers," the person injured need not have been the purchaser of the product and need not have been the one who relied on the

---

[87] Restatement (Second) of Torts § 402B cmt. *j* (1965). *See* Evans v. Toyota Motor Corp., Burton v. Danel Medical, Inc., 1999 U.S. Dist. LEXIS 2619 (E.D. Pa. Mar. 1, 1999) (applying Pennsylvania law).

[88] 773 F. Supp.2d 561 (E.D. Pa. 2011) (applying Pennsylvania law).

[89] *Id.* at 573.

[90] Westlye v. Look Sports, Inc., 22 Cal. Rptr. 2d 781 (Ct. App. 1993).

[91] Baughn v. Honda Motor Co., 727 P.2d 655 (Wash. 1986); American Safety Equipment Corp. v. Winkler, 640 P.2d 216 (Colo. 1982).

advertising before using it.[92] An example of this is *Ladd v. Honda Motor Co.*,[93] in which a man who purchased an all-terrain vehicle admitted that he did not rely on the defendant's advertising in deciding whether to buy it. Instead, he bought it because his brother had the same vehicle. However, he did rely on the company's advertising showing children riding all-terrain vehicles in deciding to let the plaintiff (the 12-year-old son of friends) ride it. According to the Tennessee appellate court, "the reliance required by § 402B need not be that of the injured consumer but may be that of the purchaser who passes the product along to the ultimate consumer."[94]

[F] Damages

Finally, a plaintiff in an action under § 402B must have suffered "physical harm" caused by the misrepresentation. However, the second caveat to § 402B leaves open the question of whether the section applies "where physical harm is caused to one who is not a consumer of the chattel."[95] Liability under this section is limited to physical harm to a person or property and does not include economic loss unaccompanied by physical damage.[96]

§ 3.05 RESTATEMENT (THIRD) OF TORTS: PRODUCTS LIABILITY

Section 9 of the Restatement (Third) of Torts: Products Liability deals with the liability of a manufacturer or seller for harm caused by misrepresentation. The section states:

> One engaged in the business of selling or otherwise distributing products who, in connection with the sale of a product, makes a fraudulent, negligent or innocent misrepresentation of material fact concerning the product is subject to liability for harm to persons or property caused by the misrepresentation.

This section, which is based on §§ 310, 311, and 402B of the Restatement (Second) of Torts, imposes strict liability on a seller and applies to fraudulent, negligent, and innocent misrepresentations. The section does not require the plaintiff to show that the product was defective at the time of sale or distribution.[97] The Restatement (Third) § 9 has received little attention from the courts.[98]

---

[92] RESTATEMENT (SECOND) OF TORTS § 402B cmt. *i* (1965).

[93] 939 S.W.2d 83 (Tenn. Ct. App. 1996).

[94] *Id.* at 101.

[95] There are no cases discussing this caveat. *See* RESTATEMENT (THIRD) OF TORTS § 9 Reporters Note 2 (1998).

[96] ExxonMobil Oil Corp. v. Amex Const. Co., Inc., 702 F. Supp.2d 942 (N.D. Ill. 2010) (applying Illinois law); Ritter v. Custom Chemicides, Inc., 912 S.W.2d 128 (Tenn. 1995).

[97] For a discussion of this section by a court that did not adopt it, see Miller v. Pfizer Inc., 196 F. Supp. 2d 1095 (D. Kan. 2002).

[98] See Giddings & Lewis, Inc. v. Industrial Risk Insurers, 348 S.W.3d 729 (Ky. 2011), in which the Kentucky Supreme Court mentioned § 9 but did not adopt it, and Freeman v. Hoffman-La-Roche, Inc.,

§ 3.06   DECEPTIVE TRADE PRACTICES STATUTES

[A]   Introduction

In addition to common law misrepresentation, the federal government, all 50 states, and the District of Columbia have enacted "consumer protection," "consumer fraud," "unfair trade practices" or "deceptive trade practices" statutes that provide an additional basis for products liability actions.[99] Many of the state consumer protection statutes date from the early 1960s when the national consumer protection movement expanded governmental regulation and oversight of consumer goods. Examples of the state statutes are the New York laws that prohibit "deceptive acts or practices in the conduct of any business, trade or commerce"[100] as well as all "false advertising in the conduct of any business, trade or commerce."[101]

Most of the state statutes provide for a private cause of action. As with common law misrepresentation, the language and details of the statutes differ from state-to-state. However, there are three elements that are similar in all of the statutes: (1) a deceptive act or practice must be part of a business transaction; (2) an intent that the consumer rely on the deception; and (3) damages to the consumer as a result of that reliance.[102] Many of the statutes permit successful plaintiffs to recover not only compensatory damages (and, in some instances, treble damages[103]), but also attorneys' fees and costs.[104] Some statutes also permit the recovery of punitive damages.[105]

Many of the trade practices statutes make it easier for plaintiffs to recover than under common law fraud. In *Suminski v. Rohrman Midwest Motors, Inc.*,[106] the buyer of a used automobile asked the dealer whether the vehicle "had a lot of repairs done to it, or if it had been in an accident." Although the vehicle had been

---

618 N.W.2d 827 (Neb. 2000) in which the Nebraska Supreme Court declined to adopt § 9.

[99] At the federal level, the agency with the principal responsibility for "consumer protection" is the Federal Trade Commission, which was established in 1914. Within the Commission, the Bureau of Consumer Protection is charged with protecting consumers from unfair or deceptive trade practices. 15 U.S.C. § 45.

[100] N.Y. Gen. Bus. Law § 349.

[101] *Id.* at § 350.

[102] *See* Goudy v. Yamaha Motor Corp., 782 N.W.2d 114 (Wis. Ct. App. 2010); Pappas v. Pella Corp., 844 N.E.2d 995 (Ill. App. Ct. 2006).

[103] In Two Old Hippies, LLC v. Catch the Bus, LLC, 807 F. Supp. 2d 1059 (D.N.M. 2011), the federal court held that the evidence did not support an award of treble damage under the New Mexico Unfair Practices Act.

[104] For examples of consumer protection statutes, see the Illinois Consumer Fraud and Deceptive Business Practices Act (815 Ill. Comp. Stat. 505/1 *et seq.*); the New Jersey Consumer Fraud Act (N.J. Stat. Ann. § 56:8-1 *et seq.*; the Texas Deceptive Trade Practices-Consumer Protection Act (Tex. Bus. & Com. § 17.41 *et seq.*); the Wisconsin Deceptive Trade Practices Act (Wis. Stat. § 100.18).

[105] *See* Keeling v. Esurance Insurance Co., 660 F.3d 273 (7th Cir. 2011) (punitive damages are available under the Illinois Consumer Fraud and Deceptive Practices Act, 815 Ill. Comp. Stat. 505/1 *et seq.*).

[106] 898 N.E.2d 194 (Ill. App. Ct. 2008).

in a rollover accident four months earlier, the dealer replied: "No, it's fine."[107] The buyer alleged that the dealer's statement was a violation of common law fraud and the Illinois Consumer Fraud and Deceptive Business Practices Act.[108] The jury found for the buyer under the Illinois statute and awarded him an amount that represented the diminished value of the vehicle and required the dealer to pay the buyer's attorneys' fees.[109]

In affirming the jury's verdict and award of damages,[110] the Illinois appellate court noted a number of differences between common law and statutory claims. First, although a plaintiff must establish common law fraud by clear and convincing evidence, the standard for a claim of statutory fraud is a preponderance of the evidence.[111] Second, a plaintiff under the Illinois consumer fraud act is not required to show actual reliance.[112] Third, despite the title of the Illinois act, the buyer is not required to show fraudulent intent on the part of the seller. It is sufficient to show that the statement "was untrue, without regard to defendant's knowledge."[113]

[B]   The Food Industry and Deceptive Trade Practices Statutes

Since the late 1960s, one target of the Federal Trade Commission, as well as state governments and plaintiffs' attorneys, has been the tobacco industry. However, with settlements between the tobacco industry and state governments and the decline of tobacco litigation, the focus of government regulators and plaintiffs has shifted to manufacturers and sellers of food products. Government, individual, and class action suits have alleged that food companies are misleading consumers and violating state and federal regulations in the labeling and contents of their products and with claims about the nutrition and ingredients in those products.[114]

The most highly publicized and controversial case against the food industry is *Pelman v. McDonald's Corporation*,[115] in which the parents of two teenagers filed a lawsuit against McDonald's restaurants on behalf of their children. The lawsuit is

---

[107]   *Id.* at 198–99.

[108]   815 ILL. COMP. STAT. 505/1 *et seq.*

[109]   898 N.E.2d at 201.

[110]   *Id.* at 204–05, 207.

[111]   *Id.* at 203. *See* Kremers v. Cocoa-Cola Co., 712 F. Supp. 2d 759 (S.D. Ill. 2010) (plaintiffs were unable to show that they actually were deceived by the label setting out the ingredients in a soft drink).

[112]   898 N.E.2d at 203.

[113]   *Id.*

[114]   Sugawara v. Pepsico, Inc., 2009 U.S. Dist. LEXIS 43127 (E.D. Cal. May 20, 2009). In April 2012, Ferrero, the maker of Nutella, agreed to settle a class action claim for $3 million. *See Nutella Consumer Class Action Settlements, available at* https://nutellaclassactionsettlement.com. For a discussion of the suits against food manufacturers, see Stephanie Strom, *Lawyers From Suits Against Big Tobacco Target Food Makers*, THE NEW YORK TIMES, Aug. 18, 2012, *available at* http://www.nytimes.com/2012/08/19/business/lawyers-of-big-tobacco-lawsuits-take-aim-at-food-industry.html?pagewanted=all.

[115]   396 F.3d 508 (2d Cir. 2005).

based on three counts that allege that: (1) McDonald's promotional representations created the false impression that its food products were nutritional and part of a healthy lifestyle if consumed daily; (2) McDonald's failed to disclose adequately that the use of certain food additives and processing techniques made its food less healthy than represented; and (3) McDonald's deceptively represented that nutritional information was readily available to its customers when, in fact, the information was not available at a significant number of its restaurants in New York.[116] The complaint also asserted that as a result of the children eating at McDonald's three to five times a week between 1987 and 2002, they developed "obesity, diabetes, coronary heart disease, high blood pressure, elevated cholesterol intake, related cancer, and/or other detrimental and adverse health effects."[117]

As in other states, the New York consumer protection statutes require a plaintiff to show that the statements were consumer-oriented, that they were misleading in a material respect, and that the plaintiff was injured as a result of them. In cases of false advertising under § 350 of the New York statute, a plaintiff also must show that he or she relied upon the allegedly false advertisement.[118] In *Pelman*, the District Court judge granted McDonald's motion to dismiss the complaint. The judge held that the customers failed to allege that the plaintiffs specifically relied to their detriment upon any particular representation made in any McDonald's advertisement or promotional material. The judge also dismissed the same claims under § 349 on the ground that the plaintiffs failed to make a sufficient causal connection between their consumption of McDonald's food and their alleged injuries.

On appeal of the dismissal of the action under § 349, the Second Circuit in 2005 reversed and reinstated the plaintiffs' claims. According to the court, no showing of reliance is required in an action based on § 349, since it goes beyond common law fraud and covers other deceptive practices. In particular, the Second Circuit focused on the District Court judge's statement that he dismissed the complaint for failure to answer a series of questions about other factors that may have played a role in their weight gain and health problems:

> What else did the plaintiffs eat? How much did they exercise? Is there a family history of the diseases which are alleged to have been caused by McDonald's products? Without this additional information, McDonald's does not have sufficient information to determine if the foods are the cause of the plaintiffs' obesity or if instead McDonald's foods are only a contributing factor.[119]

The Second Circuit felt that these questions were more appropriate to the discovery stage than to the pleading stage and that the complaint should not have been dismissed for the failure to answer them.

---

[116] *Id.* at 510.

[117] *Id.*

[118] *Id.* at 511.

[119] *Id.* at 511–12.

Upon remand of the case, McDonald's moved for a more definite statement of the plaintiffs' amended complaint.[120] Ruling on that motion, the District Court ordered the plaintiffs to "identify the advertisements that collectively amount to the alleged deceptive nutritional schemes," and to explain "why the advertisements are materially deceptive to an objective consumer."[121] Following the plaintiffs' second amended complaint, McDonald's moved to dismiss the case in 2006. However, the District Court held that (1) the plaintiffs sufficiently had described how they were aware of the nutritional schemes alleged to be defective; (2) the plaintiffs sufficiently described the injuries they suffered; and (3) the plaintiffs' claims were limited to the specific advertisements identified in their second amended complaint.[122] In 2010, the plaintiffs moved for class certification, which the District Court refused.[123] In the judge's view, the individual causation issues predominated over the common ones and the plaintiffs had failed to show, even for the common issues, that the putative class was sufficiently numerous for the court to certify an issues class.

In response to *Pelman* and to lawsuits filed by consumers in other states against the food industry for obesity, Congress and a number of state legislatures introduced "commonsense consumption acts" to protect producers and retailers of foods. The legislation provides that a "manufacturer, packer, distributor, carrier, holder, seller, marketer or advertiser of food" is exempt from civil liability arising out of "weight gain, obesity, a health condition associated with weight gain or obesity, or other generally known condition allegedly caused by or allegedly likely to result from long-term consumption of food."[124] Although a *Commonsense Consumption Act* was introduced in Congress in 2003, 2005, 2007, and 2009, it died each time in committee. However, legislatures in approximately half of the states have enacted laws to protect food manufacturers, marketers, distributors, advertisers, sellers, and trade associations in their states from claims of injury relating to a person's weight gain, obesity, or any health condition associated with weight gain or obesity.[125] None of these laws, however, prohibits suits based on false or deceptive advertising or on negligence resulting from tainted food.

[C]   Helmets and Deceptive Advertising

In response to growing number of high school football players who are suffering brain injuries as the result of concussions, the *Children's Sports Athletic Equipment Safety Act*[126] was introduced in Congress in March 2011. The legislation places the blame for these injuries on football helmet manufacturers who allegedly used misleading concussion safety claims in order to sell football helmets to children. As a result, the legislation proposes that all helmets contain

---

[120] Pelman v. McDonald's Corp., 396 F. Supp. 2d 439 (S.D.N.Y. 2005) (applying New York law).

[121] *Id.* at 445.

[122] Pelman v. McDonald's Corp., 452 F. Supp. 2d 320 (S.D.N.Y. 2006) (applying New York law).

[123] Pelman v. McDonald's Corp., 272 F.R.D. 82 (S.D.N.Y. 2010) (applying New York law).

[124] MODEL COMMONSENSE CONSUMPTION ACT § 2.

[125] For an example, *see* the ILLINOIS COMMONSENSE CONSUMPTION ACT, 745 ILL. COMP. STAT. 43/1.

[126] This Act is available at www.govtrack.us/congress/bills/112/hr1127/text. As of 2012, the bill had been referred to committee, with little chance of action on it. For a discussion of concussions in sports, see John M. Parisi and Douglas R. Bradley, *Ringing the Bell on Concussions*, TRIAL (Aug. 2012), 15.

clearly legible and visible statements warning of the limited protection afforded by helmets. It also makes it unlawful to any person to sell a football helmet with "false or misleading claim[s] with respect to the safety benefits" of the helmet.

One of the first cases dealing with advertising statements about football helmets was *Riddell, Inc. v. Schutt Sports, Inc.*,[127] in which Schutt Sports, a helmet manufacturer, alleged that Riddell, a competitor, engaged in false advertising and misrepresentation under the *Lanham Act* and the *Wisconsin Deceptive Trade Practices Act*. The basis of Schutt's claim was a 2002 study funded, in part, by Riddell. Riddell advertised that (1) "research shows a 31% reduction in concussions in players wearing Riddell Revolution Helmets"; (2) the Riddell Revolution Helmet was the "[o]nly helmet shown to reduce risk of concussion on the playing field"; and (3) "research shows that wearers of Riddell Revolution Youth helmets were 31% less likely to suffer a concussion than traditional helmet wearers."[128]

Most of the court's opinion focused on false advertising under the *Lanham Act*[129] and applied a standard that the false statements must be "literally false" and not just misleading. As a result, the only advertising statement that was shown to be "literally false" was the statement that wearers of the youth helmet were 31% less likely to suffer a concussion than wearers of traditional helmets. According to the court, the statement was false because the test subjects were not wearing youth helmets.[130] The court also dismissed Schutt's claim under Wisconsin's *Deceptive Trade Practices Act* since Schutt was unable to demonstrate that the misrepresentation caused any pecuniary loss and because the Act does not provide a cause of action for misrepresentations made to non-parties.[131]

Although suits by users of football helmets against manufacturers have not yet reached the appellate courts, there have been suits involving motorcycle helmets. In *Fabian v. Fulmer Helmets, Inc.*,[132] a motorcyclist sued a helmet manufacturer for fraudulent and negligent misrepresentation. The National Highway Traffic Safety Administration (NHTSA) has the responsibility for certifying motorcycle helmets but relies on manufacturers to conduct safety tests on their own helmets. When a manufacturer considers one of its helmets has passed the safety tests, its places a "DOT" label on the helmet. In 2000 the NHTSA tested Fulmer's large "AF-50" helmet, which passed, and in 2002 it tested Fulmer's small "AF-50" helmet, which failed the test. When the plaintiff purchased the large AF-50 helmet in 2004, the DOT symbol had not been removed. The plaintiff claimed that Fulmer's misrepresentation caused him to purchase an "unsafe," "interior-quality" helmet that created a "heightened risk of serious physical injury or death."[133] Although Fulmer moved for summary judgment, the court denied the motion, reasoning that

---

[127] 724 F. Supp. 2d 963 (W.D. Wis. 2010) (applying federal and Wisconsin law).

[128] *Id.* at 970.

[129] *Id.* at 971.

[130] *Id.* at 976.

[131] *Id.* at 980.

[132] 628 F.3d 278 (6th Cir. 2010) (applying Tennessee law).

[133] *Id.* at 280.

the size difference did not preclude the plaintiff's claim, and that the 2002 test was potentially the more accurate one.[134]

---

[134] *Id.* at 281.

Chapter 4

NEGLIGENCE AND STRICT LIABILITY: POLICIES, PARTIES, AND PRODUCTS

SYNOPSIS

§ 4.01   INTRODUCTION

§ 4.02   AN OVERVIEW OF NEGLIGENCE AND STRICT LIABILITY

[A]   Negligence

[B]   Strict Liability

[C]   Policy Reasons Underlying Strict Liability

§ 4.03   POTENTIAL PLAINTIFFS

[A]   The Duty Issue in Negligence

[B]   The "User or Consumer" in Strict Liability

[C]   Bystanders

[D]   Unintended Users and Uses of Products

§ 4.04   POTENTIAL DEFENDANTS

[A]   Persons "Engaged in the Business of Selling"

[B]   Special Categories of Sellers

[1]   Component Part Manufacturers

[2]   Sellers of Used Products

[3]   Successor Corporations

[C]   Persons Not Covered by Strict Liability

[D]   Distributor Statutes

§ 4.05   WHAT IS A PRODUCT?

[A]   Introduction

[B]   Animals

[C]   Blood and Human Tissue

[D]   Electricity

[E]   Information

[F]   Raw Materials

[G]   Real Estate

§ 4.01 INTRODUCTION

The theories of liability used most frequently by plaintiffs in products liability cases are those based on tort: negligence and strict liability. Because of the historic evolution of products liability law, these two theories have come to share many common elements and plaintiffs frequently include counts alleging both in their complaints.[1] Despite their similarities, however, there are a number of important differences between negligence and strict liability. This chapter begins an examination of the use of negligence and strict liability in products liability cases by focusing on the elements of proof required for each theory, the underlying policies that support them, the scope of persons who may be plaintiffs and defendants, and the range of items that courts have held to be a "product." The following six chapters examine the application of negligence and strict liability theory to the three different types of product defects (design, manufacturing, and failure to warn), the methods of proving that a product was defective, the requirement that a product defect have been both the factual and proximate cause of the plaintiff's injuries, the various defenses available to a manufacturer or seller, and the types of damages that an injured person may recover.

§ 4.02 AN OVERVIEW OF NEGLIGENCE AND STRICT LIABILITY

[A] Negligence

When Judge Benjamin Cardozo wrote in 1916, in *MacPherson v. Buick Motor Co.*,[2] that the liability of a manufacturer was not limited to the immediate buyer of its product if that product was "reasonably certain to place life and limb in peril when negligently made,"[3] he did more than reject the traditional privity requirement that had limited recovery in negligence actions. His opinion began a revolution that, first, made it possible to judge the liability of a manufacturer or seller of a defective product according to the principles of negligence law[4] and, later, led to strict liability.[5]

As used by lawyers and judges, the term "negligence" applies both to conduct and to a complex cause of action. The most common definition of negligent conduct is "the failure to do something which a reasonably careful person would do, or the doing of something which a reasonably careful person would not do"[6] under the

---

[1] For an example, see Cooper v. Zimmer Holdings, Inc., 320 F. Supp. 2d 1154 (D. Kan. 2004) in which the plaintiff asserted claims based not only on negligence and strict liability but also on breach of express and implied warranties and a violation of the Kansas Consumer Protection Act. For a view that negligence and strict liability no longer should be separate and distinct theories, see Bugosh v. I.U. North America, Inc., 971 A.2d 1228 (Pa. 2009).

[2] 111 N.E. 1050 (N.Y. 1916).

[3] *Id.* at 1053.

[4] *See* RESTATEMENT (SECOND) OF TORTS § 395 (1965).

[5] *Id.* at § 402A.

[6] Mangrum v. Pigue, 198 S.W.3d 496, 501–02 (Ark. 2004).

particular circumstances of the case. Thus, in a negligence action, the plaintiff must focus on the conduct of the manufacturer or seller and prove that the defect in the product, that was the cause of the injuries, was the result of their failure to use reasonable skill or care, *that is*, fault.[7] The evidentiary difficulties that a plaintiff faces in establishing that the conduct of the manufacturer or seller fell below the requisite standard of care for a reasonable person have been mitigated in some situations by the development of the concepts of negligence *per se*[8] and *res ipsa loquitur.*[9] However, the fact that the situations in which those doctrines are available to a plaintiff are limited was an important argument used by supporters of strict liability beginning in the 1960s.

Another widely cited formula for the negligence standard is that articulated by Judge Learned Hand in *United States v. Carroll Towing Co.*[10] Under what has come to be known as the "Hand formula," liability depends upon whether the burden ("B") of taking adequate precautions to prevent the harm is less than the probability ("P") that the injury-causing act will occur "discounted by" the gravity of the injury ("L") if it does occur. According to Judge Richard Posner, "[t]he [Hand] formula translates into economic terms the conventional test for negligence. . . . Unreasonable conduct is merely the failure to take precautions that would generate greater benefits in avoiding accidents than the precautions would cost."[11] Although the Hand formula has not been adopted explicitly by courts, its cost-benefit analysis underlies the way most lawyers and judges approach the question of whether conduct was negligent. In products liability cases, it is used to determine whether the design of a product was negligent and whether the manufacturer or seller should have warned, or provided more or different warnings, of dangers in using the product. An example of this is *In re Asbestos Litigation*,[12] in which the wife of an employee of an asbestos manufacturer, who developed asbestosis, alleged that the manufacturer was negligent in not warning her or her husband of the dangers of "take home" asbestos exposure. The Delaware court said that it was appropriate, when a court

---

[7] Berrier v. Simplicity Mfg., Inc., 563 F.3d 38 (3d Cir. 2007) (applying Pennsylvania law); Coons v. A.F. Chapman Corp., 460 F. Supp. 2d 209 (D. Mass. 2006) (applying Massachusetts law); Branham v. Ford Motor Co., 701 S.E.2d 5, 9 (S.C. 2010); Cronin v. J.B.E. Olson Corp., 501 P.2d 1153 (Cal. 1972).

[8] *See* Reed v. Landstar Ligon, Inc., 314 F.3d 447 (10th Cir. 2002) (applying Oklahoma law); Kemp v. Medtronic, Inc., 2001 U.S. App. LEXIS 1344 (6th Cir. 2001) (applying Ohio law); Obendorf v. Hug Spray Co., Inc., 188 P.3d 834 (Idaho 2008).

[9] Escola v. Coca Cola Bottling Co., 150 P.2d 436 (Cal. 1944). In Lawson v. Mitsubishi Sales of America, Inc., 938 So.2d 35 (La. 2006), the Louisiana Supreme Court held that, since all products liability actions in the state are governed by the Louisiana Products Liability Act (LA. REV. STAT. §§ 9:2800.51–60), the *res ipsa loquitur* doctrine could be used by a plaintiff as circumstantial evidence that a product was unreasonably dangerous when it left a manufacturer's control (as required by the Act). However, the court found that the trial judge erroneously applied the doctrine in the case. *See* Louisiana Citizens Property Ins. Co. v. General Electric Co., 2010 U.S. Dist. LEXIS 38348 (M.D. La. Apr. 19, 2010); Moore v. Anesthesia Services, P.A., 966 A.2d 830 (Del. Super. Ct. 2008).

[10] 159 F.2d 169 (2d Cir. 1947). For a discussion of the case, see Stephen G. Gilles, *United States v. Carroll Towing Co.: The Hand Formula's Home Port*, in ROBERT L. RABIN & STEPHEN D. SUGARMAN (eds.), TORT STORIES, 11 (2003).

[11] McCarty v. Pheasant Run, Inc., 826 F.2d 1554, 1557 (7th Cir. 1987).

[12] 2007 Del. Super. LEXIS 413 (Dec. 21, 2007).

engaged in the duty analysis, to measure the risk to the plaintiff caused by the defendant's conduct, and the cost or burden to the defendant in minimizing the risk.[13] Allying the formula, the court concluded that the defendant would face too high a burden to protect every foreseeable victim of off-premises exposure to asbestos and thus owed no duty to protect its employee's wife from exposure to asbestos dust.[14]

In addition to conduct, the term "negligence" also is used by lawyers and judges to describe a cause of action that requires a plaintiff to establish four interrelated elements. In a products liability action, a plaintiff first must establish that the manufacturer or seller owed her a duty to use reasonable care in the design, manufacture, or sale of its product. Second, a plaintiff must prove that the manufacturer or seller breached that duty of care. A breach of a duty of care is defined as the failure to exercise the standard of care of a "reasonable person" under the circumstances of the case.[15] In a products liability case, this requires a determination of whether the conduct of the manufacturer or seller fell below the acceptable standard of care in the design, manufacture, or distribution of the product or in providing warnings regarding the use of the product. Third, a plaintiff must establish that she suffered personal injury or property damage. If the only harm was to the product itself, a plaintiff is unable to recover in negligence and must rely on warranty theory. Finally, a plaintiff must prove that the breach of the duty was the factual and proximate cause of her injuries or damages.[16]

Despite the development of strict liability beginning in the 1960s, negligence remains an important theory for plaintiffs to consider in products liability cases. There are a number of reasons for this. First, five states (Delaware,[17] Massachusetts,[18] Michigan,[19] North Carolina[20] and Virginia)[21] have not adopted strict liability in tort. For a plaintiff in these states, negligence is the only tort theory available in a products liability case. Second, proving that a manufacturer or seller was "at fault" in designing, manufacturing, or failing to warn of the dangers associated with the use of a product may make a jury more sympathetic to a plaintiff's claims and increase the damages it awards. Third, in some situations the expiration of the statute of limitations or statute of repose may prevent a plaintiff from bringing an action in strict liability, leaving only a negligence count.[22] Fourth, negligence provides an additional net for a plaintiff during the discovery process and may result in more information about a defendant's product that would not be

---

[13] *Id.* at 24–25.

[14] *Id.* at 39–44.

[15] Trull v. Volkswagen of America, Inc., 320 F.3d 1 (1st Cir. 2002) ("reasonably prudent automobile manufacturer").

[16] Stahlecker v. Ford Motor Co., 667 N.W.2d 244 (Neb. 2003); Merrill v. Navegar, Inc., 28 P.3d 116 (Cal. 2001); Sims v. General Motors Corp., 751 P.2d 357 (Wyo. 1988).

[17] Cline v. Prowler Indus. Of Md., Inc., 418 A.2d 968 (Del. 1980).

[18] Coons v. A.F. Chapman Corp., 460 F. Supp. 2d 209 (D. Mass. 2006).

[19] Curry v. Meijer, Inc., 780 N.W.2d 603 (Mich. Ct. App. 2009).

[20] N.C. Gen. Stat. § 99B-1.1.

[21] *See* Garrett v. I.R. Witzer Co., 258 Va. 264 (1999).

[22] Blue v. Environmental Engineering, Inc., 828 N.E.2d 1128 (Ill. 2005).

available solely under a strict liability theory. Finally, many plaintiffs' attorneys feel that there is no disadvantage to including a negligence count in their complaints since they can dismiss the claim voluntarily at a later date if they do not have enough evidence to support their negligence count. On the other side, the principal reasons why a plaintiff may not plead negligence in a products liability action include the additional proof required to establish "fault" and the ability of a defendant, in many states, to raise contributory negligence as a defense.

[B]   Strict Liability

California Supreme Court Justice Roger Traynor articulated a number of reasons for holding a manufacturer "absolutely liable" in tort in his concurring opinion in the 1944 case of *Escola v. Coca Cola Bottling Co.*[23] However, his rationale was not adopted by that court, or by any court, until almost 20 years later in *Greenman v. Yuba Power Products, Inc.*,[24] an opinion also written by Justice Traynor. The framework for the system of strict liability in a products liability case was established two years later when the ALI adopted § 402A of the Restatement (Second) of Torts. That system was revised in 1998 with the adoption of the Restatement (Third) of Torts: Products Liability.

Although in some aspects strict liability is similar to warranty theory,[25] an action based on § 402A does not require any representation about the product by the seller or reliance by the buyer on the skill or judgment of the seller. In addition, strict liability does not depend upon a contract, nor is it affected by the specific requirements of a warranty action such as privity, notice or by disclaimers.[26] Strict liability, however, is not intended to be what one court has called "an enveloping net of absolute liability"[27] that entitles an injured person to recover from any member of the production or distribution chain. Instead, the defendant must have manufactured or placed a defective product in the stream of commerce and that defective product must have caused the plaintiff's injury.[28] Thus, a manufacturer generally is not strictly liable for harm caused by another manufacture's product. The exceptions to this are when the manufacturer's own product contributed substantially to the harm or when the manufacturer

---

[23]   150 P.2d 436 (Cal. 1944).

[24]   377 P.2d 897 (Cal. 1963).

[25]   Crickenberger v. Hyundai Motor Amer., 944 A.2d 1136, 1143–44 (Md. 2008) ("[T]he plaintiff in a breach of warranty claim must establish 'three product litigation basics': the existence of a defect, attribution of the defect to the seller, and a causal relationship between the defect and plaintiff's damages.").

[26]   *See* RESTATEMENT (SECOND) OF TORTS § 402A cmt. *m* (1965).

[27]   Nesselrode v. Executive Beechcraft, Inc., 707 S.W.2d 371, 375 (Mo. 1986). *See* Potter v. Chicago Pneumatic Tool Co., 694 A.2d 1319, 1328–29 (Conn. 1997) in which the Connecticut Supreme Court stated that "strict liability does not transform manufacturers into insurers, nor does it impose absolute liability. . . . Strict tort liability merely relieves the plaintiff from proving that the manufacturer was negligent and allows the plaintiff to establish instead the defective condition of the product as the principal basis of liability."

[28]   In Peterson v. Superior Court, 899 P.2d 905 (Cal. 1995), the plaintiff was injured when she fell in a hotel bathtub. The California Supreme Court refused to hold the hotel proprietor strictly liable for an alleged defect in the hotel premises that the proprietor did not build or market.

participated substantially in creating a harmful combination of the products.[29]

The purpose of the system of strict liability created by § 402A is to permit an injured party to recover without the requirement of proving negligence.[30] Liability depends upon a number of conditions.[31] For example, Nebraska has four requirements for strict liability. First, the defendant must have placed the product on the market for use and must have known, or should have known (in the exercise of reasonable care), that the product would be used without inspection for defects. Second, the product must have been in a defective condition unreasonably dangerous when it left the control of the defendant. Third, the defective condition of the product must have been the proximate cause of the plaintiff's injury while it was being used in a way and for the general purpose for which it was designed and intended. Fourth, the defective condition must have made the product unreasonably dangerous and unsafe for its intended use.[32]

According to one court, requiring the plaintiff to prove that the product was in a "defective condition unreasonably dangerous" "serves the useful function of placing some limits on the liability of a manufacturer or seller."[33] Other states construe the language of § 402A as creating a single standard and interpret the term "unreasonably dangerous" as the definition of a "defective condition."[34] Still other states have rephrased the requirements of § 402A and state that a plaintiff must prove that the injury resulted from a "condition of the product" and that condition was "an unreasonably dangerous one."[35] A few states, however, have rejected the "unreasonably dangerous" language in § 402A.[36] In *Cronin v. J. B. E. Olson Corp.*,[37] the California Supreme Court chose to adopt, instead, only the "defective" language of *Greenman v. Yuba Power Products, Inc.*[38] The court criticized the "unreasonably dangerous" phrase of the Restatement (Second) as introducing the negligence concept of foreseeability into strict liability analysis. The court then went on to state:

---

[29] O'Neil v. Crane Co., 266 P.3d 987, 1005 (Cal. 2012).

[30] Adeyinka v. Yankee Fiber Control, Inc., 564 F. Supp. 2d 265, 274 (S.D.N.Y. 2008); Mohammad v. Toyota Motor Sales, U.S.A., Inc., 947 A.2d 598 (Md. Ct. Spec. App. 2008).

[31] *See* Ruminer v. General Motors Corp., 483 F.3d 561 (8th Cir. 2007) (applying Arkansas law).

[32] In a products liability action in South Carolina, liability in a products liability action depends upon the plaintiff establishing three elements, regardless of whether the suit is based on strict liability or negligence: (1) the plaintiff was injured by the product; (2) the injury occurred because the product was in a defective condition, unreasonably dangerous to the user; and (3) the product, at the time of the accident, was in essentially the same condition as when it left the hands of the defendant. Rife v. Hitachi Constr. Mach. Co., 609 S.E.2d 565, 568 (S.C. Ct. App. 2005). For similar statements, see Vondra v. Chevron, U.S.A., 652 F. Supp. 2d 999 (D. Neb. 2009) (applying Nebraska law); O'Neil v. Crane Co., 266 P.3d 987 (Cal. 2012); Dicosolo v. Janssen Pharmaceuticals, Inc., 951 N.E.2d 1238, 1243 (Ill. App. Ct. 2011).

[33] The Union Supply Co. v. Pust, 583 P.2d 276, 282 (Colo. 1978).

[34] McAlpine v. Rhone-Poulenc Ag Co., 16 P.3d 1054 (Mont. 2000); Seattle-First National Bank v. Tabert, 542 P.2d 774 (Wash. 1975).

[35] Sollami v. Eaton, 772 N.E.2d 215 (Ill. 2002).

[36] Caterpillar Tractor Co. v. Beck 593 P.2d 871 (Alaska 1979); Berkebile v. Brandtly Helicopter Corp., 337 A.2d 893 (Pa. 1975).

[37] 501 P.2d 1153 (Cal. 1972).

[38] 377 P.2d 897 (Cal. 1963).

A bifurcated standard is of necessity more difficult to prove than a unitary one. But merely proclaiming that the phrase "defective condition unreasonably dangerous" requires only a single finding would not purge that phrase of its negligence complexion. We think that a requirement that a plaintiff also prove that the defect made the product "unreasonably dangerous" places upon him a significantly increased burden and represents a step backward in the area pioneered by this court.[39]

Although *Cronin* is widely cited in opinions and in the literature, the vast majority of courts have declined to follow its elimination of the "unreasonably dangerous" portion of § 402A's definition of strict liability. However, the Restatement (Third), §§ 1 and 2, supports the position taken in *Cronin* by stating that anyone who sells a "defective product" is liable for the harm it causes.[40]

The elements required to establish strict liability highlight the important similarities and differences between that theory and negligence. Common to strict liability and negligence is the requirement that the user or consumer show that the product was defective and unreasonably dangerous when it left the control of the manufacturer or seller. As will be discussed in detail in the next three chapters, a product may be defective because of its design, the way in which it was manufactured, or because of the failure to warn of dangers associated with the use of the product. In a negligence action, fault on the part of the manufacturer or seller in creating or passing on the defect is an essential element that an injured person must establish in order to recover.[41] In an action under § 402A, however, the focus is on the condition of the product itself.[42] A manufacturer or seller is liable for the injury or loss resulting from a defective product that it puts into the stream of commerce even in the absence of any fault. Thus, while users and consumers often include separate counts of negligence and strict liability in the same complaint, they rely on strict liability in those cases in which it is difficult or impossible to prove fault.

[C] Policy Reasons Underlying Strict Liability

Although Judge Cardozo's opinion in *MacPherson* abolished the privity requirement in negligence cases, it did not create a new theory of recovery. Instead, it brought products liability cases within the orbit of the existing negligence theory. However, Justice Traynor's opinions in *Escola* and *Greenman* and the adoption of § 402A created a new, and what has become highly controversial, tort theory of recovery for products liability cases. Since almost every word in § 402A has been the subject of debate and litigation, it is necessary to examine briefly the policy considerations underlying strict liability.

---

[39] Cronin v. J. B. E. Olson Corp., 501 P.2d 1153, 1162 (Cal. 1972).

[40] Giehl v. Terex Utilities, 2012 U.S. Dist. LEXIS 49354 (M.D. Pa. Apr. 9, 2012) (applying Pennsylvania law) (to survive a motion to dismiss in Pennsylvania, plaintiffs must adequately plead the elements of a strict liability claim set out in the RESTATEMENT (THIRD) §§ 1 and 2).

[41] East River S.S. Corp. v. Transamerica Delaval, Inc., 476 U.S. 858 (1986); Phillips v. Kimwood Mach. Co., 525 P.2d 1033 (Or. 1974); Greenman v. Yuba Power Prods., 377 P.2d 897 (Cal. 1963).

[42] Gonzales v. Caterpillar Tractor Co., 571 S.W.2d 867 (Tex. 1978).

Comment *c* to § 402A sets out four policy justifications to support the adoption of the doctrine of strict liability:

> [T]he seller, by marketing his product for use and consumption, has undertaken and assumed a special responsibility toward any member of the consuming public who may be injured by it; the public has the right to and does expect, in the case of products which it needs and for which it is forced to rely upon the seller, that reputable sellers will stand behind their goods; that public policy demands that the burden of accidental injuries caused by products intended for consumption be placed upon those who market them, and be treated as a cost of production against which liability insurance can be obtained; and that the consumer of such products is entitled to the maximum protection and the proper persons to afford it are those who market the products.[43]

These justifications for strict liability — the assumption of a duty to the public that uses the product, consumer expectations, loss shifting, and the need to protect consumers — are not new to comment *c*. Two of them — the need to protect consumers and the idea that losses caused by defective products should be shifted to manufacturers and sellers who are better able to bear the losses — echo the reasons given by Justice Traynor in his concurring opinion in *Escola*. The first of the reasons offered by Justice Traynor in that case was loss minimization. "Even if there is no negligence, . . . public policy demands that responsibility be fixed wherever it will most effectively reduce the hazards to life and health inherent in defective products that reach the market."[44] Unlike the old maxim of *caveat emptor* that held it was the buyer's responsibility to determine the quality of a product before purchasing it, Justice Traynor took the view that the manufacturer is in the best position to reduce injuries and losses caused by its defective products. Strict liability would provide the required incentive for manufacturers to produce safer products.

A second justification for strict liability found both in comment *c* to § 402A and in Justice Traynor's concurring opinion is that it places the losses that result from defects in manufactured products on those best able to bear those losses. "The cost of an injury and the loss of time or health may be an overwhelming misfortune to the person injured and a needless one, for the risk of injury can be insured by the manufacturer and distributed among the public as a cost of doing business."[45] According to this rationale, a manufacturer is in the best position to distribute the costs of the risks created by its defective products. It can self-insure or purchase insurance from a third party and then either spread the cost of that insurance among all consumers by charging a proportionately higher price for its product or absorb the cost of that insurance and reduce the profit it would otherwise make from the sale of its product. Under such a system, consumers will be less likely to

---

[43] Comment *c* has been cited by courts in support of their adoption of § 402A. *See* O.S. Stapley Co. v. Miller, 447 P.2d 248, 251–52 (Ariz. 1968). For two other discussions of the policy reasons supporting strict liability, see Harber v. Altec Industries, Inc., 812 F. Supp. 954, 957–58 (W.D. Mo., 1993) (applying Missouri law); FRANK J. VANDALL, STRICT LIABILITY: LEGAL AND ECONOMIC ANALYSIS, 20–22 (1989).

[44] Escola v. Coca Cola Bottling Co., 150 P.2d 436, 440 (Cal. 1944).

[45] *Id.* at 441.

have to bear the full burden of the losses they suffer from defective products.

The Pennsylvania Supreme Court has spoken about the policy that led it to adopt strict liability and of the need to recognize that "strict liability is not a type of mongrel derivative of negligence."[46] According to the court:

> Strict liability was intended to be a cause of action separate and distinct from negligence, designed to fill a perceived gap in our tort law. . . . This court recognized that in a modern industrial society, liability should not necessarily be predicated only on a finding that the defendant failed to exercise due care. Rather, we adopted the strict liability cause of action, finding "that the risk of loss must be placed upon the supplier of the defective product without regard to fault . . ."[47]

These risk reduction, loss spreading and consumer expectations rationales have been cited by numerous courts in support of their adoption of strict liability.[48] In addition to these justifications, another policy reason has been cited by courts in support of strict liability. In *Escola*, Justice Traynor stated that a system of strict liability would eliminate the problems of proof that result from negligence. "An injured person . . . is not ordinarily in a position to refute [evidence of negligence] or identify the cause of the defect, for he can hardly be familiar with the manufacturing process as the manufacturer himself is."[49] This rationale has found support as the complexity of modern products and the methods of manufacturing has come to mean that, frequently, only the manufacturer is in a position to know whether a product is properly designed and safe for its intended use.[50] Because of the costs involved in proving whether a product was negligently designed, manufactured, or marketed, strict liability has been put forward as a means of reducing the litigation costs incurred by a plaintiff and ensuring that a manufacturer or seller that places a defective product on the market does not escape liability because the plaintiff is unable to prove negligence.[51] This view is reflected in comment *a* to § 2 of the Restatement (Third) which states:

> By eliminating the issue of manufacturer fault from plaintiff's case, strict liability reduces the transaction costs involved in litigating that issue. . . . In many cases manufacturing defects are in fact caused by manufacturer negligence but plaintiffs have difficulty proving it. Strict liability therefore performs a function similar to the concept of res ipsa loquitur, allowing deserving plaintiffs to succeed notwithstanding what would otherwise be difficult or insuperable problems of proof.

---

[46] Phillips v. Cricket Lighters, 841 A.2d 1000, 1007 (Pa. 2003).

[47] *Id.* (quoting Azzarello v. Black Bros. Co., Inc., 391 A.2d 1020, 1024 (Pa. 1978)).

[48] *See* Fuchsgruber v. Custom Accessories, Inc., 628 N.W.2d 833 (Wis. 2001); Leong v. Sears Roebuck and Co, 970 P.2d 972 (Haw. 1998); Queen City Terminals, Inc. v. General American Transportation Corp., 653 N.E.2d 661 (Ohio 1995).

[49] Escola v. Coca Cola Bottling Co., 150 P.2d 436, 441 (Cal. 1944).

[50] Sprung v. MTR Ravensburg, Inc., 788 N.E.2d 620 (N.Y. 2003).

[51] Harber v. Altec Industries, Inc., 812 F. Supp. 954 (W.D. Mo. 1993) (applying Missouri law).

In response to the cost-savings rationale, a counter-argument can be made that strict liability does not make recovery any easier for a plaintiff or reduce economic and resource costs. Instead, strict liability simply substitutes a different set of elements of proof from those required in a negligence action. While the negligence concept of fault is not among those elements, proving and defending against the numerous elements required for strict liability can be as complex and expensive for plaintiffs and defendants as those required for negligence.

§ 4.03 POTENTIAL PLAINTIFFS

In deciding whether to bring a products liability action in negligence or strict liability, the first question a potential plaintiff must ask is whether he or she meets the test for who can be a plaintiff. In a negligence action, this means that a plaintiff must establish that the manufacturer or seller owed him or her a duty of care. In a case based on strict liability, a plaintiff must show that he or she was a "user or consumer" of the product within the meaning of § 402A. Although these tests usually result in the same group of persons being able to bring actions under both theories, the different approaches taken by the two theories require separate examination.

[A] The Duty Issue in Negligence

The duty to act with "reasonable care" imposed by negligence law does not extend to the world at large. In cases where the existence of a duty of care is an issue, it is a question of law that must be decided by the judge.[52] This requires the judge to determine, usually in the context of a motion for summary judgment, whether the plaintiff and defendant stood in such a relationship to one another that the law imposes an obligation on the defendant to act reasonably for the protection of the particular plaintiff.[53] The question of duty is the threshold issue that precedes consideration of breach and causation. A trial judge can dismiss, as a matter of law, a complaint based on negligence if he or she determines that the defendant did not owe a duty to the plaintiff under the facts of the case.

With the fall of privity as a requirement in negligence cases, the scope of the duty owed by manufacturers and sellers is very broad. By marketing their products to the public, they owe a duty of care not only to the purchasers of those products but also to all foreseeable consumers, users, and persons in possession of the products.[54] However, a new fact situation may create a question of the existence of a duty to a particular person (i.e., bystander, unintended user of a product). In such cases, courts consider a number of often vague factors. The most frequently cited of these factors is the foreseeability of an injury to the plaintiff.[55]

---

[52] Gamradt v. Federal Laboratories, Inc., 380 F.3d 416 (8th Cir. 2004) (applying Minnesota law) Carter Lincoln-Mercury, Inc. v. Emar Group, Inc., 638 A.2d 1288 (N.J. 1994).

[53] National Bank of Bloomington v. Westinghouse Electric Corp., 600 N.E.2d 1275 (Ill. App. Ct. 1992).

[54] Hopkins v. Chip-In-Saw, Inc. 630 F.2d 616 (8th Cir. 1980) (applying Arkansas law); Rossell v. Volkswagen of America, 709 P.2d 517 (Ariz. 1985).

[55] Kirk v. Hanes Corp., 771 F. Supp. 856 (E.D. Mich. 1991) (applying Michigan law); Haase v. Badger Mining Corp., 682 N.W.2d 389 (Wis. 2004).

Although courts do not require plaintiffs to prove that the particular injury they suffered was foreseeable, some injury to persons in their class must have been likely to result from the negligent design, manufacture, or marketing of the product. However, more than a mere possibility of injury is required since, with hindsight, everything is foreseeable. According to the California Supreme Court, "[f]oreseeability is not to be measured by what is more probable than not, but includes whatever is likely enough in the setting of modern life that a reasonably thoughtful [person] would take account of it in guiding practical conduct."[56] In addition to foreseeability, other factors that guide courts in their duty analysis include the likelihood of injury; the closeness of the connection between the injury and the conduct; the moral blame attached to the conduct; the magnitude of the burden on the defendant in guarding against the injury; the consequences of placing the burden on the defendant; and public policy and social requirements.[57] However, these factors rarely are independently determinative of a duty and courts give them different weight depending upon the facts of the particular case.

An example of a court analyzing all of these factors to determine whether manufacturers and sellers owed a duty to a plaintiff in a products liability case is *Halbrook v. Honda Motor Co., Ltd,*[58] in which two children were killed when a motorcycle struck the automobile in which they were riding as passengers. The parents of the children brought a wrongful death action against the companies that manufactured and sold the motorcycle. Because Michigan is one of the five states that has not adopted strict liability in tort, the parents alleged negligence in the design, manufacture, marketing and distribution of the product. The basis of their claim was that the companies manufactured and marketed a motorcycle that was dangerous and unsuitable for highways since it could travel too fast and neither an inexperienced rider nor other drivers could appreciate its capabilities. The trial court granted summary judgment to the companies based on a finding that they did not owe the children a duty.

In affirming to grant the summary judgment, the Michigan court of appeals reviewed five factors that it considered relevant to the determination of a duty of care. First, the court felt that it was foreseeable to the manufacturer both that motorists speed and that excessive speed can cause accidents. That was true particularly in this case where the manufacturer and sellers advertised the speed and acceleration abilities of the motorcycle as part of their marketing campaign. However, even though the foreseeability of injury factor weighed in favor of the plaintiffs, the court stated that a duty of care does not depend solely on foreseeability.[59]

The court looked to a second factor — the degree of certainty of the injury — and found that, unlike foreseeability, it weighed against the plaintiffs. That was because the court concluded that it was not certain that a motorcycle designed to

---

[56] Bigbee v. Pacific Tel. & Tel., 665 P.2d 947, 952 (Cal. 1983) (quoting 2 HARPER & JAMES, LAW OF TORTS, § 18.2 at p. 1020).

[57] Lamkin v. Towner, 563 N.E.2d 449 (Ill. 1990); J.S. v. R.T.H., 714 A.2d 924 (N.J. 1998).

[58] 569 N.W.2d 836 (Mich. Ct. App. 1997).

[59] *Id.* at 839.

travel at high speeds would cause injury to persons other than those riding on it. The risk of harm also depended upon the way in which the driver handled the motorcycle. Even if the motorcycle had been designed to travel no faster than the maximum speed limit, the court felt it was not certain that the accident and injuries would have been prevented.[60]

The third factor considered by the court — the closeness of the connection between the defendants' conduct and the deaths of the children — also weighed in favor of the defendants. The deaths of the children were not closely connected to the fact that the motorcycle could be driven in excess of the speed limit. Instead, the Michigan court found that the accident was more closely connected to the failure of driver of the automobile to yield the right of way and the motorcycle driver's reckless driving.[61]

The fourth factor — the moral blame attached to the conduct — required the Michigan court to look at the participants in the accident and determine who was the most blameworthy. The court found that the manufacturer and sellers were the least blameworthy since they did not cause the motorcycle driver to speed or the driver of the automobile to ignore the oncoming motorcycle. The court felt that the policy of preventing future harm could be promoted by imposing a duty on motorcycle manufacturers to design and market vehicles with limited speed and acceleration capabilities. However, the danger of a motorcycle depends heavily on its driver. In addition, the court felt that the legislature, not the courts, should determine what speed limitations should be set for motorcycles.[62]

Finally, the Michigan court considered the burdens and consequences of imposing a duty on the defendants. It held that motorcycle manufacturers should not be liable to persons in this type of case. The court felt that if it imposed a duty on manufacturers to protect persons who could be injured by the misuse of their products, the result would be a significant increase in litigation. Although, in some situations, a manufacturer is in a better position to bear the costs of litigation and redistribute them to the general public, the court found that, in this case, the burden would be too great.[63]

[B] The "User or Consumer" in Strict Liability

In order for a plaintiff to recover in an action based upon strict liability under § 402A, the person must have been the "ultimate user or consumer of the defective product." According to comment *l* to § 402A, this term is not limited to the purchaser of the product but also may be a member of the family of the purchaser, his or her employee, a guest, or a donee from the purchaser. In addition, the comment states that "it is not necessary that the ultimate user or consumer have acquired the product directly from the seller . . . [or even] have purchased the product at all." The comment goes on to define "consumers" to include not only

---

[60] *Id.*

[61] *Id.* at 839–40.

[62] *Id.* at 840.

[63] *Id.*

those who consume the product but also a person who prepares it for consumption, which it defines as "all ultimate uses for which the product is intended."[64] A "user" includes those who passively enjoy the benefits of the product, such as passengers in automobiles and in airplanes, as well as those who use the product by working on it.[65] Comment *l*'s definitions have been adopted by state products liability statutes[66] and by court decisions.[67]

[C] Bystanders

In addition to persons who are "users or consumers" of products, nonusers and nonconsumers of products, such as bystanders, passers-by, rescuers, and pedestrians, also may be injured by defective products.[68] The issue of whether a bystander can recover has arisen both in negligence and strict liability cases. Every court that has considered the question in a negligence case has held that the duty of care owed by manufacturers extends to bystanders injured by their products.[69]

Section 402A states that it expresses no opinion as to whether the section should apply to "persons other than users or consumers." However, comment *o* to that section takes the position that there may be "no essential reason why such plaintiffs should not be brought within the scope of the protection afforded, other than that they do not have the same reasons for expecting such protection as the consumer who buys a marketed product." One of the first cases holding that § 402A was available to bystanders was *Elmore v. American Motors Corp.*,[70] in which a defective automobile manufactured by the defendant went out of control and struck the plaintiff's on-coming vehicle. The California Supreme Court based its decision on what it viewed as the principal policy reason for strict liability: "to insure that

---

[64] For a discussion of the term "consumer," see Patch v. Hillerich & Bradsby & Co., 257 P.3d 383 (Mont. 2011).

[65] Mullaney v. Hilton Hotels Corp., 634 F. Supp. 2d 1130 (D. Haw. 2009); Bray v. Marathon Corp., 588 S.E.2d 93 (S.C. 2003). In Patch v. Hillerich & Bradsby Co., 257 P.3d 383 (Mont. 2011), the Montana Supreme Court held that the risk of harm from using an aluminum baseball bat extends beyond the player who actually holds the bat and includes the fielders, since they were users or consumers placed at risk by the increased exit speed caused by the bat.

[66] For an example, the INDIANA CODE § 34-6-2-29, defines a "user" for purposes of the state's products liability act as:

(1) a purchaser;

(2) any individual who uses or consumes the product;

(3) any person who, while acting for or on behalf of the injured party, was in possession and control of the product in question; or

(4) any bystander injured by the product who would reasonably be expected to be in the vicinity of the product during its reasonably foreseeable use.

[67] *See* Anderson v. Smith, 514 N.W.2d 54 (Wis. Ct. App. 1993).

[68] For cases involving the liability of manufacturers to rescuers, see McCoy v. American Suzuki Motor Corp., 961 P.2d 952 (Wash. 1998); Govich v. North American Systems, Inc., 814 P.2d 94 (N.M. 1991); Guarino v. Mine Safety Appliance Co., 255 N.E.2d 173 (N.Y. 1969).

[69] For examples, see Moning v. Alfono, 254 N.W.2d 759 (Mich. 1977); Ragin v. Porter Hayden Co., 754 A.2d 503 (Md. Ct. Spec. App. 2000). *See also* RESTATEMENT (SECOND) OF TORTS § 395 cmt. *i* (1965).

[70] 451 P.2d 84 (Cal. 1969).

the costs of injuries resulting from defective products are borne by the manufacturers that put such products on the market rather than by the injured persons who are powerless to protect themselves."[71] The court concluded by saying:

> If anything, bystanders should be entitled to greater protection than the consumer or user where injury to bystanders from the defect is reasonably foreseeable. Consumers and users, at least have the opportunity to inspect for defects and to limit their purchases to articles manufactured by reputable manufacturers and sold by reputable dealers, whereas the bystander ordinarily has no such opportunities.[72]

Other state courts also have extended strict liability to include bystanders.[73] In addition, some state statutes specifically include bystanders within the definition of "consumers" who are entitled to recover.[74] In *Horst v. Deere & Co*,[75] the Wisconsin Supreme Court held that, in determining whether a product was "unreasonably dangerous," the "consumer contemplation test," and not a "bystander contemplation test," governs all strict liability cases in Wisconsin, including those where a bystander is injured.[76] According to the court, this is because bystanders cannot have an objective expectation regarding the use of a product and, without such an objective test, a bystander expectations would be impossible to put into practice.[77]

The term "bystander" usually applies to persons in the immediate vicinity of the product during its use. However, a few courts have expanded its scope to include "domestic bystanders"[78] such as a wife who contracted cancer from inhaling asbestos fibers brought home over many years on the clothes of her husband who worked with the product.[79] By including the cleaning of the clothes, which took place away from the site where the asbestos was used, for purposes of determining who is a bystander, the courts recognizing "domestic bystanders" have expanded recovery to include activities not related to the actual use of the product.

Like § 402, the Restatement (Third) does not state explicitly whether bystanders are entitled to recover. However, the language of § 1 of the Restatement (Third), which states that sellers are liable "for harm to persons or property caused by the

---

[71] *Id.* at 88.

[72] *Id.* at 89.

[73] For examples, see Moss v. Polyco, Inc., 522 P.2d 622 (Okla. 1974); Howes v. Hansen, 201 N.W.2d 825 (Wis. 1972); Darryl v. Ford Motor Co., 440 S.W.2d 630 (Tex. 1969); Threats v. General Motors Corp., 890 S.W.2d 327 (Mo. Ct. App. 1994).

[74] *See* Ind. Code § 34-6-2-29.

[75] 769 N.W.2d 536 (Wis. 2009).

[76] *Id.* at 538.

[77] *Id.* at 550–51.

[78] Dube v. Pittsburgh Corning, 870 F.2d 790 (1st Cir. 1989).

[79] Stegemoller v. ACandS, Inc., 767 N.E.2d 974 (Ind. 2002). For a review of the cases, see Lunsford v. Saberhagen Holdings, Inc., 106 P.3d 808 (Wash. Ct. App. 2005) (plaintiff alleged that his cancer was caused by his childhood exposure to asbestos dust brought home by his father, who worked as an insulation installer).

defect," does not limit liability to consumers or users and arguably is broad enough to include bystanders.

[D]   Unintended Users and Uses of Products

Although courts agree that a broad group of persons may recover under negligence and strict liability theories in products liability cases, they are divided over whether the duty owed by manufacturers and sellers in negligence and the definition of "user and consumer" in § 402A extends to unforeseeable or unintended users of a product. Most products liability cases involve injuries to persons who were both the foreseeable and the intended users of the products. However, in some cases, a product may have been used by someone who was foreseeable but was not an intended user. An example of this are products such as disposable cigarette lighters that are marketed to adults and intended for their use that fall into the hands of small children, resulting in injuries to them or to other persons.[80] While some courts permit recovery if the plaintiff was a foreseeable user of the product, others require the plaintiff to have been the intended user.

One the first cases to consider the question of an unintended user of a product was *Winnett v. Winnett*,[81] in which the Illinois Supreme Court used the foreseeability of harm test to determine who is entitled to recover in an action based on § 402A:

> In our judgment the liability of a manufacturer properly encompasses only those individuals to whom injury from a defective product may reasonably be foreseen and only those situations where the product is being used for the purpose for which it was intended or for which it is reasonably foreseeable that it may be used."[82]

According to the court, foreseeability means not only what might occur but also what is objectively reasonable to expect.[83] In *Winnett*, a four-year-old was injured when her fingers were caught in the conveyor belt of a forage wagon. The Illinois Supreme Court held the scope of the forage wagon's "intended use" did not include use by a four-year-old child. Because the child was not a "user or consumer" of the product, the court applied a foreseeability test and concluded that it was not "objectively reasonable to expect" the child to place her fingers in the moving screen or belt of the forage wagon.[84] Thus, the court affirmed the dismissal of the plaintiff's complaint.

The same foreseeability test resulted in a plaintiff being able to recover in another Illinois case, *Palmer v. Avco Distributing Corp.*,[85] in which an 11-year-old child was injured when his leg was caught in the agitator mechanism of a fertilizer spreader designed and manufactured by the defendant. In that case, the Illinois

---

[80] *See* Palmer v. Avco Distributing Corp, 841 A.2d 1000 (Pa. 2003).

[81] 310 N.E.2d 1 (Ill. 1974).

[82] *Id.* at 4.

[83] *Id.* at 5.

[84] *Id.* at 5.

[85] 412 N.E.2d 959 (Ill. 1980).

Supreme Court found evidence that farmers customarily allowed people to ride on their farm equipment and that children often accompany their parents by riding on vehicles for pleasure and for work. The court concluded that it was "objectively foreseeable that children of plaintiff's age might ride inside fertilizer spreaders."[86] The court distinguished *Winnett*, which it said contained no allegation that it was customary for young children to roam unattended near operating farm machinery.[87]

§ 4.04 POTENTIAL DEFENDANTS

[A] Persons "Engaged in the Business of Selling"

The question of who is a proper defendant in a products liability action arises more often in strict liability actions than it does in negligence cases. This is because the language of § 402A imposes liability only on a person who "sells" a product in a "defective condition unreasonably dangerous to the user or consumer." However, § 402A does not define a "seller;" it requires only that such a person must be "engaged in the business of selling" the product that injured the plaintiff.[88] According to one federal court, the broader rationale for strict liability explains the specific requirement that the defendant must be a "seller" of the product:

> If the defendant is not engaged in the business of selling the product, then it cannot be said to have "undertaken and assumed [the] special responsibility toward . . . the consuming public." Furthermore, such a defendant has not been afforded the opportunity to treat the risk of producing the product "as a cost of production against which liability insurance [could have been] obtained." Finally, a defendant . . . that did not place the product in commerce has no ability to control the quality of the product or the conformance of the product with its design. The public should not expect to rely upon someone who has not placed the product in the stream of commerce.[89]

Comment *f* to § 402A states that, since the section "applies to any person engaged in the business of selling products for use or consumption," it therefore applies to any manufacturer of such a product, to any wholesale or retail dealer or distributor, and to the operator of a restaurant." A number of states have statutes[90]

---

[86] *Id.* at 962.

[87] *Id.* at 962.

[88] A North Dakota statute defines a "seller" as "any individual or entity, including a manufacturer, wholesaler, distributor, or retailer, who is engaged in the business of selling or leasing any product for resale, use, or consumption." N.D.C.C. § 28-01.3-01(3).

[89] Goldsmith v. Olon Andrews, Inc., 941 F.2d 423, 426 (6th Cir. 1991). In Burnett v. Covell, 191 P.3d 985 (Alaska, 2008), the Alaska Supreme Court refused to extend strict liability beyond those who place a product into the stream of commerce. Thus, an attorney was not liable in strict liability after a chair in his office collapsed when a client attempted to sit in it. The court felt that, as a landowner, the attorney already owed a duty of care to guests on his premises. *Id.* at 988–89.

[90] See the statutes in the following states: Delaware (DEL. CODE ANN. tit. 18 § 7001); Idaho (IDAHO CODE § 6-1407); Illinois (735 ILCS 5/2-621); Indiana (IND. CODE § 34-20-1); Iowa (IOWA CODE § 613.18); Kansas (KAN. STAT. ANN. § 60-3306); Kentucky (KY. REV. STAT. ANN. § 411.340) Maryland (MD. CODE ANN., CTS. &

or decisions[91] that limit strict liability to the manufacturer of the product or its component part and exclude the wholesaler and retailer. However, courts and products liability statutes that have adopted the views expressed in comment *f* apply strict liability to everyone in the chain of production and distribution.[92] These persons include: manufacturers,[93] apparent manufacturers,[94] wholesalers and distributors,[95] assemblers,[96] retailers,[97] dealers,[98] persons who sell or distribute as their own products manufactured by another;[99] trademark licensors,[100] and lessors and bailors.[101] These same groups of defendants are found in negligence actions as well. Interpreting § 402A to include a broad group of nonmanufacturing sellers who are not responsible for creating the defect has been justified on a number of grounds. Among the reasons that courts have given are: the integral role nonmanu-

---

JUD. PRO. § 5-311) Minnesota (MINN. STAT. ANN. § 544.41); Missouri (MO. REV. STAT. § 537.762); Nebraska (NEB. REV. STAT. § 25-21, 181); North Carolina (N.C. GEN. STAT. § 99B-2); North Dakota (NDCC, § 28-01.3-04); Ohio (OHIO REV. CODE ANN. § 2307.78); South Dakota (SDCL § 20-9-9); Tennessee (TENN. CODE ANN. § 29-28-106); Washington (WASH. REV. CODE ANN. § 7.72.040).

[91] *See* Sam Shainberg Co. of Jackson v. Barlow, 258 So. 2d 242 (Miss. 1972).

[92] *See* the Kansas Products Liability Act, KAN. STAT. ANN. § 60-3302(s), which defines a "product seller" as "any person or entity that is engaged in the business of selling products, whether the sale is for resale, or for use or consumption."

[93] Greenman v. Yuba Power Products, Inc., 377 P.2d 897 (Cal. 1962). A North Dakota statute defines a "manufacturer" as "a person or entity who designs, assembles, fabricates, produces, constructs, or otherwise prepares a product or a component part of a product prior to sale of the product to a user or consumer. The term includes any seller of a product who is owned in whole or significant part by the manufacturer or who owns, in whole or significant part, the manufacturer." N.D.C.C. § 28-01.3-01(1). *See* Reiss v. Komatsu Amer. Corp., 735 F. Supp. 2d 1125 (D.N.D. 2010).

[94] Long v. United States Brass Corp., 333 F. Supp. 2d 999 (D. Colo. 2004) (applying Colorado law).

[95] Fuchsgruber v. Custom Accessories, Inc., 628 N.W.2d 833 (Wis. 2001); Giuffrida v. Panasonic Industrial Co., 607 N.Y.S.2d 72 (N.Y. App. Div. 1994).

[96] Weyerhaeuser Co. v. Thermogas Co., 620 N.W.2d 819 (Iowa 2000). However, in Nationwide Agribusiness Ins. Co. v. SMA Elevator Const. Inc., 816 F. Supp. 2d 631 (N.D. Iowa 2011) (applying Iowa law), the court held that a grain elevator was not a product within the meaning of Iowa law and the general contractor was not an assembler of the allegedly defective bearing that caused an explosion.

[97] Moss v. Polyco, 522 P.2d 622 (Okla. 1974); Vandermark v. Ford Motor Co., 391 P.2d 168 (Cal. 1964).

[98] Sabloff v. Yamaha Motor Co., Ltd., 273 A.2d 606 (N.J. App. Div.), *aff'd*, 283 A.2d 321 (N.J. 1971).

[99] RESTATEMENT (SECOND) OF TORTS, § 400 (1965). RESTATEMENT (THIRD) OF TORTS § 14 (1998) is based on the RESTATEMENT (SECOND) and states:

> One engaged in the business of selling or otherwise distributing products who sells or distributes as its own a product manufactured by another is subject to the same liability as though the seller or distributor were the product's manufacturer.

In Lou v. Otis Elevator Co., 933 N.E.2d 140 (Mass. App. Ct. 2010), the appellate court held that the trial judge correctly instructed the jury following the Restatement (Third) § 14. For a list of states that have adopted apparent manufacturer doctrine, see Reiss v. Komatsu Amer. Corp., 735 F. Supp. 2d 1125, 1132–33 (D.N.D. 2010).

[100] Torres v. Goodyear Tire & Rubber Co., 786 P.2d 939 (Ariz. 1990); Connelly v. Uniroyal, Inc., 389 N.E.2d 155 (Ill. 1979); Lou v. Otis Elevator Co., 933 N.E.2d 140 (Mass. App. Ct. 2010).

[101] *See* Mullaney v. Hilton Hotels Corp., 634 F.Supp.2d 1130 (D.HI 2009); Friedland Family Enterprises v. Amoroso, 630 So.2d 1067 (Fla. 1994); Kemp v. Miller, 453 N.W.2d 872 (Wis. 1990); Francioni v. Gibsonia Truck Corp., 372 A.2d 736 (Pa. 1977). Section 20(b) of the Restatement (Third) applies strict liability to lessors and bailors who "in a commercial transaction . . . [provide a] product to another either for use or consumption or as a preliminary step leading to ultimate use or consumption." Comments *c* and *f* to § 20 state that it applies to commercial product leases and product bailments.

facturing parties play in the production and marketing of defective products; the fact that nonmanufacturing parties often can shift the loss, through indemnification, to the party who, in fact, created the defect; a feeling that nonmanufacturers are in a position to exert pressure on manufacturers for safer products; and the public policy rationale that those in the chain of distribution are involved in, and derive a profit from, placing the defective product in the stream of commerce.[102]

The Restatement (Third) reflects the expansive view of who should be liable for defective products. Section 1 imposes liability on "[o]ne engaged in the business of selling or otherwise distributing products who sells or distributes a defective product." Comment *e* states that:

> [A]ll commercial sellers and distributors of products, including nonmanu-facturing sellers and distributors such as wholesalers and retailers, are subject to liability for selling products that are defective. Liability attaches even when such nonmanufacturing sellers or distributors do not themselves render the products defective and regardless of whether they are in a position to prevent defects from occurring.

Section 20(b) defines the term "otherwise distributes":

> One otherwise distributes a product when in a commercial transaction other than a sale, one provides the product to another either for use of consumption or as a preliminary step leading to ultimate sale or consumption. Commercial nonsale product distributors include, but are not limited to, lessors, bailors, and those who provide products to others as a means of promoting either the use or consumption of such products or some other commercial activity.

Although retailers are strictly liable for defects in the products they sell, an actual sale is not required before strict liability attaches.[103] Thus, an automobile dealer that supplied vehicles to its sales staff as a means of promoting the vehicles was held strictly liable for an injury to a third party caused by one of those vehicles.[104] Similarly, sellers who distribute free samples of their products in the hope of making future sales have been held strictly liable for defects in those products.[105] In addition, sellers that hold out products for sale to potential customers[106] or provide a product to a customer for a trial period before the actual sale may be strictly liable for an injury caused by the product during that time.[107] In *Mulhern v. Outboard Marine Corp*,[108] the Wisconsin Supreme Court held that the terms "sell" and "seller" in § 402A were merely descriptive and that a product

---

[102] Zamora v. Mobil Corp., 704 P.2d 584 (Wash. 1985); Francioni v. Gibsonia Truck Corp., 372 A.2d 736 (Pa. 1977); Dunham v. Vaughan & Bushnell Manufacturing Co., 247 N.E.2d 401 (Ill. 1969).

[103] Perfection Paint & Color Co. v. Konduris, 258 N.E.2d 681 (Ind. Ct. App. 1970).

[104] Beattie v. Beattie, 786 A.2d 549 (Del. Super. Ct. 2001).

[105] Levondosky v. Marina Assoc., 731 F. Supp. 1210 (D.N.J. 1990); McKisson v. Sales Affiliates, Inc., 416 S.W.2d 787 (Tex. 1967). *See also* RESTATEMENT (THIRD) OF TORTS: PRODUCTS LIABILITY § 20 cmt. *b* (1998).

[106] Ribera-Emerling v. M. Fortunoff of Westbury Corp., 721 N.Y.S.2d 653 (2001).

[107] Robert F. Bullock, Inc. v. Thorpe, 353 S.E.2d 340 (Ga. 1987).

[108] 432 N.W.2d 130 (Wis. 1988).

need not actually be sold if it is injected into the "stream of commerce" by other means.[109] The court reasoned that the stream of commerce requirement was consistent with the application of § 402A. The court concluded that the actual sale of the product was not important as long as the defendant was in the business of selling such a product and placed the product in the stream of commerce.[110] The Restatement (Third) continues this approach. Comment *b* to § 1 states that the section applies "not only to sale transactions but also to other forms of commercial product distribution that are the functional equivalent of product sales."

[B] Special Categories of Sellers

Courts have given a broad interpretation to § 402A's requirement that the defendant be "engaged in the business of selling." However, there are some areas where courts either are divided as to whether a particular group that participates in placing a product in the stream of commerce should be strictly liable[111] or impose special requirements for liability. The following subsections examine three of those groups.

[1] Component Part Manufacturers

Most products today are composed of a number of component parts produced by different manufacturers and then assembled by the final product manufacturer. Because they no longer are limited by privity, plaintiffs frequently include component part manufacturers as defendants in their suits claiming that the finished product was defective. Section 402A and comment *q* to it take no position on the extent of the liability of a component part manufacturer for a defect in the finished product. In response to this silence, courts have held that a component part manufacturer is liable for an injury caused by a finished product if the injury was caused by a component part that was defective at the time it left the control of the part manufacturer. A component part manufacturer also may be liable if it participated in the design of the final product or in the integration of its part into the final product and that part caused the finished product to be defective.[112] However, a component part manufacturer is not liable for supplying a non-defective part or a non-defective part that becomes defective because of substantial change by the assembler of the finished product. These positions are reflected in § 5 of the Restatement (Third) which states:

> One engaged in the business of selling or otherwise distributing components who sells or distributes a component is subject to liability for harm to

---

[109] *Id.* at 134.

[110] *Id.*

[111] An example of an area where courts are divided is the liability of trade associations that voluntarily create and set safety standards. For a discussion of the cases dealing with trade associations, see Padilla v. Hunter Douglas Window Coverings, 2010 U.S. Dist. LEXIS 2808 (N.D. Ill. 2012).

[112] For a review of the cases dealing with component part manufacturers, see Thorndike v. DaimlerChrysler Corp., 2003 U.S. Dist. LEXIS 8626 (D. Me. May 21), *aff'd*, 288 F. Supp. 2d 50 (D. Me 2003); Taylor v. Elliott Turbomachinery Co., Inc., 90 Cal. Rptr. 3d 414 (Ct. App. 2009); Ranger Conveying & Supply Co. v. Davis, 254 S.W.3d 471 (Tex. App. 2007).

persons or property caused by a product into which the component is integrated if:

(a) the component is defective in itself . . . and the defect causes the harm; or

(b)(1) the seller or distributor of the component substantially participates in the integration of the component into the design of the product; and

(b)(2) the integration of the component causes the product to be defective . . . and

(b)(3) the defect in the product causes the harm.[113]

The rationale for the Restatement (Third)'s position is stated in comment *a* to § 5:

If the component is not itself defective, it would be unjust and inefficient to impose liability solely on the ground that the manufacturer of the integrated product utilizes the component in a manner that renders the integrated product defective. Imposing liability would require the component seller to scrutinize another's product which the component seller has no role in developing.

Thus, a plaintiff must show that the component part was defective when it left the control of the component part manufacturer, that the defect in the component part was the cause of her injury, and that the final product manufacturer did not change the component part substantially.

An example of the liability of a component part manufacturer is *Jimenez v. Superior Court*,[114] in which the California Supreme Court held that a window manufacturer could be held strictly liable for damages that its defective windows caused to other parts of the homes in which they were installed. The court rejected the window manufacturer's argument that it merely supplied component parts of the mass-produced homes, which were the finished products sold to consumers. According to the court:

The policies underlying strict products liability in tort . . . are equally applicable to component manufacturers and suppliers. . . . For purposes of strict products liability, there are 'no meaningful distinctions' between, on the one hand, component manufacturers and suppliers and, on the other hand, manufacturers and distributors of complete products; for both groups, the 'overriding policy considerations are the same.'[115]

---

[113] For a discussion of the Restatement's position, see Gudmundson v. Del Ozone, 232 P.3d 1059, 1072–74 (Utah 2010); Davis v. Komatsu America Industries, Corp., 42 S.W.3d 34 (Tenn. 2001); Kohler Co. v. Marcotte, 907 So. 2d 596 (Fla. Dist. Ct. App. 2005) and David A. Fischer, *Product Liability: A Commentary on the Liability of Suppliers of Component Parts and Raw Materials*, 53 S.C. L. Rev. 1137 (2002); Hildy Bowbeer, *Liability for Component Parts and Raw Materials*, 10 Kan. J.L. & Pub. Pol'y 110 (2000).

[114] 58 P.3d 450 (Cal. 2002).

[115] *Id.* at 454.

According to the court, the "overriding policy considerations" that justified strict liability were: first, component part manufacturers are "an integral part of the overall producing and marketing enterprise"; second, they may be "the only member of that enterprise reasonably available to the injured plaintiff"; and, finally, they may be in the best position to ensure product safety, and can adjust the costs of liability in the course of their continuing business relationship with other participants in the manufacturing and marketing process.[116]

In order to overcome the policy arguments in favor of strict liability, the window manufacturer in *Jimenez* raised two arguments. First, it contended that, since the windows were shipped in parts and assembled and installed by the home builder, they underwent "substantial change" from the time they left the control of the manufacturer. The court answered that argument by stating that "[t]he mere assembly of a product that is sold in parts is not a 'substantial change' in the product."[117] Second, the window manufacturer claimed that it did have physical control over the windows when they were installed in the homes. In response, the court stated: "Rarely, if ever, are defective products still in the control of a manufacturer, distributor, or retailer at the time of injury to the consumer. What matters is whether the windows were defective when they left the factory, and whether these alleged defects caused the injuries."[118]

[2] Sellers of Used Products

Courts are divided on the question of whether a commercial seller of used goods can be strictly liable if the product is defective. The majority of states hold that § 402A is not applicable to commercial sellers of used products in the absence of an allegation that the seller created the defect in the product.[119] One of the first cases to deal with the question of liability for the sale of used products was *Peterson v. Lou Bachrodt Chevrolet Co.*[120] In that case, the Illinois Supreme Court refused to extend strict liability to a used car dealer and restricted the "creation of the risk" to the actual creation of a defect. The court justified the exemption of sellers of used products from strict liability on four grounds: first, unlike sellers and distributors of new products, sellers of used products are outside the original chain of production and marketing that placed the product in the stream of commerce; second, sellers of used products lack the ability to exert pressure upon manufacturers to produce safe products; third, sellers of used products are not entitled to indemnification from the party who actually created the defect; and finally, if strict liability were imposed upon sellers of used products, they would become, in effect, insurers against defects that came into existence after the chain of distribution was completed and while the product was under the control of one or more consumers.[121]

---

[116] *Id.*

[117] *Id.*

[118] *Id.*

[119] For a review of the cases and arguments for and against extending strict liability to sellers of used products, see Allenberg v. Bentley Hedges Travel Service, Inc., 22 P.3d 223 (Okla. 2001).

[120] 329 N.E.2d 785 (Ill. 1975).

[121] *Id.* at 787. *See* Arriaga v. CitiCapital Commercial Corp., 85 Cal. Rptr. 3d 143 (Cal. Ct. App. 2008).

Almost 20 years after *Peterson*, a federal district court in Missouri, in *Harber v. Altec Industries, Inc.*,[122] reviewed the cases and policy considerations both for and against imposing strict liability on commercial sellers of used goods. The court concluded that extending strict liability to sellers of used goods would not further the rationales behind strict liability: risk spreading, risk reduction through increased inspection, risk reduction through market pressure, and meeting consumer expectations.[123] The only factor that it found weighed in favor of strict liability of sellers of used goods was victim compensation.[124] Although that is an important goal, the court felt that it did not outweigh all of the factors that weighed heavily against strict liability in such cases.[125]

Courts that have held dealers in used goods liable under § 402A also have appealed to the policy justifications behind the adoption of strict liability.[126] They have pointed out that the term "seller" does not require that the person be the first in the chain of sellers. They also have reasoned that strict liability would encourage risk reduction because dealers would increase their inspection and maintenance before resale.[127] Thus, some courts have imposed strict liability on sellers of used goods that rebuild or recondition the used goods.[128] Section 8 of the Restatement (Third) also imposes liability for personal injury or property damage on commercial sellers or distributors of used products but only if the defect:

(a)   arises from the seller's failure to exercise reasonable care; or

(b)   is a manufacturing defect . . . and the seller's marketing of the product would cause a reasonable person in the position of the buyer to expect the used product to present no greater risk of defect than if the product were new; or

(c)   is a defect . . . in a used product remanufactured by the seller or a predecessor in the commercial chain of distribution of the used product; or

(d)   arises from a used product's noncompliance . . . with a product safety statute or regulation applicable to the used product.

---

[122] 812 F. Supp. 954 (W.D. Mo.), *aff'd*, 5 F.3d 339 (8th Cir. 1993).

[123] *Id.* at 961–65.

[124] *Id.* at 965.

[125] *Id.* at 965–66.

[126] *See* Galindo v. Precision American Corp., 754 F.2d 1212 (5th Cir. 1985) (applying Texas law); Nelson v. Nelson Hardware, Inc., 467 N.W.2d 518 (Wis. 1991). Although the federal court in Harber v. Altec Industries, Inc., 812 F. Supp. 954 (W.D. Mo. 1993) (applying Missouri law) did not extend strict liability to the seller, the court analyzed the policy consideration for imposing strict liability on a seller of a used product.

[127] *See* Stanton v. Carlson Sales, Inc., 728 A.2d 534 (Conn. Super. Ct. 1998); Jordan v. Sunnyslope Appliance Propane & Plumbing Supplies Co., 660 P.2d 1236 (Ariz. Ct. App. 1983).

[128] Crandell v. Larkin and Jones Appliance Co., 334 N.W.2d 31 (S.D. 1983); Gentile v. MacGregor Mfg. Co., 493 A.2d 647 (N.J. Super. Ct. Law Div. 1985). In Cataldo v. Lazy Days R.V. Center, Inc., 920 So. 2d 174 (Fla. Dist. Ct. App. 2006), the Florida Court of Appeals refused to impose strict liability on the seller of a reconditioned motor vehicle. Although the appellate court certified the question to the Florida Supreme Court, that court denied the Petition for Review. In Malen v. MTD Products, Inc., 628 F.3d 296 (7th Cir. 2010) (applying Illinois law), the Seventh Circuit held that Illinois courts likely would not make a distinction between reconditioned products and new products.

[3]   Successor Corporations

One of the most litigated, and controversial, issues in products liability law is the liability of a successor corporation for injuries caused by a product manufactured and marketed by its predecessor company, the total assets of which have been acquired by merger or purchase by the successor corporation.[129] Courts deal with this problem by holding that a corporation that merges with another corporation assumes the latter corporation's liabilities;[130] however, a corporation that purchases all of its assets to another corporation is not liable for the liabilities of the transferor.[131] Courts recognize four exceptions to this general rule of nonliability of a successor corporation: (1) the transaction amounts to a consolidation or merger of the purchaser and seller corporation; (2) the purchaser corporation is merely a continuation of the seller corporation; (3) there is an express or implied agreement to assume the selling corporation's liabilities; or (4) the transaction is for the fraudulent purpose of escaping liability for the seller's obligations.[132] In those four situations, a corporation that purchases the assets of the other corporation assumes the latter's debts and liabilities.[133] Section 12 of the Restatement (Third) adopts this approach to the liability of a successor corporation.[134]

The first two of the above exceptions to the general rule of nonliability of a successor corporation, which involve the most commonly litigated situations, are based on the concept that a successor corporation that effectively takes over a company in its entirety should carry the predecessor's liabilities as a concomitant to the benefits it derives from the goodwill purchased. Courts reason that allowing recovery in tort against a successor corporation is merely an extension of the concept of products liability, which calls for the burden of consumer injuries to be borne by the manufacturer, who can transfer the costs to the general public as a component of the selling price. Strict liability assures that a responsible source is available to compensate the injured party.[135]

When a *de facto* merger or consolidation is alleged, a court must determine the substance of the agreement, regardless of the title put on it by the parties.[136] If the

---

[129]   For a discussion of successor liability, see Marie T. Reilly, *Making Sense of Successor Liability*, 31 Hofstra L. Rev. 745 (2003); Note: *Successor Liability, Mass Tort, and Mandatory-Litigation Class Action*, 118 Harv. L. Rev. 2357 (2005).

[130]   Myers v. Putzmeister, Inc., 596 N.E.2d 754 (Ill. App. Ct. 1992).

[131]   Crutchfield v. Marine Power Engine Co., 209 P.3d 295 (Okla. 2009).

[132]   Crutchfield v. Marine Power Engine Co., 209 P.3d 295 (Okla. 2009); Semenetz v. Sherling & Walden, Inc., 851 N.E.2d 1170 (N.Y. 2006); Savage Arms, Inc. v. Western Auto Supply Co., 18 P.3d 49 (Alaska 2001).

[133]   *See* Arnold Graphics Indus. v. Independent Agent Center, 775 F.2d 38, 42 (2d Cir. 1985) (applying New York law); Dayton v. Peck, Stow & Wilcox Co., 739 F.2d 690, 692 (1st Cir. 1984) (applying Massachusetts law); Tucker v. Paxson Mach. Co., 645 F.2d 620, 622 (8th Cir. 1981) (citing Missouri law).

[134]   For a discussion of the history and rational for these exceptions, see Restatement (Third) of Torts: Products Liability § 12 cmts. *a* and *b* (1998); Tabor v. Metal Ware Corp., 168 P.3d 814 (Utah 2007).

[135]   *See* Dayton v. Peck, Stow & Wilcox Co., 739 F.2d 690 (1st Cir. 1984) (applying Massachusetts law); Tucker v. Paxson Machine Co., 645 F.2d 620 (8th Cir. 1981) (applying Missouri law).

[136]   Philadelphia Electric Co. v. Hercules, Inc., 762 F.2d 303 (3d Cir. 1985) (applying Pennsylvania law).

parties have not complied with the statutory requirements for a *de jure* merger, but still have achieved virtually all the results of a merger, a court may hold the surviving corporation liable for the conduct of the transferor corporation as if the merger were de jure. Courts generally impose four requirements for the recognition of the purported sale of assets as a *de facto* merger: (1) continuity of the business enterprise between the seller and buyer, including continuity of management, personnel, physical location, assets, and general business operations; (2) continuity of shareholders which results from the purchasing corporation paying for the acquired assets with shares of its own stock, this stock ultimately coming to be held by the shareholders of the seller corporation so that they become a constituent part of the purchasing corporation; (3) the seller corporation ceases its ordinary business operations, liquidates, and dissolves as soon as legally and practically possible; and (4) the purchasing corporation assumes those obligations of the seller ordinarily necessary for the uninterrupted continuation of normal business operations of the seller corporation.[137]

Since a successor corporation often continues to manufacture and market the products of its predecessor, courts have considered whether to adopt an additional "product line" exception for successor corporations. Under this exception, a successor corporation that continues to manufacture a product of the business it acquires, regardless of the method of acquisition or any possible attribution of fault, assumes strict liability for products manufactured and sold before the change of corporate ownership. In *Ray v. Alad Corp.*,[138] the first decision to adopt the product line exception, the California Supreme Court set out three justifications for imposing strict liability upon a successor to a manufacturer:

> (1) the virtual destruction of the plaintiff's remedies against the original manufacturer caused by the successor's acquisition of the business, (2) the successor's ability to assume the original manufacturer's risk-spreading role, and (3) the fairness of requiring the successor to assume a responsibility for defective products that was a burden necessarily attached to the original manufacturer's good will being enjoyed by the successor in the continued operation of the business.[139]

Although some courts recognize the "product line" exception in products liability cases,[140] a majority of states,[141] and the Restatement (Third),[142] reject the exception as incompatible with the doctrine of strict liability in tort. These courts

---

[137] *See* Arnold Graphics Industries v. Independent Agent Center, 775 F.2d 38 (2d Cir. 1985) (applying New York law); Keller v. Clark Equipment Co., 715 F.2d 1280 (8th Cir. 1983) (applying North Dakota law); U.S. Automatic Sprinkler Co. v. Reliable Automatic Sprinkler Co., 719 F. Supp. 2d 1020 (S.D. Ind. 2010) (applying Indiana law); American Paper Recycling Corp. v. IHC Corp., 707 F. Supp. 2d 114 (D. Mass. 2010) (applying Massachusetts law); Tabor v. The Metal Ware Corp., 168 P.3d 814 (Utah 2007); Village Builders 96, L.P. v. U.S.Laboratories, Inc., 112 P.3d 1082 (Nev. 2005).

[138] 560 P.2d 3 (Cal. 1977).

[139] *Id.* at 9.

[140] *See* Schmidt v. Boardman Co., 11 A.3d 924 (Pa. 2011); Garcia v. Coe Mfg. Co. 933 P.2d 243 (N.M. 1997).

[141] For examples, see Tabor v. Metal Ware Corp., 168 P.3d 814 (Utah 2007); Semenetz v. Sherling & Walden, Inc., 851 N.E.2d 1170 (N.Y. 2006); Nissen Corp. v. Miller, 594 A.2d 564 (Md. 1991); Guzman v. MRM.Elgin, 567 N.E.2d 929 (Mass. 1991); Fish v. Amsted Indus., Inc., 376 N.W.2d 820 (Wis. 1985);

base their rejection of a product line exception on one or more of three arguments: (1) the exception is inconsistent with elementary products liability principles, and strict liability principles in particular, in that it results in an imposition of liability without a corresponding duty; (2) the exception threatens small successor businesses with economic annihilation because of the difficulty involved in obtaining insurance for defects in a predecessor's product; and (3) the exception is essentially a radical change in the principles of corporation law, and, as such, should be left to legislative action.[143]

[C] Persons Not Covered by Strict Liability

Despite the broad scope of potential defendants in a products liability action, courts have not imposed strict liability on everyone involved with the manufacture or distribution of a defective product. Parties that have been held not to be strictly liable for a defective product include:

Employers: A large number of products liability cases involve workers who were injured by machinery during their course of their employment. Because of state workers' compensation laws are the exclusive remedy for employees who suffer personal injuries in the course of their employment, these workers are not able to bring negligence or strict liability actions against their employers, even where their employers designed and manufactured the product for the use of their employees.[144] However, injured employees may bring products liability suits against the manufacturers and sellers of the machines that caused their injuries.

Government Contractors: The government contractor defense protects suppliers and contractors from liability for design defects where the United States approved reasonably precise specifications, the equipment conformed to those specifications, and the supplier warned the United States about the dangers in the use of the equipment.[145]

Installers and Repairers: A person who simply installs a product manufactured by someone else is not strictly liable under § 402A.[146] Similarly, a person who repairs a product after it has been manufactured and sold is not strictly liable.[147] The reason for this is that the policy behind strict liability does not apply to a person who is not involved in the sale of the product, receives no profit from placing

---

Bernard v. Kee Mfg. Co., 409 So. 2d 1047 (Fla. 1982).

[142] Under the RESTATEMENT (THIRD) OF TORTS: PRODUCTS LIABILITY § 12 (1998), the liability of a successor corporation does not include the product line exception.

[143] *See* Conn v. Fales Division of Mathewson Corp., 835 F.2d 145 (6th Cir. 1987) (applying Kentucky law); Niccum v. Hydra Tool Corp., 438 N.W.2d 96 (Minn. 1989); Ray v. Alad, 560 P.2d 3 (Cal. 1977).

[144] However, an employer's immunity does not apply to intentional torts. Wise v. CNH America, LLC. 142 P.3d 774 (Mont. 2006); Vermett v. Fred Christen & Sons Co., 741 N.E.2d 954 (Ohio 2000). For a discussion of workers' compensation statutes, see Chapter 9.

[145] Boyle v. United Technologies Corp., 487 U.S. 500 (1988). The government contractor defense is discussed in detail in Chapter 9.

[146] Winters v. Fru-Con Inc., 498 F.3d 734 (7th Cir. 2007) (applying Illinois law); Rotshteyn v. Klos Const., Inc., 2004 U.S. Dist. LEXIS 9416 (E.D. Pa. May 20, 2004) (applying Pennsylvania law); Counts v. MK-Ferguson Co., 862 F.2d 1338 (8th Cir. 1988) (applying Missouri law).

[147] Caine v. Tech Air of CT, Inc., 2003 Conn. Super. LEXIS 2645 (Sept. 25, 2003).

it in the stream of commerce and thus has no influence over the manufacturer.[148] However, an installer or repairer who also manufacturers or supplies the defective product may be strictly liable.[149] Similarly, an installer or repairer may be liable in negligence for their work.[150]

Occasional Sellers: An occasional seller that is not engaged in selling the product as regular part of its business is not strictly liable unless it actually created the defect.[151] This includes both the individual who makes an isolated sale of an item and a company that sells equipment if its primary business is not selling such equipment.[152] According to comment *f* to § 402A, the reason for excluding occasional sellers from strict liability is

> the ancient one of the special responsibility for the safety of the public undertaken by one who enters into the business of supplying human beings with products which may endanger the safety of their persons and property, and the forced reliance upon that undertaking on the part of those who purchase such goods. This basis is lacking in the case of the ordinary individual who makes the isolated sale, and he is not liable to a third person, or even to his buyer, in the absence of his negligence.[153]

The Restatement (Third) also applies only to manufacturers and other commercial sellers and distributors who are engaged in the business of selling or distributing the type of product that harmed the plaintiff. Since it does not apply to a noncommercial seller or distributor, "it does not apply to one sells foodstuffs to a neighbor, nor does it apply to the private owner of an automobile who sells it to another."[154]

Auctioneers: Auctioneers have no relationship to the manufacture of products or with the manufacturer. They act as the agent of the seller of the product for the immediate sale of the product. Thus, courts have not treated auctioneers as sellers for purposes of strict liability.[155]

---

[148] Winters v. Fru-Con, Inc., 498 F.3d 734 (7th Cir. 2007 (applying Illinois law).

[149] Jones v. A Best Products Co., 2003-Ohio-6612 (8th Dist.); Lukowski v. Vecta Educational Corp., 401 N.E.2d 781 (Ind. Ct. App. 1980).

[150] Ayala v. V. & O. Press Co., 512 N.Y.S.2d 704 (App. Div. 1987).

[151] Worrell v. Elliott & Frantz, 799 F. Supp. 2d 343 (D.N.J. 2011) (applying New Jersey law); Jaramillo v. Weyerhaeuser Co., 906 N.E.2d 387 (N.Y. 2009) (a company that sold one of its used machines (which it purchased used) to a different company was not strictly liable for a workplace accident involving that machine, which occurred 16 years later); Engel v. Corrigan Company-Mechanical Contractors, Inc., 148 S.W.3d 28 (Mo. Ct. App. 2004).

[152] Geboy v. TRL, Inc., 159 F.2d 993 (7th Cir. 1998) (applying Wisconsin law); Breidenstein v. Ludlow Corp., 498 N.Y.S.2d 639 (App. Div. 1986) (occasional seller was not liable for negligent failure to warn).

[153] For a discussion of the policy reasons involved in deciding whether an occasional seller is strictly liable, see Carollo v. Al Warren Oil Co., 820 N.E.2d 994 (Ill. App. Ct. 2004).

[154] RESTATEMENT (THIRD) OF TORTS: PRODUCTS LIABILITY § 1, cmt. *c* (1998).

[155] New Texas Auto Auction Services, L.P. v. Gomez de Hernandez. 249 S.W. 3d 400 (Tex. 2008); Musser v. Vilsmeier Auction co., 562 A.2d 279 (Pa. 1989); Brejcha v. Wilson Machery, Inc., 206 Cal. Rptr. 688 (Ct. App. 1984).

Premises Owners: Courts have refused to hold that someone who simply owns the premises on which a defective product was located is strictly liable.[156]

Service Providers: Strict liability does not apply to transactions that involve both a "service," such as those provided by physicians, dentists, and hospitals, and a "sale" of a product, if the service is the primary purpose of the transaction and the transfer of the product is secondary.[157] Thus, courts have held that the sale/service exempts pharmacist from strict liability for dispensing prescription drugs.[158] This exception from strict liability applies not only to those in the medical field but also to architects and contractors,[159] to engineers,[160] and to those that provide transportation.[161]

The Restatement (Third) adopts this position as well, stating that "[s]ervices, even when provided commercially, are not products."[162] However, as with installers and repairers, suppliers of product-related services may be liable in negligence.

[D] Distributor Statutes

In order to help nonmanufacturing sellers avoid the expenses of defending products liability suits, approximately half of the states have enacted statutes permitting their dismissal under certain conditions. While some of these statutes apply only to suits based on strict liability,[163] other statutes apply to negligence actions as well.[164] Although each statute is different, one example is the North Dakota Product Liability Act.[165] The statute provides that, in any products liability action against a defendant who did not manufacture the product, the nonmanufacturing defendant must, when answering or otherwise pleading, "file an affidavit certifying the correct identity of the manufacturer of the product allegedly

---

[156] Peterson v. Superior Court, 899 P.2d 905 (Cal. 1995); Armstrong v. Cione, 738 P.2d 79 (Haw. 1987); Siciliano v. Capitol City Shows, Inc., 475 A.2d 19 (N.H. 1984).

[157] *See* Budding v. SSM Healthcare System, 19 S.W.3d 678 (Mo. 2000); Royer v. Catholic Medical Center, 741 A.2d 74 (N.H. 1999); Cafazzo v. Central Medical Health Services, Inc., 668 A.2d 521 (Pa. 1995); Pierson v. Sharp Memorial Hosp., 264 Cal. Rptr. 673 (Ct. App. 1989). However, if there is a clear "sale" of a product, courts have been willing to impose strict liability, at least on non-medical workers who also provide a "service" to their customers. *See* Newmark v. Gimbel's Inc., 258 A.2d 697 (N.J. 1969). For a discussion of the two most widely used tests for how the primary purpose of a transaction is determined, see Linden v. Cascade Stone Co., Inc., 699 N.W.2d 189 (Wis. 2005).

[158] *See* Madison v. American Home Products Corp., 595 S.E.2d 493 (S.C. 2004); Makripodis by Makripodis v. Merrell-Dow Pharmaceuticals, 523 A.2d 374 (Pa. Super. Ct. 1987); Docken v. Ciba-Geigy, 739 P.2d 591 (Or. Ct. App. 1987).

[159] Bruzga v. PMR Architects, 693 A.2d 401 (N.H. 1997).

[160] Industrial Risk Insurers v. Creole Production Serv. Inc., 746 F.2d 526 (9th Cir. 1984) (applying Alaska law).

[161] Although Amtrak provides seats for its customs on its trains, the purpose of the trains is transportation. Haynes v. National R.R. Passenger Corp., 423 F. Supp. 2d 1073 (C.D. Cal. 2006).

[162] Restatement (Third) of Torts: Products Liability § 19(b) (1998).

[163] *See* the Illinois Distributor Statute, 735 Ill. Comp. Stat. 5/2-621; Whelchel v. Briggs & Stratton Corp., 850 F. Supp. 2d 926 (N.D. Ill. 2012) (applying Illinois law).

[164] *See* Ala. Code § 6-5-501(2) and § 6-5-521; N.J. Stat. Ann. § 2A:58C-9; Tenn Code Ann. § 29-28-106; Tex. Civ. Prac. & Rem. Code § 82.003.

[165] N.D. Cent. Code, § 28-01.3 *et seq.*

causing the personal injury, death, or damage to property."[166] Defendants who file an uncontroverted affidavit certifying the identity of the manufacturer then are dismissed from the action unless the plaintiff can show:

(a) That the certifying seller exercised some significant control over the design or manufacture of the product, or provided instructions or warnings to the manufacturer relative to the alleged defect in the product which caused the personal injury, death, or damage to property.

(b) That the certifying seller had actual knowledge of the defect in the product which caused the personal injury, death, or damage to property.

(c) That the certifying seller created the defect in the product which caused the personal injury, death, or damage to property.[167]

At any time before the trial begins, however, the plaintiff may move to vacate the dismissal order and reinstate the certifying seller if the plaintiff can show either that the applicable statute of limitation bars a products liability action against the manufacturer of the product or that the identity of the manufacturer given to the plaintiff by the certifying defendant was incorrect.[168]

The North Dakota statute also provides for indemnification of the seller for damages and costs in certain situations where a suit is filed against it. Thus, if an action is filed against a seller and the plaintiff alleges that

a product was defectively designed, contained defectively manufactured parts, had insufficient safety guards, or had inaccurate or insufficient warnings; that the condition existed when the product left the manufacturer's control;

the seller has not substantially altered the product; and

the defective condition or lack of safety guards or adequate warnings caused the plaintiff's injury or damage,

then, the manufacturer of the product must assume the cost of defense of the action, and any liability that may be imposed on the seller. The obligation to assume the seller's cost of defense also extends to actions in which the manufacturer and seller ultimately are found not liable.[169] This is in keeping with the purpose of the statute which is to relieve retailers when they are sued only because they sold the

---

[166] *Id.* at § 28-01.3-04 (1).

[167] *Id.* at § 28-01.3-04(2). *See* Reiss v. Komatsu Amer. Corp., 735 F. Supp. 2d 1125 (D.N.D. 2010) (applying North Dakota law); Paracelsus Healthcare Corp. v. Philips Electronics North America, 2000 U.S. Dist. LEXIS 20607 (D.N.D. May 7, 2000) (applying North Dakota law). Almost all distributor statutes will not release an innocent seller from liability if the court is unable to obtain jurisdiction over the manufacturer. The reason for this is that, while sellers should be excused from liability if the manufacturer, who is liable for the defect, can be sued, an injured consumer should not be denied recovery simply because a court has no jurisdiction over the manufacturer. However, North Dakota's statute contains no such provision.

[168] N.D. Cent. Code at § 28-01.3-04(3).

[169] *Id.* at § 28-01.3-05.

product.[170]

§ 4.05 WHAT IS A PRODUCT?

[A] Introduction

Essential to the application of § 402A is a finding that the plaintiff was injured by a "product" that was in a "defective condition unreasonably dangerous" to the user or consumer when it left the control of the manufacturer or seller.[171] A determination that the item that injured the plaintiff was a "product" is not an issue in negligence cases since the focus is on whether the manufacturer or seller owed a duty to the plaintiff and the causal connection between the conduct of the manufacturer or seller and the harm.

Section 402A and its comments do not define a "product." However, comment *d* provides a list of some examples of products where strict liability applies. According to the comment:

> The rule stated in this section is not limited to the sale of food for human consumption or other products for intimate body use, although it will obviously include them. It extends to any product sold in the condition, or substantially the same condition, in which it is expected to reach the ultimate user or consumer. Thus the rule stated applied to an automobile, a tire, an airplane, a grinding wheel, a water heater, a gas stove, a power tool, a riveting machine, a chair and an insecticide.[172]

The common element to all of the examples of "products" in comment *d* is that they are tangible. Thus, in *Holland v. TD Ameritrade*,[173] a federal court held that, under California law, strict liability does not apply to intangible "goods" and services. Since the plaintiff in *Holland* was claiming strict liability on a securities transaction, the claim did not relate to a tangible product and could not stand.[174]

Many states that have products liability statutes include very broad definitions of a "product" within those statutes. For example, Arkansas and Tennessee define a "product" simply as "any tangible object or good produced."[175] However, other states are more specific. Ohio, for example, defines a "product" as

---

[170] Kaylor v. Iseman Mobile Homes, 369 N.W.2d 101 (N.D. 1985).

[171] Courts have stated that strict liability applies only to a "product" that is in a finished condition when it left the manufacturer's control. Ettinger v. Triangle-Pacific Corp., 799 A.2d 95 (Pa. Super. Ct. 2002).

[172] *See* Brian A. Comer, *Products Liability Claims in South Carolina: What Exactly Does "Essentially the Same Condition" Mean?* SOUTH CAROLINA LAWYER (November 2009), 24.

[173] 2012 U.S. Dist. LEXIS 22470 (E.D. Cal. Feb. 21, 2012) (applying California law).

[174] *Id.* at *6.

[175] ARK. CODE ANN. § 16-116-102(4). In *Engelhardt v. Rogers Group, Inc.*, 132 F. Supp. 2d 757 (E.D. Ark. 2001), a federal district court applied the Arkansas statute and concluded that a resurfaced highway was not a "product."

any object, substance, mixture, or raw material that constitutes tangible personal property and that satisfies all of the following: (i) It is capable of delivery itself, or as an assembled whole in a mixed or combined state, or as a component or ingredient. (ii) It is produced, manufactured, or supplied for introduction into trade or commerce. (iii) It is intended for sale or lease to persons for commercial or personal use.[176]

The Ohio statute also specifically excludes blood, human tissue, and organs from its definition of a product.[177]

Since only a few states have products liability statutes, it is up to the courts to determine whether specific items are a "product" within the meaning of § 402A.[178] In making their decisions, courts have stated that "the policy reasons underlying the strict products liability concept should be considered in determining whether something is a product . . . rather than . . . focus[ing] on the dictionary definition of the word."[179] According to the Illinois appellate court, the policy reasons to be considered in determining whether something constitutes a "product" for purposes of strict liability are: (1) the public interest in human life and health; (2) the invitations and solicitations of the manufacturer to purchase the product; (3) the justice of imposing the loss on the manufacturer who created the risk and reaped the profit; and (4) the superior ability of the commercial enterprise to distribute the risk of injury proximately caused by the defective condition of its product by passing the loss on to the public as a cost of doing business.[180]

The definition of a "product" in the Restatement (Third) reflects the comments to § 402A, state statutes such as the one in Arkansas, and the decisions of state courts. According to § 19 of the Restatement (Third), "[a] product is tangible personal property distributed commercially for use or consumption." Because of the breadth of this definition, the specific question of what constitutes a "product" is not an issue in most situations. However, there have been a number of cases in which courts have been required to decide whether the particular item that was the source of the plaintiff's injuries or damages was a "product" within the meaning of § 402A. The following subsections briefly examine six of those areas.

[B] Animals

In the debate over whether animals, such as household pets and commercial livestock, are "products" for purposes of § 402A, courts are divided between those that follow the New York approach or the Illinois approach. In *Beyer v. Aquarium*

---

[176] Ohio Rev. Code Ann. § 2307.71.

[177] *Id.*

[178] The California appellate court, for example, has defined a "product" as "a physical article which results from a manufacturing process and is ultimately delivered to a consumer." Pierson v. Sharp Memorial Hosp., 264 Cal. Rptr. 673, 676 (Ct. App. 1989).

[179] Lowrie v. City of Evanston, 365 N.E.2d 923, 928 (Ill. App. Ct. 1977). *See* Kaneko v. Hilo Coast Processing, 654 P.2d 343 (Haw. 1982); Perez v. Fidelity Container Corp., 682 N.E.2d 1150 (Ill. App. Ct. 1997).

[180] Boddie v. Litton Unit Handling Systems, 455 N.E.2d 142, 147 (Ill. App. Ct. 1983).

Supply Co.,[181] a store employee became ill after coming in contact with allegedly diseased hamsters that had been distributed by the defendant. In a suit based on strict liability, a New York court rejected the defendant's argument that the doctrine of strict liability should be limited to cases involving manufactured products. Since the court viewed the purposes of strict liability as distributing the inevitable losses of commercial activity and promoting the marketing of safe products, it stated that "[t]here is no reason why a breeder, distributor or vendor who places a diseased animal in the stream of commerce should be less accountable for his actions than one who markets a defective manufactured product."[182] Connecticut[183] and Oregon[184] courts also have taken the position that animals are "products."

The opposite position is taken by those states that follow the Illinois approach that animals are not "products" within the meaning of § 402A.[185] In *Whitmer v. Schneble*[186] the owners of a dog that bit a young child sought indemnification under strict liability from the seller of the animal. The Illinois appellate court refused to apply strict liability, saying that the nature of the item must be fixed when it leaves the manufacturer's control and that it must reach the consumer without substantial change.[187] The court concluded that a dog's character is shaped by the purchaser who creates the risk and should bear the liability.[188] Similarly, in *Anderson v. Farmers Hybrid Co.*,[189] the Illinois appellate court held that pigs were not products under § 402A. In *Anderson*, pigs purchased from the defendant arrived in a diseased condition that spread to the plaintiff's other pigs. The court denied the plaintiff's claim for damage in strict liability, saying:

> While a "product" may be unchanged from its natural state, viable and not the result of manufacturing processes, it must also be of a fixed nature at the time it leaves the seller's control. . . . Living creatures . . . are by their nature in a constant process of internal development and growth and they are also participants in a constant interaction with the environment around them as part of the development. . . . [N]owhere in the commentary to section 402A are living things brought within the definition of a "product," nor have the plaintiffs been able to cite us to any case from any jurisdiction which has held a living creature to be a "product."[190]

---

[181] 404 N.Y.S.2d 778 (1977).

[182] *Id.* at 779.

[183] Worrell v. Sachs, 563 A.2d 1387 (Conn. Super. Ct. 1989) (puppy).

[184] Sease v. Taylor's Pets, Inc., 700 P.2d 1054 (Or. Ct. App. 1985) (rabid pet skunk).

[185] *See* Kaplan v. C Lazy U Ranch, 615 F. Supp. 234 (D. Col. 1985) (applying Colorado law) (horse ride); Blaha v. Stuard, 640 N.W.2d 85 (S.D. 2002) (dog), Coogle v. Jahangard, 609 S.E.2d 151 (Ga. Ct. App. 2005) (dog); Malicki v. Koci, 700 N.E.2d 913 (Ohio Ct. App. 1997) (parakeet); Latham v. Wal-Mart Stores, Inc., 818 S.W.2d 673 (Mo. Ct. App. 1991) (parrot).

[186] 331 N.E.2d 115 (Ill. App. Ct. 1975).

[187] *Id.* at 119.

[188] *Id.*

[189] 408 N.E.2d 1194 (Ill. App. Ct. 1980).

[190] *Id.* at 1199.

Although an animal may not be a "product" for purposes of strict liability, a retailer still may be liable under a theory of negligence for the failure to warn of diseases in the animal.[191]

[C] Blood and Human Tissue

Each year thousands of persons suffer injury or death as the result of blood borne pathogens resulting from transfusions. These pathogens include malaria, syphilis, brucellosis, hepatitis and the human immunodeficiency virus (HIV). Some courts initially held that the hospitals that performed blood transfusions were strictly liable on the grounds that blood was a "product" for purposes of § 402A.[192] However, state legislatures quickly overruled those decisions by enacting blood shield statutes which provide that hospitals and distributors of blood products are not strictly liable for injuries caused by blood transfusions.[193] Some of these statutes, and the cases interpreting them, hold that blood is not a "product" for purposes of strict liability,[194] while others classify the transfusion of blood as a medical "service" rather than a "sale,"[195] or hold that blood is an unavoidably unsafe product.[196] Courts have used the same rationales to hold that tissue banks are not strictly liable for providing human tissue for use in medical procedures.[197] The Restatement (Third) reflects these views by stating that "[h]uman blood and human tissue, even when provided commercially, are not subject to the rules of this Restatement."[198]

The question of liability for human tissue arose in a new context in 2010 in a lawsuit alleging strict liability against a sperm bank. In *D.D. v. Idant Laboratories*,[199] a woman was actinically inseminated with donor sperm obtained from a sperm bank. After the woman gave birth, her daughter began to show signs of a severe developmental disorder. Eventually, the young girl was diagnosed with

---

[191] Malicki v. Koci, 700 N.E.2d 913 (Ohio Ct. App. 1997) (parakeet).

[192] DeBattista v. Argonaut-Southwest Ins. Co., 403 So. 2d 26 (La. 1981); Rostocki v. Southwest Florida Blood Bank, Inc., 276 So. 2d 475 (Fla. 1973); Cunningham v. MacNeal Memorial Hosp., 266 N.E.2d 897 (Ill. 1970).

[193] For examples of these statutes, see ALA. CODE § 7-2-314(4); ARIZ. REV. STAT. § 32-1481; HAW. REV. STAT. § 327-51; 745 ILL. COMP. STAT. 40/1; IND. CODE § 16-41-12-11; IOWA CODE ANN. § 142C.12; KY. REV. STAT. ANN. § 139.125; LA. STAT.ANN. § 9:2797; MD. CODE § 5-630; MONT. CODE ANN. § 50-33-104; N.M. STAT. ANN. § 24-10-5; R.I. GEN. LAW § 23-17-30; S.C. CODE ANN. § 44-43-10.

[194] OHIO REV. CODE ANN. § 2307.71; Samson v. The Greenville Hosp. Sys., 377 S.E.2d 311 (S.C. 1989).

[195] For examples, see ALA. CODE § 7-2-314(4); CAL. HEALTH AND SAFETY CODE § 1606; KY. REV. STAT. ANN. § 139.125. *See* McKee v. Cutter Laboratories, Inc., 866 F.2d 219 (6th Cir. 1989) (applying Kentucky law); Brandt v. Boston Scientific, 792 N.E.2d 296 (Ill. 2003); McCombs v Southern Regional Medical Center, 504 S.E.2d 747 (Ga. Ct. App. 1998).

[196] Doe v. Miles Laboratories, Inc., 927 F.2d 187 (4th Cir. 1991) (applying Maryland law); Chauvin v. Sisters of Mercy Health System, 818 So. 2d 833 (La. Ct. App. 2002).

[197] Condos v. Musculoskeletal Transplant Foundation, 208 F. Supp. 2d 1226 (D. Utah 2002) (applying Utah law); Cryolife, Inc. v. Superior Court of Santa Cruz County, 2 Cal. Rptr. 3d 396 (Ct. App. 2003).

[198] RESTATEMENT (THIRD) OF TORTS: PRODUCTS LIABILITY § 19(c) (1998). *See also* the discussion of "human blood and human tissue" in § 19, cmt. c.

[199] 2010 U.S. App. LEXIS 6815 (3d Cir. Apr. 1, 2010) (applying New York law). Under the rules of the Third Circuit, the opinion is not a precedent that binds the court.

Fragile X, a genetic syndrome that results in various physical, intellectual, emotional, and behavioral disorders.[200] In a suit that sought to recover the expenses associated with care that her daughter would require throughout her life, the woman argued that the sperm bank should be held strictly liable for providing defective sperm. Although the Third Circuit acknowledged that the difficulties the child will face in her life were "tragic," the court held that the child lacked a cognizable injury since, under New York law, a child "does not have a protected right to be born free of genetic defects."[201]

[D] Electricity

Another subject that has given rise to a number of cases is electricity. Many of these cases have arisen as the result of accidental contact with allegedly defective high voltage transmission lines. These cases raise two questions for the courts: first, is electricity a "product" for purposes of § 402A and, second, if it is a "product," have the elements of strict liability been met when the injury results from contact with transmission lines?

As to the first issue, most courts have held that electricity can be a "product" for purposes of § 402A.[202] The rationale for this position was stated in *Elgin Airport Inn v. Commonwealth Edison Co.*[203] in which the plaintiff sought recovery for damages sustained by its air-conditioning system when the defendant delivered dangerous low-voltage electricity. According to the Illinois appellate court: "[E]lectrical energy is artificially manufactured, can be measured, bought and sold, exchanged in quantity and quality, delivered wherever desired and has been held by our Supreme Court to be personal property whose unlawful transportation is larceny."[204] Although the Illinois Supreme Court later reversed on the grounds that the level of current was not unreasonably dangerous, the court accepted the appellate court's finding that electricity is a "product" within the meaning of § 402A.[205] However, the opposite position is taken by courts that hold that electricity is a "service," not a "product" and that strict liability does not apply to services. According to the Ohio Supreme Court: "Consumers . . . are not paying for individual products but for the privilege of using [the electric company's] service."[206]

---

[200] *Id.* at *2–*3.

[201] *Id.* at *14.

[202] *See* Smith v. Home Light & Power Co., 734 P.2d 1051 (Colo. 1987); Ransome v. Wisconsin Electric Power Co., 275 N.W.2d 641, 643 (Wis. 1979); Hanus v. Texas Utilities Co., 71 S.W.3d 874 (Tex. App. 2002). In Butler v. City of Peru, 733 N.E.2d. 912, 919 (Ind. Ct. App. 2000), the Indiana Appellate Court stated, without deciding the question, that "electricity may be a product under" the Indiana Product Liability Act.

[203] 410 N.E.2d 620 (Ill. App. Ct. 1980).

[204] *Id.* at 624.

[205] Elgin Airport Inn, Inc. v. Commonwealth Edison Co., 432 N.E.2d 259 (Ill. 1982).

[206] Otte v. Dayton Power & Light Co., 523 N.E.2d 835, 839 (Ohio 1988). *See also* Wyrulec Co. v. Schutt, 866 P.2d 756 (Wyo. 1993); Balke v. Central Missouri Elec. Coop., 966 S.W.2d 15 (Mo. Ct. App. 1997); Bowen v. Niagara Mohawk Power Corp., 590 N.Y.S.2d 628 (App. Div. 1992).

Although courts are not in complete agreement as to whether electricity is a "product" or a "service," they do agree that personal injury or property damage caused by contact with a high voltage transmission line does not fall within § 402A.[207] Courts have given a number of reasons for their position that electricity is not a "product" prior to delivery to the consumer: (1) the electricity flowing through the power line was not in a "marketable" condition at the time of the injury;[208] (2) defects in the transmission lines carrying the electrical current are not sufficient to create liability since the lines are not "packaging" for the current, are not sold to the consumer, and remain owned by and under the exclusive control of the electric company at the time of the injury;[209] and (3) until the electricity has passed through the customer's electric meter, it has not been placed in the "stream of commerce."[210] The Restatement (Third) retains the distinction between pre-and post-delivery. According to § 19, electricity is a product when "the context of [its] distribution and use is sufficiently analogous to the distribution and use of tangible personal property that it is appropriate to apply the rules stated in this Restatement."

[E] Information

Another question that has confronted courts is whether "information" contained in books, maps, charts and the electronic media is a "product" for purposes of § 402A. Courts have been unwilling to extend strict liability to publishers for ideas contained in books or magazines.[211] The leading case in this area is *Winter v. G. P. Putnam's Sons*,[212] in which the plaintiff became ill from eating mushrooms after relying on information in *The Encyclopedia of Mushrooms* published by the defendant. Although the physical book was a "product," the Ninth Circuit refused to apply § 402A to the information contained in the book on the ground that the language of strict liability reflects its focus on tangible items. The court also felt that the "cost" of applying strict liability to words and idea in books would be too high. According to the court:

> We place a high priority on the unfettered exchange of ideas. We accept the risk that words and ideas have winds we cannot clip and which carry them we know not where. The threat of liability without fault (financial respon-

---

[207] *See* Smith v. Home Light and Power Co., 734 P.2d 1051 (Colo. 1987); Wirth v. Mayrath Industries, Inc. 278 N.W.2d 789 (N.D. 1979); Wood v. Public Service Company of New Hampshire, 317 A.2d 576 (N.H. 1974).

[208] Genaust v. Illinois Power Co. 343 N.E.2d 465 (Ill. 1976).

[209] Monroe v. Savannah Elec. & Power Co., 471 S.E.2d 854 (Ga. 1996).

[210] For a discussion of the tests used by courts to determine whether electricity has been "sold," see Darling v. Central Vermont Public Service Corp., 762 A.2d 826 (Vt. 2000). *See also* Bryant v. Tri-County Electric Membership Corp., 844 F. Supp. 347 (W.D. Ky. 1994) (applying Kentucky law); Bowen v. Niagara Mohawk Power Corp., 590 N.Y.S.2d 628 (App. Div. 1992).

[211] Gorran v. Atkins Nutritionals, Inc., 464 F. Supp. 2d 315 (S.D.N.Y. 2006) (applying Florida law); Russo v. NCS Pearson, Inc., 462 F. Supp. 2d 981 (D. Minn. 2006) (applying Minnesota law); Jones v. J. B. Lippincott, 694 F. Supp. 1216 (D. Md. 1988); Herceg v. Hustler Magazine, 565 F. Supp. 802 (S.D. Tex. 1983); Appleby v. Miller, 554 N.E.2d 773 (Ill. App. Ct. 1990).

[212] 938 F.2d 1033 (9th Cir. 1991) (applying California law).

sibility for our words and ideas in the absence of fault or a special undertaking or responsibility) could serious inhibit those who wish to share thoughts and theories.[213]

Although the plaintiff in *Winter* argued that strict liability be applied only to books that give instruction on how to accomplish a physical activity and that are intended to be used as part of an activity that is inherently dangerous, the Ninth Circuit felt that the such a limitation was "illusory."[214] However, one area where courts have been willing to impose strict liability is to nautical and airline maps and charts. Courts have justified this on the grounds that maps and charts are analogous to other navigational instruments such as a compass or radar which, when defective, will be dangerous[215] and that maps and charts are used for their physical characteristics rather than for ideas.[216]

In recent years, the rise of new forms of communication has confronted courts with the question whether video games, movies, and internet sites are "products."[217] In *James v. Meow Media, Inc.,*[218] a high school student shot several of his fellow students, killing three and wounding a number of others. The parents of the victims brought suit in negligence and strict liability, alleging that the shooter regularly watched video games, movies and internet sites produced by the defendant firms that "desensitized" him to violence and caused him to kill his fellow students. The federal district court in Kentucky held that the firms owed no duty in negligence to protect third parties from how viewers or players processed the ideas and images in their games, movies and internet sites. This is consistent with the approach of courts which uniformly have refused to expand the scope of negligence to media broadcasters and publishers for allegedly defective information.[219] The court also held that, while the video game cartridges and movie cassettes were tangible "products," the "words and pictures" they contained were not "products" for purposes of § 402A.[220] Other courts have followed this approach and have held that intangible thoughts, ideas, and expressive content are not "products" within the meaning of strict liability.[221]

---

[213] *Id.* at 1035.

[214] *Id.*

[215] Way v. Boy Scouts of America, 856 S.W.2d 230 (Tex. App. 1993).

[216] Fluor Corp. v. Jeppesen & Co., 216 Cal. Rptr. 68 (Ct. App. 1985).

[217] Wilson v. Midway Games, Inc., 198 F. Supp. 2d 167 (D. Conn. 2002) (apply Connecticut law). For a discussion of the applicability of § 402A to information sold and distributed on the internet, see Nathan D. Leadstrom, *Note: Internet Web Sites as Products Under Strict Products Liability: A Call for an Expanded Definition of Product,* 40 WASHBURN L.J. 532 (2001).

[218] 300 F.3d 683 (6th Cir. 2002) (applying Kentucky law).

[219] Brandt v. The Weather Channel, 42 F. Supp. 2d 1344 (S.D. Fla. 1999) (applying Florida law); Birmingham v. Fodor's Travel Publications, Inc., 833 P.2d 70 (Haw. 1992).

[220] *See* Richard C. Ausness, *The Application of Product Liability Principles to Publishers of Violent or Sexually Explicit Material,* 3 FLA. L. REV. 603 (2000).

[221] Wilson v. Midway Games, Inc., 198 F. Supp. 2d 167 (D. Conn. 2002) (applying Connecticut law).

[F]   Raw Materials

Section 402A contains a "caveat" that "[t]he Institute expresses no opinion as to whether the rules stated in this Section may not apply . . . (2) to the seller of a product expected to be processed or otherwise substantially changed before it reaches the user or consumer." While comment *e* states that § 402A normally will apply to articles that have undergone processing before sale, courts have not limited strict liability to such items. Their position is supported by comment *p* which provides that "the mere fact that the product is to undergo processing, or other substantial change, will not in all cases relieve the seller of liability." In a number of cases, courts have held that items that have not been manufactured or processed before sale can be products. These include such materials as aluminum,[222] asbestos,[223] lumber.[224] However, in *Apperson v. E. I. DuPont de Nemours & Co.*,[225] the Seventh Circuit held that raw material, Teflon, manufactured by one company and incorporated into a dental implant by another company was not a "product" within the meaning of § 402A. The court distinguished inherently dangerous raw materials, such as asbestos, from raw materials with safe uses, such as Teflon, which only become dangerous when incorporated into specialized devices.[226]

Although the Restatement (Third) does not explicitly mention raw materials, comment *c* to § 5 states that "[p]roduct components include raw materials. . . . Thus, when raw materials are contaminated or otherwise defective within the meaning of § 2(a), the seller of the raw materials is subject to liability for harm caused by such defects." However, the comment also states that a "basic raw material such as sand, gravel, or kerosene cannot be defectively designed." Liability for the use of such materials lies not with the supplier but with the person who incorporates them into the finished product.

[G]   Real Estate

Although most products liability cases involve items of personal property, courts also have considered whether strict liability applies to real property. In a case from California,[227] the state's appellate court held that "in terms of today's society, there are no meaningful distinctions between . . . mass production and the sale of homes and the mass production and sale of automobiles and that the pertinent overriding policy considerations are the same."[228] In keeping with that view, the California

---

[222] Davis v. Wells Aluminum Southeast, Inc., 323 S.E.2d 215 (Ga. Ct. App. 1984).

[223] Griffin v. Allis-Chalmers Corp. Product Liability Trust, 246 P.3d 483 (Or. Ct. App. 2010); Jenkins v. T & N PLC, 53 Cal. Rptr. 2d 642 (Ct. App. 1996).

[224] Wilkinson v. Bayshore Lumber Co., 227 Cal. Rptr. 327 (Ct. App. 1986); Housman v. C. A. Dawson & Co., 245 N.E.2d 886 (Ill. App. Ct. 1969).

[225] 41 F.3d 1103 (7th Cir. 1994) (applying Illinois law).

[226] *Id.* at 1107. *See* Haase v. Badger Mining Corp., 669 N.W.2d 737 (Wis. Ct. App. 2003) (sand).

[227] Kriegler v. Eichler Homes, Inc., 74 Cal. Rptr. 749 (Ct. App. 1969).

[228] *Id.* at 752. *See also* Kaneko v. Hilo Coast Processing, 654 P.2d 343 (Haw. 1982) (a manufacturer could be strictly liable for a defective component part in a prefabricated building that had to be assembled); Avner v. Longridge Estates, 77 Cal. Rptr. 633 (Ct. App. 1969) (developers of homes on

court of appeals, in *Del Mar Beach Club Owners v. Imperial Contracting*,[229] held that a developer could be held strictly liable for the defective design and construction of a multi-unit residential project. Since the homeowners did not have the opportunity to participate in the design or construction of the project, the court felt that their individual units appeared to "fit the classic mold of buyers of mass-produced housing."[230]

Despite the view of the California courts, courts and legislatures in other states have looked to the specific requirements of strict liability and held that buildings and similar structures are not "products" within the meaning of § 402A.[231] In *Papp v. Rocky Mountain Oil*,[232] the Montana Supreme Court found that an oil "treater" or "separator" facility was not a product. In *Papp*, the widow of an oil and gas worker brought a strict liability action against the lessee of a "separator" facility when her husband was killed after inhaling sulphide gas while completing work on an auxiliary flow line in the facility. In affirming summary judgment for the defendants, who were in the business of extracting oil and gas for refinement, the court held that the facility was not a "product" for purposes of strict liability: (1) the defendants were not in the business of selling separator facilities; (2) the separator facility did not reach the stream of commerce but, instead, passed "from one lessee to another;"[233] and (3) the decedent was not a consumer using the facility after it reached the stream of commerce.[234] In addition to Montana, Illinois courts have held that a condominium unit,[235] a multilevel open-air parking garage,[236] and a sheltered-care facility[237] were not products for purposes of strict liability. The courts offered three justifications for their decisions: (1) the drafters of the § 402A did not contemplate a structure such as a building to be a proper subject for a strict liability action;[238] (2) other remedies are available against those responsible for faulty construction on the theories of negligence and implied warranty;[239] and (3) there is no difficulty of access to a remote manufacturer or supplier and no mass production over which to distribute the risk of injury.[240]

Just as courts are divided over whether buildings are products, there is no single view as to whether their component parts are products. The Illinois

---

hillside property could be strictly liable for damages caused by inadequate drainage and improper compaction of the fill on the development); Schipper v. Levitt & Sons, Inc., 207 A.2d 314 (N.J. 1965).

[229]   176 Cal. Rptr. 886 (Ct. App. 1981).

[230]   *Id.* at 893. *See* Acosta v. Glenfed Development Corp., 28 Cal. Rptr. 3d 92 (Ct. App. 2005).

[231]   In 2007 Arkansas enacted a statute exempting real estate and improvements on them from the definition of a "product" if the real estate was supplied by a lawfully registered entity. Ark. Code § 4-86-102(c). *See* Plaza v. Fisher Development, Inc., 971 So. 2d 918 (Fla. Dist. Ct. App. 2007).

[232]   769 P.2d 1249 (Mont. 1989).

[233]   *Id.* at 1256.

[234]   *Id.* at 1255.

[235]   Heller v. Cadral Corp., 406 N.E.2d 88 (Ill. App. Ct. 1980).

[236]   Lowrie v. City of Evanston, 365 N.E.2d 923 (Ill. App. Ct. 1977).

[237]   Immergluck v. Ridgeview House, Inc., 368 N.E.2d 803 (Ill. App. Ct. 1977).

[238]   Lowrie v. City of Evanston, 365 N.E.2d 923, 928 (Ill. App. Ct. 1977).

[239]   *Id.* at 929.

[240]   Immergluck v. Ridgeview House, Inc., 368 N.E.2d 803, 805 (Ill. App. Ct. 1977).

appellate court in *Boddie v. Litton Unit Handling Systems*,[241] for example, cited with approval cases from a number of states that applied strict liability "to products which would be clearly classifiable as real estate fixtures or have specifically held such items to be products for strict liability purposes."[242] The court held these cases were in accord with comment *d* to § 402A, which lists such fixtures as a water heater and a gas stove as examples of products.[243] However, subsequent decisions from the Illinois appellate court and the Seventh Circuit have held that specific parts of structures become an integral part of those structures and thus were no longer products for purposes for strict liability.[244]

The Restatement (Third) takes the same approach to real property that it does to electricity. According to § 19, real property may be a product when "the context of [its] distribution and use is sufficiently analogous to the distribution and use of tangible personal property that it is appropriate to apply the rules stated in this Restatement."

---

[241] 455 N.E.2d 142 (Ill. App. Ct. 1983).

[242] *Id.*

[243] *Id.*

[244] *See* Hilliard v. Lummus Co., Inc., 834 F.2d 1352, 1354 (7th Cir. 1987) (applying Illinois law); St. Louis v. Rockwell Graphic Systems, 581 N.E.2d 93 (Ill. App. Ct. 1991); Billman v. Crown-Trygg Corp., 563 N.E.2d 903 (Ill. App. Ct. 1990); Cross v. Ainsworth Seed Co., 557 N.E.2d 906 (Ill. App. Ct. 1990); Duncavage v. Allen, 497 N.E.2d 433 (Ill. App. Ct. 1986); Calumet Country Club v. Roberts Environmental Control Corp., 483 N.E.2d 613 (Ill. App. Ct. 1985); Hubbard v. Chicago Housing Authority, 487 N.E.2d 20 (Ill. App. Ct. 1985).

Chapter 5

DESIGN DEFECTS

SYNOPSIS

§ 5.01 PRODUCT DEFECTS

§ 5.02 DESIGN DEFECT

    [A] Characteristics of a Design Defect

    [B] Negligence, Strict Liability, and Product Designs

        [1] Introduction

        [2] Negligent Design

        [3] Strict Liability

    [C] Crashworthiness Doctrine

§ 5.03 TESTS FOR DETERMINING A DESIGN DEFECT

    [A] Introduction

    [B] Consumer Expectation Test

        [1] Introduction

        [2] Who is an Ordinary Consumer?

        [3] What Does an Ordinary Consumer Expect of a Product?

        [4] When Does the Consumer Expectations Test Apply?

    [C] Risk-Utility Analysis

        [1] Introduction

        [2] Factors Used in Risk-Utility Analysis

        [3] Reasonable Alternative Design

        [4] Burden of Proof

    [D] Alternative Tests

§ 5.04 OPEN AND OBVIOUS DANGERS

§ 5.05 STATE-OF-THE-ART

§ 5.01   PRODUCT DEFECTS

Almost any product is capable of causing injuries when used in certain ways. However, the fact that a product "caused" the plaintiff's injuries is not enough, in itself, to hold a manufacturer or seller liable for those injuries.[1] Instead, before an injured person can recover in an action based upon either negligence or strict liability, he or she must prove that there was a "defect" in the product at the time it left the control of the manufacturer or seller and that the defect caused the plaintiff's injuries.[2] In addition, most states follow § 402A of the Restatement (Second) of Torts and require a plaintiff to show that the particular "defect" made the product "unreasonably dangerous."[3] Whether or not a product was in a defective condition that made it unreasonably dangerous when it left the defendant's control is at the heart of products liability law and is the subject of almost all litigation.[4] This litigation not only involves issues about what makes a product "defective" and "unreasonably dangerous" and the proof required to establish those requirements, it also raises questions about the economic and societal consequences of a finding that a product was defective.[5]

Courts and statutes define a product "defect" in very broad language: an "imperfection";[6] an "injury-producing hazard accompanying normal use of a product";[7] "a condition of a product that renders it unsafe for normal or anticipated handling and consumption."[8] Because a defect is not limited to the mechanics or the function of a product but includes anything that makes it "unreasonably dangerous,"[9] it is impossible to list all of the types of imperfections or hazards that can constitute a defect.[10] Although § 402A requires a product to be in a "defective condition," neither that section nor the comments to it define a "defect." Instead, § 402A, comment *h*, states simply that a "product is not in a defective condition when it is safe for normal handling and consumption." However, the comments to § 402A list a number of sources that can give rise to a defective condition in a product. These include harmful ingredients that are not characteristic of the product, either as to their presence or quantity; foreign objects in a product; decay

---

[1] Seattle-First National Bank v. Tabert, 542 P.2d 774 (Wash. 1975); Kutzler v. AMF Harley-Davidson, 550 N.E.2d 1236 (Ill. App. Ct. 1990).

[2] Pritchett v. Cottrell, Inc., 512 F.3d 1057 (8th Cir. 2008) (applying Kansas and Missouri law).

[3] Bourne v. Marty Gilman, Inc., 452 F.3d 632 (7th Cir. 2006) (applying Indiana law) (a football goalpost was not "unreasonably dangerous" since a reasonable person should have realized the risk posed by a falling goalpost); Kinser v. Gehl Co., 184 F.3d 1259 (10th Cir. 1999) (applying Kansas law); Farnham v. Bombardier, Inc., 640 A.2d 47 (Vt. 1994).

[4] Smith v. Brown & Williamson Tobacco Corp., 275 S.W.3d 748, 792 (Mo. Ct. App. 2008) ("The 'heart and soul' of a strict liability design defect case is unreasonable danger and causation.").

[5] For one expression of "uneasiness" over the economic and societal "impact" of products liability law, see the "Conclusion" to Judge Arlin Adams' opinion for the court in *Dawson v. Chrysler Corp.*, 630 F.2d 950, 962–63 (3d Cir. 1980).

[6] Singleton v. Manitowoc Co., Inc., 727 F. Supp. 217, 221 (D. Md. 1989) (applying Maryland law).

[7] Boudreau v. Baughman, 368 S.E.2d 849, 860 (N.C. 1988).

[8] TENN. CODE ANN. § 29-28-102(2).

[9] Anderson v. M.W. Kellogg Co., 766 P.2d 637, 643 (Colo. 1988).

[10] *See* W. Page Keeton, *The Meaning of Defect in Products Liability Law*, 45 Mo. L. REV. 579 (1980).

or deterioration of a product before sale; the way in which a product is prepared or packaged; or the failure to provide adequate directions or warnings about a product.[11] A product also may be defective because of the absence of a safety device[12] or because it was not "crashworthy."[13] Whether a product is defective for purposes of negligence and strict liability also depends upon whether it is unavoidably unsafe, whether the risk of the harm is "open and obvious" to the consumer or user, whether the product has been altered, and whether the product was being used for its intended or foreseeable purpose. Determining whether a product is defective is complicated further by the wide range of products which have been subject to litigation. Among the products are asbestos,[14] automobiles,[15] cell phones,[16] chemicals,[17] drugs and medical devices,[18] fire arms,[19] lawn mowers,[20] medical implants,[21] table saws,[22] tobacco,[23] and trampolines.[24]

Although the comments to § 402A list some of the sources of product defects, the section does not categorize the types of defects. According to Professor Twerski and Henderson, this was because the drafters of the section had in mind only manufacturing defects and, thus, saw no reason to distinguish between other types of defects.[25] Despite the failure of § 402A to classify the forms that a defect can take, courts, as well as the Restatement (Third), have divided the types of product defects into three broad categories:[26] (1) design defects; (2) manufacturing defects; and (3) inadequate instructions or warnings concerning the use or risks of a product. These three categories are used in analyzing defects both in strict liability

---

[11] RESTATEMENT (SECOND) OF TORTS § 402A cmts. *h* and *j* (1965). See also the discussion of the various ways a product may be defective in *Barker v. Lull Engineering Co.*, 573 P.2d 443, 453 (Cal. 1978).

[12] *See* Shreve v. Sears, Roebuck & Co., 166 F. Supp. 2d 378 (D. Md. 2001) (applying Maryland law); Ogletree v. Navistar International Transportation Corp., 522 S.E.2d 467 (Ga. 1999); Prentis v. Yale Manufacturing Co., 365 N.W.2d 176 (Mich. 1984).

[13] Huff v. White Motor Corp., 565 F.2d 104 (7th Cir. 1977) (applying Indiana law); Larsen v. General Motors Corp., 391 F.2d 495 (8th Cir. 1968) (applying Minnesota law); Sumnicht v. Toyota Motor Sales, U.S.A., Inc., 360 N.W.2d 2 (Wis. 1984).

[14] Saller v. Crown Cork & Seal Co., 115 Cal. Rptr. 3d 151 (Ct. App. 2010).

[15] Goodner v. Hyundai Motor Co., 650 F.3d 1034 (5th Cir. 2011) (applying Texas law).

[16] *See, e.g.,* Pinney v. Nokia, Inc., 402 F.3d 430 (4th Cir. 2005); Newman v. Motorola, Inc., 2003 U.S. App. LEXIS 21367 (4th Cir. Oct. 22, 2003).

[17] Agrofollajes, S.A. v. E.I. Du Pont De Nemours & Co., 48 So. 3d 976 (Fla. Dist. Ct. App. 2010).

[18] Beard v. Johnson & Johnson, Inc., 41 A.3d 823 (Pa. 2012); Grundberg v. Upjohn Co., 813 P.2d 89 (Utah 1991).

[19] Williams v. Bennett, 921 So. 2d 1269 (Miss. 2006).

[20] Horst v. Deere & Co., 769 N.W.2d 536 (Wis. 2009).

[21] Metronic, Inc. v. Lohr, 518 U.S. 470 (1996).

[22] Osorio v. One World Technologies, 659 F.3d 81 (1st Cir. 2011) (applying Massachusetts law).

[23] Adamo v. Brown & Williamson Tobacco Co., 900 N.E.2d 966 (N.Y. 2008).

[24] Parish v. Health & Fitness, Inc., 719 N.W.2d 540 (Iowa 2006).

[25] Aaron D. Twerski & James A. Henderson, *Manufacturers' Liability for Defective Product Designs: The Triumph of Risk-Utility*, 74 BROOK. L. REV. 1061, 1063 (2009).

[26] *See, e.g.,* O'Neil v. Crane Co., 266 P.3d 987 (Cal. 2012); Gorton v. American Cyanamid Co., 533 N.W.2d 746 (Wis. 1995); Banks v. ICI Americas, Inc., 450 S.E.2d 671 (Ga. 1994); RESTATEMENT (THIRD) OF TORTS: PRODUCTS LIABILITY § 2 (1998).

cases and in negligence cases. Each category not only has its own characteristics and tests for determining whether the product was defective, it also presents its own unique problems of proof. The remainder of this chapter focuses on design defects. The following two chapters examine manufacturing defects and the failure to warn about dangers associated with a product or to provide adequate instructions about the use of a product.

§ 5.02 DESIGN DEFECT

[A] Characteristics of a Design Defect

The largest number of products liability cases that reach trial involve an allegation that the plaintiff's injuries were caused by a design defect in the product in question. The design of a product includes the manufacturer's specifications, choice of materials, as well as the structure of the product.[27] Despite the volume of litigation, design defects are the most difficult for a plaintiff to identify and to prove. In part this is because, unlike manufacturing defects, which are unintended and often can be identified by comparing the particular product alleged to have caused the plaintiff's injuries with the manufacturer's own design for the product or with other units of the same product line produced by the manufacturer, there are no objective standards by which to judge a design defect.[28] The aspect of a design that makes a product defective is not the result of a mistake on the part of the manufacturer. Instead, "[a] design defect exists when the product is built in accordance with its intended specifications but the design itself is inherently defective."[29] The manufacturer's intentional choice of the specifications or materials used for the product is inherent in every unit of the particular model produced by the manufacturer. The design choice makes all of those products unsafe when put to their intended or foreseeable use. Because of the economic and societal consequences of finding that a manufacturer's entire product line was defective,[30] courts and commentators continually seek to devise appropriate standards for judging whether a product's design made it unreasonably dangerous. As will be discussed in detail in § 5.03, the most frequently used of the standards that courts have developed to determine whether a defect in a product makes it unreasonably dangerous are the "consumer expectations test" and the "risk-utility analysis."

---

[27] Boudreau v. Baughman, 368 S.E.2d 849 (N.C. 1988); Husky Industries v. Black, 434 So. 2d 988 (Fla. Dist. Ct. App. 1983); Jones v. White Motor Corp., 401 N.E.2d 223 (Ohio Ct. App. 1978). In most cases, the manufacturer of a product also designed it. However, in some situations, the purchaser provided the design specifications to the manufacturer. In such a situation, the court in Sepulveda-Esquivel v. Central Machine Works, 84 P.3d 895 (Wash. Ct. App. 2004), held that the manufacturer was not liable.

[28] Prentis v. Yale Manufacturing Co., 365 N.W.2d 176 (Mich. 1984); O'Brien v. Muskin Corp., 463 A.2d 298 (N.J. 1983); Caterpillar Tractor Co. v. Beck, 593 P.2d 871 (Alaska 1979).

[29] Chavez v. Glock, Inc., 144 Cal. Rptr. 3d 326, 342–43 (App. Ct. 2012). *See* Boudreau v. Baughman, 368 S.E.2d 849, 860 (N.C. 1988); Leichtamer v. American Motors Co., 424 N.E.2d 568 (Ohio 1981); Caterpillar Tractor Co. v. Beck, 593 P.2d 871 (Alaska 1979).

[30] In Thibault v. Sears, Roebuck & Co., 395 A.2d 843, 846 (N.H. 1978), the New Hampshire Supreme Court expressed this concern when it stated: "The utility of the product must be evaluated from the point of view of the public as a whole, because a finding of liability for defective design could result in the removal of an entire product line from the market."

[B]   Negligence, Strict Liability, and Product Designs

[1]   Introduction

Plaintiffs frequently include separate counts of negligence and strict liability in their design defect complaints.[31] In recent years, some courts have fused negligence theory with strict liability theory to determine whether a product was defective.[32] As a result, one court has said of a design defect case that "there is almost no difference between a prima facie case in negligence and one in strict liability."[33] Reflecting the approach developed by many state courts, § 2 of the Restatement (Third) applies a negligence (i.e., risk-utility) analysis as the standard for judging design defect and failure to warn cases,[34] while retaining strict liability (i.e., consumer expectations) as the test for manufacturing defects. However, despite the shift from strict liability to negligence in design defect cases,[35] there is a fundamental distinction between the two theories: "Negligence theory concerns itself with determining whether the conduct of the defendant was reasonable in view of the foreseeable risk of injury; strict liability is concerned with whether the product itself was unreasonably dangerous."[36]

[2]   Negligent Design

The elements that a plaintiff must establish in an action alleging negligence in the design of a product are the same as those in other negligence cases. According to one court, a negligent design claim has three basic requirements: "(1) a duty to anticipate and design against reasonably foreseeable hazards; (2) breach of that duty; and (3) injury proximately caused by the breach."[37] The standard of care imposed by the duty in a negligence action does not require the manufacturer to

---

[31] *See* Malen v. MTD Prod., Inc., 628 F.3d 296 (7th Cir. 2010) (applying Illinois law); Mullaney v. Hilton Hotels Corp., 634 F. Supp. 2d 1130 (D. Haw. 2009) (applying Hawai'i law); Branham v. Ford Motor Co., 701 S.E.2d 5 (S.C. 2010).

[32] *See* Solo v. Trus Joist MacMillan, 2004 U.S. Dist. LEXIS 4107 (D. Minn. Mar. 15, 2004) (applying Minnesota law); Jones v. Amazing Products, Inc., 231 F. Supp. 2d 1228 (N.D. Ga. 2002) (applying Georgia law).

[33] Colon v. BIC USA, Inc., 199 F. Supp. 2d 53, 83 (S.D.N.Y. 2001) (quoting Denny v. Ford Motor Co., 662 N.E.2d 730 (N.Y. 1995)). *See* Sheila Birnbaum, *Unmasking the Test for Design Defect: from Negligence [to Warranty] to Strict Liability to Negligence*, 33 VAND. L. REV. 539 (1980).

[34] RESTATEMENT (THIRD) OF TORTS: PRODUCTS LIABILITY § 2 (1998). This section was adopted by the Iowa Supreme Court in Wright v. Brooke Group, 652 N.W.2d 159 (Iowa 2002). New Jersey also generally follows § 2. Indian Brand Farms, Inc. v. Novartis Crop Prot., Inc., 617 F.3d 207 (3d Cir. 2010). *See* Aaron D. Twerski & James A. Henderson, *Manufacturers' Liability for Defective Product Designs: The Triumph of Risk-Utility*, 74 BROOK. L. REV. 1061 (2009).

[35] *See* TRW Vehicle Safety Sys., Inc., v. Moore, 936 N.E.2d 201, 209 (Ind. 2010) (Under the Indiana Products Liability Act,. IND. CODE § 34-20-2-2, a plaintiff alleging a design defect must show negligence: the manufacturer or seller "failed to exercise reasonable care under the circumstances in designing the product.")

[36] Dart v. Wiebe Manufacturing, Inc., 709 P.2d 876, 880 (Ariz. 1985). *See also* Syrie v. Knoll International, 748 F.2d 304 (5th Cir. 1984) (applying Texas law); Slisze v. Stanley-Bostitch, 979 P.2d 317 (Utah 1999); Bilotta v. Kelley Co., 346 N.W.2d 616 (Minn. 1984).

[37] Jablonski v. Ford Motor Co., 955 N.E.2d 1138 (Ill. 2011). *See* Kirk v. Hanes Corporation of North Carolina, 771 F. Supp. 856 (E.D. Mich. 1991) (applying Michigan law).

design a product that is accident-proof, is incapable of causing injury, or that incorporates every available safety device.[38] Instead, a manufacturer has a duty to use ordinary or reasonable care so that the design will make the product reasonably safe for its intended use[39] or for a use that was reasonably foreseeable.[40] In deciding whether the design of a product is reasonably safe, some courts have adopted the definition used by the consumer expectations test discussed in the next section: a product is "unreasonably dangerous" if it is "dangerous to an extent beyond which would be expected by the ordinary consumer who purchases it."[41]

In a negligent case, the focus is on the manufacturer's conduct and whether the manufacturer acted reasonably in choosing the specifications, materials, or structure for the product, in light of the risks it knew about or should have known about.[42] In determining whether a manufacturer acted reasonably in designing a product, courts hold a manufacturer to the standard of "an expert in the field." As such, the manufacturer is required it to "keep reasonably abreast of scientific knowledge and discoveries touching his product and of techniques and devices used by practical men in his field."[43] Deciding what such an expert would do in choosing a design for a product has led many plaintiffs, manufacturers, and courts to abandon reliance on consumer expectations and to analyze the purpose, costs, and the risks and utility of the manufacturer's design, as well as reasonable alternative designs, by examining a series of factors.[44] These include: the likelihood and gravity of the potential harm and the burden of precautions that effectively would avoid the harm; the style, type, and particular purpose of the product; the cost of an alternative design, since the product's marketability may be adversely affected by a cost factor

---

[38] Westinghouse Electric Corp. v. Nutt, 407 A.2d 606 (D.C. 1979); Morrell v. Precise Engineering, Inc., 630 N.E.2d 291 (Mass. App. Ct. 1994).

[39] Messer v. Amway Corp., 210 F. Supp. 2d 1217 (D. Kan. 2002) (citing Garst v. General Motors Corp., 484 P.2d 47 (Kan. 1971)).

[40] Henrie v. Northrop Gruman Corp., 502 F.3d 1228 (10th Cir 2007) (applying Utah law); Burt v. Makita USA, Inc., 212 F. Supp. 2d 893 (N.D. Ind. 2002) (applying the Indiana Products Liability Act); Hillrichs v. Avco Corp., 514 N.W.2d 94 (Iowa 1994); Micallef v. Miehle Co., 348 N.E.2d 571 (N.Y. 1976). This standard has been adopted by § 395 of the RESTATEMENT (SECOND) OF TORTS which states:

> A manufacturer of a chattel made under a plan or design which makes it dangerous for the uses for which it is manufactured is subject to liability to others whom he should expect to use the chattel or to be endangered by its probable use for physical harm caused by his failure to exercise reasonable care in the adoption of a safe plan or design.

[41] Messer v. Amway Corp., 210 F. Supp. 2d 1217, 1233 (D. Kan. 2002) (applying Kansas law).

[42] Trull v. Volkswagen of America, Inc., 320 F.3d 1 (1st Cir. 2002) (applying New Hampshire law); Enrich v. Windmere Corp., 616 N.E.2d 1081 (Mass. 1993); McLaughlin v. Michelin Tire Corp., 778 P.2d 59 (Wyo. 1989).

[43] Feldman v. Lederle Laboratories, 479 A.2d 374, 386–87 (N.J. 1984), quoting 2 FOWLER HARPER & FLEMING JAMES, THE LAW OF TORTS § 28.4 (1956). In Jablonski v. Ford Motor Co., 955 N.E.2d 1138, 1156 (Ill. 2011), the Illinois Supreme Court held that compliance with all relevant industry standards may be relevant in deciding whether a manufacturer exercised reasonable care in design a product but is not dispositive on the issue of negligent design.

[44] The RESTATEMENT (SECOND) OF TORTS § 291, adopts a risk-utility analysis, saying that the determination of whether a manufacturer exercised reasonable care in its product design involves "balancing of the risks inherent in the product design with the utility of benefit derived from the product." See Jablonski v. Ford Motor Co., 955 N.E.2d 1138 (Ill. 2011).

that greatly outweighs the added safety of the product; and the price of the product itself.[45]

[3] Strict Liability

In contrast to a negligent case, which focuses on whether the manufacturer took reasonable care in selecting the design of the product, the emphasis in a design defect case based on § 402A is on the design of the product itself and whether the design made it unreasonably dangerous at the time it left the control of the manufacturer.[46] Since § 402A does not mention design defects specifically, in order to establish a *prima facie* case in a design defect case, a plaintiff must establish the general elements for liability under the section. In most states, these elements require proof that (1) the design of product resulted in a "defective condition unreasonably dangerous" to the ultimate user or consumer of the product; (2) the product was expected to and did reach the user or consumer "without substantial change in the condition in which it was sold;" (3) the defective design must have been the cause of the plaintiff's injuries; (4) the defendant that sold the product was engaged in the business of selling such products; and (5) the plaintiff suffered injuries as a result.[47]

Some courts have held that a product is not in a "defective condition unreasonably dangerous" if it performed as intended by its design. This position has been very controversial in cases involving firearms. In *McCarthy v. Olin*,[48] for example, a gunman killed six people and wounded 19 when he entered a commuter train and opened fire, using a gun loaded with Winchester "Black Talon" hollow point bullets that are designed to "bend upon impact into six ninety-degree angle razor-sharp petals . . . that increase the wounding power of the bullet by stretching, cutting and tearing tissue and bone as it travels through the victim."[49] The plaintiffs brought suit against the manufacturer of the bullets in strict liability, alleging that the bullets were "unreasonably designed and ultrahazardous."[50] The Second Circuit, however, affirmed the lower court's dismissal of the design defect claim, stating that "[t]he bullets were not in defective condition nor were they unreasonably dangerous for their intended use because the Black Talons were purposely designed to expand on impact and cause severe wounding."[51]

---

[45] Wagatsuma v. Patch, 879 P.2d 572, 584 (Haw. 1994). *See* Malen v. MTD Prod., Inc., 628 F.3d 296 (7th Cir. 2010) (applying Illinois law); Peck v. Bridgeport Machines, 237 F.3d 614 (6th Cir. 2001) (applying Michigan law); Metzgar v. Playskool Inc., 30 F.3d 459 (3d Cir. 1994) (applying Pennsylvania law); Chavez v. Glock, Inc., 144 Cal. Rptr. 3d 326 (App. Ct. 2012).

[46] Freeman v. Hoffman-La Roche, Inc., 618 N.W.2d 827 (Neb. 2000); Denny v. Ford Motor Co., 662 N.E.2d 730 (N.Y. 1995); Caterpillar Tractor Co. v. Beck, 593 P.2d 871 (Alaska, 1979). In Branham v. Ford Motor Co., 701 S.E.2d 5 (S.C. 2010), the South Carolina Supreme Court rejected the use of post-distribution evidence to evaluation a products a product's design.

[47] The Union Supply Company v. Pust, 583 P. 2d 276, 282–83 (Colo. 1978). *See* Mullaney v. Hilton Hotels Corp., 634 F. Supp. 2d 1130 (D. Haw. 2009) (applying Hawai'i law).

[48] 119 F.3d 148 (2d Cir. 1997) (applying New York law).

[49] *Id.* at 152. *See also* Halliday v. Sturm, Ruger & Co., 770 A.2d 1072 (Md. Ct. Spec. App. 2001) (applying Maryland law).

[50] *Id.* at 151.

[51] *Id.* at 155.

[C] Crashworthiness Doctrine

In most design defect cases, the plaintiff alleges that the defective design was the cause both of the accident and of his or her injuries. However, in some motor vehicle accident cases, the defective design was not the cause of the initial accident. Instead, the design defect was the cause of a "second collision" in which the plaintiff suffered separate injuries or injuries more severe than they would have been had the design of the product not been defective.[52] The defect that causes or enhances the plaintiff's injuries in an automobile may be in the design of the airbags, dashboard, door locks, fuel system, restrain system, roof, or side impact protection. In *Richardson v. Volkswagenwerk, A.G.*,[53] for example, the plaintiff was the driver of a Volkswagen involved in a head-on collision with a Ford Mustang. Although the design of the Volkswagen was not responsible for the initial collision, that accident resulted in a "second collision" in which the plaintiff's body struck the Volkswagen's allegedly defective dashboard and assist grip. In his suit against the automobile manufacturer, the plaintiff was able to seek damages only for those injuries that resulted from him striking the dashboard or for his enhanced injuries resulting from the collision.[54] Evidence about the cause of the initial accident was not relevant.[55]

The crashworthiness, or second collision, doctrine[56] has its origins in a 1968 decision, *Larsen v. General Motors Corp.*,[57] in which the Eighth Circuit held that, where the plaintiff's injuries or enhanced injuries are due to the manufacturer's failure to use reasonable care to avoid subjecting the user of its products to an unreasonable risk of injury, negligence principles are applicable.[58] In *Larsen*, the plaintiff alleged that the automobile manufacturer's negligent design of a steering assembly caused his injuries in an automobile accident. In reply, General Motors argued that it had "no duty whatsoever to design and manufacture a vehicle which is otherwise 'safe' or 'safer' to occupy during a collision."[59] According to the court, however, although "automobiles are not made for the purpose of colliding with each

---

[52] Whitted v. General Motors Corp., 58 F.3d 1200 (8th Cir. 1995). For a discussion of the crashworthiness in the context of drunk driving cases, see Ellen M. Bublick, *The Tort-Proof Plaintiff: The Drunk in the Automobile, Crashworthiness Claims, and the Restatement (Third) of Torts*, 74 BROOK. L. REV. 708 (2009).

[53] 552 F. Supp. 73 (W.D. Mo. 1982).

[54] *See* Mickle v. Blackmon, 166 S.E.2d 173 (S.C. 1969).

[55] *See* Thomas Harris, *Enhanced Injury Theory: An Analytic Framework*, 62 N.C. L. REV. 643 (1984) ("In enhanced injury [crashworthiness] cases, . . . a claimant's fault in causing the accident is not a basis for reducing his recovery. . . . [A] manufacturer's duty is that of minimizing the injurious effects of contact however caused."). *See also* Reed v. Chrysler Corp., 494 N.W.2d 224 (Iowa 1992).

[56] In Caiazzo v. Volkswagenwerk A. G., 647 F.2d 241, 243 fn.2 (2d Cir. 1981), the court distinguished between "crashworthiness," which it defined as "the protection that a passenger motor vehicle affords its passengers against personal injury or death as a result of a motor vehicle accident" and "second collision," which it said "usually refers to the collision between a passenger and an interior part of the vehicle following an impact or collision. The term has also been applied to ejection cases . . . in which the second collision is between an occupant of the car and the ground."

[57] 391 F.2d 495 (8th Cir. 1968).

[58] *Id.* at 502.

[59] *Id.* at 497.

other, a frequent and inevitable contingency of normal automobile use will result in collisions and injury-producing impacts."[60] Given the reality of automobile accidents, the court concluded:

> No rational basis exists for limiting recovery to situations where the defect in design or manufacture was the causative factor of the accident, as the accident and the resulting injury, usually caused by the so-called "second collision" of the passenger with the interior part of the automobile, all are foreseeable. Where the injuries or enhanced injuries are due to the manufacturer's failure to use reasonable care to avoid subjecting the user of its products to an unreasonable risk of injury, general negligence principles should be applicable. The sole function of an automobile is not just to provide a means of transportation, it is to provide a means of safe transportation or as safe as is reasonably possible under the present state of the art.[61]

Under the crashworthiness doctrine, as formulated by *Larsen* and applied by courts claims, a "manufacturer is under a duty to use reasonable care in the design of its vehicle to minimize the unreasonable risk of injuries in the event of collisions."[62] This duty means that a manufacturer is liable not only for a design defect that causes an initial accident, but also for the damage or injury that would not have occurred as a result of the initial accident if the design had not been defective. The crashworthiness doctrine now has been adopted in every state and is applicable both in negligence and in strict liability cases.[63] The doctrine is not limited to manufacturers of automobiles.[64]

In some enhanced injury cases, the plaintiff or the weather, rather than a third party, was responsible for the initial accident. In such a case, the manufacturer is liable only for the injuries or enhanced injuries caused by the defect in the product. In other cases, however, a third party was responsible for the initial accident while the defective design caused the enhanced injuries. If it is possible to separate the plaintiff's injuries between those caused by the initial collision and those that resulted from the second collision, the jury will apportion liability between the manufacturer and all others whose fault combined to cause the plaintiff's injuries. However, if the plaintiff's injuries cannot be divided between the first collision and the second collision, the manufacturer and third parties are jointly and severally liable for all of the plaintiff's injuries, unless the jurisdiction has eliminated joint and several liability.[65]

---

[60] *Id.* at 502.

[61] *Id.* For a similar statement of the "premise underlying the crashworthiness doctrine," see Malen v. MTD Prods., Inc., 628 F.3d 296, 311 (7th Cir. 2010) (applying Illinois law).

[62] 391 F.2d at 502.

[63] *See* Polk v. Ford Motor Company, 529 F.2d 259 (8th Cir. 1976) (applying Missouri law); Miller v. Todd, 551 N.E.2d 1139 (Ind. 1990); Leichtamer v. American Motors Co., 424 N.E.2d 568 (Ohio 1981).

[64] For a discussion of the range of products to which the crashworthiness doctrine has been applied, see Malen v. MTD Prod., Inc., 628 F.3d 296, 311–12 (7th Cir. 2010) (applying Illinois law).

[65] For a discussion of joint and several liability, see Chapter 10.

More difficult for the courts is the question of who bears the burden of proof for purposes of apportioning the damages. The majority of states follow the Restatement (Second) of Torts[66] and hold that the plaintiff must prove only that the design defect was a "substantial factor in producing damages over and above those which were probably caused as a result of the original impact or collision."[67] Under this approach, once the plaintiff meets the burden of proving that the defective design was a substantial factor in causing or enhancing his or her injuries, the burden of proof shifts to the manufacturer to show which injuries were the result of the initial collision and those attributable to the defective design.[68] However, a minority of states follow the approach set out in *Huddell v. Levin*[69] and require the plaintiff to prove precisely and exactly the injuries attributable to the initial collision and those caused by the alleged design defect.[70]

Unlike § 402A, the Restatement (Third) states that "a manufacturer has a duty to design and manufacture its product so as reasonably to deduce the foreseeable harm that may occur in an accident brought about by causes other than a product itself."[71] According to § 16 of the Restatement (Third), the plaintiff in an "enhanced injury case" must prove that the defect was a substantial factor in increasing the harm he or she suffered when compared to potential harm from other causes. If that proof supports a finding that the plaintiff would have suffered harm from other causes despite the product defect, then the seller's liability is limited to the increased harm that is due only to the product defect. However, if the proof does not support such a conclusion, the seller is liable for all of the plaintiff's harm due to the defect and to other causes. Finally, a seller of a defective product, who is liable for all or part of the plaintiff's harm, is jointly and severally liable with other parties who are responsible for causing the harm.

§ 5.03 TESTS FOR DETERMINING A DESIGN DEFECT

[A] Introduction

Negligence and strict liability set out, in broad terms, what a plaintiff must prove in a design defect case. Ordinarily, the determination of whether the plaintiff has met its requirement of showing that a product was defective and unreasonably dangerous is a question of fact for the jury.[72] However, an exception to this is Pennsylvania, which holds that it is for the trial judge, not the jury, to make a social

---

[66] *See* RESTATEMENT (SECOND) OF TORTS §§ 433, 433A & 433B (1965).

[67] Mitchell v. Volkswagenwerk, A.G., 669 F.2d 1199, 1206 (8th Cir. 1982).

[68] Trull v. Volkswagen of America, Inc., 187 F.3d 88, 101–02 (1st Cir. 1999) (applying New Hampshire law).

[69] 537 F.2d 726, 737–38 (3d Cir. 1976).

[70] *See also* Caiazzo v. Volkswagenwerk, A. G., 647 F.2d 241 (2d Cir. 1981) (applying New York law); Stonehocker v. General Motors Corp., 587 F.2d 151, 158 (4th Cir. 1978) (applying South Carolina law); Yetter v. Rajeski, 364 F. Supp. 105, 109 (D.N.J. 1973) (applying New Jersey law).

[71] RESTATEMENT (THIRD) OF TORTS: PRODUCTS LIABILITY § 16 cmt. *a* (1998). Iowa adopted §§ 16 and 17 in Jahn v. Hyundai Motor Co., 773 N.W.2d 550 (Iowa 2009).

[72] *See* Goodner v. Hyundai Motor Co., 650 F.3d 1034 (5th Cir. 2011) (applying Texas law); Korando v.

policy determination whether a product was unreasonably dangerous.[73]

In negligence actions, juries and judges use the multifactored risk-utility analysis mentioned above to determine whether the manufacturer acted reasonably in selecting the design of the product. In deciding whether a product is unreasonably dangerous for purposes of § 402A, states initially followed the "consumer expectations test," and examined the operation and safety of a product from the perspective of the expectations of an ordinary consumer.[74] However, that test has been criticized by those who point out that it asks only whether an ordinary consumer expected the harm. These critics suggest that the test protects poor manufacturing standards since, if a dangerous design is widespread, it comes to be expected by consumers and cannot be unreasonably dangerous.[75] This has led the majority of states to adopt some form of a "risk-utility" analysis.[76] As its name indicates, this analysis examines whether the benefits of having the product with the particular design outweigh its risks of harm and the costs of a safer product. The shift from the consumer expectations test to the risk-utility analysis has been more than a simple change in the applicable test. Since the risk-utility analysis is a negligence-based test with its origins in the Learned Hand formula,[77] the move to such an analysis has resulted in a pull-back from strict liability in design defect cases.

Although there are differences in the details, states now permit plaintiffs in strict liability actions to show that the design resulted in a product that was unreasonably dangerous by using some form of four different approaches. First, five states continue to follow the consumer expectations test in all strict liability cases.[78] Second, most states permit a plaintiff to use either the consumer expectations test or the risk-utility analysis.[79] One result of this is that a product

---

Uniroyal Goodrich Tire Co., 637 N.E.2d 1020 (Ill. 1994); Cole v. Lantis Corp., 714 N.E.2d 194 (Ind. Ct. App. 1999).

[73] Azzarello v. Black Brothers Co., Inc., 391 A.2d 1020 (Pa. 1978). For a discussion of the factors a court may consider in making its determination, see Martinez v. Triad Controls, Inc., 593 F. Supp. 2d 741 (E.D. Pa. 2009) (applying Pennsylvania law). *See also* Moyer v. United Dominion Indus. Inc., 473 F.3d 532 (3d Cir. 2007) (applying Pennsylvania law) for a discussion of the standards for the admissibility of evidence at trial.

[74] For an analysis of the consumer expectations test, see Douglas A. Kysar, *The Expectations of Consumers*, 103 COLUM. L. REV. 1700 (2003) and Jerry J. Phillips, *Consumer Expectations*, 53 S.C. L. REV. 1047 (2002).

[75] For a list of articles critical of the consumer expectations test, see Aaron D. Twerski & James A. Henderson, *Manufacturers' Liability for Defective Product Designs: The Triumph of Risk-Utility*, 74 BROOK. L. REV. 1061, 1067, fn.34 (2009).

[76] For a discussion of the debate over the consumer expectations test and the risk-utility analysis in one state, see Andrew Meade, *A Reasonable Alternative to the Reasonable Alternative Design Requirement in Products Liability Law: A Look at Pennsylvania*, 62 HASTINGS L.J. 155 (2010).

[77] United States v. Carroll Towing Co., 159 F.2d 169 (2d Cir. 1947).

[78] Horst v. Deere & Co., 769 N.W.2d 536 (Wis. 2009). However, the justices in *Horst* disagreed whether Wisconsin should adopted the RESTATEMENT (THIRD), § 2(b). *See also* Halliday v. Sturm, Ruger & Co., 792 A.2d 1145 (Md. 2002); Delaney v. Deere & Co., 999 P.2d 930 (Kan. 2000); Haag v. Bongers, 589 N.W.2d 318 (Neb. 1999); Kirkland v. General Motors corp., 521 P.2d 1353 (Okla. 1974).

[79] Hawai'i permits plaintiffs to use three approaches in negligence and strict liability cases: the consumer expectations test; the risk-utility analysis, or the latent danger test. Mullaney v. Hilton Hotels

may be found to be defectively designed under the consumer expectations test but not under the risk-utility analysis.[80] Third, some states have incorporated the risk-utility factors into the consumer expectation analysis of the design of the product.[81] Finally, a few states have adopted the Restatement (Third) and rejected the consumer expectations test as an independent basis for finding a design defect.[82] Because the consumer expectations test and the risk-utility analysis remain the tests for establishing a design defect, the following sections will examine them separately.

[B] Consumer Expectation Test

[1] Introduction

Under the consumer expectation test (sometimes referred to as the "consumer contemplation" test,[83] or the "reasonable expectations" test,[84]), the question of whether the defect in the design of the product makes it "unreasonably dangerous" depends upon whether the danger posed by the design is greater than an ordinary consumer would expect when using the product in an intended or reasonably foreseeable manner.[85] The focus of the test is on the reasonable safety expectations of an "ordinary consumer" concerning the product, rather than on the product itself or any negligence in the design decision of the manufacturer.[86] The consumer expectations test has its genesis not only in the UCC's principles of implied warranty of merchantability and implied warranty of fitness for a particular purpose but also in § 402A, comment *g*, which states that a product is in a "defective condition" if it is, "at the time it leaves the seller's hands, in a condition not contemplated by the ultimate consumer, which will be unreasonably dangerous to him." Although the drafters of § 402A originally was meant the consumer expecta-

---

Corp., 634 F. Supp. 2d 1130 (D. Haw. 2009) (applying Hawai'i law). Under the "latent-danger" test, "a product is defective in design, even if faultlessly made, if the use of the product in a manner that is intended or reasonably foreseeable, including reasonably foreseeable misuses, involves a substantial danger that would not be readily recognized by the ordinary user of the product and the manufacturer fails to give adequate warnings of the danger." *Id.* at 1148, quoting, Tabieros v. Clark Equip. Co., 944 P.2d 1279, 1310 (1997).

[80] Cunningham v. Mitsubishi Motors Corp., 1993 U.S. Dist. LEXIS 21299 (S.D. Ohio June 16, 1993) (applying Ohio law).

[81] *See* Potter v. Chicago Pneumatic Tool Co., 694 A.2d 1319 (Conn. 1997); Seattle-First National Bank v. Tabert, 542 P.2d 774 (Wash. 1975).

[82] Branham v. Ford Motor Co., 701 S.E.2d 5 (S.C. 2010). RESTATEMENT (THIRD) OF TORTS: PRODUCTS LIABILITY § 2 cmt. *g*. One state that has applied the RESTATEMENT (THIRD) is Florida. *See* Agrofollajes, S.A. v. E.I. Du Pont De Nemours & Co., 48 So. 3d 976 (Fla. Dist. Ct. App. 2010).

[83] *See* Horst v. Deere & Co., 769 N.W.2d 536 (Wis. 2009).

[84] Vincer v. Esther Williams All-Aluminum Swimming Pool Co., 230 N.W.2d 794, 798 (Wis. 1975).

[85] Newell Rubbermaid, Inc. v. The Raymond Corp., 676 F.3d 521 (6th Cir. 2012) (applying Ohio law); Pritchett v. Cottrell, Inc., 512 F.3d 1057 (8th Cir. 2008) (applying Kansas law); Bourne v. Marty Gilman, Inc., 452 F.3d 632 (7th Cir. 2006) (applying Illinois law); Chavez v. Glock, Inc., 144 Cal. Rptr. 3d 326 (App. Ct. 2012).

[86] Mullaney v. Hilton Hotels Corp., 634 F. Supp. 2d 1130 (D. Haw. 2009) (applying Hawai'i law); Calles v. Scripto-Tokai Corp., 864 N.E.2d 249 (Ill. 2007).

tions test to apply only to manufacturing defects, courts gradually applied it to design defect cases as well.

An example of the use of the consumer expectations test is *Hansen v. Baxter Healthcare Corp.*,[87] in which a friction-fit IV catheter that had been inserted into a patient's jugular vein became detached, resulting in her death. In a suit against the manufacturer of the catheter, the estate of the patient alleged, among other things, that the tubing on the catheter was unreasonably dangerous because it was designed without a Luer-lock connection and that the friction-fit connection failed when the catheter was used in a reasonably foreseeable manner.[88] In response, the manufacturer contended that, consistent with the learned intermediary doctrine,[89] the healthcare professionals who inserted the catheter, rather than the patient herself, should be considered the "consumer" of the product for purposes of the consumer expectations test. In addition, the manufacturer argued that, as in the case of a prescription medical device, the patient was not familiar enough with the catheter to have any "expectations" about how it would work or about its safety. The Illinois Supreme Court, however, rejected both of the manufacturer'sarguments. According to the court, the evidence showed that the decision to purchase the catheter was made solely by the nursing products committee at the hospital, that the chair of the committee relied upon the manufacturer to advise him about the proper uses for the catheter, and that the person who purchased the device from the manufacturer's sales representative was not a physician. Thus, the court concluded that the catheter was more like atypical prescription products such as contraceptives where courts have held that the ordinary consumer expectation test is applicable. In addition, the court found that a patient, who was conscious after surgery, reasonably could have expected that her IV catheter connection, if properly designed and manufactured, would be safe for its intended purpose. Since the patient was the person who used the catheter and would be harmed by the product if it failed, the court held that her expectations of the product performance and safety should be the test.[90]

The consumer expectations test has been called a "simple test"[91] that is "reliable and easy to administer."[92] However, while all states apply the test in manufacturing defect cases, most states now use the consumer expectations test as an alternative to the risk-utility analysis in design defect cases. In states that use the consumer expectations test, either alone or as an alternative to the risk-utility analysis, there are four related questions that may arise when the test is used.

---

[87] 764 N.E.2d 35 (Ill. 2002).

[88] *Id.* at 38.

[89] The learned intermediary doctrine is discussed in detail in Chapter 7.

[90] *Id.* at 43–45.

[91] Todd v. Societe BIC, S.A., 21 F.3d 1402, 1406 (7th Cir. 1994) (applying Illinois law).

[92] Rebecca Tustin Rutherford, Comment: *Changes in the Landscape of Products Liability Law: An Analysis of the Restatement (Third) of Torts*, 63 J. Air L. & Com. 209, 224 (1997).

[2] Who is an Ordinary Consumer?

As in the *Hanson* case, one question that may arise in a design defect case is whether the person using the product at the time of the injury was an "ordinary consumer." Most juries and judges determine a consumer's expectations of a product not by those of the particular consumer of the product but by the objective test set out in § 402A, comment *i*: "The article sold must be dangerous to an extent beyond that which would be contemplated by the ordinary consumer who purchases it, with the ordinary knowledge common to the community as to its characteristics."[93] In *Horst v. Deere & Co.*,[94] the Wisconsin Supreme Court rejected substituting an ordinary "bystander" test when the person injured by the product was not the user of the product but a bystander.

In the vast majority of cases, whether the plaintiff was, in fact, an ordinary consumer of the product is not an issue. However, in some cases, the person who used the product was not the purchaser or an intended user of it. An example of this is a small child who, without parental permission, uses a product designed for use by adults. In *Calles v. Scripto-Tokai Corp.*,[95] a three-year-old child died in a fire after playing with a lighter. Although the lighter was not used in its intended manner (by an adult), the Illinois Supreme Court held that an ordinary consumer would expect that a child could obtain possession of the lighter and attempt to use it. Thus, a child was a reasonably foreseeable user of the lighter and an ordinary consumer would understand the possible consequences if a child obtained possession of one. Based on the facts of the case, the lighter performed as an ordinary consumer would expect when used in a foreseeable manner — by a child.[96]

[3] What Does an Ordinary Consumer Expect of a Product?

Hansen points to a second question that can arise when the consumer expectations test is used: does an ordinary consumer have sufficient knowledge or familiarity with the design of the product to have reasonable expectations about its safety or performance in the given situation? Two examples of the "ordinary knowledge" and expectations that consumers have about products were given by the

---

[93] In Heaton v. Ford Motor Co., 435 P.2d 806, 808 (Or. 1967), the Oregon Supreme Court stated:

In deciding what a reasonable consumer expects, the jury is not permitted to decide how strong products should be, nor even what consumers should expect. . . . The jury is supposed to determine the basically factual question of what reasonable consumers do expect.

See also Sigler v. Amer. Honda Motor Co., 532 F.3d 469 (6th Cir. 2008) (applying Tennessee law); Brown v. Sears, Roebuck & Co. 328 F.3d 1274 (10th Cir. 2003) (applying Utah law); Jenkins v. Amchem Prods. Inc., 886 P.2d 869 (Kan. 1994); Dart v. Wiebe Manufacturing Co., 709 P.2d 876 (Ariz. 1985); Vincer v. Esther Williams All-Aluminum Swimming Pool Co., 230 N.W.2d 794 (Wis. 1975).

[94] 769 N.W.2d 536 (Wis. 2009). In *Horst*, a two-year-old boy's feet were severed when his father accidentally ran over him with a riding lawn mower. The father had engaged a manual override switch that permitted the blades to turn while he was driving the mower in reverse.

[95] 864 N.E.2d 249 (Ill. 2007).

[96] *Id.* at 257–58. Although the lighter satisfied the consumer-expectations test, the court held that it could be considered unreasonably dangerous under the risk-utility test.

court in *Todd v. Societe BIC, S.A.*:[97]

> [A] pair of rubber soled shoes are not unreasonably dangerous simply because the person wearing them slips on a wet floor, because "it is a matter or common knowledge that shoes are more likely to slip when wet than dry. . . ." But if a hammer breaks when striking a steel peg, sending a metal fragment into the user's eye, the hammer is unreasonably dangerous because ordinary consumers do not expect hammers to chip on impact.

Similarly, in *Anderson v. Weslo, Inc.*,[98] the Washington appellate court stated:

> The ordinary consumer buys a trampoline in order to jump on it. Anytime a person jumps on a trampoline, he or she could fall and be injured. The dangers of jumping are therefore obvious enough to be contemplated by the ordinary consumer.

Unfortunately, the dangers of many products are not as obvious to consumers as rubber shoes and trampolines. An example of an increasingly complex product that frequently tests the limits of consumers' expectations is the automobile. In *Soule v. General Motors Corp.*,[99] the California Supreme Court gave some simple examples of what it felt an ordinary consumer could expect of automobiles: "[T]he ordinary consumers of modern automobiles may and do expect that such vehicles will be designed so as not to explode while idling at stoplights, experience sudden steering or brake failure as they leave the dealership, or roll over and catch fire in two-mile-per-hour collisions."[100] More difficult, however, was the situation in *Heaton v. Ford Motor Co.*,[101] in which the Oregon Supreme Court stated that a truck traveling 35 miles an hour and hitting a five or six inch rock was not so common an occurrence that the average person would know from personal experience what to expect of a truck under the circumstances. This led the court to affirm the involuntary nonsuit in the case, saying that to allow the jury to decide on its own intuition how strong a truck wheel should be would convert the concept of strict liability into absolute liability.

When dealing with consumer expectations about the safety of specific internal systems of an automobile such as airbags and seatbelts, courts increasingly look to "the expectation of performance, not the technical considerations of the product."[102] That was the attitude of the Sixth Circuit in *Hisrich v. Volvo Cars of North America, Inc.*,[103] in which an air-bag deployed and killed a six-year-old girl after a low-speed collision. In reversing the jury verdict for the manufacturer, the Sixth Circuit held that it was not necessary that an ordinary consumer know "the technical consider-

---

[97] 21 F.3d 1402, 1407 (7th Cir. 1994) (applying Illinois law).

[98] 906 P.2d 336 (Wash. Ct. App. 1995).

[99] 882 P.2d 298 (Cal. 1994).

[100] *Id.* at 308, n.3.

[101] 435 P.2d 806 (Or. 1967).

[102] Hisrich v. Volvo Cars of North America, Inc., 226 F.3d 445, 455 (6th Cir. 2000) (applying Ohio law).

[103] 226 F.3d 445 (6 *th* Cir. 2000) (applying Ohio law).

ations that influence the design of the airbag system in [the plaintiff's] Volvo."[104] Instead, a consumer needs to have only an expectation of the normal operation and safety of the product to satisfy the test. Similarly, in *Force v. Ford Motor Co.*,[105] the Florida appellate court held that, while ordinary consumers may not know the technical aspects of how seatbelts work, they are familiar enough with the item to have developed expectations about the function they perform and their safety.[106] That was sufficient for application of the consumer expectations test.

Since the consumer's expectations are a question of fact, courts favor leaving the question to the general experience of the jury.[107] According to the Connecticut Supreme Court: " 'The jury can draw their own reasonable conclusions as to the expectations of the ordinary consumer and the knowledge common in the community at large.' "[108] An example of leaving this question to the jury, even in a case involving a complicated medical device, is *Mele v. Howmedica, Inc.*,[109] in which the plaintiff alleged injury resulting from a device that was implanted during hip replacement surgery. The device used a cable that passed through the bone and created a risk of chafing off bone particles. As in *Hansen*, the manufacturer claimed that the plaintiff did not know of the particular device when he had the hip replacement and thus did not have any expectations about the safety of the system. However, the Illinois appellate court held that, even if implantees did not have expectations specific to the particular part of the artificial hip, they may have had relevant expectations about the safety of the artificial hip as a whole. Although jurors are entitled to use their own experiences to determine what an ordinary consumer would expect in such a situation, plaintiffs and manufacturers often attempt to influence that decision by presenting evidence going to the ordinary purpose of the product, the characteristics of the product, and any representations the manufacturer made about the product in advertisements.[110]

[4]   When Does the Consumer Expectations Test Apply?

Closely related to the issue of whether an ordinary consumer has sufficient knowledge of a product to have expectations about its safety is the question whether the facts of a case are appropriate for the test.[111] The question arises because the

---

[104] *Id.* at 455.

[105] 879 So.2d 103 (Fla. Dist. Ct. App. 2004).

[106] *Id.* at 109.

[107] In Buehler v. Whalen, 70 Ill. 2d 51 (Ill. 1977), for example, the Illinois Supreme Court held that a jury did not need testimony from consumers to reach its conclusion that car buyers do not expect their cars to burst into flames in collisions.

[108] Giglio v. Connecticut Light & Power Co., 429 A.2d 486, 489 (Conn. 1980), quoting Slepski v. Williams Ford, Inc., 364 A.2d 175, 178 (Conn. 1975).

[109] 808 N.E.2d 1026 (Ill. Ct. App. 2004).

[110] Charles E. Cantú, *Distinguishing the Concept of Strict Liability for Ultra-Hazardous Activities from Strict Products Liability Under Section 402A of the Restatement (Second) of Torts: Two Parallel Lines of Reasoning That Never Should Meet*, 35 Akron L. Rev. 31, 45–47 (2001).

[111] In Chavez v. Glock, Inc., 144 Cal. Rptr. 3d 326, 349–50 (App. Ct. 2012), the California appellate court stated that the initial determination whether the consumer expectations test is properly applied to a particular case is for the court.

consumer expectations test and risk-utility analysis are used as alternative tests. Some states limit the consumer expectations test to what two leading commentators have called "res-ipsa like cases that do not require the application of a general standard to determine defective design. For all the rest . . . risk-utility balancing is mandated."[112] In those states, the consumer expectations test is used in cases involving "a simple product which poses an obvious danger,"[113] a design that is "self-evident[ly] . . . not reasonably suitable and safe,"[114] cases where the failure of the product was simple,[115] or cases where the everyday experience of the product's users permits a conclusion that the design of the product did not meet minimum safety standards without the need for expert opinion.[116] When those standards are within the experience and common knowledge of jurors, expert witnesses either are not required[117] or may not be called[118] to establish what an ordinary consumer would or should expect. While the amount of proof necessary to establish a design defect under the consumer-expectations test is not subject to a formula, it generally is sufficient if the plaintiff provides evidence of (1) his or her use of the product; (2) the circumstances surrounding the injury; and (3) the objective features of the product that are relevant to an evaluation of its safety.[119]

Other courts take the position that the consumer expectations test is not negated automatically by a product's complexity.[120] In *Cunningham v. Mitsubishi Motors Corp.*,[121] for example, the issue arose in the context of consumers' expectations about automobile seatbelts. The Ohio federal court concluded that consumer expectations test was appropriate because consumers had been "bombarded with information regarding the importance of wearing seat belts because of the

---

[112] James A. Henderson & Aaron D. Twerski, *Achieving Consensus on Defective Product Design*, 83 CORNELL L. REV. 867, 899–900 (1998).

[113] Haddix v. Playtex Family Products Corp., 138 F.3d 681, 684 (7th Cir. 1998) (applying Illinois law) (since tampons are a simple product and pose an obvious danger, the consumer expectations test, not the risk-utility analysis, was the proper test to use in a motion for summary judgment). Similarly, in Miles v. S. C. Johnson & Son, Inc., 2002 U.S. Dist. LEXIS 10511 (N.D. Ill. 2002) (applying Illinois law), the district court found that Crystal Drano drain cleaner was a simple, obviously dangerous product and that only the consumer expectations test applied.

[114] Suter v. San Angelo Foundry & Machine Co., 406 A.2d 140, 150 (N.J. 1979).

[115] Morson v. Superior Court, 109 Cal. Rptr. 2d 343 (Ct. App. 2001).

[116] Soule v. General Motors Corp., 882 P.2d 298, 308 (Cal. 1994) ("[T]he consumer expectations test is reserved for cases in which the everyday experience of the product's users permits a conclusion that the product's design violated minimum safety assumptions, and is thus defective regardless of expert opinion about the merits of the design."). Using this test, the California appellate court held that the consumer expectations test is applicable in asbestos litigation, even though expert testimony may be required to establish legal causation. Jones v. John Crane, Inc., 35 Cal. Rptr. 3d 144, 153–54 (Ct. App. 2005).

[117] Newell Rubbermaid, Inc. Vv. The Raymond Corp., 676 F.3d 521 (6th Cir. 2012) (applying Ohio law).

[118] Howard v. Omni Hotels Management, 136 Cal. Rptr. 3d 739 (Cal. Ct. App. 2012).

[119] Mansur v. Ford Motor Co., 129 Cal. Rptr. 3d 200, 208 (Ct. App. 2011).

[120] *See* Hansen v. Baxter Healthcare Corp., 764 N.E.2d 35 (Ill. 2002) (medical device); Jackson v. General Motors Corp., 60 S.W.3d 800 (Tenn. 2001) (seatbelt).

[121] 1993 U.S. Dist. LEXIS 21299 (S.D. Ohio June 16, 1993) (applying Ohio law). *See also* Force v. Ford Motor Co., 879 So. 2d 103 (Fla. Dist. Ct. App. 2004).

protection which they provide."[122] The court stated that it was not willing to preclude the use of the consumer expectation test

> in a situation involving a familiar consumer product which is technically complex or uses a new process to accomplish a familiar function. Many familiar consumer products involve complex technology. In addition, manufacturers are constantly altering the methods in which products perform familiar functions. Thus, to conclude that the consumer expectation test cannot be used because a product is technologically complex or because a new process is used to achieve a familiar result would be to significantly reduce the use of that test. . . . Because of their long usage and consumer familiarity with the measure of safety which seat belts provide, consumer expectations do provide useful guidance.[123]

[C] Risk-Utility Analysis

[1] Introduction

The consumer expectations test is the standard used by § 402A to determine whether a product is unreasonably dangerous. However, manufacturers frequently make choices in the design of their products that involve weighing a number of factors and alternatives. By the 1980s, this led many courts and commentators to criticize the consumer expectations test as unsatisfactory for determining whether the design of a product created a defective condition that made it unreasonably dangerous.[124] In *Soule v. General Motors Corp.*,[125] for example, the defendant argued that the consumer expectations test was an "unworkable, amorphic, fleeting standard" that was "deficient and unfair in several respects." The defendant set out five reasons to support its contention.

> First, it defies definition. Second, it focuses not on the objective condition of products, but on the subjective, unstable, and often unreasonable opinions of consumers. Third, it ignores the reality that ordinary consumers know little about how safe the complex products they use can or should be made. Fourth, it invites the jury to isolate the particular consumer, component, accident and injury before it instead of considering whether the whole product fairly accommodates the competing expectations of all consumers in all situations. Fifth, it eliminates the careful balancing of risks and benefits which is essential to any design issue.[126]

---

[122] 1993 U.S. Dist. LEXIS 21299, at *14.

[123] *Id.* at 14–15.

[124] *See* Sheila Birnbaum, *Unmasking the Test for Design Defect: From Negligence [to Warranty] to Strict Liability to Negligence*, 33 VAND. L. REV. 593 (1980). For judicial expressions of the limitations of the consumer expectations test, see Turner v. General Motors, Camacho v. Honda Motor Co., 741 P.2d 1240 (Colo. 1987).

[125] 882 P.2d 298 (Cal. 1994).

[126] *Id.* at 309–10. In the early years of strict liability, Professor John Wade criticized the consumer expectations test as the exclusive test for determining a design defect on the ground that in "many situations . . . the consumer would not know what to expect, because he would have no idea how safe the

In response to earlier criticisms of the consumer expectations test, the California Supreme Court, in *Barker v. Lull Engineering Co., Inc.*,[127] developed a "risk-utility analysis" for design defect cases. In *Barker*, a construction worker was injured seriously when the lift truck he was operating became unbalanced on a steep grade and dropped the lumber it was carrying. Although the worker jumped out of the cab of the truck when it started to tip, he jumped directly into the path of the falling lumber. The worker sued the truck manufacturer, claiming that the truck should have been equipped with "outriggers," large mechanical arms extending from the sides of the machine, to provide stability on steep grades. The trial court judge instructed the jury under the consumer expectation test and the jury returned a verdict for the manufacturer on the grounds that an ordinary consumer would expect the lift truck to tip on steep terrain. On appeal, however, the California Supreme Court reversed, holding that the consumer expectations test was an "undue restriction on the application of strict liability principles."[128] The court stated that, previously, it had "flatly rejected the suggestion that recovery in a products liability action should be permitted only if a product is more dangerous than contemplated by the average consumer, refusing to permit the low esteem in which the public might hold a dangerous product to diminish the manufacturer's liability for injuries caused by the product."[129] To deal with the inadequacy of the consumer expectations test, the court did not reject it but, instead, adopted a new approach that permitted a plaintiff to show that a design was defective by using either of two alternative tests: consumer expectations and risk-utility analysis.

> First, a product may be found defective in design if the plaintiff establishes that the product failed to perform as safely as an ordinary consumer would expect when used in an intended or reasonably foreseeable manner. Second, a product may alternatively be found defective in design if the plaintiff demonstrates that the product's design proximately cause his injury and the defendant fails to establish, in light of the relevant, factors, that, on balance, the benefits of the challenged design outweigh the risks of danger inherent in such design.[130]

In response to the second alternative of the *Barker* test, the majority of courts have adopted some form of a risk-utility analysis (sometimes referred to as the "risk-benefit" analysis,[131] the "danger-utility" analysis,[132] or the "cost-benefit"

---

product could be made." John Wade, *On the Nature of Strict Liability for Products*, 44 Miss. L.J. 825, 829 (1973).

[127] 573 P.2d 443 (Cal. 1978). *See* Soule v. General Motors Corp., 882 P.2d 298 (Cal. 1994).

[128] 573 P.2d at 451.

[129] *Id.*

[130] *Id.* at 456. The California Supreme Court reconsidered the first consumer expectations portion of the *Barker* test in Soule v. General Motors Corp., 882 P.2d 298 (Cal. 1994). In *Pannu v. Land Rover North America*, 120 Cal. Rptr. 3d 605, 615 (Ct. App. 2011), a California court used both the consumer expectation test and the risk-utility test to hold that the evidence supported a finding that the design of an SUV presented excessive preventable danger of a rollover. *See* Saller v. Crown Cork & Seal Co., 115 Cal. Rptr. 3d 151 (Ct. App. 2010) (plaintiff presented sufficient evidence to use the consumer expectations test).

[131] Hisrich v. Volvo Cars of North America, Inc., 226 F.3d 445 (6th Cir. 2000) (applying Ohio law); Jennings v. BIC Corp., 181 F.3d 1250 (11th Cir. 1999) (applying Florida law).

analysis[133]) to determine whether the design of a product made it unreasonably dangerous.[134]

The risk-utility analysis recognizes that there are benefits as well as risks in almost every product. In order to determine whether the risks make the product unreasonably dangerous, it is necessary to weigh those risks against the benefits.[135] This requires expert testimony if the risks and utility of the design are technically complex and outside the understanding of lay jurors.[136] In design defect cases, a product is unreasonably dangerous when the evidence establishes that the risk of the challenged design outweighs the benefits from the design.[137] This is a policy judgment that involves a "balancing the likelihood and gravity of harm . . . against the burden of the precaution which would be effective to avoid the harm,"[138] a process that is similar to the formula articulated by Judge Learned Hand in *United States v. Carroll Towing Co.*[139] The effect of this process, according to the New York Court of Appeals, has been to bring

> the inquiry in design defect cases closer to that used in traditional negligence cases, where the reasonableness of an actor's conduct is considered in light of a number of situational and policy-driver factors. While efforts have been made to steer away from the fault-oriented negligence principles by characterizing the design defect cause of action in terms of a product-based rather than a conduct based analysis . . . , the reality is that the risk/utility balancing test is a 'negligence-inspired' approach, since it invites the parties to adduce proof about the manufac-

---

[132] Espeaignnette v. Gene Tierney Co., 43 F.3d 1 (1st Cir. 1994) (applying Maine law); Camacho v. Honda Motor Co., 741 P.2d 1240 (Colo. 1987).

[133] Tokio Marine & Fire Ins. Co., Ltd. v. Grove Manufacturing Co., 958 F.2d 1169 (1st Cir. 1992) (applying Puerto Rican law).

[134] For a review and analysis of the approaches of courts to design defects between 1999 and 2009, see Aaron D. Twerski & James A. Henderson, *Manufacturers' Liability for Defective Product Designs: The Triumph of Risk-Utility*, 74 BROOK. L. REV. 1061, 1073–108 (2009).

[135] Lamkin v. Towner, 563 N.E.2d 449 (Ill. 1990).

[136] Newell Rubbermaid, Inc. v.The Raymond Corp., 676 F.3d 521 (6th Cir. 2012) (applying Ohio law).

[137] Metzgar v. Playskool Inc., 30 F.3d 459 (3d Dist. 1994); Sperry-New Holland v. Prestage, 617 So. 2d 248 (Miss. 1993); Voss v. Black & Decker Manufacturing Co., 450 N.E.2d 204 (N.Y. 1983).

[138] Burke v. Illinois Power Co., 373 N.E.2d 1354, 1367 (Ill. App. Ct. 1978). *See* Indian Brand Farms, Inc. v. Novartis Crop Prot., Inc., 617 F.3d 207 (3d Cir. 2010) (applying New Jersey law).

[139] 159 F.2d 169 (2d Cir. 1947). Under the Hand formula, liability depends upon whether the burden of adequate precautions (B) is less than the probability of injury (P) x the gravity of the injury if it does occur (L). According to one commentator:

> When a jury decides that the risk of harm outweighs the utility of a particular design that the product is not as safe as it could be, it is saying that in choosing the particular design and cost trade-offs, the manufacturers exposed the consumer to greater risk of danger than he should have. Conceptually and analytically, this approach bespeaks negligence.

Birnbaum, *Unmasking the Test for Design Defect: Negligence [to Warranty] to Strict Liability to Negligence*, 33 VAND. L. REV. 593, 610 (1980). For examples of judicial decisions taking this view, see Nunnally v. R.J. Reynolds Tobacco Co., 869 So.2d 373 (Miss. 2004) and Banks v. ICI Americas, Inc., 450 S.E.2d 671 (Ga. 1994).

turer's choices and ultimately requires the fact finder to make 'a judgment about the [manufacturer's] judgment.'[140]

[2] Factors Used in Risk-Utility Analysis

In balancing the risks inherent in a product's design against the utility or benefit derived from the challenged design, the fact-finder weighs a number of factors.[141] One of the most frequently cited list of factors are the seven set out by Dean John W. Wade in a 1973 law review article.[142] These factors are:

(1) The usefulness and desirability of the product, i.e., its utility to the user and to the public as a whole.

(2) The safety aspect of the product, i.e., the likelihood that it will cause injury and the probable seriousness of the injury.

(3) The availability of a substitute product which will meet the same need and not be as unsafe.

(4) The manufacturer's ability to eliminate the unsafe character of the product without impairing its usefulness or making it too expensive to maintain its utility.

(5) The user's ability to avoid danger by the exercise of care in the use of the product.

(6) The user's anticipated awareness of the dangers inherent in the product and their avoidability because of public general knowledge of the obvious condition of the product, or the exercise of suitable warnings or instructions.

(7) The feasibility, on the part of the manufacturer, of spreading the loss by setting the price of the product or carrying liability insurance.

Courts rarely analyze in detail all seven of the Wade factors in a single decision. One case that did discuss each factor is *Van Doren v. Coe Press Equip. Corp.*[143] In *Van Doren*, the plaintiff was the operator of machines used to make housings for

---

[140] Denny v. Ford Motor Co., 662 N.E.2d 730, 735 (N.Y. 1995). *See* Banks v. ICI Americas, Inc., 450 S.E.2d 671, 674 (Ga. 1994) ("The balancing test that forms the risk-utility analysis is this consistent with Georgia law, which has long applied negligence principles in making the determination whether a product was defectively designed.").

[141] For some of the factors considered by courts, see Osorio v. One World Technologies, Inc., 659 F.3d 81 (1st Cir. 2011) (applying Massachusetts law, which uses warranty law instead of strict liability theory); Thompson v. Sunbeam Products, Inc., 2011 U.S. Dist. LEXIS 110677 (S.D. Ohio Sept. 28, 2011) (applying Ohio law); Timpte Industries, Inc. v. Gish, 286 S.W.3d 306, 311 (Tex. 2009); Williams v. Bennett, 921 So.2d 1269 (Miss. 2006).

[142] John Wade, *On the Nature of Strict Tort Liability for Products*, 44 Miss. L.J. 825, 837–38 (1973). *See* Calles v. Scripto-Tokai Corp., 864 N.E.2d 249, 261 (Ill. 2007) which sets out the jurisdictions that have adopted and relied on the Wade factors. For a criticism of the Wade factors, see David G. Owen, *Design Defect Ghosts*, 74 Brook. L. Rev. 927, 953 (2009).

[143] 592 F. Supp. 2d 776 (E.D. Pa. 2008) (applying Pennsylvania law). All seven of the Wade factors also were discussed in detail in Riley v. Becton Dickinson Vascular Access, Inc., 913 F. Supp. 879 (E.D. Pa. 1995) (applying Pennsylvania law).

lights. One of the machines he operated was a machine used to straighten large coils of metal. The machine had two large metal rolls between which the metal would be pulled in order to be straightened. On returning from a break, the plaintiff was walking in front of the machine when his right hand suddenly became trapped between the rolls of the machine. The machine lifted him off the ground and pulled him in. As he attempted to free his right hand using his left hand, his left hand also became caught in the machine. As a result, it was necessary to amputate both of the plaintiff's arms.

The machine originally was built with a metal attachment called a stock support, which was used to guide material into the straightener. According to the manufacturer, the stock support also acted as a guard by ensuring that the operator remained approximately 18 inches away from the "pinch point," the space between the machine's two rolls. The Operator's Maintenance Manual did not identify the stock support as a guard or safety feature. However, 25 years before the original purchaser of the machine removed the stock support and replaced it with a feeder tray. Four years before the accident, the original purchaser transferred the machine to the plaintiff's employer without the stock support or the feeder tray.[144]

In considering the manufacturer's motion for summary judgment, the Pennsylvania federal court analyzed the seven Wade factors. Under the first factor, the court concluded that it was undisputed that the machine was useful, desirable, and specially designed to meet the specific needs of the user.[145] The third Wade factor is the availability of a substitute product that would meet the same need and not be as unsafe. However, since the plaintiff did not present any evidence that there was an alternate, safer machine available to achieve the same purposes, the court found that factors one and three weighed in favor of not finding the design of the machine defective.[146]

Under the second of Wade factor, the court considered the likelihood and seriousness of any potential injury caused by the machine. The plaintiff presented evidence that the top pinch roll of the machine was unguarded. The plaintiff's expert testified that, because of the design, it was inevitable that workers would, at times, be injured. Given the large size and high power of the machine, and that there was no emergency off-switch near the nip point, any injury would be serious. Thus, the court found that the risk and potential seriousness of the injury suffered by the

---

[144] 592 F. Supp. 2d at 780–81.

[145] In Beard v. Johnson & Johnson, 41 A.3d 823, 836–37 (Pa. 2012), the Pennsylvania Supreme Court did not limit the focus of risk-utility analysis to the intended use of a product — the use that was alleged to have caused the injury – in determining its utility. According to the court, "a product's utility obviously may be enhanced by multi-functionality, so that it would be imprudent to deny trial courts the ability to assign some weight to this factor in assessing product design." In Adamo v. Brown & Williamson Tobacco Corp., 900 N.E.2d 966 (N.Y. 2008), the New York Court of Appeals held that the plaintiff failed to show that regular cigarettes and "light" cigarettes have the same utility to a smoker, since the only "utility" of a cigarette is to gratify a smokers desire for a certain experience. Although not an issue in *Van Doren*, the aesthetic attractiveness of a product also may be relevant in assessing the utility of a product. Calles v. Scripto-Tokai Corp., 864 N.E.2d 249, 261 (Ill. 2007); Bell v. Bayerische Motoren Werke Aktiengesellschaft, 105 Cal. Rptr.3d 485, 504 (Ct. App. 2010).

[146] 592 F. Supp. 2d at 791.

plaintiff weighed in favor of finding the machine defective under the second factor.[147]

The fourth Wade factor is the manufacturer's ability to eliminate the unsafe character of the product without impairing its usefulness or making it too expensive to maintain its utility. The plaintiff argue that two of the main aspects of the machine that made it unsafe were the inadequate guarding of the rolls and the lack of warnings and instructions related to the stock support and the cleaning of the rolls. He presented evidence that the machine's manual contained neither warnings regarding the purported guarding function of the stock support nor any instructions on how to clean the machine safely. He also presented evidence that such warnings and instructions would not be costly and would help eliminate the unsafe character of the product by making consumers aware of the need to keep the stock support in place and of the appropriate safety precautions that they should take when cleaning the machine. The plaintiff also presented evidence that the stock support left the top roll exposed and that the machine was operable when that stock support was removed. According to the plaintiffs, the main safety measure that would have eliminated the dangerous aspect of the machine would be the installation of interlocked top and bottom guards. These guards would have prevented workers from accidentally coming too close to either roll and being drawn into the pinch point between the two rolls. The plaintiff presented evidence that these guards were available and feasible. The manufacturer argued, however, that the plaintiff admitted he had never seen a straightener with the alleged alternative features. Given that they argue that the machine stock support was a guard for the bottom roll, the court found that it was reasonable that the top roll could have a similar guard. Thus, the court found that the manufacturer had the ability to install a top guard and to provide adequate warnings and explanations as to the guarding feature of the stock support. The manufacturer also had the ability to provide instructions for safe cleaning of the rolls. Since the defendants make no argument that these safety features would have been excessively expensive or that they would have diminished the machine's utility, the court concluded that the fourth Wade factor weighed in favor of finding the machine was defective.[148]

The fifth factor in the Wade analysis is the user's ability to avoid danger by the exercise of care in the use of the product. The manufacturer argued that this factor should weigh in its favor because the plaintiff knew and understood the dangers presented by the machine and could have anticipated and avoided the risk of getting his hand stuck in the machine. However, under the fifth factor, the focus is not on whether the particular plaintiff could have avoided the injury but on whether the class of ordinary purchasers of the product could avoid injury through the exercise of care in use of the product. Because the top roller was exposed, a person working with the machine would not have been able to avoid the possibility of coming into accidental contact with it. Finally, the plaintiff testified that his arm became trapped while walking in front of the machine, which he had turned off prior to taking his break. Given that the machine operator's job involved standing in front of the roller area to put the metal into the rollers before beginning a job, the operator would not

---

[147] *Id.* at 791–92.

[148] *Id.* at 792.

have been able to avoid being in front of the rollers in the course of his work when he thought the machine was off. Thus, the court found that an objective user would not have been able to completely avoid the danger presented by the exposed rollers.[149]

The sixth Wade factor is the user's anticipated awareness of the dangers inherent in the product and their ability to avoid the dangers because of public general knowledge of the obvious condition of the product, or the exercise of suitable warnings or instructions. The focus inquiry under this factor is on the product. The manufacturer alleged that the plaintiff's experts admitted that the danger was open and obvious. However, the expert testified that the danger was open and obvious to the plaintiff, not necessarily to the general public. In addition, nothing in the machine's manual indicated that the stock support was a safety feature or provided any warnings regarding its removal. Thus, due to the lack of suitable warnings or instruction regarding the function of the stock support, it would not be obvious to the general public that the machine was missing an original safety feature. Again, the federal court found that the plaintiff presented sufficient evidence that a user would not necessarily be aware of the machine's dangerous conditions.[150]

The final factor in the Wade analysis is the feasibility, on the part of the manufacturer, of spreading the loss by setting the price of the product or carrying liability insurance. Using this factor, the court weighed the manufacturer's ability to spread the risk of loss by adjusting the price of the product or carrying liability insurance. The manufacturer did not argue that it lacked that ability. Instead, it argued that manufacturers should not be required to spread the economic loss of an accident that was caused "not by any defect in the product, but rather by an inattentive user." In addition, it argued that it was against public policy to hold manufacturers responsible for such a "bizarre" accident. The court, however, concluded that, under Pennsylvania law, a plaintiff's failure to exercise care in the use of a product is not relevant to whether a product is unreasonably dangerous. It also found that, as the party in the best position to determine the potential risks and costs, the manufacturer had the ability to spread the risk of loss. As a result, the seventh factor also weighed in favor of finding the product defective.[151] Based on balancing the risk and utility of the machine using the seven Wade factors, the federal district court found, as a matter of law, that the machine was unreasonably dangerous and defective.[152]

[3] Reasonable Alternative Design

Of all the factors used in risk-utility analysis, the one that has received the most attention is whether, in Professor Wade's words, a "substitute product" was available at the time of manufacture that would meet the same need as the challenged product and not be as unsafe. In *Hansen v. Baxter Healthcare Corp.*,[153]

---

[149] *Id.* at 792–93.

[150] *Id.* at 793.

[151] *Id.* at 793-94.

[152] *Id.*

[153] 764 N.E.2d 35 (Ill. 2002).

discussed above in connection with the consumer expectations test, the Illinois Supreme Court also affirmed the jury's finding for the plaintiff based on a risk-utility analysis. According to the court, there was sufficient evidence that, first, a connector existed that would have prevented an unintentional disconnection of the catheter and that, second, the cost of the connector would have been only between three and five cents per unit.[154] For many other products, however, there is no alternative design that will reduce the risk of injury without drastically altering the nature of the product. In *Anderson v. Weslo, Inc*,[155] for example, the Washington appellate court held that the risk-utility analysis was not applicable in a case involving a teenager injured while using a trampoline because, "[g]iven the nature and purpose of a trampoline, it is impossible to imagine an alternative design that would have prevented [the plaintiff's] harm."[156]

One of the most important sections of the Restatement (Third) is § 2(b) which requires a plaintiff to show a reasonable alternative design in a design defect case. According to the section, a product

> is defective in design when the foreseeable risks of harm posed by the product could have been reduced or avoided by the adoption of a reasonable alternative design by the seller or by other distributor, or a predecessor in the commercial chain of distribution, and the omission of the alternative design renders the product not reasonably safe.[157]

According to comment *d* to § 2:

> Subsection (b) adopts a reasonableness ("risk-utility balancing") test as the standard for judging the defectiveness of product designs. Mores specifically, the test is whether a reasonable alternative design would, at reasonable cost, have reduced the foreseeable risk of harm posed by the product and, if so, whether the omission of the alternative design by the seller . . . rendered the product not reasonably safe. . . . Under prevailing rules concerning allocation of burden of proof, the plaintiff must prove that such a reasonable alternative was, or reasonably could have been, available at the time of sale or distribution.

State statutes[158] and judicial decisions[159] in many the states also require a plaintiff to prove the existence of a feasible (reasonable) alternative design that

---

[154] *Id.* at 45. *See also* Honda of America Manufacturing, Inc. v. Norman, 104 S.W.3d 600 (Tex. App. 2003). In *Colon v. BIC USA, Inc.*, 199 F. Supp. 2d 53 (S.D.N.Y. 2001) (applying New York law), the court held that there was insufficient evidence that the design of a disposable cigarette lighter was unreasonably dangerous since there was no evidence of a feasible alternative design.

[155] 906 P.2d 336 (Wash. Ct. App. 1995).

[156] *Id.* at 340.

[157] Restatement (Third) of Torts: Products Liability § 2(b) (1998). This section was cited with approval in *Berrier v. Simplicity Mfg.*, 563 F.3d 38 (3d Cir. 2009) (applying Pennsylvania law). Wisconsin also has moved to the Restatement (Third) approach. Wis. Stat. Ann. § 895.047(1)(a) ("A product is defective in design if the foreseeable risks of harm posed by the product could have been reduced or avoided by the adoption of a reasonable alternative design by the manufacturer and the omission of the alternative design renders the product not reasonably safe.").

[158] Among the statutes are Tex. Civ. Prac. & Rem. Code Ann. § 82.005 (in a design defect case, "the

would have provided greater overall safety to consumers than the design the manufacturer actually used. An example of the failure to meet this requirement is *Allen v. Minnstar*,[160] in which the Tenth Circuit affirmed summary judgment in favor of manufacturer of a boat engine that the plaintiff alleged was defective because of the absence of a propeller guard on the boat. According to the court, the plaintiff failed to show "an alternative, safer design, practicable under the circumstances and available at the time of the defendants' placing the boat and engine in the stream of commerce."[161]

One state that has rejected the Restatement (Third) and its requirement that the plaintiff establish a reasonable alternative design is Connecticut. In *Potter v. Chicago Pneumatic Tool Co.*,[162] the plaintiffs were shipyard workers who alleged that defects in the pneumatic hand tools they used created excessive vibrations that caused their injuries. The jury returned a verdict for the plaintiffs and the defendant argued that it was time for the court to abandon the consumer expectation test and to adopt the requirement that the plaintiff must prove the existence of a reasonable alternative design in order to prevail on a design defect claim.[163] The Connecticut Supreme Court rejected the defendant's argument for two reasons. First, the court felt that requiring proof of a feasible alternative design imposed an undue burden on plaintiffs that could prevent preclude otherwise valid claims from jury consideration. The reason for that was that such proof would require plaintiffs to retain an expert witness even in cases in which jurors could infer a design defect from circumstantial evidence.[164] Second, the court felt that, in some situations, a product may be in a "defective condition unreasonably dangerous" even though there is no feasible alternative design. In such cases, the manufacturer is strictly liable despite the fact that there is no reasonable alternative design.[165]

---

burden is on the claimant to prove by a preponderance of the evidence that there was a safer alternative design."); LA. REV. STAT. § 9:2800.56; MISS. CODE ANN. § 11-1-63(a), (f); N.J. STAT. ANN. § 2A:58c-3; N.C. GEN. STAT. ANN. § 99B-6; WIS. STAT. ANN. § 895.047. However, proof of a safer alternative design is not enough for liability. The plaintiff also must show that the alleged defect in the existing product made it unreasonably dangerous. Zavala v. Burlington Northern Santa Fe Corp., 355 S.W.3d 359, 370 (Tex. App. 2011).

[159] For examples, *see* Malen v. MTD Prod., Inc., 628 F.3d 296 (7th Cir. 2010) (applying Illinois law); Wankier v. Crown Equipment Corp., 353 F.3d 862 (10th Cir. 2003) (applying Utah law); Burt v. Makita Corp., 212 F. Supp. 2d 893 (N.D. Ind. 2002) (applying Indiana law); Branham v. Ford Motor Co., 701 S.E.2d 5 (S.C. 2010); Voss v. Black & Decker Mfg. Co., 450 N.E.2d 204 (N.Y. 1983); Jenkins v. International Paper Co., 945 So.2d 144 (La. Ct. App. 2006). Although the Minnesota Supreme Court does not require evidence of a feasible alternative design in every case, it has stated that it can conceive only of "rare cases" in which "the product may be judge unreasonably dangerous because it should be removed from the market rather than redesigned." Kallio v. Ford Motor Co., 407 N.W.2d 92. 97 (Minn. 1987); Wagner v. Hesston Corp., 450 F.3d 756 (8th Cir. 2006) (applying Minnesota law).

[160] 8 F.3d 1470 (10th Cir. 1993) (applying Utah law).

[161] *Id.* at 1479.

[162] 694 A.2d 1319 (Conn. 1997).

[163] 694 A.2d at 1331.

[164] *Id.* at 1332.

[165] *Id.* For a discussion of the reaction of states to the RESTATEMENT (THIRD), § 2(b), after *Potter*, see

Although the Restatement (Third) requires the plaintiff to show a reasonable alternative design, it recognizes one exception to the requirement: the design is "manifestly unreasonable."[166] In *Parish v. ICON Health & Fitness, Inc.*,[167] the plaintiff, who was paralyzed when he was attempting flips on a trampoline, argued that a backyard trampoline is so inherently dangerous that a reasonable alternative design is not available. Since application of the exception was an issue of first impression for the Iowa Supreme Court, it looked to the language of the Restatement (Third) (which it adopted), law review articles, and an analogous situation in another state and concluded that the exception was not appropriate in the case. Trampolines are common and widely used products, the number of injuries is very low, and the product has health benefits in terms of exercise and entertainment.[168]

[4] Burden of Proof

As with many areas of products liability law, there is a disagreement among the courts as to who bears the burden of proving that the risks of the design of a product outweigh its benefits. In *Barker v. Lull Engineering Co.*,[169] the California Supreme Court did more than establish two alternative tests for determining design defect liability. The court concluded that, in a strict liability action using risk-utility analysis, a plaintiff may recover if he "demonstrates that the product's design proximately caused his injury and the defendant fails to establish, in light of the relevant factors, that, on balance, the benefits of the challenged design do not outweigh the risk of danger inherent in such design."[170] Under the *Barker* court's assignment of the burden of proof, once a plaintiff makes a *prima facie* showing that the product's design proximately caused the injuries, the burden shifts to the defendant to prove that the benefits outweigh the risks.[171] Although the majority of states have adopted *Barker's* two-prong approach to proving whether the design of a product made it unreasonably dangerous, only three other states have followed its lead in shifting the burden of proof to the defendant.[172] The majority of states have chosen, instead, to follow the traditional approach to burden of proof and require the plaintiff to show: (1) there was a defect in the design of the product manufactured or sold by the defendant; (2) the design defect existed at the time the product left the defendant's control; and (3) the defect in the design was the direct and proximate cause of the plaintiff's injuries.[173] If the plaintiff relies on the

---

Larry S. Stewart, *Strict Liability for Defective Product Design: The Quest for a Well-Ordered Regime*, 74 BROOK. L. REV. 1039 (2009).

[166] According to the RESTATEMENT (THIRD) § 2(b), cmt. *e*, "the designs of some products are so manifestly unreasonable, in that they have low social utility and high degree of danger, that liability should attach even absent proof of a reasonable alternative design."

[167] 719 N.W.2d 540 (Iowa 2006).

[168] *Id.* at 544–45.

[169] 573 P.2d 443 (Cal. 1978).

[170] *Id.* at 456.

[171] Pannu v. Land Rover North America, 120 Cal. Rptr. 3d 605 (Ct. App. 2011).

[172] Lamkin v. Towner, 563 N.E.2d 449 (Ill. 1990); Ontai v. Straub Clinic & Hospital, Inc., 659 P.2d 734 (Haw. 1983); Caterpillar Tractor Co. v. Beck, 593 P.2d 884 (Alaska 1979).

[173] Donegal Mutual Ins. v. White Consolidated Indus., 852 N.E.2d 215 (Ohio Ct. App. 2006).

consumer expectation test, he or she has the burden of showing some aspect of the design made the product's performance less safe than an ordinary consumer would expect it.[174] Similarly, under the risk-benefit analysis, the plaintiff must produce evidence that the risk of harm posed by the product's design, the likelihood that harm will occur, the gravity of the harm if it occurs, and, if required, the feasibility of a safer alternative design, outweigh the utility of the challenged design of the product.[175]

[D]   Alternative Tests

The previous sections have shown that states use a variety of approaches to determine whether the design of a product is defective. While a few states define a design defect solely in terms of the consumer expectations theory[176] or solely in terms of risk-utility analysis,[177] most state statutes and judicial decisions follow the lead of the California Supreme Court in *Barker v. Lull Engineering Co.*[178] and adopted an integrated test which permits use of the two tests as alternatives.[179] In most situations, the two tests are not mutually exclusive and either or both can be used in a case.[180] An example of this is *Glenn v. Overhead Door Corp.*,[181] in which a mother left her three-year-old daughter in a car with the engine running while it was parked in her garage with the garage door closed. The daughter died of carbon monoxide poisoning. In a suit against the manufacturer of the electronic garage door opener, the father alleged that the design of the product was defective since it did not include a technologically feasible sensor that would cause the door's motor to engage and the door to rise if the level of carbon monoxide reached a potentially dangerous level. However, the Mississippi court of appeals affirmed summary judgment for the manufacturer on the ground that, under the consumer expectation test, the mother appreciated the danger that led to their daughter's death. The court also held that the father could not prevail under risk-utility

---

[174] Bouher v. Aramark Services, Inc., 910 N.E.2d 40 (Ohio Ct. App. 2009).

[175] Austin v. Mitsubishi Electronics America, Inc., 966 F. Supp. 506 (E.D. Mich. 1997) (applying Michigan law): Armentrout v. FMC Corp., 842 P.2d 175 (Colo. 1992); Dart v. Wiebe Manufacturing Inc., 709 P.2d 876 (Ariz. 1985); Knitz v. Minster Machine Co., 432 N.E.2d 814 (Ohio 1982); Wilson v. Piper Aircraft Corp., 579 P.2d 1287 (Or. 1978).

[176] *See* Green v. Smith & Nephew AHP, Inc., 629 N.W.2d 727 (Wis. 2001); Rojas v. Lindsay Mfg. Co., 701 P.2d 210, 212 (Idaho 1985); Ritter v. Narragansett Elec. Co., 283 A.2d 255, 263 (R.I. 1971).

[177] *See* Branham v. Ford Motor Co., 701 S.E.2d 5 (S.C. 2010); Banks v. ICI Americas, Inc., 450 S.E.2d 671 (Ga. 1994).

[178] 573 P.2d 443 (1978). *See* Mansur v. Ford Motor Co., 129 Cal. Rptr. 3d 200 (Ct. App. 2011).

[179] For examples, *see* OHIO REV. CODE § 2307.75(A); Peck v. Bridgeport Machines, Inc., 237 F. 3d 614 (6th Cir. 2001) (applying Michigan law); Branham v. Ford Motor Co., 701 S.E.2d 5 (S.C. 2010); Mikolajczyk v. Ford Motor Co., 901 N.E.2d 329 (Ill. 2008); Halliday v. Sturm, Ruger & Co., 792 A.2d 1145 (Md. 2002).

[180] Newell Rubbermaid, Inc. v. The Raymond Corp., 676 F.3d 521, 529 (6th Cir. 2012) (applying Ohio law). However, in Kokins v. Teleflex, Inc., 621 F.3d 1290 (10th Cir. 2010), the court held, that under Colorado law, complex cases involving primarily technical and scientific information require the use of the risk-utility analysis rather than the consumer expectations test.

[181] 935 So. 2d 1074 (Miss. 2006).

analysis since the daughter's death could have been avoided by the exercise of reasonable care on the mother's part.[182]

Other states have developed variations on the consumer expectations test and risk-utility analysis. In *Potter v. Chicago Pneumatic Tool Co.*,[183] the Connecticut Supreme Court restated its support for the consumer expectations test, while recognizing that there are situations in which the complex design of a product makes it difficult or impossible for the ordinary consumer to have any expectations of safety about it.[184] To deal with these cases, the court adopted a modified consumer expectations, under which

> a consumer's expectations may be viewed in light of various factors that balance the utility of the product's design with the magnitude of its risks. We find persuasive the reasoning of those jurisdictions that have modified their formulation of the consumer expectation test by incorporation of the risk-utility factors into the ordinary consumer expectation analysis. . . . Thus, the modified consumer expectation test provides the jury with the product's risks and utility and then inquires whether a reasonable consumer would consider the product unreasonably dangerous.[185]

Under the *Potter* approach, the consumer expectation test establishes the product's risks and utility. The inquiry then is whether a reasonable consumer, with that information, would consider the product's design unreasonably dangerous. The Connecticut court listed a number of factors — basically those set out earlier by Professor John Wade — the jury could consider in weighing the risk and utility.[186]

Although the Connecticut court in *Potter* adopted a modified consumer expectation test, it did not require the plaintiff to present evidence of the product's risks and benefits in every case. Instead, it said that the ordinary consumer expectations test should be used in situations where "the everyday experience of the particular product's users permits the inference that the product did not meet minimum safety expectations."[187] In contrast, the court stated that risk-utility balancing of the modified test should be reserved for cases where "the particular facts do not reasonably permit the inference that the product did not meet the safety expectations of the ordinary consumer."[188] Under this approach, it is the function of the court to determine when a jury instruction on the ordinary consumer expectation test or the modified test is appropriate.[189]

States with products liability statutes also use two tests for determining whether the design of a product makes it unreasonably dangerous. An example of this is the

---

[182] *Id.* at 1080–81.

[183] 694 A.2d 1319 (Conn. 1997).

[184] *Id.* at 1333.

[185] *Id.*

[186] *Id.* at 1333–34.

[187] *Id.* at 1334.

[188] *Id.*

[189] *Id.*

Tennessee Products Liability Act[190] which uses the consumer expectations test and the "prudent manufacturer" test.[191] The consumer expectations test looks at whether a product was unreasonably dangerous from the perspective of the expectations of an ordinary consumer who uses it. The prudent manufacturer test requires the determination of whether a prudent manufacturer would have marketed the product knowing its dangerous condition. Application of the prudent manufacturer test requires a balancing of factors used in the risk-utility analysis.[192]

Unlike the position taken by many other states, Tennessee requires expert testimony to support both types of design defect claims.[193] In addition, unlike the modified consumer expectation test developed in *Potter*, which asks whether a reasonable consumer, knowing the product's risks and utility, would consider the product unreasonably dangerous, the Tennessee test assumes that a prudent manufacturer would engage in the risk-utility analysis and consider such factors as the product's usefulness, the costs involved with an alternative design, and the seriousness and likelihood of potential harm in making its decision whether to market the product.

A recent refinement in the use of the consumer expectations test and the risk-utility analysis has been provided by the Illinois Supreme Court in *Mikolajczyk v. Ford Motor Co.*[194] In that case, the court rejected treating the consumer-expectations test and the risk-utility analysis as an either/or approach to liability in design defect cases. Instead, the court held that the defendant was entitled to a jury instruction on the risk-utility analysis, even though the plaintiff had relied on the consumer-expectations test.[195] According to the court, "both the consumer-expectation test and the risk-utility test may be utilized in a strict liability design defect case to prove that the product is 'unreasonably dangerous.' "[196] The court further held that, "[w]hen both tests are employed, consumer expectation is to be treated as one factor in the multifactor risk-utility analysis."[197] The ability of the parties to choose which test to use is illustrated by *Jablonski v. Ford Motor Co.*,[198] in which both parties used only the risk-utility analysis. In its decision, the Illinois Supreme Court did not mention the consumer-expectation test.

---

[190] TENN. CODE ANN. § 29-28-101 *et seq.*

[191] *Id.* at § 29-28-102(8). *See* Sigler v. Amer. Honda Motor Co., 532 F.3d 469 (6th Cir. 2008) (applying Tennessee law); Brown v. Crown Equipment Co., 181 S.W.3d 268 (Tenn. 2005); Clinton H. Scott, *Defective Condition or Unreasonably Dangerous Under the Tennessee Products Liability Act: Just What Does It Mean?* 33 U. MEM. L. REV. 945 (2003).

[192] Ray *ex rel.* Holman v. BIC Corp., 925 S.W.2d 527, 530–33 (Tenn. 1996). *See* Brown v. The Raymond Corp., 432 F.3d 640 (6th Cir. 2005) (applying the prudent manufacturer test under Tennessee law).

[193] Newell Rubbermaid, Inc. v. The Raymond Corp., 676 F.3d 521, 526 (6th Cir. 2012) (applying Tennessee law).

[194] 901 N.E.2d 329 (Ill. 2008).

[195] *Id.* at 359.

[196] *Id.* at 360.

[197] *Id. See* Show v. Ford Motor Co., 659 F.3d 584 (7th Cir. 2011) (applying Illinois law).

[198] 955 N.E.2d 1138 (Ill. 2011).

§ 5.04   OPEN AND OBVIOUS DANGERS

One question that arises both in negligence and strict liability cases is whether a plaintiff should be barred from recovery if the risk created by the design of the product, such as the absence of a safety device, was "open and obvious."[199] An "open and obvious," or "patent," danger is defined as "an unsafe aspect of the product that is an inherent characteristic of the product and that would be recognized by the ordinary person who uses or consumes the product with the ordinary knowledge common to the class of persons for whom the product is intended. . . ."[200] In negligence cases, using a product that contains an open and obvious danger is treated as factor in considering whether the plaintiff was contributorily negligent.[201] In strict liability cases, the consumer expectations test and risk-utility analysis take different approaches to such a danger. In most states that apply the consumer expectations test, an open and obvious danger created by the design of a product bars recovery because the consumer did not expect the product to be safe.[202] An example of this is *Kutzler v. AMF Harley-Davidson*[203] in which the plaintiff suffered multiple fractures and severe injuries to his leg when the motorcycle he was riding was sideswiped by an automobile that crossed the center line of the highway. The plaintiff brought suit against the manufacturer of the motorcycle alleging it was unreasonably dangerous because it was designed with extra-wide gas tanks and not equipped with crash bars. The Illinois appellate court, however, dismissed the case on the ground that the extra-wide gas tank and absence of crash bars were obvious both to someone who looked at the motorcycle as well as to a rider who sat down on it. Since the motorcycle could not be expected to protect the rider from sideswipes, the design was not unreasonably dangerous and the motorcycle did not failure to perform in a manner reasonably to be expected in light of its design.

A majority of states now reject the idea that the open and obvious dangers of a product is an absolute defense to a defective design claim based on strict liability. However, this does not preclude use of the risk-utility test and the obviousness of the risk is an issue in determining the product's risks, the reasonable expectations of consumers, and the expected uses of the product.[204] An open and obvious risk will bar recovery only when it outweighs the other factors that are considered in

---

[199] For a justification of the "open and obvious" rule, see Campo v. Scofield, 95 N.E.2d 802 (N.Y. 1950). *Campo* was overruled by Micallef v. Miehle Co., 348 N.E.2d 571 (N.Y. 1976).

[200] N.J. Stat. Ann. § 2A:58C-3(a)(2).

[201] Restatement (Second) of Torts § 398 cmt. *b* (1965) states: "If the dangerous character of the plan or design is known to the user of the chattel, he may be in contributory fault if the risk involved in using it is unreasonably great or if he fails to take those special precautions which the known dangerous character of the chattel requires."

[202] Sandage v. Bankhead Enterprises, Inc., 177 F.3d 670 (8th Cir. 1999) (applying Missouri law); Brewer v. Harley-Davidson, Inc., 1999 U.S. App. LEXIS 2962 (10th Cir. Feb. 24, 1999) (applying Oklahoma law); Kirk v. Hanes Corporation of North Carolina, 771 F. Supp. 856 (E.D. Mich. 1991) (applying Michigan law).

[203] 550 N.E.2d 1236 (Ill. App. Ct. 1990). *See also* Shaffer v. AMF Inc., 842 F.2d 893 (6th Cir. 1988) (applying Ohio law).

[204] Calles v. Scripto-Tokai Corp., 864 N.E.2d 249, 260 (Ill. 2007).

weighing the risks against the benefits of the product as designed.[205] The Restatement (Third) takes this position based on the drafters' view that, in the strong majority of states, the open and obvious nature of a product is not necessarily an absolute bar to recovery.[206]

Although recognized by the majority of states, a few states have abolished the open and obvious danger rule. In *Smith ex. rel. Smith v. Bryco Arms*,[207] a 15-year-old accidentally shot his 14-year-old friend with a.22 caliber handgun. The plaintiffs argued that the gun was defective because its design did not incorporate safety devices and warnings designed to prevent foreseeable unintentional shooting accidents. In reversing the trial court's grant of summary judgment for the manufacturer, the New Mexico Supreme Court noted that, although the dangers of a gun may be open and obvious, the state had abolished the doctrine. As a result, "a risk is not reasonable simply because it is open and obvious to persons using ordinary care."[208]

§ 5.05 STATE-OF-THE-ART

In many products liability cases, the manufacturer will attempt to show that the design of its product was not defective because it was the "state-of-the-art" at the time of manufacture.[209] In *Potter v. Chicago Pneumatic Tool Co.*,[210] the plaintiffs alleged that defects in the design of the pneumatic hand tools they used in their work created excessive vibrations that caused their injuries. The manufacturer presented testimony that they "produced the safest and highest quality tools that they were able to design." A representative of one of the defendant's customers also testified that the defendant's tools were the best for his company's purposes and that his company would be in a "tough situation" if it had to replace the defendant.[211] The plaintiff, however, presented evidence that one of the manufacturer's competitors had produced a tool since 1976 that reduced vibration and that the manufacturer has been aware of the tool.[212] Thus, in order to make their case, both the plaintiff and the manufacturer presented evidence of the "state-of-the-art" at the time the manufacturer produced its hand tools.

The concept of the state-of-the-art has two separate but related meanings in products liability cases. In one sense, the state-of-the-art is more than just the

---

[205] *See* Swix v. Daisy Manufacturing Co., 373 F.3d 678 (6th Cir. 2004) (applying Michigan law); Ogeltree v. Navistar International Transportation Corp., 500 S.E.2d 570 (Ga. 1998); Sperry-Holland v. Prestage, 617 So.2d 248 (Miss. 1993).

[206] RESTATEMENT (THIRD) OF TORTS: PRODUCTS LIABILITY § 2 cmt. *d* (1998). See Blue v. Environmental Engineering, Inc., 828 N.E.2d 1128 (Ill. 2005), adopting the RESTATEMENT (THIRD) position.

[207] 33 P.3d 638 (N.M. Ct. App. 2001).

[208] *Id.* at 650.

[209] The INDIANA PRODUCT LIABILITY ACT (IND. CODE § 34-20-5-1) provides a rebuttable presumption that a product is not defective if it was manufactured in conformity with the state-of-the art.

[210] 694 A.2d 1319 (Conn. 1997).

[211] *Id.* at 1344.

[212] *Id.*

industry custom.[213] It is the level of relevant "technical, mechanical and scientific knowledge of manufacturing, designing, testing, or labeling the same or similar products which was in existence and reasonably feasible for use at the time of manufacture."[214] In this sense, it is an elusive standard. It can be determined only by balancing a wide-ranging pool of data from academic, professional, and industry sources.[215] These, in turn, must be analyzed in light not only of basic consumer expectations but also technological and financial realities. In this sense, the totality of such materials has a direct bearing on the jury's decision on the adequacy of the challenged design.

State-of-the-art evidence must be relevant to the specific risk at issue and not simply be a general characteristic of the product. In *Wade v. Terex-Telelect, Inc.*,[216] a truck lineman was rendered a quadriplegic after he fell from a double-man bucket attached to a truck while working on the installation of a transformer approximately 30 feet off the ground. The truck lineman claimed that the design of the bucket was defective because the lack of an interior step on the dielectric liner caused the step to be covered up, resulting in his fall. The Indiana appellate court held that the evidence offered by the defendant, while proving that the liner was the best technology for dielectric insulation, did not show that the liner was the best design to prevent falls.

Although manufacturers in some cases have argued that state-of-the-art is available only in failure to warn cases, courts hold that it is available in design defect cases as well. However, it is not available in manufacturing defect cases.[217] Plaintiffs, on the other hand, often argue that while state-of-the-art is relevant in negligence cases, it should not be used in strict liability cases. Since negligence cases focus on the conduct of the manufacturer in selecting the particular design of the product, state-of-the-art evidence is relevant to whether the manufacturer acted reasonably in selecting the design. If a safer design was available and feasible, a manufacturer is negligent in not adopting that design. However, plaintiffs argue that state-of-the-art should not be admissible in strict liability cases since the evidence focuses the jury's attention on the manufacturer's conduct in choosing the

---

[213] According to Arizona courts, "[a]lthough the customs of an industry may be relevant, because those customs may lag behind technological development, they are not identical with state of the art. . . . [C]ustom refers to what was being done in the industry; state of the art refers to what feasibly could have been done." Bauerline v. Equity Residential Properties Management Corp., 2006 U.S. Dist. LEXIS 94182, at *8 (D. Ariz. Dec. 29, 2006) (applying Arizona law).

[214] *See* Ariz. Rev. Stat. § 12-681(10); Potter v. Chicago Pneumatic Tool Co., 694 A.2d 1319, 1346 (Conn. 1997). Although the Indiana Product Liability Act does not define "state-of-the-art," Indiana courts have defined the term to mean "the best technology reasonably feasible" at the time the defendant designed, manufactured, packaged, or labeled the product. Wade v. Terex-Telelect, Inc., 966 N.E.2d 186, 192 (Ind. Ct. App. 2012).

[215] South Dakota recognizes that evidence of industry standards is proper as a state of the art defense. Cullison v. Hilti, Inc., 2011 U.S. Dist. LEXIS 137663 (D.S.D. Nov. 28, 2011) (applying South Dakota law). In Indiana, a jury can consider (1) evidence of the existing level of technology, (2) industry standards; (3) the lack of other advanced technology; and (4) the product's safety record, and the lack of prior accidents. Bourke v. Ford Motor Co., 2007 U.S. Dist. LEXIS 15871 (N.D. Ind. Mar. 5, 2007) (applying Indiana law).

[216] 966 N.E.2d 186 (Ind. Ct. App. 2012).

[217] Potter v. Chicago Pneumatic Tool Co., 694 A.2d at 1346–47.

design. Although some courts take the position that state-of-the-art is not a defense to strict liability,[218] the majority of courts have rejected that argument and hold that state-of-the-art evidence is relevant to helping the jury determine whether the product was defective and unreasonably dangerous.[219] This applies both in cases using the consumer expectations test and risk-utility analysis.[220]

The most difficult question for courts has been how to treat evidence of the state-of-the- art. In some states, proof that the product conformed with the state-of-the-art when it first was sold is a complete defense to a defective design claim.[221] New Jersey has codified the state-of-the-art defense in a provision that states:

> In any products liability action against a manufacturer or seller for harm allegedly caused by a product that was designed in a defective manner, the manufacturer or seller shall not be liable if:
>
> (1) At the time the product left the control of the manufacturer, there was not a practical and technically feasible alternative design that would have prevented the harm without substantially impairing the reasonably antici- pated or intended function of the product.[222]

At the same time, however, New Jersey holds that the state-of-the-art defense is not applicable if a court finds, by clear and convincing evidence, that:

(1)   The product is egregiously unsafe or ultra-hazardous;

(2)   The ordinary user or consumer of the product cannot reasonably be expected to have knowledge of the product's risks, or the product poses a risk of serious injury to persons other than the user or consumer; and

(3)   The product has little or no usefulness.[223]

Other states take the position that compliance with the state-of-the-art does not entitle the manufacturer of a judgment in its favor. In Indiana, for example, there is a rebuttable presumption that a product was not defective if, before the sale by the manufacturer, the product: (1) was in conformity with the generally recognized state-of–the-art applicable to the safety of the product at the time the product was designed manufactured, packaged or labeled; or (2) complied with applicable codes, standards, regulations, or specifications established, adopted, promulgated, or

---

[218] *See* Green v. Kubota Tractor Corp., 2012 U.S. Dist. LEXIS 56770 (N.D. Ill. Apr. 24, 2012) (applying Illinois law).

[219] Potter v. Chicago Pneumatic Tool Co., 694 A.2d at 1347.

[220] *Id.* at 1348.

[221] *See* Ariz. Rev. Stat. § 12-683(1); Iowa Code § 668.12; Bernal v. Daewoo Motor America, Inc., 2011 U.S. Dist. LEXIS 58918 (D. Ariz. June 2, 2011). A South Dakota statute (S.D. Codified Laws § 20-9-10.1) provides that conformity with the prevailing state of the art existing at the time a product first was sold may be considered in determining whether a product was in a defective condition or unreasonably dangerous.

[222] N.J. Stat. Ann. § 2A:58C-3(a).

[223] N.J. Stat. Ann. § 2A:58C-3b.

approved by the United States or Indiana.[224]

This presumption arose in response to complaints by manufacturers that courts were giving insufficient weight to their compliance with government safety standards. As a result, the presumption is mandatory and, unless rebutted, allows the conclusion that the manufacturer was not negligent. In order to overcome the presumption, the plaintiff must show that the reasonably prudent manufacturer would have taken additional precautions even though the product complied with government regulations.[225]

---

[224] IND. CODE § 34-20-5-1. *See also* KY. REV. STAT. § 411.310(2).

[225] Schultz v. Ford Motor Co., 822 N.E.2d 645 (Ind. Ct. App. 2005).

Chapter 6

MANUFACTURING DEFECTS

SYNOPSIS

§ 6.01 MANUFACTURING DEFECTS

[A] Deviation from the Design

[B] Manufacturing Defects and Design Defects

§ 6.02 THE DIVERSITY OF MANUFACTURING DEFECTS

[A] Types of Manufacturing Defects

[B] Testing and Inspection

[C] Labeling and Packaging

§ 6.03 NEGLIGENT AND STRICT LIABILITY MANUFACTURE

[A] Negligence

[B] Strict Liability

§ 6.04 TESTS FOR DETERMINING A MANUFACTURING DEFECT

[A] Consumer Expectations Test

[B] Rejection of the Risk-Utility Analysis

§ 6.05 FOOD AND DRINK CASES

[A] Foreign-Natural Test

[B] Consumer Expectations Test

[C] Hybrid Test

[D] Proof of a Food Defect

§ 6.01 MANUFACTURING DEFECTS

[A] Deviation from the Design

Even if a product is designed properly, it still may be unreasonably dangerous due to a defect that arose during the manufacturing process. The archetypal example of such a defect is *MacPherson v. Buick Motor Co.*,[1] the first case in which a court permitted a plaintiff to recover for a manufacturing defect using ordinary negligence principles. In that case, the plaintiff did not allege that his injury was due to a design that made all Buick automobiles defective. Instead, he claimed that the particular Buick automobile that he purchased was defective because one of its

---

[1] 111 N.E. 1050 (N.Y. 1916).

wheels was manufactured with defective wood that caused the spokes to crumble. Similarly, the basis of the plaintiff's suit in *Escola v. Coca-Cola Bottling Co.*[2] was not that the design of Coca-Cola bottles was defective. Instead, the plaintiff alleged that her injuries were caused either by excessive gas in the particular bottle that exploded and injured her or by the manufacturer's negligence in failing to detect a weakness in that bottle before it refilled it.

In contrast to the complexity of a design defect, courts have referred to a manufacturing defect as "a fairly straightforward concept"[3] and stated that defining the standard and meaning of such a defect is "relatively easy."[4] The reason for this is that, unlike a design defect, which results from a condition in the product that was intended by the manufacturer and is present in every unit of the product model, a manufacturing defect is "a physical departure from a product's intended design"[5] that usually is random and affects only one or a small percentage of the products of a specific design.[6] Unless the product has been destroyed,[7] a manufacturing defect usually can be shown by an objective standard: comparing the particular product that caused the plaintiff's injuries with the manufacturer's own design specifications for that product or with a product from the same manufacturer produced according to the design.[8] This "deviation from the design" test has been adopted as the definition of a manufacturing defect by courts and by products liability statutes:

> A product is defective in manufacture or construction if, when it left the control of its manufacturer, it deviated in a material way from the design specifications, formula, or performance standards of the manufacturer, or from otherwise identical units manufactured to the same design specifications, formula, or performance standards. A product may be defective in manufacture or construction as described in this section even though its manufacturer exercised all possible care in its manufacture or construction.[9]

---

[2] 150 P.2d 436 (Cal. 1944). For a more recent version of *Escola*, see Lee v. Crookston Coca-Cola Bottling Co., 188 N.W. 2d 426 (Minn. 1971).

[3] Jones v. Amazing Products, Inc., 231 F. Supp. 2d 1228, 1236 (N.D. Ga. 2002) (applying Georgia law).

[4] O'Brien v. Muskin Corp., 463 A.2d 298, 304 (N.J. 1983).

[5] RESTATEMENT (THIRD) OF TORTS: PRODUCTS LIABILITY § 1 cmt. *a* (1998).

[6] Wood v. Old Trapper Taxi, 952 P.2d 1375 (Mont. 1997).

[7] The difficulty of proving a manufacturing defect when the product is not available for inspection by either party is illustrated by Ford Motor Co. v. Gonzalez, 9 S.W.3d 195 (Tex. App. 1999). *See* Creazzo v. Medtronic, Inc., 903 A.2d 24, 30 (Pa. 2006) ("a claim of manufacturing defect is untenable in the absence of the product itself.").

[8] In Myrlak v. Port Authority of N.Y. and N.J., 723 A.2d 45, 51 (N.J. 1999), the New Jersey supreme court defined a manufacturing defect as a deviation "from the design specifications, formulae, or performance standards of the manufacturer or from otherwise identical units manufactured to the same manufacturing specifications or formulae." (quoting the New Jersey Products Liability Act, N.J. STAT. ANN. § 2A:58C-2a). For similar definitions of a manufacturing defect, *see* Godoy *ex rel.* Gramling v. E.I. Du Pont de Nemours & Co., 768 N.W.2d 674 (Wis. 2009); Ford Motor Co. v. Ledesma, 242 S.W.3d 32 (Tex. 2007); Dierks v. Mitsubishi Motors Corp., 256 Cal. Rptr. 230 (Cal. 1989); Donegal Mut. Ins. v. White Consol. Indus., 852 N.E.2d 215 (Ohio Ct. App. 2006).

[9] OHIO REV. CODE ANN. § 2307.74. *See* Thompson v. Sunbeam Prods., 2011 U.S. Dist. LEXIS 110677

An example of a court's use of the deviation test is *In re Coordinated Latex Glove Litigation*[10] in which the plaintiff alleged that the latex gloves she used at work contained natural or artificial substances that caused her to suffer latex allergies. Although the jury found a manufacturing defect and awarded the plaintiff compensatory damages, the trial court judge granted the manufacturer's post-trial motion for judgment notwithstanding the verdict (JNOV). The California appellate court held that the trial judge properly granted the motion since the gloves "did not differ from the manufacturer's intended result, nor did they have materially significant differences among identical units from the same product line."[11] The Restatement (Third) also adopts the deviation from design test by stating that a product has a manufacturing defect "when the product departs from its intended design even though all possible care was exercised in the preparation and marketing of the product."[12] In *Wright v. Brooke Group Ltd.*,[13] in which the Iowa Supreme Court adopted § 2 and then held that a "plaintiff may not recover from a cigarette manufacturer under a manufacturing defect theory when the cigarettes smoked by the plaintiff were in the condition intended by the manufacturer."[14]

[B] Manufacturing Defects and Design Defects

Most of the early products liability cases involved only claims of manufacturing defects. Although manufacturing defects remain a source of litigation, in recent years the number of appellate court decisions involving only a manufacturing defect has been eclipsed by design and failure to warn cases.[15] In part this is because, unless the product was destroyed, it often is fairly easy to determine whether the product deviated from the manufacturer's intent. The elaborate debates over the risks and benefits of the product and alternative products that characterize design defect and failure to warn cases, and which have moved those cases away from strict liability and toward a negligence analysis, are not present in manufacturing defect cases. In manufacturing defect cases, the design and identical products can be used to show that the particular product was defective. As a result, if a product did not conform to its intended design, the manufacturer

---

(S.D. Ohio Sept. 28, 2011) (applying Ohio law); Zavala v. Burlington Northern Santa Fe Corp., 355 S.W.3d 359, 368 (Tex. Ct. App. 2011). In Barker v. Lull Engineering Co., 573 P.2d 443, 454 (Cal. 1978), the California Supreme Court stated:

> In general, a manufacturing or production defect is readily identifiable because a defective product is one that differs from the manufacturer's intended result or from other ostensibly identical units of the same product line. For example, when a product comes off the assembly line in a substandard condition it has incurred a manufacturing defect.

See also Freeman v. Hoffman-La Roche, Inc., 618 N.W.2d 827 (Neb. 2000); Corcoran v. Sears, Roebuck and Co., 711 A.2d 371 (N.J. Super. Ct. App. Div. 1998).

[10] 121 Cal. Rptr. 2d 301 (Ct. App. 2002).

[11] *Id.* at 316.

[12] RESTATEMENT (THIRD) OF TORTS: PRODUCTS LIABILITY § 2(a) (1998). Comment c to § 2 goes on to state that "a manufacturing defect is a departure from a product's unit design specifications."

[13] 652 N.W.2d 159 (Iowa 2002).

[14] *Id.* at 178.

[15] For a case in which the plaintiff alleged only a manufacturing defect, see Montez v. Ford Motor Co., 161 Cal. Rptr. 578 (Ct. App. 1980).

usually will settle the case or will contest only the issue of damages, unless it believes that the defect was not, in fact, a cause of the injury.

Another reason for the decline of cases alleging only a manufacturing defect is the sophistication of modern products. In many cases, it is difficult to determine whether the defective condition that caused the plaintiff's injury was due only to a manufacturing defect or whether it was due to the design, manufacture, or failure to warn of the dangers. As a result, plaintiffs usually allege some combination of all three theories in separate counts in their complaints.[16]

The difficulty of determining whether an injury was due to a manufacturing defect or to a design defect was discussed by the court in *In re Coordinated Latex Glove Litigation*.[17] After holding that the trial judge properly granted a JNOV to the plaintiff's claim that the latex gloves she used at work contained a manufacturing defect, the California appellate court discussed the close relationship between manufacturing and design defects and the difficulty of distinguishing between the two. For example, a defect that results from the failure of a quality control technique intended to determine the rate of flaws in a particular product may be characterized as a manufacturing defect. However, the manufacturer's choice as to the particular type of quality control technique to use frequently is made on the basis of cost considerations and thus is analogous to the choice of one design over another. This makes it difficult to distinguish the particular source of the defect.[18] As in other latex glove litigation, the plaintiffs' theories had "aspects common to both the design defect and manufacturing defect theories" in that "the materials from which the latex gloves were made contained excessive amounts of latex rubber proteins close to the surface of the gloves, causing the plaintiffs to become sensitized to them and to develop or to exacerbate an existing allergy."[19] Because determining the source of the allergic reactions involved the science of the manufacturing and preparation procedures, as well as the medical aspects of an individual's allergic reactions to various substances, the court concluded that it was useless to focus on a distinction between the raw materials from which the product was made and the actual construction of the product itself for purposes of determining whether the defect was the result of design or manufacture.[20]

---

[16] An early example of a plaintiff alleging both a design and a manufacturing defect is Greenman v. Yuba Power Products, Inc., 377 P.2d 897 (Cal. 1963). For other examples, see Medtronic v. Lohr, 518 U.S. 470 (1996); Transue v. Aesthetech Corp., 341 F.3d 911 (9th Cir. 2003) (applying California law); Mohammad v. Toyota Motor Sales, U.S.A., 947 A.2d 598 (Md. Ct. Spec. App. 2008).

[17] 121 Cal. Rptr. 2d 301 (Ct. App. 2002).

[18] *Id.* at 311 (citing 1 MARSHALL SHAPO, THE LAW OF PRODUCTS LIABILITY ¶ 9.01(2), at 9-5 to 9-6 (3d ed. 1994)).

[19] *Id.* quoting Morson v. Superior Court, 109 Cal. Rptr. 2d 343, 354 (Ct. App. 2001).

[20] *Id.*

§ 6.02   THE DIVERSITY OF MANUFACTURING DEFECTS

[A]   Types of Manufacturing Defects

As the cases in the last section illustrate, manufacturing defects can arise in products as diverse as automobiles, soft drink bottles, work gloves, and cigarettes.[21] Because the production process often involves the integration of a large number of component parts and equipment with human labor and skill, there are countless opportunities for mistakes to occur, even if the manufacturer adopts the most rigorous quality-control system.[22] Defects in finished products can result from:

- the raw materials or the component parts used in the product;[23]

- human or mechanical error in assembling the components of the product,[24]

- human or mechanical error in manufacturing the product;[25]

- missing parts in the product;[26]

- foreign objects in the product,[27]

- impure ingredients in the product.[28]

Although most manufacturing defects originate at the factory during the manufacturing process itself, they also can arise after shipment. In such a situation, the Restatement (Third) states that the commercial distributor or seller of the product is liable as if the product had been manufactured defectively.[29] This

---

[21] In recent years, cases have raised the question whether individual sperm donors and sperm banks may be liable for "manufacturing" defective sperm. *See* Jennifer M. Vagle, NOTE: *Putting the "Product" in Reproduction: The Viability of a Products Liability Action for Genetically Defective Sperm*, 38 PEPP. L. REV. 1175 (2011).

[22] *See* John W. Wade, *On the Nature of Strict Tort Liability for Products*, 44 MISS. L.J. 825, 825 (1973) ("The prototype [products liability] case was that in which something went wrong in the manufacturing process, so that the product had a loose screw or a defective or missing part or a deleterious element, and was not the safe product it was intended to be.").

[23] Bell v. T.R. Miller Mill Co., Inc., 768 So.2d 953 (Ala. 2000); Magnuson v. Kelsey-Hayes Co., 844 S.W.2d 448 (Mo. Ct. App. 1992). *See* Lewis L. Laska, *What Every Personal Injury Lawyer Should Know About Nanotechnoogy*, TRIAL (Sept. 2012), 26.

[24] Jenkins v. General Motors Corp., 446 F.2d 377 (5th Cir. 1971) (applying Georgia law); Price v. Wilson Sporting Goods Co., 2005 U.S. Dist. LEXIS 35739 (D. Colo. July 18, 2005) (applying Colorado law); DeWitt v. Eveready Battery Co., 565 S.E.2d 140 (N.C. 2002); USX Corp. v. Salinas, 818 S.W.2d 473 (Tex. App. 1991).

[25] Keeler v. Richards Manufacturing Co., Inc., 817 F.2d 1197 (5th Cir. 1987) (applying Texas law); Doupnik v. General Motors Corp., 275 Cal. Rptr. 715 (Ct. App. 1990).

[26] Yamaha Motor Co., Ltd. v. Thornton, 579 So. 2d 619 (Ala. 1991); Morris v. Chrysler Corp., 303 N.W.2d 500 (Neb. 1981).

[27] See the discussion of these defects in the context of food and drink cases at § 6.05, *infra. See also* Glover v. BIC Corp., 6 F.3d 1318 (9th Cir. 1993) (applying Oregon law).

[28] See the discussion of these defects in the context of food and drink cases at § 6.05, *infra. See also* Van Wyk v. Norden Laboratories, 345 N.W.2d 81 (Iowa 1984).

[29] RESTATEMENT (THIRD) OF TORTS: PRODUCTS LIABILITY § 2 (1998).

is because the test for strict liability under the Restatement (Third) is whether "the product was defective when it left the hands of the given seller in the distributive chain."[30]

[B] Testing and Inspection

Two important aspects of the manufacturing process that can result in defects in a product are the testing and inspection of a product before it is distributed and the labeling and packaging of a product. The failure to test arises in two types of situations: first, where adequate tests for defects were not conducted either during or after the production process and a product containing a defect was placed on the market and, second, where the particular product was not defective but the properties of the product in general were not tested adequately before it was placed on the market.[31] The extent of testing and inspecting that a manufacturer must perform is an issue where the necessary equipment and processes require considerable time and expense. In negligence cases, courts have held that manufacturers have a duty to conduct those tests and inspections that are reasonably necessary to ensure that the product is safe.[32] In order to establish what tests or inspections are reasonably necessary, the plaintiff must establish a standard of care and show the manufacturer's deviation from it.[33] The standard of care may be based on the industry-wide custom of testing or inspections, the past practices of the manufacturer, or expert testimony.[34] However, in order to succeed, the plaintiff must establish not only what tests or inspections should have been performed but that those tests or inspections would have detected the defect.[35] Although most testing and inspection cases involve manufacturers, a seller also may be liable if it is customary to inspect the particular product, such as an automobile, prior to delivering it to the buyer.[36]

---

[30] *Id.* at cmt. *c.*

[31] Borel v. Fiberboard Paper Products Corp., 493 F.2d 1076 (5th Cir. 1973) (applying Texas law); Ford Motor Co. v. Zahn, 265 F.2d 729 (8th Cir. 1959) (applying Minnesota law); Mercer v. Pittway Corp., 616 N.W.2d 602 (Iowa 2000). Oregon defines a "product liability civil action" as "a civil action brought against a manufacturer, distributor, seller or lessor of a product for damages for personal injury, death or property damage arising out of: (1) Any design, inspection, testing, manufacturing or other defect in a product." Or. Rev. Stat. § 30.900. However, in Branham v. Ford Motor Co., 701 S.E.2d 5 (S.C. 2010), the court has held that, in South Carolina, there is no separate "failure to test claim" apart from the duty to design and manufacture a product that is not defective and unreasonably dangerous.

[32] Nicklaus v. Hughes Tool Co., 417 F.2d 983 (8th Cir. 1969) (according to the court, it was not necessary to determine whether the law of California, the place of manufacturing and testing, or Arkansas, the place of the accident, applied in the case, since there was no significant difference in the law of the two states that was applicable to the case); Lindquist v. Ayerst Laboratories, Inc., 607 P.2d 1339 (Kan. 1980).

[33] Scittarelli v. The Providence Gas Co., 415 A.2d 1040 (R.I. 1980).

[34] *See* Bogosian v. Mercedes-Benz of North America, Inc., 104 F.3d 472 (1st Cir. 1996) (applying Rhode Island law); 1836 Callowhill St. v. Johnson Controls, Inc., 819 F. Supp. 460 (E.D. Pa. 1993) (applying Pennsylvania law); West v. Broderick & Bascom Rope Co., 197 N.W.2d 202 (Iowa 1972).

[35] Messer v. Amway Corp., 2004 U.S. App. LEXIS 16445 (10th Cir. Aug. 10, 2004) (applying Kansas law); Weiss v. Chrysler Motors Corp., 515 F.2d 449 (5th Cir. 1975).

[36] Langford v. Chrysler Motors Corp., 513 F.2d 1121 (2d Cir. 1975) (applying New York law); Bass v. General Motors Corp., 447 S.W.2d 443 (Tex. App. 1968).

[C] Labeling and Packaging

A product also may be defective because of the labeling and packaging used for its distribution. Examples of this are a number of cases in which glass soft drink or beer bottles exploded in the hands of those who had purchased them or who were stacking them in restaurants.[37] Comment *h* to § 402A sets out the reasons for imposing liability for defective packaging:

> No reason is apparent for distinguishing between the product itself and the container in which it is supplied; and the two are purchased by the user or consumer as an integrated whole. Where the container is itself dangerous, the product is sold in a defective condition. Thus a carbonated beverage in a bottle which is so weak or cracked, or jagged at the edges, or bottled under such excessive pressure that it may explode or otherwise cause harm to the person who handles it, is in a defective and dangerous condition. The container cannot logically be separated from the contents where the two are sold as a unit, and the liability stated in this section arises not only when the consumer drinks the beverage and is poisoned by it, but also when he is injured by the bottle while he is handling it in preparatory to consumption.

Packaging cases are as diverse as the products they contain.[38] Many of the labeling and packaging cases involve the containers in which chemicals are sold.[39] Although manufacturers owe a duty of care to those who purchase or work near chemicals to exercise reasonable care in packaging them,[40] the issue in many of these cases has not been whether the chemicals were packaged in a reasonable manner but whether the claim of negligent packaging was preempted by federal statutes.[41]

---

[37] *See* Bredberg v. Pepsico, 551 N.W.2d 321 (Iowa 1996); Van Duzer v. Shoshone Coca Cola Bottling Co., 741 P.2d 811 (Nev. 1987); Falstaff Brewing Corp. v. Williams, 234 So. 2d 620 (Miss. 1970); Escola v. Coca-Cola Bottling Co., 150 P.2d 436 (Cal. 1944).

[38] Welge v. Planters Lifesavers Co., 17 F.3d 209 (7th Cir. 1994) (applying Illinois law) (glass jar containing peanuts); McGregor v. The Scotts Co., LLC, 2011 U.S. Dist. LEXIS 87412 (E.D. Mo. Aug. 8, 2011) (applying Missouri law) (bag of potting soil containing a snake); Corbin v. Camden Coca-Cola Bottling Co., 290 A.2d 441 (N.J. 1972) (carton containing soft-drink bottles); Tenaglia v. Procter & Gamble, Inc., 737 A.2d 306 (Pa. Super. Ct. 1999) (cardboard box of diapers); Martin v. Burger King, 1998 Mass. Super. LEXIS 607 (Oct. 9, 1998) (packages in which french fries were sold).

[39] Chandler v. Moreland Chemical Co., 154 S.E.2d 502 (N.C. 1967).

[40] Waering v. BASF Corp., 146 F. Supp. 2d 675 (M.D. Pa. 2001) (applying Pennsylvania law).

[41] See the Federal Insecticide, Fungicide and Rodenticide Act (FIFRA), 7 U.S.C. §§ 136-136y, and the Hazardous Materials Transportation Act, 49 U.S.C. § 5125. *See also* Hawkins v. Leslie's Pool Mart, Inc., 184 F.3d 244 (3d Cir. 1999); Jeffers v. Wal-Mart Stores, Inc., 171 F. Supp. 2d 617 (S.D.W. Va. 2001); Lucas v. Bio-Lab, Inc., 108 F. Supp. 2d 518 (E.D. Va. 2000); Lyall v. Leslie's Poolmart, 984 F. Supp. 587 (E.D. Mich. 1997).

§ 6.03　NEGLIGENT AND STRICT LIABILITY MANUFACTURE

As in design defect cases, a plaintiff can bring a manufacturing defect case based upon an allegation of negligence and/or strict liability. In order to establish a *prima facie* case under either theory, a plaintiff must establish:[42] (1) a defect in the manufacture of the product that made it unreasonably dangerous;[43] (2) the defect existed at the time the product left the control of the manufacturer or seller;[44] (3) the defect was the cause in fact and proximate cause of the plaintiff's injuries.[45] In addition, in a negligence action, the plaintiff must prove not only that there was a manufacturing defect but also that the defect was the result of the failure of the defendant to exercise reasonable skill and care in the manufacturing process.[46] One advantage of alleging both negligence and strict liability in a manufacturing defect case is that, if the manufacturer is found to be not liable under one of the theories, it still may be liable under the other.

[A]　Negligence

There is little distinction between a negligent manufacturing claim and other types of common law negligence.[47] A plaintiff must establish first that the manufacturer owed him or her a duty of care. A duty arises if the nature of the product is such that it is reasonably certain to endanger human life if it is not manufactured properly and the plaintiff was the purchaser or a foreseeable user of the product. The plaintiff also must prove that the manufacturer's fault, *that is*, it failed to use reasonable skill and care in the construction, testing, or inspection of the product, and that the defect in the product that resulted from the lack of due care was the cause-in-fact as well as the proximate cause of his or her injuries.[48] The standard of care by which the manufacturer's conduct is measured in a negligence case is that of a reasonably prudent manufacturer.[49] In *MacPherson v. Buick Motor Co.*,[50] Judge Cardozo stated that the manufacturer owed the user of the automobile a duty since the very nature of an automobile is a warning that, unless its wheels are constructed properly, injury is almost certain to occur. The standard of reasonable care in the manufacture of products was reflected in § 395 of the Restatement of Torts, adopted in 1934, which has been carried over into the

---

[42] Johnson v. Michelin Tire Corp., 812 F.2d 200 (5th Cir. 1987) (applying Texas law); Myrlak v. Port Authority of N.Y. and N.J., 723 A.2d 45 (N.J. 1999); State Farm Fire & Casualty Co. v. Chrysler Corp., 523 N.E.2d 489 (Ohio 1988).

[43] Mixon v. Chrysler Corp., 663 S.W.2d 713 (Ark. 1984).

[44] Welge v. Planters Lifesavers Co., 17 F.3d 209 (7th Cir. 1994) (applying Illinois law); Kerr v. Corning Glass Works, 169 N.W.2d 587 (Minn. 1969).

[45] Johnson v. Michelin Tire Corp., 812 F.2d 200 (5th Cir. 1987) (applying Texas law); Lee v. Crookston Coca-Cola Bottling Co., 188 N.W.2d 426 (Minn. 1971).

[46] Larsen v. General Motors Corp., 391 F.2d 495 (8th Cir. 1968) (applying Minnesota law).

[47] Doe v. Solvay Pharmacies, Inc., 350 F. Supp. 2d 257 (D. Me. 2004) (applying Maine law).

[48] Pouncey v. Ford Motor Co., 464 F.2d 957 (5th Cir. 1972) (applying Alabama law); Willis v. Floyd Brace Co., 309 S.E.2d 295 (S.C. Ct. App. 1983).

[49] Holder v. Keller Industries, Inc., 2000 Tex. App. LEXIS 910 (Feb. 9, 2000).

[50] 111 N.E. 1050 (N.Y. 1916).

Restatement (Second) of Torts, adopted in 1965. That section provides in part:

> A manufacturer who fails to exercise reasonable care in the manufacture of a chattel which, unless carefully made, he should recognize as involving an unreasonable risk of causing physical harm to those who use it . . . is subject to liability for physical harm caused to them by its lawful use in a manner and for a purpose for which it is supplied.[51]

Because of the difficulties of proving that a manufacturing defect in a product was the result of a breach of a duty on the part of the manufacturer, even with the help of the doctrine of *res ipsa loquitur*, most plaintiffs bring their manufacturing defect claims in strict liability as well as negligence.

[B] Strict Liability

Section 402A provides for strict liability when a product is in a "defective condition unreasonably dangerous to the user or consumer" and applies it even though the manufacturer or seller "has exercised all possible care in the preparation" of the product. The Restatement (Third) goes beyond § 402A and asks only whether the manufacturing defect departed from the product's "intended design."[52] Comment *a* to § 2 states that imposing strict liability for a manufacturing defect that departs from the "intended design" furthers several broad objectives. First, it encourages manufacturers to invest more in product safety than does a system based on negligence. Second, strict liability discourages the use of defective products by making the purchase price of such products reflect the cost of the defect. Third, plaintiffs often have difficulty proving that a manufacturing defect was due to negligence. Strict liability helps plaintiffs overcome the difficulties in proving fault by performing a function similar to *res ipsa loquitur*. Finally, strict liability helps promote the fulfillment of reasonable consumer expectations.[53]

§ 6.04   TESTS FOR DETERMINING A MANUFACTURING DEFECT

[A] Consumer Expectations Test

Definitions of a manufacturing defect are based on the idea that such a defect is a deviation from the intended design of the product. However, these definitions do not state how to determine whether the deviation from the design is so serious as to make the product unreasonably dangerous for purposes of liability. Although manufacturers sometimes attempt to convince courts to adopt a risk-benefit analysis to determine whether the manufacturing defect is actionable, state courts, in keeping with § 402A, comment *g*, use the consumer expectations test in

---

[51] RESTATEMENT (SECOND) OF TORTS § 395 (1965).

[52] RESTATEMENT (THIRD) OF TORTS: PRODUCTS LIABILITY § 2(a) (1998).

[53] RESTATEMENT (THIRD) OF TORTS: PRODUCTS LIABILITY § 2 cmt. *a* (1998).

manufacturing defect cases.[54] According to one court, the reason for the continuing use of this test is that

> [m]anufacturing defect cases involve products which are flawed, i.e., which do not conform to the manufacturer's own specifications, and are not identical to their mass-produced siblings. The flaw theory is based upon a fundamental consumer expectancy: that a mass-produced product will not differ from its siblings in a manner that makes it more dangerous than the others.[55]

The consumer expectations test requires the consumer to show that, at the time the product left the seller's hands, it was "in a condition not contemplated by the ultimate consumer, which will be unreasonably dangerous to him." Thus, a product is defective only if it does not meet the safety standards existing at the time of sale or reasonable consumer expectations held at the time of sale.[56] Even those states that have adopted the risk-utility analysis for design defect and failure-to-warn cases retain the consumer expectations test in manufacturing defect cases. An example of the consumer expectations test is *Ridgway v. Ford Motor Co.*,[57] in which the plaintiff suffered severe burns when his truck burst into flames while he was driving it. In his action against the manufacturer of the truck, the plaintiff alleged both negligence and strict liability due to a manufacturing defect in the fuel system and/or the electrical system. In reversing the grant of summary judgment on the plaintiff's strict liability claim, the Texas appellate court stated: "The manufacturing defect theory is based upon a consumer expectancy that a mass-produced product will not differ from its counterparts in a manner which makes it more dangerous than the others."[58]

Crucial to the consumer expectations test is that the product was being used as intended at the time of the injury. In *Fitzgerald Marine Sales v. LeUnes*,[59] the plaintiff alleged that a defect in the manufacture of the steering wheel of his motorboat was the cause of his injury. The plaintiff and another man were riding in the boat when it took a sharp turn to the right. The plaintiff attempted to use the steering wheel as a restrain but it broke in his hand and he was thrown into the water. In his suit against the boat manufacturer, the plaintiff alleged that the steering wheel was unreasonably dangerous because it was not strong enough to prevent him from being thrown into the water. The jury was instructed that a product is "unreasonably dangerous" when it is "dangerous to an extent beyond that which would be contemplated by the ordinary user of the product, with the

---

[54] *See, e. g.*, Branham v. Ford Motor Co., 701 S.E.2d 5 (S.C. 2010).

[55] Ford Motor Co. v. Pool, 688 S.W. 2d 879, 881 (Tex. App. 1985), *aff'd in part and rev'd in part*, 715 S.W.2d 629 (Tex. 1986).

[56] Robinson v. S.D. Brandtjen & Kluge, Inc., 500 F.3d 691 (8th Cir. 2007) (applying South Dakota law). The Kansas Product Liability Act (KAN. STAT. ANN. § 60-3304(a)) provides that when an injury-causing product was in compliance with regulatory safety standards, the product is not defective unless "a reasonably prudent product seller could and would have taken additional precautions." *See* Newton v. Standard Candy Co., 2008 U.S. Dist. LEXIS 69183 (D. Neb. Sept. 12, 2008) (applying Kansas law).

[57] 82 S.W.3d 26 (Tex. App. 2002).

[58] *Id.* at 30.

[59] 659 S.W.2d 917 (Tex. App. 1983).

ordinary knowledge common to the community of such users as to the product's characteristics."[60] The Texas court looked to the "purpose of a steering wheel on a motorboat" and said that it was to steer the boat, not to serve as a restraining device. Since there was no evidence that the steering wheel was unreasonably dangerous for its intended purpose of steering the boat, the court held that the steering wheel was not defective as a matter of law.[61]

Although the consumer expectations test has been criticized widely in design defect and failure-to-warn cases, and has been replaced by the risk-utility analysis by states and by the Restatement (Third), the test has been retained for manufacturing defects. The reason for this, according to one critic, is that

> [t]he consumer expectations test for strict liability operates effectively when the product defect is a construction or manufacturing defect. . . . An internal standard exists against which to measure the product's condition — the manufacturer's own design standard. In essence, a product flawed in manufacture frustrates the manufacturer's own design objectives. Liability is imposed on manufacturers in these cases even if the manufacturer shows it acted reasonably in making the product.[62]

[B] Rejection of the Risk-Utility Analysis

Although courts have not adopted the risk-utility analysis in manufacturing defect cases, this has not stopped some manufacturers using it in negligence cases in an attempt to show that the risk of injury was low enough that their manufacturing process was reasonable. An example of this is *Ford Motor Co. v. Zahn*,[63] in which the plaintiff was a passenger in an automobile. When the driver applied the brakes suddenly to avoid a collision, the plaintiff was thrown forward, causing his head to hit the dashboard ash-tray. The plaintiff alleged that the ash-tray was defective because its upper right-hand corner was sharp and it had a jagged protrusion, caused by a dull cutting die. The manufacturer argued that the sampling process used to inspect the ash-trays was not negligent because of the nature, position, and size of the defect and because the foreseeability of the occurrence and the injury were low. According to the manufacturer, the only harm that could be anticipated from the defect was a cut finger or torn clothes and that since, the foreseeable risk was low, its inspection was reasonable. The Eighth Circuit, however, rejected the manufacturer's argument and affirmed the jury's verdict for the plaintiff. According to the court, while the risk of danger from the defective ash tray was not as great as other risks, the plaintiff did suffer a serious injury. The jury was entitled to consider that automobiles are fast moving and that emergencies frequently arise which require the sudden application of the brakes that throw passengers against the dashboard.[64] Passengers expect that they will

---

[60] *Id.* at 918.

[61] *Id.*

[62] Keith Miller, *Design Defect Litigation in Iowa: The Myths of Strict Liability*, 40 Drake L. Rev. 465, 473 (1991).

[63] 265 F.2d 729 (8th Cir. 1959) (applying Minnesota law).

[64] *Id.* at 731–32.

not be injured by sharp objects on the dashboard.

§ 6.05　FOOD AND DRINK CASES

A frequent source of claims against food processors and restaurants are harmful substances in food and drink products that make them defective.[65] The basis of these claims, which can be based on breach of warranty, negligence, or strict liability,[66] is that the presence of the harm ingredient was due to a defect in the manufacture or preparation of the food products.[67] In analyzing these claims, courts use two different tests: the "foreign-natural" test and the "consumer expectations" test.

[A]　Foreign-Natural Test

The first test used by courts in cases involving harmful substances in food is the foreign-natural test. Using this test, courts distinguish between an injury caused by a harmful object or substance that is "foreign" to the food product and an injury caused by an item that is "natural" to the product. If the injury was caused by a "foreign" substance in the food, courts have no difficulty holding the manufacturer or restaurant liable for breach of warranty, negligence, or strict liability. Among the items that courts have held to be a "foreign" substance in food are: a condom in a soft drink;[68] a decomposed housefly in a soft drink;[69] a dead mouse in a soft drink bottle;[70] a decomposed human toe in chewing tobacco;[71] rocks in breakfast cereal;[72] metal in a soup can;[73] glass in ice cream;[74] and a small metal screw in chewing gum.[75] A consumer is barred, however, from recovery if the injury was caused by an object that occurs "naturally" in any ingredient in the food. Among the items that courts have held are found "naturally" in food products are a fish bone in fish chowder;[76] and a turkey bone in a creamed turkey dish.[77]

---

[65]　In this section, the word "food" is used to include both food and drink products.

[66]　Doyle v. The Pillsbury Co., 476 So. 2d 1271 (Fla. 1985).

[67]　In addition to foreign substances in food and drink products are cases involving bottles that exploded during handling. The classic example of this was Escola v. Coca-Cola Bottling Co., 150 P.2d 436 (Cal. 1944) in which the California Supreme Court expanded the doctrine of *res ipsa loquitur* a situation where the bottle had been out of the control of the defendant for a considerable period of time. Cases now are brought using strict liability. *See* Bredberg v. PepsiCo, 551 N.W.2d 321 (Iowa 1996); Tyler v. Natchitoches Coca-Cola Bottling Co., 491 So. 2d 358 (La. 1986).

[68]　Hagan v. Coca-Cola Bottling Co., 804 So.2d 1234 (Fla. 2001).

[69]　LeBlanc v. Louisiana Coca-Cola Bottling Co., 60 So.2d 873 (La. 1952).

[70]　Anderson v. Tyler, 274 N.W. 48 (Iowa 1937); Paul v. Rodgers Bottling Co., 6 Cal. Rptr. 867 (Cal Ct. App. 1960).

[71]　Pillars v. R. J. Reynolds Tobacco Co., 78 So. 365 (Miss. 1918).

[72]　Elliott v. Kraft Foods North America, Inc., 118 S.W.3d 50 (Tex. App. 2003).

[73]　Campbell Soup Co. v. Dusek, 135 So.2d 414 (Miss. 1961).

[74]　Amdal v. F. W. Woolworth Co., 84 F. Supp 657 (N.D. Iowa 1949) (applying Iowa law).

[75]　Hickman v. William Wrigley, Jr. Co., 768 So.2d 812 (La. Ct. App. 2000).

[76]　Webster v. Blue Ship Tea Room, 198 N.E.2d 309 (Mass. 1964). In defending the tradition of fish chowder and the occasional presence of fish bones in it, the judge in the case stated:

The first case to articulate the "foreign-natural" test was *Mix v. Ingersoll Candy Co.*,[78] in which a restaurant customer who ordered a chicken pot pie was injured when he swallowed a fragment of a chicken bone contained in the pie. In affirming the dismissal of the customer's complaint against the restaurant for negligence and breach of implied warranty, the California Supreme Court distinguished earlier cases where plaintiffs had been permitted to recover:

> All of the cases are instances in which the food was found not to be reasonably fit for human consumption, either by reason of the presence of a foreign substance, or an impure and noxious condition of the food itself, such as for example, glass, stones, wires or nails in food served, or tainted, decayed, diseased, or infected meats or vegetables. . . . [D]espite the fact that a chicken bone may occasionally be encountered in a chicken pie, such chicken pie, in the absence of some further defect, is reasonably fit for human consumption. Bones which are natural to the type of meant served cannot legitimately be called a foreign substance, and a consumer who eats meat dishes ought to anticipate and be on his guard against the presence of such bones. At least he cannot hold the restaurant keeper whose representation implied by law is that the meat dish is reasonably fit for human consumption, liable for any injury occurring as a result of the presence of a chicken bone in such chicken pie.[79]

Although the "foreign-natural" test has been used by many courts,[80] it has been criticized by courts and commentators on a number of grounds. First, it sometimes can be difficult to make a bright line distinction between ingredients that are "foreign" or "natural" to a product. For example, is a bone "foreign" to a meat dish or soup or is it a "natural" part of the food? This difficulty has led commentators and courts to a second criticism that there is no logical basis for treating the two types of substances differently if they cause injury.[81] According to one court, a "nutshell

---

> It is not too much to say that a person, sitting down in New England to consume a good New England fish chowder, embarks on the gustatory adventure which may entail the removal of some fish bones from his bowl as he proceeds. . . . We should be prepared to cope with the hazards of fish bones, the occasional presence of which in chowders is, it seems to us, to be anticipated, and which, in light of a hallowed tradition, do not impair their fitness or merchantability. *Id.* at 312.

[77] Goodwin v. Country Club of Peoria, 54 N.E.2d 612 (Ill. App. Ct 1944).

[78] 59 P.2d 144 (Cal. 1936). In Mexicali Rose v. Superior Court, 822 P.2d 1292, 1304 (Cal. 1992), the California Supreme Court overruled *Mix* "to the extent" that it "precludes a cause of action in negligence when injuries are caused by substances natural to the preparation of the food served."

[79] *Id.* at 148. *See also* Brown v. Nebiker, 296 N.W. 366 (Iowa 1941) (a pork chop contained a bone sliver).

[80] Webster v. Blue Ship Tea Room, 198 N.E.2d 309 (Mass. 1964); Lewis v. Handel's Homemade Ice Cream & Yogurt, 2003 Ohio App. LEXIS 3196 (June 30, 2003); Leigh A. Aughenbaugh, Note: *The Demise of the Foreign-Natural Test in North Carolina - Goodman v. Wenco Foods*, 16 Campbell L. Rev. 275, 289 (1994).

[81] According to one commentator:

> The distinction makes bad sense. It makes even worse law. If the *Mix* court were taken seriously, one is confronted by the ludicrous spectacle of the chef in the local hashhouse carefully culling the chicken chow mein to remove any ground glass, tacks or other debris he might encounter while disdainfully ignoring the serrated chicken bones therein on the assumption that the *Mix* decision immunizes him from liability.

natural to nut meat can cause as much harm as a foreign substance, such as a pebble, piece of wire or glass."[82] Courts also have criticized the "foreign-natural" test for not meeting the expectations of consumers who purchase and consume food and drink products. According to the Illinois Supreme Court:

> In an era of consumerism, the foreign-natural standard is an anachronism. It flatly and unjustifiably protects food processors and sellers from liability even when the technology may be readily available to remove injurious natural objects from foods. The consumer expectation test, on the other hand, imposes no greater burden upon processors or sellers than to guarantee that their food products meet the standards of safety that consumers customarily and reasonably have come to expect from the food industry.[83]

[B] Consumer Expectations Test

In response to the criticisms of the foreign-natural test, most states have turned to the consumer expectations test.[84] Under this test, whether the injurious substance is "foreign" or "natural" is irrelevant. Instead, liability is based on whether the consumer had a reasonable expectation that the harmful substance would not be found in the food product.[85] However, if the manufacturer or restaurant can show that the customer reasonably should have expected the substance in his food, the customer is barred from recovery.[86] A frequently cited example of the consumer expectation test is *Jackson v. Nestle-Beich, Inc.*,[87] in which the plaintiff broke a tooth on a pecan shell when she bit into a piece of chocolate-covered candy. In rejecting the foreign-natural test, the Illinois Supreme Court stated:

Mitchel J. Ezer, *The Impact of the Uniform Commercial Code on the California Law of Sales Warranties*, 8 UCLA L. REV. 281, 304 (1961). *See also* O'Dell v. De Jean's Packing co., 585 P.2d 399 (Okla. Ct. App. 1978). However, for a defense of the "foreign-natural" test, see the dissent of Justice James Heiple in Jackson v. Nestle-Beich, Inc., 589 N.W.2d 546, 552–53 (Ill. 1992).

[82] Zabner v. Howard Johnson's, Inc. 201 So. 2d 824, 826 (Fla. Dist. Ct. App. 1967).

[83] Jackson v. Nestle-Beich, Inc., 589 N.E.2d 547, 551 (Ill. 1992) (quoting Note, *Products Liability — The Test of Consumer Expectation for "Natural" Defects in Food Products*, 37 OHIO ST. L.J. 634, 651–52 (1976). In *Jackson*, the plaintiff broke his tooth on a pecan shell embedded in candy.

[84] In Yong v. Marriott Corp., 656 F. Supp. 445, 448 (D. Md. 1987) (applying Maryland law), the district court stated that the " 'reasonable expectation' test has largely displaced the natural/foreign test." *See also* Schafer v. JLC Food Systems, Inc., 695 N.W.2d 570 (Minn. 2005); Harris-Teeter, Inc. v. Burroughs, 399 S.E.2d 801 (Va. 1991); Phillips v. Town of West Springfield, 540 N.E.2d 1331 (Mass. 1989). For a discussion of the evolution from the foreign/natural test to the consumer expectations test, see Clime v. Dewey Beach Enters., 831 F. Supp. 341 (D. Del. 1993); Porteous v. St. Ann's Cafe & Deli, 713 So. 2d 454 (La. 1998).

[85] Mitchell v. Fridays, 748 N.E.2d 89 (Ohio Ct. App. 2000) (clam shell in a clam strip); Goodman v. Wenco Foods, Inc., 423 S.E.2d 444 (N.C. 1992) (bone in a hamburger); Hochberg v. O'Donnell's Restaurant, Inc., 272 A.2d 846 (D.C. 1971) (unpitted olive in a martini); Zabner v. Howard Johnson's, Inc., 201 So. 2d 824 (Fla. Dist. Ct. App. 1967) (walnut shell in maple walnut ice cream).

[86] Vitiello v. Captain Bill's Restaurant, 594 N.Y.S.2d 295 (App. Div. 1993) (customer should expect small bones in fish).

[87] 589 N.E.2d 547 (Ill. 1992).

[W]e do not find that manufacturers of products such as Nestle describes serve so important a public service that they merit treatment substantially different from that of manufacturers of other products. In this regard, we believe the consumer's reasonable expectations as to the contents of food products, as the gauge of strict liability, adequately balances consumers' interest in the defect-free products and such manufactures' interest in reasonable cost of doing business.

With an awareness of that test, consumers and their attorneys need ask themselves only one question before deciding to bring an action of this type: Would a reasonable consumer expect that a given product might contain the substance or matter causing a particular injury? . . . The test thus provides a reasonable and concrete standard to govern actions of this sort.[88]

Similarly, in *Kolarik v. Cory International Corp.*,[89] a consumer fractured a tooth when he bit down on a pit in a pimento-stuffed olive in a salad. The Iowa Supreme Court applied the consumer expectations test, stating:

[C]onsumers may develop reasonable expectations that certain components of food products in their natural state that serve to impede human consumption will be removed. Specifically, we believe that the purchaser of pimento-stuffed olives may reasonably anticipate that the olive pits have been removed.[90]

The Restatement (Third) also rejects the "foreign-natural" test and adopts the consumer expectations test for food cases. According to § 7 of the Restatement, "[o]ne engaged in the business of selling or otherwise distributing food products who sells or distributes a food product that is defective . . . is subject to liability for harm to persons or property caused by the defect." The section goes on to state that "a harm-causing ingredient of the food product constitutes a defect if a reasonable consumer would not expect the food product to contain that ingredient."[91]

---

[88] *Id.* at 550. The position adopted by the Illinois court in *Jackson* echoed the position taken thirty years earlier by the Wisconsin Supreme Court in *Betehia v. Cape Cod Corp.*, 103 N.W.2d 64, 68-69 (Wis. 1960), in which the plaintiff encountered a chicken bone in a sandwich.

> There is a distinction between what a consumer expects to find in a fish stick and in a baked or fried fish, or in a chicken sandwich made from sliced white meat and in roast chicken. The test should be what is reasonably expected by the consumer in the good as served, not what might be natural to the ingredients of that food prior to preparation. What is to be reasonably expected by the consumer is a jury question in most cases; at least we cannot say as a matter of law that a patron in a restaurant must expect a bone in a chicken sandwich wither because chicken bones are occasionally found there or are natural to chicken.

[89] 721 N.W.2d 159 (Iowa 2006). A New York court also rejected the foreign-natural test and applied the consumer expectations test (which it referred to as the "reasonable expectation" test) in the case of a restaurant patron who suffered a broken tooth as the result of an alleged injurious object in a hamburger. Rudloff v. Wendy's Restaurant of Rochester, 821 N.Y.S.2d 358 (N.Y.Sup.Ct. 2006).

[90] 721 N.W.2d at 166.

[91] The rationale for the consumer expectations test in food cases is discussed in the RESTATEMENT (THIRD) § 7 cmt. *b* (1998). *See* Schafer v. JLC Food Systems, 695 N.W.2d 570 (Minn. 2005).

[C]   Hybrid Test

Although most states use either the foreign/natural test or the consumer expectations test in food cases, California has adopted an approach that combines the two tests. In *Mexicali Rose v. Superior Court*,[92] a restaurant patron suffered throat injury after he swallowed a one-inch bone contained in an enchilada. Although the California Supreme Court rejected the "foreign-natural" test of *Mix* as the exclusive test for determining liability when a substance causes injuries, it was unwilling to adopt the pure consumer expectations test. Instead, the court said that liability should be based on the consumer's expectations within the context of the foreign-natural test. In dismissing the patron's warranty and strict liability claim, the court stated its new approach:

> If the injury-producing substance is natural to the preparation of the food served, it can be said that it was reasonably expected by its very nature and the food cannot be determined unfit or defective. A plaintiff in such a case has no cause of action in strict liability or implied warranty. If, however, the presence of the natural substance is due to a restauranteur's failure to exercise due care in food preparation, the injured patron may sue under a negligence theory.

> If the injury-causing substance is foreign to the food served, then the injured patron may also state a cause of action in implied warranty and strict liability, and the trier of fact will determine whether the substance (i) could be reasonably expected by the average consumer and (ii) rendered the food unfit or defective.[93]

[D]   Proof of a Food Defect

As with all products liability cases, a consumer in a food case must prove that the food or drink was in fact defective, that the harmful ingredient or condition existed when the product left the control of the manufacturer or seller, and that the harmful ingredient or condition was the cause of the injuries. The difficulties that a plaintiff can face in proving that food was defective and the cause of the injuries are illustrated by *Anderson v. Piccadilly Cafeteria, Inc.*,[94] in which a restaurant customer became very ill shortly after eating a fruit salad that she said was discolored and "didn't look good."[95] However, no one else who ate salads in the restaurant that day became ill and one of the customer's doctor testified that she did not have any symptom usually associated with food borne diseases. Since there was no proof that the salad was contaminated, the Louisiana court held that the customer's illness may have been due to the fact that different people reacted differently to the appearance, taste, or smell of foods, whether wholesome or contaminated. Since courts hold that an emotional response is not a basis for liability without proof that the food was harmful, the court held that the restaurant

---

[92]   822 P.2d 1292 (Cal. 1992).

[93]   *Id.* at 1303–04.

[94]   804 So. 2d 75 (La. Ct. App. 2001).

[95]   *Id.* at 76.

was not liable. Although the customer in *Anderson* was unable to recover for the reasons stated above, she had eaten some of the salad that was the subject of the litigation. If she had not, her recovery would have been barred by the "impact rule." In order to recover for physical and psychological injuries caused by food products, a plaintiff must have consumed at least a portion of the food or drink.[96] Merely seeing unwholesome food is not sufficient.[97]

Proving that the harmful condition existed at the time it left the control of the manufacturer was also can be a problem for the plaintiff. In *Shoshone Coca-Cola Bottling Co. v. Dolinski*,[98] the plaintiff suffered physical and mental distress when he partially consumed the contents of a bottle of soft drink that contained a decomposed mouse. The bottler argued that the plaintiff failed to present sufficient proof to establish that the mouse was in the bottle when it left the bottler's possession. However, the plaintiff offered the expert testimony of a toxicologist who examined the bottle and contents on the day the plaintiff drank from it. It was his opinion that the mouse "had been dead for a long time" and that the dark stains (mouse feces) that he found on the bottom of the bottle must have been there before the soft drink was added to the bottle. The jury accepted that evidence and the Nevada Supreme Court affirmed the verdict and judgment.

The requirement of proof can be a particular problem if the plaintiff is unable to identify the object in the food product that caused the injury.[99] That was the issue in *Schafer v. JLC Food Systems, Inc.*,[100] in which the plaintiff experienced a sharp pain to her throat immediately after swallowing a bite of a muffin. Although the specific cause of the pain never was found because the muffin was not saved, the Minnesota Supreme Court held that circumstantial evidence, within limits, could be used to establish to make a *prima facie* showing that the muffin was defective. The limits on the use of circumstantial evidence are:

> (1) the injury-causing event was of a kind that would ordinarily only occur as a result of a defective condition in the food product; (2) the defendant was responsible for a condition that was the cause of the injury; and (3) the injury-causing event was not caused by anything other than a food product defect existing at the time of the food product's sale.[101]

In *Schafer*, the fact that a cut was found on the plaintiff's throat immediately after the event made it more probable than not that the muffin was defective and permitted the case to be submitted to the jury.

---

[96] Coca-Cola Bottling Co. of Plainview v. White, 545 S.W.2d 279 (Tex. Civ. App. 1977).

[97] Doyle v. The Pillsbury Co., 476 So. 2d 1271 (Fla. 1985).

[98] 420 P.2d 855 (Nev. 1966).

[99] Wieland v. C. A. Swanson & Sons, 223 F.2d 26 (2d Cir. 1955); Kneibel v. RRM Enterprises, 506 N.W.2d 664 (Minn. Ct. App. 1993).

[100] 695 N.W.2d 570 (Minn. 2005).

[101] *Id.* at 17.

Chapter 7

WARNING DEFECTS

SYNOPSIS

§ 7.01 CHARACTERISTICS OF A WARNING DEFECT

    [A] Warnings and Instructions

    [B] Persons Who Have a Duty to Warn

    [C] Negligence and Strict Liability

    [D] Design Defects and the Failure to Warn

§ 7.02 WHEN A WARNING MUST BE GIVEN

    [A] Introduction

    [B] Unavoidably Unsafe Products

    [C] Open and Obvious Dangers

§ 7.03 PERSONS WHO MUST BE WARNED

    [A] Users, Consumers, and Bystanders

    [B] Persons with Allergic Reactions

    [C] Bulk Supplier/Sophisticated User/Sophisticated Supplier Doctrine

§ 7.04 ADEQUACY OF THE WARNING

    [A] Criteria for Determining the Scope and Adequacy of a Warning

    [B] Form of the Warning

    [C] Content of the Warning

§ 7.05 POST-SALE DUTY TO WARN OR RECALL

    [A] Post-Sale Duty to Warn

    [B] Product Recalls

        [1] Judicially Mandated Product Recalls

        [2] Legislative Product Recalls

§ 7.06 THE LEARNED INTERMEDIARY DOCTRINE

    [A] Origin and Scope of the Learned Intermediary Doctrine

    [B] When a Warning Must Be Given to Physicians

    [C] Adequacy of the Warning

    [D] Causation

    [E] Exceptions to the Learned Intermediary Doctrine

        [1] Mass Immunization

        [2] Oral Contraceptives and Contraceptive Devices

[3]   FDA Mandate

[4]   Direct-to-Consumer Advertising

§ 7.01   CHARACTERISTICS OF A WARNING DEFECT

[A]   Warnings and Instructions

Manufacturers have a duty to design and to manufacture products that are reasonably safe for their intended purposes and foreseeable uses. However, even if a product is not defective in its design or manufacture, it still may be unreasonably dangerous if the manufacturer fails to warn or to provide adequate warnings about a product's dangers or fails to provide instructions or to provide adequate instructions about how to use a product safely.[1] An over-the-counter medicine, for example, may be designed and manufactured in a manner that makes it safe and beneficial for use by a large number of people. At the same time, however, that medicine may cause serious side-effects if taken by certain groups of persons, such as pregnant women or those with high blood pressure, or if taken too frequently, for too long a period of time, in too large a dose, or in connection with certain other medicines. Courts have held that a manufacturer has an obligation to warn users and consumers of over-the-counter medicines directly of the foreseeable risks associated with such products and to give them adequate instructions about how to use the medicines in a safe manner.[2]

Courts often use the term "failure to warn" to include both the failure to provide adequate warnings about the dangers of a product and the failure to supply adequate instructions about a product's use.[3] The reason for this is that the purpose of both warnings and instructions is the same: to prevent a product from being unreasonably dangerous by giving consumers information about the product of which they are not aware.[4] In the case of an over-the-counter medicine, for example, a warning must inform users of any ingredients in the product that might pose an unreasonable risk of harm to certain types of persons (*i.e.*, children) or to persons with certain conditions (*i.e.*, high blood pressure). By making consumers aware of the risks, an effective warning permits them to decide whether or not the potential benefits of the medicine outweigh its risks.[5] Requiring the manufacturer to provide instructions or directions with a medicine enables consumers who use the product to do so safely and effectively by knowing the recommended dosage,

---

[1] Thompson v. Sunbeam Prods., 2011 U.S. Dist. LEXIS 110677 (S.D. Ohio Sept. 28, 2011) (applying Ohio law); Moore v. Ford Motor Co., 332 S.W.3d 749 (Mo. 2011); Flax v. Daimlerchrysler Corp., 272 S.W.3d 521 (Tenn. 2008); Lewis v. Sea Ray Boats, Inc., 65 P.3d 245 (Nev. 2003); Feldman v. Lederle Laboratories, 479 A.2d 374 (N.J. 1984). The failure to warn of a product's potential dangers when warnings are required is a type of marketing defect. Zavala v. Burlington Northern Santa Fe Corp., 355 S.W.3d 359, 374 (Tex. Ct. App. 2011).

[2] The "learned intermediary doctrine," which applies to prescription drugs, does not apply to over-the-counter medicines. For a discussion of the doctrine, see § 7.06.

[3] Delaney v. Deere and Co., 999 P.2d 930 (Kan. 2000).

[4] RESTATEMENT (SECOND) OF TORTS § 402A cmt. *j* (1965). *See* Seibel v. Symons Corp. 221 N.W.2d 50 (N.D. 1974).

[5] Ontai v. Straub Clinic and Hospital, Inc., 659 P.2d 734 (Haw. 1983).

how often to take the medicine, and what activities or other medicines to avoid while taking it.[6]

Although warnings and instructions involve different types of information about a product, there is a close relationship between the two. This is because, in some situations, a manufacturer or seller that provides a warning about the risks of the use of a product also must provide adequate instructions about how to use the product safely.[7] Similarly, a manufacturer or seller that provides instructions for the use if a product must include a warning of the risks of the failure to follow those instructions.[8] An example of this is *Midgley v. S.S. Kresge Co.*,[9] in which a store sold, under its own label, a telescope for viewing the sun. The accompanying instruction book contained a warning that stated: "Caution: Please refrain from looking up the sun [*sic*] without attaching the sun glass. Also the sun should not be seen through the finderscope."[10] However, the accompanying manual did not provide adequate instructions for the use of the telescope since it contained no diagrams or illustrations for the proper installation of the sun filer. As a result, a 13-year-old user who purchased a telescope suffered irreparable solar burn to the retina of his eye as a result of improper assembly of the sun filter on the telescope. In holding that the jury should have considered the manufacturer's liability for failure to warn under a theory of strict liability as well as negligence, the court discussed the interrelationship between instructions and a warning:

> [A] product requiring assembly and use in conformity with the supplier's directions is defective if the supplier fails to warn adequately of conditions and circumstances created by such assembly or use which would render the product dangerous to the user. Therefore, the supplier is strictly liable for injury proximately from composing and furnishing a set of instructions for assembly and use which does not adequately avoid the danger of injury.[11]

[B] Persons Who Have a Duty to Warn

In most cases, the duty to warn is imposed on the manufacturer of a product,[12] as well as on the manufacturer of specific component parts incorporated into a finished product.[13] In *Walton v. AVCO Corp.*,[14] for example, the manufacturer of a

---

[6] Salinas v. Amteck of Kentucky, Inc., 682 F. Supp. 2d 1022 (N.D. Cal. 2010) (applying California law); Veil v. Vitek, Inc., 803 F. Supp. 229 (D.N.D. 1992) (applying North Dakota law).

[7] Texsun Feed Yards, Inc. v. Ralston Purina Co., 447 F.2d 660 (5th Cir. 1971) (applying Texas law).

[8] Hiigel v. General Motors Corp., 544 P.2d 983 (Colo. 1975); Oberg v. Advanced Transformer Company, Inc., 569 N.E.2d 50 (Ill. App. Ct. 1991).

[9] 127 Cal. Rptr. 217 (Ct. App. 1976).

[10] *Id.* at 219.

[11] *Id.* at 221.

[12] Germann v. F.L. Smithe Machine Co., 395 N.W.2d 922 (Minn. 1986). However, in California, "a manufacturer has no duty to warn of defects in products supplied by others and used in conjunction with the manufacturer's product unless the manufacturer's product itself causes or creates the risk of harm." Taylor v. Elliott Turbomachinery Co., Inc., 90 Cal. Rptr. 3d 414, 421 (Ct. App. 2009). Under § 12 of the RESTATEMENT (THIRD), a corporation that acquires assets from another corporation is liable for harm caused by defective products sold by the predecessor only in limited situations. However, under § 13, a successor corporation is liable for its own failure to warn after acquiring the assets of another

helicopter had an independent duty to warn service centers and owners of the defective engine, even though the engine was manufactured by another company that had issued a "Service Instruction" to service centers when it learned of the defect. The liability of the helicopter manufacturer was based on three factors: it had incorporated a defective part into the helicopter; it had subsequent knowledge of the engine's defect; and the manufacturer of a product is considered to be an expert concerning its products and to know of the risks connected with their use. Component part manufacturers, such as the one that produced the engine in *Walton*, also may have a duty to warn of known dangers in the use of the products they sell.[15]

In addition to manufacturers, those in the chain of distribution of a product also may have a duty to warn. This is the position taken by the Restatement (Third) which states that "sellers down the chain of distribution must warn when doing so is feasible and reasonable."[16] One example of "sellers down the chain of distribution" who have a duty to warn is automobile dealers. Since they have an opportunity to inspect their vehicles before the sale, they have a duty to warn potential buyers of the dangers posed by such features as airbags.[17] Another example of someone who may have a duty to warn is a lessor of a product. According to the New York Court of Appeals, a lessor has a duty to warn "against latent dangers resulting from foreseeable uses of [a leased] product of which it knew or should have known."[18]

[C] Negligence and Strict Liability

A claim alleging a failure to warn may be brought in implied warranty of merchantability, negligence, and/or strict liability.[19] However, a reading of § 388 of the Restatement (Second) of Torts, the comments to § 402A, and § 2 of the

---

corporation when certain conditions are met and when a reasonable person in the successor corporation's position would warn. The Utah Supreme Court has adopted § 13 of the RESTATEMENT (THIRD). Tabor v. Metal Ware Corp., 168 P.3d 814 (Utah 2007).

[13] For a discussion of the component parts doctrine, see Taylor v. Elliott Turbomachinery Co., Inc., 90 Cal. Rptr. 3d 414, 429–31 (Ct. App. 2009).

[14] 610 A.2d 454 (Pa. 1992).

[15] However, when a component part of an integrated product is not defective, the manufacturer of the component part is not liable for an injury that results from a defect in the integrated product. *See* Coons v. A. F. Chapman Corp., 460 F. Supp. 2d 209 (D. Mass. 2006) (applying Massachusetts law); Brennaman v. R.M.I. Co., 639 N.E.2d 425 (Ohio 1994).

[16] RESTATEMENT (THIRD) OF TORTS: PRODUCTS LIABILITY § 2 cmt. *i* (1998). *See* Santoro v. Donnelly, 2004 U.S. Dist. LEXIS 22849 (S.D.N.Y. Nov. 12, 2004) (applying New York law); Tellez-Cordova v. Campbell Hausfeld/Scott Fetzger Co., 28 Cal. Rptr. 3d 744 (Ct. App. 2004); Grady v. American Optical Corp., 702 S.W.2d 911 (Mo. Ct. App. 1985).

[17] *See* Juliano v. Toyota Motor Sales, U.S.A., Inc., 20 F. Supp. 2d 573 (S.D.N.Y. 1998) (applying New York law).

[18] Liriano v. Hobart Corp., 700 N.E.2d 303, 305 (N.Y. 1998). *See* Adeyinka v. Yankee Fiber Control, Inc, 564 F. Supp. 2d 265 (S.D.N.Y. 2008) (applying New York law).

[19] In Richter v. Limax International, Inc., 45 F.3d 1464 (10th Cir. 1995) (applying Kansas law), the jury found a manufacturer liable both in negligence and in strict liability for its failure to warn of the dangers of a trampoline. *See* Stupak v. Hoffman-La Roche, Inc., 2009 U.S. App. LEXIS 12482 (11th Cir.

Restatement (Third) shows that, in practice, there is no real difference between negligence and strict liability in failure to warn cases and the analysis is basically the same.[20] As a result, most states use a negligence analysis in failure to warn cases, whether the claim is brought in negligence or strict liability.[21]

The basis of negligence analysis is § 388 of the Restatement (Second) of Torts. This section, which focuses on what the component part manufacturer, knew, rather than the product itself, sets out the criteria for determining when there is a duty to warn and the standard of reasonable care required for a warning. Section 388, which has been cited widely by courts,[22] provides:

> One who supplies directly or through a third person a chattel for another to use is subject to liability to those whom the supplier should expect to use the chattel with the consent of the other or to be endangered by its probable use, for physical harm caused by the use of the chattel in the manner for which and by which a person for whose use it is supplied, if the supplier
>
> (a)   knows or has reasons to know that the chattel is or is likely to be dangerous for the use for which it is supplied, and
>
> (b)   has no reason to believe that those for whose use the chattel is supplied will realize its dangerous condition, and
>
> (c)   fails to exercise reasonable care to inform them of its dangerous condition or the facts which make it likely to be dangerous.

However, liability under § 388 is limited to those in the chain of the distribution of the product. The duty to warn does not apply to someone who does not manufacture, sell, or supply the product.[23]

June 10, 2009) (discussing the duty to warn in negligence and strict liability under Wisconsin law); Salinas v. Amteck of Kentucky, Inc., 682 F. Supp. 2d 1022 (N.D. Cal. 2010) (applying California law).

[20] *See* Koken v. Black & Veatch Construction, Inc., 426 F.3d 39 (1st Cir. 2005) (applying Maine law); Taylor v. Monsanto Co., 150 F.3d 806 (7th Cir. 1998) (applying Indiana law); Perlmutter v. United States Gypsum Co., 54 F.3d 659 (10th Cir. 1995) (applying Colorado law).

[21] *See* Richter v. Limax International, 45 F.3d 1464, 1468 (10th Cir. 1995) ("Kansas applies the same test to whether a manufacturer met his duty to warn under negligence as it does under strict liability."); Johnson v. Zimmer, Inc., 2004 U.S. Dist. LEXIS 6007 (D. Minn. Mar. 31, 2004) (applying Minnesota law); Roberts v. Performance Site Management, Inc., 2004-Ohio-2820 (10th Dist.); Olson v. Prosoco, Inc., 522 N.W.2d 284 (Iowa 1994). In Moore v. Ford Motor Co., 332 S.W.3d 749, 764 (Mo. 2011), the Missouri Supreme Court set out four elements for a claim for failure to warn based in negligence: "(1) the defendant designed the product at issue; (2) the product did not contain an adequate warning of the alleged defect or hazard; (3) the defendant failed to use ordinary care to warn of the risk of harm from the alleged defect or hazard; and (4) as a direct result of the defendant's failure to adequately warn, the plaintiff sustained damage."

[22] Among the cases that have endorsed this section are Roney v. Gencorp., 654 F. Supp. 2d 501 (S.D. W. Va. 2009) (applying West Virginia law); Reiss v. Komatsu Am. Corp., 735 F. Supp. 2d 1125 (D.N.D. 2010) (applying North Dakota law); Vondra v. Chevron, U.S.A., 652 F. Supp. 2d 999 (D. Neb. 2009) (applying Nebraska law); Johnson v. American Standard, Inc., 179 P.3d 905 (Cal. 2008); Gray v. Badger Mining Corp., 676 N.W.2d 268 (Minn. 2004).

[23] Simonetta v. Viad Corp., 197 P.3d 127 (Wash. 2008).

Section 402A does not mention warning defects explicitly. However, as in negligence cases, the comments to the section state that liability is based on the failure to exercise reasonable care in discovering and warning of a risk of harm. Comment *h* to § 402A provides that, where a seller "has reason to anticipate that danger may result from a particular use, as where a drug is sold which is safe only in limited doses, he may be required to give adequate warning of the danger (see comment *j*) and a product sold without such warning is in a defective condition." Comment *j* then states that, because many products cannot be made entirely safe for all of their uses, "[i]n order to prevent the product from being unreasonably dangerous, the seller may be required to give directions or warning . . . as to its use."[24] Unlike § 402A, section 2(c) of the Restatement (Third) lists "inadequate instructions or warnings" as one of three categories of a product defect. It then states that a product

> is defective because of inadequate instructions or warnings when the foreseeable risks of harm posed by the product could have been reduced or avoided by the provision of reasonable instructions or warnings by the seller or other distributor . . . and the omission of the instructions or warnings renders the product not reasonably safe.[25]

[D] Design Defects and the Failure to Warn

In many cases, a plaintiff alleges that a product was defective both in its design and because the manufacturer or seller failed to provide adequate warnings.[26] In jurisdictions that use a risk-utility analysis for design defect cases, courts often consider whether as warning was given as one of the factors that weighs in the balance of risk against utility.[27] However, the Restatement (Third) takes the position that, where a safer alternative design is available and reasonable for a

---

[24] For a discussion of these sections of the Restatement, see *Simonetta v. Viad Corp.*, 197 P.3d 127 (Wash. 2008). In In Moore v. Ford Motor Co., 332 S.W.3d 749, 756 (Mo. 2011), the Missouri Supreme Court set out five elements of a cause of action for strict liability failure to warn: "(1) the defendant sold the product in question in the course of its business; (2) the product was unreasonably dangerous at the time of sale when used as reasonably anticipated without knowledge of its characteristics; (3) the defendant did not give adequate warning of the danger; (4) the product was used in a reasonably anticipated manner; and (5) the plaintiff was damaged as a direct result of the product being sold without an adequate warning." *See also* Koken v. Black & Veatch Construction, Inc., 426 F.3d 39, 45 (1st Cir. 2005) (applying Maine law). Other courts also have stressed the need for the plaintiff to establish that the product was " 'defective due to inadequate warning or instruction' and that this defect was the proximate cause of [the plaintiff's] injuries." McConnell v. Cosco, Inc., 238 F. Supp. 2d 970, 976 (S.D. Ohio 2003) (applying Ohio law). *See* Adeyinka v. Yankee Fiber Control, Inc., 564 F. Supp. 2d 265, 280 (S.D.N.Y. 2008) (applying New York law); Kirkland v. Emhart Glass S.A., 805 F. Supp. 2d 1072 (W.D. Wash. 2011) (applying Washington law); Merck & Co. Inc. v. Garza, 347 S.W.3d 256 (Tex. 2011); Patch v. Hillerich & Bradsby Co., 257 P.3d 383 (Mont. 2011).

[25] For a discussion of § 2(c), see RESTATEMENT (THIRD) OF TORTS: PRODUCTS LIABILITY § 2 cmts. *i–o* (1998). *See also* Krummel v. Bombardier Corp., 206 F.3d 548 (5th Cir. 2000) (applying Louisiana law); Nationwide Agribusiness Ins. Co. v. SMA Elevator Const. Inc., 816 F. Supp. 2d 631 (N.D. Iowa 2011) (applying Iowa law); Blue v. Environmental Engineering, Inc., 828 N.E.2d 1128 (Ill. 2005).

[26] *See* Rivera v. Philip Morris, Inc., 395 F.3d 1142 (9th Cir. 2005) (applying Nevada law); Unrein v. Timesavers, Inc., 394 F.3d 1008 (8th Cir. 2005).

[27] Rogers v. Ingersoll-Rand Co., 144 F.3d 841 (D.C. Cir. 1998) (applying D.C. law).

product, the manufacturer must adopt that safer design rather than simply warn consumers of the dangers that exist in the design. Only in situations where there is no reasonable alternative design may warnings or instructions be sufficient to make the product reasonably safe.[28] An example of a case alleging that the design of a product was unreasonably dangerous because it did not contain an adequate warning of the dangers or provide an instruction on how to use it is *Strum, Ruger & Company, Inc. v. Bloyd*,[29] in which the plaintiff was struck in the ankle by a bullet that was fired from a revolver that accidentally was dropped on a concrete floor. The revolver had been hidden under the floor mat of the car by its owner and fell out when the plaintiff removed the mat to clean the inside of the car. The Kentucky Supreme Court held that a gun was not designed defectively because, when it was sold new, the gun was accompanied by a pamphlet warning of its unsafe mechanism and advising a user how the gun should be carried.[30] The manufacturer was under a duty only to design a gun that was safe for its anticipated reasonable use and that use was covered by the warning that accompanied the sale. Since the manufacturer could not have anticipated the way in which the accident occurred, there was no defect in the design or in the warning.

Although some cases analyze a warning as part of the design of a product, the two defects are different conceptually. As was discussed in Chapter 5, a product contains a design defect if it fails to meet consumer expectations or if the risks of the design outweigh its benefits. In a failure to warn case, the design and the manufacturer of the product meet all of the design requirements yet the product still contains a danger that is known to the manufacturer but is not obvious to the ordinary user or consumer.[31] Although § 2(c) of the Restatement (Third) recognizes the failure to warn as a category of product defects, it does not set out explicitly the elements of a failure to warn case. However, within the section are many of the questions that must be analyzed in a failure to warn case. First, when does a manufacturer or seller have a duty to provide a warning or instructions to consumers? Although § 2(c) of the Restatement (Third) defines a product as defective when "foreseeable risks of harm" could be reduced or avoided by instructions or warnings, it does not define when "foreseeable risks of harm" trigger a duty to warn. Is there a duty to warn if the "foreseeable risks of harm" are "open and obvious"? Second, if there is a duty to provide warnings or instructions, to whom must they be given? Third, what constitutes "reasonable instructions or warnings"? What is the effect of "reasonable instructions or warnings?" Finally, does the duty to provide warnings end with the sale of the product or must a warning be given to consumers if the risk of harm was not known until after the sale of the product? When, if ever, does the duty extend to recalling and retrofitting a product? The remainder of this chapter examines these questions and others related to warning defects.

---

[28] RESTATEMENT (THIRD) OF TORTS: PRODUCTS LIABILITY § 2 cmt. *l* (1998).

[29] 586 S.W.2d 19 (Ky. 1979).

[30] *Id.* at 20–21.

[31] For a discussion of the differences between design defect claims and failure to warn claims, see Hollister v. Dayton Hudson Corp., 201 F.3d 731 (6th Cir. 2000) (applying Michigan law).

§ 7.02 WHEN A WARNING MUST BE GIVEN

[A] Introduction

Even if a product is designed and manufactured properly, it is impossible to eliminate all of the dangers or risks that can result from every possible use.[32] In order that the risks not make a product unreasonably dangerous, it may be necessary for the manufacturer to provide a warning or to include instructions for the proper use of the product. Thus, the first question that must be asked in every case alleging inadequate warnings or instructions about the dangers of a product is: Did the manufacturer or seller have a duty to warn of the particular dangers connected with the use of the product? This is a question of law for the court to decide.[33]

The easiest cases to decide are those involving products such as alcohol, cigarettes, medicines, and some food items where the question of when a warning must be provided has been answered by government regulations mandating that the products carry health warnings about their contents or specific dangers in their use.[34] Since there is no issue of a duty to warn in those cases, the question becomes whether the plaintiff's injuries were within the scope of the dangers covered by the warning.[35] More difficult, however, are the cases involving products where a warning is not required by government regulations. Since it is impossible to warn of every possible danger in every product, whether a duty to warn exists is "a question of law that generally depends on mixed considerations of logic, common sense, justice, policy, and precedent."[36] In addition, warnings are not cost free. There is a monetary cost in labeling, package inserts, and instruction manuals, as well as a psychological cost. If a manufacturer includes too many warnings along with a product, the value of the warnings to users and consumers may be depreciated. In *Scott v. Black and Decker, Inc.*,[37] the plaintiff alleged that the manufacturer was liable for failing to warn that its electric portable band saw was dangerous if used in a flammable atmosphere. Although the Fifth Circuit upheld the warnings as adequate, the extensive list of warnings may have resulted in "warning overload" that made the product less safe by causing the buyer to ignore the warnings.

> The owner's manual, which Black & Decker issues with each saw, lists twenty safety warnings on the first inside page, including instructions to ground the tool adequately, to wear proper apparel, to keep guards in place, to maintain properly, etc., in addition to an explicit warning about use of the

---

[32] Wolfe v. Ford Motor Co., 376 N.E.2d 143 (Mass. App. Ct. 1978).

[33] Daniel v. Coleman Company Inc., 599 F.3d 1045 (9th Cir. 2010) (applying Washington law); Stringer v. National Football League, 749 F. Supp. 2d 680 (S.D. Ohio 2009) (applying Ohio law).

[34] For a discussion of the warnings required by the FDA, see In re Avandia Marketing Sales Practices and Products Liability Litigation, 817 F. Supp. 2d 535 (E.D. Pa. 2011); Schedin v. Ortho-McNeil-Janssen Pharmaceuticals, Inc., 808 F. Supp. 2d 1125 (D. Minn. 2011).

[35] Thongchoom v. Graco Children's Products, Inc., 71 P.3d 214 (Wash. Ct. App. 2003).

[36] Simonetta v. Viad Corp., 197 P.3d 127 (Wash. 2008).

[37] 717 F.2d 251 (5th Cir. 1983) (applying Louisiana law).

saw in explosive atmospheres. The saw itself had a label instructing the user to read the owner's manual before using the tool.[38]

Because most states use a negligence analysis in failure to warn cases, whether they are brought in negligence or strict liability,[39] the focus is on what the manufacturer knew or should have known about the risk of harm at the time the product was sold or distributed.[40] A duty to warn is imposed when a manufacturer: (1) knew or should have known that the product posed a sufficiently serious risk of harm when used for its intended or reasonably foreseeable purposes, and (2) had no reason to believe that the users or consumers of the product would be aware of and understand the risk of harm.[41] Foreseeability means a serious risk of harm that is objectively reasonable to expect, not just what conceivably might occur.[42] What is objectively "reasonable" to expect means that the manufacturer is required to warn not only of dangers from the intended use of its product but also of the dangers from the foreseeable unintended of the product.[43] In deciding what risks were foreseeable, courts hold manufacturers to the standard of an expert regarding its products.[44]

Since the duty to warn is based on the foreseeability of the risk of harm, a manufacturer is liable only for risks that were known or knowable at the time of manufacture of the product. It is not liable for failing to warn of unknowable risks.[45] The California Supreme Court's decision in *Anderson v. Owens Corning Fiberglass Corp.*[46] is illustrative of this principle. In *Anderson*, the court said that, in order to establish strict liability for failure to warn, a plaintiff must prove that the defendant "did not adequately warn of a particular risk that was known or knowable in light of the generally recognized and prevailing best scientific and medical knowledge

---

[38] *Id.* at 254. After setting out the extent of the warnings, the court stated of the manufacturer: "More it cannot do; to require it to place a specific warning encompassing these facts on the saw is beyond the 'reasonable steps' " demanded by earlier cases. *Id.*

[39] Varano v. Jabar, 197 F.3d 1 (1st Cir. 1999) (applying Maine law); O'Flynn v. Owens-Corning Fiberglas, 759 So. 2d 526 (Miss. Ct. App. 2000).

[40] *See* Strasser v. Transtech Mobile Fleet Service, Inc., 613 N.W.2d 142 (Wis. 2000); Moore v. Vanderloo, 386 N.W.2d 108, 116 (Iowa 1986); Woodill v. Parke Davis & Co., 402 N.E.2d 194 (Ill. 1980). A few states hold that it is irrelevant whether the manufacturer knew of the danger or should have known of the risk of danger. *See* Halphen v. Johns-Manville Sales Corp., 484 So. 2d 110 (La. 1986); Elmore v. Owens-Illinois, Inc., 673 S.W.2d 434 (Mo. 1984); Phillips v. Kimwood Machine Co., 525 P.2d 1033 (Or. 1974).

[41] Stupak v. Hoffman-La Roche, Inc., 2009 U.S. App. LEXIS 12482 (11th Cir. June 10, 2009) (applying Wisconsin law); Stringer v. National Football League, 749 F. Supp. 2d 680 (S.D. Ohio 2009) (applying Ohio law); Glittenberg v. Doughboy Recreational Industries, 491 N.W.2d 208 (Mich. 1992).

[42] Sollami v. Eaton, 772 N.E.2d 215 (Ill. 2002).

[43] RESTATEMENT (SECOND) OF TORTS § 402A cmt. *h* (1965); RESTATEMENT (THIRD) OF TORTS: PRODUCTS LIABILITY § 2 cmt. *p* (1998); Lugo v. LJN Toys, 552 N.E.2d 162 (N.Y. 1990).

[44] Borel v. Fiberboard Paper Products Corp., 493 F.2d 1076 (5th Cir. 1973) (applying Texas law); Feldman v. Lederle Laboratories, 479 A.2d 374 (N.J. 1984); Garlock, Inc. v. Gallagher, 814 A.2d 1007 (Md. Ct. Spec. App. 2003).

[45] *See* Rosa v. City of Seaside, 675 F. Supp. 2d 1006 (N.D.Cal. 2009) (applying California law) in which the court held that the manufacturer of a taser gun did not have to warn of risk of cardiac failure since the evidence showed that the risk was not "known or knowable" at the time the gun was manufactured.

[46] 810 P.2d 549 (Cal. 1991). *See* Chavez v. Glock, Inc., 2012 Cal. App. LEXIS 832 (Ct. App. 2012).

available at the time of the manufacture and distribution. . . . [T]he reasonableness of the defendant's failure to warn is immaterial."[47] Based on this test, the court held that a defendant could present evidence of the "state of the art," that is, evidence that the particular risk was neither known nor knowable by application of scientific knowledge available at the time of the manufacture or distribution of the product. The court stated, "exclusion of state of the art evidence, when the basis of liability is a failure to warn, would make a manufacturer the virtual insurer of its product's safe use, a result that is not consonant with established principals of strict liability."[48] The overwhelming majority of jurisdictions accept this premise, which is consistent with comment *j* to the Restatement § 402A, which confines a duty to warn to a situation in which a seller "has knowledge or by the application of reasonable, developed human skill and foresight should have knowledge of?the danger."[49]

In *O'Neil v. Crane Co.*,[50] the California Supreme Court confronted another question of foreseeability and the duty to warn. In *O'Neil*, the defendants manufactured valves and pumps used on Navy ships. The plaintiff's decedent was exposed to asbestos released from external insulation and internal gaskets and packing, all of which were made by third parties and added to the pumps and valves after their sale by the defendants to the Navy. The defendants played no part in the manufacture or distribution of those replacement products and did not participate in their integration into its products after the sale. However, the plaintiffs argued that it was foreseeable that workers would be exposed to asbestos in replacements parts. The California Supreme Court held that there was no case law in the state to support the idea that a manufacturer, after selling a completed product to a purchaser, remains under a duty to warn that purchaser of potentially defective additional pieces of equipment that the purchaser may add to the product.[51] Since there was no showing that the defendants' original products contributed substantially to the death, the defendants were not liable in strict liability or negligence for failing to warn of any dangers in the replacement parts.[52]

[B]   Unavoidably Unsafe Products

Even if a product is manufactured according to the "state of the art," it may be "unavoidably unsafe" or "inherently dangerous" because of the present limits of knowledge about the design or manufacture of the product. Firearms, knives, and explosives are examples of such products. In some situation, the inability to produce a reasonably safe product is a sufficient reason not to manufacture and sell it. However, many other products, particularly drugs and medical devices, are a

---

[47] *Id.* at 558.

[48] *Id.* at 550. *See also* Woodill v. Parke Davis & Co., 402 N.E.2d 194 (Ill. 1980).

[49] *See* RESTATEMENT (SECOND) OF TORTS § 402A, cmt. *j* (1965). However, some states take the position that is not necessary that a manufacturer appreciate the specific nature of the hazard posed by the product to create the duty to warn. Instead, there is a duty to warn if the manufacturer had a general awareness of the risk. *See* Boyd v. Lincoln Elec. Co., 902 N.E.2d 1023 (Ohio Ct. App. 2008).

[50] 266 P.3d 987 (Cal. 2012).

[51] *Id.* at 998.

[52] Delaware took the same position in *In re Asbestos Litigation: Thomas Milstead*, 2012 Del. Super. LEXIS 258 (June 1, 2012).

great benefit to a large number of people despite being "unavoidably unsafe." If the product is useful and it is beneficial to have it on the market, comment *k* to § 402A provides that it will not be considered "defective" or "unreasonably dangerous" and the manufacturer will not be strictly liable for the unfortunate consequences of its use provided the product is "properly prepared, and accompanied by proper directions and warning."[53]

Although comment *k* has been adopted in the overwhelming majority of states that have considered the matter,[54] states interpret comment *k* in a number of different ways and there is considerable disagreement concerning its application. A few states interpret comment *k* to make all prescription drugs exempt from strict liability. Under this view, a prescription drug that is properly manufactured and accompanied by an adequate warning of the risks known to the manufacturer at the time of sale is not defectively designed as a matter of law.[55] The majority of states, however, apply it on a case-by-case basis, holding that the interests developing and marketing prescription drugs can be met with giving manufacturers blanket immunity.[56] Thus, in *Castrignano v. E.R. Squibb & Sons*,[57] the Rhode Island Supreme Court held that a case-by- case method of determining the applicability of comment *k* in drug products cases was the most appropriate method.[58] The court also held that comment *k* is not applicable to allegations that a prescription drug manufacturer failed adequately to warn of risks associated with its drug. In such cases, the court held, where the basis of the plaintiff's complaint is the failure to warn adequately, strict liability theory is a properly pled cause of action. The court observed that, although comment *k* cites examples, its language does not establish definitely the boundaries of its exemption.[59] The comment suggests that a drug properly prepared and marketed, and accompanied by proper warnings when the situation calls for it, could not be subject to strict liability when it satisfies the risk-benefit analysis. Satisfying this standard qualifies a drug as unavoidably unsafe. Although the comment speaks of proper warnings, its language does not address exempting drugs from strict liability for failure to warn of the dangers created by their use. Thus, the *Castrignano* court concluded that the exemption applies only to allegations of a defective design. In order to avoid liability for failure to warn, the manufacturer must pass the test set out in comment *j* of the Restatement.

---

[53] RESTATEMENT (SECOND) OF TORTS § 402A cmt. *k* (1965).

[54] *See* Schwartz, *Unavoidably Unsafe Products: Clarifying the Meaning and Policy Behind Comment*, 42 WASH. & LEE L. REV. 1139 (1985).

[55] Young v. Key Pharmaceuticals, 922 P.2d 59 (Wyo. 1996); Grundberg v. Upjohn Co., 813 P.2d 89 (Utah 1991); Brown v. Superior Court (Abbott Laboratories), 751 P.2d 470 (Cal. 1988).

[56] *See* Hill v. Searle Laboratories, 884 F.2d 1064 (8th Cir. 1989) (applying Arkansas law); Castrignano v. E.R. Squibb & Sons, Inc., 546 A.2d 775 (R.I. 1988).

[57] Castrignano v. E.R. Squibb, 546 A.2d 775 (R.I. 1988).

[58] *Id.* at 781.

[59] *Id.* at 780.

[C]   Open and Obvious Dangers

An essential element for a duty to warn is unequal knowledge between the manufacturer and the user about the dangers posed by the product.[60] Thus, the Restatements and state court decisions make it clear that a manufacturer has no duty to warn if, from an objective point of view, the knowledge of the risk posed by a product is open, obvious, and generally appreciated by users of the product. Section 388(b) of the Restatement (Second) of Torts states that, in negligence cases, there is a duty to warn only if the manufacturer "has no reason to believe that those for whose use the chattel is supplied will realize its dangerous condition."[61] Similarly, comment *j* to § 402A states that, in cases based on strict liability, the seller is not required to warn when the danger or potential danger in a product "is generally known and recognized."[62] Comment *j* to § 2 of the Restatement (Third) provides:

> In general, a product seller is not subject to liability for failing to warn or instruct regarding risks and risk-avoidance measures that should be obvious to, or generally known by, foreseeable product users. When a risk is obvious or generally known, the prospective addressee of a warning will or should already know of its existence. Warning of an obvious or generally known risk in most instances will not provide an effective additional measure of safety.[63]

In keeping with the position taken by the Restatements, the vast majority of courts also have adopted an "open and obvious" exception to the duty to warn.[64] According to one court, "nothing of value is gained by a warning regarding a dangerous condition that already is obvious to the average consumer and is generally appreciated."[65] A few states, however, either reject the open and obvious doctrine[66] or have rejected an all-or-nothing approach and, instead, treat the obviousness of the risk as a factor for the trier of fact to consider in determining liability.[67] In *Chow*

---

[60] Seegers Grain Co. v. United States Steel Corp., 577 N.E.2d 1364 (Ill. App. Ct. 1991). In Illinois, a seller of used goods also has a duty to warn of dangerous conditions of which it knows or if it had unequal knowledge and reason to believe that the buyer will not perceive the danger. Whelchel v. Briggs & Stratton Corp., 2012 U.S. Dist. LEXIS 15278 (N.D. Ill. Feb. 7, 2012) (applying Illinois law).

[61] *See also* RESTATEMENT (SECOND) OF TORTS § 388 cmt. *k* (1965).

[62] RESTATEMENT (SECOND) OF TORTS § 388 cmt *j* (1965).

[63] RESTATEMENT (THIRD) OF TORTS: PRODUCTS LIABILITY § 2 cmt. *j* (1998).

[64] *See* Robinson v. South Dakota Brandtjen & Kluge, Inc., 500 F.3d 691 (8th Cir. 2007) (applying North Dakota law); Ahrens v. Ford Motor Co., 340 F.3d 1142 (10th Cir. 2003) (applying Oklahoma law); Koken v. Black & Veatch Construction Co., 426 F.3d 39 (1st Cir. 2005) (applying Maine law); Burke v, Spartanics, Ltd., 252 F.3d 131 (2d Cir. 2001) (applying New York law); Caterpillar, Inc. v. Shears, 911 S.W.2d 379, 382 (Tex. 1995).

[65] Blue v. Environmental Engineering, Inc., 803 N.E.2d 187, 194 (Ill. App. Ct. 2002). *See also* Jamieson v. Woodward & Lothrop, 247 F.2d 23 (D.C. Cir. 1957); Caterpillar, Inc. v. Shears, 911 S.W.2d 379 (Tex. 1995).

[66] *See* Harris v. Karri-On Campers, Inc., 640 F.2d 65 (7th Cir. 1981) (applying West Virginia law); Tacke v. Vermeer Manufacturing Co., 713 P.2d 527 (Mont. 1986).

[67] *See* Horton v. American Tobacco Co., 667 So. 2d 1289 (Miss. 1995); Armentrout v. FMC Corp., 842 P.2d 175 (Colo. 1992): House v. Armour of America, Inc., 886 P.2d 542 (Utah Ct. App. 1994).

v. Rickitt & Colman, Inc.,[68] the New York Court of Appeals adopted a risk-benefit analysis when a defendant seeks summary judgment on the ground that the risk is open and obvious. In *Chow*, the plaintiff was injured while using a chemical, which was 100% lye, to clean a clogged floor drain in the kitchen of a restaurant where he worked. According to the court, the defendant/manufacturer must do more than allege that the product was inherently dangerous and that the danger was open and obvious. It must show that the benefits of the product outweighed the risks of its intended use.

> [D]efendants cannot rely simply on the fact that their product is what they say it is and that everyone knows that lye is dangerous; that only begs the question. . . . [K]nowing how dangerous lye is, was it reasonable for defendants to place [the product] into the stream of commerce as a drain cleaning product for use by a lay person? Defendants offered no answer to this question, and thus did not demonstrate their entitlement to judgment as a matter of law.[69]

The problem for courts is determining what risks are open and obvious. The test is an objective one based upon whether a "reasonable person"[70] could recognize and appreciate the risk. Although this requirement is easy to state, its application depends upon the facts of each case. Because of the great variety of products, the ways in which they are used, and the risks they may present, it is impossible to give an exact definition of when a risk is open and obvious to a reasonable person. Whether a particular danger is open and obvious depends on a number of factors: (1) the complexity of the product; (2) the knowledge, age, background, experience, intelligence, and training of the injured person; (3) the extent to which the required contact of the injured person with the device is routine and repetitive; and (4) whether the injured person was distracted.[71] The complexity of these factors makes it a question of fact for the jury to decide. Among the various dangers that have been held to be open and obvious to a reasonable person are:

- burns from water hot enough to brew tea,[72]

- a disposable butane lighter,[73]

- dangers of consuming alcohol,[74]

- diving into a shallow swimming pool,[75]

---

[68] 950 N.E.2d 113 (N.Y. 2011).

[69] *Id.* at 116.

[70] Sollami v. Eaton, 772 N.E.2d 215 (Ill. 2002); Sauder Custom Fabrication, Inc. v. Boyd, 967 S.W.2d 349 (Tex. 1998).

[71] Figgie International, Inc., Snorke-Economy Div. v. Tognocchi, 624 A.2d 1285 (Md. Ct. Spec. App. 1993).

[72] Bouher v. Aramark Services, Inc., 910 N.E.2d 40 (Ohio Ct. App. 2009).

[73] Adams v. Perry Furniture Co., 497 N.W.2d 514 (Mich. Ct. App. 1993).

[74] Brown Forman Corp. v. Brune, 893 S.W.2d 640 (Tex. App. 1994).

[75] Spaulding v. Lesco International Corp., 451 N.W.2d 603 (Mich. Ct. App. 1990).

- driving with a foot sticking out of a golf cart,[76]
- a handgun,[77]
- a meat grinder,[78]
- operating a front-end loader without a roll bar,[79]
- riding on a motorcycle,[80]
- riding unrestrained in an open cargo bed of a pickup truck,[81]
- smoking,[82]
- jumping on a trampoline.[83]

However, courts have held that it was not open and obvious to a reasonable person that:

- a fire-causing electrical problem also could knock out a smoke alarm,[84]
- a body-care product could be fatal if ingested by a child,[85]
- a small child could chock on a marshmallow[86] or a toy block.[87]

In deciding whether a risk was open and obvious, courts also have drawn a distinction between an reasonable adult's ability to recognize and appreciate certain risks and a child's ability. In *Bunch v. Hoffinger Industries, Inc.*,[88] an 11-year old became a quadriplegic after diving into four-foot deep above-ground swimming pool. In her suit against the manufacturer of the pool liner, the plaintiff alleged a failure to warn of the dangers of diving into a shallow pool. At trial, the plaintiff stated that she vaguely remembered stickers on the pool liner that said: "No diving in shallow water" and showed a man making a "pike," or vertical, dive with the word "caution." The plaintiff said she believed the label warned her "[n]ot to dive like that."[89] After an extensive review of diving cases involving adults and children, the

---

[76] Vela v. Yamaha Motor Corp., 2002 Tex. App. LEXIS 3185 (May 8, 2002).

[77] *See* Perkins v. F.I.E. Corp., 762 F.2d 1250 (5th Cir. 1980) (applying Louisiana law); Mavilia v. Stoeger Industries, 574 F. Supp. 107 (D. Mass. 1983) (applying Massachusetts law); Resteiner v. Sturm, Ruger & Co., 566 N.W.2d 53 (Mich. Ct. App. 1997); Richardson v. Holland, 741 S.W.2d 751 (Mo. Ct. App. 1987); Riordan v. Int'l Armament Corp., 477 N.E.2d 1293 (Ill. App. Ct. 1985).

[78] Liriano v. Hobart Corp., 170 F.3d 264 (2d Cir. 1999) (applying New York law).

[79] Bates v. Richland Sales Corp., 803 N.E.2d 977 (Ill. App. Ct. 2004).

[80] Shaffer v. AMF Inc., 842 F.2d 893 (6th Cir. 1988) (applying Ohio law).

[81] Josue v. Isuzu Motors America, Inc., 958 P.2d 535 (Haw. 1998).

[82] Gibbs v. Republic Tobacco, L.P., 119 F. Supp. 2d 1288 (M.D. Fla. 2000) (applying Florida law).

[83] Sollami v. Eaton, 772 N.E.2d 215 (Ill. 2002).

[84] Laaperi v. Sears, Roebuck & Co., 787 F.2d 726 (1st Cir. 1986) (applying Massachusetts law).

[85] Greene v. A.P. Products, Ltd., 691 N.W.2d 38 (Mich. Ct. App. 2004).

[86] Emery v. Federated Foods, Inc., 863 P.2d 426 (Mont. 1993).

[87] Metzgar v. Playskool, Inc., 30 F.3d 459 (3d Cir. 1994) (applying Pennsylvania law).

[88] 20 Cal. Rptr. 3d 780 (Ct. App. 2004).

[89] *Id.* at 785.

California appellate court concluded it was not evident that, "as a matter of law, the dangers of 'shallow' or surface diving into a shallow pool are open and obvious to minors."[90] Since other courts had considered prior swimming and diving experience, familiarity with the pool in question, and the public's general awareness of diving dangers in determining whether the danger is open and obvious to adults, the court felt that it was "absurd and somewhat illogical to consider these factors in determining an awareness of danger but to ignore or exclude the age of the diver."[91]

Although it was foreseeable that the swimming pool in *Bunch* would be used by an 11 year old, the product was not marketed specifically to children. In cases where a product's primary marketing target is children, courts have required that whether a risk is open and obvious be determined by a "reasonable child" standard rather than an adult "reasonable person" test. In *Swix v. Daisy Manufacturing Co., Inc.*,[92] a child who used an air rifle and his parents brought an action against the rifle's manufacturer alleging defective design and failure to warn of known danger. The Sixth Circuit stated that in determining whether a danger was open and obvious, "the focus is the typical user's perception and knowledge of whether the relevant condition or feature that creates the danger associated with use is fully apparent, widely known, commonly recognized, and anticipated by the ordinary user or consumer."[93] The court reasoned that, since the median age of the purchasers of the gun was 12 years old, the objective "reasonable child standard" applied with respect to the manufactures' duty to warn, even though the air rifle was used under the direct supervision of any adult.[94]

Some courts permit manufacturers in strict liability failure to warn cases to present evidence of the plaintiff's knowledge of the risk based on common knowledge in the particular industry. In *Campos v. Firestone Tire & Rubber Co.*,[95] a tire mechanic brought a products liability action against the manufacturer of the rim assembly, alleging product defect and failure to warn. The New Jersey Supreme Court held the manufacturer had a duty to warn the tire mechanic of the danger of inserting his hand into the protective cage while the tire was being inflated.[96] However, the court also held that the tire mechanic's knowledge of the danger as a result of prior accident which occurred when he inserted his hand into cage while the tire was being inflated was relevant to the question of causation, i.e., whether manufacturer's failure to warn of danger was the cause of mechanic's injury.[97]

---

[90] *Id.* at 796 (quoting Klen v. Doughboy Recreational, Inc., 643 N.E.2d, 1360, 1369-1370 (Ill. App. Ct. 1994).

[91] *Id.*

[92] 373 F.3d 678 (6th Cir. 2004).

[93] *Id.* at 686.

[94] *Id.* at 686–88. *See also* Klen v. Asahi Pool, Inc., 643 N.E.2d 1360, 1366 (Ill. Ct. 1993) (when a 14-year-old was injured after diving into an swimming pool, the Illinois appellate court held that the question of whether the risk was open and obvious must be judged by the "reasonable or objective class of 14-year olds.").

[95] 485 A.2d 305 (N.J. 1984).

[96] *Id.* at 310.

[97] *Id.* at 311.

Similarly, in *ExParte Chevron Chemical Co.*,[98] employees of a gas company sued the manufacturer of a plastic pipe after the pipeline exploded during an installation, alleging negligent failure to warn of danger of static electricity and alleging liability under the Alabama Extended Manufacturer's Liability Doctrine (AEMLD). However, the Alabama Supreme Court held the manufacturer did not have duty to warn the gas company or its employees of a danger that was common knowledge in the industry, and published in a manual given to the very employees who were injured.[99]

§ 7.03 PERSONS WHO MUST BE WARNED

[A] Users, Consumers, and Bystanders

Once it is determined that a manufacturer or seller has a duty to provide a warning or instructions about the use of a product, the next question that must be asked is: to whom must the warning be provided? The Restatements and cases take the position that, a manufacturer has a duty "to warn those persons it should reasonably foresee would be likely to use its product or who are likely to come into contact with a latent danger inherent in the product's use."[100] In negligence cases, section 388 of the Restatement (Second) of Torts requires that a warning be given to those who should be expected to use the product or to be endangered by its probable use. The comments to § 402A state that, in strict liability cases, the warning must be given to the "ultimate user or consumer."[101] In the case of consumer goods that are sold to the general public, these sections mean the same thing: the manufacturer must provide the warning directly to the users along with the product.[102] Depending upon the product, these warnings can be printed directly on the product package or they may be placed on package inserts or in instruction manuals.

The purpose of such warnings is to inform consumers about the dangers of a product of which they are unaware so that they can make an informed decision about whether and how to use it.[103] However, if warning would not facilitate a user's decision process, the manufacturer has no duty to provide one to the user. In *Stevens v. Cessna Aircraft Co.*,[104] a California court held that the manufacturer of a small airplane had no duty to warn the passengers of the plane's load capacity. According to the court, whether the plane could fly safely with a particular total weight of passengers depended on too many factors for the passengers to make an informed decision based on a warning. In such a situation, passengers depend on

---

[98] 720 So. 2d 922 (Ala. 1998).

[99] *Id.* at 926.

[100] Taylor v. Monsanto Co., 150 F.3d 806, 808 (7th Cir. 1998) (applying Indiana law).

[101] RESTATEMENT (SECOND) OF TORTS § 402A cmt. *j* (1965).

[102] Johnson v. Harley-Davidson Motor Company Group, Inc., 2004 Iowa App. LEXIS 344 (Feb. 27, 2004); RESTATEMENT (SECOND) OF TORTS § 388 (1965).

[103] O'Neil v. Crane Co., 266 P.3d 987 (Cal. 2012).

[104] 170 Cal. Rptr. 925 (Ct. App. 1981).

the pilot to determine the safe load capacity.[105]

The duty to warn also may extend to persons other than user or consumers. According to the Restatement (Third), it may be necessary to provide instructions and warnings "to others who a reasonable seller should know will be in a position to reduce or avoid the risk of harm."[106] An example of persons who are "in a position to reduce or avoid the risk of harm" from a product are physicians who act as learned intermediaries between drug manufacturers and patients. In some situations, a manufacturer also may have a duty to warn bystanders. However, before a court will impose a duty to warn a bystander, it must determine who the primary recipient of the warning was, whether a warning would have been seen by the bystander, and whether the lack of the warning was the cause of the bystander's injury.[107]

[B] Persons with Allergic Reactions

In a number of cases, the question has arisen whether manufacturers must provide warnings to persons who have allergic reactions to nonprescription drugs, chemicals used in consumer goods, or ingredients in food products.[108] The comments to § 402A,[109] the Restatement (Third),[110] and the cases[111] all agree that whether manufacturers have a duty to warn these persons depends on three factors. First, the product must contain an ingredient to which a "substantial number of persons" in the general population are allergic. Although courts have not quantified what constitutes a "substantial number," the plaintiff must show that the reaction was not unique. However, if the risk posed by the allergic reaction is a severe harm, the "substantial number" required for a warning is less than if the potential harm is not serious. Second, the ingredient must be one whose danger is not generally known to consumers or one that consumers would not expect to find in the product. If it generally is known that the particular product contains an ingredient to which a substantial number of persons are allergic, there is no duty to warn. Finally, the manufacturer must have known, or should have known, at the time of sale, that the product contained an ingredient to which a "substantial number" of persons were allergic.

---

[105] *Id.* at 926.

[106] RESTATEMENT (THIRD) OF TORTS: PRODUCTS LIABILITY § 2 cmt. *i* (1998).

[107] Scordino v. Hopeman Brothers, Inc., 662 So. 2d 640 (Miss. 1995); Daniels v. Bucyrus-Erie Corp., 516 S.E.2d 848 (Ga. Ct. App. 1999). For a discussion of the learned intermediary doctrine, see § 7.06.

[108] Livingston v. Marie Callenders, Inc., 85 Cal. Rptr. 2d 528 (Ct. App. 1999) (MSG in soup); Kaempfe v. Lehn & Fink Products. Corp., 249 N.Y.S.2d 840 (App. Div. 1964) (aluminum sulphate in spray-on deodorant).

[109] RESTATEMENT (SECOND) OF TORTS § 402A cmt. *j* (1965).

[110] RESTATEMENT (THIRD) OF TORTS: PRODUCTS LIABILITY § 2 cmt. *k* (1998).

[111] *See, e.g.,* Guilbeau v. W. W. Henry Co., 85 F.3d 1149 (5th Cir. 1996) (applying Louisiana law); Guevara v. Dorsey Laboratories, 845 F.2d 364 (1st Cir. 1988) (applying Puerto Rican law); Griggs v. Combe, Inc., 456 So. 2d 790 (Ala. 1984).

[C]   Bulk Supplier/Sophisticated User/Sophisticated Supplier Doctrine

Despite the broad duty imposed on manufacturers to provide warnings and instructions about their products, there are some situations where they may not be required to provide the warnings directly to the ultimate users and consumers of products. One of these, products covered by the "learned intermediary doctrine," is discussed in detail in § 7.06. Three others — the "bulk supplier" doctrine, the "sophisticated intermediary" doctrine and the "sophisticated user" doctrine — are closely related affirmative defenses.[112]

The "bulk supplier" doctrine holds that the manufacturer of products that are sold in bulk, such as asbestos or industrial chemicals, may fulfill its duty to warn the employees who use the products by relying on an intermediary distributor that has knowledge of the risks to warn the ultimate users.[113] There are two rationales behind this doctrine. First, where a manufacturer delivers a product in a bulk container to an intermediary, the intermediary repackages the product and then resells it. This makes it impossible for the manufacturer to warn the ultimate users directly of the risks since the product is not provided to those users in the manufacturer's own packages.[114] Second, products provided in bulk often have a number of uses and are reformulated by the intermediary for those uses. This results in the manufacturer not knowing of the particular risks since it may not know exactly how its product will be used.[115]

Although the intermediary to whom the bulk goods are sold has its own obligation to warn, one court has pointed out that there is no "bright line rule" to determine whether the manufacturer's reliance on the intermediary to provide the necessary warning was reasonable.[116] Instead, it depends upon

> (1) the dangerous condition of the product; (2) the purpose for which the product is used; (3) the form of any warnings given; (4) the reliability of the third party as a conduit of necessary information about the product; (5) the magnitude of the risk involved; and (6) the burdens imposed on the supplier by requiring that he directly warn all users.[117]

Even when the bulk supplier is entitled to rely on the intermediary to provide the necessary warnings about a product, the manufacturer still must provide adequate information to the intermediary so that it is informed of the potential dangers and

---

[112] For a detailed discussion of these three doctrines, see Gray v. Badger Mining Corp., 676 N.W.2d 268 (Minn. 2004).

[113] Hoffman v. Houghton Chemical Corp., 751 N.E.2d 848 (Mass. 2001). The doctrine has its origins in the Restatement (Second) of Torts § 388 cmt. *n* (1965). Roney v. Gencorp., 654 F. Supp. 2d 501 (S.D.W. Va. 2009) (applying West Virginia law).

[114] Wood v. Phillips Petroleum, 119 S.W.3d 874 (Tex. App. 2003).

[115] Genereux v. American Beryllia Corp., 577 F.3d 350, 374 (1st Cir. 2009) (applying Massachusetts law).

[116] *Id.* at 856.

[117] *Id.* (quoting Goodbar v. Whitehead Brothers, 591 F. Supp. 552, 557 (D.W. Va. 1984)).

is in a position to pass on the warnings to the ultimate users.[118]

The "sophisticated user" doctrine provides that a manufacturer has no duty to warn the ultimate user of a product if it has reason to believe that the user knows or should know of the particular dangers involved with the product.[119] The rationale for this doctrine is that, if the risks of the product already are known by the user, an additional warning will have little deterrent effect.[120] In *House v. Armour of America, Inc.*,[121] the plaintiff's husband, a corrections officer who was a member of a SWAT team, was killed while carrying out an arrest. The plaintiff alleged that the manufacturer of the fabric used in the body armor vest her husband had been wearing at the time was strictly liable for failing to warn him of the limitations and capabilities of the vest. In its reply, the manufacturer argued that the husband was a sophisticated user since he had been "a highly and specially trained prison officer" who was "clearly knowledgeable regarding the characteristics of soft body armor vests."[122] However, after reviewing the record, the Utah Supreme Court concluded that there was insufficient evidence that any training given to the husband and SWAT team involved the use and capabilities of body armor. Since the SWAT team had purchased body armor only a few years before the incident, the court stated that, when the husband was killed, his SWAT team "not only lacked knowledge about the capabilities of body armor, but also lacked experience in using the product."[123]

Closely related to the "sophisticated user" doctrine is the "sophisticated intermediary" doctrine. Under this doctrine the duty to warn is satisfied when the manufacturer provides a product directly to an intermediary such as an employer who then passes on the information about the dangers to the employee/users.[124] In such a situation, the manufacturer of the product does not have a duty to warn the ultimate user directly of the risks from use of the product if: (1) the product is sold to an intermediary that has knowledge or sophistication equal to the manufacturer's; (2) the manufacturer adequately warned the intermediary; and (3) the manufacturer reasonably can rely on the intermediary to warn the ultimate user.[125]

---

[118] Donahue v. Phillips Petroleum Co., 866 F.2d 1008, 1012 (8th Cir. 1989) (applying Missouri law).

[119] *Id. See* Irrer v. Milacron, Inc., 484 F. Supp. 2d 677 (E.D. Mich. 2007) (applying the Michigan statute defining a "sophisticated user"); Johnson v. American Standard, Inc., 179 P.3d 905 (Cal. 2008); Carrel v. National Cord & Braid Corp., 852 N.E.2d 100 (Mass. 2006). The doctrine is sometimes explained as a corollary to the open and obvious doctrine. Genereux v. Am. Beryllia Corp., 577 F.3d 350, 364 (1st Cir. 2009) (applying Massachusetts law).

[120] Hall v. Ashland Oil, 625 F. Supp. 1515 (D. Conn. 1986) (applying Connecticut law); Hill v. Wilmington Chemical Corp., 156 N.W.2d 898 (Minn. 1968).

[121] 929 P.2d 340 (Utah 1996).

[122] *Id.* at 345.

[123] *Id.*

[124] Conley v. Lift-All Company, Inc., 2005 U.S. Dist. LEXIS 15468 (S.D. Ind. July 25, 2005) (applying Indiana law); Cotton v. Buckeye Gas Products Co., 840 F.2d 935 (D.C. Cir. 1988) (applying Virginia law).

[125] *See* First National Bank & Trust Co. v. American Eurocopter Corp., 378 F.3d 682 (7th Cir. 2004) (applying Indiana law). Courts apply the defense when (1) the employer maintained full knowledge of the ranger of dangers equal to that of the manufacturer; or (2) the manufacturer made the employer knowledgeable by providing adequate warnings and safety instructions to the employer. Gray v. Badger Mining Corp., 676 N.W.2d 268 (Minn. 2004).

In deciding whether the supplier's reliance on an intermediary to warn ultimate users was reasonable, courts consider (1) the dangerous condition of the product; (2) the purpose for which the product is used; (3) the form of any warning given; (4) the reliability of the third party as a conduit of necessary information about the product; (5) the magnitude of the risk involved; and (6) the burdens imposed on the supplier by requiring that he directly warn all users.[126] Unlike the "bulk supplier" doctrine, the "sophisticated user" doctrine and the "sophisticated intermediary" doctrine do not require the product to be supplied to the ultimate user through an intermediary or that the product be supplied in bulk.

In some situations, courts have refused to apply the bulk supplier/sophisticated user doctrines. An example of this is *Oman v. Johns-Mansville Corp.*,[127] in which the Fourth Circuit found that the product (asbestos) was very dangerous, that the burden on the manufacturer in placing a warning on the product was not great, that the employer was unaware of the danger for a long time, and that, when the employer became aware of the danger, it failed to warn its employees.[128]

§ 7.04 ADEQUACY OF THE WARNING

[A] Criteria for Determining the Scope and Adequacy of a Warning

Once it is determined that a manufacturer has a duty to warn of the dangers of a product and to whom the warning must be given, the next question is whether the warning was "one calculated to bring home to a reasonably prudent user of the product the nature and extent of the danger involved in using the product."[129] Whether a warning was adequate to inform "a reasonably prudent user of the product" of the risks o the product is an issue for the trier of fact.[130] However, a manufacturer does not have to warn of every possible danger involving the use of the product. In *Anderson v. Weslo, Inc.*,[131] the plaintiff, a 16-year-old who was a "very experienced, although self-taught, trampoline user" was injured while attempting to do a double flip on a trampoline manufactured by the defendant. He

---

[126] Vondra v. Chevron U.S.A., Inc., 652 F. Supp. 2d 999, 1008 (D. Neb. 2009) (citing Eagle-Picher Industries, Inc. v. Balbos, 604 A.2d 445, 464 (Md. 1992).

[127] 764 F.2d 224 (4th Cir. 1985) (applying Virginia law).

[128] *Id.* at 233. *See also* Hunnings v. Texaco, Inc., 29 F.3d 1480 (11th Cir. 1994) (applying Florida law); Fisher v. Professional Compounding Centers of America, Inc., 311 F. Supp. 2d 1008 (D. Nev. 2004) (applying Nevada law); Union Carbide Corp. v. Kavanaugh, 879 So. 2d 42 (Fla. Dist. Ct. App. 2004) (applying Florida law).

[129] Gerber v. Hoffman-La Roche Inc., 392 F. Supp. 2d 907 (S.D. Tex. 2005) (applying Texas law) (drug insert warnings "specifically and unambiguously" warned of the plaintiff of the dangers of using the product); Banner v. Hoffmann-La Roche Inc., 891 A.2d 1229, 1239 (N.J. Super. App. Div. 2006) (warnings given to the plaintiff were "accurate, clear, and unambiguous").

[130] Huff v. Elmhurst-Chicago Stone Co., 419 N.E.2d 561 (Ill. App. Ct. 1981). However, the adequacy of a warning is a matter of law for the court to decide if reasonable minds cannot differ as to its sufficiency. Jacobs v. E.I. du Pont de Nemours & Co., 67 F.3d 1219 (6th Cir. 1995) (applying Tennessee law).

[131] 906 P.2d 336 (Wash. Ct. App. 1995).

brought an action in negligence and strict liability action against the manufacturer, alleging, among other things, that the user's manual failed to warn him of the kinds of injuries that could result from doing somersaults on the trampoline. The Washington appellate court affirmed the grant of summary judgment for the manufacturer. Although the warnings on the trampoline did not inform the plaintiff of every possible injury that could occur while using the product, they did warn of the general risk of injury and of the serious risk of injury when doing somersaults. The court also felt that it was obvious to an ordinary person that they could land on any part of their body, including their head, neck, or back, and suffer serious injury. Thus, the court held that the manufacturer's warnings adequately informed users of the risk, and that proximate cause had not been established as a matter of law.

In order to help juries and courts decide whether a warning was adequate, the New Mexico appellate court set out five general criteria.[132] According to the court: (1) a warning must indicate adequately the scope of the danger; (2) a warning must communicate reasonably the extent or seriousness of the harm that could result from the danger; (3) the physical aspects of the warning — conspicuousness, prominence, relative size of print, — must be adequate to alert a reasonably prudent person to the danger; (4) a simple directive warning (i.e., "Do not use") may be inadequate, without some indication of consequences from failure to follow the directive; and (5) the means to convey the warning must be adequate.[133] In applying these factors, courts require that the form of the warning was such that it was able to catch the attention of reasonable users or consumers in the circumstances of their use of the product.[134] However, even if the form of the warning was sufficient, the content also must be understandable to ordinary users of the product and give them a reasonable indication of the nature and extent of the danger posed by the product.[135]

[B] Form of the Warning

In most cases a warning about the dangers associated with the use of a product will be placed on the product itself and/or in a package insert along with any instructions for the user to read before using the product. An example of the use of warnings on the label, product inserts, and direct mailings is *Barnes v. The Kerr Corp.*[136] In *Barnes* warnings that mixing dental amalgam presented a health risk were printed on the jars in which the capsules were sent. The labels stated in

---

[132] First National Bank in Albuquerque v. Nor-Am Agricultural Products, Inc., 537 P.2d 682 (N.M. Ct. App. 1975).

[133] *Id.* at 691–92. For similar statements of the criteria for an adequate warning, see Oman v. Johns-Manville Corp., 764 F.2d 224 (4th Cir. 1985) (applying Virginia law); Great Lakes Reinsurance v. City of Fort Pierce, 2008 U.S. Dist. LEXIS 33026 (S.D. Fla. Jan. 10, 2008) (applying Florida law); Lewis v. Sea Ray Boats, Inc., 65 P.3d 245 (Nev. 2003); Bergeron v. Pac. Food, Inc., 2011 Conn. Super. LEXIS 366 (Feb. 14, 2011).

[134] White v. ABCO Engineering Corp., 221 F.3d 293 (2d Cir. 2000) (applying New Jersey law).

[135] Cottam v. CVS Pharmacy, 764 N.E.2d 814 (Mass. 2002); DaimlerChrysler Corp. v. Hillhouse, 161 S.W.3d 541 (Tex. App. 2004).

[136] 418 F.3d 583 (6th Cir. 2005) (applying Tennessee law).

capital letters that the product CONTAINED METALLIC MERCURY and featured an image of a skull and crossbones next to the word POISON. On a chart of different hazards, including flammability, reactivity, and health hazards, the labels also warned that metallic mercury presented a "serious health hazard." The labels recommended using protective gear such as glasses, gloves, and a face mask when handling the amalgams, and warned that ingesting the mercury could cause "Neurotoxic/Nephrotoxic effects," that the inhalation of mercury could cause "Bronchiolitis, Pneumonitis and Pulmonary Edema," and that even skin contact could have harmful effects, including "redness and irritation to the eyes and skin."[137] In addition to the warnings on the label, each jar contained an insert with directions and additional detailed warnings. After the instructions about how to use the product, the word WARNING appeared in bold, capital letters, followed by a paragraph setting out the dangers of, and precautions against, mercury poisoning.[138] A third warning was provided to users of the product in the Material Safety Data Sheet (MSDS), a regularly updated document that was mailed to dentists who purchased the defendant's products. The MSDS described mercury as a "hazardous ingredient" and stated that chronic mercury poisoning could cause a number of medical problems.[139] The Sixth Circuit concluded that the warnings provided to users by the manufacturer were sufficient as a matter of law. Specifically, the court stated that the warnings (1) adequately indicated the scope of the danger; (2) gave detailed advice on how to use the dental amalgam capsules in order to avoid mercury poisoning; and (3) openly displayed and presented the warning in three separate media.[140]

Not only must the warning be on the product or in package inserts, it must be in a form designed to catch the attention of a reasonable user of the product.[141] In deciding whether the form of a warning was adequate, a jury often will consider the position of warning, its color, the size of print, and the symbols used to call the user's attention to the warning or cause the user to be more likely to read the label and warning than not.[142] In *Barnes*, for example, the court was influenced in its holding that the warnings were adequate as a matter of law by the fact that they were in capital letters on the labels and were accompanied by a skull and crossbones.[143] In most cases, however, the form of the warning does not rise to the

---

[137] *Id.* at 586.

[138] *Id.*

[139] *Id.*

[140] *Id.* at 591.

[141] Henry v. General Motors Corp., 60 F.3d 1545 (11th Cir. 1995) (applying Georgia law) (yellow sticker on a truck jack was adequate since the plaintiff, who was illiterate, knew that it signified a warning and did not ask anyone to read it to him).

[142] Pavlik v. Lane Ltd./Tobacco Exporters International, 135 F.3d 876 (3d Cir. 1998) (applying Pennsylvania law); Jones v. Amazing Products, 231 F. Supp. 2d 1228, 1247 (N.D. Ga. 2002) (applying Georgia law).

[143] For other examples of pictorial symbols, see O'Neil v. Electrolux Home Prod., Inc., 2008 U.S. Dist. LEXIS 39998 (D. Mass. May 14, 2008) (applying Massachusetts law); Koruba v. American Honda Motor Co., Inc., 935 A.2d 787, 791 (N.J. Super. App. Div. 2007) ("in certain situations, such as where the product is likely to be used by unskilled industrial workers illiterate in English, pictorial symbols may be required to adequately convey safety warnings.").

level of "a matter of law" and is, instead, a question for the jury. An example of a court leaving to the jury the question of whether the size of a warning and its location on a product were sufficient to communicate the risks is *Casey v. Pactiv,*[144] in which the manufacturer of a turkey roasting pan placed a notice on the side of the pan that it could hold a turkey weighing up to 20 pounds. The plaintiff cooked an 18-pound turkey in the pan. However, when the plaintiff lifted the sides of the pan to remove the finished turkey from the oven, the pan collapsed, spilling hot juices onto his legs and feet. The plaintiff suffered severe second- and third-degree burns, requiring several surgeries and skin grafts. In his suit against the manufacturer, the plaintiff alleged negligent design and failure to give an adequate warning. The manufacturer filed a motion for summary judgment, arguing that the warnings on the pan were adequate to avoid the type of accident that the plaintiff suffered.

The Massachusetts court noted that the roasting pan contained two warnings. First, in "very small print," the pan's label said:

> Perfect for roasts up to 20 lbs when bottom of pan is properly supported. Caution: do not lift by sides only. To avoid spilling *always* support bottom of pan with a cookie sheet.[145]

Second, embossed on the bottom of the pan, the manufacturer directed the user to "SUPPORT THE BOTTOM." The court noted, however, that the label for the product also stated that the pan was "reusable" and "sturdy."[146] These words appeared in large print, immediately above the fine print indicating that the pan should be supported with a cookie sheet. The court concluded that it could not hold that the statement "caution: do not lift by sides" was adequate as a matter of law, particularly since the label was not permanent. The label was placed on a wrapper that had to be removed and thrown away before the pan could be used.[147] Thus, the court denied the manufacturer's motion for summary judgment, holding that "the inconspicuous nature of the caution on the label, the size of the print, its contradictory words, its failure to be complete and accurate regarding the inherent dangers in the use of this pan, and its failure to mention the possibility of the pan 'collapsing' may all be considered by the jury."[148]

[C]   Content of the Warning

In addition to providing a warning in a form that reaches the attention of the user of the product, a manufacturer also must ensure that the content of the warning "convey[s] a fair indication of the nature and extent of the danger to the mind of a reasonably prudent person."[149] The extent of the content of the warning

---

[144] 2004 Mass. Super. LEXIS 200 (June 7, 2004).

[145] *Id.* at *3 (emphasis in original).

[146] *Id.* at *3–*4 (capitalization in original).

[147] *Id.* at *9.

[148] *Id.* at *11.

[149] Spruill v. Boyle-Midway, Inc., 308 F.2d 79, 85 (4th Cir. 1962) (applying Virginia law). *See also* Smith v. Louisville Ladder Co., 237 F.3d 515 (5th Cir. 2001) (applying Texas law); Johnson v. Colt

depends on the foreseeability of the use of the product and the type of danger involved.[150] An example of a warning for an otherwise safe product is *Kelso v. Bayer Corp.*,[151] in which the plaintiff used a 12 hours extra moisturizing nasal spray continuously for three years. At the end of that time, he learned that his continued use of the product had caused permanent nasal tissue damage that would require multiple sinus surgeries. The plaintiff sued the manufacturer of the spray in strict liability, alleging that it failed to warn him adequately of the dangers associated with the product. The warning on the spray package read:

> Do not exceed recommended dosage.

> ***Stop use and ask a doctor if symptoms persist. Do not use this product for more than 3 days. Use only as directed. Frequent or prolonged use may cause nasal congestion to recur or worsen.[152]

In affirming the district court's grant of summary judgment to the manufacturer, the Seventh Circuit stated that the warning against prolonged use was adequate since it was "unequivocal:"[153] "the plain, clear and unambiguous language of the warning states: 'Do not use this product for more than 3 days.' Period. . . . Moreover, the warning clearly informs users to: 'Stop use and ask a physician if symptoms persist.' The warning was clear."[154] In addition, the court held that the warning was adequate even though it did not warn that the product could cause permanent nasal tissue damage and had a risk of habituation since a manufacturer need not warn of all possible consequences of failing to follow a warning.[155]

With the growing linguistic diversity in the United States, some cases have raised the question of whether the content of a warning was adequate if it was only in English.[156] Courts have deferred to the requirements of state and federal statutes to determine whether such warnings were adequate. In *Ramirez v. Plough, Inc.*,[157] the mother of a four months old child gave him a nonprescription aspirin manufactured by the defendant to relieve the symptoms of his cold. Although the label stated that the dosage for a child under two years old was "as directed by doctor," the mother did not consult a doctor before giving her child the aspirin. Over a two-day period, she gave the child three tablets. When she finally took her child

---

Industries Operating corp., 797 F.2d 1530 (10th Cir. 1986) (applying Kansas law).

[150] Hood v. Ryobi America Corp., 181 F.3d 608 (4th Cir. 1999) (applying Maryland law); Pottle v. Up-Right, Inc., 628 A.2d 672 (Me. 1993); Johnson v. Harley-Davidson Motor Co. Group. Inc., 2004 Iowa App. LEXIS 344 (Feb. 27, 2004).

[151] 398 F.3d 640 (7th Cir. 2005) (applying Illinois law). For other examples, see Torsiello v. Whitehall Laboratories, Division of Home Products Corp., 398 A.2d 132 (N.J. Super. Ct. 1979) (the plaintiff, who took eight aspirin tablets a day for 14 months to relieve the pain of arthritis; as a result of the prolonged use, he suffered an attack of gastrointestinal hemorrhaging, that was diagnosed as "GI bleeding secondary to aspirin gastritis)"; Michael v. Warner/Chilcott, 579 P.2d 183 (N.M. Ct. App. 1978) (the plaintiff developed kidney failure after using sinus tablets daily for eight years).

[152] *Id.* at 641.

[153] *Id.* at 642.

[154] *Id.*

[155] *Id.*

[156] *See* Torres-Rio v. LPS Laboratories, Inc., 152 F.3d 11 (1st Cir. 1998).

[157] 863 P.2d 167 (Cal. 1993).

to the hospital, a doctor advised her to give the child nonprescription medicines that did not contain aspirin. However, she disregarded the advice and continued to give her child aspirin. The child later developed Reye's syndrome, resulting in severe neurological damage, including cortical blindness, spastic quadriplegia, and mental retardation. In her suit against the drug manufacturer, the child alleged negligence because the manufacturer distributed the product with warnings in English only. The California Supreme Court, however, affirmed summary judgment in favor of the manufacturer, holding that it had no duty to provide warnings in Spanish since applicable state and federal statutes required warnings to be only in English.[158] The court felt that deciding if and when warnings or other information should be in a language other than English was a task for which legislative and administrative agencies were better suited.[159]

Where a manufacturer provides a warning, it is entitled to assume that users and consumers will read it and follow it.[160] Thus, even if a warning was inadequate, courts usually will bar the plaintiff from recovering if it can be shown that he or she failed to read the warning.[161] That was the situation in *Ramirez* where the plaintiff asserted an alternative basis of liability that the label in English provided defective warnings of the risks of giving young children aspirin. The California court also rejected that argument because the plaintiff's mother "neither read nor obtained translation of the product labeling. Thus, there is no conceivable causal connection between the representations or omissions that accompanied the product and plaintiff's injury."[162] Similarly, in *Daniel v. Ben E. Keith Co.*,[163] the plaintiff was unable to recover on her failure to warn claim against the manufacturer of a chlorine bleach product. The plaintiff there was injured when her coworker mistakenly used the defendant's bleach to clean deep fat fryers in the restaurant where they worked. Adding the bleach to the fryer caused the bleach to boil, producing chlorine gas. The plaintiff inhaled the chlorine gas, which caused her to suffer from Reactive Airway Dysfunction Syndrome. The plaintiff brought suit against the defendant, alleging that their failure to warn of the risks of chlorine bleach caused her injuries.[164] The jury found for the defendant, and the plaintiff appealed. Amongst other issues, the plaintiff argued that the court erred by not

---

[158] *Id.* at 173–74. *See* Medina v. Louisville Ladder, Inc., 496 F. Supp. 2d 1324, 1329 (M.D. Fla. 2007) ("[T]here is no indication that Florida law imposes a duty on manufacturers and sellers to provide bilingual warnings on consumer products, and this Court is unwilling to extend the concept of duty that far. [T]here is no indication that a product may be found unreasonably dangerous under Florida law merely because it lacks bilingual warnings and instructions. [T]his Court is unwilling to extend the bounds of strict product liability law and negligence that far.").

[159] 863 P.2d at 174–75.

[160] E.R. Squibb & Sons, Inc. v. Cox, 477 So. 2d 963 (Ala. 1985).

[161] This is because, when the plaintiff does not read the instructions on a product before using it, many courts hold that an inadequate warning cannot be the proximate cause of the resulting injury. Robinson v. McNeil Consumer Healthcare, 671 F. Supp. 2d 975 (N.D. Ill. 2009) (applying Illinois law); Cooper v. Old Williamsburg Candle Corp., 653 F. Supp. 2d 1220 (M.D. Fla. 2009) (applying Florida law).

[162] 863 P.2d at 177.

[163] 97 F.3d 1329 (10th Cir. 1996) (applying Oklahoma law).

[164] *Id.* at 1331.

giving an instruction to the jury regarding the heeding presumption.[165]

The Tenth Circuit, applying Oklahoma law, affirmed the decision of the district court and the findings of the jury. The court noted the rule that there is a rebuttable presumption that the users of a product will read and heed an adequate warning.[166] In *Daniel*, however, the defendant successfully rebutted that presumption. The defendant elicited testimony from the plaintiff's coworker that on the morning of the accident, "he was in a hurry and did not look at the label."[167] It was because he failed to look at the label that he mistakenly used bleach instead of fryer cleaner. Because the plaintiff's coworker completely ignored the product's label, "any presumption that a different warning would have been heeded disappeared, and plaintiffs continued to carry the burden of proving that the allegedly inadequate warning caused her injury."[168] Thus, the Tenth Circuit ruled that the district court properly refused to give a heeding presumption instruction.

§ 7.05   POST-SALE DUTY TO WARN OR RECALL

[A]   Post-Sale Duty to Warn

Although every state recognizes a duty on the part of a manufacturer to warn consumers or users of dangers it knew about or should have known about at the time of the sale of a product, this duty traditionally did not extend past the sale. However, more than half of the states now also recognize a duty on a manufacturer to warn users and consumers in some situations of dangers that come to its attention after the sale of the product.[169] The underlying goal of requiring both pre- and post-sale warnings is the same: reduce the chance of injury by equalizing the information between the manufacturer and consumers about product risks. However, while the rationale for both duties is identical, the parameters in which they are applied are different.

For states recognizing a post-sale duty to warn, the duty may arise in two situations: first, when the manufacturer becomes aware of a defective that makes the product unreasonably dangerous and that condition was unknown to the seller

---

[165] *Id.*

[166] *Id. See also* Menz v. New Holland N.A., Inc., 507 F.3d 1107 (8th Cir. 2007) (applying Missouri law); Broyles v. Kasper Machine Co. 865 F. Supp. 2d 887 (S.D. Ohio 2012) (applying Ohio law); Rivera v. Philip Morris, Inc., 209 P.3d 271 (Nev. 2009); Lightolier v. Hoon, 876 A.2d 100 (Md. 2005).

[167] 97 F.3d at 1333.

[168] *Id. See* Smith v. Brown & Williamson Tobacco Corp., 275 S.W.3d 748 (Mo. Ct. App. 2008).

[169] For examples, see Bryant v. Giacomini, S.P.A., 391 F. Supp. 2d 495 (N.D. Tex. 2005) (Texas recognizes a post-sale duty to warn where the manufacturer regains some significant control over the product and where a manufacturer assumed a post-sale duty and then did not use reasonable means to discharge that duty); Patton v. Hutchinson Wil-Rich Manufacturing Co., 861 P.2d 1299 (Kan. 1993) (drug manufacturers); Walton v. Avco Corp., 610 A.2d 454 (Pa. 1992) (limited post-sale duty to warn). *See also* Cigna Insurance Co. v. Oy Saunatec, Ltd., 241 F.3d 1 (1st Cir. 2001) (applying Massachusetts law); Densberger v. United Technologies Corp., 125 F. Supp. 2d 585 (D. Conn. 2000) (applying Connecticut law); Flax v. Daimlerchrysler Corp., 272 S.W.3d 521 (Tenn. 2008); Ford Motor Co. V. Reese, 684 S.E.2d 279 (Ga. Ct. App. 2009).

at the time of sale but was discovered after the sale,[170] and, second, when the danger comes to the attention of the manufacturer as a result of advancements in the state of the art, with which it is expected to stay current.[171] An early example of a court recognizing such a duty to warn in such a situation is *Comstock v. General Motors Corp.*,[172] in which an automobile manufacturer learned of brake problems only weeks after releasing several of its 1953 models but failed to take action to warn buyers of the defect. The Michigan court extended its rule requiring manufacturers to warn of dangers known at the time of sale by holding that "a like duty to give prompt warning exists when a latent defect which makes the product hazardous to life becomes known to the manufacturer shortly after the product has been put on the market."[173]

Most states hold that there may be a post-sale duty to warn whether the plaintiff brought the claim in negligence or strict liability. However, states that recognize a post-sale duty to warn use a negligence analysis based on a "reasonableness standard" that takes a variety of factors into consideration in determining when and to whom a post-sale warning must be given, as well as the nature of the warning.[174] Although a crucial factor is whether the manufacturer had sufficient notice that the product posed a risk of serious harm,[175] the analysis is dependent on the facts in each case and includes: (1) the nature of the harm that may result unless notice is given; (2) the likelihood that harm will occur; (3) the number of persons who must be warned; (4) the economic burden on the manufacturer of identifying and notifying product users; (5) the nature of the industry; (6) the type of product involved; (7) the number of product units manufactured or sold; and (8) steps taken other than giving of notice to correct the problem.[176] In limited situations, section 10 of the Restatement (Third) also imposes a post-sale duty to warn. The section uses a "reasonable person" test to determine when a post-sale warning should be given and sets out four conditions that would lead a "reasonable person" to provide such a warning:

> (a) One engaged in the business of selling or otherwise distributing products is subject to liability for harm to persons or property caused by the seller's failure to provide a warning after the time of sale or distribution of a product if a reasonable person in the seller's position would provide such a warning.

Section 10 goes on to state that a *reasonable person in the seller's position* would provide a post-sale warning if four conditions are present. First, he knows or

---

[170] *See* Padilla v. Black & Decker Corp., 2005 U.S. Dist. LEXIS 4720 (E.D. Pa. Mar. 24, 2005) (applying Pennsylvania law); Mercer v. Pittway Corp., 616 N.W.2d 602 (Iowa 2000).

[171] Cover v. Cohen, 461 N.E.2d 864 (1984).

[172] 99 N.W.2d 627 (Mich. 1959).

[173] *Id.* at 634. *See also* Gregory v. Cincinnati, Inc, 538 N.W.2d 325 (Mich. 1995).

[174] Lovick v. Wil-Rich, 588 N.W.2d 688 (Iowa 1999).

[175] Post-sale accidents involving the product are one factor that may provide a manufacturer's with the notice required to create a post-sale duty to warn. *See* Cover v. Cohen, 461 N.E.2d 864 (N.Y. 1984).

[176] Patton v. Hutchinson Wil-Rich Manufacturing Co., 861 P.2d 1299, 1314–15 (Kan. 1993). *See* Padilla v. Black & Decker Corp., 2005 U.S. Dist. LEXIS 4720 (E.D. Pa. Mar. 25, 2005) (applying Pennsylvania law); Cover v. Cohen, 461 N.E.2d 864 (N.Y. 1984).

should know that the product poses a *substantial risk of harm* to persons or property. Second, those to whom the warning should be given can be identified and are assumed to be unaware of the risk of harm. Third, a warning can be provided effectively and acted upon by those who receive it. And, finally, the risk of harm is great enough to justify the burden of providing the warning.[177]

Regardless of the factors, however, courts exempt manufacturers from warning an owner who has purchased a product second-hand. Such a person becomes part of a universe of people too large and too diffuse for manufacturers and sellers to identify.[178]

Despite the trend toward recognizing a post-sale duty to warn, a few jurisdictions have rejected imposing such a duty. Generally, the states that do not recognize a post-sale duty to warn believe that requiring the duty would inject negligence principles into strict liability claims when products are defective and would eliminate the requirement under strict liability that the defect existed before the manufacturer sold the product. In *Collins v. Hyster Co.*,[179] the Illinois appellate court reasoned that "the law does not contemplate placing the onerous duty on manufacturers to subsequently warn all foreseeable users of products based on increased design or manufacture expertise that was not present at the time the product left its control."[180] In addition, even states that recognize a post-sale duty to warn hold that the duty does not apply where the danger is open and obvious or the consumer is a sophisticated user of the product.

[B] Product Recalls

[1] Judicially Mandated Product Recalls

In addition to alleging that a manufacturer has a post-sale duty to warn of a danger that came to its attention after the product left its control, some plaintiffs have asserted that a manufacturer had a duty to recall and retrofit a product, after its sale, with a safety device. Unless mandated by a statute, however, courts have rejected imposing such an obligation on manufacturers.[181] Although most of the cases have dealt with the issue briefly in a motion for summary judgment, the

---

[177] RESTATEMENT (THIRD) OF TORTS: PRODUCTS LIABILITY § 10 (1998). *See* Kendall v. Bausch & Lomb, Inc., 2009 U.S. Dist. LEXIS 52454 (D.S.D. June 17, 2009) (applying South Dakota law); Jablonski v. Ford Motor Co., 955 N.E.2d 1138 (Ill. 2011); Lovick v. Wil-Rich, 588 N.W.2d 688 (Iowa 1999); Hanlan v. Chandler, 2008 Mass. Super. LEXIS 368 (Nov. 6, 2008) (there is no duty to warn subsequent purchasers of a product if the manufacturer is unable to reasonably identify those purchasers). Although Maine recognizes that, in limited circumstances, there can be a post-sale duty to warn known indirect purchasers, it has not adopted § 10 of the RESTATEMENT (THIRD) OF TORTS. Brown v. Crown Equip. Corp., 960 A.2d 1188 (Me. 2008).

[178] Lewis v. Ariens Co., 751 N.E.2d 862 (Mass. 2001).

[179] 529 N.E.2d 303 (Ill. App. Ct. 1988).

[180] *Id.* at 306.

[181] *See* Morales v. E.D. Etnyre & Co., 382 F. Supp. 2d 1285 (D.N.M. 2005) (applying New Mexico law); Padilla v. Black & Decker Corp., 2005 U.S. Dist. LEXIS 4720 (E.D. Pa. Mar. 25, 2005) (applying Pennsylvania law); Eberts v. Kawasaki Motors Corp., U.S.A., 2004 U.S. Dist. LEXIS 1294 (D.N.D. Feb. 2, 2004) (applying North Dakota law); Flock v. Scripto-Tokai Corp., 2001 U.S. Dist. LEXIS 23885 (S.D. Tex. Aug. 2, 2001) (applying Texas law); Ford Motor Co. V. Reese, 684 S.E.2d 279 (Ga. Ct. App. 2009).

Illinois appellate court, in *Modelski v. Navistar International Transportation Corp.*,[182] set out its reasons for holding there was no duty in detail. In *Modelski* the plaintiff alleged that the manufacturer was negligent in failing to retrofit a tractor, after its sale, with a safety device that would have eliminated the danger created by the unexpected loss of the bolts on the battery box cover. However, the Illinois court held that, in the absence of a statutory obligation or voluntary undertaking, the manufacturer had no duty to recall or retrofit the product to remedy a danger of which it did not know, nor should have known.[183] According to the court, its holding was in keeping with the position taken by most state courts.[184]

> The consequences of imposing upon manufacturers an extrastatutory duty to recall and retrofit used products to incorporate post-sale state of the art designs would be the equivalent of mandating that manufacturers insure their products will always comply with current safety standards. This we are unwilling to do. If such a continuing duty is to be imposed, it is legislature that is better suited to the task. In a legislative setting, due consideration can be given to the type of products to which such a duty would apply and to whether a statute of repose should be enacted to limit the potentially indefinite duration of the duty.[185]

The holding of the court in *Modelskis* is supported by § 11 of the Restatement (Third) which deals with the "Liability of Commercial Product Seller or Distributor for Harm Caused by Post-Sale Failure to Recall Product." According to the Restatement:

> One engaged in the business of selling or otherwise distributing products is subject to liability for harm to persons or property caused by the seller's failure to recall a product after the time of sale or distribution if:
>
> (a)
>
> > (1) a governmental directive issued pursuant to a statute or administrative regulation specifically requires the seller or distributor to recall the product; or
> >
> > (2) the seller or distributor, in the absence of a recall requirement under Subsection (a)(1), undertakes to recall the product; and
>
> (b) (b) the seller or distributor fails to act as a reasonable person in recalling the product.[186]

---

[182] 707 N.E.2d 239 (Ill. App. Ct. 1999).

[183] However, there may be a continuing duty if, at the time of the manufacture of the product, the manufacturer knew or should have known of the hazard. Jablonski v. Ford Motor Co., 955 N.E.2d 1138 (Ill. 2011).

[184] *See* Horstmyer v. Black & Decker, (U.S.), Inc., 151 F.3d 765 (8th Cir. 1998) (applying Missouri law); Tabieros v. Clark Equipment Co., 944 P.2d 1279 (Haw. 1999); Gregory v. Cincinnati Inc., 538 N.W.2d 325 (Mich. 1995); Patton v. Hutchinson Wil-Rich Manufacturing Co., 861 P.2d 1299 (Kan. 1993).

[185] *Id.* at 247.

[186] RESTATEMENT (THIRD) OF TORTS: PRODUCTS LIABILITY § 11 (1998). For a critique of § 11, see James T. O'Reilly, *Product Recalls and the Third Restatement: Consumers Lose Twice from Defects in Products and in the Restatement*, 33 U. MEM. L. REV. 883 (2003).

In support of this limited duty to recall a product, comment a to § 11 speaks of the burdens that the recall of a product places on manufacturers.

Duties to recall products impose significant burdens on manufacturers. Many product lines are periodically redesigned so that they become safer over time. If every improvement in product safety were to trigger a common-law duty to recall, manufacturers would face incalculable costs every time they sought to make their product lines better and safer.[187]

[2] Legislative Product Recalls

Although courts have refused to impose a general duty to recall products whose defects become known only after sale, a number of government agencies have the power to impose product recalls. Among these agencies are: the Consumer Protection Safety Commission ("CPSC"), the Federal Trade Commission ("FTC"), the Food and Drug Administration ('FDA"),[188] and the National Highway Traffic Safety Administration (NTSA"). Because of the broad authority of the CPSC (it has jurisdiction over 15,000 types of products), its importance to attorneys who represent manufacturers, distributors, and retailers in products liability actions, and the controversy surrounding some of the agency's actions,[189] this subsection briefly examines Consumer Product Safety Act ("CPSA")[190] as an example of scope and procedure of legislative recalls.

Under § 15(d) of the CPSA,[191] a manufacturer, importer, distributor, or retailer of a consumer product distributed in the United States that receives information from which a person could "reasonably conclude" that one of its products contains a defect that "could" create a "substantial product hazard"[192] or create "an unreasonable risk of serious injury or death"[193] must make a report to the CPSC[194]

---

[187] *Id.* at cmt. *a.*

[188] The range of items for which the FDA has issued warnings or recalled includes bone putty, cantaloupes, dietary supplements, medical devices, romaine lettuce, and tracheostomy tubes.

[189] *See* Andrew Martin, *Fateful Attractions: For Rare-Earth Magnets, Child Safety Is a Growing Issue,* THE NEW YORK TIMES, Aug.17, 2012, *available at* http://www.nytimes.com/2012/08/17/business/for-buckyballs-toys-child-safety-is-a-growing-issue.html?pagewanted=all.

[190] 15 U.S.C.S. §§ 2051 *et seq.* The CPSA was enacted by Congress in 1972. The CPSA gives the CPSC a mandate to protect the public against "unreasonable risks of injury associated with consumer products." The CPSA defines a "consumer product" as "any article, or component part thereof, produced or distributed (i) for sale to a consumer for use in or around a permanent or temporary household or residence, a school, in recreation, or otherwise, or (ii) for the personal use, consumption or enjoyment of a consumer in or around a permanent or temporary household or residence, a school, in recreation, or otherwise." *Id.* at § 2052(a)(1). "Children's products" (16 C.F.R. 1200.2) are subject to enhanced regulations and reporting requirements under the CPSA and Consumer Product Safety Improvements Act of 2008 (CPSIA). The CPSIA defines a "children's product" as a product designed or intended primarily for children 12 years of age and younger. The CPSIA adds a number of standards for such products, such as maximum levels of lead and a ban on certain phthalates.

[191] *Id.* at § 2064(d).

[192] 15 U.S.C. § 2064(b)(2).

[193] *Id.* at § 2064(b)(3).

[194] The CPSC has five Commissioners and about 500 employees (compliance/field investigators, scientists and engineers, customs agents, and attorneys). In 2011 its budget was about $122 million.

of the defect within 24 hours of receiving the information.[195] The CPSA does not define terms such as "defect," "substantial product hazard," "unreasonable risk," or "serious injury." The reporting requirements of the CPSA are implemented by regulations adopted by the CPSC.

Defect: CPSC regulations state that the term "defect" includes the dictionary or commonly accepted meaning of the word. Thus, a defect is a fault, flaw, or irregularity that causes weakness, failure, or inadequacy in form or function.[196] A defect may result from an error in the design or manufacture of a product. In addition, the regulations state that

> a product may contain a defect even if the product is manufactured exactly in accordance with its design and specifications, if the design presents a risk of injury to the public. A design defect may also be present if the risk of injury occurs as a result of the operation or use of the product or the failure of the product to operate as intended. A defect can also occur in a product's contents, construction, finish, packaging, warnings, and/or instructions. With respect to instructions, a consumer product may contain a defect if the instructions for assembly or use could allow the product, otherwise safely designed and manufactured, to present a risk of injury.[197]

Substantial product hazard: The regulations define "substantial product hazard" as either (1) A failure to comply with an applicable consumer product safety rule, which failure creates a substantial risk of injury to the public, or (2) A product defect which (because of the pattern of defect, the number of defective products distributed in commerce, the severity of the risk, or otherwise) creates a substantial risk of injury to the public.[198]

Unreasonable risk: The regulations set out the following explanation of what constitutes an unreasonable risk:

> In determining whether a product presents an unreasonable risk, the firm should examine the utility of the product, or the utility of the aspect of the product that causes the risk, the level of exposure of consumers to the risk, the nature and severity of the hazard presented, and the likelihood of resulting serious injury or death.[199]

Serious injury: The regulations provide the following guidance with those events that constitute a serious injury:

> The Commission believes that the term includes not only the concept of "grievous bodily injury," defined at § 1115.12(d), but also any other significant injury. Injuries necessitating hospitalization which require actual

---

[195] Although the legal obligation to report is placed upon the manufacturer, importer, distributor, and retailer, they may agree among themselves who will file the report and who will be responsible for the recall. If the other parties know that the CPSC has been informed, they do not have to file a second report.

[196] 16 C.F.R. § 1115.4.

[197] *Id.*

[198] *Id.* at § 1115.2(a).

[199] *Id.* at § 1115.6(b).

medical or surgical treatment, fractures, lacerations requiring sutures, concussions, injuries to the eye, ear, or internal organs requiring medical treatment, and injuries necessitating absence from school or work of more than one day are examples of situations in which the Commission shall presume that such a serious injury has occurred.[200]

Under § 6(b) of the CPSA, the CPSC must give a manufacturer 15 days notice before it discloses information that will "permit the public to ascertain readily the identity of the manufacturer or private labeler of a consumer product." The manufacturer then has an opportunity to provide comments, and its comments may be included with the information that is disclosed. During those 15 days, the CPSC must take steps to ensure that the information to be disclosed is accurate and fair. In 2011, pursuant to the CPSIA, the CPSC launched SaferProducts.gov, a public database that posts reports involving consumer products.

There are two main routes to the recall of a product. First, after receiving a report, the CPSC may determine that the product contains a defect that creates a "substantial product hazard" or an "unreasonable risk." The company then may voluntarily recall the product. However, if the company disagrees with the CPSC's decision, it can refuse to recall. In that situation, the CPSC can initiate an administrative proceeding to require the company to recall the product. Second, a company can agree to announce publicly a recall program acceptable to the CPSC within 20 days of the initial report. Recalls usually include some combination of replacement of the product with another product, a repair program, a refund, a public recall announcement, a direct letter campaign, notice on the company's website, and posters at retailer.

Under § 12 of the CPSA, if the CPSC determines that a product "presents imminent and reasonable risk of death, serious illness, or severe personal injury," it can file an action in U.S. District Court, asking the court to declare the product an "imminently hazardous product." The court has jurisdiction to grant temporary or permanent relief to protect the public from the product. The CPSC also can seek civil penalties in federal court against a company for "knowingly" violating the CPSA reporting requirements. The maximum penalty for individual violations is $100,000. The maximum total penalty per violation or series of related violations is $15 million. Knowing and willful violations of the CPSA also can lead to criminal penalties of up to five years imprisonment and/or a fine.

§ 7.06 THE LEARNED INTERMEDIARY DOCTRINE

[A] Origin and Scope of the Learned Intermediary Doctrine

The purpose of products liability law is to place the cost of injuries caused by products that are "unreasonably dangerous" on the manufacturers or suppliers of those products.[201] At the same time, however, some products, such as prescription drugs and medical devices, may be unavoidably unsafe yet not be unreasonably

---

[200] *Id.* at § 1115.6(c).

[201] Hill v. Searle Laboratories, 884 F.2d 1064 (8th Cir. 1989).

dangerous because they provide a great benefit to a large number of people. In order to encourage the production of prescription drugs and medical devices, the drafters of § 402A included an exception to the rule of strict liability for manufacturers of prescription drugs from strict liability provided that the drugs are "properly prepared and accompanied by proper directions and warnings."[202]

Although manufacturers are protected from strict liability for "properly prepared" prescription drugs and medical devices if they provide "proper directions and warnings," section 402A does not state to whom the "directions and warnings" must be given. Although products liability law generally requires that warnings be given to the "ultimate user or consumer" of the product, courts in almost every state have created an exception for prescription drugs in the form of the "learned intermediary doctrine."[203] This doctrine provides that prescription drug and medical device manufacturers satisfy their duty to warn if they provide complete, accurate, and timely warnings to proscribing physicians, or other health professionals who may prescribe their products, of the risks or contraindications associated with their drugs and devices of which they know or should have reason to know.[204] Courts have not expanded the application of the learned intermediary doctrine beyond the pharmaceutical or medical arena.[205] The doctrine applies with both to strict liability and negligence claims.[206]

Courts have given a number of reasons for the learned intermediary doctrine: patients rely on their physician's advice and warnings for prescription drugs; drug manufactures lack effective means to communicate to the specific risks to each patient; the ordinary consumer is unable to understand complex medical warnings while a doctor can; imposing a duty to warn patients would interfere with the physician-patient relationship.[207] However, the primary rationale behind the

---

[202] See RESTATEMENT (SECOND) OF TORTS § 402A cmt. k (1965).

[203] See Murthy v. Abbott Labs., 2012 U.S. Dist. LEXIS 29683 (S.D. Tex. Mar. 6, 2012) (applying Texas law); Smith v. Pfizer Inc., 688 F. Supp. 2d 735 (M.D. Tenn. 2010) (applying Tennessee law); Rimbert v. Eli Lilly and Co., 577 F. Supp. 2d 1174 (D.N.M. 2008) (applying New Mexico law); Rohde v. Smiths Medical, 165 P.3d 433 (Wyo. 2007). However, after examining the history of the doctrine and the current state of the pharmaceutical industry, the West Virginia Supreme Court decided not to adopt the rule in State ex. rel. Johnson & Johnson Corp. V. Karl, 647 S.E.2d 899 (W. Va. 2007).

[204] Ehlis v. Shire Richwood, Inc., 367 F.3d 1013 (8th Cir. 2004) (applying North Dakota law); Greaves v. Eli Lilly & Co., 277 F.R.D. 243 (E.D.N.Y. 2011) (applying Rhode Island law); Rite Aid Corp. v. Levy-Gray, 894 A.2d 563 (Md. 2006). Using their medical judgment, physicians then have a duty to convey the warning to their patients. Kirk v. Michael Reese Hospital & Medical Center, 513 N.E.2d 387 (Ill. 1987).

[205] Nye v. Bayer Cropscience, Inc., 347 S.W.3d 686 (Tenn. 2011). Courts also have limited the learned intermediary doctrine in cases involving pharmacists. See Downing v. Hyland Pharmacy, 194 P.3d 944 (Utah 2008), in which the Utah Supreme Court held that a pharmacist could be liable in negligence for filling prescriptions for a drug that had been withdrawn from the market at the request of the FDA and Rite Aid Corp. v. Levy-Gray, 894 A.2d 563 (Md. 2006), in which the Maryland court declined to extend the doctrine to cases in which pharmacy disseminates information about the properties and efficacy of a prescription drug.

[206] For a list of states that have done so, see Downing v. Hyland Pharmacy, 194 P.3d 944, 946–47 (Utah 2008).

[207] Larkin v. Pfizer, Inc., 153 S.W.3d 758, 763–64 (Ky. 2004). See also Bernard J. Garbutt III & Melinda E. Hofmann, Recent Developments in Pharmaceutical Products Liability Law: Failure to

doctrine is the assumption that physicians or other health professionals, as the persons who prescribe the drugs, are a "learned intermediary" between the manufacturer and the consumers. As such, they are in the best position to give an individualized warning to their patients, based upon the physicians' knowledge of their patients and the inherent risks of the drugs, which are likely to be complex and vary in the effects they have on users.[208] As a medical expert, the prescribing physician can take into account the propensities of the drug as well as the susceptibilities of the patient and weigh the benefits of any medication against its potential dangers. The choice the physician makes is an individualized medical judgment based on his or her knowledge both of the patient and the drug or device.[209] The scope of the learned intermediary doctrine is illustrated by *Hernandez v. Schering Corp.*,[210] in which a patient suffered permanent vision loss after using a drug prescribed by his physician. The patient also attended a class sponsored by the drug manufacturer which dealt with how to use the drug and possible side effects. Although a document given to those who attended the class mentioned blindness, the nurse who taught the class did not mention any vision-related side effects.[211] In a suit against the drug manufacturer, the Illinois appellate court held that the physician undertook to warn the patient of the side-effects of the drug and that the manufacturer did not voluntarily undertake to warn by sponsoring the class.[212]

Although the learned intermediary concept has been recognized since the late 1940s,[213] it was not until 1966, in *Sterling Drug v. Cornish*[214] that a court first used the term "learned intermediary" when the Eight Circuit recognized that a "purchaser's doctor is a learned intermediary between the purchaser and the manufacturer."[215] In recent years, courts have extended the doctrine from prescription drugs to include prescription medical implants and devices as well.[216] Discussing a cardiac pacemaker, the Fourth Circuit stated:

> The decision to prescribe a cardiac pacemaker involves precisely the sort of individualized medical balancing contemplated by the drug exception. Unlike polio vaccines, pacemakers are not dispensed indiscriminately in mass clinics, but instead are prescribed only after a physician balances the

---

Warn, the Learned Intermediary Defense, and Other Issues in the New Millennium, 58 FOOD DRUG L.J. 269, 272–73 (2003).

[208] Ackermann v. Wyeth Pharmaceuticals, 526 F.3d 203 (5th Cir. 2008) (applying Texas law); Jacobs v. Dista Prods. Co., 693 F. Supp. 1029 (D. Wyo. 1988).

[209] *See* Beale v. Biomet, Inc., 492 F.Supp.2d 1360 (S.D. Fla. 2007 (applying Florida law); Vitanza v. Upjohn Co., 778 A.2d 829 (Conn. 2001).

[210] 958 N.E.2d 447 (Ill. App. Ct. 2011).

[211] *Id.* at 449–51.

[212] *Id.* at 452–55.

[213] *See* Marcus v. Specific Pharmaceuticals, 77 N.Y.S.2d 508 (1948).

[214] 370 F.2d 82 (8th Cir. 1966).

[215] *Id.* at 85.

[216] *See* Ellis v. C.R. Bard, Inc., 311 F.3d 1272, 1280 (11th Cir. 2002) (applying Georgia law); Willett v. Baxter International, Inc., 929 F.2d 1094 (5th Cir. 1991) (applying Louisiana law); Phelps v. Sherwood Med. Indus., 836 F.2d 296 (7th Cir. 1987) (applying Indiana law).

individual's needs against the known risks. Indeed, expert testimony in the present case indicated that each pacemaker candidate presents different problems requiring individualized professional judgments about lead models and generator units.[217]

This evolution is reflected in the Restatement (Third). Although §§ 6(a) and 6(b) hold manufacturers of prescription drugs and medical devices liable if their products are defective in their design, manufacture or inadequate warnings, sections 6 (c) and 6(d) codify the learned intermediary doctrine in § 6:

> (c) A prescription drug or medical device is not reasonably safe due to defective design if the foreseeable risks of harm posed by the drug or medical device are sufficiently great in relation to its foreseeable therapeutic benefits that reasonable health-care providers, knowing of such foreseeable risks and therapeutic benefits, would not prescribe the drug or medical device for any class of patients.

> (d) A prescription drug or medical device is not reasonably safe due to inadequate instructions or warnings if reasonable instructions or warnings regarding foreseeable risks of harm are not provided to:

> (1) prescribing and other health care providers who are in a position to reduce the risks or harm in accordance with the instructions or warnings.[218]

Although the learned intermediary doctrine answers the question of who must provide a warning about prescription drugs, it does not address the issue of when a drug manufacturer must warn physicians, what constitutes an adequate warning, and any exceptions to the doctrine. Those issues have been left to the courts.

[B] When a Warning Must Be Given to Physicians

The learned intermediary doctrine applies only to prescription drugs and medical devices.[219] Manufacturers do not have to provide warnings to physicians for over-the-counter drugs and medical devices because the rationales supporting the doctrine do not apply when a physician does not individually balance the risks involved in a patient using a particular product.[220] The doctrine also applies only to warning physicians about drugs' known dangerous propensities.[221] However, since manufacturers are held to the standard of an expert in their field, they have a continuing duty to keep informed of scientific developments that affect the safety of their products and to notify physicians of risks they discover from the use of their

---

[217] Brooks v. Medtronic, Inc., 750 F.2d 1227, 1232 (4th Cir. 1984).

[218] RESTATEMENT (THIRD) OF TORTS: PRODUCTS LIABILITY §§ 6(c) and 6(d)(1) (1998). *See also* RESTATEMENT (THIRD) OF TORTS: PRODUCTS LIABILITY § (2) cmt. *i* and § 6(d)(1) cmt. *b*.

[219] Reyes v. Wyeth Laboratories, 498 F.2d 1264 (5th Cir. 1974); Beale v. Biomet, Inc., 492 F. Supp. 2d 1360 (S.D. Fla. 2007) (applying Florida law).

[220] In the case of nonprescription drugs and devices, the manufacturer has a duty to provide the warning directly to the purchaser of the product.

[221] Kirk v. Michael Reese Hospital and Medical Center, 513 N.E.2d 387 (Ill. 1987).

products.[222] Manufacturers may have a duty to warn physicians of very rare, idiosyncratic, adverse reactions to their products if the potential harm is likely to be severe.[223] In warning physicians, manufacturer must use methods that are reasonably calculated to bring the dangers to their attention.[224]

A corollary of the learned intermediary doctrine is the principle that the manufacturer of a prescription drug or medical device does not have a duty to warn physicians of risks that are well known to the medical community. However, if there is any question of whether the drug manufacturer's knowledge is superior to that of the medical community, it is an issue for the jury to decide.[225]

[C] Adequacy of the Warning

Under the learned intermediary doctrine, a manufacturer is not liable if it provides adequate warnings to prescribing physicians or other health professionals.[226] However, if the warning to the intermediary is inadequate or misleading, the manufacturer remains liable for injuries suffered by the user.[227] In order to constitute an adequate warning, courts have adopted varying forms of a reasonableness standard.[228] According to the California Supreme Court, this "infuses some negligence concepts" into the strict liability claim.[229] Some courts also have held that an otherwise adequate warning may become inadequate if a drug manufacturer over-promotes a drug to physicians.[230]

Although whether a warning is adequate usually is a question for the trier of fact,[231] courts are likely to hold that a warning to physicians is adequate as a matter of law when the warning is clear, accurate, and unambiguous.[232] In *Thom v. Bristol-Myers Squibb*,[233] the Tenth Circuit listed five factors for determining whether a warning is adequate as a matter of law: (1) the warning must adequately indicate the scope of danger; (2) the warning must reasonably communicate the

---

[222] Proctor v. Davis, 682 N.E.2d 1203 (Ill. App. Ct. 1997).

[223] *See* Wright v. Carter Prods., 244 F.2d 53 (2d Cir. 1957) (applying New York law); Tomer v. American Home Prods. Corp., 170 Conn. 681, 368 A.2d 35 (1976); Crocker v. Winthrop Laboratories, 514 S.W.2d 429 (Tex. 1974).

[224] McEwen v. Ortho Pharmaceutical Corp., 528 P.2d 522 (Or. 1974).

[225] Hansen v. Baxter Healthcare Corp., 764 N.E.2d 35 (Ill. 2002).

[226] Rohde v. Smiths Medical, 165 P.3d 433 (Wyo. 2007).

[227] Ackermann v. Wyeth Pharmaceuticals, 526 F.3d 203 (5th Cir. 2008) (applying Texas law); Colville v. Pharmacia & Upjohn Co., 565 F. Supp. 2d 1314 (N.D. Fla. 2008) (applying Florida law). *See* Brown v. Glaxo, Inc., 790 So. 2d 35 (La. Ct. App. 2000) (a misleading oral statement by a pharmaceutical sale representative may supersede an otherwise adequate written warning to a physician).

[228] *See* Stahl v. Novartis Pharmaceuticals Corp., 283 F.3d 254, 267 (5th Cir. 2002) (applying Louisiana law); Ralston v. Smith & Nephew Richards, Inc., 275 F.3d 965, 974 (10th Cir. 2001) (applying Kansas law).

[229] Carlin v. Superior Court, 962 P.2d 1347, 1350 (Cal. 1996).

[230] *See* Salmon v. Parke, Davis, & Co., 520 F.2d 1359 (4th Cir. 1975); Stevens v. Parke, Davis & Co., 507 P.2d 653 (Cal. 1973); Whitley v. Cubberly, 210 S.E.2d 289 (N.C. Ct. App. 1974).

[231] Bukowski v. CooperVision Inc., 592 N.Y.S.2d 807, 807 (1993); MacDonald v. Ortho Pharmaceuticals, 475 N.E.2d 65, 71 (Mass. 1985).

[232] Stahl v. Novartis Pharmaceuticals Corp., 283 F.3d 254, 267 (5th Cir. 2002).

[233] Thom v. Bristol-Myers Squibb Co., 353 F.3d 848 (10th Cir. 2003).

extent or seriousness of harm that could result from misuse of the drug; (3) the physical layout of the warning must adequately alert a reasonably prudent person of the dangers; (4) a simple directive may be inadequate if it fails to detail possible consequences due to failure to follow it; and, (5) the means to convey the warning must be adequate.[234] Warnings provided by drug manufacturers may be inadequate even though all government regulations and requirements were met in the production and marketing of the drug and in the changes to the literature.[235] In addition, if a manufacturer does not change a warning it knows is widely disregarded, a jury may infer that the warning was insufficient.[236]

In *Swayze v. McNeil Laboratories*,[237] the Fifth Circuit addressed the appropriate methods of informing a learned intermediary. The court stated that drug manufacturers use three methods for disseminating information about the benefits and dangers of their products: (1) printed warnings and detailed information on packet inserts enclosed in packages containing the drug; (2) publication of identical warnings in the Physician's Desk Reference (PDR), a "dictionary" of drugs routinely relied upon by physicians; and (3) the dispatch of "detail men," who are part salespersons and part educators, to speak with practicing physicians in their offices. The court ruled that if the warnings provided to health care practitioners, through the PDR, package inserts, and detail men, were adequate, then the drug was not unreasonably dangerous, and the manufacturer's conduct was neither unreasonable nor negligent.[238]

Courts have held that even a package insert, which has been approved by the Food and Drug Administration and published in the Physicians' Desk Reference, does not, as a matter of law, relieve the manufacturer of its obligation to communicate an adequate warning to the users of a dangerous drug, where it was alleged that the approved insert did not adequately warn of potential dangers to users.[239]

[D] Causation

In addition to showing that a drug manufacturer provided an inadequate warning about a prescription drug or medical device, a plaintiff also must show that the inadequate warning was a substantial cause of the injury.[240] A majority of

---

[234] *Id.* at 852.

[235] *See* Yarrow v. Sterling Drug, 263 F. Supp. 159, 162 (D.S.D. 1967); Stegall v. Catawba Oil Co., 133 S.E.2d 138 (N.C. 1963).

[236] Incollingo v. Ewing, 282 A.2d 206 (Pa. 1971).

[237] 807 F.2d 464 (5th Cir. 1987).

[238] *Id.* at 471. *See also* Tatum v. Schering Corp., 795 F.2d 925 (11th Cir. 1986); Jacobs v. Dista Prods. Co., 693 F. Supp. 1029 (D. Wyo. 1988). State and federal courts have been uniform in holding that the PDR is the recognized authority to which doctors turn to obtain adverse reaction and precautions information respecting prescription drugs. *See* United States v. Schuster, 777 F.2d 264 (5th Cir. 1985); Stanton v. Astra Pharmaceutical, 718 F.2d 553 (3d Cir. 1983); DeLuryea v. Winthrop Laboratories, 697 F.2d 222 (8th Cir. 1983).

[239] In re Avandia Marketing, Sales Practices and Products Liability Litigation, 817 F. Supp. 2d 535 (E.D. Pa. 2011) Bristol-Myers Co. v. Gonzales, 561 S.W.2d 801 (Tex. 1978).

[240] *See* Pustejovsky v. Pliva, Inc., 623 F.3d 271 (5th Cir. 2010) (applying Texas law); In re Prempro

states hold that, if the plaintiff proves that the warning was inadequate, there is a rebuttable presumption that an adequate warning will be read and heeded once it is given. However, if the drug manufacturer can prove that an adequate warning would not have changed the doctor's decision to prescribe a particular drug, the drug manufacturer is not liable due to lack of causation.[241] Thus, a majority of courts have held that a manufacturer's inadequate warnings were not the proximate cause of the plaintiff's injuries where the prescribing physician failed to read the manufacturer's warnings. In such cases, the doctor's negligence constituted an intervening cause.[242]

[E] Exceptions to the Learned Intermediary Doctrine

Section 6(d)(2) of the Restatement (Third) limits the applicability of the learned intermediary doctrine by providing that manufacturers must warn the patient directly "when the manufacturer knows or has reason to know that health-care providers will not be in a position to reduce the risks of harm in accordance with the instructions or warnings." The drafters created this limitation to the learned intermediary doctrine because existing case law supported the idea that warnings should be given directly to patients when a manufacturer knows a health care provider will not act as a learned intermediary.[243] However, the drafters of the Restatement (Third) refrained from taking a position on what other exceptions courts should adopt when it stated that it left it to developing case law to decide whether exceptions to the learned intermediary doctrine should be adopted.[244] Over the years, courts have adopted four major exceptions to the learned intermediary doctrine.

[1] Mass Immunization

Although a manufacturer's duty to warn of the risks of prescription drugs usually extends only to the physician, if the manufacturer knows or should know that the drug will be sold, distributed, or administered without the intervention of individualized medical judgment to balance the risks, as in a mass immunization, the duty to warn may run directly to the product user.[245] In *Reyes v. Wyeth*,[246] an

---

Products Liability Litigation, 586 F.3d 547 (8th Cir. 2009) (the evidence on causation was sufficient to permit the jury to find that a failure to warn was the proximate cause of the plaintiff's injuries).

[241] Ehlis v. Shire Richwood, Inc., 367 F.3d 1013 (8th Cir. 2004); Motus v. Pfizer Inc., 358 F.3d 659, 661 (9th Cir. 2004).

[242] Hall v. Elkins Sinn, Inc., 2004 U.S. App. LEXIS 12255 (5th Cir. 2004); Thom v. Bristol-Myers Squibb Co., 353 F.3d 848 (10th Cir. 2003).

[243] *See* RESTATEMENT (THIRD) OF TORTS: PRODUCTS LIABILITY § 6 cmt. *e* (1998).

[244] *Id.* For a discussion of exceptions to the learned intermediary rule, *see* Murthy v. Abbott Labs., 2012 U.S. Dist. LEXIS 29683 (S.D.Tex. 2012) (applying Texas law); Vitanza v. Upjohn Co., 48 F. Supp. 2d 124 (D. Conn. 1999); Edwards v. Basel Pharmaceuticals, 933 P.2d 298 (Okla. 1997).

[245] *See* Davis v. Wyeth Laboratories, 399 F.2d 121 (9th Cir. 1968) (applying Montana law). However, in Brazzell v. United States, 788 F.2d 1352 (8th Cir. 1986) (applying Iowa law), the Eight Circuit held that a doctor's participation in administering the swine flu vaccine was did not overcome the manufacturer's duty to warn the ultimate consumer, since vaccination program was designed to be at emergency pace, which gave physicians little opportunity to investigate the vaccine they were administering. *See also* Hurley v. Lederle Laboratories, 863 F.2d 1173 (5th Cir. 1988).

eight-month-old child received an oral polio vaccination from a health clinic and two weeks later was diagnosed with polio. The Fifth Circuit held that the learned intermediary doctrine did not insulate the manufacturer from liability and that the manufacturer had a duty to warn the ultimate consumer of risks involved in taking the vaccination.[247] The court reasoned that the rationale behind the learned intermediary doctrine vanished because the manufacturer had reason to know that a physician would not make an individual balancing of the risks and benefits before administering the vaccine.[248]

Courts have limited the applicability of the mass immunization exception by providing that the exception does not apply in situations where a physician-patient relationship exists.[249] Thus, where a physician administers a vaccination to his patient, the learned intermediary doctrine still applies. In *Niemiera v. Schneider*,[250] the parents of a child who suffered a disabling convulsive episode which left him brain damaged brought an action against a physician, a hospital, and the manufacturer of the vaccine alleged to have caused the episode. The New Jersey Supreme Court held that the learned intermediary doctrine relieved the manufacturer of a duty to warn the parents directly of the vaccine's potentially dangerous side effects, since the role of the physician required an exercise in medical judgment concerning when and under what circumstances the vaccine should be administered.

[2]   Oral Contraceptives and Contraceptive Devices

Some states have also carved out an exception to the learned intermediary doctrine for oral contraceptives and contraceptive devices.[251] Unlike most other prescription drugs, contraceptives generally are not therapeutic, curative, or diagnostic. Their use usually is initiated by the patient rather than the physician. A woman's heightened participation in the decision-making process as to whether she wants a specific contraceptive encourages manufacturers of contraceptives to pursue public relations campaigns directed towards potential users. Plaintiffs argue that this outreach to the ultimate consumer justifies an exception to the learned

---

[246] Reyes v. Wyeth Laboratories, 498 F.2d 1264 (5th Cir. 1974) (applying Texas law).

[247] *Id.* at 1276.

[248] *Id.* at 1269. The situation in *Reyes* is now covered by the National Childhood Vaccine Injury Act of 1986 which provides in part:

> No vaccine manufacturer shall be liable in a civil action for damages arising from a vaccine-related injury or death associated with the administration of a vaccine after October 1, 1988, solely due to the manufacturer's failure to provide direct warnings to the injured party (or the injured party's legal representative) of the potential dangers arising from the administration of the vaccine manufactured by the manufacturer.

[249] Hurley v. Lederle Laboratories, 863 F.2d 1173, 1179 (5th Cir. 1988); Niemiera v. Schneider, 114 N.J. 550 (1989).

[250] 555 A.2d 1112 (N.J. 1989).

[251] Gurski v. Wyeth-Ayerst Div. Of American Home Products Products Corp., 953 F. Supp. 412 (D. Mass. 420) (applying Massachusetts law); Stephens v. G.D. Searle & Co., 602 F. Supp. 379 (E.D. Mich. 1985). *See* Yonni D. Fushman, *Perez v. Wyeth Labs., Inc.: Toward Creating a Direct-to-Consumer Advertisement Exception to the Learned Intermediary Doctrine*, 80 B.U.L. Rev. 1161, 1167 (2000) (the oral contraceptives exception is less prevalent than the mass immunization exception).

intermediary rule. In *MacDonald v. Ortho Pharmaceutical Corp.*,[252] the Massachusetts Supreme Court adopted an exception for oral contraceptives saying that, unlike other prescription drugs where patients play a passive role in determining what is prescribed to them, the patient usually plays an active role in determining what form of birth control she will use. The doctor's role as a learned intermediary is lessened because women may take oral contraceptives for an extended period of time without seeing their doctor and do not necessarily have to consult their physicians before every refill.[253]

The question of whether a manufacturer must provide a direct warning to consumers also has been raised in a number of cases involving intrauterine devices (IUDs). Although a few courts have treated IUDs like oral contraceptives,[254] the majority of courts hold the learned intermediary doctrine applies to them.[255] These courts reason that there is no reason to believe that the learned intermediary doctrine applies with any less force to a case involving the use of a prescription device as to a prescription drug. The physician performs an individualized balancing of the benefits and risks to the patient before prescribing the device. The doctor's prescription for the device is followed by periodic checkups and physician-patient consultations. Thus, the doctor is no less a learned intermediary between the manufacturer of the IUD and the patient than a physician who prescribes oral contraceptives. As with prescription drugs, the manufacturer of an IUD must give timely and adequate warnings to the medical profession of any dangerous side effects from the use of the device.

[3] FDA Mandate

A third exception to the learned intermediary doctrine, recognized only in Oklahoma, applies where the FDA has mandated direct warnings be provided to patients.[256] In *Edwards v. Basel Pharmaceuticals*,[257] an FDA mandate required that prescription nicotine patches be accompanied by warnings to the physician as well as to the ultimate consumer. The Oklahoma Supreme Court held that when the FDA requires manufacturers to issue warnings directly to the patient, the "manufacturer is not automatically shielded from liability by properly warning the prescribing physician."[258] In addition, the court found that the manufacturer does not necessarily satisfy its duty to warn the consumer simply by complying with

---

[252] 475 N.E.2d 65 (Mass. 1985).

[253] Stephens v. G.D. Searle & Co., 602 F. Supp. 379 (E.D. Mich. 1985).

[254] *See* Hill v. Searle Laboratories, 884 F.2d 1064, 1071 (8th Cir. 1989); MacDonald v. Ortho Pharmaceutical Corp., 475 N.E.2d 65 (Mass. 1985); Odgers v. Ortho Pharmaceutical Corp., 609 F. Supp. 867 (E.D. Mich. 1985) (applying Michigan law).

[255] *See* Beyette v. Ortho Pharmaceutical Corp., 823 F.2d 990 (6th Cir. 1987); Allen v. G.D. Searle & Co., 708 F. Supp. 1142 (D. Or. 1989); Lacy v. G.D. Searle & Co., 567 A.2d 398, 398 (Del. 1989); Tetuan v. A.H. Robins Co., 738 P.2d 1210 (Kan. 1987); Terhune v. A.H. Robins Co., 577 P.2d 975 (Wash. 1978).

[256] *See* Catherine A. Paytash, Note: *The Learned Intermediary Doctrine and Patient Package Inserts: A Balanced Approach to Preventing Drug-Related Injury*, 51 STAN. L. REV. 1343, 1353 (1999).

[257] 933 P.2d 298 (Okla. 1997).

[258] *Id.* at 303.

minimum FDA warning requirements.[259]

[4]   Direct-to-Consumer Advertising

A fourth exception to the learned intermediary doctrine results from the growth of direct-to-consumer advertising for drugs and medical devices.[260] Several courts have alluded to the fact that direct-to-consumer advertising by manufacturers has lessened the role of the learned intermediary.[261] The Restatement (Third) also notes that arguments have been made in support of adopting an exception when manufacturers advertise a prescription drug in the mass media.[262] However, only the New Jersey Supreme Court explicitly has adopted a direct-to-consumer advertising exception to the learned intermediary doctrine.[263] The court felt that when manufacturers advertise directly to consumers the rationales behind the learned intermediary doctrine do not apply because the advertising does not preserve the doctor-patient relationship, indicates that drug manufacturers do have the means to communicate with patients, and indicates that the information is not too complex to convey to consumers.[264] Thus, manufacturers that advertise their prescription drugs and medical devices directly to consumers must provide adequate warnings to consumers.

---

[259] *Id.*

[260] *See* Sheryl Calabro, *Breaking the Shield of the Learned Intermediary Doctrine: Placing the Blame Where It Belongs*, 25 Cardozo L. Rev. 2241, 2255 (2004); Ozlem A. Bordes, Article: *The Learned Intermediary Doctrine and Direct-to-Consumer Advertising: Should the Pharmaceutical Manufacturer Be Shielded From Liability?* 81 U. Det. Mercy L. Rev. 267 (2004).

[261] *See* Hill v. Searle Laboratories, 884 F.2d 1064, 1071 (8th Cir. 1989) (the learned intermediary doctrine should not apply to IUDs, in part because the manufacturer marketed the product to women); Murthy v. Abbott Labs., 2012 U.S. Dist. LEXIS 29683 (S.D. Tex. Mar. 6, 2012) (applying Texas law); Garside v. Osco Drug, Inc., 764 F. Supp. 208, 211 (D.C. Mass 1991) (in addition to the mass immunization and oral contraceptives exception, "in an appropriate case, the advertising of a prescription drug to the consuming public may constitute a third exception to the learned intermediary rule"); Stephens v. G.D. Searle & Co., 602 F. Supp. 379, 380 (E.D. Mich. 1985) (differentiated oral contraceptives from other drugs by stating that manufacturers use "zealous marketing practices" to encourage women to specifically request birth control drugs).

[262] Restatement (Third) of Torts: Products Liability § 6d cmt. e (1998).

[263] Perez v. Wyeth, 734 A.2d 1245 (N.J. 1999). *See* Yonni D. Fushman, Perez v. Wyeth Labs. Inc.: Toward Creating a Direct-to-Consumer Advertisement Exception to the Learned Intermediary Doctrine, 80 B.U.L. Rev. 1161 (2000). See, however, In re Norplant Products Liability Litigation, 165 F.3d 374 (5th Cir. 1999) and Lennon v. Wyeth-Ayerst Laboratories, Inc., 779 A.2d 1228 (Pa. Super. Ct. 2001) which rejected adopting a direct-to-consumer advertising exception.

[264] *Id.* at 1255.

Chapter 8

PROBLEMS OF PROOF: DEFECT AND CAUSATION

SYNOPSIS

§ 8.01   INTRODUCTION

§ 8.02   PROOF OF A DEFECT

    [A]   Direct and Circumstantial Evidence

    [B]   *Res Ipsa Loquitur* and "An Inference of a Product Defect"

    [C]   Product Testing and Spoliation of Evidence

        [1]   Product Testing

        [2]   Spoliation of Evidence

§ 8.03   EXPERT WITNESSES

    [A]   Introduction

    [B]   The Standards for the Admissibility of Expert Testimony

        [1]   The *Frye* Test

        [2]   The *Daubert* Test

        [3]   *Daubert* and Opinion Testimony

        [4]   The Scope of *Daubert*

        [5]   The District Court Judge as "Gatekeeper"

         [a]   Reliability

         [b]   Relevance

        [6]   Review of the District Court Decision

    [C]   The Qualifications for an Expert

    [D]   The Permissible Scope of Expert Testimony

§ 8.04   CAUSE-IN-FACT

    [A]   Introduction

    [B]   "But For" and "Substantial Factor" Tests

    [C]   Establishing the Identity of the Manufacturer

    [D]   Exposure to Risk of Future Injury

§ 8.05   PROXIMATE CAUSE

    [A]   Introduction

    [B]   Foreseeability

    [C]   Natural and Probable Consequences

    [D]   Condition v. Cause

§ 8.01   INTRODUCTION

In every products liability case, the plaintiff faces a number of problems of proof. In a strict liability action, one of the most difficult elements to establish is that the product was in a "defective condition unreasonably dangerous" when it left the manufacturer's control. In a negligence action, the hardest issue for a plaintiff to prove usually is that the defect in the product was the result of conduct by the manufacturer or seller that fell below the required standard of care. In addition, even if the plaintiff establishes that the product was in a "defective condition unreasonably dangerous" or that the manufacturer was negligent, he or she also must prove, by a preponderance of the evidence, that there was a causal connection between the defective condition of the product or the negligence and the injuries or damages.[1] Causation also is an essential element in breach of warranty actions.[2] Courts often use the term "proximate cause" to describe this connection, although causation analysis involves two separate and very different concepts: cause-in-fact and legal cause.[3] This chapter examines the methods a plaintiff can use to prove that a product was defective. It also analyzes some of the issues that a plaintiff may face in establishing that the defect was the cause-in-fact and the proximate cause of the injury or damage.

§ 8.02   PROOF OF A DEFECT

[A]   Direct and Circumstantial Evidence

Whether a claim is based on negligence or strict liability, the foundation of a plaintiff's cause of action is proof of the existence of a defect in the product at the time it left the control of the manufacturer or seller. Without such proof, the manufacturer or seller is entitled to summary judgment[4] or a directed verdict.[5] A plaintiff may prove that a product was defective either by direct evidence or by circumstantial evidence from which reasonable inferences of a defect may be drawn.[6] Direct evidence usually takes the form of the allegedly defective product

---

[1] In re Methyl Tertiary Butyl Ether ("MTBE") Products Liability Litigation, 591 F. Supp. 2d 259, 266 (S.D.N.Y. 2008) (applying New York law); Virgil v. "Kash n' Karry" Service Corp., 484 A.2d 652 (Md. Ct. Spec. App. 1984).

[2] Allstate Ins. Co. v. Hamilton Beach/Proctor Silex, Inc., 473 F.3d 450 (2d Cir. 2007) (applying Vermont law); Coons v. A. F. Chapman Corp., 460 F. Supp. 2d 209 (D. Mass. 2006) (applying Massachusetts law).

[3] Kirkland v. Emhart Glass, S.A., 805 F. Supp. 2d 1072 (W.D. Wash. 2011) (applying Washington law); Mitchell v. Gonzales, 819 P.2d 872, 876 (Cal. 1991). However, because of the confusion with using the term "proximate cause" to describe both factual and legal causation, the RESTATEMENT (THIRD) OF TORTS: LIABILITY FOR PHYSICAL HARM AND EMOTIONAL HARM (2010), Ch. 6, Special Note on Proximate Cause, has separate chapters for factual causation and that it calls the "scope of liability" (i.e., legal causation). See June v. Union Carbide Corp., 577 F.3d 1234, 1239–44 (2009) (applying Colorado law).

[4] Humphreys v. General Motors Corp., 839 F. Supp. 822 (N.D. Fla. 1993) (applying Florida law); Parsons v. Ford Motor Co., 85 S.W.3d 323 (Tex. App. 2002).

[5] Wernimont v. International Harvestor Corp., 309 N.W.2d 137 (Iowa Ct. App. 1981).

[6] Lozano v. Lozano, 52 S.W.3d 141 (Tex. 2001); Tweedy v. Wright Ford Sales, Inc., 357 N.E.2d 449 (Ill. 1976).

itself and/or the testimony of an expert who has examined the product and who offers an opinion on the product's design, manufacture, or warnings.[7] In a manufacturing defect case, the defect in the product usually results from faulty materials or faulty assembly of the parts.[8] The presence of the product permits the parties and their experts to compare its condition with the requirements specified in the design or with similar products of the same model manufactured by the defendant.[9] In a design defect case, the plaintiff's expert witnesses often will compare the product with similar products from other manufacturers in an attempt to show that there was a reasonable alternative design to the one used by the manufacturer and that it would have been safer. This will require the experts used by the plaintiff and the defendant to testify about technological feasibility, cost, and the likelihood of consumer acceptance of an alternative design.[10]

Because a determination of whether a product was defective cannot be based on conjecture or speculation, direct evidence is the desired means of proof. However, direct evidence is not required to establish a *prima facie* case for a defect. This is because, in some cases, the plaintiff is unable to identify the specific defect due to the destruction or loss of the product that caused the injuries.[11] In other cases, the product may be available but the plaintiff may be unable to identify a specific defect in it.[12] In cases where the absence of direct evidence prevents the plaintiff from proving the specific defect in the design or manufacture of the product, the plaintiff can rely on the facts and circumstantial evidence of the accident to argue that a reasonable jury could conclude that the product was defective.[13] Circumstantial evidence has been defined as "the proof of certain facts and circumstances in a given case from which the jury may infer other connected facts which usually and reasonably follow according to the common experience of mankind."[14] An example of the types of circumstantial evidence that can lead to the inference of a product defect is *Daniel v. Indiana Mills & Manufacturing, Inc.*,[15] in which the plaintiff

---

[7] Pouncey v. Ford Motor Co., 464 F.2d 957 (5th Cir. 1972) (applying Alabama law). In some case, a defect may be established by a direct eyewitness of the product malfunction. In such cases, expert testimony is not necessary to defeat a motion for summary judgment. Perez-Trujillo v. Volvo Car Corp., 137 F.3d 50 (1st Cir. 1998) (applying Puerto Rican law).

[8] Willis v. Floyd Brace Co., Inc., 309 S.E.2d 295 (S.C. Ct. App. 1983); Harris v. Bardwell, 373 So. 2d 777 (La. Ct. App. 1979).

[9] Keeler v. Richards Manufacturing Co., Inc., 817 F.2d 1197 (5th Cir. 1987) (applying Texas law). For a discussion of the inspection process for defective products, see § 8.02(C)[1].

[10] The role of expert witnesses is discussed in § 8.03.

[11] In Greene v. B.F. Goodrich Avionics Systems, 409 F.3d 784 (6th Cir. 2005) (applying Kentucky law), the plaintiff alleged that a defective gyroscope caused a helicopter crash in which her husband, the pilot, died. Since the vertical gyroscopes were destroyed in the crash, there was no direct evidence of their failure. The plaintiffs were able to introduce circumstantial evidence that would allow the jury to infer a design or manufacturing defect in the product. *See also* Lindsay v. McDonnell Douglas Aircraft Corp., 460 F.2d 631 (8th Cir. 1972) (an admiralty suit) (airplane crashed in the ocean and never was recovered).

[12] *See* Motley v. Fluid Power of Memphis, Inc., 640 S.W.2d 222 (Tenn. Ct. App. 1982).

[13] *See* Worsham v. A.H. Robins Co., 734 F.2d 676 (11th Cir. 1984) (applying Florida law); Ford Motor Co. v. Gonzalez, 9 S.W.3d 195 (Tex. App. 1999).

[14] Pace v. McClow, 458 N.E.2d 4, 8 (Ill. App. Ct. 1983). *See* Allstate Ins. Co. v. Hamilton Beach/Proctor Silex, Inc., 473 F.3d 450 (2d Cir. 2007) (applying Vermont law).

[15] 103 S.W.3d 302 (Mo. Ct. App. 2003).

was injured when a truck he was driving jackknifed and left the highway. The plaintiff alleged that his injuries resulted when his seat belt failed, causing him to be thrown from the truck during the accident. On appeal from a jury verdict in favor of the plaintiff, the manufacturer of the seat belt assembly argued that the plaintiff failed to produce sufficient evidence that to prove: (1) the seatbelt was worn and released during the accident, (2) he was wearing his seatbelt, or (3) he did not unlatch it himself during the accident to avoid becoming trapped with the flammable gasoline tanker he was pulling. The Missouri appellate court held that the jury could infer the existence of a defect in the seatbelt from five types of circumstantial evidence: testimony from the plaintiff and any witnesses; testimony of medical personnel who treated the plaintiff at the scene of the accident; the circumstances of the accident; testimony from experts about the seatbelt and the accident; and tests duplicating the conditions of the accident.[16]

In some states, the use of circumstantial evidence to draw an inference of a product defect is known as the "general defect" or "indeterminate defect" theory.[17] Other states use a variation of this called "malfunction theory."[18] In Pennsylvania, for example, courts have held that, to prevail on a malfunction theory, a plaintiff must present sufficient evidence that: (1) the product malfunctioned; (2) the plaintiff used the product in a manner that was intended or reasonably expected by the manufacturer; and (3) there were no other reasonable secondary causes of the defect.[19] An example of the malfunction theory is *Dominquez v. Bohn Ford, Inc.*,[20] in which the Louisiana Supreme Court held that the failure of brakes on a van to function within a few weeks after its purchase created a *prima facie* case that the van was defective and that the defect existed when the product left the manufacturer's control. There also was no evidence of abnormal use of the van during the time the plaintiff had driven it. Underlying all of these theories of circumstantial evidence for establishing an inference that a product was defective is the idea that "common experience indicates that certain accidents do not occur

---

[16] *Id.* at 309–10.

[17] In Riley v. De'Longhi Corp., 2000 U.S. App. LEXIS 27082 (4th Cir. Oct. 30, 2000) (applying Maryland law), the court determined that a product defect could be inferred from circumstantial evidence by analyzing five factors: (1) expert testimony as to possible causes; (2) the occurrence of the accident a short time after the sale; (3) same accidents in similar products; (4) the elimination of other causes of the accident; and (5) the types of accident that does not happen without a defect.

[18] *See* Edic v. Century Products Co., 364 F.3d 1276 (11th Cir. 2004) (applying Florida law); Liberty Mut. Fire Ins. Co. v. Sharp Electronics Corp., 2011 U.S. Dist. LEXIS 71890 (M.D. Pa. July 5, 2011) (sufficient circumstantial evidence to permit the plaintiffs to assert a malfunction theory). In Metropolitan Property & Casualty Ins. Co. v. Deere & Co., 25 A.3d 571 (Conn. 2011), the Connecticut Supreme Court said that, although the malfunction theory is based on the idea that the fact of an accident can support an inference of a defect, proof of an accident alone is not sufficient to establish a manufacturer's liability. Instead, there must be evidence that the product, and not some other cause apart from the product, was more likely than not the cause of the plaintiff's injury and that the defect existed when the product left the manufacturer's control. Texas, however, generally does not recognize a product malfunction as sufficient proof of a product defect. Instead, the plaintiff must identify a specific defect and rule out other possible causes. Ford Motor Co. v. Ledesma, 242 S.W.3d 32, 42 (Tex. 2007).

[19] Booth v. Black & Decker, Inc., 166 F. Supp. 2d 215, 220 (E.D. Pa. 2001) (applying Pennsylvania law); Tweedy v. Wright Ford Sales, Inc., 357 N.E.2d 449 (Ill. 1976).

[20] 483 So. 2d 934 (La. 1986).

absent some defect," and that an inference of a defect under specific circumstances should be permitted.[21]

There are other types of circumstantial evidence that may or may not be admissible to prove that a product was defective. Federal courts and most states follow the "subsequent repairs" doctrine and exclude evidence of subsequent remedial measures, at least when such evidence is offered to establish fault on the part of the manufacturer.[22] However, courts permit plaintiffs to present evidence of prior substantially similar accidents or incidents to show the unreasonably dangerous condition of a product.[23] Evidence of similar post-accident occurrences or injuries involving the same product also is admissible to refute testimony from defense witness that the design of a product was not defective.[24] Evidence of either prior accidents or subsequent accidents usually is proper if, at the relevant times, the product involved was in substantially the same condition and the accidents were sufficiently similar.[25] The defendant also may introduce evidence of the lack of prior accidents if it can show that the same product was used and the product was used under conditions substantially similar to those in which the plaintiff used the product.[26]

---

[21] Williams v. Smart Chevrolet Co., 730 S.W.2d 479, 482 (Ark. 1987). *See also* Heaton v. Ford Motor Co., 435 P.2d 806, 808 (Or. 1967) (if a product fails in unusual, unexpected circumstances, "the inference is that there was some sort of defect, a precise definition of which is unnecessary"); Crump v. MacNaught P.T.Y. Ltd., 743 S.W.2d 532, 535 (Mo. Ct. App. 1987) (common sense suggests handles do not usually fly off pumps); Bombardi v. Pochel's Appliance & TV Co., 518 P.2d 202, 204 (Wash. Ct. App. 1973) (common sense would lead jury to conclude that television set was defective because it caught on fire).

[22] *See* the FEDERAL RULES OF EVIDENCE, Rule 407 (2005):

When, after an injury or harm allegedly caused by an event, measures are taken that, if previously taken, would have made the injury or harm less likely to occur, evidence of the subsequent measures is not admissible to prove negligence, culpable conduct, a defect in a product, a defect in a product's design, or a need for a warning or instruction. This rule does not require the exclusion of evidence of subsequent measures when offered for another purpose, such as proving ownership, control or feasibility of precautionary measures, if controverted, or impeachment.

Rule 407 does not bar evidence of measures taken after the design or manufacture of a product, but before the injury allegedly caused by the event. In re Air Crash Disaster, 86 F.3d 498 (6th Cir. 1996). In addition, the rule does not bar evidence of subsequent remedial measures if the evidence is offered for purposes of impeachment.

States also have adopted provisions barring evidence of subsequent remedial measures. Wisconsin legislation (WIS. STAT. ANN. § 895.047(4)), for example, provides that evidence of remedial measures taken subsequent to the sale of the product is not admissible for the purpose of showing a manufacturing defect in the product, a defect in the design of the product, or the need for a warning or instruction. This subsection does not prohibit the admission of such evidence to show a reasonable alternative design that existed at the time when the product was sold.

[23] Croskey v. BMW of North Amer., Inc., 532 F.3d 511 (6th Cir. 2008) (applying Michigan law); Shatz v. Ford Motor Co., 412 F. Supp. 2d 581 (N.D. W. Va. 2006); Branham v. Ford Motor Co., 701 S.E.2d 5 (S.C. 2010).

[24] Koehn v. R.D. Werner Co., 809 P.2d 1045 (Colo. Ct. App. 1990); Bass v. Cincinnati, Inc., 536 N.E.2d 831 (Ill. App. Ct. 1989).

[25] Johnson v. Ford Motor Co., 988 F.2d 573 (5th Cir. 1993) (applying Mississippi law); Mercer v. Pittway Corp., 616 N.W.2d 602 (Iowa 2000).

[26] *See* McKenzie v. SK Hand Tool Corp., 650 N.E.2d 612 (Ill. App. Ct. 1995).

When using circumstantial evidence, a plaintiff must negate other reasonable causes for the defect in the product, such as misuse or alteration, for which the defendant would not be responsible. This is necessary to establish a reasonable inference that the dangerous condition was present in the product when it left the control of the manufacturer or seller[27] and justify the jury inferring the probability of a defect.[28] An inference of a defect cannot be drawn simply from evidence that the product failed and an injury resulted.[29] Instead, the evidence must be sufficient to make a defect reasonably probable and more probable than any other theory based on the evidence.[30] Circumstantial evidence that relates to whether an inference of a defect can be drawn includes the product's age, the product's purpose, the expected useful life of the product, the occurrence of the accident a short time after the sale, and the maintenance of the product before the accident.[31] In most cases, the longer a product has been out of the manufacturer's control and the older that it is, the more likely that someone else or some other factor was responsible for the product's failure. The key to whether the circumstantial evidence is sufficient is whether the jury, which must weigh all the evidence presented to it and determine what evidence offers the more plausible explanation of the events that cause the plaintiff's injuries, properly can draw an inference that the product was defective in its design, manufacture, or lack of warnings.

[B] *Res Ipsa Loquitur* and "An Inference of a Product Defect"

In negligence cases, the burden of proof is difficult where the plaintiff has been injured but has no direct evidence of the events that led to the accident. To help the plaintiff meet the burden of establishing a *prima facie* case and avoid summary judgment, courts use the doctrine of *res ipsa loquitur*, which literally means "the thing speaks for itself."[32] Res ipsa loquitur is not a separate cause of action or a theory of liability. Instead, it is a rule of evidence that allows a jury to infer negligence from the circumstances of an accident.[33] However, since the mere fact of an accident is not enough to create an assumption that a product was defective, res ipsa loquitur requires the plaintiff to prove that: (1) the accident was one that

---

[27] Ruminer v. General Motors Corp., 483 F.3d 561 (8th Cir. 2007) (applying Arkansas law).

[28] *See* Yielding v. Chrysler Motor Co., 783 S.W.2d 353 (Ark. 1990); Motley v. Fluid Power of Memphis, Inc., 640 S.W.2d 222 (Tenn. Ct. App. 1982).

[29] Hernandez v. Nissan Motor Corp., 740 S.W.2d 894 (Tex. App. 1987).

[30] Scanlon v. General Motors Corp., 326 A.2d 673 (N.J. 1974); Wernimont v. International Harvester, Inc., 309 N.W.2d 137 (Iowa Ct. App. 1981).

[31] Harrison v. Bill Cairns Pontiac of Marlow Heights, Inc., 549 A.2d 385 (Md. Ct. Spec. App. 1988); Shramek v. General Motors Corp., 216 N.E.2d 244 (Ill. App. Ct. 1966).

[32] Res ipsa loquitur was used in Escola v. Coca Cola Bottling Co., 150 P.2d 436 (Cal. 1944), in which the California Supreme Court held that the plaintiff could use the doctrine to establish a prima facie case of a manufacturer's breach of duty.

[33] Haddock v. Arnspiger, 793 S.W.2d 948, 950 (Tex. 1990). For a lengthy discussion of the rule, see Lawson v. Mitsubishi Motor Sales of Amer., Inc., 938 So. 2d 35 (La. 2006). However, the doctrine cannot be used if the plaintiff identifies two or more products that potentially could have caused the accident. Depositors Ins. Co. v. Wal-Mart Stores, Inc., 506 F.3d 1092 (8th Cir. 2007) (applying Iowa law).

ordinarily does not occur in the absence of negligence[34] and (2) the defendant had exclusive management and control of the product that caused the injury.[35] Whether res ipsa loquitur is applicable in a particular case is a question of law that must be decided by the court.[36] If the court decides that the doctrine of res ipsa loquitur is applicable, then it is the jury's function to weigh the evidence and to determine whether the circumstantial evidence of negligence has been overcome by any proof offered by the manufacturer. Because res ipsa loquitur is a rule of circumstantial evidence, the jury is permitted but not compelled to find for the plaintiff.[37] Any presumption raised by res ipsa loquitur in favor of the plaintiff will give way to contrary proof offered by the manufacturer. Such proof may consist of testimony about its due care in the design or manufacture of the product or proof that the accident was caused by the plaintiff's misuse of the product or by a third person.

Although res ipsa loquitur is used in products liability cases based on negligence, most courts have held that the doctrine is not applicable in strict liability cases.[38] The reasons for this were set out by the New Jersey Supreme Court in *Myrlak v. Port Authority*,[39] in which the plaintiff was injured when a chair he was using at work collapsed. No one other than the plaintiff saw the accident and there was no evidence that the chair had been misused by the plaintiff or anyone else. However, the chair was not used exclusively by the plaintiff. The plaintiff brought suit against the manufacturer of the chair based on strict liability and alleging a manufacturing defect and a failure to warn. However, at trial, the plaintiff's expert was unable to identify a specific defect in the chair or even to state that a defect had caused the accident. The New Jersey Supreme Court rejected the use of res ipsa loquitur in cases based on strict liability saying that it was a rule of evidence that allows a plaintiff in a negligence case to meet its requirement of showing that the defendant breached its duty of care. Strict liability, however, is a theory of allocating responsibility regardless of the manufacturer's fault.

Although most courts have rejected the use of res ipsa loquitur in strict liability cases, many states and the Restatement (Third) has adopted an "indeterminate defect test" that permits circumstantial evidence to support an inference of a product defect in such cases. According to § 3 of the Restatement:

---

[34] Balistreri v. Richard E. Jacobs Group, Inc., 322 F. Supp. 2d 972 (E.D. Wis. 2004) (applying Wisconsin law) (automatic sliding glass doors, activated by motion sensors, ordinarily do not malfunction in the absence of negligence).

[35] Depositors Ins. Co. v. Wal-Mart Stores, Inc., 506 F.3d 1092 (8th Cir. 2007) (applying Iowa law); Mohammad v. Toyota Motor Sales, U.S.A., Inc., 947 A.2d 598 (Md. Ct. Spec. App. 2008); Williams v. American Medical Systems, 548 S.E.2d 371 (Ga. Ct. App. 2001). Some courts do not apply the "exclusive control" requirement literally. *See* Condiff v. R.D. Werner Co., Inc., 2003 U.S. Dist. LEXIS 14288 (E.D. La. Aug. 15, 2003) (applying Louisiana law).

[36] Gould v. Motel 6 Operating L.P., 2005 Wash. App. LEXIS 244 (Feb. 7, 2005); Nutting v. Northern Energy, 874 P.2d 482 (Colo. Ct. App. 1994).

[37] McGuire v. Stein's Gift & Garden Center, 504 N.W.2d 385 (Wis. Ct. App. 1993).

[38] One state in which res ipsa loquitur can be used in a strict liability case is Wisconsin. *See* Smoot v. Mazda Motors of America, Inc., 469 F.3d 675 (7th Cir. 2006) (applying Wisconsin law).

[39] 723 A.2d 45 (N.J. 1999).

It may be inferred that the harm sustained by the plaintiff was caused by a product defect existing at the time of sale or distribution, without proof of a specific defect, when the incident that harmed the plaintiff:

  (a)   was of a kind that ordinarily occurs as a result of a product defect; and

  (b)   was not, in the particular case, solely the result of causes other than product defect existing at the time of sale or distribution.[40]

Comment *b* to this section states that "[s]ection 3 claims are limited to situations in which a product fails to perform its manifestly intended function, this supporting a conclusion that a defect of some kind is the most probable explanation." Comment *c* provides that there is "[n]o requirement that [the] plaintiff prove what aspect of the product was defective. The inference of defect may be drawn under this Section without proof of the specific defect. Furthermore, quite apart from the question of what type of defect was involved, the plaintiff need not explain specifically what constituent part of the product failed."

Section 3, which is based on res ipsa loquitur, it permits the jury to draw two inferences: (1) that the harmful incident was caused by a product defect, and (2) that the defect was present when the product left the manufacturer's control. In contrast, res ipsa loquitur creates a single inference that the defendant breached its duty of care. Despite this difference, § 3 parallels the elements of res ipsa loquitur requirements that (1) the product was in the defendant's exclusive control at the time of the accident and (2) the defect occurred before the product left the control of the manufacturer. These elements can be satisfied through direct or circumstantial evidence as well as by evidence that negates causes other than product defect. In addition, even those states that hold that res ipsa loquitur is not applicable to a strict products liability action have recognized that the inferences and principles that form the core of res ipsa loquitur "merely instantiates the broader principle, which is as applicable to a products case as to any other tort case, that an accident can itself be evidence of liability[,] . . . if it is reasonably plain that the defect was not introduced after the product was sold."[41]

Because § 3 of the Restatement (Third) has its origins in res ipsa loquitur, the drafters of the section were aware of the parallel between drawing an inference of negligence in an appropriate case and drawing an inference of a product defect under similar circumstances. The section was adopted to "set forth the formal requisites for drawing an inference" in some product defect cases.[42] Thus, § 3 of the Restatement (Third) does in a strict liability case what res ipsa loquitur does in a negligence case.

---

[40] Restatement (Third) of Torts: Products Liability, § 3 (1998). New York follows this section. Speller v. Sears, Roebuck & Co., 790 N.E.2d 252 (N.Y. 2003).

[41] Welge v. Planters Lifesavers Co., 17 F.3d 209, 211 (7th Cir. 1994) (applying Illinois law). *See also* Williams v. Smart Chevrolet Co., 730 S.W.2d 479 (Ark. 1987); Lang v. Federated Department Stores, 287 S.E.2d 729, 731 (Ga. Ct. App. 1982).

[42] Restatement (Third), § 3 cmt. *a* (1998).

[C]   Product Testing and Spoliation of Evidence

[1]   Product Testing

If the product that allegedly caused the plaintiff's injuries was not destroyed in the accident, the plaintiff and the defendant will want to conduct thorough tests on it before trial to determine whether it was defective and whether it was the product that caused the injuries. Although product testing is expensive, it is a critical means of determining whether the product was defective and, if so, whether it could have been a cause of the plaintiff's injuries. However, before either side can conduct tests on the product (which usually is in the physical control of the plaintiff), it is necessary for the parties to draft, agree upon, and sign an "Inspection Protocol," that is, a memorandum setting out the ground rules for the inspection. Because of the importance of product testing to all parties, the sensitive nature of the testing, and the potential for disagreements, it is necessary to have as detailed an Inspection Protocol as possible. Although the specific provisions of each Inspection Protocol will differ depending upon the nature of the accident, the particular product, and where the testing is conducted, a sample protocol is set out below.

1. The inspection shall begin at 9:00 a.m. on every workday and shall end at 6:00 p.m. unless the Team Leaders agree to a continuation.

2. The inspection shall recess for lunch from 12:00–1:00 p.m. Team Leaders may adjust lunch time as necessary to the prompt completion of the task.

3. The monitor cameras, if used, shall continue without interruption during lunch.

4. No work shall be performed at the scene during lunch.

5. [The plaintiff's attorney or law firm] or its representations shall act as host.

6. The systematic investigation of [the product or the scene of the accident] precludes "jumping ahead" to facilitate a particular goal of an interested party.

7. Each party shall be allowed one photographer who shall take their photographs and then the video shall be taken using the same method. The photographers shall perform the task as a team. After the initial documentation of [the product or the scene of the accident] by a photographer designated by each party is completed, other representatives of the parties then may photograph or video [the product or scene of the accident] as they believe necessary.

8. The goal is to photograph [the product or the scene of the accident]. Photographs of the parties shall be avoided if at all possible. Before photographing a party, it is appropriate to give notice and opportunity to move out of the photograph.

9. All parties shall have the right to engage their own engineers, scientists, chemists, or other professionals.

10. The parties shall properly identify themselves and sign the "Scene Poster."

11. Each party shall recognize a single Team Leader who shall represent his or her party in Protocol matters such as Team Leader meetings.

12. Only the Team Leaders, their representative or attorney shall be allowed to voice the position of their client.

13. There shall be a Team Leader meeting to discuss issues or concerns. Any participating party may attend the Team Leader meeting. Only the Team Leaders, attorney, or client shall be authorized to speak during this meeting.

14. Any video camera used shall not record audio. The master tape shall have no audio.

15. A single copy of all photographs and videotapes taken during the evidence inspection shall be exchanged between the parties without charge to the parties. Additional photographs can be acquired by request and compensation to their parties. This exchange does not include monitor tapes.

16. This Protocol is addressed to a [product or scene of the accident] investigation, that is, Phase I Analysis. If it becomes necessary to conduct a more detailed examination of the [product or scene], a Phase II Analysis will be coordinated by the attorneys or claim representatives.

17. Task Protocols shall be used as necessary.

18. The Task Protocol documents the basic steps, rationale, and goal of the task. Each Team Leader must approve the Task Protocol before the task is attempted. All team Leaders must be notified before the evaluation is executed so that they may be present during the event.

19. Only a single Task Protocol can be undertaken during the same time period except as agreed upon by all Team Leaders.

20. Once documented by all parties and with an approved Task Protocol, the specific Interested Parties may assist with the manipulation or movement of their products.

21. Samples shall be numbered sequentially. There shall be no duplication of evidence numbers.

22. [Product Liability, Inc.] has been retained to receive evidence secured by the parties. Any evidence secured by interested parties shall be immediately transmitted to [Product Liability, Inc.].

23. Parties shall secure evidence they select.

24. Parties shall be responsible for their own safety.

25. Parties all bring all necessary tools for the completion of their investigation.

26. No sample, artifact, or item of evidence may be secured in violation of applicable criminal laws. The parties are responsible for verifying proper licensing of their representatives.

27. The evidence shall remain in the custody of [Product Liability, Inc.]. An "evidence list" shall be provided to each party before the scene investigation is complete.

28. Once all the evidence has been secured, it shall not be inspected without notice to all of the parties.

29. Any measurements taken must not be destructive.[43]

30. There shall be no evidence secured without notice to the Team Leaders.

31. The surface of the evidence must not be altered. Such alteration would include, but not be limited to scratching, cutting, or wiping surface coating without a Task protocol being established first.

32. Any tests not delineated within the Protocol document must first have a written protocol submitted to the Team Leaders for approval.

33. By signature to this Protocol all parties agree to allow any other participating party to observe each test and inspection at [the site of the testing].

34. There shall be no surreptitious recordings of any type.

35. Any change in the established Protocol shall require unanimous agreement.

36. Participants using recording devices to document personal notes shall make diligent effort to maintain custody and control of their recorders.

37. Participants shall give notice before using recording devices.

38. Investigators, engineers, and other participants must adhere to all applicable criminal laws.

[2] Spoliation of Evidence

Although both the plaintiff and defendant want to conduct tests on any product involved in an accident that may lead to litigation, in some situations the product is lost, destroyed, or altered before it is possible to examine it.[44] This may be the result of intentional or negligent conduct. Thus, if the plaintiff has control of the product, it is important that he or she retain it and make sure that the product is not discarded, lost, destroyed, or altered before the manufacturer has an opportunity to conduct tests on it. Similarly, manufacturers should have a formal product retention policy to establish a uniform means by which items involved in product

---

[43] For discussion of when a court will permit destructive testing, the four factors a court considers when deciding whether to permit it, and the conditions that one court placed on such testing, see White v. Cooper Tools, Inc., 2010 U.S. Dist. LEXIS 33815 (D.S.D. Apr. 6, 2010).

[44] See Hirsch v. General Motors Corp., 628 A.2d 1108 (N.J. Super. Ct. 1993), in which the plaintiffs' insurance company inspected their automobile that had been damaged severely by a fire. However, the day after the insurance company declared the automobile a "total loss," but before the defendants had an opportunity to test it, the automobile was given to a salvage company. See also Brown v. Stone Manufacturing Co., 660 F. Supp. 454 (S.D. Miss. 1986); Drayton v. Jiffee Chemical Corp., 395 F. Supp. 1081 (N.D. Ohio 1975); Kambylis v. Ford Motor Co., 788 N.E.2d 1 (Ill. App. Ct. 2003).

liability cases are stored. If not, plaintiffs and manufacturers risk an allegation of spoliation.

Spoliation consists of the destruction, significant alteration, concealment, or failure to preserve evidence relevant to litigation that will affect adversely the ability of a plaintiff or defendant to prove the claim or defense.[45] Although claims of spoliation arise most often in cases involving documents or medical records, they also may be an issue in products liability cases, particularly those based on claims of manufacturing defects.[46] If the plaintiff alleges that his or her damages were caused by a design defect and the product is not available or has been altered, another product of the same model can be tested. However, if the basis of the claim is a manufacturing defect, the loss, destruction, or alteration of the product will harm the ability of the plaintiff or the defendant to prove their case since it is unlikely that another product with the same "manufacturing defect" can be found.

The question for courts since the mid-1980s has been whether to treat spoliation as an independent tort subject to an award of damages or to deal with it through judicial sanctions. Currently, courts in about half-a-dozen states expressly recognize a cause of action in tort for intentional[47] and/or negligent[48] spoliation of evidence. One state that recognizes a cause of action in tort for spoliation of evidence is West Virginia. According to the Supreme Court in that state, a spoliation claim requires proof of six elements: (1) the existence of a pending or potential civil action; (2) the alleged spoliator had actual knowledge of the pending or potential civil action; (3) a duty to preserve evidence arising from a contract, agreement, statute, administrative rule, voluntary assumption of duty, or other special circumstances; (4) a spoliation of evidence; (5) the spoliated evidence was vital to a party's ability to prevail in the pending or potential civil action; and (6) damages.[49] Although many states do not recognize a common law duty to preserve evidence, the Illinois Supreme Court, in *Boyd v. Travelers Insurance Co.*,[50] held that such a duty may arise by agreement, a contract, a statute, a special circumstance, or the defendant's voluntary assumption of a duty by affirmative conduct. Under this test, a "special circumstance" includes a party's knowledge of pending litigation or

---

[45] Allstate Ins. Co. v. Hamilton Beach/Proctor Silex, Inc., 473 F.3d 450 (2d Cir. 2007) (applying Vermont law); Rizzuto v. Davidson Ladders, Inc., 905 A.2d 1165 (Conn. 2006); Goff v. Harold Ives Trucking Co., Inc., 27 S.W.3d 387 (Ark. 2000).

[46] Allstate Ins. Co. v. Hamilton Beach/Proctor Silex, Inc., 473 F.3d 450 (2d Cir. 2007) (applying Vermont law) (coffee maker).

[47] *See* Hazen v. Municipality of Anchorage, 718 P.2d 456 (Alaska 1986); Hirsch v. General Motors Corp., 628 A.2d 1108 (N.J. Super. Ct. Law Div. 1993).

[48] *See* Holmes v. Amerex Rent-A-Car, 180 F.3d 294 (D.C. Cir. 1999) (applying District of Columbia law); St. Mary's Hospital, Inc. v. Brinson, 685 So. 2d 33 (Fla. Dist. Ct. App. 1996). For a list of states that recognize a cause of action for spoliation, see Fletcher v. Dorchester Mutual Insurance Co., 773 N.E.2d 420, 424 (Mass. 2002).

[49] Mace v. Ford Motor Co., 653 S.E.2d 660, 664 (W. Va. 2007). In *Mace*, the claim for negligent spoliation failed since there was no evidence of a pending or potential civil action or evidence that the defendant had actual knowledge of any pending or potential civil action. For a similar statement of the elements for the tort, see Rizzuto v. Davidson Ladders, Inc., 905 A.2d 1165 (Conn. 2006); Continental Insurance Co. v. Herman, 576 So. 2d 313 (Fla. Dist. Ct. App. 1990).

[50] 652 N.E.2d 267 (Ill. 1995). *See also* Denton v. Northeast Illinois Regional Commuter Railroad Corp., 2004 U.S. Dist. LEXIS 7234 (N.D. Ill. Apr. 23, 2004) (applying Illinois law).

reasonable knowledge that specific evidence may be relevant to anticipated litigation.[51] The assumption of a duty to preserve evidence may result from a company's voluntary adoption of a product retention policy that creates a duty that otherwise would not exist.

The vast majority of courts that have considered spoliation have declined to treat it as a tort.[52] Among the reasons given by the courts for their refusal is that sanctions for discovery violations already exist and that the costs and burdens that would be imposed on courts outweigh the benefits of permitting a tort claim for spoliation.[53] Instead of treating spoliation as a tort, these courts rely on the traditional judicial sanctions of (1) dismissal of the action; (2) barring the spoliator from using evidence about the product acquired before its destruction; (3) jury instructions permitting it to infer that the missing evidence would have been unfavorable to the party responsible for its loss.[54] However, under a test adopted by a number of courts, the trial court judge must analyze three factors in determining what sanctions to impose because of spoliation of evidence: (1) the degree of fault of the party who altered or destroyed the evidence; (2) the degree of prejudice suffered by the opposing party; and (3) the availability of a lesser sanction that will protect the opposing party's rights and deter future similar conduct.[55]

---

[51] Kambylis v. Ford Motor Co., 788 N.E.2d 1 (Ill. App. Ct. 2003). *See also* Hirsch v. General Motors Corp., 628 A.2d 1108 (N.J. Super. Ct. 1993).

[52] *See* MetLife Auto & Home v. Joe Basil Chevrolet, Inc., 807 N.E.2d 865 (N.Y. 2004); Lueter v. California, 115 Cal. Rptr. 2d 68 (Ct. App. 2002). For lists of states that do not recognize a cause of action for spoliation, see Fletcher v. Dorchester Mutual Insurance Co., 773 N.E.2d 420, 424, n.9 (Mass. 2002) and Timber Tech Engineered Building Products v. The Home Insurance Co., 55 P.3d 952, 954, n.5 (Nev. 2002).

[53] Cedars-Sinai Medical Center v. Superior Court, 954 P.2d 511 (Cal. 1998); Reilly v. D'Errico, 1994 Conn. Super. LEXIS 2450 (Sept. 21, 1994).

[54] Workman v. AB Electrolux Corp., 2005 U.S. Dist. LEXIS 16306 (D. Kan. Aug. 8, 2005) (applying Kansas law); Davis v. Ford Motor Co., 375 F. Supp. 2d 518 (S.D. Miss. 2005) (applying Mississippi law); Aetna Life and Casualty Co. v. Imet Mason Contractors, 707 A.2d 180 (N.J. Super. Ct. App. Div. 1998); Kirkland v.New York City Housing Authority, 666 N.Y.S.2d 609 (App. Div. 1997). Fed. R. Civ. P. 37(b)(2) give federal courts the authority to enter sanctions for discovery abuses. See, however, Stringer v. Packaging Corporation of America, 815 N.E.2d 476 (Ill. App. Ct. 2004), in which the court denied judicial sanctions where the product was discarded by a co-worker of the plaintiff while the plaintiff was in the hospital and without his knowledge.

[55] Schmid v. Milwaukee Electric Tool Corp., 13 F.3d 76 (3d Cir. 1994) (applying Pennsylvania law); Lafayette Insurance Company v. CMA Dishmachines, 2005 U.S. Dist. LEXIS 8026 (E.D. La. Apr. 26, 2005) (applying Louisiana law); Tracy v. General Motors Corp., 524 S.E.2d 879 (W. Va. 1999); Trevino v. Ortega, 969 S.W.2d 950 (Tex. 1998). In deciding whether a party is entitled to a jury instruction directing a spoliation inference, the court in Veloso v. Western Bedding Supply Co., 281 F. Supp. 2d 743, 746 (D.N.J. 2003) (applying New Jersey law), a products liability case involving documents allegedly lost by the defendants, stated that four factors are necessary: (1) the evidence must be under the adverse party's control; (2) there must be intentional suppression or withholding of the evidence (i.e., there is no inference where the evidence was lost or accidently destroyed); (3) the evidence must be relevant; and (4) it must have been reasonably foreseeable at the time the document was created that it later would be discoverable.

§ 8.03 EXPERT WITNESSES

[A] Introduction

The complexity of modern products frequently makes it difficult for juries (and judges) to determine whether they were defective. The question turns on the intricacies of the design and manufacture of the products and when and what type of warnings should be given concerning their use. The answer may require knowledge of such diverse topics as chemistry, the principles and materials of construction, engineering, medicine, and pharmacology. As a result, evidence supporting or challenging an allegation that a product was defective may mean little or nothing to the trier of fact without the assistance of expert testimony.[56] The findings and opinions of experts not only help the trier of fact decide whether the product was defective, they also are crucial in establishing whether the defect was the cause of the plaintiff's injuries.[57] Although expert testimony is not required in every products liability case,[58] such testimony may be necessary in cases where the jury does not have the experience or expertise that allows it to reach an informed decision.[59] The crucial role that expert witnesses play in most products liability cases requires an understanding of three important questions: (1) What are the standards for the admissibility of expert testimony? (2) What are the qualifications for an expert? (3) What is the permissible scope of expert testimony? In federal courts, expert testimony is governed by Rules 702 through 706 of the Federal Rules of Evidence.[60] Since almost all states have adopted a similar approach to expert testimony,[61] this section examines the issues of expert testimony in products liability cases by focusing on the Federal Rules.

---

[56] For a detailed discussion of expert testimony, see PAUL C. GIANNELLI, UNDERSTANDING EVIDENCE Chs. 24–25 (3d ed. 2009).

[57] For examples of cases that could not be decided without expert testimony, see Allison v. McGhan Medical Corp., 184 F.3d 1300 (11th Cir. 1999) (whether the plaintiff's complex medical problems were caused by silicon breast implants); Blanchard v. Eli Lilly & Co., 207 F. Supp. 2d 308 (D. Vt. 2002) (applying Vermont law) (whether murder/suicide was caused by antidepressant drug). *See also* Derienzo v. Trek Bicycle Corp., 376 F. Supp. 2d 537 (S.D.N.Y. 2005) (applying New York law).

[58] Flight International v. Allied Signal, 1995 U.S. App. LEXIS 15599 (9th Cir. June 20, 1995) (applying California law); Harrell Motors, Inc. v. Flanery, 612 S.W.2d 727 (Ark. 1981).

[59] Show v. Ford Motor Co., 659 F.3d 584 (7th Cir. 2011) (applying Illinois law) (expert testimony for claims based on the risk-utility analysis and the consumer expectations test); Menz v. New Holland North America, Inc., 507 F.3d 1107 (8th Cir. 2007) (applying Missouri law) (necessity of expert testimony in a failure to warn case involving the stability of a tractor); Burley v. Kytec Innovative Sports Equip., Inc., 737 N.W.2d 397 (S.D. 2007) (expert testimony required for issues of design defect and causation); Mohammad v. Toyota Motor Sales, U.S.A., Inc., 947 A.2d 598 (Md. Ct. Spec. App. 2008) (expert testimony is required when the question of whether a product is defective is beyond the understanding of the average lay person; an expert is not required when the issue is one of common knowledge).

[60] *See* GLEN WEISSENBERGER & JAMES J. DUANE, FEDERAL RULES OF EVIDENCE: RULES, LEGISLATIVE HISTORY, COMMENTARY AND AUTHORITY (2001 & 2005-06 Supp.). For a detailed discussion of Rules 702 to 706, see JACK B. WEINSTEIN & MARGARET A. BERGER, WEINSTEIN'S EVIDENCE MANUAL STUDENT EDITION Ch. 13 (7th ed. 2005).

[61] For an example, see TEX. R. EVID. §§ 702–706; WIS. STAT. ANN. § 907.02.

[B] The Standards for the Admissibility of Expert Testimony

The most controversial question surrounding expert testimony is: What are the standards for its admissibility? At the present time, there are two principal tests for the admission of expert evidence: the *Frye* test and the *Daubert* test.

[1] The *Frye* Test

In order to determine the reliability, and the admissibility, of novel scientific evidence, many federal and state courts have based their decision on *Frye v. United States.*[62] In that case, the United States Court of Appeals for the District of Columbia stated:

Just when a scientific principle or discovery crosses the line between the experimental and demonstrable stages is difficult to define. Somewhere in this twilight zone the evidential force of the principle must be recognized, and while courts will go a long way in admitting expert testimony deduced from a well-recognized scientific principle or discovery, the thing from which the deduction is made must be sufficiently established to have gained general acceptance in the particular field in which it belongs.[63]

One commentator has written that the *Frye* test is designed to accomplish six goals. These are:

(1) ensure that a minimal reserve of experts exist who can critically examine the validity of a scientific determination in a particular case, (2) promote a degree of uniformity in decision, (3) avoid the interjection of a time consuming and often misleading determination of the reliability of a scientific technique in litigation, (4) assure that scientific evidence introduced will be reliable . . . and thus relevant, (5) provide a preliminary screening to protect against the natural inclination of the jury to assign significant weight to scientific techniques presented under circumstances where the trier of fact is in a poor position to place an accurate evaluation upon reliability, and (6) impose a threshold standard of reliability, in light of the fact that cross-examination by opposing counsel is unlikely to bring inaccuracies to the attention of the jury.[64]

In practice, the *Frye* test means that novel techniques of product testing that have not been peer reviewed and gained "general acceptance" within the particular scientific community are inadmissible. Only when the procedures have gained such acceptance are they admissible. Critics point out, however, that *Frye* does not provide judges with guidelines as to what constitutes "general acceptance" in a particular scientific community and does not permit judges to keep up with the

---

[62] 293 F. 1013 (D.C. Cir. 1923).

[63] *Id.* at 1014. A *Frye* hearing is not required unless the evidence involves a novel theory or methodology. Parker v. Mobil Oil Corp., 857 N.E.2d 1114 (N.Y. 2006); Moore v. Harley-Davidson Motor Co., 241 P.3d 808 (Wash. Ct. App. 2010).

[64] Michael Graham, Cleary & Graham's Handbook of Illinois Evidence § 702.4, at 565 (6th ed. 1994).

rapid changes in scientific fields.[65] Because of these criticisms, the federal courts and more than half of the states no longer use the *Frye* standard. However, the states that continue to follow *Frye* are among those with the largest populations: California, Florida, Illinois, New York, New Jersey, Michigan, Pennsylvania, and Washington. Thus, while *Frye* no longer applies in federal courts and in the majority of the states, it continues to be the test for the admissibility of expert testimony in the states with the most products liability litigation.

[2]   The *Daubert* Test

In 1975, Congress adopted the Federal Rules of Evidence. The version of Rule 702 of the Rules that was into effect from 1975 to 2000 defined an expert and the situations when expert testimony was admissible. Although the Rule was meant to expand the admissibility of evidence, it did not set out any standards for evaluating its admissibility. As a result, federal and state courts continued to use the *Frye* test of "general acceptance" in the relevant scientific community. However, the Supreme Court adopted a different test for federal courts in 1993 with its decision in *Daubert v. Merrell Dow Pharaceuticals, Inc.*,[66] a products liability case involving a claim that the birth defects of two children had been caused by their mother's prenatal ingestion of the prescription drug Bendectin. The defendant drug manufacturer argued that the affidavits, submitted by the plaintiffs' medical experts to establish a causal connection between Bendectin and the children's birth defects, were inadmissible because they did not meet the *Frye* test.[67] The Supreme Court, however, held that the adoption of Federal Rules of Evidence in 1975 superceded *Frye* as the basis for the admission of scientific evidence.[68] According to the Court, there is nothing in the text of the Federal Rules or in the drafting history of Rule 702 that gives any indication that the "general acceptance" test of *Frye* is a necessary precondition for the admission of scientific evidence.[69] The Court also felt that the "general acceptance" test conflicted with the liberal language of Rule 402 of the Federal Rules of Evidence which states: "All relevant evidence is admissible, except as otherwise provided. . . . Evidence which is not relevant is inadmissible."[70]

Although the Federal Rules of Evidence replaced *Frye*, the Supreme Court stated that does not mean that the Federal Rules do not place limits on the admissibility of scientific evidence.[71] The Court stated that, under Rule 104(a) of the Federal Rule of Evidence, dealing with questions of admissibility generally, a judge must make a preliminary assessment as to whether the underlying reasoning or methodology of the proposed testimony is scientifically valid and properly can be

---

[65] For a critical discussion of *Frye*, see Robert J. Goodwin, *Fifty Years of Frye in Alabama: The Continuing Debate Over Adopting the Test Established in* Daubert v. Merrell Dow Pharmaceuticals, Inc., 35 Cumb. L. Rev. 231 (2005); Clark Hedger, *Daubert and the States: A Critical Analysis of Emerging Trends*, 49 St. Louis U. L.J. 177 (2004).

[66] 509 U.S. 579 (1993).

[67] *Id.* at 583–84.

[68] *Id.* at 587.

[69] *Id.* at 587–89.

[70] *Id.* at 588.

[71] *Id.* at 589.

applied to the facts at issue.[72] When faced with potential expert scientific testimony, the trial judge no longer uses a single "general acceptance" test as in *Frye*. Instead, the Court stated that the judge must ask a series of questions such as:

- Can the theory or technique be tested and has it been tested?

- Has the theory or technique been subjected to peer review and publication?

- In the case of a particular scientific technique, what was the known or potential error rate discovered during the testing?

- What is the "general acceptance" of the theory or technique within the relevant scientific community?[73]

As a result of *Daubert*, a witness must do more than establish an area of expertise to qualify as an expert. The witness must substantiate his or her conclusions and opinions with scientific or technical findings that meet the case's criteria for relevance and reliability.[74] While the jury is free to reach judgments on the scientific evidence that the witness presents and the judge permits it to consider, the role of the judge is that of an initial "gatekeeper." Under the Federal Rules of Evidence, the judge's job is to determine if the evidence is sufficient to help a reasonable jury to reach a conclusion.[75] An indication of the attractiveness of this approach to the admission of expert testimony is that more than half of the states have adopted *Daubert* or some variation of it since 1993.[76]

[3] *Daubert* and Opinion Testimony

In products liability cases, an expert witness' opinion testimony frequently is crucial in establishing whether a product was defective and whether it was the cause of the plaintiff's injuries. In *General Electric Co. v. Joiner*,[77] the plaintiff alleged that his lung cancer was "promoted" by his exposure to chemical PCBs in the

---

[72] *Id.* at 592–93. *See* Sigler v. Amer. Honda Motor Corp., 532 F.3d 469 (6th Cir. 2008); Bitler v. A.O. Smith Corp., 400 F.3d 1227 (10th Cir. 2004); Masters v. Hesston Corp., 291 F.3d 985 (7th Cir. 2002).

[73] 509 U.S. at 593–94. For the application of these factors in other products liability cases, see Bielskis v. Louisville Ladder, Inc., 663 F.3d 887 (7th Cir. 2011) (portable scaffold); Miller v. Pfizer, Inc., 356 F.3d 1326 (10th Cir. 2004); Ford Motor Co. v. Ledesma, 242 S.W.3d 32 (Tex. 2007); Brown v. Crown Equipment Corp., 181 S.W.3d 268 (Tenn. 2005).

[74] Huey v. United Parcel Service Inc., 165 F.3d 1084 (7th Cir. 1999). *See* Guinn v. AstraZeneca Pharmaceuticals LP, 602 F.3d 1245 (11th Cir. 2010) (at the *Daubert* hearing, the plaintiff's expert failed to establish a genuine issue of material fact on the issue of specific causation).

[75] For cases in which a court held that proffered expert testimony was admissible, see Primiano v. Cook, 598 F.3d 558, 565 (9th Cir. 2010) ("When considering the applicability of *Daubert* criteria . . . , the inquiry must be flexible."). For cases in which a court excluded expert testimony as unreliable, see Bielskis v. Louisville Ladder, Inc., 663 F.3d 887 (7th Cir. 2011); Dunn v. Nexgrill Indus., 636 F.3d 1049 (8th Cir. 2011); Tamraz v. Lincoln Electric Co., 620 F.3d 665 (6th Cir. 2010); Buck v. Ford Motor Co., 810 F. Supp. 2d 815 (N.D. Ohio 2011).

[76] The most recent state to adopt *Daubert* is Wisconsin which, in 2011, amended WIS. STAT. § 907.02 to adopt the *Daubert* reliability standard with respect to expert testimony in all actions filed in state on or after February 1, 2011.

[77] 522 U.S. 136 (1997).

workplace.[78] Although the plaintiff's experts sought to rely on animal studies linking PCBs to cancer in mice, the Supreme Court held that the district court judge did not abuse his discretion in holding that the studies were not a sufficient basis for the experts' opinions that the plaintiff's cancer was caused by exposure to the PCBs. Of importance to the use of opinion testimony in products liability cases was the Court's statement that, just because an expert has an opinion does not mean that the court has to admit it. According to the Court: "A court may conclude that there is simply too great an analytical gap between the data and the opinion proffered."[79] Just as the willingness of an expert to testify does not create the necessary link between certain *alleged* scientific data and the admissibility of the expert's opinion based on this data, the presence of the necessary link between the data and the proffered opinion may require the admission of the opinion.

[4] The Scope of *Daubert*

For purposes of products liability cases, the most important question raised by *Daubert* was whether the decision applies to all expert testimony or only to scientific expert testimony. In 1999, the Supreme Court answered that question, holding in *Kumho Tire Co. v. Carmichael*[80] that the *Daubert* "gatekeeping" duties of district court judges apply to all expert testimony, not just to scientific testimony. This means that everyone in a products liability case whose testimony is presented as that of an expert is subject to challenge on the *Daubert* factors.

In *Kumho Tire*, the plaintiffs brought a products liability suit against a tire manufacturer and its distributor as the result of a tire blow out which caused a minivan to overturn. The plaintiffs based a significant part of their case on the deposition of a "tire failure analyst" who would testify that, in his opinion, a manufacturing or design defect caused the tire to blow out and the vehicle to overturn. His opinion was based on a visual and tactile inspection of the tire and upon the theory that, in the absence of at least two of four specific, physical symptoms indicating tire abuse, the tire failure was of the sort that occurred when there was a defect.[81] The tire manufacturer sought to exclude the testimony on the ground that his methodology failed to satisfy Rule 702 of the Federal Rules of Evidence.[82] Although the Eleventh Circuit held that *Daubert* was limited to scientific testimony and that, since the testimony of the plaintiffs' expert was skill-or experience-based, it was not subject to *Daubert*,[83] the Supreme Court reversed. According to the Court, the obligation to ensure that expert testimony is not only relevant but reliable applies to the testimony of engineers and to other experts who are not scientists.[84] The Court gave a number of reasons for its holding. First, the language of Rule 702 does not distinguish between "scientific" knowledge and

---

[78] Joiner v. General Electric Co., 864 F. Supp. 1310, 1312 (N.D. Ga. 1994).

[79] 522 U.S. 136, 146 (1997).

[80] 526 U.S. 137 (1999).

[81] *Id.* at 143–45.

[82] *Id.* at 145.

[83] Carmichael v. Samyang Tire, Inc., 131 F.3d 1433 (11th Cir. 1997).

[84] Kumho Tire Co. v. Carmichael, 526 U.S. 137, 147 (1999).

"technical" or "other specialized" knowledge[85] This is because it is the word "knowledge" in Rule 702, not the words that modify it, that establishes a standard for evidentiary reliability.[86] *Daubert* referred only to "scientific" knowledge because that was the nature of the expertise in the case.[87] Second, Rules 702 and 703 give all expert witnesses, not just "scientific" ones testimonial latitude unavailable to other witnesses on the assumption that their opinion will have a reliable basis in the knowledge and experience of the discipline.[88] Finally, the Court felt that it would be difficult, if not impossible for judges to administer a gatekeeping system that depended upon a distinction between "scientific" knowledge and "technical" or "other specialized' knowledge since there is no clear dividing line between the two types.[89] Thus, all expert witnesses in products liability cases now are subject to the *Daubert* factors in the admissibility of their testimony.[90]

[5] The District Court Judge as "Gatekeeper"

The Supreme Court's trilogy of *Daubert*, *Joiner*, and *Kumho Tire* created a new framework for determining the admissibility of expert testimony.[91] In response to those decisions, Rule 702 of the Federal Rules of Evidence was amended in 2000.[92] The current Rule "reflects" the broad latitude the Supreme Court has given to district court judges to determine the admissibility of expert testimony. Under Rule 702 and the *Daubert* trilogy, district court judges must act as "gatekeepers" for the admission of expert testimony. The purpose of this role is to prevent what one court has called "speculative, unreliable expert testimony" from being presented to the jury under the "mantle of reliability" that attaches to the label "expert testimony."[93] Under *Daubert* and its progeny, the trial court judge, as the "gatekeeper," makes a "preliminary assessment of whether the reasoning or methodology underlying the [expert] testimony is scientifically valid and of whether that reasoning or methodology can be applied to the facts at issue."[94] This requires the judge to conduct an inquiry to ensure that the testimony or evidence

---

[85] *Id.*

[86] *Id.* at 147.

[87] *Id.* at 147–48.

[88] *Id.* at 148.

[89] *Id.*

[90] It is the responsibility of the parties to present expert testimony, where necessary, that meets the *Daubert* requirements for admissibility. *See* Weisgram v. Marley Co., 528 U.S. 440 (2000).

[91] Truck Insurance Exchange v. MagneTek, Inc., 360 F.3d 1206, 1209 (10th Cir. 2004).

[92] Rule 702 now provides:

> If scientific, technical, or other specialized knowledge will assist the trier of fact to understand the evidence or to determine a fact in issue, a witness qualified as an expert by knowledge, skill, experience, training, or education, may testify thereto in the form of an opinion or otherwise, if (1) the testimony is based upon sufficient facts or data, (2) the testimony is the product of reliable principles and methods, and (3) the witness has applied the principles and methods reliably to the facts of the case.

[93] McCorvey v. Baxter Healthcare Corp., 298 F.3d 1253, 1256 (11th Cir. 2002).

[94] Daubert v. Merrell Dow Pharmaceuticals, 509 U.S. 579, 592–93 (1993). *See* Newell Rubbermail, Inc. v. The Raymond Corp., 676 F.3d 521 (6th Cir. 2012).

is "both reliable and relevant."[95] However, there is no single requirement for admissibility of expert testimony.[96] The Supreme Court in *Kumho Tire* said that the goal of the reliability and relevance requirement

> is to make certain that an expert, whether basing testimony upon professional studies or personal experience, employs in the courtroom the same level of intellectual rigor that characterizes the practice of an expert in the relevant field. Nor is it denied that the particular questions that it mentioned will often be appropriate for use in determining the reliability of challenged expert testimony. Rather, the trial judge must have considerable leeway in deciding in a particular case how to go about determining whether particular expert testimony is reliable. A trial court should consider the specific factors identified in *Daubert* where they are reasonable measures of the reliability of expert testimony.[97]

[a]   Reliability

The first task facing a district court judge is to evaluate whether the expert's proposed testimony has a reliable basis in the expert's discipline.[98] This requires an examination of whether the expert's opinions are based on the "methods and procedures of science" or are "subjective belief or unsupported speculation."[99] In order to meet the test for reliability, the expert must have " 'good grounds' for his or her belief."[100] However, reliability does not require the plaintiff to prove that the expert is "undisputably correct."[101] Instead, the plaintiff's burden is to show that the "method employed by the expert in reaching the conclusion is scientifically sound."[102]

To determine reliability, the Supreme Court in *Daubert* suggested that the district court consider four factors. These factors remain relevant after the adoption of amended Rule 702.[103] However, the *Daubert* factors are not definitive or exhaustive and a judge has wide discretion in making a determination an expert's reliability.[104] Depending on the issue, the expert's particular expertise, and the subject of the expert's testimony, these factors may or may not be applicable in

---

[95] Junk v. Terminix Int'l Co., 628 F.3d 439, 448 (8th Cir. 2010).

[96] "[*Daubert*] made clear that its list of factors was meant to be helpful, not definitive. . . . The trial judge must have considerable leeway in deciding in a particular case how to go about determining whether particular expert testimony is reliable." Kumho Tire Co., Ltd. v. Carmichael, 526 U.S. 137, 151–52 (1999).

[97] *Id.* at 152.

[98] Bitler v. A.O. Smith Corp., 400 F.3d 1227 (10th Cir. 2004).

[99] Calhoun v. Yamaha Motor Corp., U.S.A., 350 F.3d 316, 321 (3d Cir. 2003) (quoting *Daubert*, 509 U.S. at 590).

[100] *Id.*

[101] Mitchell v. Gencorp, Inc., 165 F.3d 778, 781 (10th Cir. 1999).

[102] *Id.*

[103] Guy v. Crown Equipment, 394 F.3d 320 (5th Cir. 2004).

[104] Bitler v. A.O. Smith Corp., 400 F.3d 1227 (10th Cir. 2004).

determining reliability.[105] According to the Supreme Court in *Kumho Tire*, "[f]ailure to consider one, or even any, of these factors?will not be dispositive of a district court's failure to fulfill its gatekeeping role."[106] Instead, the inquiry into an expert's reliability "is meant to be flexible and fact specific, and a court should use, adapt, or reject *Daubert* factors as the particular case demands."[107]

Although the judge evaluates the reliability of an expert's testimony, the gatekeeper role is not intended to replace the role of the jury. The "believability or persuasiveness" of the testimony remains a matter for the trier of fact and the judge cannot exclude an expert because he or she believes one expert is more persuasive than another expert.[108] According to the Fifth Circuit, *Daubert* makes it clear that " '[v]igorous cross-examination, presentation of contrary evidence, and careful instruction on the burden of proof are the traditional and appropriate means of attacking shaky but admissible evidence.' "[109] Thus, in exercising its role as gatekeeper, a district court judge cannot transform a *Daubert* hearing into a trial on the merits.[110]

[b] Relevance

For the second part of the *Daubert* test, the district court judge must determine whether the proposed testimony is relevant to the issue in question. As stated in the Federal Rules of Evidence, relevant evidence "means evidence having any tendency to make the existence of any fact that is of consequence to the determination of the action more probable or less probable than it would be without the evidence."[111] *Daubert* described the consideration of relevant evidence as one of "fit."[112] Thus, even if the expert's evidence satisfies the test for reliability, it may not have a sufficient bearing on the issue in the case to justify a determination that it has relevant "fit."[113] In addition, if an expert offers only an "equivocal opinion," and "does not make any fact more or less probable," the testimony will be held irrelevant and inadmissible.[114]

The district court judge's discretion as to relevance also applies the admissibility of experimental tests as evidence in products liability cases.[115] When the science underlying an expert testimony is sound, the expert usually will not need testing to

---

[105] Pipitone v. Biomatrix, Inc., 288 F.3d 239 (5th Cir. 2002).

[106] Kumho Tire v. Carmichael, 526 U.S. 137, 152 (1999).

[107] *Id.* at 141. *See also* Pipitone v. Biomatrix, Inc., 288 F.3d 239, 245 (5th Cir. 2002) ("It is a fact-specific inquiry.").

[108] Rink v. Cheminova, Inc., 400 F.3d 1286, 1287 (11th Cir. 2005).

[109] Pipitone v. Biomatrix, Inc., 288 F.3d 239, 250 (5th Cir. 2002).

[110] *Id.*

[111] FEDERAL RULES OF EVIDENCE Rule 401. For a discussion of the standards for the exclusion of evidence in strict liability cases, see Moyer v. Dominion Indus., Inc., 473 F.3d 532 (3d Cir. 2007) (applying Pennsylvania law).

[112] Daubert v. Merrell Dow Pharmaceuticals, Inc., 509 U.S. 579, 591 (1993).

[113] Garlinger v. Hardee's Foodsystems, Inc., 2001 U.S. App. LEXIS 18559 (4th Cir. Aug. 16, 2001).

[114] Pipitone v. Biomatrix, Inc., 288 F.3d 239, 245 (5th Cir. 2002).

[115] McKnight v. Johnson Controls, Inc., 36 F.3d 1396 (8th Cir. 1994).

establish reliability under *Daubert*. However, if an expert proposes a theory that modifies well-established knowledge about regularly occurring phenomenon, the importance of testing in determining the reliability of the expert's testimony will "be at its highest."[116] A district court judge can exclude relevant evidence if its probative value is "substantially outweighed" by its likelihood to confuse the issue or mislead the jury.[117] This is an issue when a party introduces evidence that attempts to reconstruct an accident or evidence to show an example of the product. Courts will construe the evidence to determine if it is "sufficiently close in appearance to the original accident to create the risk of misunderstanding by the jury."[118] To avoid the exclusion of accident reconstruction evidence, the party may need to show a "substantial similarity in circumstances" between the reconstruction and the original accident.[119] In contrast, a party may introduce evidence that simply illustrates "general scientific principles" without a showing of substantial similarity in circumstances.[120] However, a court may admit an expert's experimental test into evidence to demonstrate an event could occur, if it is necessary as a basis to the expert's opinion that the event occurred during the accident.[121]

[6] Review of the District Court Decision

Under *Daubert*, evaluating the reliability and relevance of expert testimony is entrusted to the district court judge who has "wide discretion" both in deciding how to assess and determine an expert's reliability. An appellate court will give the district court judge "considerable leeway" in exercising its discretion.[122] An appellate court reviews *de novo* whether the district court judge properly admitted or excluded expert testimony,[123] and the standard of review is abuse of discretion.[124]

---

[116] Bitler v. A.O. Smith Corp., 400 F.3d 1227, 1235–36 (10th Cir. 2004).

[117] *See* Fireman's Fund Ins. Co. v. Canon U.S.A., Inc., 394 F.3d 1054 (8th Cir. 2005); Jodoin v. Toyota Motor Corp., 284 F.3d 272 (1st Cir. 2002).

[118] Jodoin v. Toyota Motor Corp., 284 F.3d 272, 278–79 (1st Cir. 2002).

[119] *Id.* at 278.

[120] *Id.*

[121] Nemir v. Mitsubishi Motors Corp., 381 F.3d 540, 544 (6th Cir. 2004).

[122] Rink v. Cheminova, Inc., 400 F.3d 1286, 1291 (11th Cir. 2005). *See also* Norris v. Baxter Healthcare Corp., 397 F.3d 878, 883 (10th Cir 2005) ("[W]e recognize the wide latitude a district court has in exercising its discretion to admit or exclude expert testimony.").

[123] Bitler v. A.O. Smith Corp., 400 F.3d 1227 (10th Cir. 2004).

[124] Newell Rubbermaid, Inc. v. The Raymond Corp., 676 F.3d 521 (6th Cir. 2012); Rink v. Cheminova, Inc., 400 F.3d 1286 (11th Cir. 2005). The standard also applies in many state courts. *See* Green v. Alpharma, Inc., 284 S.W.3d 29 (Ark. 2008); Exxon Pipeline v. Zwahr, 88 S.W.3d 623 (Tex. 2002); Donegal Mutual Ins. v. White Consolidated Indus., Inc., 852 N.E.2d 215 (Ohio Ct. App. 2006); Miller v. Bernard, 957 N.E.2d 685, 693 (Ind. Ct. App. 2011) ("The admission or exclusion of expert testimony lies within the sound discretion of the trial court, and will not be reversed absent an abuse of that discretion.").

[C] The Qualifications for an Expert

In order to strengthen the credibility of some witnesses and to permit them to give opinion testimony about the cause of the injuries, plaintiffs and defendants in products liability actions seek to qualify them as *experts*.[125] Rule 702 of the Federal Rules of Evidence states that a witness may be "qualified as an expert" if the witness has "scientific, technical, or other specialized knowledge" that "will assist the trier of fact to understand the evidence or to determine a fact in issue."[126] This determination is made by the trial court judge after listening to the qualifications of the person and appellate courts will affirm the decision to admit or exclude expert testimony unless the decision was "manifestly erroneous."[127] State rules define the qualifications for an expert witness in much the same way as the Federal Rules of Evidence. For example, Illinois Supreme Court Rule 220 provides that

> an expert is a person who, because of education, training or experience, possesses knowledge of a specialized nature beyond that of the average person on a factual matter material to a claim or defense in pending litigation and who may be expected to render an opinion within his expertise at trial.

Although there are no federal or state rules that explicitly require expert testimony, courts have stated that such testimony is required to assist the trier of fact when the issue "cannot be determined by common knowledge and experience."[128] Thus, expert testimony is necessary when the subject matter of an inquiry is such that only a person with particular skills or experience in the area is capable of forming an opinion. The determinative factor for the competency of an expert witness is whether the person has sufficient skills or experience in the particular field so that his or her testimony will assist the jury in reaching its conclusion.[129] "Special expertise" is interpreted liberally and does not depend on the person being a member of a particular profession. Instead, courts look at a number of factors in assessing whether a person is qualified as an expert. These include not only the broad categories of education, training, and experience, but also such factors as education in particular areas, attendance at related continuing education programs, teaching experience, publications, and professional organization memberships. In

---

[125] In selecting a person to testify as an expert, the attorneys for the plaintiff and the defendant want someone who has the time to devote to the case, with whom they are comfortable working, and who knows how to communicate with members of a jury in a language they can understand.

[126] For a case in which the court determined that witnesses training and experience as a mechanical engineer and his experience in accident investigation qualified him as an expert witness, see Galloway v. Big G. Express, Inc., 590 F. Supp. 2d 989 (E.D. Tenn. 2008).

[127] General Electric Co. v. Joiner, 522 U.S. 136, 142 (1997).

[128] Wilson v. Stilwill, 309 N.W.2d 898, 907 (Mich. 1981).

[129] Chavez v. Glock, Inc., 2012 Cal. App. LEXIS 832, at *68 (July 24, 2012). See Sigler v. American Honda Motor Corp., 532 F.3d 469 (6th Cir. 2008), in which the court properly excluded the testimony of the plaintiff's expert mechanic since he lacked expertise in the field of accident reconstruction and Pineda v. Ford Motor Co., 520 F.3d 237 (3d Cir. 2008), in which the Court of Appeals reversed a District Court finding that the plaintiff's engineer was not qualified as an expert. The court concluded that his methodology was reliable.

Calhoun v. Yamaha Motor Corp., U.S.A.,[130] the plaintiff's 14-year-old daughter was killed while riding a jet ski manufactured by the defendant. The plaintiff, who alleged a design defect in the jet ski's accelerating mechanism, offered an expert to testify that the jet ski's accelerating mechanism was not as safe as other alternative designs. The expert was "a lieutenant for San Diego's Marine Safety Services for sixteen years," "had extensive experience with jet skis," and had conducted "aquatic related accident investigations."[131] The defendants sought to exclude the expert's testimony because he lacked "formal education or training in engineering?or human factors."[132] However, the Virginia court allowed his testimony about "how jet skis operate," the differences between defendant's jet ski and other brands and models, and how each type of "various accelerating mechanisms" works.[133]

Although background, education, and training usually qualify an expert as having general knowledge to testify about general matters, "specific knowledge" is required to support a specific opinion.[134] Thus, in *Calhoun*, the appellate court found that the expert had "no education or experience in product design of jet skis or accelerating mechanisms," and held that he "had neither the general background nor the specific knowledge to support his proffered testimony that the 'squeeze finger throttle' was less safe than other designs."[135] In addition, an expert witness cannot offer testimony on matters "outside" his or her "area of expertise." In *Calhoun*, the plaintiff offered a second expert to testify that the jet ski's warnings were inadequate. The expert had "a bachelor's degree in naval architecture and marine engineering, as well as higher degrees in other fields," and had "worked with the Navy and the Department of Defense and served as an accident reconstruction consultant with a focus on marine engineering and boat accidents."[136] The court upheld the exclusion of the expert's testimony finding that, "in contrast to his background in naval architecture and marine engineering" which allowed him to testify generally about mechanical issues, "he possessed no expertise with regard to warning design."[137]

[D]   The Permissible Scope of Expert Testimony

Once a witness is qualified as an expert, the final question for courts is: What is the permissible scope of the expert's testimony? Rule 702 of the Federal Rules of Evidence states that an expert may testify "in the form of an opinion or otherwise." Rule 704 gives broad scope to such testimony by stating that opinion testimony "otherwise admissible is not objectionable because it embraces an ultimate issue to be decided by the trier of fact." Thus, in addition to giving opinion testimony, an

---

[130]   350 F.3d 316 (3d Cir. 2003).

[131]   *Id.* at 321.

[132]   *Id.* at 323.

[133]   *Id.*

[134]   *See* Calhoun v. Yamaha Motor Co., U.S.A., 350 F.3d 316, 322 (3d Cir. 2003).

[135]   *Id.* at 324.

[136]   *Id.*

[137]   *Id.*

expert is given special latitude to testify based upon certain hearsay and third-party observations that normally would not be admissible.

§ 8.04   CAUSE-IN-FACT

[A]   Introduction

A *prima facie* case of negligence or strict liability requires proof of more than the existence of a defect in a product. The plaintiff also must present proof that permits the trier of fact to conclude that it is more likely than not that the allegedly defective condition in the product caused the plaintiff's injuries. The proof of causation must be by a probability and the trier of fact is not permitted to speculate among several possible causes of plaintiff's injuries.[138] In many cases, this is not difficult. However, with some products, causation presents serious problems. For example, proving that a particular drug or chemical caused the plaintiff's injury requires expert medical testimony. Proof that a defect in a machine was the cause of the injuries may require engineering evidence. In reply, the manufacturer or seller will offer its own expert testimony and will argue that the injuries were caused by factors unrelated to the condition of the product. Normally, cause-in-fact is a question for the jury.[139] However, when the material facts are undisputed, and there can be no difference in the judgment of reasonable persons as to the inferences to be drawn from them, cause-in-fact becomes a question of law and the court may grant summary judgment or direct a verdict for the plaintiff or the defendant.[140]

This section examines three issues that can arise in establishing the necessary causal connection between the product defect and the plaintiff's injuries: (1) What tests do plaintiffs and defendants and courts use to prove causation? (2) How can a plaintiff establish causation if he or she does not know the identity of the manufacturer or seller of the product? (3) Can a plaintiff establish the necessary causal connection between the product and an injury that has not yet occurred?

---

[138] Hickey v. Otis Elevator Co., 840 N.E.2d 637 (Ohio Ct. App. 2005). For an analysis of the historical development causation, see Union Pump Co. v. Allbritton, 898 S.W.2d 773, 777–79 (Tex. 1995) (Cornyn, J., concurring opinion). Under § 15 of the RESTATEMENT (THIRD), "[w]hether a product defect caused harm to persons or property is determined by the prevailing rules and principles governing causation in tort." In In re Methyl Tertiary Butyl Ether ("MTBE") Products Liability Litigation, 591 F. Supp. 2d 259, 266 (S.D.N.Y. 2008) (applying New York law), a federal district court took that position.

[139] Reynolds v. Strauss Veal, Inc., 519 N.E.2d 226 (Ind. Ct. App. 1988).

[140] See Tiner v. General Motors Corp., 909 F. Supp. 112, 119 (N.D.N.Y. 1995) (applying New York law), in which the court granted summary judgment when the plaintiff "wholly failed to show her injuries were caused or enhanced by any defect in the air bag" in her automobile. See also Wright v. St. Mary's Medical Center of Evansville, Inc., 59 F. Supp. 2d 794 (S.D. Ind. 1999) (applying Indiana law).

[B]   "But For" and "Substantial Factor" Tests

In order to determine whether a product was the cause-in-fact of the plaintiff's injury, courts use two tests: the *but for* test (sometimes referred to as a *sine qua non* test) and the substantial factor test.[141] Under the *but for* test, "an act is a factual cause of an outcome if, in the absence of the act, the outcome would not have occurred."[142] Thus, the plaintiff must show that his or her injury would not have occurred without the defect in the product. An example of the use and effect of this test in a products liability case is *Gordon v. Goldman Brothers Inc.*,[143] in which a novice hiker was injured when he slipped on the side of a steep hill. The hiker brought suit against the manufacturer and retailer of the boots he was wearing at the time of the accident, alleging breach of warranty, negligence, and strict liability failure to warn. In dismissing the complaint, the New York court stated:

> Assuming that the boots in question were not designed for use on rocky or mountainous terrain, the circumstances of the accident do not on their face establish that the boots were in any way responsible for the fall. Noticeably missing from the plaintiffs' papers is any expert's affidavit or other evidence attesting to the fact that different boots might have prevented the accident.[144]

While the *but for* test can be used in many cases to determine what, in fact, has occurred, the idea of a single cause of an injury is not appropriate in the complex society of the 21st century. Instead, an injury is more likely to have multiple or concurring causes. Application of the *but for* test in such a case relieves both tortfeasors of liability on the ground that *but for* the conduct of one, the incident would still have occurred.[145] For these reasons, most states now accept the definition of causal connection set out in § 431 of the Restatement (Second) of Torts: "The actor's negligent conduct is a legal cause of harm to another if (a) his conduct is a substantial factor in bringing about the harm . . ."[146] According to one court,

---

[141] Sometimes courts use both tests. In Ford Motor Co. v. Ledesma, 242 S.W.3d 32, 46 (Tex. 2007), the Texas Supreme Court said that the jury should have been instructed that the "producing cause" of the accident was both the "substantial cause of the event and the "but-for cause," one without which the event would not have occurred.

[142] RESTATEMENT (THIRD) OF TORTS: LIABILITY FOR PHYSICAL HARM, § 26 (2005). *See also* Rudeck v. Wright, 709 P.2d 621, 628 (Mont. 1985) ("The defendant's conduct is a cause of the event if the event would not have occurred but for that conduct; or conversely, the defendant's conduct is not a cause of the event, if the event would have occurred without it."); and John D. Rue, *Note: Returning to the Roots of the Bramble Bush: The "But For" Test Regains Primacy in Causal Analysis in the American Law Institute's Proposed Restatement (Third) of Torts*, 71 FORDHAM L. REV. 2679 (2003).

[143] 515 N.Y.S.2d 39 (App. Div. 1987).

[144] *Id.* at 40.

[145] Rutherford v. Owens-Illinois, Inc., 941 P.2d 1203 (Cal. 1997).

[146] *See* Malen v. MYD Products, Inc., 628 F.3d 296 (7th Cir. 2010) (applying Illinois law); Xavier v. Philip Morris USA Inc., 787 F. Supp. 2d 1075 (N.D. Cal. 2011) (applying California law); Donovan v. Philip Morris USA, Inc., 268 F.R.D. 1 (D. Mass. 2010) (applying Massachusetts law). For a discussion of the use of the substantial factor test to prove causation in asbestos cases, see In re Asbestos Products Liability Litigation, 2011 U.S. Dist. LEXIS 101081 (E.D. Pa. July 27, 2011) (applying New York law); Borg-Warner Corp. v. Flores, 232 S.W.3d 765 (Tex. 2007); Jane Stapleton, *The Two Explosive*

the phrase "substantial factor" is used to "denote the fact that the defendant's conduct has such an effect in producing the harm as to lead reasonable men to regard it as a cause, using that word in the popular sense, in which there always lurks the idea of responsibility."[147] The substantial factor test has been criticized as not going far enough and as being too general. However, courts and commentators appear convinced that "substantial factor" is a phrase sufficiently intelligible to furnish an adequate guide in instructions to juries and that it is neither possible nor desirable to reduce it to any more specific terms.[148]

In most products liability cases, the issues faced by plaintiffs and defendants in proving and disproving factual causation are no different from those in other torts cases. Plaintiffs and defendants will rely on expert witnesses and any questions of causation will turn on the admissibility and believability of their testimony. However, in cases involving drugs and medical devices,[149] some states require plaintiffs to prove two forms of causation: general causation and specific causation.[150] What is required to prove general and specific causation in medical cases is illustrated by *Norris v. Baxter Heathcare Corp.*,[151] in which the plaintiff alleged that she suffered a systemic disease that was caused by a silicone gel breast implant. In upholding the grant of summary judgment in favor of the manufacturer of the implant, the Tenth Circuit stated that, in silicone breast implant litigation, a plaintiff must show both general and specific causation. "General causation" requires proof that the product is capable of causing a particular injury, disease, or condition in the general population. "Specific causation" focuses on whether the substance caused the particular plaintiff's injury.[152] To establish specific causation in a case involving drugs, the plaintiff must present expert testimony showing "a specific train of medical evidence connecting the illness to the product."[153] One method of determining specific causation is differential diagnosis, a process whereby doctors experienced in diagnostic techniques provide testimony, after physical examinations, taking medical histories, and reviewing clinical and laboratory tests, countering other possible causes.[154] Since the plaintiff in *Norris* presented no epidemiological evidence of any causal connection between silicone

---

Proof-of-Causation Doctrine Central to Asbestos Claims, 74 Brook. L. Rev. 1011 (2009).

[147] Lear Siegler, Inc. v. Perez, 819 S.W.2d 470, 472 (Tex. 1991). *See* Clark v. Leisure Vehicles, Inc., 292 N.W.2d 630, 635 (Wis. 1980).

[148] Bidar v. Amfac, Inc., 669 P.2d 154 (Haw. 1983).

[149] Easter v. Aventis Pasteur, Inc., 358 F. Supp. 2d 574 (E.D. Tex. 2005) (applying Texas law).

[150] *See* Merck & Co. v. Garza, 347 S.W.3d 256 (Tex. 2011). According to the Kansas Supreme Court, proof of general causation ordinarily is required only in mass tort litigation with large existing epidemiological records. *See* Kuhn v. Sandoz Pharmaceuticals, Corp., 14 P.3d 1170 (Kan. 2000). However, in Donaldson v. Central Illinois Public Service Corp., 767 N.E.2d 314 (Ill. 2002), the Illinois Supreme Court stated that Illinois law does not define causation in terms of "generic" or "specific" causation. Instead, a plaintiff must prove "cause in fact" and "legal cause."

[151] 397 F.3d 878 (10th Cir. 2005) (applying Colorado law).

[152] *See* Merck & Co. v. Garza, 347 S.W.3d 256, 262 (Tex. 2011) (in drug cases, causation can be proved directly, with evidence of controlled scientific experiments, or indirectly, with epidemiological studies).

[153] Newton v. Roche Laboratories, Inc., 243 F. Supp. 2d 672, 682 (W.D. Tex. 2002).

[154] *See* Westberry v. Gislaved Gummi AB, 178 F.3d 257 (4th Cir. 1999); Hines v. Conrail, 926 F.2d 262 (3d Cir. 1991).

breasts implants and systemic disease, the court held that the product could not have caused the plaintiff's injuries.[155]

Proof of general and specific causation also may be required cases not involving drugs or medical devices.[156] In *McCoy v. Whirlpool Corp.*,[157] the plaintiffs brought a strict liability suit alleging manufacturing defects against the manufacturer of a dishwasher which caught on fire, destroying their home and killing their daughter. The district court judge held that, on the issue of general causation, the plaintiffs were required to show that a manufacturing defect that caused excessive resistance heating in the door latch switch assembly was a scientifically plausible cause of a fire in the brand of dishwasher they had purchased. On the issue of specific causation, the plaintiffs had to show that excessive resistance heating due to one of the two alleged defects in their machine raised the temperature high enough to cause the specific fire. Since the plaintiffs did not present sufficient evidence of general causation, the district court judge granted the manufacturer's motion for judgment as a matter of law.

[C]   Establishing the Identity of the Manufacturer

In addition to proving that the defective product was the cause-in-fact of the injuries, the plaintiff also must establish that the defendant was the manufacturer or supplier of that product.[158] It is not sufficient to identify a defendant as one of several manufacturers or suppliers of the product that caused the injury. In order to establish the necessary causal connection between the defendant and the injury, the plaintiff must establish that the defendant, in fact, manufactured or supplied the defective product.[159] The failure to do so will result in summary judgment for the defendant.[160] An example of the problems a plaintiff can face in identifying the manufacturer of an allegedly defective product, particularly if there has been a long delay between the date of the accident and the date of filing suit, is *Moore v. Mississippi Valley Gas Co.*,[161] in which the plaintiff's daughter was burned badly when she fell into a bathtub full of hot water in 1989. By the time the plaintiff filed suit against the defendant/manufacturer of water heaters in 1996, her landlord had replaced and discarded the one involved in the accident. There were no witnesses who could identify the make, model, or manufacturer of the allegedly defective hot water heater. The only evidence of any involvement by the defendant/manufacturer was a sales invoice stating that Cornelius Williams, who had lived at the address of

---

[155] 397 F.3d 878, 881 (10th Cir. 2005).

[156] Smith v. General Motors Corp., 376 F. Supp. 2d 664 (W.D. Va. 2005) (applying Virginia law) (seatbelt).

[157] 379 F. Supp. 2d 1187 (D. Kan. 2005) (applying Kansas law).

[158] Coons v. A. F. Chapman Corp., 460 F. Supp. 2d 209 (D. Mass. 2006) (applying Massachusetts law) (negligence action); Sheffield v. Owens-Corning Fiberglass Corp., 595 So. 2d 443, 450 (Ala. 1992) (the "threshold requirement of any products liability action is identification of the injury-causing product and its manufacturer").

[159] Mulcahy v. Eli Lilly & Co., 386 N.W.2d 67, 76 (Iowa 1986).

[160] Brown v. Stone Manufacturing Co., 660 F. Supp. 454, 458 (S.D. Miss. 1986) (applying Mississippi law).

[161] 863 So. 2d 43 (Miss. 2003).

the accident, had purchased a 40-gallon hot water heater, Serial # 0181M17815 in 1981. However, the receipt did not indicate at what address that hot water heater was installed. Williams had since died and the company that installed the hot water heater no longer existed. Since the defendant/manufacturer did not have the opportunity to identify, inspect, or test the water heater involved in the accident, no one was certain whether the 1981 hot water heater was the defendant's. Thus, the Mississippi court refused to leave the issue to the jury's speculation or conjecture and granted summary judgment.

In *Moore* part of the problem was that the plaintiff waited seven years to bring her claim, even though she was aware of her daughter's injury and the cause of it. However, in cases involving products such as drugs, asbestos, or lead paint, the plaintiff may not know that he or she has a claim because the harmful effects may not become evident for decades. By that time, the plaintiff may not be able to identify the manufacturer or seller of the product. Examples of this are the DES cases, where the plaintiffs were the daughters of women who took the drug in the early 1950s. At the time, DES was a generic drug and a large number of manufacturers produced the drug. By the time the connection between DES and the plaintiffs' cancer was established and the plaintiffs brought their suits in the 1970s, the specific manufacturers of the DES taken by their mothers often were unknown or had gone out of business. This made it impossible for the plaintiffs to identify the specific manufacturer of the DES taken by their mothers during their pregnancies more than two decades earlier. In *Sindell v. Abbott Laboratories*,[162] the California Supreme Court developed a new approach to the problem by basing liability on a market share theory that apportions liability among the defendant manufacturers of a fungible product based on their respective shares of the relevant market, unless a particular defendant can prove that it did not manufacture the product that caused the plaintiff's injuries.[163] In order to establish market share liability under *Sindell*, a plaintiff must show: (1) the injury causing product is fungible; (2) the inability to identify the manufacturer is not due to the plaintiff's own action or inaction; and (3) the plaintiff has joined the manufacturers of a "substantial share" of the product market. Although market-share liability initially attracted wide-spread attention,[164] the majority of courts now reject it.[165] An example of this attitude is *Smith v. Eli Lilly & Co.*,[166] in which the Illinois Supreme Court referred to market share liability as a "radical departure" from the

---

[162] 607 P.2d 924 (Cal. 1980).

[163] *Id.* at 937.

[164] For courts that adopted market share liability, see Hymowitz v. Eli Lilly & Co., 539 N.E.2d 1069 (N.Y. 1989); Collins v. Eli Lilly Co., 342 N.W.2d 37 (Wis. 1984); Martin v. Abbott Laboratories, 689 P.2d 368 (Wash. 1984).

[165] *See, e.g.*, Fields v. Wyeth, Inc., 613 F. Supp. 2d 1056 (W.D. Ark. 2009) (applying Arkansas law) (Arkansas has retained the traditional requirement of proximate cause in all tort cases: Sutowski v. Eli Lilly & Co., 696 N.E.2d 187 (Ohio 1998); Shackil v. Lederle Laboratories, 561 A.2d 511 (N.J. 1989)). Although the Florida Supreme Court has recognized the limited availability of market share liability, it has held that a pharmaceutical manufacturer cannot be liable where it could prove that it did not manufacture the drug that caused the injury. Conley v. Boyle Drug Co., 570 So. 2d 275 (Fla. 1990).

[166] 560 N.E.2d 324 (Ill. 1990).

traditional tort principle of causation.[167] The Restatement (Third) lists the cases and articles on both sides of the question.[168] In recent years, a new series of cases involving lead paint have raised the same issue as in the DES cases: the inability of the plaintiffs, due to no fault of their own, to identify the manufacturer of the paint in their building. As in the post-*Sindell* DES cases, most courts have rejected the use of the market share liability theory to establish causation.[169] In a controversial 2005 decision, *Thomas v. Mallett*,[170] the Wisconsin Supreme Court extended the risk-contribution theory it adopted for DES cases[171] to a minor who suffered lead poisoning as a result of ingesting lead-based paint from homes in which he live. As a result, the seven named manufacturers could be held jointly and severally liable, despite the plaintiff's inability to identify the precise producer of the white lead carbonate pigment he ingested, due to its generic nature. However, legislation went into effect in Wisconsin in 2011 that limits *Thomas* and provides that, if a claimant cannot identify the specific manufacturer, distributor, seller, or promoter of a product, the claimant can recover only if

(a)   [He or she] proves all of the following:

1.   That no other lawful process exists for the claimant to seek any redress from any other person for the injury or harm.

2.   That the claimant has suffered an injury or harm that can be caused only by a manufactured product chemically and physically identical to the specific product that allegedly caused the claimants injury or harm.

3.   That the manufacturer, distributor, seller, or promoter of a product manufactured, distributed, sold, or promoted a complete integrated product, in the form used by the claimant or to which the claimant was exposed, and that meets all of the following criteria:

a.   Is chemically and physically identical to the specific product that allegedly caused the claimants injury or harm.

b.   Was manufactured, distributed, sold, or promoted in the geographic market where the injury or harm is alleged to have occurred during the time period in which the specific product that allegedly caused the claimants injury or harm was manufactured, distributed, sold, or promoted.

c.   Was distributed or sold without labeling or any distinctive characteristic that identified the manufacturer, distributor,

---

[167] *Id.* at 334.

[168] RESTATEMENT (THIRD) OF TORTS: PRODUCTS LIABILITY, § 15, cmt. *c* (1998).

[169] *See, e.g.*, Santiago v. Sherwin Williams Co., 3 F.3d 546 (1st Cir. 1993) (applying Massachusetts law); Jefferson v. Lead Paint Industries, 930 F. Supp. 241 (E.D. La. 1996) (applying Louisiana law); Abbasi v. Paraskevoulakos, 718 N.E.2d 181 (Ill. 1999); Brenner v. American Cyanamid Co., 699 N.Y.S.2d 848 (App. Div. 1999).

[170] 701 N.W.2d 523 (Wis. 2005).

[171] Collins v. Eli Lilly Co., 342 N.W.2d 37 (Wis. 1984). "Risk-contribution theory" is Wisconsin's version of market share liability.

seller, or promoter.

(b)   The action names, as defendants, those manufacturers of a product who collectively manufactured at least 80 percent of all products sold in this state during the relevant production period by all manufacturers of the product in existence during the relevant production period that are chemically identical to the specific product that allegedly caused the claimants injury or harm.[172]

[D]   Exposure to Risk of Future Injury

The challenge for plaintiffs in most products liability cases is to draw the necessary causal connection between the defective product and their existing injuries. However, in some cases, plaintiffs allege that, although the product has not caused them any present injury, it has created an increased risk for harm in the future. Claims alleging an increased risk of future harm usually result from the use or exposure to one of three types of products: asbestos,[173] drugs,[174] and medical devices.[175] In these cases, plaintiffs often make three allegations in their complaints: (1) the product was defective and unreasonably dangerous; (2) the product places the plaintiff at a substantially greater risk of a specific future harm; and (3) the increased risk of future harm requires current and future medical testing and monitoring.[176]

Plaintiffs in increased risk of future harm cases must present evidence that establishes, with "reasonable probability," that the product increased the risk of a specific future medical problem.[177] An example of the issues involved in these cases is *Mauro v. Raymark Industries, Inc.,*[178] in which the plaintiff worked as a repairman and plumber-steamfitter from 1964 until the mid-to-late 1970s. In 1981 the plaintiff discovered, as the result of a physical examination, that, although his lungs were "normal" at the time, his exposure to asbestos during his employment might increase his risk of developing lung cancer. That was because he had bilateral thickening of both chest walls and calcification of the diaphragm.[179] In the plaintiff's action against the manufacturer of the asbestos, the trial court judge charged the jury that it could award the plaintiff damages for his present medical condition, the cost of medical surveillance, and for his emotional distress. Proof of an increased risk of cancer requires expert testimony and, in *Mauro*, the plaintiff's expert testified that there was a "high probability" that the plaintiff had "an

---

[172] WIS. STAT. ANN. § 895.046(4).

[173] Herber v. Johns-Manville Corp., 785 F.2d 79 (3d Cir. 1986) (applying New Jersey law); Mauro v. Raymark Industries, Inc., 561 A.2d 257 (N.J. 1989).

[174] In re Propulsid Products Liability Litigation, 208 F.R.D. 133 (E.D. La. 2002).

[175] Sutton v. St. Jude Medical S.C., Inc., 419 F.3d 568 (6th Cir. 2005) (applying Tennessee law); In re St. Jude Med., Inc. Silzone Heart Valves Products Liability Litigation, 2004 U.S. Dist. LEXIS 13965 (D. Minn. July 15, 2004).

[176] Sutton v. St. Jude Medical S.C., Inc., 419 F.3d 568, 571 (6th Cir. 2005) (applying Tennessee law).

[177] *See* Coll v. Sherry, 148 A.2d 481, 486 (N.J. 1959).

[178] 561 A.2d 257 (N.J. 1989).

[179] *Id.* at 258.

increased risk" of contracting cancer during his lifetime.[180] However, the expert was unable to testify that it was "probable" that plaintiff would contract cancer, and the statistical studies the expert wanted to use to show a correlation between asbestos-related disease and cancer were excluded because they were not referred to during discovery or in the witnesses expert report. Since there was no evidence in the record of the likelihood that plaintiff would contract cancer, the judge refused to submit the increased risk claim to the jury.[181] The New Jersey Supreme Court affirmed the trial court's decision, stating that "prospective damages are not recoverable unless they are reasonably probable to occur."[182]

Mauro followed the approach taken by the majority of courts that requires the plaintiff to prove the increased risk of future harm as a reasonable medical probability. One way of establishing this is with statistical studies evidence comparing the plaintiff's future risk of the specific harm with those who were not exposed to the product.[183] However, many commentators have urged recognition of a cause of action for an enhanced risk of future harm where the risk is less than probable. In *Mauro*, the New Jersey Supreme Court reviewed a number of the articles taking that position[184] as well as the arguments in favor of and opposed to recognizing enhanced-risk damages.[185] Although not a products liability case, the Illinois Supreme Court, in *Dillon v. Evanston Hospital*,[186] came down on the side of those who argue that the reasonable probability standard is too stringent when it held that a plaintiff can recover for an increased risk of future harm, even if the injury is improbable. However, the amount of damages must reflect the probability of the occurrence of the future injury.

Plaintiffs in increased risk cases may seek two types of damages. As in the *Dillon* case, they may treat the anticipated harm as the injury and seek damages based on the statistical probability of the harm occurring in the future. In *Herber v. Johns-Manville Corp.*,[187] a case also involving an increased risk of cancer as the result of exposure to asbestos in the workplace, the plaintiff argued that the increase in risk was an element of the damage he already had suffered and should be considered in the calculation of his damage award. According to the plaintiff, he should receive an amount equal to the amount that a person having an asbestos-caused cancer would receive, reduced proportionately to reflect the probability that he would not develop cancer.[188] However, even with expert testimony such a determination is very speculative. Thus, in addition, or in the alternative, plaintiffs

---

[180] *Id.* at 258.

[181] *Id.* at 259–60.

[182] *Id.* at 261.

[183] In Sutton v. St. Jude Medical S.C., Inc., 419 F.3d 568 (6th Cir. 2005), the plaintiff alleged an increased risk of harm from a medical device inserted in his chest after bypass surgery when compared with persons who underwent traditional surgery. The Sixth Circuit accepted the allegation as true and remanded the case.

[184] *Id.* at 264–67.

[185] *Id.* at 266.

[186] 771 N.E.2d 357 (Ill. 2002).

[187] 785 F.2d 79 (3d Cir. 1986) (applying New Jersey law).

[188] *Id.* at 82. The Third Circuit in *Herber* refused to permit the plaintiff to litigate the issue of

may view their injury as the cost of future periodic medical testing and monitoring in order to detect the future physical harm.[189] In order to recover these costs, plaintiffs must establish a number of elements: (1) exposure to a defective product; (2) creating a significantly increased risk of future harm; (3) an existing monitoring procedure that makes detection of the future harm possible; (4) the monitoring procedure is different from the normally recommended in the absence of the exposure; (5) the monitoring is reasonably necessary in light of current scientific principles.[190] Recovery for medical monitoring for future harm is recognized by a number of states.[191] One state that is opposed to medical monitoring is Louisiana, which has enacted a statute preventing plaintiffs from recovering such damages. According to the Louisiana statute: "Damages do not include costs for future medical treatment, services, surveillance, or procedures of any kind unless such treatment, services, surveillance, or procedures are directly related to a manifest physical or mental injury or disease."[192]

§ 8.05   PROXIMATE CAUSE

[A]   Introduction

Proof that the defendant's product was defective and was the cause-in-fact of the plaintiff's injury does not mean necessarily that the defendant will be liable for the plaintiff's injuries. As in other areas of tort law, it also is necessary for the plaintiff to establish that the product was the "proximate cause" or "legal cause" of the injuries.[193] A plaintiff must establish proximate cause in all products liability actions: negligence, strict liability,[194] and misrepresentation.[195] Proximate cause is not an issue of "causation" since there is no question that the product, in fact, caused the plaintiff's injuries. Instead, proximate cause is a policy question: How far should the legal responsibility of a manufacturer or seller extend for a defective product that, in fact, has caused harm?[196] The answer to this question is one of the

---

increased risk on the ground that he did not present evidence of the required medical probability of future cancer.

[189] *See* Friends for All Children Inc. v. Lockheed Aircraft Corp., 746 F.2d 816 (D.C. Cir. 1984). However, in Metro-North Commuter Railroad v. Buckley, 521 U.S. 424 (1997), the Supreme Court held that a plaintiff cannot recover costs for medical monitoring in a Federal Employers' Liability Act case on the basis that there was a lack of support in the common law. For a discussion of medical monitoring in products liability cases, see Sutton v. St. Jude Medical S.C., Inc., 419 F.3d 568, 571–75 (6th Cir. 2005).

[190] *See* Redland Soccer Club v. Department of the Army, 696 A.2d 137, 145–46 (Pa. 1997).

[191] *See* Xavier v. Philip Morris USA Inc., 787 F. Supp. 2d 1075 (N.D. Cal. 2011) (applying California law); Gibbs v. E.I. DuPont De Nemours & Co., 876 F. Supp. 475 (W.D.N.Y. 1995) (applying New York law).

[192] LA. REV. STAT. ANN. art. 2315.

[193] *See* Burley v. Kytec Innovative Sports Equip. Inc., 737 N.W.2d 397, 409 (S.D. 2007).

[194] *See* Broyles v. Kasper Machine Co., 2012 U.S. Dist. LEXIS 44508 (S.D. Ohio Mar. 30, 2012 (applying Ohio law). For a lengthy analysis of all aspects of proximate cause in products liability cases alleging negligence, see Collins v. Li, 933 A.2d 528 (Md. Ct. App. 2007).

[195] *See* Hollenbeck v. Selectone Corp., 476 N.E.2d 746 (Ill. App. Ct. 1985).

[196] In Caputzal v. Lindsay Co., 222 A.2d 513, 517 (N.J. 1966), the New Jersey Supreme Court said that the answer to the question was based "upon mixed considerations of logic, common sense, justice,

most debated in tort law and, over the years, has produced a number of different approaches. Most courts now hold that a defect in a product was the proximate cause of the plaintiff's injuries if the cause was "foreseeable in light of the attending circumstances" and was "the natural and probable consequence" of the defective product.[197] However, foreseeability does not require that the manufacturer or seller should have foreseen the precise risk or exact result that occurred. Instead, the essential factor is that the defendant should have anticipated the general kind of consequences that occurred.[198] Similarly, whether the injury was the "natural and probable consequence" of a defect in the product requires consideration of any intervening or superseding causes such as product misuse or alteration and whether they were foreseeable.[199] The effect of proximate cause is to limit the responsibility of a manufacturer or seller for the consequences of defective products and prevent strict liability from becoming absolute liability.[200] This section examines three tests courts have used to determine how far legal responsibility should extend.

[B]   Foreseeability

An analysis to determine foreseeability has been called "the touchstone of any determination of proximate cause."[201] Issues of foreseeability arise in a variety of contexts: foreseeability of the plaintiff; foreseeability of the use of the product;[202] foreseeability of the harm; and foreseeability of intervening factors. For example, because of the abolition of privity in negligence and strict liability actions, the liability of a manufacturer or seller extends not only to users and consumers of the product[203] but also to foreseeable bystanders injured by a product.[204] However,

---

policy and precedent." *See* E.J. Stewart, Inc. v. Aitken Products, 607 F. Supp. 883 (E.D. Pa. 1985) (applying Pennsylvania law); Lear Siegler, Inc. v. Perez, 819 S.W.2d 470 (Tex. 1991); Ferguson v. Lieff, Cabraser, Heimann & Bernstein, 69 P.3d 965 (Cal. Ct. App. 2003). For an overview of proximate cause, see *Symposium: Legal Cause: Cause-in-Fact and the Scope of Liability for Consequences*, 54 VAND. L. REV. 941 (2001).

[197] White v. Ford Motor Co., 312 F.3d 998, 1006 (9th Cir. 2002) (applying California law). According to another court, proximate cause is defined as that cause which "in natural and continuous sequence, unbroken by an efficient intervening cause, produces the injury, and without which the injury would not have occurred, the injury being the natural and probable consequences of the wrongful act." Yount v. Deibert, 147 P.3d 1065, 1070 (Kan. 2006). Under this test, there may be more than one proximate cause of an event. Miller v. Bernard, 957 N.E.2d 685 (Ind. Ct. App. 2011).

[198] Petition of Kinsman Transit Co., 338 F.2d 708 (2d Cir. 1964); Timmons v. Ford Motor Co., 982 F. Supp. 1475 (S.D. Ga. 1997) (applying Georgia law).

[199] Buckley v. Bell, 703 P.2d 1089 (Wyo. 1985); Hutto v. McNeil-PPC, Inc., 79 So. 3d 1199 (La. Ct. App. 2011).

[200] Helene Curtis Industries, Inc. v. Pruitt, 385 F.2d 841 (5th Cir. 1967).

[201] Collins v. Li, 933 A.2d 528, 549 (Md. Ct. App. 2007).

[202] *See* Gay v. O. F. Mossberg & Sons, Inc., 2009-Ohio-2954, 2009 Ohio App. LEXIS 2520.

[203] In duty to warn cases, for example, courts state that the warning must be sufficient to adequately protect all foreseeable users of the product from any hidden dangers presented by it. *See* Whitehead v. St. Joe Lead Co., 729 F.2d 238 (3d Cir. 1984); Freas v. Prater Construction Corp., 573 N.E.2d 27 (Ohio 1991).

[204] Peck v. Ford Motor Co., 603 F.2d 1240 (7th Cir. 1979) (applying Indiana law); Rivers v. Great Dane Trailers, Inc., 816 F. Supp. 1525 (M.D. Ala. 1993) (applying Florida law).

even if the manufacturer owed a duty to the plaintiff, the manufacturer or seller may allege that it is not legally responsible for the plaintiff's particular injury because it was the result of a use of the product that was not foreseeable at the time of manufacture. Courts speak of a manufacturer having a duty to produce products that are safe when used for their "intended purpose"[205] or for a "reasonably foreseeable purpose."[206] However, the "intended" or "foreseeable" use of a product depends upon the specific facts and circumstance of each case. Statements by courts as to what was the "intended purpose" or a "reasonably foreseeable purpose" of a product was in previous cases is of little help in predicting what courts will do in the future.

Because foreseeability is fact specific, it is only possible to provide an example of facts that have led a court to conclude that the use of a product was foreseeable. An illustration of the extent of the foreseeable intended use of a product is *Ayers v. Johnson & Johnson Baby Products Co.*,[207] in which the parents of a 15-month-old baby brought a product liability action against the manufacturer of baby oil, after the baby swallowed the oil and suffered brain damage aspiration. The parents alleged that if they had known of the risks of the product, they would have treated it more carefully.[208] The Washington Supreme Court concluded the parents had presented sufficient evidence of causation and inadequacy of warnings on the bottle of baby oil to support the jury's verdict in their favor. The evidence included testimony from the mother that "she made a practice of reading labels on products" and shelved dangerous products high out of the reach of her 15-month-old twins. The mother also testified that, besides placing dangerous products out of reach, she specifically told her teenage daughters to keep their purses away from the twins if their purses contained anything that could harm a baby.[209] The Court held that the jury was entitled to infer that, if the parents had known of the dangers of aspiration, they would have treated the baby oil with the same caution they used with other items they recognized as highly dangerous, and that "had they done so, the accident would never have occurred," concluding that the evidence of causation presented to the jury was sufficient to sustain the jury's verdict.[210] According to the court:

> What makes baby oil unique, and what is the *sine qua non* of our decision, is that baby oil is intended for use *on babies*. When he drank the oil, David Ayers was acting in conformity with the behavior to be expected of any 15-month-old child. It is this kind of predictable infant behavior which necessitates that consumers and parents be alerted to the dangers of a product promoted for use on babies.[211]

---

[205] Port Authority of New York and New Jersey v. Arcadian Corp., 189 F.3d 305 (3d Cir. 1999) (applying New Jersey law). *See, however*, Winnett v. Winnett, 310 N.E.2d 1 (Ill. 1974) (the scope of a farm forage wagon's intended use did not include its use by a four-year-old child).

[206] Frey v. Montgomery Ward & Co., 258 N.W.2d 782, 788 (Minn. 1977).

[207] 818 P.2d 1337 (Wash. 1991).

[208] *Id.* at 1341.

[209] *Id.* at 1340–41.

[210] *Id.* at 1341.

[211] *Id.* at 1343.

The misuse of a product also may be the proximate cause of an injury if it was reasonably foreseeable.[212] As with other aspects of foreseeability, whether the misuse of a product was foreseeable is fact specific and, as a result, generally is a matter for the jury to decide,[213] unless there is no evidence from which a jury reasonably could find the required causal connection between the use of the misuse of the product and the resulting injuries. An example both of the misuse of a product and a situation where that misuse was so unforeseeable that the court did not leave the issue to the jury is *Port Authority of New York and New Jersey v. Arcadian Corp.*,[214] in which the plaintiff sued the manufacturers of ammonium nitrate used by terrorists to make the explosive device used in the bombing of the World Trade Center in February 1993. The plaintiff brought the action in negligence and strict liability alleging that the product was defective because of the failure to add anti-explosive properties to it. The district court granted a manufacturers' motion to dismiss under Rule 12(b)(6) of the Federal Rule of Civil Procedure, saying that the misuse of the fertilizer for use in the bomb was not foreseeable. The fact that the manufacturers knew of the possibility that fertilizer products could be or had been used as components in bombs did not save the claim since it showed only "subjective foreseeability." According to the court, what was required was an "objective foreseeability determination."

> No jury reasonably could conclude that one accidental explosion 50 years ago, one terrorist act in this country almost 30 years ago, and scattered terrorists incidents throughout the world over the course of the last 30 years would make an incident like the World Trade Center bombing anything more than a remote or theoretical possibility.[215]

Proximate cause extends not only to the foreseeable uses of a products but also to the foreseeable risks of harm from those uses. However, because the foreseeable use of a product and the foreseeable harm resulting from that use are closely tied, the Oregon Supreme Court, in *Newman v. Utility Trailer & Equipment Co., Inc.*,[216] used two hypotheticals involving a shovel to illustrate difference between the two. In the first hypothetical, a person used a shovel to prop open a heavy door. Because of the way the shovel was designed, it was not capable of holding the door open and it slammed shut, crushing the person's hand. The court said the manufacturer of the shovel would not be liable for the person's injury since it was not reasonably foreseeable that the shovel would be used in that manner. In the second hypothetical, the shovel was used to dig a ditch, and, while it was being used for that purpose, the blade struck a rock in the soil and a piece of steel from the blade flew up and injured user's eye. In that situation, the manufacturer or seller would be assumed

---

[212] "Product misuse, an affirmative defense, is a superseding cause of injury that absolves a tortfeasor of his or her own wrongful conduct only when the misuse was 'so highly extraordinary as to be unforeseeable.'" Chavez v. Glock Inc., 207 Cal. App. 4th 1283, 1308 (2012). *See* Morales v. American Honda Motor Co., 71 F.3d 531 (6th Cir. 1995); Belleville v. Rockford Mfg. Group, Inc., 172 F. Supp. 2d 913 (E.D. Mich. 2001); Palmer v. Avco Distributing Corp., 412 N.E.2d 959 (Ill. 1980).

[213] Sanders v. Lull International, Inc., 411 F.3d 1266 (11th Cir. 2005) (applying Florida law); Heatherly v. Alexander, 421 F.3d 638 (8th Cir. 2005) (applying Nebraska law).

[214] 991 F. Supp. 390 (D.N.J. 1997) (applying New Jersey law), *aff'd* 189 F.3d 305 (3d Cir. 1999).

[215] *Id.* at 402–03.

[216] 564 P.2d 674 (Or. 1977).

to have had knowledge of the risk of injury to the user caused by the use of the shovel. Since the shovel was being used for a purpose for which it was manufactured, the liability of the manufacturer would extend to the harm that a reasonable manufacturer knew or should have known was presented by the shovel.[217] That knowledge is assumed regardless of whether the particular manufacturer actually "foresaw or reasonably should have foreseen the danger."[218] It also is immaterial that the manufacturer could not foresee the precise manner or anticipate the particular chain of events that resulted in plaintiff's injury.[219] The plaintiff would be entitled to recover for the harm actually suffered, even though the extent of the injuries were more severe than manufacturer could have foreseen and even if the injuries were aggravated by plaintiff's "predisposition or weakness"[220]

[C] Natural and Probable Consequences

In approaching proximate cause, the focus is on the effect of the defect on the circumstances surrounding the accident. The question is whether the plaintiff's injury was a "natural and probable consequence" of the defect in the design or manufacture of the product or the failure to warn about the dangers associated with the use of the product. This becomes an issue when, after a product has left the control of the manufacturer or seller, an intervening act results in an injury to the plaintiff.[221] In order for the intervening act to break the causal connection, the intervening act must have been independent of the defective product, adequate by itself to cause the plaintiff's injury, and not reasonably foreseeable by the manufacturer.[222] In other words, the intervening act must become the superseding by being the new proximate cause of the injury.[223]

An intervening cause may result from actions of the plaintiff or a third party. Although an intervening act will not become a superseding cause unless it was unforeseeable,[224] it is not necessary that the precise injury was foreseeable.[225] In *Wallace v. Owens-Illinois, Inc.*,[226] the intervening cause of the injury was the

---

[217] *Id.* at 675–76.

[218] *Id.* at 677. *See also* Green v. Smith & Nephew AHP, Inc., 629 N.W.2d 727 (Wis. 2001).

[219] Katz v. Swift & Co., 276 F.2d 905 (2d Cir. 1960) (applying New York law); Stazenski v. Tennant Co., 617 So. 2d 344 (Fla. Dist. Ct. App. 1993); Anderson v. Dreis & Krump Mfg. Corp., 739 P.2d 1177 (Wash. Ct. App. 1987).

[220] Poplar v. Bourjois, Inc., 80 N.E.2d 334, 337 (N.Y. 1948).

[221] Wallace v. Owens-Illinois, Inc., 389 S.E.2d 155 (S.C. Ct. App. 1989); Dugan by Dugan v. Sears, Roebuck & Co., 454 N.E.2d 64 (Ill. App. Ct. 1983).

[222] Hurt v. Coyne Cylinder Co., 956 F.2d 1319 (6th Cir. 1992) (applying Tennessee law); Kuras v. International Harvester Co., 820 F.2d 15 (1st Cir. 1987) (applying Rhode Island law); Smith v. Pfizer, Inc., 688 F. Supp. 2d 735 (M.D. Tenn. 2010) (applying Tennessee law) (husband's suicide was not an intervening cause that relieved the drug manufacturer of liability).

[223] Rossell v. Volkswagen of America, 709 P.2d 517 (Ariz. 1985).

[224] "[A]n intervening cause becomes a superseding cause, thereby relieving the defendant of liability for the original conduct, 'when [the] intervening force was unforeseeable and may be described, with the benefit of hindsight, as extraordinary.'" Barrett v. Harris, 86 P.3d 954, 958 (Ariz. Ct. App. 2004).

[225] Achin v. Begg Tire Center, 694 F.2d 226 (10th Cir. 1982) (applying New Mexico law).

[226] 389 S.E.2d 155 (S.C. Ct. App. 1989).

plaintiff's actions. In that case, the plaintiff was opening a glass soft drink bottle in his kitchen when it exploded because of a defect in its manufacture. Pieces of glass and the liquid contents of the bottle fell on the floor. However, the explosion did not injure the plaintiff. He left the kitchen and returned about five minutes later to clean up the floor. In the course of cleaning-up, the plaintiff got liquid on the smooth leather soles of his bedroom slippers, which caused him to slip, fall, and suffer bodily injuries. The South Carolina appellate court held that the plaintiff's intervening actions did not break the chain of causation and become a superseding cause. Instead, the explosion created a hazardous condition on the kitchen floor and the plaintiff's attempt to clean-up the spill was a normal and foreseeable response to the situation. The fact that his actions may have been negligent did eliminate the defendants' liability since the plaintiff's negligence is not a question of proximate causation but of contributory negligence.[227]

The same approach is taken by courts if the intervening cause was the act of a third party. In *Price v. Blaine Kern Artista, Inc.*,[228] the plaintiff was an entertainer who wore a caricature mask of George Bush manufactured by the defendant covering his entire head. He alleged he was injured when a patron pushed him causing the weight of the mask to injure his neck as he fell to the ground. The plaintiff claimed the mask was defective due to the absence of a safety harness to support his head and neck. The manufacturer argued that the act of the patron in pushing the plaintiff was an intervening, superseding cause of the injuries. However, the Nevada Supreme Court said that the risk of the fall and the resulting strain on the plaintiff's head and neck were within the realm of risks that should have been considered and addressed by the manufacturer in the design of the product. Thus, the initial cause of the plaintiff's fall was not important, considering that it was foreseeable that, among the users of the defendant's products, some would fall for a variety of reasons.[229]

Manufacturers often allege that the alteration of the product by the plaintiff or a third party constituted a superseding cause of the injury. As with other types of intervening acts, an alteration of product that was reasonably foreseeable by the manufacturer is not a superseding cause.[230] However, an alteration of a product that reasonably could not have been anticipated is a superseding cause.[231] An example of a product alteration that was an intervening act is *Rios v. Niagara Machine & Tool Works*,[232] in which a punch press was manufactured without any safety devices. After purchasing the machine, the plaintiff's employer installed a

---

[227] *Id.* at 157 (It is not the "quality" of plaintiff's actions but their foreseeability that determines proximate cause. The test is the probable consequences reasonably to be anticipated, not "character" of subsequent or intervening events.).

[228] 893 P.2d 367 (Nev. 1995).

[229] *Id.* at 370. *See also* Anderson v. Dreis & Krump Mfg. Corp., 739 P.2d 1177, 1186 (Wash. Ct. App. 1987).

[230] Anderson v. Dreis & Krump Mfg. Corp., 739 P.2d 1177, 1184 (Wash. Ct. App. 1987). This normally is a question for the jury. Piper v. Bear Medical Systems, Inc., 883 P.2d 407, 413 (Ariz. Ct. App. 1994).

[231] Hood v. Ryobi America Corp., 181 F.3d 608 (4th Cir. 1999) (applying Maryland law); McDaniel v. French Oil Mill Machine Co., 623 So. 2d 1146 (Ala. 1993).

[232] 319 N.E.2d 232 (Ill. 1974).

safety device that failed, resulting in the plaintiff's injury. The Illinois Supreme Court held that whatever unreasonably dangerous condition existed when the punch press left the manufacturer's control was corrected by the employer's alteration.[233] Thus, in determining whether the alteration was sufficient to relieve the manufacturer of liability, the focus is on whether the plaintiff's injury was caused by a defective condition in the original product or by an unforeseeable subsequent alteration.[234]

[D] Condition v. Cause

Another method of determining the scope of a manufacturer's liability is based on a distinction between the *cause* of the injury and a *condition* that permitted the injury to occur. The *cause* of an injury is that which actually produced it. However, if the defect in the product simply created a condition by which an injury was made possible by some subsequent, independent act of a third party, the creation of the condition was not a proximate cause of the injury.[235] According to one court:

> A circumstance is a condition if the forces set in operation by the defendant have come to rest in a position of apparent safety and some new force intervenes. . . . Relevant factors include the kind of hazard that was created, its gravity, its relation in time and space to the injury, and whether the defendant could reasonably foresee that an injury would be a likely result of his conduct.[236]

Two cases illustrate the use of the cause/condition distinction to hold that a defect in a product was not the proximate cause of the plaintiff's injuries. In *Union Pump Co. v. Allbritton*,[237] the defendant's pump caught fire and, two hours after the fire was extinguished, the plaintiff was injured walking across a pipe rack wet with water and foam from the fire. The Texas Supreme Court held that the pump fire did no more than create the condition that made the plaintiff's injuries possible. The court concluded that "the circumstances surrounding her injuries are too remotely connected with Union Pump's conduct or pump to constitute a legal cause of her injuries." Similarly, in *Kleen v. Homak Manufacturing Co., Inc.*,[238] a 15-year-old broke into his father's locked gun safe, removed a gun, and shot himself. The Illinois appellate court held that the suicide was entirely the boy's own decision and was not foreseeable to the gun safe manufacturer. The court found that the allegedly defective condition of the gun safe provided a condition that allowed the boy access to the gun but did not cause his suicide.

---

[233] *Id.* at 236.

[234] Medina v. Air-Mite Devices, Inc., 515 N.E.2d 770 (Ill. App. Ct. 1987).

[235] *See* Port Authority of New York and New Jersey v. Arcadian Corp., 189 F.3d 305 (3d Cir. 1999) (applying New Jersey law).

[236] First Springfield Bank & Trust v. Galman, 702 N.E.2d 1002, 1007 (Ill. App. Ct. 1998).

[237] 898 S.W.2d 773, 776 (Tex. 1995).

[238] 749 N.E.2d 26 (Ill. App. Ct. 2001).

Chapter 9

DEFENSES

SYNOPSIS

§ 9.01 INTRODUCTION

§ 9.02 CONDUCT-BASED DEFENSES

    [A] Introduction

    [B] Contributory Negligence

    [C] Assumption of Risk

    [D] Alteration of a Product

    [E] Misuse of the Product

    [F] Comparative Fault

§ 9.03 STATUS-BASED DEFENSES

    [A] Employer Immunity

        [1] Employer Liability to Employees

        [2] Employer Liability to Third Parties

    [B] Government Contractor Defense

        [1] Framework for the Defense

        [2] The Three Prongs of the Defense

        [3] Expansion of the Defense

§ 9.04 TIMES-BASED DEFENSES

    [A] Statutes of Limitations

    [B] Statute of Repose

    [C] Useful Shelf-Life

§ 9.05 GOVERNMENT AND INDUSTRY STANDARDS

    [A] Government Standards

    [B] Government Standards and the Pharmaceutical Industry

    [C] Industry Standards

§ 9.06 PREEMPTION

    [A] Introduction

    [B] Express Preemption

    [C] Field Preemption

    [D] Conflict Preemption

§ 9.01 INTRODUCTION

In a products liability action, a manufacturer or seller may raise a number of defenses. Many of these defenses are based on the specific requirements for negligence, strict liability, or a state's products liability statute. In a strict liability action, for example, the plaintiff has the burden of proving all of the elements of § 402A: (1) the plaintiff was injured by a "product"; (2) the product was in a "defective condition unreasonably dangerous" at the time it left the defendant's control; (3) the defendant was a "seller" of the product; (4) the plaintiff was a "user or consumer" of the product; (5) the plaintiff suffered physical injury or property damage; and (6) the defect in the product was the cause-in-fact and proximate cause of the plaintiff's injury or damage. Since a claim will fail if the manufacturer or seller can show that the plaintiff did not prove any one of those essential elements, the starting point for the defense of a strict liability action is the language of § 402A itself.[1]

In addition to the defenses based on the specific requirements of warranty, negligence, and strict liability, a manufacturer or seller in a product liability action has a number of other potential defenses. Some of these defenses, such as the danger created by the product was "open and obvious,"[2] the product was "unavoidably dangerous," or the product was "state of the art," were discussed in the chapters dealing with the different types of product defects. In a few situations, legislation provides manufacturers or sellers with immunity from liability. For example, the *Protection of Lawful Commerce in Arms Act*[3] gives makers, dealers, and distributors of firearms immunity from civil lawsuits by cities and individuals seeking to hold them liable for the unlawful use of guns by third persons. Similarly, the *Biomaterials Access Assurance Act of 1998*[4] states that companies that provide biomaterials that are used to manufacture implantable medical devices are immune from civil liability. Although the manufacturer of the medical device may be liable, the company that provided the raw materials or component parts is immune.

This chapter examines five broad categories of defenses available in products liability actions. First, a manufacturer or seller may base its defense on the plaintiff's conduct. In addition to the traditional tort defenses of contributory negligence and assumption of the risk, this category includes product alteration and misuse of the product. Second, a defendant may show that its status gives it immunity from the plaintiff's products liability suit against it. Such immunity is

---

[1] Similarly, the starting point for the defense of a negligence action are the four requirements of that tort: (1) a duty; (2) a breach of that duty; (3) personal injury or property damage; and (4) a causal connection between the breach of the duty and the plaintiff's injury or damage. The failure to prove any one of these elements will result in a decision for the defendant.

[2] Wisconsin has adopted legislation that states that a court must dismiss an action brought in strict liability "if the damage was caused by an inherent characteristic of the product that would be recognized by an ordinary person with ordinary knowledge common to the community that uses or consumes the product." Wis. Stat. Ann. § 895.047(3)(d).

[3] 15 U.S.C. § 7901 *et seq.* Chavez v. Glock, Inc., 207 Cal. App. 4th 1283, 1316–18 (2012). The constitutionality of the Act was upheld in Ileto v. Glock, Inc., 565 F.3d 1126 (9th Cir. 2009). *See* Adames v. Sheahan, 909 N.E.2d 742 (Ill. 2009).

[4] 21 U.S.C. 1601 *et seq.*

found in state workers' compensation statutes and in the government contractor defense. Third, a manufacturer or seller may show that the plaintiff failed to file the lawsuit within the time period required by the statute of limitations, the statute of repose, or the useful safe life of the product. Fourth, a manufacturer or seller may allege that the product's conformity with governmental or industry safety standards bars liability. Finally, a manufacturer or seller may show that a federal statute preempts any state product liability claim. Most of these defenses are a complete bar to a plaintiff's recovery. However, in the case of the conduct-based defenses of contributory negligence, assumption of risk, and misuse, whether the defense bars the plaintiff's recovery or reduces the amount of the plaintiff's damages depends on whether the particular state has adopted comparative fault and whether the action is based on negligence or strict liability.

§ 9.02 CONDUCT-BASED DEFENSES

[A] Introduction

At common law, conduct on the part of a plaintiff that amounted to contributory negligence, assumption of risk, alteration, or misuse of a product was a total bar to recovery. However, since the 1960s, almost every state has adopted some form of comparative fault that has changed the effect that some of the conduct-based defenses have on the plaintiff's recovery. Depending on the state and on the particular type of conduct, these defenses either may bar the plaintiff's recovery or they may reduce the amount of the plaintiff's damages, based upon the trier of fact's apportionment of the percentage of the fault among the parties.[5] Since the adoption of comparative fault has not lessened the importance of the plaintiff's conduct as a defense in a products liability action, this section analyzes contributory negligence, assumption of risk, alteration, and misuse of a product separately and then examines the various forms of comparative fault and their effect upon recovery.

[B] Contributory Negligence

At common law, a plaintiff's contributory negligence was a complete bar to recovery in a negligence action.[6] Contributory negligence consists of conduct on the part of the plaintiff that "falls below the standard to which he should conform for his own protection, and which is a legally contributing cause co-operating with the negligence of the defendant in bringing about the plaintiff's harm."[7] Unlike the

---

[5] Among the factors that determine the percentage of fault assigned to the parties are: (1) whether the conduct resulted from inadvertence or involved an awareness of the danger; (2) how great a risk was created by the conduct; (3) the significance of what was sought by the conduct; (4) the capacities of the actor, whether superior or inferior and (5) any extenuating circumstances which might require the actor to proceed in haste without proper thought. Hutto v. McNeil-PPC, Inc., 79 So. 3d 1199 (La. Ct. App. 2011).

[6] Butterfield v. Forrester, 103 Eng. Rep. 926 (K.B. 1809). The *Butterfield* rule entered American law in Smith v. Smith, 18 Mass. (2 Pick. 621) (1824). *See* John Wade, *Comparative Negligence — Its Development in the United States and Its Present Status in Louisiana*, 40 La. L. Rev. 299 (1980).

[7] Restatement (Second) of Torts, § 463 (1965). See § 464 which applies the reasonable person standard

defense of misuse, which involves the plaintiff's deliberate use of a product in a manner that was unintended or unforeseeable by the manufacturer, a plaintiff is contributorily negligent if they fail to discover a defect in a product which they should have discovered if they had been reasonably diligent.[8] The almost universal acceptance of contributory negligence as a bar to recovery in the early 1960s,[9] even when the plaintiff's fault was slight when compared to the defendant's, was one of the reasons that led to the adoption of strict liability for products liability cases. According to comment *n* of § 402A:

> Since the liability with which this Section deals is not based upon negligence of the seller, but is strict liability, the rule applied to strict liability cases (§ 524) applies. Contributory negligence of the plaintiff is not a defense when such negligence consists merely in a failure to discover the defect in the product, or to guard against the possibility of its existence.[10]

In the early years of § 402A, the effect of contributory negligence was one of the defining differences between negligence and strict liability in products liability actions. In negligence cases contributory negligence remained a bar to the plaintiff's recovery,[11] subject to some limited exceptions such as the extreme youth of the plaintiff[12] or a statute creating the defendant's duty.[13] In contrast, courts ignored a plaintiff's contributory negligence in strict liability actions when it consisted of the failure to discover the defect in the product or to guard against the possibility of its existence.[14] However, as part of broadening the scope of tort liability in the late 1960s and early 1970s that led to the adoption of strict liability for products liability cases, courts and legislatures began to abandon contributory negligence as a complete bar to recovery in negligence cases and to create a system of "comparative negligence." As a result, all but five jurisdictions[15] now have adopted, either by legislation or judicial decision, some form of comparative fault under which the plaintiff's negligence is not necessarily an absolute bar to recovery

---

in contributory negligence cases. Under legislation adopted in Wisconsin, if the defendant, in an action based on strict liability, proves that the plaintiff was under the influence of illegal drugs or was intoxicated at the time of the injury, it is a rebuttable presumption that the drug or intoxication was the cause of the injury. WIS. STAT. ANN. § 895.047(3)(a).

[8] J.H.O.C. v. Volvo Trucks, N.Amer., 2008 U.S. App. LEXIS 25660 (11th Cir. Dec. 18, 2008) (applying Alabama law); Jimenez v. Sears Roebuck & Co., 904 P.2d 861, 865 (Ariz. 1995).

[9] Section 467 of the RESTATEMENT (SECOND) OF TORTS, adopted in 1965, states that "the plaintiff's contributory negligence bars recovery against a defendant whose negligent conduct would otherwise make him liable to the plaintiff for the harm sustained by him."

[10] RESTATEMENT (SECOND) OF TORTS, § 402A cmt. *n* (1965).

[11] *See* Parris v. M.A. Bruder & Sons, Inc., 261 F. Supp. 406 (E.D. Pa. 1966) (applying Pennsylvania law); Reed v. Carlyle & Martin, Inc., 202 S.E.2d 874 (Va. 1974).

[12] *See* Porter v. United Steel & Wire Co., 436 F. Supp. 1376 (N.D. Iowa 1977) (applying Iowa law).

[13] *See* Zerby v. Warren, 210 N.W.2d 58 (Minn. 1973).

[14] McCown v. International Harvester Co., 342 A.2d 381 (Pa. 1975); Williams v. Brown Manufacturing Co., 261 N.E.2d 305 (Ill. 1970).

[15] Alabama, the District of Columbia, Maryland, North Carolina and Virginia have not adopted comparative fault and make the plaintiff's contributory negligence a complete bar to recovery. *See* Ray v. Ford Motor Co., 2011 U.S. Dist. LEXIS 147880 (D. Ala. Dec. 22, 2011); Dennis v. Jones, 928 A.2d 672 (D.C. Ct. App. 2007); Duncan v. U.S., 2011 U.S. Dist. LEXIS 74665 (D. Md. July11, 2011); Sorrells v. M.Y.B. Hospitality Ventures, 423 S.E.2d 72 (N.C. 1992); Chilton v. Homestead, 79 Va. Cir. 708 (2008).

in negligence cases. Instead, the jury determines the percentage of the plaintiff's negligence and the defendant's negligence in order to decide whether the plaintiff can recover and, if so, the amount damages he or she should receive.

The adoption of comparative negligence forced states to consider whether, in cases based on strict liability, they should continue to follow comment *n* and ignore the plaintiff's contributory negligence or to take a plaintiff's contributory negligence into consideration in determining liability and damages. Some courts have refused to import comparative negligence into cases based on strict liability.[16] Among the reasons for their hesitation are the language of comment *n* to § 402A, the perceived difficulty of comparing the plaintiff's negligence with the defendant's strict liability for the product defect, and the feeling that it was not appropriate to use negligence principles in strict liability cases.[17] Despite these concerns, however, the majority of states now treat the plaintiff's ordinary negligence as a factor to be taken into consideration in apportioning liability and in determining the amount of damages in strict liability cases as well as those based on negligence.[18] This approach is contained in the Connecticut products liability statute which states that "[i]n causes of action based on strict tort liability, contributory negligence or comparative negligence shall not be a bar to recovery."[19] The statute then provides that "the comparative responsibility of, or attributed to, the claimant, shall not bar recovery but shall diminish the award of compensatory damages proportionately, according to the measure of responsibility attributed to the claimant."[20]

The type of conduct that will reduce a plaintiff's recovery in a products liability case is illustrated by *General Motors Corp. v. Saint.*[21] In that case a woman was injured when the automobile she was driving hit a low shoulder on a road, went out of control, and hit a tree. The woman sued General Motors, claiming that the car was not crashworthy because its seat belt assembly failed to protect her adequately from the enhanced injuries she suffered in the accident. Specifically, she alleged that the seat belt's "comfort feature," which General Motors designed and installed in its cars, allowed extensive slack to develop and, as a result, caused the seat belt

---

[16] Two states that refuse to admit evidence concerning a plaintiff's ordinary contributory negligence in a strict liability are Oregon (Mason v. Mt. St. Joseph, Inc., 203 P.3d 329 (Or. 2009)) and Pennsylvania (Pa. Dept. Of Gen. Servs. v. U.S. Mineral Prods. Co., 898 A.2d 590 (Pa. 2006)).

[17] *See* Bowling v. Heil Co., 511 N.E.2d 373 (Ohio 1987); Beshada v. Johns-Manville Products Corp., 447 A.2d 539 (N.J. 1982); Sheehan v. Anthony Pools, 440 A.2d 1085 (Md. Ct. Spec. App. 1982).

[18] See Whitehead v. Toyota Motor Corp., 897 S.W.2d 684, 691–92 (Tenn. 1995) for a list of the "overwhelming majority of states [that] have adopted the view that comparative fault should apply to products liability actions based on strict liability." *See also* Bostick v. Flex Equip. Co., Inc., 54 Cal. Rptr. 3d 28, 68 (Ct. App. 2007) (Croskey, J., concurring). The Restatement (Third) also states that a "strong majority" of courts now apply comparative negligence principles in strict products liability cases. *See* Restatement (Third) of Torts: Products Liability § 17, cmt. *a* (1998).

[19] Conn. Gen. Stat. § 52-572l.

[20] *Id.* at § 52-572o(a). *See* Barry v. Quality Steel Prods., Inc., 905 A.2d 55, 61 (Conn. 2006) ("Section 52-572o accomplishes two goals. It requires the fact finder to determine the total amount of damages, irrespective of the plaintiff's fault, that is, the amount of damages the plaintiff 'would receive if comparative responsibility were disregarded. . . . It also requires the fact finder to allocate that total amount of damages among the parties, including the plaintiff, according to their respective percentages of responsibility.").

[21] 646 So. 2d 564 (Ala. 1994).

not to restrain properly the occupant.[22] The Alabama Supreme Court reversed a jury verdict in favor of the woman. According to the court, there was evidence from the woman's own expert that she was aware of the slack and allowed it to remain in her seat belt when wearing it. General Motors foresaw the danger that would result from someone's doing so and warned against it in its owner's manual. The court held that a jury could find that, although the woman did not use her seat belt in an unintended or unforeseen manner, she nonetheless was negligent in failing to use reasonable care in wearing it. The court remanded the case, saying that General Motors was entitled to a jury charge on contributory negligence.[23]

[C] Assumption of Risk

Like contributory negligence, assumption of risk was a complete bar to a plaintiff's recovery in a negligence action at common law.[24] Courts recognize two types of assumption of risk. Primary or express assumption of risk arises where the "parties have voluntarily entered a relationship in which plaintiff assumes well-known, incidental risks."[25] As a condition of the relationship, plaintiffs often sign a written agreement in which they expressly assume some or all of the risks of the relationship.[26] In products liability cases, the defense of primary assumption of risk often is raised when persons are injured while engaging in sporting activities.[27] Secondary or implied assumption of risk is defined as "a type of contributory negligence where the plaintiff voluntarily encounters a known and appreciated hazard created by the defendant without relieving the defendant of his duty of care with respect to such hazard."[28] Although the drafters of § 402A felt that courts should ignore a plaintiff's ordinary contributory negligence in determining liability and damages, they took a different position concerning secondary or implied assumption of risk. According to comment n:

> [T]he form of contributory negligence which consists in voluntarily and unreasonably proceeding to encounter a known danger, and commonly passes under the name of assumption of risk, is a defense under this Section as in other cases of strict liability. If the user or consumer discovers the defect and is aware of the danger, and nevertheless proceeds unrea-

---

[22] *Id.* at 565.

[23] *Id.* at 568.

[24] Nally v. Charbonneau, 362 A.2d 494 (Conn. 1975); Murphy v. Steeplechase Amusement Co., 166 N.E. 173 (N.Y. 1929).

[25] Olson v. Hansen, 216 N.W.2d 124, 127 (Minn. 1974).

[26] *See* Neumann v. Gloria Marshall Figure Salon, 500 N.E.2d 1011 (Ill. App. Ct. 1986) (a woman who was injured by an exercise machine at a health club had signed a contract with the health center containing an exculpatory clause). The ability of a manufacturer or seller to disclaim liability for personal injuries.

[27] *See, e.g.*, Ford v. Polaris Indus., Inc., 43 Cal. Rptr. 3d 215 (Ct. App. 2006) (since the design defect in a watercraft escalated the risk of harm beyond the inherent risk of falling into the water, the plaintiff's assumption of that risk did not bar the plaintiff's suit).

[28] *See, e.g.*, Andren v. White-Rodgers Company, 465 N.W.2d 102, 104 (Minn. Ct. App. 1991).

sonably to make use of the product and is injured by it, he is barred from recovery.[29]

Although the drafters of § 402A were willing to permit primary or express assumption of risk remain a defense in strict liability actions, section 18 of the Restatement (Third) also takes the position that "contractual exculpations, oral or written, do not bar or reduce otherwise valid products liability claims against sellers or other distributors of new products for harm to persons."[30]

Contained within comment *n* to § 402A are both the definition of assumption of risk and the three elements that a manufacturer or seller must show to establish both primary and secondary assumption of risk.[31] First, courts hold that the plaintiff must have had knowledge of the particular risk or danger in the product. It is not sufficient for the defendant to show simply that the plaintiff was aware generally that the product exposed him or her to danger. Instead, the defendant must prove that the plaintiff was aware of the specific defect which caused his injury. Second, the plaintiff must have understood the unreasonably dangerous risk created by the product. Finally, the plaintiff must have chosen voluntarily and unreasonably to use the product after discovering the defect and its danger.[32] Thus, unlike contributory negligence, which is based on a showing that the plaintiff failed to use ordinary care in dealing with the product and does not require that the plaintiff was aware of the risk or even have thought about it, assumption of risk requires that the plaintiff knew, understood, and voluntarily accepted the specific danger created by the product.

An example of the application of the three requirements for assumption of risk is *Haugen v. Minnesota Mining & Manufacturing Co.*,[33] in which the plaintiff was blinded when the grinding wheel on which he was working exploded and a piece from the wheel struck him in the eye. The Washington appellate court affirmed the trial court's finding for the plaintiff and held that the jury instructions given by the trial court were proper. The instruction read:

> It is not enough to bar recovery . . . on the defense of assumption of the risk that the plaintiff knew that there was a general danger connected with the use of the product, but rather it must be shown that the plaintiff

---

[29] RESTATEMENT (SECOND) OF TORTS § 402A cmt. *n* (1965). Many states continue to treat assumption of risk as a complete defense both in negligence and strict liability actions. *See* Ciocca v. BJ's Wholesale Club, Inc., 2011 U.S. Dist. LEXIS 130931 (E.D. Pa. 2011) (applying Pennsylvania law).

[30] RESTATEMENT (THIRD) OF TORTS: PRODUCTS LIABILITY § 18 (1998). *See* Boles v. Sun Ergoline, Inc., 223 P.3d 724, 726–27 (Colo. 2010) (citing § 18).

[31] Little v. Liquid Air Corp., 37 F.3d 1069 (5th Cir. 1994) (applying Mississippi law); Sobolik v. Briggs & Stratton Power Products Group. Inc., 2011 U.S. Dist. LEXIS 33911 (D. Minn. 2011) (applying Minnesota law); Ellsworth v. Sherne Lingerie, Inc., 495 A.2d 348 (Md. 1985).

[32] In Lutz v. Nat'l Crane Corp., 884 P.2d 455, 461–62 (Mont. 1994), the Montana Supreme Court held that the defense of assumption of risk is not applicable without evidence that the victim actually knew he or she would suffer serious injury or death and, knowing that, the victim voluntarily exposed himself or herself to the risk. *See* Sheehan v. The North Amer. Marketing Corp., 610 F.3d 144 (1st Cir. 2010) (applying Rhode Island law); Krajewski v. Enderes Tool Co., 396 F. Supp. 2d 1045 (D. Neb. 2005) (applying Nebraska law); Eastman v. Stanley Works, 907 N.E.2d 768 (Ohio Ct. App. 2009); Bowen v. Cochran, 556 S.E.2d 530, 531–32 (Ga. Ct. App. 2001).

[33] 550 P.2d 71 (Wash. Ct. App. 1976).

actually knew, appreciated, and voluntarily and unreasonably exposed himself to the specific defect and danger which caused his injuries.[34]

Although the court in *Haugen* allowed the manufacturer to raise assumption of risk, courts are divided over whether a worker can "voluntarily" assume a risk of injury from a product in the workplace. Some courts take the position that the exposure to the risk is not voluntary when it occurs in the workplace, even if workers could have chosen not to do their job.[35] Other courts, however, view the employees' voluntary exposure to a known risk in the workplace as assumption of risk.[36]

The test for determining whether the plaintiff assumed the risk is subjective rather than objective.[37] It is the particular plaintiff's understanding and appreciation of the danger presented by the product that must be assessed, rather than that of the reasonably prudent person under similar circumstances. In making this determining, the jury is entitled to consider all of the facts. It is not required to accept the plaintiff's testimony that he or she was unaware of the danger if, in light of all of the evidence, the plaintiff could not have been unaware of the hazard. In making that determination, the plaintiff's age, experience, knowledge, and under-standing, as well as the obviousness of the defect and the danger it poses, are relevant factors for the jury to consider.[38] The application of the subjective test in product liability cases is illustrated by *Thomas v. Kaiser Agricultural Chemicals*[39] in which the plaintiff suffered an eye injury when liquid nitrogen fertilizer sprayed into his face while he was attempting to fill a fertilizer applicator. His injury occurred after he inadvertently opened the air pressure relief valve on the applicator, which released pent-up pressure and the remaining liquid nitrogen. The plaintiff alleged that the machine contained a defective attachment called an adaptor. He testified that he had read the conspicuous and detailed warning label cautioning users to bleed off all the air pressure in the tank before refilling the applicator. However, he attempted to refill the applicator without verifying that the air pressure gauge read zero as the instructions directed. The Illinois Supreme Court held that the plaintiff assumed the risk only if he was actually aware of the defective nature of the product and appreciated its unreasonably dangerous condition but voluntarily chose to act in disregard of the danger.[40] The court found insufficient evidence of such awareness, despite the plaintiff's 18 years as a farmer, because he had used the particular machine only once before.

---

[34] *Id.* at 74. *See,* however, Lonon v. Pep Boys, Manny, Moe & Jack, 538 A.2d 22 (Pa. Super. Ct. 1988) for a decision approving "general" assumption of risk.

[35] Chauncey v. Peco, Inc., 2010 U.S. Dist. LEXIS 13037, at *13 (E.D. Pa. Feb. 16, 2010) (applying Pennsylvania law); Routzahn v. Garrison, 2006 Ohio App. LEXIS 3602, at *P53 (Ohio Ct. App. 2006).

[36] Green v. Allendale Planting Co, 954 So. 2d 1032 (Miss. 2007) (whether an employee assumed the risk is a question for the jury).

[37] Country Mut. Ins. Co. v. Sunbeam Prods., 500 F. Supp. 2d 986, 990 (N.D. Ill. 2007) (applying Illinois law); Patters Enters. v. Johnson, 272 P.3d 93 (Mont. 2012). This differs from contributory negligent where juries apply the objective reasonable person standard in judging the plaintiff's conduct.

[38] Moran v. Raymond Corp., 484 F.2d 1008 (7th Cir. 1973) (applying Illinois law); Johnson v. Clark Equipment Co., 547 P.2d 132 (Or. 1976); Staymates v. ITT Holub Industries, 527 A.2d 140 (Pa. Super. Ct. 1987).

[39] 407 N.E.2d 32 (Ill. 1980).

[40] *Id.* at 36.

[D] Alteration of a Product

Under warranty, negligence, and strict liability theories, a manufacturer is liable for a defect in a product that existed at the time the product left its control. At the same time, the plaintiff has the burden of proving that the product "was expect to, and did, reach the user without substantial change in the condition in which it was sold."[41] In some cases, however, the buyer alters or modifies the product after purchase. The Idaho Code states that:

"Alteration or modification" occurs when a person or entity other than the product seller changes the design, construction, or formula of the product, or changes or removes warnings or instructions that accompanied or were displayed on the product. "Alteration or modification" of a product includes the failure to observe routine care and maintenance, but does not include ordinary wear and tear.[42]

In order for a manufacturer to succeed on the alteration defense, it must establish four elements:[43] (1) there was a substantial alternation or modification of the product; (2) the alteration or modification occurred after it left the manufacturer's control; (3) the alteration or modification was the proximate cause of the plaintiff's injury;[44] and (4) the alteration or modification was not made with the manufacturer's express or implied consent or was not reasonably foreseeable.[45] "Foreseeability" is defined as an alteration that, objectively, is foreseeable, not merely one that conceivably might occur. Thus, "[i]f a product is capable of easily being modified by its operator, and if the operator has a known incentive to effect the modification, then it is objectively reasonable for a manufacturer to anticipate the modification. Conversely, if the alteration of the product requires special expertise, or otherwise is not accomplished easily, then it is not objectively reasonable for a defendant to foresee the modification."[46]

The fact that a product was altered by the buyer after the sale does not necessarily relieve the manufacturer of liability.[47] Instead, the alternation in the product must have been "substantial."[48] What constitutes a substantial alteration is left to the legislatures and courts to decide. North Dakota, for example, states that

---

[41] RESTATEMENT (SECOND) OF TORTS § 402A (1965).

[42] IDAHO CODE § 6-1405(4)(a). These sections are taken from the Model Uniform Products Liability Act § 112(D)(1).

[43] Kinsey v. Louisville Ladder, Inc., 2011 U.S. Dist. LEXIS 93272 (E.D. Pa. Aug. 19, 2011) (applying Pennsylvania law); Islam v. Modern Tour, Inc., 2004 U.S. Dist. LEXIS 19768 (S.D.N.Y. Sept. 30, 2004) (applying New York law); Tober v. Graco Children's Products, 2004 U.S. Dist. LEXIS 18254 (S.D. Ind. July 28, 2004) (applying Indiana law).

[44] Gaskin v.Sharp Elecs. Corp., 2007 U.S. Dist. LEXIS 72347 (N.D. Ind. Sept. 26, 2007) (applying Indiana law).

[45] Torno v. 2SI, LLC, 2006 U.S. Dist. LEXIS 27856 (E. D. Mich. May 10, 2006) (applying Michigan law).

[46] Davis v. Pak-Mor Mfg. Co., 672 N.E.2d 771, 775 (Ill. App. Ct. 1996). See Perez v. Sunbelt Rentals, Inc., 968 N.E.2d 1082, 1085 (Ill. App. Ct. 2012).

[47] Johnson v. Niagara Machine & Tool Co., 555 So. 2d 88 (Ala. 1989).

[48] See Almazan v. CTB, Inc., 2000 U.S. Dist. LEXIS 21434 (W. D. Tex. Apr. 27, 2000) (applying Texas

the alteration or modification must have "changed the purpose, use, function, design, or intended use or manner of use of the product from that for which the product was originally designed, tested, or intended."[49] Thus, a change in a product that does not affect its operation is not a substantial alteration.[50]

Before a court can make the determination that the alteration was substantial, it must decide whether the design or manufacture of the product was defective before its alteration. If the product was not defective when it left the control of the manufacturer or seller, but became so because of the alteration, then the alteration was "substantial" and the manufacturer is not liable.[51] The alteration, rather than the design or manufacture, made the product more dangerous than a consumer would expect the product to be.[52] However, if the product was defective when it left the manufacturer's control and there was a substantial modification after the sale, then it is a question of fact whether the original defect or the subsequent modification was the cause of the plaintiff's injuries.

In order to succeed on an alteration defense, a manufacturer must show a substantial alteration or modification after the product left its control and prove that the change "proximately caused the claimant's harm."[53] For most courts this showing of a causal connection between the modification of the product and the injury is the heart of the alteration defense. Connecticut, for example, requires proof that the injury would not have occurred "but for" the alternation in the product.[54]

Finally, a manufacturer will not be able to succeed on the alteration defense if the changes were made according to the manufacturer's instructions or specification or with its express or implied consent. In addition, a modification or alteration that was part of the anticipated use of the product is considered foreseeable and is not sufficient to apply the alteration defense.[55] The more difficult an alteration or modification is to make, the less foreseeable it is to the manufacturer.[56] Thus, where a manufacturer was aware that heavy-equipment users sometimes installed twelve-volt accessories in their machines made the installation of a twelve-volt harness a

---

law); CNH America, Inc. v. Roebuck, 41 So. 3d 41 (Ala. 2009); Banner Welders, Inc. v. Knighton, 425 So. 2d 441 (Ala. 1982).

[49] N.D. Rev. Stat. § 28-01.3-03.

[50] Banner Welders, Inc. v. Knighton, 425 So. 2d 441, 450 (Ala. 1982).

[51] Amatulli v. Delhi Construction Corp., 571 N.E.2d 645 (N.Y. 1991).

[52] See the discussion of the "substantial" requirement in Hiner v. Deere and Co., Inc., 340 F.3d 1190, 1198–99 (10th Cir. 2003) (applying Kansas law).

[53] Idaho Code § 6-1405(4)(b).

[54] Conn. Gen. Stat. § 52-572p. See Potter v. Chicago Pneumatic Tool Co., 694 A.2d 1319, 1339 (Conn. 1997). See also Tanksley v. ProSoft Automation, Inc., 982 So. 2d 1046 (Ala. 2007).

[55] Idaho Code § 6-1405(4); Hall v. Porter Paints Store, 2004 U.S. Dist. LEXIS 19590, at *23 (S.D. Ind. Aug. 20, 2004) (applying Indiana law) ("The modification or alteration of a product must be independent of the expected use of the product in order for the modification or alteration defense to apply.").

[56] See Bates v. Richland Sales Corp., 803 N.E.2d 977, 985 (Ill. App. Ct. 2004) (because the removal of a roll bar required employees to cut through eight bolts and electrical wires as well as use a hoist to lift the heavy bar from the front-end loader, the alteration was substantial and unforeseeable).

foreseeable alteration.[57] Courts determine the foreseeability of an alteration by examining the design of the product in light of its "intended and reasonably foreseeable uses, modifications, or alterations."[58] However, the effect of product modification has been changed by some states that have adopted comparative fault statutes. An example of this is a Kentucky statute which states that "in all tort actions, including product liability actions, involving the fault of more than one (1) party to the action," the jury shall decide "the percentage of the total; fault of all parties to each claim."[59] According to one court, this means that "when both the plaintiff's modification and the defendant's actions play a substantial role in causing the plaintiff's injury, the comparative fault doctrine demands that fault and thus damages be apportioned among other tortfeasors."[60] The effect of this is that manufacturers no long have complete protection in situations where the plaintiff modified or altered a product if the manufacturer also is at fault.

[E]   Misuse of the Product

In addition to contributory negligence, assumption of risk, and alteration of a product, a manufacturer or seller may not be liable if the plaintiff misused the product that caused the injuries or damage. What distinguishes misuse from the other conduct-based defenses, both in negligence and strict liability cases, is that the majority of states treat proof of the absence of misuse as an element of the plaintiff's case instead of requiring the defendant to plead misuse as an affirmative defense.[61] For those states taking the majority position, misuse goes to the issue of causation and proof by the plaintiff that the product was used in an objectively foreseeable manner is necessary to establish that a defect in the product, rather than misuse, was the cause of the injury or damages.[62] Whether part of the plaintiff's case or an affirmative defense, misuse of a product that is not reasonably foreseeable is either a bar to recovery[63] or a factor in reducing damages.[64] Misuse of a product that is foreseeable either is not a defense or is included in states' comparative fault schemes where the misuse contributed to the plaintiff's

---

[57] Welch Sand & Gravel, Inc. v. O & K Trojan, Inc., 668 N.E.2d 529, 534 (Ohio Ct. App. 1995).

[58] *Id.* at 533.

[59] KENTUCKY REVISED STATUTES § 411.182.

[60] Low v. Power Tool Specialist, Inc., 803 F. Supp. 2d 655, 658 (E.D. Ky. 2011) (applying Kentucky law).

[61] *See, e.g.*, Jurado v. Western Gear Works, 619 A.2d 1312 (N.J. 1993); Hughes v. Magic Chef, Inc., 288 N.W.2d 542 (Iowa 1980) Gourdine v. Crews, 955 A.2d 769 (Md. 2008). For a decision treating misuse as an affirmative defense, see Tellez-Cordova v. Campbell, 28 Cal. Rptr. 3d 744 (Ct. App. 2004).

[62] *See* Sanders v. Lull Int'l, Inc., 411 F.3d 1266 (11th Cir. 2005) (applying Georgia law). The facts in Gaudio v. Ford Motor Co., 976 A.2d 524 (Pa. Super. Ct. 2009) led the court to distinguish it from *Madonna. See also* Sohngen v. Home Depot USA, Inc., 2008 U.S. Dist. LEXIS 8080, at *5–*6 (W.D. Pa. Feb. 4, 2008) which found that Pennsylvania courts hold that evidence of a plaintiff's misuse of a product consisting of his ordinary negligence is not admissible with regard to causation in a strict liability case unless the misuse was the sole cause of the accident.

[63] Andrews v. Harley-Davidson, Inc., 796 P.2d 1092 (Nev. 1990).

[64] Wallis v. Townsend Vision, Inc., 2009 U.S. Dist. LEXIS 82007 (C.D. Ill. Sept. 9, 2009) (applying Illinois law).

injuries.[65]

Statutes, courts, and § 402A define misuse as the use of a product by the plaintiff "in a way not reasonably foreseeable by the manufacturer or seller"[66] that was a cause of the plaintiff's injury or damages.[67] Under this definition, there is no misuse simply because the plaintiff used the product in a way that the manufacturer did not intend (*i.e.*, inattention, carelessness or foreseeable misuse). Instead, the manufacturer must show that the plaintiff's injuries were caused by a misuse that was not foreseeable, *that is*, that the plaintiff intentionally used the product in a way that was not reasonably related to its intended uses.[68] The Restatement (Third) also defines the scope of liability for design defects and defects due to inadequate warnings in terms of "the foreseeable risks of harm posed by the product."[69] According to comment *m* to § 2:

> Subsections (b) and (c) impose liability only when the product is put to uses that it is reasonable to expect a seller or distributor to foresee. Product sellers and distributors are not required to foresee and take precautions against every conceivable mode of use and abuse to which their products might be put. Increasing the costs of designing and marketing products in order to avoid the consequences of unreasonable modes of use is not required.[70]

It is the use of the product in a manner that is not reasonable for the seller to expect that separates misuse from contributor negligence and assumption of the risk. In *O.S. Stapley Co. v. Miller*,[71] the Arizona Supreme Court distinguished the

---

[65] Horn v. Fadal Machining Ctrs., LLC, 972 So. 2d 63, 78 (Ala. 2007) ("[W]hen asserting misuse as a defense . . . the defendant must establish that the plaintiff used the product in some manner different from that intended by the manufacturer. Stated differently, the plaintiff's misuse of the product must not have been 'reasonably foreseeable by the seller or manufacturer.' "). *See* Chairez v. James Hamilton Constr. Co., 215 P.3d 732 (N.M. Ct. App. 2009); Smith v. Ingersoll-Rand Co., 14 P.3d 990 (Alaska 2000); Jimenez v. Sears, Roebuck & Co., 904 P.2d 861 (Ariz. 1995); Elliott v. Sears, Roebuck & Co., Inc., 642 A.2d 709 (Conn. 1994).

[66] Rahmig v. Mosley Manufacturing Co., 412 N.W.2d 56, 74 (Neb. 1987). *See* COL. REV. STAT. § 13-21-402.5. According to comment *h* to § 402A:

> A product is not in a defective condition when it is safe for normal handling and consumption. If the injury results from abnormal handling, as where a bottled beverage is knocked against a radiator to remove a cap; or from abnormal preparation for use, as where too much salt is added to food; or from abnormal consumption, as where a child eats too much candy and is made is, the seller is not liable.

[67] Wisconsin legislation provides that "[t]he damages for which a manufacturer, seller, or distributor would otherwise be liable shall be reduced by the percentage of causal responsibility for the claimants harm attributable to the claimants misuse, alteration, or modification of the product." WIS. STAT. ANN. § 895.047(3)(c). In Perez v. VAS S.p.A., 115 Cal. Rptr. 3d 590, 611 (Ct. App. 2010), the court held that the plaintiff's "misuse of the product was so extreme as to be the sole cause of his injury."

[68] Cigna Ins. Co. v. Oy Saunatec, Ltd., 241 F.3d 1 (1st Cir. 2001) (applying Massachusetts law). If a plaintiff's alteration or modification of a product in a way that, although foreseeable, goes against the express warnings of the manufacturer, also may be misuse that bars recovery. *See* Prince v. B.F. Ascher Co., Inc., 90 P.3d 1020 (Okla. 2004).

[69] RESTATEMENT (THIRD) OF TORTS: PRODUCTS LIABILITY, §§ 2(b) and 2(c) (1998).

[70] *Id.* at cmt. *m.*

[71] 447 P.2d 248, 253 (Ariz. 1968).

three forms of conduct by defining contributory negligence as the "[f]ailure to discover a defect in the product which the plaintiff should, if he was reasonably diligent, have discovered." The court went on to state that, "notwithstanding the discovery of such a defect, [if] the plaintiff nevertheless uses the article" the conduct is assumption of the risk. Finally, the court said that the plaintiff's use of a product "for certain purposes or in a manner not reasonably foreseen by the manufacturer is misuse."[72]

Because the use of each product is different and many products have more than one foreseeable use, it is impossible for courts to set out a formula for determining what uses of a product are and are not "reasonably foreseeable." An example of a use that a court held was foreseeable is *Ellsworth v. Sherne Lingerie*,[73] in which the plaintiff was severely burned when the nightgown she was wearing ignited as a result of its coming in contact with a burner on the stove in her kitchen. The plaintiff brought an action based in breach of warranty, negligence, and strict liability against the manufacturer.[74] At the time of the accident, the plaintiff admitted that she was wearing the nightgown inside out and that the two pockets were protruding. At trial, the defendant argued that the plaintiff's use of the gown "in effect draping it over a hot burner for an appreciable period of time, cannot seriously be considered a reasonably foreseeable manner of use."[75] However, the Maryland appellate court held that, while the plaintiff's use of the nightgown may have been careless, it was reasonably foreseeable that loosely fitting clothes such as a nightgown occasionally will be worn inside out and thus could come in contact with a stove while worn in the kitchen (which also was foreseeable).[76] Thus, the court concluded that her use of the product was reasonably foreseeable.[77]

A number of misuse cases involve foreseeable misuse of a product by persons for whom the product was not intended. For example, in a long line of cases involving disposable cigarette lighters, courts have sought to determine whether manufacturers must include childproof latches on their products, even though they are intended to be used only by adults. Even though the number of accidents involving children makes the risk of their setting fires foreseeable, most courts hold that manufacturers do not have a duty to design a product intended for adults in a way that will make it safe for children just because it is foreseeable that the product might fall into the hands of children.[78]

---

[72] *Id.* at 253.

[73] 495 A.2d 348 (Md. Ct. Spec. App. 1985).

[74] *Id.* at 351.

[75] *Id.*

[76] *Id.* at 356–57. *See* Johnson v. Medtronic, Inc., 2012 Mo. App. LEXIS 294, at *30 (Mar. 6, 2012) (applying Missouri law) ("the concept of reasonably anticipated use . . . includes misuse and abnormal use which is objectively foreseeable").

[77] For other cases holding that the misuse was foreseeable, see Chronister v. Bryco Arms, 125 F.3d 624, 627 (8th Cir. 1997) (applying Missouri law) ("in applying strict liability in tort for design defects, manufacturers cannot escape liability on grounds of misuse or abnormal use if the actual use proximate to the injury was objectively foreseeable"); Threats v. General Motors, Corp., 890 S.W.2d 327 (Mo. Ct. App. 1994) (since speeding, although illegal, is foreseeable, the manufacturer should have designed the automobile airbag to deploy in such circumstances).

[78] *See, e.g.*, Hernandez v. Tokai Corp., 2 S.W.3d 251 (Tex. 1999).

[F] Comparative Fault

Although a few states adopted comparative negligence as early as the middle of the 19th century,[79] the doctrine did not become widespread until the early 1970s. As of 2012, all but five jurisdictions – Alabama, the District of Columbia, Maryland, North Carolina, and Virginia – had adopted some form of comparative fault, either by legislation or judicial decision.[80] Many states go beyond simply comparing the plaintiff's negligence with that of the defendant and weigh the fault of the plaintiff when it consists of assumption of the risk or alteration of the product. States also take the fault of the plaintiff into account in assessing damages when the defendant is strictly liable.[81] A few states also have incorporated misuse of the product into their comparative fault systems.[82] This is reflected in the Uniform Comparative Fault Act (UCFA).[83] The effect of the UCFA and the state statutes and decisions is to ease the harsh effect of contributory negligence under which any degree of fault on the part of a plaintiff barred recovery.

Comparative fault takes one of two different forms.[84] First, about one-quarter of the states have adopted "pure" comparative fault, either for all theories of recovery or only for negligence or strict liability cases. For these states, the pure comparative fault is the only system that truly apportions damages according to the relative fault of the parties.[85] An example of pure comparative fault is the New York statute which provides that, in actions for personal injury, property damage, and wrongful death,

> the culpable conduct attributable to the claimant or to the decedent including contributory negligence or assumption of risk, shall not bar recovery, but the amount of damages otherwise recoverable shall be diminished in the proportion which the culpable conduct attributable to the

---

[79] *See* Galena & Chicago Union Ry. v. Jacobs, 20 Ill. 478 (1858). However, in 1885 Illinois returned to contributory negligence. Calumet Iron & Steel Co. v. Martin, 3 N.E. 456 (Ill. 1885).

[80] For a discussion of comparative fault in products liability cases, see Richard C. Henke, *Comparative Fault in Products Liability: Comparing California and New Jersey*, 19 T.M. Cooley L. Rev. 301 (2002). *See also* Burleson v. RSR Group Fla., Inc., 981 So. 2d 1109 (Ala. 2007).

[81] Whitehead v. Toyota Motor Corp., 897 S.W.2d 684 (Tenn. 1995).

[82] For example, see Jimenez v. Sears Roebuck & Co, 904 P.2d 861 (Ariz. 1995), in which the Arizona Supreme Court held that comparative fault principles apply to the defense misuse of a product in a strict liability action, and N.D. Cent. Code § 32.03.2.

[83] Section 1(b) of the Uniform Comparative Fault Act defines "fault" as:

> [A]cts or omissions that are in any measure negligent or reckless toward the person or property of the actor or others, or that subject a person to strict tort liability. The term also includes breach of warranty, unreasonable assumption of risk not constituting an enforceable express consent, misuse of a product for which the defendant otherwise would be liable, and unreasonable failure to avoid an injury or to mitigate damages. Legal requirements of causal relation apply both to fault as the basis for liability and to contributory fault.

See Thompson v. Brown & Williamson Tobacco Corp., 207 S.W.3d 76 (Mo. Ct. App. 2006).

[84] For a summary of the different approaches to "comparative responsibility," see Restatement (Third) of Torts: Apportionment of Liability, § 7 Reporters' Notes (2000).

[85] *See* Alvis v. Ribar, 421 N.E.2d 886, 898 (Ill. 1981).

claimant or decedent bears to the culpable conduct which caused the damages.[86]

Under the New York statute, and in other states that use the pure form of comparative fault, plaintiffs who are 1%, 50% or even 99% at fault for their injuries, whether resulting from contributory negligence or assumption of risk, recover the amount of their damages less the percentage of their fault. In *Ocampo v. Paper Converting Mach. Co.*,[87] the plaintiff was maintaining and inspecting an aluminum foil interfolder machine when her hair became caught in the machine, resulting in a portion of her scalp being torn from her head. In a suit against the manufacturer of the machine, the jury found that the plaintiff's damages for medical care, pain and suffering, disfigurement and loss of normal life totaled $6.1 million. In apportioning responsibility for the plaintiff's injuries, the jury concluded that she was 8% responsible, the manufacturer of the machine was 67% responsible, and the plaintiff's employer was 37% responsible. The jury reduced the plaintiff's total damages by her percentage of fault (8%).

Second, the states that have adopted comparative fault use one of two forms of the "modified rule." Under the modified rule, the amount of the plaintiff's damages is reduced by the percentage of his or her fault. However, unlike the pure form of comparative fault, if the plaintiff's fault exceeds a stated percentage of the total fault, the plaintiff is barred from recovering any damages. There are two forms of modified comparative fault. First, under the "50% rule," the plaintiff's fault is a complete bar to recovery if the plaintiff was 50% or more at fault. This means that, if the fact-finder determines that the plaintiff and defendant each were 50% at fault, the plaintiff is barred from all recovery. However, if a plaintiff is found to be less than 50% at fault, the award is reduced by the percentage of the plaintiff's fault. An example of this form of comparative fault is the Arkansas statute which states, in part:

    (a)   In all actions for damages for personal injuries or wrongful death or injury to property in which recovery is predicated upon fault, liability shall be determined by comparing the fault chargeable to a claiming party with the fault chargeable to the party or parties from whom the claiming party seeks to recover damages.

    (b)

        (1)   If the fault chargeable to a party claiming damages is of a lesser degree than the fault chargeable to the party or parties from whom the claiming party seeks to recover damages, then the claiming party is entitled to recover the amount of his or her damages after they have been diminished in proportion to the degree of his or her own fault.

        (2)   If the fault chargeable to a party claiming damages is equal to or greater in degree than any fault chargeable to the party or parties from whom the claiming party seeks to recover damages, then the

---

[86] N.Y. C.P.L.R. § 1411.

[87] 2005 U.S. Dist. LEXIS 17107 (N.D. Ill. Aug. 12, 2005) (applying Illinois law).

claiming party is not entitled to recover such damages.[88]

Under the second form of modified comparative fault, often referred to as the "51% rule" or the "more than 50% rule," the plaintiff's contributory fault will be a complete bar to recovery only if it exceeds that of the defendant. An example of this approach is the Illinois statute which states:

> In all actions on account of bodily injury or death or physical damage to property based on . . . product liability based on strict tort liability, the court shall instruct the jury in writing that the defendant shall be found not liable if the jury finds that the contributory fault of the plaintiff is more than 50% of the proximate cause of the injury or damage for which recovery is sought.[89]

Under this form of comparative fault, if the fact-finder determines that the plaintiff and defendant were each 50% at fault, the plaintiff still recovers 50% of his or her damages.[90] An example of the "more than 50% rule" is *Tidemann v. Nadler Gold Co.*,[91] in which the plaintiff was severely injured when a golf car that she was attempting to operate suddenly lurched forward and crashed into a garage door. The plaintiff's strict liability theory was dismissed as a matter of law, but her negligence claim went to the jury. The jury returned a verdict in which it apportioned 82% of the fault for the accident to the plaintiff and 18% to the defendant that had reconditioned and sold the gold cart. Since the plaintiff's fault for the accident was more than 50%, she recovered no damages.

The Restatement (Third) does not follow comment *n* to § 402A. Instead, section 17 adopts the position followed by the majority of states and does not distinguish between contributory negligence, assumption of risk, alteration, and misuse as defenses. According to the section:

> A plaintiff's recovery of damages for harm caused by a product defect may be reduced if the conduct of the plaintiff combines with the product to cause the harm and the plaintiff's conduct fails to conform to generally applicable rules establishing appropriate standards of care.[92]

---

[88] Ark. Code Ann. § 16-64-122.

[89] 735 Ill. Comp. Stat. 5/2-1116. *See* Wallis v. Townsend Vision, Inc., 2009 U.S. Dist. LEXIS 82007 (C.D. Ill. Sept. 9, 2009) (applying Illinois law).

[90] *See* General Motors Corp. v. Sanchez, 997 S.W.2d 584 (Tex. 1999).

[91] 224 F.3d 719 (7th Cir. 2000) (applying Illinois law). *See also* Malen v. MTD Products, Inc., 628 F.3d 296 (7th Cir. 2010) (applying Illinois law).

[92] Restatement (Third) of Torts: Products Liability, § 17 (1998).

§ 9.03 STATUS-BASED DEFENSES

[A] Employer Immunity

[1] Employer Liability to Employees

According to the Bureau of Labor Statistics, 4,690 persons were killed and over 3 million persons suffered injuries or illnesses in workplace incidents in the U.S. in 2010.[93] Although many of these deaths and injuries resulted from falls, fires, homicides, and vehicle accidents, a large number of the accidents involved machine tools, such as punch presses, drills, saws, and meat cutters, and exposure to harmful substances such as chemicals and asbestos. Many of the victims of these accidents or their survivors were able to bring negligence or strict liability suits against the manufacturers of the machines or the harmful substances. However, every state has adopted a workers' compensation statute that bars "employees" who suffer injuries "arising out of" and "in the course of employment" from bringing tort suits against their employers.[94] In the place of the common law right of employees to sue their employers, workers' compensation statutes establish an administrative system of no-fault liability for employers that removes the defense of the workers' contributory negligence and imposes statutory limits on the amount injured employees may recover.[95] These statutes not only provide compensation for medical care and lost income to workers and death benefits to the families of workers killed "in the course of employment" (although, in many cases, in a lower amount that they could recover in a tort action), they also give immunity to employers from lawsuits brought by workers. The procedure and compensation provided by the workers' compensation statutes are the exclusive remedy for all claims against employers, subject to limited exceptions. Although those exceptions vary among the states, one example is the California worker's compensation statute which, after stating that it is "the sole and exclusive remedy of the employee or his or her dependents against the employer,"[96] provides that an employee, or his or her dependents in the case of death, may bring a tort action for damages against the employer in three situations:

> (1) Where the employee's injury or death is proximately caused by a willful physical assault by the employer. (2) Where the employee's injury is aggravated by the employer's fraudulent concealment of the existence of the injury and its connection with the employment. . . . (3) Where the employee's injury or death is proximately caused by a defective product manufactured by the employer and sold, leased, or otherwise transferred

---

[93] U.S. Department of Labor, Bureau of Labor Statistics, Injuries, Illnesses, and Fatalities (last visited June 28, 2012) http://www.bls.gov/iif/oshwc/cfoi/worker_memorial.htm.

[94] For examples, *see* 820 ILL. COMP. STAT. 305/1 *et seq.*; N.J. STAT. ANN. § 34:15-8. *See also* Marshall v. H. K. Ferguson Co., 623 F.2d 882 (4th Cir. 1980) (under the Virginia Workmens' Compensation Act, the employer was immune from any common law action by an employee injured on the job).

[95] Participation in the workers' compensation system is mandatory in every state except Texas, which permits employers to choose whether or not to provide workers' compensation, although public employers and employers that enter into a building or construction contract with a governmental entity must provide workers' compensation to their employees.

[96] CAL. LAB. CODE § 3602(a).

for valuable consideration to an independent third person, and that product is thereafter provided for the employee's use by a third person.[97]

California also permits an exception to the exclusive remedy provision of its workers' compensation statute where the injury or death resulted from the employer's knowing removal of, or failure to provide, a guard on a power press.[98]

Another exception to the exclusive remedy provisions is the "dual capacity" or "dual persona" doctrine. Under this doctrine, "an employer may become a third person, vulnerable to tort suit by an employee, if — and only if — it possesses a second personal liable so completely independent from and unrelated to its status as an employer that by established standards the law recognizes that persona as a separate legal person."[99] In order to invoke the doctrine, an employee must show that the employer acted in two distinct capacities and that he or she was injured as a result of conduct in which the employer engaged while acting in its capacity other than that of employer.[100] However, where the duties of the employer under both capacities are intertwined to the extent that its conduct in the second capacity cannot be held to create obligations unrelated to its capacity as an employer, the dual capacity doctrine is inapplicable.[101] Despite the attention that it has received, the dual capacity doctrine is recognized only by about half-a-dozen states. The two states that initially adopted it, California and Ohio, since have rejected it.[102]

In recent years the exclusive remedy provision has been challenged on constitutional grounds.[103] The only successful case has been *Smothers v. Gresham Transfer*,[104] in which an employee claimed that his respiratory problems were work-related. When the employee was denied worker's compensation, the Oregon trial court permitted him to bring a negligence action against his employer. In upholding the employee's suit, the Oregon Supreme Court held that, because the state's workers' compensation statute provided the exclusive remedy for all work-related injuries, the statute violated the state constitution. The court found that the exclusive remedy provision's bar to employer liability violate the remedy

---

[97] *Id.* at § 3602(b). *See also* Rainer v. Union Carbide Corp., 402 F.3d 608 (6th Cir. 2004) (applying Kentucky law); Perry v. Heavenly Valley, 209 Cal. Rptr. 771 (Ct. App. 1985).

[98] CAL. LAB. CODE § 4558.

[99] Stayton v. Clariant Corp., 10 A.3d 597 (Del. 2010) (citing Arthur Larson, Larson's Workers' Compensation Law, § 113.01[1], p. 113.2 (2000). For discussion of the dual capacity exception, see Van Doren v. Coe Press Equip. Corp., 592 F. Supp. 2d 776, 797–804 (E.D. Pa. 2008) (applying Pennsylvania law); Dyke v. St. Francis Hospital, 861 P.2d 295 (Okla. 1993). Although Pennsylvania has applied the doctrine, a court interpreted the exception strictly and held that it did not apply in Soto v. Nabisco, Inc., 32 A.3d 787 (Pa. 2011).

[100] For examples of the use of the dual capacity doctrine, see Stayton v. Clariant Corp., 10 A.3d 597 (Del. 2010); Rosales v. Verson Allsteel Press Co., 354 N.E.2d 553 (Ill. App. Ct. 1976).

[101] McCormick v. Caterpillar Tractor Co., 423 N.E.2d 876 (Ill. 1981).

[102] See Bell v. Industrial Vangas, Inc., 637 P.2d 266 (Cal. 1981), which was overturned by legislation (CAL. LAB. CODE § 3602(a) and Mercer v. Uniroyal, Inc., 361 N.E.2d 492 (Ohio Ct. App. 1976) which was rejected by Schump v. Firestone Tire and Rubber Co., 541 N.E.2d 1040 (Ohio 1989).

[103] In Engel v. Workers' Compensation Appeals Board, 1998 Cal. LEXIS 4199 (June 24, 1998), the California Supreme Court denied a petition to review the constitutionality of that state's workers' compensation act.

[104] 23 P.3d 333 (Or. 2001).

clause of the Oregon constitution which provides that "every [person] shall have remedy by due course of law for injury done him in his person, property, or reputation."[105]

[2] Employer Liability to Third Parties

Employees injured in the course of employment are barred by workers' compensation laws from suing their employers in negligence or strict liability for their injuries. If the employees were injured by machinery or a work-place substance, they will sue the manufacturer of the product. However, the manufacturer may bring a third-party action against the employer seeking indemnification or contribution.[106] Such claims by the manufacturer may be based on allegations that the employer failed to provide the employee with a safe working environment, failed to adequately instruct the employee on how to use the product, failed to adequately supervise the employee while using the product, or failed to maintain the product properly.[107] The vast majority of states extend the immunity of the employer from torts suits by its employees to include immunity from claims for contribution by third-parties for contribution.[108] Only one state, New York, permits a defendant to recover unlimited contribution from negligent employers. In addition, a few states allow limited contribution from the employer.[109] In Illinois, for example, the Contribution Act[110] requires employers to contribute to tort judgments when they are found to be responsible for any part of an employee's injuries. However, the amount that an employer can be required to contribute is limited to the amount of its statutory liability under the state's workers' compensation statute.[111]

[B] Government Contractor Defense

[1] Framework for the Defense

The government contract defense provides an affirmative defense in products liability actions to contractors that manufacture equipment for the federal government. Although the source of the defense is the federal government's sovereign immunity, courts have stated that "the government contractor defense does not confer sovereign immunity on contractors."[112] Instead, according to the Ninth Circuit, the government contractor defense is "only a corollary financial benefit

---

[105] Or. Const. art. 1, § 10.

[106] *See* Coello v. Tug Manufacturing Corp., 756 F. Supp. 1258 (W.D. Mo. 1991) (applying Missouri law).

[107] *See* Ocampo v. Paper Converting Machine Co., 2005 U.S. Dist. LEXIS 17107 (N.D. Ill. Aug. 12, 2005) (applying Illinois law).

[108] *See, e.g.,* Oaklawn Jockey Club v. Pickens-Bond Construction, 477 S.W.2d 477 (Ark. 1972).

[109] *See* Kotecki v. Cyclops Welding Corp., 585 N.E.2d 1023 (Ill. 1991); Lambertson v. Cincinnati Corp., 257 N.W.2d 679 (Minn. 1977).

[110] 740 Ill. Comp. Stat. 100/0.01 *et seq.*

[111] *See* Kotecki v. Cyclops Welding Corp., 585 N.E.2d 1023 (Ill. 1991).

[112] U.S. *ex rel.* Ali v. Daniel, Mann, Johnson & Mendenhall, 355 F.3d 1140, 1147 (9th Cir. 2004).

flowing from *the government's* sovereign immunity."[113]

The framework for the government contractor defense was laid out by the Supreme Court in *Boyle v. United Technologies Corp.*,[114] in which a Marine helicopter crashed off the Virginia coast during a training exercise. Although Boyle, the copilot, survived the impact of the crash, he was unable to escape from the helicopter and drowned. His father brought an action against the manufacturer of the helicopter, alleging that it had defectively designed the copilot's emergency escape-hatch system since the hatch opened out instead of in. Although there is no federal legislation specifically giving immunity to government contractors, the Supreme Court held that there are a few situations involving "uniquely federal interests" where state law may be pre-empted and replaced by federal law prescribed by the courts.[115] According to the Court, the procurement of equipment by the United States is an area of uniquely federal interest.[116] However, rather than give government contractors blanket immunity from liability, the Court formulated a "government contractor defense." Under this defense, state law imposing liability for design defects in military equipment is displaced where: (1) the United States approved reasonably precise specifications for the product; (2) the product conformed to those specifications; and (3) the supplier warned the United States about dangers in the use of the product known to the supplier but not to the United States.[117] In *Boyle*, the Court held that the state-imposed duty of care, as an asserted basis for a contractor's liability, was in direct conflict with the duty imposed by the government contract and thus the state tort law had to be displaced.

[2] The Three Prongs of the Defense

The first prong of the government contractor defense set out in *Boyle* requires a showing that the government "approved reasonably precise specifications" for the product. Courts have interpreted the term "approved" as requiring actual review and evaluation of the specifications for the equipment rather than simply a "rubber stamp."[118] The approval must constitute a "discretionary function" of the government, which is defined as government acts involving "the use of policy judgment."[119] Courts have reinforced the importance of actual review, stating that only "genuine consideration and informed judgment satisfies the first prong of *Boyle*."[120] The requirement that the specifications be "reasonably precise" means that the government will exercise its discretion over "significant details and all critical design choices" unless it approves only general guidelines; the contractor then will have discretion over design choices.[121] On the other hand, the government is not

---

[113] Rodriguez v. Lockheed Martin Corp., 627 F.3d 1259, 1262 (9th Cir. 2010) (italics in the original).

[114] 487 U.S. 500 (1988).

[115] *Id.* at 504–05.

[116] *Id.* at 505–07.

[117] *Id.* at 512. *See* Rodriguez v. Lockheed Martin Corp., 627 F.3d 1259 (9th Cir. 2010).

[118] *See* Trevino v. General Dynamics Corp., 865 F.2d 1474, 1480 (5th Cir. 1989).

[119] *Id.*

[120] Haltiwanger v. Unisys Corp., 949 F. Supp. 898, 902–03 (D.D.C. 1996).

[121] Trevino v. General Dynamics Corp., 865 F.2d 1474, 1481 (5th Cir. 1989). *See also* Kerstetter v.

required to instruct the manufacturer on how to make the product and can approve a design for which it provided no input.[122]

One issue that has arisen in recent years is whether the first prong of *Boyle* is met if the allegedly defective product was modeled off a "stock" or "off the shelf" product that had been manufactured previously. In *In re "Agent Orange" Product Liability Litigation*,[123] the plaintiffs, who were either U.S. military veterans or their relatives, alleged that various forms of cancer were caused by the veteran's exposure to the chemical defoliant "Agent Orange" during service in Vietnam. The plaintiffs argued that the government "rubber stamped" its approval of the defendant/manufacturer's specifications for the defoliant. They also alleged that "Agent Orange" was simply a combination of off-the-shelf, commercially available herbicides, rather than products specifically tailored to the government's needs.[124] In addition, the plaintiffs argued that, while the government may have had some input in developing the defoliant, the input was not significant because the component chemicals were not developed originally for military use, aspects of the components' composition already were patented, and the defendants may have proposed certain specifications.[125]

In holding that the first prong was met, the Second Circuit found that the government exercised adequate discretion and was the agent of the decision.[126] The court noted that *Boyle* "explicitly contemplated government reliance on manufacturers' expertise in making a fully informed decision as to what to order." In addition, evidence showed that the Army specifically requested that a specific component have a 98% purity level, instead of the standard 50% level in commercial products.[127] According to the court, this demonstrated that the government utilized sufficient discretion, making the government the "agent of the decision."[128]

The second prong of the government contractor defense requires a manufacturer to establish that the product conformed to the reasonably precise specifications approved by the government. In *Elmore v. Rockwell Automation*,[129] a Postal Service worker suffered a severe injury when his arm became entangled in a mail conveyer system. The worker brought suit against the builder of the conveyer system and the subcontractor that provided its electrical control boxes. The defendants relied on the government contractor defense, asserting that the

---

Pacific Scientific Co., 210 F.3d 431, 438 (5th Cir. 2000) (" 'the reasonably precise' standard is satisfied so long as the specifications address, in reasonable detail, the product design feature, alleged to be defective); Bailey v. McDonnell Douglas Corp., 989 F.2d 794, 799 (5th Cir. 1993) (specifications need not address the specific defect alleged, just the specific feature)).

[122] *Id.* at 1480.

[123] 517 F.3d 76 (2d Cir. 2008).

[124] *Id.* at 90.

[125] *Id.* at 91.

[126] *Id.* at 91–92.

[127] *Id.*

[128] *See* Brinson v. Raytheon Co., 571 F.3d 1348 (11th Cir. 2009) (in assessing whether the first prong is met, a contractor may rely on post-design, post-production evidence to show that the government approved reasonably precise specifications); Getz v. Boeing Co., 690 F. Supp. 2d 982 (N.D. Cal. 2010).

[129] 306 F. Supp. 2d 751 (N.D. Ill. 2004).

conveyor system conformed to government specifications.[130] However, the worker offered expert testimony that the system violated Occupational Safety and Health Administration (OSHA) safety guidelines, that the machine did not have a warning where it was required, and that the emergency stop button was too far from the nip point. Since conformity with OSHA guidelines was a requirement in the Postal Service's specifications, the district court denied the defendants' motion for summary judgment on its government contractor defense.[131]

The third prong of the government contractor defense requires proof that the contractor warned the United States government about known dangers associated with the use of the product.[132] Under this prong, the contractor must disclose information when the government knows less about the danger than the contractor. However, a contractor is not required to warn about latent defects, only those about which it has actual knowledge.[133] The party asserting the government contract defense must prove either that "the contractor lacked actual knowledge of the danger or that the government was independently aware of the defect" in order to demonstrate that the government was as aware of the danger as the contractor.[134] Thus, "if the government was already independently aware of a risk and chose to act regardless of the knowledge, [a] defendant may still employ the government contractor defense without further warning the government."[135]

In *Boyle*, the Supreme Court applied the government contractor defense in the context of a design defect. Federal courts are split as to whether the defense applies only to design defects or to manufacturing defects as well.[136] In *Bailey v. McDonnell Douglas Corporation*,[137] for example, the Fifth Circuit held that the defense is not limited to design defect claims. The court stated that the defense will apply when the three conditions laid out in *Boyle* are satisfied with respect to "the particular product feature upon which the claim is based."[138] Many courts also have held the defense applies to failure to warn claims.[139] In *Kerstetter v. Pacific*

---

[130] *Id.* at 753.

[131] *Id.*

[132] *See* Haltiwanger v. Unisys Corp., 949 F. Supp. 898, 904 (D.D.C. 1996); Niemann v. McDonnell Douglas Corp., 721 F. Supp. 1019, 1028 (S.D. Ill.1989).

[133] Kerstetter v. Pacific Scientific Co., 210 F.3d 431 (5th Cir. 2000).

[134] Haltiwanger v. Unisys Corp., 949 F. Supp. 898, 904 (D.D.C. 1996); Niemann v. McDonnell Douglas Corp., 721 F. Supp. 1019, 1028 (S.D. Ill.1989).

[135] Stout v. Borg-Warner Corp. 933 F.2d 331, 336–37 (5th Cir. 1991).

[136] *See, e.g.*, Mitchell v. Lone Star Ammunition, Inc., 913 F.2d 242 (5th Cir. 1990) (the defense only applies in cases of defective design); Bentzlin v. Hughes Aircraft Co., 833 F. Supp. 1486 (C.D. Cal. 1993) (the defense applies to manufacturing defect claims); Torrington Co. v. Stutzman, 46 S.W.3d 829 (Tex. 2000) (upholding refusal to submit the defense to the jury because the defect originated in the products manufacture, not in its design).

[137] 989 F.2d 794 (5th Cir. 1993).

[138] *Id.* at 801–02.

[139] In Tate v. Boeing Helicopters, 55 F.3d 1150, 1157 (6th Cir. 1995), the court outlined the elements a contractor must establish in a failure to warn case: (1) the federal government exercised its discretion and approved any warnings; (2) the contractor's warnings conformed those approved by the government; and (3) the contractor warned the government of any dangers known to the contractor but not to the

Scientific Company,[140] the Fifth Circuit held that, since the Navy knew of the danger of the uncommanded seat release on the T-34C aircraft's pilot restraint system, the contractor did not have a duty of warn it of that danger. In addition, even if the government was unaware of the defect, a contractor's failure to warn the government about latent defects would not preclude the use of the defense.[141] In *Densberger v. United Technologies*,[142] the Second Circuit held that a helicopter manufacturer was liable in negligence for deaths arising out of the company's post-sale failure to warn the Army that its helicopter could become uncontrollable. According to the court, the government contractor defense makes sense only if the government limited the warnings that the contractor was permitted to give to the users. However, in *Densberger*, the manufacturer failed to warn the Army of the problems with the helicopter, not the pilots. Thus, the defense did not apply and the survivors were permitted to bring their action.

[3] Expansion of the Defense

Although the government contractor defense once was limited to manufacturers and suppliers that did business with the government, Congress expanded the defense and gave it new importance in 2002 with the enactment of the Homeland Security Act. Contained within that Act is the Support Anti-Terrorism by Fostering Effective Technologies Act of 2002 (the "Safety Act"),[143] under which the Secretary of the Department of Homeland Security can designate certain products as "qualified anti-terrorism technology."[144] These include "any product, equipment, service, device, or technology designed, developed, modified, or procured for the specific purpose of preventing, detecting, identifying, or deterring acts of terrorism or limiting the harm such acts might otherwise cause."[145] If a claim arises from an act of terrorism when "qualified anti-terrorism technology" has been used in defense against the terrorism, there is a federal cause of action.[146] In addition, the Act creates a rebuttable presumption that the government contractor defense applies to the sellers of these technologies.[147] However, in a change from the past application of the defense, the presumption applies not only when a plaintiff's claims arises from the sale of the technology to the federal government but also when the sale was to private parties.[148] Before the presumption arises, the Secretary, who has the exclusive responsibility for reviewing and approving anti-terrorism technology, must certify that the technology: (1) will perform as intended; (2) conforms with the

---

government. *See also* Emory v. McDonnell Douglas Corp., 148 F.3d 347 (4th Cir. 1998); Oliver v. Oshkosh Truck Corp., 96 F.3d 992 (7th Cir. 1996).

[140] 210 F.3d 431 (5th Cir. 2000).

[141] *Id.* at 436.

[142] 297 F.3d 66 (2d Cir. 2002).

[143] 6 U.S.C. §§ 441–444.

[144] *Id.* at § 441(b).

[145] *Id.* at § 444(1).

[146] *Id.* at § 442.

[147] *Id.* at § 442(d)(1).

[148] *Id.*

seller's specifications; and (3) is safe for use as intended.[149]

§ 9.04   TIMES-BASED DEFENSES

[A]   Statute of Limitations

Every state has enacted a statute of limitations that establishes specific time limits for filing products liability actions based on warranty, negligence, and strict liability. These statutes provide an affirmative defense that the manufacturer or seller must plead. These statutes are an attempt to strike a balance between giving injured plaintiffs adequate time to bring their claims and the need to protect manufacturers and sellers by making sure that the evidence and witnesses' memories are fresh. If a defendant fails to raise the defense, the action will proceed.

The time periods set out in the statutes of limitations vary from state to state and depend on whether the claim is for personal injury, property damage, or wrongful death. They can be as short as one year, as in Kentucky,[150] Louisiana,[151] and Tennessee,[152] or as long as six years, as in Maine,[153] Minnesota,[154] and North Dakota.[155] However, the most common limitation periods are four years for breach of warranty actions[156] and two or three years for negligence[157] and strict liability[158] claims.

In most states, the statute of limitations begins to run from the date "the cause of action accrues." Usually, this is the date on which the personal injury or property damage occurred.[159] However, because that can frustrate the goal of giving the injured plaintiff adequate time to bring his or her claim, courts have held that the running of the statute of limitations may be tolled by certain situations. Thus, if a child is injured by a defective product, the statute is tolled during the

---

[149]   *Id.* at 442(d)(2). Another example is the Public Readiness and Emergency Preparedness Act (42 U.S.C. § 247d-6(d)), which authorizes the Secretary of the Department of Health and Human Services to issue a declaration that provides immunity from tort liability (except for willful misconduct) for claims of loss caused, arising out of, relating to, or resulting from the administration or the use of countermeasures to diseases, threats and conditions determined by the Secretary to constitute a present, or credible risk of a future public health emergency to entities and individuals involved in the development, manufacture, testing, distribution, administration, and use of such countermeasures.

[150]   Ky. Rev. Stat. Ann. §§ 413.140(1)(a) (personal injury) 413.180 (wrongful death and survival actions).

[151]   La. Code Civ. Pro. Art. 3492.

[152]   Tenn. Code Ann. § 28-3-104(b) (personal injury).

[153]   Me. Rev. Stat. Ann. tit. 14, § 752 (personal injury).

[154]   Minn. Stat. Ann. § 541.05, Subd. 1 (personal injury or property damage).

[155]   N.D. Cent. Code § 28-01-16(5).

[156]   *See* Fla. Stat. Ann. § 95.11(3)(k); N.H. Rev. Stat. § 382-A:2-725(1) (four years). *See also* Kelleher v. Marvin Lumber and Cedar Co., 891 A.2d 477 (N.H. 2005).

[157]   *See, e.g.,* Ga. Code Ann. § 9-3-33 (two years) and Md. Code Ann., Cts. and Jud. Pro. § 5-101 (three years).

[158]   *See, e.g.,* N.J. Stat. Ann. § 2A:14-2 (two years) and Miss. Code Ann. § 15-1-49 (three years).

[159]   Genereux v. Amer. Beryllia Corp., 577 F.3d 350 (1st Cir. 2009) (applying Massachusetts law).

period that he or she is a minor.[160] In addition, courts in most states have created some form of a discovery rule.[161] Under this rule, the statute of limitations does not begin to run until the plaintiff knows, or reasonably should have known, of an injury and knows or reasonably should have known that the injury was caused by the wrongful action of another.[162] In *Fox v. Ethicon Endo-Surgery, Inc.*,[163] the plaintiff brought a medical malpractice action resulting when she discovered that, after gastric bypass surgery, there was a perforation at the stapled closure of her small intestine, causing fluid to leak into her abdominal cavity. Almost a year after filing suit against her doctor, and two years after the surgery, the plaintiff learned, during the deposition of her doctor, that her bowel had been stapled with an "Ethicon GIA-type stapler." The plaintiff then sought to amend her complaint, adding the manufacturer as a defendant, and alleging strict liability in the design, manufacture, and assembly of the stapler.[164]

In *Fox*, the manufacturer asserted that the plaintiff's products liability claim was time-barred by the one year statute of limitations. The plaintiff, however, argued that, under the discovery rule, the statute of limitations for her products liability claim did not begin to run until the doctor's deposition.[165] Although the manufacturer argued for a restrictive rule that would make the statute of limitations in a products liability action begin to run at the same time the statute of limitations for the medical malpractice action commenced, the California Supreme Court reject the argument as inconsistent with the discovery rule. According to the court, "if a plaintiff's reasonable and diligent investigation disclosed only one kind of wrongdoing when the injury was actually caused by tortious conduct of a wholly different sort, the discovery rule postpones accrual of the statute of limitations on the newly discovered claim."[166] Thus, the statute of limitations on the plaintiff's products liability claim did not begin to run until the date of her doctor's deposition and the plaintiff was permitted to amend her complaint.

[B] Statute of Repose

In addition to statutes of limitation, states in the late 1960s began to enact statutes of repose. Regardless of when the cause of action accrued, these statutes bar a plaintiff's claim unless it is brought within a specific number of years from the date the defendant manufactured or sold the product.[167] These statutes have

---

[160] *See* Cox v. McDonnell-Douglas Corp., 665 F.2d 566 (5th Cir.1982) (applying Texas law); Miles v. S.C. Johnson & Son, Inc., 2001 U.S. Dist. LEXIS 12904 (N.D. Ill. May 23, 2001) (applying Illinois law).

[161] *See* John's Heating Service v. Lamb, 46 P.2d 1024 (Alaska 2002); Lawhon v. L.B.J. Institutional Supply, Inc., 765 P.2d 1003 (Ariz. Ct. App. 1988).

[162] *See* In re Prempro Products Liability Litigation, 586 F.3d 547 (8th Cir. 2009) (applying Arkansas law); Kelleher v. Marvin Lumber and Cedar Co, 891 A.2d 477 (N.H. 2005).

[163] 110 P.3d 914 (Cal. 2005).

[164] *Id.* at 917–918.

[165] *Id.* at 918–923.

[166] *Id.* at 924.

[167] *See* McGovern, *The Variety, Policy and Constitutionality of Product Liability Statutes of Repose*, 30 Am. U.L. Rev. 579 (1981).

been criticized as unfair to plaintiffs,[168] since they may bar claims before they have arisen, and challenged on constitutional grounds.[169] As a result, more than 30 states do not have statutes of repose. In those state that do, the goal of the statute is the same as with statutes of limitations: give plaintiffs time to prepare their claims while giving manufacturers and sellers certainty that, after a specific period of time, they will not have to worry about suits involving their products.[170]

Among the states that have adopted statutes of repose, the statutes are state specific and the time varies greatly. In Illinois, for example, the statute of repose states that, a "product liability action based on the doctrine of strict liability in tort" must be commenced "within 12 years from the date of first sale, lease or delivery of possession by a seller or 10 years from the date of first sale, lease or delivery of possession to its initial user, consumer, or other non-seller, whichever period expires earlier."[171] Some states also limit the application of their statutes of repose. For example, although Connecticut has no general statute of repose, a statute of repose bars all claims arising out of workplace accidents brought more than 10 years after the date the seller parted with possession of the product.[172] Georgia's statute of repose does not apply to failure to warn claims,[173] actions in negligence against manufacturers of products implicated in birth defects, or actions against manufacturers that arise out of negligence.[174] Wisconsin's statute states that, in claims based on strict liability, "a defendant is not liable to a claimant for damages if the product alleged to have caused the damage was manufactured 15 years or more before the claim accrues, unless the manufacturer makes a specific representation that the product will last for a period beyond 15 years. This subsection does not apply to an action based on a claim for damages caused by a latent disease."[175] In Massachusetts and Minnesota, states without a statute of repose in products liability actions, some products liability claims still may be subject to the states' statutes of repose applicable to tort actions arising out of improvements to real property.[176]

---

[168] *See* Comment, *Due Process Challenges to Statutes to Repose*, 40 Sw. L.J. 997 (1986).

[169] The constitutionality of most state statutes of repose has been upheld. *See, e.g.*, Barwick v. Celotex Corp., 736 F.2d 946 (4th Cir. 1984) (upholding the constitutionality of the North Carolina statute) and McIntosh v. Melroe Co., 729 N.E.2d 972 (Ind. 2000) (upholding the constitutionality of the Indiana statute). However, a number of statutes have been struck down as violating state constitutions. For examples, *see* Dickie v. Farmers Union Oil Co., 611 N.E.2d 168 (N.D. 2000); Hazine v, Montgomery Elevator Co., 861 P.2d 625 (Ariz. 1993); and Kennedy v. Cumberland Engineering Co., 471 A.2d 195 (R.I. 1984).

[170] Goad v. Celotex Corp., 831 F.2d 508 (4th Cir. 1987) (applying Texas law).

[171] 735 Ill. Comp. Stat. 5/13-213(b). In Davis v. Toshiba Machine Co., America, 710 N.E.2d 399 (Ill. 1999), the Illinois Supreme Court held that an action can be filed within two years of an injury, so long as the injury occurred within the period of the statute of repose, regardless of whether the time within the statute has expired.

[172] Conn. Gen. Stat. § 52-577a(c).

[173] Chrysler Corp. v. Batten, 450 S.E.2d 208 (Ga. 1994).

[174] Ga. Code Ann. § 51-1-11(c); Vickery v. Waste Management of Georgia, Inc., 549 S.E.2d 482 (Ga. Ct. App. 2001).

[175] Wis. Stat. Ann. § 895.047(5).

[176] Mass. Gen. Laws Ann. ch. 260, § 2B; Minn. Stat. Ann. § 541.051.

[C] Useful Shelf-Life

In 2005 DaimlerChrysler and Ford Motor Company began advising their automobile and truck customers: "Tires and spare tire should be replaced after six years, regardless of the remaining tread. Failure to follow this warning can result in sudden tire failure. You could lose control and have an accident resulting in serious injury or death."[177] The companies were responding to research that suggested tires can degrade rapidly as they get older, regardless of how much they are used. This raises the question of whether, independently of the statute of repose, a manufacturer has a defense that the product has exceeded its "useful safe life."[178]

The source of useful safe life analysis is the Model Uniform Product Liability Act (MUPLA), created by the Department of Commerce in 1979.[179] Section 110(A)(1) of the Act states that "a product seller shall not be subject to liability to a claimant for harm under this Act if the product seller proves by a preponderance of the evidence that the harm, was caused after the product's 'useful safe life' had expired."[180] The Act states that the "useful safe life" of a product begins "at the time of delivery of the product and extends for the time during which the product would normally be likely to perform or be stored in a safe manner."[181] The Act then sets out a number of factors that help determine whether a product's useful safe life has expired. These include: (1) the amount of "wear and tear" to which the product has been subject; (2) the effect of deterioration from the user, similar users, and from climate or other conditions under which the product was used or stored; (3) the normal practices of the user, similar users, and the product seller with respect to the circumstances, frequency, and purposes of the product's use, and with respect to repairs, renewals, and replacements; (4) any representations, instruction, or warnings made by the product seller concerning proper maintenance, storage, and use of the product or the expected useful safe life of the product; and (5) any modification or alteration of the product by a user or third party.[182]

Statutes of repose and the concept of useful safe life are similar in that they provide a period of time beyond which a manufacturer or seller will not be liable for a product. However, useful life statutes are more advantageous to plaintiffs since that they are more flexible and do not contain the rigid periods of time imposed by statutes of repose. For example, instead of a fixed statute of repose, Idaho provides that a manufacturer or seller is not liable for harm if it can prove that the harm occurred after the product's "useful safe life" had expired.[183] The statute states,

---

[177] *Chrysler: Change Tires After 6 years*, The Detroit News, May 27, 2005, *available at* http://www.gminsidenews.com/forums/f58/chrysler-change-tires-after-6-years-15220/.

[178] *See* Charles E. Cantu, *The Useful Life Defense: Embracing the Idea That All Products Eventually Grow Old and Die*, 80 Neb. L. Rev. 1 (2001).

[179] 44 Fed. Reg. 62, 714 (1979).

[180] *Id.* at 62, 732.

[181] *Id.*

[182] *Id.*

[183] Idaho Code § 6-1403(1).

however, that the manufacturer can be liable if it expressly warranted the product for a longer period of time. For claims involving harm caused more than ten years after the time of the delivery of the product, there is a rebuttable presumption that the harm was caused after the useful safe life expired. Kansas also has a useful life statute that is almost to the one in Idaho.[184] However, the Kansas statute lists the five factors in the MUPLA to help the fact-finder determine whether the product's safe life has expired.[185] In Washington, the useful safe statute has many similarities to those in other states as well as a few important differences.[186] Although a product seller generally is not liable for harm after the product's useful safe life has expired, it may be liable if: (1) it told the buyer the product had a longer warranty than the useful safe life; (2) it intentionally misrepresented facts about the product or concealed information about it and such conduct led to the plaintiff's injury; or (3) the injury was caused by exposure to a defective product, which the plaintiff received and used for the first time within the product's safe life bit the harm did not manifest itself until after the safe life had expired. In addition, the Washington statute states that if the injury occurred more than twelve years after the buyer received the product, there is a presumption that the useful life had expired.[187]

§ 9.05 GOVERNMENT AND INDUSTRY STANDARDS

In products liability cases, plaintiffs often attempt to show that the manufacturer or seller was negligent per se or that the product was unreasonably dangerous by reference to government or industry standards. Similarly, manufacturers frequently attempt to rebut allegations of negligence and product defectiveness by basing their defense on compliance with those same standards.[188] In addition, many state consumer protection statutes provide some type of regulatory compliance defense if a product complied with applicable codes, standards, and regulations relating to its design, performance, and warnings. However, the states differ as to how much weight they giver to such evidence.[189]

[A] Government Standards

In addition to the standards imposed by common law negligence and strict liability, manufacturers of products as diverse as airplanes, automobiles, drugs, food, and toys are subject to state and federal statutes and administrative regulations intended to promote product safety. These regulations may apply to the design, inspection, testing, manufacture, labeling, warnings, or instructions for

---

[184] KAN. STAT. ANN. § 60-3303; Hiner v. Deere & Co., 161 F. Supp. 2d 1279 (D. Kan. 2001) (applying Kansas law)

[185] *Id.* at § 60-3303(a).

[186] WASH. REV. CODE § 7.72.060(1).

[187] *Id.* at § 7.72.060(2).

[188] *See* Victor Schwartz & Cary Silverman, *Preemption of State Common Law by Federal Agency Action: Striking the Appropriate Balance that Protects Public Safety*, 84 TUL. L. REV. 1203, 1226–31 (2010).

[189] *Id.* at 1229–30.

use of the product. In a negligence case, the violation of a government regulation may result in a finding that the manufacturer was negligent *per se*, helping the plaintiff to establish a *prima facie* case of negligence.[190] This approach first was articulated in *Martin v. Herzog*[191] when Judge Benjamin Cardozo stated that the "unexcused omission" of a statutory requirement was "more than some evidence of negligence. It *is* negligence in itself . . . Jurors have no dispensing power by which they may relax the duty."[192] This position was adopted by the Restatement (Second) of Torts which states: "The unexcused violation of the legislative enactment of an administrative regulation which is adopted by the court as defining the standard of conduct of a reasonable man, is negligence in itself."[193] Thus, if a manufacturer is found to have violated a statute or regulation, the questions for the jury are: (1) was the statute or regulation in effect at the time of the sale of the product? (2) was the plaintiff within the class of persons intended to be protected by the statute or regulation? (3) was the violation of the statute or regulation a cause of the plaintiff's injury? and (4) was the violation of the statute an "excused omission"?[194]

A manufacturer also may raise compliance with a government statute or regulation as a defense to an allegation that its product was defective.[195] Although, in negligence cases, the fact that a product complied with an applicable statute is evidence that the product was not defective, it is not conclusive and does not shield a manufacturer from liability.[196] One reason for this is that government standards are considered to be a minimum standard for a product and, in some situations, the product is expected to meet more than that minimum standard. The Restatement (Second) of Torts, for example, states that "[c]ompliance with a legislative enactment or an administrative regulation does not prevent a finding of negligence where a reasonable man would take additional precautions."[197] In strict liability actions, a few states also hold that compliance with government standards is relevant but not conclusive as to whether the product was defective.[198] However, the majority of states hold that compliance with a government regulation should not be considered "where the product's condition and consumer expectations are

---

[190] *See* Baxley v. Fischer, 134 S.E.2d 291 (Va. 1964).

[191] 126 N.E. 814 (N.Y. 1920).

[192] *Id.* at 815 (emphasis in the original).

[193] RESTATEMENT (SECOND) OF TORTS, § 288B (1965).

[194] Although Judge Cardozo did not discuss when an omission of a statute might be excused, § 288A of the RESTATEMENT (SECOND) OF TORTS, lists five situations when a "violation is excused."

[195] *See Symposium: Regulatory Compliance as a Defense to Products Liability*, 88 GA. L.J. 2049 (2000).

[196] Woodell v. Proctor & Gamble Manufacturing Co., 1999 U.S. Dist. LEXIS 12850 (N.D. Tex. Aug. 16, 1999) (applying Texas law); Abadie v. Metropolitan Life Insurance Co., 784 So.2d 46 (La. Ct. App. 2001); Barry v. Don Hall Laboratories, 642 P.2d 685 (Or. Ct. App. 1982).

[197] RESTATEMENT (SECOND) OF TORTS § 288C (1965).

[198] *See* Lorenz v. Celotex Corp., 896 F.2d 148 (5th Cir. 1990) (applying Texas law). In some states, such a Nevada, proof of compliance with government standards does not bar recovery in a breach of warranty or strict liability action but is admissible as evidence of a product's defectiveness. Rader v. Teva Parental Medications, Inc., 795 F. Supp. 2d 1143 (D. Nev. 2011) (applying Nevada law).

the central inquiries and liability may be imposed regardless of the degree of care exercised by the manufacturer."[199]

Some states have codified a rebuttable presumption that a product is not in a defective condition if it is in "conformity with government standards established for that industry."[200] *Niemela v. Imperial Manufacturing, Inc.*,[201] is an example of Utah's application of such a statute.[202] In *Niemela*, the plaintiff, a postal worker, alleged that she was injured by opening and closing Imperial's mailboxes over one million times. Part of the plaintiff's mail route included a subdivision of approximately 600 homes, all of which were required to use Imperial's mailboxes. The plaintiff claimed that the Imperial mailbox doors did not align properly, making them difficult to open and close especially in inclement weather. Ultimately, her struggles with the Imperial mailboxes caused her serious and permanent injury when she attempted to open one of the mailboxes with a screwdriver.[203] Imperial moved for summary judgment, alleging that the mailboxes were presumed not to be defective because they complied with federal mailbox regulations in effect when they were designed and manufactured.[204] The Utah Court of Appeals concluded that Imperil was entitled to a presumption of non-defectiveness because the mailboxes conformed to government standards at the time they were installed.[205]

The Restatement (Third) takes the same position in strict liability cases as that taken by the majority of states in negligence cases toward the noncompliance and compliance with safety statutes and regulations. Section 4, which applies "[i]n connection with liability for defective design or inadequate instructions or warnings," states:

(a) a product's noncompliance with an applicable product safety statute or administrative regulation renders the product defective with respect to the risks sought to be reduced by the statute or regulation; and

(b) a product's compliance with an applicable product safety statute or administrative regulation is properly considered in determining whether

---

[199] Bailey v. V & O Press, 770 F.2d 601, 607–09 (6th Cir. 1985 (applying Ohio law). *See also* Harsh v. Petroll & Hac, 840 A.2d 404 (Pa. 2003).

[200] *See* N.D. Cent. Code § 28-01.3-09. Wisconsin legislation provides that, in actions based on strict liability, "[e]vidence that the product, at the time of sale, complied with material respects with relevant standards, conditions, or specifications adopted or approved by federal or state law or agency shall create a rebuttable presumption that the product is not defective." Wis. Stat. Ann. § 895.047(3)(b). *See* Ind. Code § 34-20-5-1 and Wade v. Terex-Telelect, Inc., 966 N.E.2d 186 (Ind. Ct. App. 2012).

[201] 263 P.3d 1191 (Utah Ct. App. 2011).

[202] Utah Code Ann. § 78B-6-703(2). This section states: "There is a rebuttable presumption that a product is free from any defect or defective condition where the alleged defect in the plans or designs for the product or the methods and techniques of manufacturing, inspecting and testing the product were in conformity with government standards established for that industry which were in existence at the time the plans or designs for the product or the methods and techniques of manufacturing, inspecting and testing the product were adopted."

[203] *Id.* at 1194.

[204] *Id.* at 1195.

[205] *Id.* at 1199.

the product is defective with respect to the risks sought to be reduced by the statute or regulation, but such compliance does not preclude as a matter of law a finding of product defect.[206]

[B] Government Standards and the Pharmaceutical Industry

One industry that has received special attention from a few states for compliance with government standards is the pharmaceutical industry. Six state legislatures have enacted or considered enacting laws that provide immunity or a limitation on damages to the manufacturers and seller of prescription drugs whose products comply with FDA standards.[207] The broadest of these laws is the one contained in a 1996 amendment to Michigan's products liability statute.[208]

> In a products liability action against a manufacturer or seller, a product that is a drug is not defective or unreasonably dangerous, and the manufacturer or seller is not liable, if the drug was approved for safety and efficacy by the United States food and drug administration, and the drug and labeling were in compliance with the United States food and drug administration's approval at the time the drug left the control of the manufacturer or seller. . . . This subsection does not apply if the defendant at any time before the event that allegedly caused the injury does any of the following:
>
> (a) Intentionally withholds or misrepresents to the United States food and drug administration information concerning the drug that is required to be submitted under the federal food, drug, and cosmetic act;
>
> (b) Makes an illegal payment to an official or employee of the United States food and drug administration for the purpose of securing or maintaining approval of the drug.[209]

Michigan law defines a "product liability action" as "an action based in a legal or equitable theory of liability brought for the death of a person or for injury to a person or damage to property caused by or resulting from the production of a product."[210]

---

[206] RESTATEMENT (THIRD) OF TORTS: PRODUCTS LIABILITY § 4 (1998).

[207] The Michigan statute (MICH. COMP. LAWS § 600.2946(5)) is discussed in the following paragraphs. The Texas statute, TEX. CIV. PRAC. & REM. CODE § 82.007, applies to failure to warn cases. See Murthy v. Abbott Laboratories, 847 F. Supp. 2d 958 (S.D.Tex. 2012) (applying Texas law). The New Jersey statute (N.J. STAT. ANN. § 2A:15-5.14(b)) prohibits punitive damages if the drug was approved by the FDA. Similar legislation also has been proposed in Georgia, North Carolina, and Wisconsin.

[208] MICH. COMP. LAWS § 600.2946. For a discussion of the reasons for the law, see Garcia v. Wyeth-Ayerst Labs., 385 F.3d 961, 967 (6th Cir. 2004) (applying Michigan law).

[209] MICH. COMP. LAWS § 600.2946(5). The constitutionality of this amendment was upheld in Taylor v. Smithkline Beecham Corp., 658 N.W.2d 127 (Mich. 2003).

[210] Id. at § 600.2945(h).

The scope of the Michigan statute is illustrated by *White v. SmithKline Beecham Corp.*,[211] in which the parents of an adolescent who committed suicide after taking the anti-depressant drug Paxil filed suit against the drug's manufacturer. In 1992, the FDA approved Paxil for treating depression in adult patients. However, Paxil never was approved by the FDA for use by children or adolescents. Studies conducted by the manufacturer showed that Paxil was ineffective for the treatment of depression in children and adolescents and was associated with an increased risk of suicide. However, the manufacturer told its sales representatives that Paxil was safe for the treatment of adolescent depression but did not tell them of the risk of suicide. In 2003, the FDA recommended that Paxil not be prescribed to children or adolescents and a year later requested that the manufacturer place a black-box warning on the label regarding the risks. The manufacturer complied with the request. However, in *White*, the plaintiff's 16-year-old daughter committed suicide in 2001, four years before the manufacturer placed a warning on the label.[212]

The central issue for the federal court in *White* was whether the plaintiffs could maintain their claim alleging negligence, strict liability, breach of express warranty, and fraud on the basis that, since the FDA never approved the use of Paxil for children or adolescents, the immunity provided by the Michigan statute did not apply.[213] Although the plaintiffs admitted that Paxil had been approved for adults and that the drug complied with FDA labeling requirements, they alleged that the manufacturer had attempted to influence physicians to prescribe Praxil "off-label" for adolescents. The court, however, held that the plaintiff had not provided any evidence that the FDA had found fraud or bribery within the first of the two exceptions to the Michigan statute.[214] The plaintiffs also argued that the statute did not apply since the FDA had never approved the use of Paxil by children and adolescents. However, the court interpreted the statute as providing immunity to drug manufacturers for products approved by the FDA. Since, the statute does not limit the immunity to situations where the drug is used for its approved purposes, the court concluded that it was up to the legislature to limit the protection available to "off-label" uses of a drug.[215]

[C] Industry Standards

In addition to government safety regulations, there are numerous industry standards for the design and use of products.[216] Compliance with these standards and with the custom in the industry is an issue in design defect cases more often than those involving manufacturing defects and the failure to warn. Although industry standards and custom do not have the force of law, courts tend to treat

---

[211] 538 F. Supp. 2d 1023 (W.D. Mich. 2008) (applying Michigan law).

[212] *Id.* at 1025–26.

[213] *Id.* at 1026.

[214] *Id.* at 1029–39.

[215] *Id.* at 1030. *See also* Attorney General v. Merck Sharp & Dohme Corp., 807 N.W.2d 343 (Mich. Ct. App. 2011) (application for leave to appeal to the Michigan Supreme Court was denied (803 N.W.2d 696 (Mich. 2011)).

[216] Among these are the American National Standards Institute (ANSI) codes and the Underwriter Laboratories (UL) Standards.

them in the same way that they do government standards. Thus, in a negligence case, if the manufacturer did not comply with an industry standard for the design of the product, the trier of fact may find that it breached its duty of care to the plaintiff. Conversely, manufacturers introduce evidence of their compliance with industry standards and custom in the hope of showing that they acted like reasonable manufacturers in the selection of the design and thus met the requirement of due care.[217] However, as with government regulations, compliance with industry standards and custom, while evidence of what is the reasonable standard in the industry in negligence cases, does not establish conclusively that the standard of care the manufacturer is expected to meet.[218] If an industry has adopted careless methods, it is not permitted to set its own uncontrolled standard.[219] Similarly, although compliance with industry standards is used in negligence cases, is not admissible in strict liability cases[220] Finally, Pennsylvania takes the position that evidence of compliance with industry standards injects negligence concepts into strict liability where the focus is on the product and not on the manufacturer's conduct.[221]

§ 9.06 PREEMPTION

[A] Introduction

In 2000 a group of peanut farmers in western Texas sprayed their crops with pesticide manufactured by Dow Agrosciences. Although the chemical killed the weeds, it also stunted the growth of their crops, resulting in millions of dollars in losses. The farmers notified Dow of their intent to sue for false advertising, breach of warranty, and frzuau8lent trade practices under the Texas Deceptive Trade Practices Act (DTPA), on the grounds that they were misled by the retailers of the pesticide and were not warned that it was harmful in soils with high pH levels. In response, Dow filed a declaratory judgment action in federal court, asserting that the farmers' claims expressly or impliedly were pre-empted by the Federal Insecticide, Fungicide, and Rodenticide Act (FIFRA).[222] The farmers then counterclaimed, alleging strict liability, negligence, fraud, breach of warranty, and

---

[217] Wade v. Terex-Telelect, Inc., 966 N.E.2d 186 (Ind. Ct. App. 2012); Bragg v. Hi-Ranger, Inc., 462 S.E.2d 321 (S.C. Ct. App. 1995).

[218] Masters v. Hesston Corp., 291 F.3d 985 (7th Cir. 2002) (applying Illinois law); McKee v. Cutter Laboratories, Inc., 866 F.2d 219 (6th Cir. 1989) (applying Kentucky law); Condos v. Musculoskeletal Transplant Foundation, 208 F. Supp. 2d 1226 (D. Utah 2002) (applying Utah law); Dunn v. Wixom Brothers, 493 So. 2d 1356 (Ala. 1986); Howard v. Omni Hotels Management, Corp., 136 Cal. Rptr. 3d 739 (Ct. App. 2012).

[219] Jones v. Hutchinson Manufacturing, Inc., 502 S.W.2d 66, 70 (Ky. Ct. App. 1973).

[220] See Grimshaw v. Ford Motor Co., 174 Cal. Rptr. 348, 378 (Ct. App. 1981) ("In a strict products liability case, industry custom or usage is irrelevant to the issue of defect.").

[221] In Lewis v. Coffing Hoist Division, Duff-Norton Co., Inc., 528 A.2d 590 (Pa. 1987), the Pennsylvania Supreme Court held that the question of whether or not the defendant complied with industry standards improperly focuses on the quality of the defendant's conduct in making its design choice, and not on the attributes of the product itself. See Estate of Hicks v. Dana Companies, 984 A.2d 943 (Pa. Super. Ct. 2009).

[222] 7 U.S.C. § 136.

a violation of the Texas DTPA. The federal district court granted Dow's motion for summary judgment on the ground that the claims expressly were pre-empted by § 136v(b) of the FIFRA, which provides that states "shall not impose or continue to affect any requirements under this subchapter."[223] The Fifth Circuit affirmed, saying that the FIFRA overrides state laws that either directly or indirectly impose different labeling requirements.[224] In June 2004 the Supreme Court granted certiorari in the case and agreed to decide whether the farmers' claims of defective design, defective manufacture, negligent testing, and breach of express warranty were preempted by the FIFRA.[225]

Although the question of when a federal statute preempts state common law has become a frequent source of litigation and scholarly attention, it was not until 1992 that the Supreme Court began to address the issue in the context of products liability cases.[226] Because the decisions still are evolving, they are difficult to reconcile, making preemption the most confusing of all of the defenses in products liability cases. The basis of the power of the federal government to preempt state products liability laws is the Supremacy Clause of the Constitution, which provides that the "Constitution and the Laws of the United States . . . shall be the supreme Law of the Land; and the Judges in every State shall be bound thereby, any Thing in the Constitution or Laws of any State to the Contrary notwithstanding."[227] As a result, when a state law conflicts with a federal statute or regulations promulgated by a federal agency, the state law is "without effect.[228] However, the Supremacy Clause itself conflicts with the traditional powers of the states to regulate and to decide disputes involving their citizens. In an attempt to balance the Supremacy Clause with the concerns for state powers, the Supreme Court in 1947 instructed federal courts that state police powers were not to be superseded by federal law unless "that was the clear and manifest purpose of Congress.[229] Despite these concerns about interfering with state regulatory powers, a number of product-related federal statutes contain preemption provisions. Preemption clauses can be found in such diverse legislation as the Public Health Cigarette Smoking Act of 1969,[230] the Federal Hazardous Substances Act,[231] the Locomotive Inspection Act,[232] and the Medical Device Amendments to the Food, Drug and Cosmetic Act.[233] In recent years, courts also have sought to determine the extent to which the federal preemption provisions bar state common law products liability actions.

---

[223] Dow Agrosciences, LLC v. Bates, 205 F. Supp. 2d 623 (N.D. Tex. 2002).

[224] Dow Agrosciences, LLC v. Bates, 332 F.3d 323 (5th Cir. 2003).

[225] Bates v. Dow Agrosciences, LLC, 2004 U.S. LEXIS 4598 (June 28, 2004).

[226] Cipollone v. Liggett Group, Inc., 505 U.S. 504 (1992).

[227] U.S. CONST., art. VI. cl. 2.

[228] Maryland v. Louisiana, 451 U.S. 725, 746 (1981).

[229] Rice v. Santa Fe Elevator Corp., 331 U.S. 218, 230 (1947).

[230] 15 U.S.C. § 1334(b).

[231] 15 U.S.C. § 1261.

[232] 49 U.S.C. § 20701 et. seq.

[233] 21 U.S.C. § 360(k).

Federal preemption of state product liability cases would not be as controversial if it was limited to situations where Congress or a federal agency[234] clearly stated its express intent to preempt state law. However, in *Louisiana Public Service Commission v. FCC*,[235] the Supreme Court set out the three different ways in which a federal statute preempts a state law:

> Pre-emption occurs when Congress, in enacting a federal statute, expresses a clear intent to preempt state law, when there is outright or actual conflict between federal and state law, where compliance with both federal and state law is in effect physically impossible, where there is implicit in federal law a barrier to state regulation, where Congress has legislated comprehensively, thus occupying an entire field of regulation and leaving no room for the states to supplement federal law, or where the state law stands as an obstacle to the accomplishment and execution of the full objectives of Congress. Preemption may result not only from action taken by Congress itself; a federal agency acting within the scope of its congressionally delegated authority may preempt state regulation.[236]

Contained within the *Louisiana Public Service Commission* opinion are the three situations in which federal preemption applies in products liability cases: (1) where Congress expressly has preempted state action (express preemption); (2) where Congress has implemented a comprehensive regulatory scheme in an area, removing the entire field from state regulation (field preemption); or (3) where state action conflicts with federal law (conflict preemption).

[B] Express Preemption

When Congress chooses expressly to preempt state law, the question for courts is whether the challenged state law is one the federal statute intends to preempt. An example of statutory language designed to preempt state laws is § 136v(b) of Federal Insecticide, Fungicide, and Rodenticide Act[237] which provides that states "shall not impose or continue in effect any requirements for labeling or packaging in addition to or different from those required under this subchapter." The problem with this section for the Supreme Court in *Bates v. Dow Agrosciences*[238] was to determine the meaning of the term "requirements" imposed by a state. Some courts had held that "requirements" included only state legislative

---

[234] In an attempt to limit the amount of express preemption language originating from federal agencies, President Barak Obama, in a policy memorandum, stated that the "general policy of [this] administration [is] that preemption of state law by executive departments and agencies should be undertaken only with full consideration of the legitimate prerogatives of the state and with a sufficient legal basis for preemption." 74 Fed. Reg. 24693 (May 20, 2009).

[235] 476 U.S. 355 (1986).

[236] *Id.* at 368–69. *See* Lorillard Tobacco Co. v. Reilly, 533 U.S. 525, 541 (2001): "State action may be foreclosed by express language in a congressional enactment, by implication from the depth and breadth of a congressional scheme that occupies the legislative field, or by implication because of a conflict with a congressional enactment."

[237] 7 U.S.C. § 136.

[238] 544 U.S. 431 (2005).

"requirements,[239] while other courts interpreted the term to include common law tort claims as well.[240]

In *Cipollone v. Liggett Group, Inc.*,[241] the Supreme Court first confronted the issue of whether or not common law tort claims could be preempted expressly. In *Cipollone*, the Court found that the preemption provision in the Public Health Cigarette Smoking Act of 1969 was broad enough to preclude common law tort actions as well regulation by state statutes.[242] Lower courts faced with the task of construing preemption provisions similar or identical to the one in *Cipollone* also have found common law claims to be preempted.[243] However, in *Medtronic, Inc. v. Lohr*,[244] the Supreme Court held that the preemption provision in § 360(k) of the Medical Device Amendments to the Food, Drug and Cosmetic Act (FDCA)[245] bars state requirements with respect to medical devices that are different from or in addition to specific federal requirements, but does not preclude state common law actions based on a breach of the general duties imposed on every manufacturer of products placed in the stream of commerce.[246] The plaintiffs also argued that common law duties are never "requirements" within the meaning of section 360(k) and thus the section never preempts common law action. The Court did not respond directly to that argument for two reasons:

> First, since none of the . . . [plaintiff's] claims is pre-empted in this case, we need not resolve hypothetical cases. . . . Second, given the critical importance of device specificity in our (and the FDA's) construction of section 360K, it is apparent that few, if any, common-law duties have been preempted by this statute. It will be rare indeed for a court hearing a common-law cause of action to issue a decree that has 'the effect of establishing a substantive requirement for a specific device.' Until such a case arises, we see no need to determine whether the statute explicitly pre-empts such a claim.[247]

Thus, under *Cipollone* and *Medtronic*, Congress has the power expressly to preempt common law claims. However, courts must read the federal statute's preemption language with care to determine exactly which common law claims are preempted and which claims can stand.

---

[239] *See* Oja v. Howmedica, Inc., 111 F.3d 782 (10th Cir. 1997).

[240] *See* Martin v. Medtronic, Inc., 254 F.3d 573 (5th Cir. 2001); Kemp v. Medtronic, 231 F.3d 216 (6th Cir. 2000); Mitchell v. Collagen Corp., 126 F.3d 902 (7th Cir. 1997).

[241] 505 U.S. 504 (1992).

[242] *Id.* at 521–22.

[243] *See* Taylor AG Industries v. Pure-Gro, 54 F.3d 555 (9th Cir. 1995) (construing the Federal Insecticide, Fungicide, and Rodenticide Act); Busch v. Graphic Color Corporation, 662 N.E.2d 397 (Ill. 1996) (construing the Federal Hazardous Substances Act).

[244] 518 U.S. 470 (1996).

[245] 21 U.S.C. § 301 *et seq.*

[246] 518 U.S. at 500–02.

[247] *Id.* at 502–03.

It was against the backdrop of *Cipollone* and *Medtronic* that the Supreme Court decided *Bates v. Dow Agrosciences.*[248] The Court noted that, unlike the language in the *Cipollone* preemption clause, FIFRA's preemption clause prohibits only requirements that are "in addition to or different from" the labeling and packaging requirements of FIFRA.[249] The Court stressed that nothing in the statute "preclude[s] States from imposing different or additional *remedies*, but only different or additional *requirements.*"[250] Thus, it held that common law "rules that require manufacturers to design reasonably safe products, to use due care in conducting appropriate testing of their products, to market products free of manufacturing defects, and to honor their express warranties . . . do not qualify as requirements for 'labeling or packaging' "[251] and were not preempted. The Court explained that, although the defendant's express warranty was written on their label, the plaintiffs' cause of action for breach of warranty only sought to enforce the defendant's voluntary contractual commitment that was created when they made their warranty. However, that did not resolve all of the plaintiffs' claims. The Court said it had insufficient information to determine whether the Texas definition of fraud imposed a broader duty on the defendant than the requirement in FIFRA that labels cannot have false or misleading statements. If so, the Texas common law would, in fact, impose an additional requirement on the defendant. Thus, the Court remanded the plaintiffs' claims for fraud and negligent failure to warn to the court of appeals to determine whether or not Texas's common law duties were equivalent to the FIFRA misbranding standards.[252]

The Supreme Court has continued to look at the specific language in statutes to determine when Congress expressly intended to preempt common law claims. In *Altria Group, Inc. v. Good,*[253] the Court found that the Federal Cigarette Labeling and Advertising Act (FCLAA)[254] "does not pre-empt state-law claims . . . that are predicated on the duty not to deceive."[255] The Court stated that, when the text of a preemption clause is ambiguous, it should be read as disfavoring preemption.[256] It reasoned that, because the FCLAA's preemption clause speaks directly to state actions concerning "requirement[s] or prohibition[s] on smoking and health" — specifically state actions that preempt warnings — the FCLAA did not expressly preempt state law claims for fraud.[257]

In other cases, the Supreme Court has found that, where a federal statute has a clear express preemption clause, it preempts state law claims on the issue.[258] In

---

[248] 544 U.S. 431 (2005).

[249] *Id.* at 444.

[250] *Id.* at 448.

[251] *Id.* at 444.

[252] *Id.* at 453–54.

[253] 555 U.S. 70 (2008).

[254] 15 U.S.C. § 1331 *et seq.*

[255] 555 U.S. at 91.

[256] *Id.* at 77.

[257] *Id.* at 77–92.

[258] For an analysis of recent express, as well as implied, and conflict, preemption decisions by the

Riegel v. Metronic, Inc.,[259] a state tort claim for failure to warn, the Court (by an 8-1 vote) followed its earlier decision in *Medtronic, Inc. v. Lohr*, noting that the Medical Device Amendments to the Food, Drug, and Cosmetic Act bar state requirements with respect to medical devices that are different from or in addition to specific federal requirements.[260] In *Riegel*, Justice Antonin Scalia, writing for the Court, adhered to the view in *Lohr* that, for premarket approval of medical devices, "common-law causes of action for negligence and strict liability do impose [state level] 'requirement[s]'" and would be pre-empted by federal requirements specific to a medical device."[261] Similarly, in *Bruesewitz v. Wyeth*,[262] the Court (by a 6-2 vote) upheld an express preemption clause in the National Childhood Vaccine Injury Act (NCVIA) of 1986, which barred state law claims against drug manufacturers over the side effects of childhood vaccines.[263] Justice Scalia, again writing for the Court, interpreted the phrase "the Act expressly eliminates liability for a vaccine's unavoidable, adverse side effects" to include injury or death, which preempted any state law liability claims against the vaccine's manufacturer.[264]

[C]   Field Preemption

Even in the absence of explicit language in a federal statute intended to preempt state law on a subject, federal preemption still may be implied. Courts recognize that implied preemption takes two forms: field preemption and conflict preemption. Field preemption occurs when the "scheme of federal regulation [is] so pervasive as to make reasonable the inference that Congress left no room for the States to supplement it.'"[265] In deciding whether there is any room left for state regulation, courts look to the pervasiveness of the federal scheme of regulation, the federal interest at stake, and the danger of frustration of federal goals in making the determination as to whether a challenged state law can stand. Because of the need to show a scheme of comprehensive federal regulation that creates a reasonable inference that Congress has left no room for supplemental state regulation, field preemption is a difficult argument to make in products liability cases.[266]

Supreme Court, see Erwin Chemerinsky, *The New Preemption Landscape*, TRIAL, 52 (May 2011).

[259] 552 U.S. 312 (2008).

[260] *Id.* at 321–22.

[261] *Id.* at 323–24. For analysis of the Court's decision in *Riegel*, see In re Medtronic, Inc., Sprint Fidelis Leads Products Liability Litigation, 623 F.3d 1200 (8th Cir. 2010); Gross v. Stryker, 2012 U.S. Dist. LEXIS 34071 (W.D. Pa. Mar. 14, 2012).

[262] 131 S. Ct. 1068 (2011).

[263] *Id.* at 1082.

[264] *Id.* at 1074.

[265] Fidelity Federal Savings & Loan Association v. De la Cuesta, 458 U.S. 141, 153 (1982). *See* English v. General Electric Co., 496 U.S. 72 (1990); Rice v. Santa Fe Elevator Corp., 331 U.S. 218 (1947); Choate v. Champion Home Builders Co., 222 F.3d 788 (10th Cir. 2000).

[266] For an argument in support of extending field preemption to drug cases, see Richard A. Epstein, *The Case for Field Preemption of State Laws in Drug Cases*, 103 Nw. U. L. REV. 463 (2009). *See also* Paul E. Stinson, *Implied Field Preemption of Aviation Claims Under the Federal Aviation Act: How the Landscape is Changing*, 11 ISSUES IN AVIATION LAW AND POLICY 67 (2011).

Although field preemption is important in other areas of the law, it has not been the subject of extensive analysis in products liability cases. An example of a court finding no field preemption in a products liability case is *Pinney v. Nokia Inc.*,[267] in which the Fourth Circuit held that five class action lawsuits brought by plaintiffs who alleged they were exposed to unsafe levels of radio frequency radiation from using wireless telephones should be heard by the state courts where they originated, because there was no federal subject-matter jurisdiction. Although Congress enacted § 332 of the Federal Communications Act[268] to ensure the development of an infrastructure necessary to provide wireless services, the court said the Act does not occupy the legislative field of wireless communications so thoroughly as to create a reasonable inference that Congress meant to leave no room for the states to supplement it.[269]

A rare example of a federal statute that occupies an entire field of regulation in products liability cases is the Federal Locomotive Inspection Act (FLIA).[270] The precursor to the FLIA was the Locomotive Boiler Inspection Act. As early as 1926, the Supreme Court ruled, in *Napier v. Atlantic Coast Line Railroad Company*,[271] that Congress intended to occupy the entire field of locomotive regulation. The original Boiler Inspection Act only covered the boiler on a train's locomotive. The Supreme Court noted, however, that in 1915 the Act was modified to "include the entire locomotive and tender and all parts and appurtenances thereof."[272] This language, in conjunction with the authority given to for the Interstate Commerce Commission to "prescribe requirements and establish rules to secure compliance" convinced the Court that the Boiler Inspection Act, as amended, occupied the entire field of locomotive safety.[273] The Supreme Court revisited field preemption under the FLIA in *Kurns v. Railroad Friction Products Corp.*,[274] in which the plaintiffs' state law claims were based on design defect and failure-to- warn of asbestos in locomotive repair parts. The exposure to the asbestos occurred while the plaintiff worked as a welder in a locomotive repair shop. Relying on *Napier*, the Court held that Congress, through the FLIA, "intended to occupy the entire field of regulating locomotive equipment" which included both locomotive equipment and repair equipment in a repair shop or on the rail line, thus preempting the plaintiffs' state-law tort claims.[275]

---

[267] 402 F.3d 430 (4th Cir. 2005).

[268] 47 U.S.C. § 151 *et seq.*

[269] 402 F.3d at 459.

[270] 49 U.S.C. § 20701 *et seq.*

[271] 272 U.S. 605, 613 (1926).

[272] *Id.* at 608.

[273] *Id.* at 608–09.

[274] 132 S. Ct. 1261 (2012).

[275] *Id.* at 1267–68.

[D] Conflict Preemption

The most common form of implied preemption is conflict preemption. Conflict preemption occurs where a state law conflicts with a federal statute or regulation, or when the state law frustrates the purposes of Congress in enacting the legislation. The Supreme Court has explained that

> even where Congress has not completely displaced state regulation in a specific area, state law is nullified to the extent that it actually conflicts with federal law. Such a conflict arises when compliance with both federal and state regulations is a physical impossibility, or when state law stands as an obstacle to the accomplishment and execution of the full purposes and objectives of Congress.[276]

Thus, state regulations that have not been preempted explicitly by Congress still may be preempted. Such preemption will occur both when it is "a physical impossibility" to comply with both state and federal law, and when "the state law stands as an obstacle to the accomplishment of the full purposes and objectives of Congress."[277]

It is within implied conflict preemption, and specifically obstacle preemption, that the Supreme Court, in *Geier American Honda Motor Co.*,[278] held (by a 5-4 vote) that state tort suits for failure to provide airbags conflicted with the purposes of Federal Motor Vehicle Safety Standard 208 (FMVSS 208). FMVSS 208 was adopted by the Department of Transportation under the powers given to it by the National Traffic and Motor Vehicle Safety Act.[279] The Act contained a saving clause which provided that "compliance with a federal safety standard does not exempt any person from any liability under common law."[280] The Court held, however, that conflict preemption may exist even when Congress includes a saving clause so that state liability is not expressly preempted by the federal statute.[281] To hold otherwise, the Court said, would allow the law "to destroy itself."[282] The Court then considered the validity of the plaintiff's common law action, which sought to hold the defendant liable for failing to install air bags in its 1987 Honda Accord. The Court noted that the Department of Transportation enacted FMVSS 208 to encourage a gradual introduction of a variety of passive restraint systems into the marketplace. The plaintiffs' action, however, would have required all automobile manufacturers to install airbags in all of their automobiles in 1987. Such a requirement would have been "an obstacle to the variety and mix of devices that the federal regulation

---

[276] Hillsborough County v. Automated Med. Labs., 471 U.S. 707, 713 (1985).

[277] *Id.*

[278] 529 U.S. 861 (2000). *See* Susan Raeker-Jordan, *A Study in Judicial Sleight of Hand: Did Geier v. American Honda Motor Co. Eradicate the Presumption Against Preemption?* 17 BYU J. PUB. L. 1 (2002).

[279] 15 U.S.C. § 1381 *et seq.* (1988) (current version at 49 U.S.C. § 30101 *et seq.*).

[280] 529 U.S. at 868.

[281] *Id.* at 869.

[282] *Id.* at 872.

sought."[283] Thus, the Court ruled that the plaintiffs' action was preempted by FMVSS 208.[284]

The 1989 version of FMVSS 208 again was at the center of a conflict preemption case in *Williamson v. Mazda Motor of America*.[285] The question posed in the case was whether FMVSS 208, in requiring automobile manufacturers to install either simple lap belts or lap-and-shoulder belts on rear inner seats of passenger vehicles, preempted a state tort suit that, if successful, would have denied manufacturers a choice of seat belts by imposing tort liability on those who choose to install a simple lap belt.[286] In an 8-0 ruling (Justice Kagan did not participate in the decision), the Supreme Court held that FMVSS 208 did not preempt state tort law suits because the choice of the seat belt was not a significant objective of the federal legislation in the case, as opposed to *Grier*, where allowing the manufacturer to choose the passive restraint system installed in the vehicle was a key objective in the federal regulation.[287]

The Court in *Williamson* found that the Department of Transportation's (DOT) reasoning for giving manufacturers a choice on seat belts was very different from the choice the DOT gave manufacturers in *Grier*.[288] In *Grier*, the DOT was trying to get consumers to accept new passive restraint systems – airbags and automatic seatbelts – and giving manufacturers a choice of the restrain system they installed in their vehicles was an important objective of the regulation.[289] However, in *Williamson*, the DOT gave the manufacturers a choice of the type of seat-belt because the agency did not see a major difference in the two seat belts as safety concerns, allowing manufacturers to make their decision based upon a cost-based analysis of their options.[290] Finally, in *Williamson*, the Court noted that the DOT and the Solicitor General agreed that the agency's regulations did not preempt the state tort claim.[291]

The Food, Drug, and Cosmetic Act again was the basis of a preemption claim in *Wyeth v Levine*,[292] a case in which the plaintiff brought common law claims of negligence and strict liability in state court against Wyeth, the manufacturer of the drug Phenergan. The plaintiff received Phenergan through an IV-push in order to stop the side-effects of nausea from severe migraine. Typically, Phenergan is administered through an IV-drip, since an IV-push creates a risk of the drug entering an artery, which occurred in *Wyeth* and led to gangrene and the amputation of part of the plaintiff's arm.[293] The plaintiff alleged that Wyeth's

---

[283] *Id.* at 881.

[284] *Id.*

[285] 131 S. Ct. 1131 (2011).

[286] *Id.* at 1134.

[287] *Id.*

[288] *Id.* at 1137.

[289] *Id.* at 1136–37.

[290] *Id.* at 1138–39.

[291] *Id.* at 1139.

[292] 555 U.S. 555 (2009).

[293] *Id.* at 559.

labeling was defective because it did not warn of the dangers of gangrene and amputation if the drug came in contact with an artery and "failed to instruct clinicians to use the IV-drip method . . . instead of the higher risk IV-push method."[294] Wyeth argued that the plaintiff's state tort claims were preempted because it was impossible for the company to comply both with state laws and with the FDCA.[295] This raised the question whether federal regulations set the minimum standards that states are free to raise or whether federal regulations make judgments about the optimal balance between risks and benefits that states must follow.

In *Wyeth*, a Vermont jury awarded the plaintiff $6 million in damages and the state supreme court upheld the verdict against the drug company. The United States Supreme Court (by a 6-3 vote) affirmed the Vermont Supreme court and held that federal law did not preempt the plaintiff's state-law claim that Wyeth's labeling of Phenergan failed to warn of the dangers of its intravenous administration. The majority rejected Wyeth's argument that, by unilaterally changing its labeling of Phenergan, it would have violated federal labeling regulations since the FDA only sets the floor for the minimum required labeling.[296] The Court noted that the drug manufacturer bears the primary responsibility to label adequately its product and the FDCA allows the manufacturer to update the labeling without FDA approval.[297] The Court also rejected Wyeth's argument that requiring it to comply with the state-law duty to provide a stronger warning would interfere with Congress' purpose of entrusting the FDA with drug labeling decisions. The Court reasoned that Congress did not intend to preempt state-law failure to warn actions when it created the Food, Drug, and Cosmetic Act.

In *Wyeth* the manufacturer also argued that the intent of Congress was that the FDCA expressly preempt any state tort law claims against manufacturers.[298] However, the Supreme Court also rejected that argument, noting that, in the 70-year history of the FDCA, Congress never had enacted an express preemption provision for prescription drugs and that it specifically chose not to when it enacted an express preemption clause for medical devices but not for prescription drugs.[299]

The Supreme Court's most recent conflict preemption decision is *Pliva, Inc. v. Mensing*,[300] in which the Court refused to extend its holding in *Wyeth* to generic drugs. The issue in *Pliva* centered on the generic version of a brand-name drug and the different labeling regulations that affect generic manufacturers.[301] Generic drug manufacturers' warning labels must be the same as the brand-name's label. The FDA stated that generic manufacturers are not allowed to unilaterally strengthen their warning labels because regulations require their labels to be the

---

[294] *Id.* at 560.

[295] *Id.* at 568.

[296] *Id.* at 571.

[297] *Id. See* Mason v. SmithKline Beecham Corp., 596 F.3d 387 (7th Cir. 2010).

[298] 555 U.S. at 573.

[299] *Id.* at 574.

[300] 131 S. Ct. 2567 (2011).

[301] *Id.* at 2574.

same as the brand-name manufacturers' label and the generic manufacturer would be in violation of the Hatch Waxman Amendments which control generic drug manufacturing, approval and labeling.[302] According to the Court, its decision in *Pliva* was not contrary to *Wyeth* since *Wyeth* involved a brand-name manufacturer who could "unilaterally strengthen its warning without prior FDA approval" and thus be in compliance with both state and federal law at the same time.[303] However, in *Pliva*, the generic drug manufacturer could not satisfy state law claims because the Hatch Waxman Act barred generic drug manufacturer from changing its labels and thus preempted the plaintiff's state law claims.

Because federal preemption provides immunity from liability to companies whose products cause injury, death, or property harm, it has become one of the most controversial issues in products liability law. Supporters of preemption based on their arguments on three grounds: it is better to give regulatory decisions to government agencies that have the expertise than to lay juries; uniform standards are preferable to 50 different standards; and the uncertainty of attempting to comply with numerous different state standards. However, critics reply that if preemption is interpreted too broadly, cases are taken away from juries and consumers go uncompensated, which conflicts with the tradition of corrective justice.[304] Because of the stakes involved and because there are so many facets to preemption — express, field, and conflict, inconsistent results and continuing debate will remain the norm for many more years as lower courts and the Supreme Court struggle to determine the scope of specific federal legislation and agency regulations.

---

[302] *Id.* at 2574–75.

[303] *Id.* at 2581.

[304] *See* Thomas O. McGarity, The Preemption War (2008).

Chapter 10

DAMAGES

SYNOPSIS

§ 10.01 INTRODUCTION

§ 10.02 COMPENSATORY DAMAGES

    [A]   Damages for Personal Injury

        [1]   General Damages and Special Damages

        [2]   Present Cash Value

        [3]   Collateral Source Rule

        [4]   Loss of Consortium

    [B]   Damages for Pain and Suffering

    [C]   Damages for Emotional Distress

        [1]   The Impact Rule

        [2]   Medical Monitoring

        [3]   Bystanders

    [D]   Limitations on Noneconomic Damages

    [E]   Wrongful Death and Survival Actions

    [F]   Damage to Property

§ 10.03 ECONOMIC LOSS DOCTRINE

§ 10.04 PUNITIVE DAMAGES

    [A]   Introduction

    [B]   Conduct and Standard of Proof Required for Punitive Damages

    [C]   Statutory Controls on Punitive Damage Awards

    [D]   The Constitutionality of Punitive Damages

§ 10.05 PRE-JUDGMENT AND POST-JUDGMENT INTEREST

§ 10.06 JOINT AND SEVERAL LIABILITY

§ 10.01 INTRODUCTION

The goal of plaintiffs in products liability actions is to recover compensation for the personal injury and/or property damage they have suffered, and may suffer in the future, as the result of defective products. As in all cases involving personal injury and property damage, there are two broad categories of damages plaintiffs may recover in products liability lawsuits: compensatory and punitive. The goal of compensatory damages is to compensate plaintiffs not only for their medical expenses, lost wages, and damage or destruction of property but also for their non-economic injuries, such as pain and suffering, loss of enjoyment of life, and emotional distress. However, if the only loss a plaintiff suffers is the damage or destruction of the product itself or economic loss from the failure of the product to perform as expected, the economic loss doctrine limits recovery to an action for breach of warranty.[1] Since defective products sometimes also cause death, the beneficiaries of a decedent may seek compensation for their economic and non-economic losses under a wrongful death statute. Finally, punitive damages are available in certain products liability actions as a means of punishing manufacturers or sellers for misrepresentation or for conduct that showed a reckless disregard for the safety of others.

§ 10.02 COMPENSATORY DAMAGES

The purpose of compensatory damages is to reimburse the plaintiff for losses caused as a result of the defendant's tortuous conduct. This goal is an integral part of all of the sections of the Restatements governing products liability. Sections 388–390, 392, 395, 397, 398 of the Restatement (Second) of Torts, which deal with the liability in negligence of persons who supply goods for the use by others, state that a supplier is liable for the "physical harm" caused by its product. The comments to those sections make it clear that "physical harm" includes both bodily harm and property damage. Similarly, § 402A provides that the seller of a defective product in a strict liability action is liable for the "physical harm . . . caused to the ultimate user or consumer, or to his property." Finally, § 1 of the Restatement (Third) states: "One engaged in the business of selling or otherwise distributing products who sells or distributes a defective product is subject to liability for harm to persons or property caused by the defect."[2] Although all of the Restatement sections allow an injured person to recover damages for personal injury and property damage, they do not discuss the specific types and amount of the damages that a plaintiff can recover. Those issues are left to the legislatures and to the courts to determine.

[A] Damages for Personal Injury

[1] General Damages and Special Damages

In a products liability action, the types of damages a plaintiff may recover for personal injury and the principles governing their recovery are the same as those in all breach of contract and tort lawsuits. However, the specific categories of those damages vary from state to state.[3] One example of the range of compensatory

---

[1] Because damages for breach of warranty are covered in Chapter 2, this chapter will discuss only damages brought under the theories of negligence and strict liability.

[2] Comment *d* to § 1 of the Restatement (Third) states that the section "applies only to harm to persons or property." Economic loss is governed by § 21 of the Restatement (Third).

[3] One category of damages that varies among the states is "loss of enjoyment of life" or "hedonic damages." These damages are meant to compensate a plaintiff for the loss of enjoyment of activities that he or she once valued but can no longer participate in because of the injuries, such as the inability to continue participating in organized sports. States often include such damages as part of loss of

damages for personal injuries is contained in the Illinois Pattern Jury Instructions[4] which, in the appropriate situation, permits a plaintiff to recover for a broad range of damages for personal injury. These include:

- The disfigurement resulting from the injury.[5]

- The disability experienced (and reasonably certain to be experienced in the future) or the loss of normal life experienced (and reasonably certain to be experienced in the future).[6]

- The increased risk of future harm resulting from the injury.[7]

- Shortened life expectancy.[8]

- The pain and suffering experienced (and reasonably certain to be experienced in the future) as a result of the injuries.[9]

- The emotional distress experienced (and reasonably certain to be experienced in the future).[10]

- The reasonable expense of necessary medical care, treatment, services received (and the present cash value of the reasonable expenses of medical care, treatment, and services reasonably certain to be received in the future).[11]

- The value of (time) (earnings) (profit) (salaries) (benefits) lost and the present cash value of the (time) (earnings) (profits) (salaries) (benefits) reasonably certain to be lost in the future.[12]

- The reasonable expense of necessary help which has been required as a result of the injury (and the present cash value of such expense reasonably certain to be required in the future).[13]

Traditionally, courts have divided compensatory damages into two broad categories — general damages and special damages — each with their own pleading and proof requirements. General damages are difficult to calculate because they are noneconomic damages. They include disfigurement, disability, pain and suffering,

---

enjoyment of life or pain and suffering. However, most states do not recognize hedonic damages as a separate category of damages. For a discussion of hedonic damages, see Frontier Ins. Co. v. Blaty, 454 F.3d 590 (6th Cir. 2006) (applying Michigan law); Flowers v. Lea Power Partners, 2012 U.S. Dist. LEXIS 67359 (D.N.M. Apr. 2, 2012) (applying New Mexico law); Matlock v. Greyhound Lines, Inc., 2010 U.S. Dist. LEXIS 92359 (D. Nev. Aug. 10, 2010) (applying Nevada law).

[4] ILLINOIS PATTERN JURY INSTRUCTIONS (CIVIL) (2012 ed.).

[5] *Id.* at No. 30.04.

[6] *Id.* at No. 30.04.01.

[7] *Id.* at No. 30.04.03.

[8] *Id.* at No. 30.04.05.

[9] *Id.* at No. 30.05.

[10] *Id.* at No. 30.05.01.

[11] *Id.* at No. 30.06.

[12] *Id.* at No. 30.07.

[13] *Id.* at No. 30.09.

and emotional distress.[14] Since an objective monetary amount cannot be awarded for general damages, a plaintiff does not have to plead or prove a specific amount in order to recover. Special damages, on the other hand, are those economic losses that are a direct result of the injury. Special damages include the plaintiff's medical expenses (past and future), lost earnings and earning capacity (past and future), and the cost of repair or value of replacement of property that has been damaged or destroyed. Since it is possible to quantify these damages by presenting bills and receipts (or, in the case of future medical expenses or future lost wages, estimates with the help of expert testimony), the plaintiff must plead and prove their specific amount in order to recover.

An example of the types and amount of compensatory damages that a jury may award in a products liability suit is *Anderson v. Sears, Roebuck & Co.*,[15] in which the plaintiff's home was destroyed completely by a fire that was ignited by a defective heater. In addition to the property loss, the plaintiff and her infant daughter were burned severely, resulting in multiple permanent injuries to the daughter. The plaintiff brought suit against the manufacturer and the retailer of the heater. The jury returned a verdict in favor of the plaintiffs for $2 million. In response to a post-trial motion that the damages were excessive, the district court judge held that the award of $600,000 for the child's past physical and mental pain was not unreasonable.[16] The child suffered extensive burns over a large portion of her body that required a number of hospitalizations, four operations and skin grafts, and resulted in a number of infections including pneumonia. The judge felt that the most tragic aspect of the case was the mental and emotional trauma suffered by the child at an age that is crucial to a child's psychological and personality formation.[17] The judge also upheld the jury's award of:

$750,000 for the future physical and mental pain that the child would undergo;[18]

$250,000 for future medical expenses including lifetime treatment and counseling by plastic surgeons, psychiatrists and sociologists;[19]

$330,000 for the permanent loss of earning capacity;[20] and

up to $1,100,000 for permanent disability and disfigurement.[21]

---

[14] McGee v. AC & S, Inc., 933 So. 2d 770 (La. 2006).

[15] 377 F. Supp. 136 (E.D. La. 1974) (applying Louisiana law). See U-Haul Int'l., Inc. v. Waldrip, 322 S.W.3d 821 (Tex. App. 2010), in which a man suffered catastrophic injuries when a truck rented by his daughter rolled backwards, knocked him down, and rolled over him. Experts agreed the truck had an inoperable parking brake and damaged transmission, although they disagreed about the extent and cause. The Texas appellate court discussed and upheld an award of damages for lost earning capacity ($169,000), past and future medical expenses ($3 million), past and future physical impairment ($3 million), and disfigurement and past and future loss of consortium ($2.76 million).

[16] 377 F. Supp. at 138–39.

[17] *Id.*

[18] *Id.* at 139.

[19] *Id.*

[20] *Id.* at 139–40.

[21] *Id.* at 140.

[2] Present Cash Value

Personal injury awards usually are paid to a plaintiff in a present lump-sum amount rather than in installments over a number of years. Because some types of special damages that a jury may award will not occur until a future date (i.e., future medical expenses, future wage losses), it is necessary for it to discount them to their "present cash value" in order to avoid giving the plaintiff a windfall.[22] This is because, due to inflation, money received in one year is worth more than the same dollar amount received 10 or 20 years in the future. "Present cash value" is defined in as "the sum of money needed now, which, when added to what that sum may reasonably be expected to earn in the future, will equal the amounts of the [expenses] [earnings] [benefits] at the times in the future when [the expenses must be paid] [or] [the earnings (benefits) would have been received]."[23]

Courts usually do not become involved in determining the actual present cash value of an award. It is for the parties to produce expert testimony, usually from economists, to project the total amount of those future economic damages for the trier of fact.[24] Since jury instructions usually do not state how inflation should be considered in projecting future losses or how to deal with anticipated future increases in the injured person's earnings, these also are matters for the parties and expert testimony in determining present value.[25] Finally, the parties must suggest to the trier of fact the appropriate percentage rate that should be used in discounting future damages. State statutes either are silent on this matter or are vague as to the amount. The Alaska statute, for example, speaks only of investment at "long-term future interest rates in the best and safest investments."[26]

[3] Collateral Source Rule

In a personal injury case, some of a plaintiff's economic losses, such as medical expenses and lost wages, may be covered by insurance policies, social security, workers' compensation, pension benefits, or the plaintiff's employer. However, under the "collateral source rule," a personal injury award may not be reduced or offset by the amount of any compensation that the injured person may receive from

---

[22] Fickle v. State of Nebraska, 735 N.W.2d 754 (Neb. 2007); Estate of Shinholster v. Annapolis Hospital, 685 N.W.2d 275 (Mich. 2004); Wagner v. Union Pacific R.R., 642 N.W.2d 821 (Neb. Ct. App. 2002). Some states hold that future damages for noneconomic damages such as pain and suffering, loss of a normal life, and loss of society are not reduced to present value. See L.G. v. United States, 2007 U.S. Dist. LEXIS 97232 (C.D. Cal. Sept. 5, 2007) (applying California law); Friedman v. C & S Car Service, 527 A.2d 871 (N.J. 1987).

[23] ILLINOIS PATTERN JURY INSTRUCTIONS (CIVIL) No. 34.02 (2012 ed.).

[24] In Jones & Laughlin Steel Corp. v. Pfeifer, 462 U.S. 523 (1983), the Supreme Court discussed the three major approaches used by courts in calculating present value: (1) simply adopting a below-market discount rate, (2) relying on market interest rates while permitting evidence of future price inflation, and (3) applying the "total offset" method. See Helpin v. Trs. of the Univ. of Pa., 10 A.3d 267 (Pa. 2010); Miller v. Pacific Trawlers, Inc., 131 P.3d 821 (Or. Ct. App. 2006); Stringham v. United Parcel Service, Inc., 536 N.E.2d 1292 (Ill. App. Ct. 1989). For an example of how an expert may establish the discount rate, see Lawson v. U.S., 454 F. Supp. 2d 373 (D. Md. 2006) (applying Maryland law in an action under the Federal Tort Claims Act).

[25] Culver v. Slater Boat Co., 722 F.2d 114 (5th Cir. 1983).

[26] ALASKA STAT. § 09.17.040(b).

a source other than the tortfeasor.[27] Instead, the plaintiff is entitled to recover the full amount of his provable damages, regardless of the amount of the compensation the person received, so long as the sources are unrelated to the defendant.[28] One purpose of the rule is to prevent the jury from being influenced or distracted in its determination of liability or damages by evidence that the plaintiff was receiving some form of compensation.[29] More importantly, there is a feeling that, if the defendant was responsible for the losses, it should not be relieved of paying compensation because the plaintiff had the foresight to purchase insurance or because some other source paid the plaintiff's expenses.[30]

As part of their tort reform legislation, more than half of the states have enacted legislation modifying the collateral source rule in limited circumstances or for certain types of cases or altering it for all personal injury cases.[31] Other states, however, have refused to change the rule of courts have struck down changes as unconstitutional.[32] The principle reason for this is a feeling that the plaintiff should not be compensated twice for the same injury. However, many of the states that have abolished or limited the collateral source rule provide that such evidence is not applicable to collateral benefits paid under federal programs, insurance policies paid for by the plaintiff, pensions, or where a right of subrogation exists.[33]

[4]　Loss of Consortium

Although most products liability suits involve a claims for compensation by the person who was injured by the defective product, states also permit the spouse of an injured person to recover for loss of consortium.[34] Loss of consortium is an injury to the marital relationship and damages are intended to compensate the spouse for a broad range of losses. The scope of loss of consortium varies among the states and can include such elements as (1) loss of love and affection, (2) loss society and companionship, (3) impairment of sexual relations, (4) loss of performance of marital services, (5) loss of financial support, (6) loss of aid and assistance, and (7)

---

[27]　Oden v. Chemung County Industrial Development Agency, 661 N.E.2d 142 (N.Y. 1995).

[28]　Lawson v. U.S., 454 F. Supp. 2d 373 (D. Md. 2006) (applying Maryland law in an action under the Federal Tort Claims Act).

[29]　Simmons v. Hoegh Lines, 784 F.2d 1234 (5th Cir. 1986); Scott v. Garfield, 912 N.E.2d 1000 (Mass. 2009).

[30]　Volunteers of Amer. Colorado Branch v. Gardenswartz, 242 P.3d 1080 (Colo. 2010); Hutchings v. Childress, 895 N.E.2d 520 (Ohio 2008); Helfend v. Southern California Rapid Transit Dist., 465 P.2d 61 (Cal. 1970).

[31]　See Graff v. Robert M. Swendra Agency, Inc., 800 N.W.2d 112 (Minn. 2011), for a discussion of the Minnesota statute.

[32]　For a list of states that have limited, abolished, or retained the collateral source rule, see Rebecca Levenson, Comment: *Allocating the Costs of Harm to Whom They Are Due: Modifying the Collateral Source Rule After Health Care Reform*, 160 U. Penn. L. Rev. 921, 926, ns. 21–23 (2012).

[33]　*See, e.g.,* Alaska Stat. § 9.17.070 and Or. Rev. Stat. § 2315.20. *See* White v. Jubitz Corp., 219 P.3d 566 (Or. 2009); Fickle v. State, 735 N.W.2d 754 (Neb. 2007).

[34]　*See* Baughn v. Eli Lilly & Co., 356 F. Supp. 2d 1177 (D. Kan. 2005) (applying Kansas law); Lillebo v. Zimmer, Inc., 2005 U.S. Dist. LEXIS 2563 (D. Minn. Feb. 16, 2005) (applying Minnesota law); Timms v. Verson Allsteel Press Co., 520 F. Supp. 1147 (N.D. Ga. 1981) (applying Georgia law); Schreiner v. Fruit, 519 P.2d 462 (Alaska 1974).

loss of fidelity caused by the injury.[35] Although spouses may recover for loss of their consortium and for the consortium of their children,[36] the majority of states refuse to permit children to recover for loss of consortium of a parent in personal injury cases.[37] The courts have given a number of reasons for their position: (1) uncertainty as to the scope of the class of plaintiff to whom the action would be available; (2) the additional economic burden placed on the public; (3) fear of multiplicity of lawsuits; (4) the difficulty in assessing damages; (5) the possibility of double recovery; and (6) the feeling that the issue is one for the legislature to resolve.[38]

[B] Damages for Pain and Suffering

The categories of special damages are capable of exact measurement or of an estimate with the help of expert witnesses. The categories of general damages, however, are much more difficult to calculate since they involve noneconomic loss.[39] Because of the amounts that juries sometimes award, the most controversial category of noneconomic damages is pain and suffering.[40] The traditional arguments in favor of such damages are that they console the victim, indicate the victim's interest in the integrity of his or her person, and provide a fund from which to pay attorney fees. Since there is no objective standard by which a jury can

---

[35] Caskey v. Merrick Constr. Co., 86 So. 3d 186 (La. Ct. App. 2012). *See* Limone v. U.S., 497 F. Supp. 2d 143 (D. Mass. 2007) (applying Massachusetts law); Hutchings v. Childress, 895 N.E.2d 520 (Ohio 2008); Thompson v. Brown & Williamson Tobacco Corp., 207 S.W.3d 76 (Mo. Ct. App. 2006).

[36] For an analysis of the law involving filial consortium, see Limone v. U.S., 497 F. Supp. 2d 143 (D. Mass. 2007) (applying Massachusetts law) (dependent minor child); Hancock v. The Chattanooga Hamilton County Hosp. Auth., 54 S.W.3d 234 (Tenn. 2001). *See also* Adams v. U.S.A., 669 F. Supp. 2d 1203 (D. Mont. 2009) (applying Montana law); Maggard v. Pemberton, 897 N.E.2d 1168 (Ohio Ct. App. 2008); Allemand v. Discovery Homes, Inc., 38 So. 3d 1183 (La. Ct. App. 2010).

[37] For cases rejecting a cause of action by a child for the loss of a parent's consortium, see Kirkland v. Sam's East, Inc., 411 F. Supp. 2d 639 (D.S.C. 2005) (applying South Carolina law); Riley v. Keenan, 967 A.2d 868 (N.J. Super. App. Div. 2009). Illinois does not recognize a cause of action for a child's loss of a parent's society due to a nonfatal injury. Hanks v. Cotler, 959 N.E.2d 728 (Ill. App. Ct. 2011). For examples of states that permit a child to recover for their loss of parental consortium in personal injury cases, see Simmons v. Christus Schumpert Med. Cntr., 71 So. 3d 407 (La. Ct. App. 2011); U-Haul Int'l., Inc. v. Waldrip, 322 S.W.3d 821 (Tex. App. 2010).

[38] *See* Jennifer C. Parker, *Comment: Torts-*Taylor v. Beard: *The Tennessee Supreme Court Declines Adoption of a Cause of Action for Loss of Parental Consortium in Personal Injury Cases*, 34 U. Mem. L. Rev. 737 (2004).

[39] Tennessee defines "noneconomic damages" to include "physical and emotional pain; suffering; inconvenience; physical impairment; disfigurement; mental anguish; emotional distress; loss of society, companionship and consortium; injury to reputation; humiliation; noneconomic effects of disability, including loss of enjoyment of normal activities, benefits and pleasures of life and loss of mental or physical health, well-being or bodily functions; and all other nonpecuniary losses of any kind or nature." Tenn. Code Ann. § 29-39-101(2).

[40] In McDougald v. Garber, 536 N.E.2d 372, 374–75 (N.Y. 1989), the New York Court of Appeals stated: "An economic loss can be compensated in kind by an economic gain; but recovery for non-economic losses such as pain and suffering and loss of enjoyment of life rests on the 'legal fiction that money damages can compensate for a victim's injury.' We accept this fiction, knowing that although money will neither ease the pain nor restore the victim's abilities, this device is as close as the law can come in its effort to right the wrong. We have no hope of evaluating what has been lost, but a monetary award may provide a measure of solace for the condition created."

determine the "value" of a plaintiff's pain and suffering, and since witnesses may not express their subjective opinion on the matter, some courts permit counsel for the plaintiff and the defendant to suggest to the jury a total amount of damages for the pain the plaintiff has suffered in the past and is likely to suffer in the future.[41] The problem with this method, however, is that there is no objective basis for such any suggestion because the "value" of the pain and suffering is only an estimate by both sides.

In order to provide the jury some guidance in determining the damages for pain and suffering, about half of the states permit a plaintiff's attorney to "suggest" to the jury that the plaintiff's damages for pain and suffering be measured in terms of a specific dollar amount for a specific period of time.[42] This method, known as the *"per diem"* or *"unit-of-time"* approach, asks the jury to think about the plaintiff's injury in terms of "$x" per day. The jury then is asked to multiply that amount by the number of days of the plaintiff's pain and suffering.[43] In making its determination, the jury can consider evidence of the plaintiff's age and life expectancy.

Many states prohibit use of the *per diem* approach to calculate damages for pain and suffering.[44] In *Caley v. Manicke*,[45] the Illinois Supreme Court held that although it is permissible, during closing arguments, for counsel to suggest to the jury a total amount to compensate for pain and suffering, it is improper for counsel to suggest a formula, such as an award of a specific sum *per diem* to calculate those damages.[46] The court held that pain and suffering has no commercial value to which a jury can refer in determining damages and that the *per diem* approach produces an illusion of certainty.[47] According to the court, the *per diem* formula, rather than encouraging reasonable and practical consideration, tends to discourage such consideration.

Whether a court uses the *per diem* method or permits counsel to suggest a total amount of damages for pain and suffering, the determination of such damages is left to the jury so long as there is adequate believable evidence to support the

---

[41]   *See* Allison v. Stalter, 621 N.E.2d 977 (Ill. App. Ct. 1993).

[42]   Debus v. Grand Union Stores, 621 A.2d 1288 (Vt. 1993); Vanlandingham v. Gartman, 367 S.W.2d 111 (Ark. 1963); Jones v. Hogan, 351 P.2d 153 (Wash. 1960).

[43]   For a discussion of the per diem approach for arguing damages for pain and suffering, see Faught v. Washam, 329 S.W.2d 588, 601–04 (Mo. 1959). For examples of the per diem approach, see Westbrook v. General Tire & Rubber Co., 754 F.2d 1233 (5th Cir. 1985); Worsley v. Corcelli, 377 A.2d 215 (R.I. 1977); Jones v. Hogan, 351 P.2d 153 (Wash. 1960); Giant Food Inc. v. Satterfield, 603 A.2d 877 (Md. Ct. Spec. App. 1992).

[44]   According to the Minnesota Supreme Court, "no amount of money per day could compensate a plaintiff reduced to plaintiff's position, and to attempt such evaluation . . . leads only to monstrous verdicts." Ahlstrom v. Minneapolis, St. Paul & Sault Ste. Marie RR, 68 N.W.2d 873, 891 (Minn. 1955). The use of mathematical formulas in calculating pain and suffering damages also was rejected by California's Supreme Court in Beagle v. Vasold, 417 P.2d 673 (Cal. 1966). *See also* Matter of New York Asbestos Litigation, 812 N.Y.S.2d 514 (App. Div. 2006); Meyers v. Southern Builders, Inc., 7 S.W.3d 507 (Mo. Ct. App. 1999).

[45]   182 N.E.2d 206 (Ill. 1962).

[46]   *Id.* at 208.

[47]   *Id.*

award. Expert testimony may be needed to support a plaintiff's claim that such damages are reasonably certain to occur in the future. In addition, a plaintiff can offer photographic evidence as proof of the nature and extent of the pain and suffering, as well as day-in-the-life videotapes.[48] Juries also may consider the plaintiff's own testimony and the testimony of family and friends about symptoms of pain and suffering they have witnessed in determining the amount of damages to award.[49]

[C] Damages for Emotional Distress

[1] The Impact Rule

Another form of noneconomic damages that plaintiffs may seek in products liability actions is emotional distress. Although plaintiffs occasionally allege intentional infliction of emotional distress,[50] most claims are based on negligent infliction of emotional distress. When the person who alleges negligent inflict of emotional distress was the user or consumer of the product, states follow the "impact rule" and require the person to establish that the emotional distress was caused by physical injury resulting from the defective product.[51] The reasons for the common law rule requiring physical injury as a prerequisite for an award for emotional distress were stated by the Texas Supreme Court:

> [M]ental anguish, standing alone, is too subtle and speculative to be measured by any known standard; mental anguish and its consequences are so intangible and peculiar and vary so much with the individual that they cannot reasonably be anticipated, hence they fall without the boundaries of any reasonably proximate causal connection with the act of the defendant; a "wide door" might thereby be opened not only to fictitious claims but to litigation over trivialities and mere bad manners as well; and finally, since mental anguish can exist only in the mind of the injured party, not only its extent but its very existence can be established only by the word of the injured party, in the absence of some objective injury.[52]

A number of emotional distress cases in products liability have resulted from finding foreign objects in food or drink products.[53] An example of what constitutes

---

[48] Bannister v. Noble, 812 F.2d 1265 (10th Cir. 1987) (applying Oklahoma law); Ellingwood v. Stevens, 564 So. 2d 932 (Ala. 1990); Jones v. City of L.A., 24 Cal. Rptr. 2d 528 (Ct. App. 1993).

[49] *See* Swift v. State Farm Mut. Auto. Ins. Co., 796 F.2d 120 (5th Cir. 1986) (applying Louisiana law); Delph v. Jenkins, 1987 Ohio App. LEXIS 8708 (Sept. 18, 1987).

[50] RESTATEMENT (SECOND) OF TORTS, § 46 (1965). For a case in which damages for intentional infliction of emotional distress were alleged, but were not successful, in a products liability suit, see Vietnam Association for Victims of Agent Orange/Dioxin v. Dow Chemical Co. (In re "Agent Orange" Products Litigation), 373 F. Supp. 2d 7 (E.D.N.Y. 2005).

[51] *See* Lewis v. CITGO Petroleum Corp., 561 F.3d 698 (7th Cir. 2009) (applying Illinois law); Ball v. Joy Technologies, Inc., 958 F.2d 36 (4th Cir. 1991) (applying Virginia and West Virginia law); Zeigler v. Fisher-Price, Inc., 261 F. Supp. 2d 1047 (N.D. Iowa 2003) (applying Iowa law).

[52] Harned v. E-Z Finance Co., 254 S.W.2d 81, 85 (Tex. 1953).

[53] *See* Palmer v. Nan King Restaurant, Inc., 798 A.2d 583 (N.H. 2002); Ellington v. Coca Cola Bottling Co., Inc., 717 P.2d 109 (Okla. 1986); Chambley v. Apple Restaurants, Inc., 504 S.E.2d 551 (Ga. Ct. App.

"physical injury" in those cases is *Kroger Co. v. Beck*,[54] in which the plaintiff was eating a piece of steak when she felt a sharp pain in the back of her throat. When she vomited, she found that it contained an inch-long piece of a hypodermic needle used for injecting animals. The Indiana appellate court affirmed an award of damages for her emotional distress even though the injury did not require medical treatment or cause permanent physical problems. According to the court, the award was justified by her physical reaction and anxiety over what could have happened if she had swallowed the needle and her resulting aversion to eating meat.

In recent decades, products liability cases have included claims of emotional distress from the threat or fear of future disease, such as AIDS or cancer. Although most courts refuse to permit recovery in the absence of present symptoms[55] or, in some cases, a "serious" or "reasonable probability" that the injury will occur,[56] some courts do permit recovery for emotional distress from the fear of contracting AIDS if the plaintiff can show actual exposure to the HIV virus.[57] Courts also deny recovery of damages for emotional distress for the fear of future injury from the use of a product. In *Khan v. Shiley Incorporated*,[58] the plaintiff, who was the recipient of an artificial heart valve, brought an action against the manufacturer of the valve alleging emotional and physical distress upon learning the valve was within a group being recalled due to a propensity to fracture. In denying relief from what the plaintiff described as, "the constant threat of imminent death or other serious physical injury and the anxiety, fear and emotional distress that results [from the defective valve],"[59] the California appellate court stated that, "a cause of action does not presently exist under any theory premised on the *risk* the valve *may* malfunction in the future."[60] The court held that, as long as the valve continued to function, the recipient stated no cause of action under strict liability, negligence, or breach of warranty.[61]

[2] Medical Monitoring

Because courts are reluctant to permit recovery for emotional distress caused by the fear of future disease or injury, plaintiffs who have been exposed to a product or a drug increasingly seek compensation for medical monitoring. A medical

---

1998); Way v. Tampa Coca Cola Bottling Co., 260 So. 2d 288 (Fla. Dist. Ct. App. 1972).

[54] 375 N.E.2d 640 (Ind. Ct. App. 1978).

[55] Metro-North Commuter Railroad Co. v. Buckley, 521 U.S. 424 (1997) (asbestos); Southern Bakeries, Inc. v. Knipp, 852 So. 2d 712 (Ala. 2002) (asbestos); Payton v. Abbott Laboratories, 437 N.E.2d 171 (Mass. 1982) (DES).

[56] *See* Gideon v. Johns-Manville Sales Corp., 761 F.2d 1129 (5th Cir. 1985) (applying Texas law); McCafferty v. Centerior Service Co., 983 F. Supp. 715 (N.D. Ohio 1997); Sullivan v. Combustion Engineering, 590 A.2d 681 (N.J. Super. Ct. App. Div. 1991).

[57] Johnson v. American National Red Cross, 578 S.E.2d 106 (Ga. 2003); Hagan v. Coca-Cola Bottling Co., 804 So. 2d 1234 (Fla. 2001).

[58] 266 Cal. Rptr. 106 (Ct. App. 1990).

[59] *Id.* at 108.

[60] *Id.* at 112.

[61] The court, however, reversed the grant of summary judgment for the manufacturer on the deceit count, saying that it was not dependent on the value malfunctioning. *Id.* at 112–13.

monitoring award covers the costs of periodic medical examinations to track the long-term effects of the plaintiff's use of a drug or medical device or exposure to chemicals.[62] In *Mauro v. Raymark*,[63] the plaintiff was unable to recover for the enhanced risk of contracting cancer due to exposure to asbestos because he did not present evidence establishing the future occurrence of cancer was a reasonable medical probability. The New Jersey Supreme Court, however, upheld the right of plaintiffs to recover medical surveillance expenses. In its opinion, the court discussed the reasons for permitting medical monitoring and the requirements that the plaintiff must establish.

> [W]e hold that the cost of medical surveillance is a compensable item of damages where the proofs demonstrate, through reliable expert testimony predicated upon the significance and extent of exposure to chemicals, the toxicity of the chemicals, the seriousness of the diseases for which individuals are at risk, the relative increase in the chance of onset of disease in those exposed, and the value of early diagnosis, that such surveillance to monitor the effect of exposure to toxic chemicals is reasonable and necessary. In our view, this holding is thoroughly consistent with our rejection of plaintiffs' claim for damages based on their enhanced risk of injury. That claim seeks damages for the impairment of plaintiffs' health, without proof of its likelihood, extent, or monetary value. In contrast, the medical surveillance claim seeks reimbursement for the specific dollar costs of periodic examinations that are medically necessary notwithstanding the fact that the extent of plaintiffs' impaired health is unquantified.[64]

Because medical monitoring can extend over a number of years, it can be expensive for defendants, particularly in class action suits or suits involving multiple plaintiffs. An example of this is *Burns v. Jaquays Mining Corp.*,[65] in which 56 residents of land adjacent to an asbestos-producing mill brought suit against the mill owner to recover for subclinical asbestos-related injuries. The residents, none of whom was diagnosed as having asbestosis, sought damages for the increased risk of developing cancer or other asbestos-related diseases and for the emotional distress caused by the knowledge and fear of these impending developments. The Arizona court held that subclinical asbestos-related injury was not sufficient to constitute the actual loss or damage required to support a cause of action. The court refused to award damages for the fear of contracting asbestos-related diseases in the future without some showing of bodily injury. However, the court awarded the

---

[62] For a discussion of medical monitoring, see Norwood v. Raytheon Co., 414 F. Supp. 2d 659 (W.D. Tex. 2006); Donovan v. Philip Morris USA, Inc., 914 N.E.2d 891 (Mass. 2009); Meyer *ex rel.* Coplin v. Fluor Corp., 220 S.W.3d 712 (Mo. 2007). However, in Metro-North Commuter R.R. v. Buckley, 521 U.S. 424 (1997), the Supreme Court held that a plaintiff exposed to asbestos could not recover for medical monitoring in an FELA case. Courts that have rejected medical monitoring include Parker v. Wellman, 2007 U.S. App. LEXIS 8805 (11th Cir. Apr. 18, 2007) (applying Georgian law) and Paz v. Brush Engineered Materials, Inc., 949 So. 2d 1 (Miss. 2007).

[63] 561 A.2d 257 (N.J. 1989).

[64] *Id.* at 263 (*quoting* Ayers v. Jackson Township, 525 A.2d 287, 312–13 (N.J. 1987). The Utah Supreme Court set out eight similar requirements that a plaintiff must prove to recover medical monitoring costs in Hansen v. Mountain Fuel Supply Co., 858 P.2d 970 (Utah 1993).

[65] 752 P.2d 28 (Ariz. Ct. App. 1987).

residents damages for "medical surveillance" of the development of cancer and other asbestos-related diseases. The court, citing policy considerations behind awarding such expenses, stated that such damages were:

> consistent with the important public health interest in fostering access to medical testing for individuals whose exposure to toxic chemicals creates an enhanced risk of disease. . . . The availability of a substantial remedy before the consequences of plaintiff's exposure have the beneficial effect of preventing or mitigating serious future illnesses and thus reduce the overall costs of the responsible parties.[66]

[3] Bystanders

States take a variety of approaches to determining when a bystander is entitled to recover damages for emotional distress resulting from witnessing the injury or death of a third person caused by a defective product. Most courts limit recovery to those bystanders who can prove that they were within the "zone of danger."[67] Under this standard, "a bystander who is in the zone of physical danger and who, because of the defendant's negligence, has reasonable fear for his own safety, is given a right of action for physical injury or illness resulting from emotional distress."[68] Although a bystander is not required to suffer physical impact or injury from the defective product, the bystander must have been in such proximity to the accident that there was a high risk that he or she would suffer physical impact.

Although the majority of states have adopted the zone of danger test for bystanders, some states have confined it to negligence and have not extended it to strict liability. In *Pasquale v. Speed Products Engineering*,[69] the plaintiff and his wife were watching an automobile race when parts from one of the cars flew into the stands, struck the wife, and killed her. Despite the plaintiff's severe emotional trauma at witnessing his wife's death, the Illinois Supreme Court held that fault is an indispensable element in an action for infliction of emotional distress. Since strict liability is not based upon fault, the court held that the manufacturer should not be liable for inflicting emotional distress.

Despite the limitation on recovery for emotional distress in *Pasquale*, about half of the states have moved beyond the "zone of danger" test and permit bystanders to recover for negligent infliction of emotional distress under a foreseeability test.[70]

---

[66] *Id.* at 33 (quoting from Ayers v. Township of Jackson, 525 A.2d 287, 311 (N.J. 1987). See Donovan v. Philip Morris USA, Inc., 914 N.E.2d 891 (Mass. 2009), permitting medical monitoring in a suit by smokers since the damage to their lungs created an increased risk of cancer.

[67] *See* Abbatiello v. Monsanto Co., 522 F. Supp. 2d 524 (S.D.N.Y. 2007) (applying New York law); Goodby v. Vetpharm, 974 A.2d 1269 (Vt. 2009); Perrotti v. Gonicberg, 877 A.2d 631 (R.I. 2005); Rickey v. Chicago Transit Authority, 457 N.E.2d 1 (Ill. 1983); Hedgepeth v. Whitman Walker Clinic, 22 A.3d 789 (D.C. 2011).

[68] Rickey v. Chicago Transit Authority, 457 N.E.2d 1, 5 (Ill. 1983).

[69] 654 N.E.2d 1365 (Ill. 1995).

[70] *See* Pearsall v. Emhart Industries, Inc., 599 F. Supp. 207 (E.D. Pa. 1984) (applying Pennsylvania law).

In *Dillon v. Legg*,[71] the California Supreme Court held that damages for mental distress could be recovered if the distress was a reasonably foreseeable result of the tortfeasor's conduct.[72] The court set out three factors to determine whether the injury was foreseeable:

(1) Whether the plaintiff was located near the scene of the accident as contrasted with one who was a distance away from it. (2) Whether the shock resulted from a direct emotional impact upon the plaintiff from the sensory and contemporaneous observance of the accident. (3) Whether plaintiff and the victim were closely related, as contrasted with an absence of any relationship or the presence of only a distant relationship.[73]

Although many states have adopted some form of the *Dillon* foreseeability guidelines for recovery for emotional distress of bystanders, few courts have had the opportunity to apply those guidelines in products liability cases. A case that did apply the *Dillon* test is *General Motors Corp. v. Burry*,[74] in which the three young daughters of a woman suffered severe brain damage as a result of an automobile accident sought compensation for the mental anguish they suffered as a result of witnessing the accident and their mother's injuries. Although Texas uses the Dillon test in claims for emotion distress brought by bystanders, the Texas court denied recovery, saying that there was no evidence that the girls experienced shock and direct emotional impact as a result of witnessing the injury to their mother at the time of the accident.[75]

Some courts have avoided the difficulties of choosing between the "zone of danger" test and the *Dillon* test by characterizing the plaintiff as a "user" of the product rather than as a "bystander." An example of this is *Gnirk v. Ford Motor Company*,[76] in which a child drowned when his mother's car rolled backwards as she was attempting to open a fence gate. The mother brought an action against Ford for the emotional distress of witnessing the death of her son caused by the allegedly defective park mechanism. She claimed the accident caused her great depression, insomnia, permanent psychological injury, and physical illness.[77] The district court viewed the mother as a "user" of Ford's product and not as a "bystander."[78] As such,

---

[71] 441 P.2d 912 (Cal. 1968). In *Dillon*, a mother was permitted to state a claim for emotional distress from witnessing the death of her child as a result of a motorist's alleged negligent driving. As a bystander, the mother was not in the "zone of danger" nor was she threatened personally with bodily harm. However, she allegedly that, as a result of witnessing the fatal accident, she "sustained great emotional disturbance and shock and injury to her nervous system which caused her great physical and mental pain and suffering." *Id.* at 914.

[72] *Id.* at 921.

[73] *Id.* at 920.

[74] 203 S.W.3d 514 (Tex. App. 2006). *See* Schmidt v. Boardman Co., 11 A.3d 924 (Pa. 2011); Walker v. Clark Equipment, 320 N.W.2d 561, 563 (Iowa 1982); Mansour v. Leviton Mfg. Co., 890 A.2d 336 (N.J. Super. Ct. App. Div. 2006).

[75] 203 S.W.3d at 547–48.

[76] 572 F. Supp. 1201 (D.S.D. 1983) (applying South Dakota law).

[77] *Id.* at 1202.

[78] *Id.*

Ford owed the mother an independent duty not to harm her.[79] In recognizing the fine line distinguishing physical from emotional injury, the court stated that Restatement (Second) of Torts § 436A, comment c,[80] was a reasonable guide for determining whether the mother suffered bodily injury proximately caused by emotional disturbance inflicted by Ford.[81] The court denied Ford's motion for summary judgment and remanded the case to determine whether the mother could make out a case on the issue of whether she sustained bodily injury proximately caused by the alleged emotional disturbance inflicted by Ford. If successful, the mother also would be entitled to recover damages for her emotional distress. However, few courts have followed the approach used in *Gnirk.*[82]

[D]   Limitations on Noneconomic Damages

Because of the uncertainty of noneconomic damages in general, and damages for pain and suffering in particular, more than half of the states have enacted some form of legislative limitation on such damages over the past three decades.[83] While many of these statutory caps on noneconomic damages apply only in medical malpractice cases,[84] a number of them apply in all cases, including products liability cases.[85] The form and amount of these limitations vary greatly. Some states, for example, simply place a limit on the total amount a plaintiff can recover for pain and suffering[86] or for all noneconomic damages in personal injury cases.[87]

---

[79] *Id.* at 1203.

[80] Restatement (Second) of Torts, § 436 A, comment c states:

[Emotional distress] accompanied by transitory, non-recurring physical phenomena, harmless in themselves, such as dizziness, vomiting, and the like, does not make the actor liable where such phenomena are in themselves inconsequential and do not amount to any substantial bodily harm. On the other hand, long continued nausea or headaches may amount to physical illness, which is bodily harm; and even long continued mental disturbance, as for example in the case of repeated hysterical attacks, or mental aberration, may be classified by the courts as illness, notwithstanding their mental character.

[81] 572 F. Supp. at 1204–05.

[82] For two other cases that treated the plaintiff as the "user" of the produce, see Bray v. Marathon Corp., 588 S.E.2d 93 (S.C. 2003); Kately v. Wilkinson, 195 Cal. Rptr. 902 (Ct. App. 1983). For a case that distinguished *Gnirk* and held that the plaintiff was not a "user," see Straub v. Fisher and Paykel Health Care, 990 P.2d 384 (Utah 1999).

[83] As of July 2012, at least 27 states had enacted limits on damages for pain and suffering. In at least 16 states, courts have held that the limits are constitutional.

[84] A 2005 Missouri statute, for example, limited noneconomic damages in medical malpractice cases to $350,000. Mo. Rev. Stat. § 538.210. However, the Missouri Supreme Court held the statute unconstitutional in Watts v. Lester E. Cox Med. Cntrs., 376 S.W.3d 633 (Mo. 2012). Other state caps in medical malpractice cases also have been struck down as violating state constitutions. *See* Broussard v. St. Edward Mercy Med. Cntr., 2012 Ark. 14; Atlanta Oculoplastic Surgery, P.C. v. Nestlehutt, 691 S.E.2d 218 (Ga. 2010); Lebron v. Gottlieb Mem'l. Hosp., 930 N.E.2d 895 (Ill. 2010); Ferdon v. Wisconsin Patients Compensation Fund, 2005 WI 125.

[85] For a discussion, in the context of a products liability case, of Ohio's general cap on noneconomic damages, see Arbino v. Johnson & Johnson, 880 N.E.2d 420 (Ohio 2007). The Ohio Supreme Court upheld the cap which was challenged on grounds of the right to a trial by jury, the open courts and right to a remedy provision of the Ohio constitution, due process, equal protection, separation of powers, and the single-subject rule of the state constitution.

[86] Kansas limits pain and suffering damages to $250,000 (Kan. Stat. Ann. § 60-19a01), while Hawaii

However, other states either have a variable limit or permit the amount of recovery for noneconomic damages to be raised in certain situations. Tennessee caps noneconomic damages at $750,000 for each "injured plaintiff," with the cap increased to $1,000,000 for "catastrophic loss/injury."[88] Idaho limits noneconomic damages to $400,000 with adjustments based on the state's average annual wage.[89] Colorado imposes a $250,000 cap on noneconomic damages but permits the court to increase the amount to $500,000 if it finds "clear and convincing evidence" to do so.[90] Alaska states that noneconomic damages may not exceed the greater of $400,000 or $8,000 times the years of the plaintiff's life expectancy. However, if the plaintiff suffers severe permanent injury, the amount increases to the greater of $1 million or $25,000 times the years of the plaintiff's life expectancy.[91] Ohio restricts noneconomic loss to $250,000 or three times the amount of economic loss, not to exceed $350,000 per plaintiff or $500,000 per occurrence. The Ohio cap is not applicable, however, in cases of catastrophic injury, which is defined as injury resulting in "permanent and substantial physical deformity, loss of use of a limb or loss of a bodily organ system"[92] or "a permanent physical functional injury that permanently prevents the injured person from being able to independently care for self and perform life sustaining activities."[93]

[E] Wrongful Death and Survival Actions

When a person is killed by a defective product, the claim for compensation must be brought under the state's wrongful death statute.[94] These statutes have been adopted in every state in response to the common law doctrine that a cause of action dies with the victim or the wrongdoer. As a result, no action for wrongful death can be brought outside of the statutes. Wrongful death actions raise difficult valuation problems and the amount of the award of damages varies from state to state.

A wrongful death action is brought by the personal representative of the deceased person in order to recover compensation for the economic and noneconomic losses suffered by the decedent's relatives as a result of the death.[95]

---

raises the limit to $375,000 (HAW. REV. STAT. § 663-8.7). *See* Samsel v. Wheeler Transportation Services, 789 P.2d 541 (Kan. 1990).

[87] Maryland limits all noneconomic damages in personal injury cases to $350,000 (MD. CODE ANN. CTS. & JUD. PROC. § 11-108), while Mississippi raises the limit to $1,000,000 in non-health care provider cases (MISS. CODE ANN. § 11-1-60).

[88] TENN. CODE ANN. §§ 29-39-102(a)(2) and 29-39-102(c)–(e).

[89] IDAHO CODE § 6-1603.

[90] COLO. REV. STAT. § 13-21-102.5.

[91] ALASKA STAT. § 9.17.010.

[92] OHIO REV. CODE ANN. § 2315.19(B)(3)(a).

[93] *Id.* at § 2315.19(B)(3)(b). *See* Arbino v. Johnson & Johnson, 880 N.E.2d 420 (Ohio 2007), upholding the constitutionality of the Ohio approach.

[94] For examples of wrongful death statutes, see DEL. CODE ANN. tit. 10, §§ 3721–3725; 740 ILL. COMP. STAT. 180/1-180/2.2; KY. REV. STAT. ANN. § 411.130; TENN. CODE ANN. § 20-5-113.

[95] For examples of products liability suits brought under wrongful death acts, see Rivera v. Philip Morris, Inc., 395 F.3d 1142 (9th Cir. 2005) (applying Nevada law); Palmer v. Volkswagen of America, Inc.,

The personal representative must bring the action for the benefit of a specific class of beneficiaries, usually limited to the surviving spouse,[96] children, parents, and siblings. There are two principal elements of compensation in a wrongful death action. The first is the reasonable expectation of the financial contributions the decedent would have made to the beneficiaries had he or she not died. This amount is based upon what the decedent earned in the past, the amount the decedent spent on his or her own personal expenses, what the decedent contributed to the beneficiaries in the past, and the earning capacity of the decedent. A court also may consider the decedent's age, heath, life expectancy, and habits of work and thrift in determining the amount he or she would have contributed to the beneficiaries.

In recent years, states have expanded the scope of recovery in wrongful death actions to include noneconomic items. A spouse, for example, is entitled to compensation for the loss of the society the deceased spouse would have contributed if he or she lived.[97] In addition, when the wrongful death involves a parent, the surviving children can recover the value of their parent's companionship, love, and affection.[98] If the decedent left young children, this also includes the value of the instruction, moral training, and supervision of education the decedent might have been expected to give the children had he or she lived. Although parents can recover wrongful death damages for the loss of services of a child, there is disagreement whether surviving parents also may recover for their loss of the child's society and companionship.[99] States also permit the recovery of funeral expenses as a part of a wrongful death action and a few courts have permitted recovery for grief and emotional distress.[100] However, punitive damages are not available in a wrongful death action.[101]

Since wrongful death statutes limit recovery to the losses suffered by the beneficiaries, states have enacted separate survival acts permitting any cause of action the decedent had at the time of his or her death to survive the death.[102]

2005 Miss. LEXIS 21 (Jan. 13, 2005); General Motors Corp. v. Hebert, 501 S.W.2d 950 (Tex. Civ. App. 1973).

[96] A few states now permit registered domestic partners to recover in a wrongful death action. *See* CAL. CIV. PROC. CODE § 377.60.

[97] *See* Hutto v. McNeil-PPC, Inc., 79 So. 3d 1199, 1217 (La. Ct. App. 2011). A claim for loss of consortium can be made only by husbands and wives who were legally married at the time of the injury. It does not permit recovery for the loss of an ex-spouse. Doerner v. Swisher International, Inc., 272 F.3d 928 (7th Cir. 2001) (applying Indiana law).

[98] Giuliani v. Guiler, 951 S.W.2d 318 (Ky. 1997); Hall v. Gillins, 147 N.E.2d 352 (Ill. 1958).

[99] For a decision permitting loss of society of a minor child, see Bullard v. Barnes, 468 N.E.2d 1228 (Ill. 1984). For a decision refusing to permit a claim by parents for the loss of companionship arising out of injury to their child, see Siciliano v. Capitol City Shows, Inc., 475 A.2d 19 (N.H. 1984).

[100] Vogler v. Blackmore, 352 F.3d 150 (5th Cir. 2003).

[101] Eisert v. Greenberg Roofing & Sheet Metal Co., 314 N.W.2d 226 (Minn. 1982).

[102] For an example of such laws, see the Pennsylvania Survival Act (42 PA. CONS. STAT. § 8302) which states simply: "All causes of action or proceedings, real or personal, shall survive the death of the plaintiff or of the defendant, or the death of one or more joint plaintiffs or defendants." *See also* 755 ILL. COMP. STAT. 5/27-6; TENN. CODE ANN. § 20-5-102.

These statutes, which can be brought along with a wrongful death action,[103] are a response to the common law which does not permit a tort action to survive the death of the victim or the tortfeasor. In a survival action, the legal representative of the decedent brings an action for the economic and noneconomic damages suffered by the decedent between the date of the injury and the date of death. Thus, any products liability action that the decedent could have brought had he or she lived survives the death, and any damages that are awarded are for the benefit of the decedent's estate.[104] The damages recoverable in a survival action include the decedent's medical expenses, conscious pain and suffering, lost earnings, and the damage or loss of the decedent's property.

[F]   Damage to Property

Finally, a plaintiff in a products liability suit may recover compensation for the damage or destruction of real or personal property caused by the defective product. The measure of compensation in products liability cases is the same as in other cases. If the property is destroyed, the plaintiff is entitled to the value of the property at the time of its destruction.[105] In cases where the property was not destroyed totally, but where the damage is not capable of being repaired, the measure of damages is the difference between the reasonable value of the property before and after the damage.[106] If the damaged personal property can be repaired, the measure of damages is the cost of those repairs plus the amount of the difference in the value of the property, if the value of the property after repair is less than its value before it was damaged.[107]

§ 10.03   ECONOMIC LOSS DOCTRINE

Of particular importance in products liability actions are cases where the plaintiff claims only "economic loss." Economic loss is defined as "damages for inadequate value, costs of repair or replacement of the defective product, or consequent loss of profits — without any claim of personal injury or damage to other property."[108] Such loss includes "the diminution in value of the product because it is inferior in quality and does not work for the general purposes in which it was manufactured

---

[103] *See* Peltz v. Sears, Roebuck and Co., 367 F. Supp. 2d 711 (E.D. Pa. 2005) (applying Pennsylvania law).

[104] Estate of Merrill v. Jerrick, 605 N.W.2d 645 (Wis. Ct. App. 1999).

[105] Gateway Foam Insulators, Inc. v. Jokerst Paving & Contracting, Inc., 279 S.W.3d 179, 184 (Mo. 2009) ("Where a property owner is the victim of a tort that destroys his property, the law seeks to restore him to his 'full actual loss' by awarding him the 'monetary equivalent' of the destroyed property so as to place him in 'as good a position as he would have enjoyed in the absence of the destruction.' ").

[106] Pennsylvania Dept. of Gen. Serv. v. U.S. Mineral Products Co., 898 A.2d 590 (Pa. 2006); Stackhouse v. Logangate Property Mgt., 872 N.E.2d 1294 (Ohio Ct. App. 2007).

[107] Behrens v. W. S. Bills & Sons, Inc., 283 N.E.2d 1 (Ill. App. Ct. 1972).

[108] Casa Clara Condominium Ass'n, Inc v. Charley Toppino & Sons, Inc., 620 So. 2d 1244, 1246 (Fla. 1993) (*quoting* Note, *Economic Loss in Products Liability Jurisprudence*, 66 COLUM. L. REV. 917, 918 (1966)). However, if there is damage to property other than the product itself, a plaintiff may bring an action for damage to that property. Aardema v. U.S. Dairy Systems, Inc., 215 P.3d 505 (Idaho 2005).

and sold."[109] Under the "economic loss doctrine," a plaintiff whose only damages are injury to the product itself cannot recover in negligence or strict liability. Instead, the plaintiff is limited to an action for breach of warranty.[110] The rationale behind the doctrine, which is followed by almost every state both in consumer and commercial transactions, is that damage to the product itself means simply that customer received "insufficient product value."[111]

The starting point for the economic loss doctrine in products liability cases is *Seely v. White Motor Co.*,[112] in which the purchaser of a defective truck sued for damages to the truck and for lost profits from his inability to use it in his hauling business. The California Supreme Court allowed the purchaser to recover against the manufacturers for breach of express warranty. The court, however, refused to allow recovery on the theory of strict liability.[113] Since there was no personal injury or damage to property other than to the product itself, the court held that strict liability was not designed "to undermine the warranty provisions of the Uniform Commercial Code but, rather, to govern the distinct problem of physical injuries."[114]

The vast majority of states follow the economic loss doctrine as articulated in *Seely*.[115] However, a few states permit an exception based on a distinction between a disappointed consumer and an endangered one. Maryland, for example, has held that a plaintiff may recover economic loss in strict products liability if the "defective product creates a situation potentially dangerous to persons or other property, and loss occurs as a result of that danger . . ."[116] A mid-flight engine failure caused by a defective product is an example of a "potentially dangerous" situation in which economic loss is recoverable.[117] Georgia permits recovery for economic loss when a "sudden and calamitous event" not only causes damages to the product but poses an

---

[109] 620 So. 2d at 1246 (*quoting* Comment, *Manufacturers' Liability to Remote Purchasers for "Economic Loss" Damages — Tort or Contract?*, 114 U. Pa. L. Rev. 539, 541 (1966).

[110] *See* In re Ford Motor Co. Speed Control Deactivation Switch Products Liab. Litig., 664 F. Supp. 2d 752 (E.D. Mich. 2009); Kelleher v. Marvin Lumber and Cedar Co., 891 A.2d 477 (N.H. 2005); Moorman Manufacturing Co. v. National Tank Co., 435 N.E.2d 443 (Ill. 1982). Some states make an exception to the economic loss rule for claims based on misrepresentation. *See* Guardian Construction Co. v. Tetra Tech Richardson, Inc., 583 A.2d 1378 (Del. Super. Ct. 1990).

[111] Oceanside at Pine Point Condominium Owners Association v. Peachtree Doors, Inc., 659 A.2d 267, 270 (Me. 1995). *See* Progressive Insurance Co. v. General Motors Corp., 749 N.E.2d 484 (Ind. 2001).

[112] 403 P.2d 145 (Cal. 1965).

[113] *Id.* at 145.

[114] *Id.* at 149.

[115] For a review of these cases, see Alloway v. General Marine Industries, L.P., 695 A.2d 264, 270–71 (N.J. 1997).

[116] Lloyd v. GMC, 916 A.2d 257, 269 (Md. 2007). *See* Morris v. Osmose Wood Preserving, 667 A.2d 624 (Md. 1995) ("serious, and unreasonable risk of death or personal injury"); Northern Power & Engineering Corp. v. Caterpillar Tractor Co., 623 P.2d 324, 329 (Alaska 1981). However, South Carolina and Tennessee are two states that have rejected the "sudden threat" exception. Sapp v. Ford Motor Corp., 687 S.E.2d 47 (S.C. 2009); Lincoln Gen. Ins. Co. v. Detroit Diesel Corp., 293 S.W.3d 487 (Tenn. 2009).

[117] Lloyd v. GMC, 916 A.2d 257, 269 (Md. 2007).

unreasonable risk of injury to persons and other property.[118] Similarly, the Iowa Supreme Court has held that a consumer can sue the manufacturer in tort if the damage to the property resulted from a "sudden or dangerous occurrence."[119] In addition to this exception, a few other states permit recovery of economic loss arising out of consumer (as opposed to commercial) transactions.[120]

In 1986, the United States Supreme Court reviewed the roles of tort and contract law in a case involving economic loss in *East River Steamship Corporation v. Transamerica Delaval, Inc.*[121] In *East River*, the plaintiffs, who were the charterers of four ships, sued the manufacturer of the turbines installed in the ships in negligence and strict liability, alleging that the turbines were defectively designed. The plaintiffs claimed that the damage to the turbines entitled them to compensation for the cost of repairs and for lost income while the ships were out of service. The Supreme Court adopted an approach similar to *Seely*, holding that "a manufacturer in a commercial relationship has no duty under either a negligence or strict products liability theory to prevent a product from injuring itself."[122] The Court stated that when a product injures only itself, "the reasons for imposing a tort duty are weak and those for leaving the party to its contractual remedies are strong."[123] The Court's decision has been very influential on state courts in their interpretation of the economic loss rule.[124]

In support of its holding, the Supreme Court reviewed the policy considerations in favor of the application of the economic loss doctrine to commercial transactions. The Court first stressed the importance of maintaining the historical distinction between tort law and contract law. According to the Court, tort liability is concerned primarily with safety and protects society's interest in freedom from harm, regardless of any agreement between the parties.[125] When a person is injured "the cost of an injury and the loss of time or health may be an overwhelming misfortune" that one person is not prepared to meet.[126] Conversely, a contractual duty arises from society's interest in the performance of promises and traditionally has been concerned with the fulfillment of reasonable economic expectations. When the only damage is to the product itself, the commercial user loses the value of the product, risks dissatisfied customers who find the product fails to meet their needs, or experiences increased costs in performing a service; all losses which can be

---

[118] Lumbermen's Underwriting Alliance v. Blount Int'l., Inc., 2007 U.S. Dist. LEXIS 102300 (N.D. Ga. Feb. 5, 2007) (applying Georgia law).

[119] American Fire and Casualty Co. v. Ford Motor Co., 588 N.W.2d 437, 439 (Iowa 1999).

[120] Franklin Grove Corp. v. Drexel, 936 A.2d 1272 (R.I. 2007).

[121] 476 U.S. 858 (1986). Although *East River* was decided under admiralty law, included in its holding was that admiralty law incorporates general principles of product liability law.

[122] *Id.* at 871.

[123] *Id.*

[124] *See* Giddings & Lewis, Inc. v. Indus. Risk Insurers, 348 S.W.3d 729 (Ky. 2011); Dobrovolny v. Ford Motor Co., 793 N.W.2d 445 (Neb. 2011); Eastwood v. Horse Harbor Found., Inc., 241 P.3d 1256 (Wash. 2010); Grams v. Milk Prods., Inc., 699 N.W.2d 167 (Wis. 2005).

[125] East River Steamship Corporation v. Transamerica Delaval, Inc., 476 U.S. 858, 871 (1986).

[126] *Id.*

insured.[127] As a result, the Court found that the tort concern with safety is reduced when an injury is only to the product itself.[128] In addition, "the increased cost to the public that would result from holding a manufacturer liable in tort for injury to the product itself is not justified."[129]

The Court also emphasized that damage to the product itself is best understood in terms of warranty since the product did not meet the consumer's expectations.[130] According to the Court, "maintenance of product value and quality is precisely the purpose of express and implied warranties."[131] A consumer's claim of a non-working product can be brought as a breach-of-warranty action, or the consumer can reject the product, or revoke its acceptance, and sue for breach of contract.[132] The Court found that when a product causes economic disappointment by not meeting a purchaser's expectations, the resulting failure to receive the benefit of the bargain is a core concern of contract law, not tort law.

Included in the Court's policy considerations governing the economic loss rule were the parties' freedom to allocate economic risk by contract. The Court stated that contract law, and specifically warranty law, is better suited for commercial controversies because "the parties may set the terms of their own agreements."[133] The economic loss doctrine encourages the party best situated to assess the risk of economic loss (usually the purchaser) to assume, allocate, or insure against that risk. For example, a manufacturer may be in a better position to absorb the risk of loss from physical injury or property damage, but a purchaser may be better situated to absorb the "risk of economic loss caused by the purchase of a defective product."[134] In addition, "the manufacturer can restrict its liability, within limits, by disclaiming warranties or limiting remedies."[135] In exchange, the Court reasoned, the purchaser pays less for the product.[136] Thus, the Court found that commercial situations are best regulated by warranty law because they generally do not involve large disparities in bargaining power and the parties are free to allocate the risk through contract.[137]

Finally, the Supreme Court emphasized that warranty law has built-in-boundaries and restraints on liability, in contrast to tort actions which may subject

---

[127] *Id.*

[128] *Id.*

[129] *Id.* at 872.

[130] *Id.*

[131] *Id. See* U.C.C. § 2-313 (express warranty), § 2-314 (implied warranty of merchantability), and § 2-315 (warranty of fitness for a particular purpose).

[132] *Id. See* U.C.C. § 2-601, 2-608, 2-612.

[133] *Id.* at 872–73.

[134] Seely v. White Motor Co., 403 P.2d 145 (Cal. 1965).

[135] East River Steamship Corporation v. Transamerica Delaval, Inc., 476 U.S. 858, 872–73 (1986).

[136] *Id.* at 873.

[137] Many state courts follow *East River* in commercial transactions and preclude tort actions when a product damages only itself. *See* Alloway v. General Marine Industries, L.P., 695 A.2d 264 (N.J. 1997); Cooperative Power Association v. Westinghouse Elec. Corp., 493 N.W.2d 661 (N.D. 1992); Koss Construction v. Caterpillar Inc., 960 P.2d 255 (Kan. Ct. App. 1998).

the manufacturer to limitless damages. "In products liability law," the Court reasoned, "where there is a duty to the public generally, forseeability is an inadequate brake . . . Permitting recovery for all foreseeable claims for purely economic loss could make a manufacturer liable for vast sums."[138] As a result, the Court found that it would be extremely difficult for a manufacturer to account for the expectations of all persons who may encounter its product. Warranty law, in contrast, places limitations on liability based on privity and the requirement of foreseeability of consequential damages as a result of breach.[139] The application of warranty law to commercial losses was necessary to prevent manufacturers from being liable for damages unknown and unlimited in scope.

In addition to state courts and the Supreme Court, the economic loss rule also is supported by § 21 of the Restatement (Third). This section codifies the economic loss rule in products liability actions and provides that:

> For purposes of this Restatement, harm to persons or property includes economic loss if caused by harm to:
>
> (a)   the plaintiff's person; or
>
> (b)   the person of another when harm to the other interferes with an interest of the plaintiff protected by tort law; or
>
> (c)   the plaintiff's property other than the defective product itself.

This section sets out the limitations courts have placed on the application of products liability law to various forms of economic loss.[140]

Although the economic loss doctrine prevents recovery of compensation in negligence or strict liability, a plaintiff can use negligence, strict liability, and warranty theories when the product causes damage to "other property."[141] One problem for courts has been defining what constitutes "other property." The Supreme Court discussed the scope of "other property" in the context of component parts in *Saratoga Fishing Co. v. J.M. Martinac & Co.*,[142] in which the primary purchaser of a ship added to a skiff, a fishing net, and spare parts to it. The vessel, with the added parts, then was sold to the plaintiff. An engine room fire, partially caused by a faulty hydraulic system, led to the sinking of the ship. The plaintiff brought a products liability suit against the manufacturer of the hydraulic system and the company that built the vessel. The Court concluded that when a manufacturer places an item into the stream of commerce by selling it to an initial user, that item is the "product itself."[143] Items added to the product by the initial user are

---

[138] East River Steamship Corporation v. Transamerica Delaval, Inc., 476 U.S. 858, 874 (1986).

[139] *Id.*

[140] *See* Flowers v. Viking Yacht Co., 840 A.2d 291, 294–95 (N.J. 2003); Bay Breeze Condominium Association, Inc. v. Norco Windows, Inc., 651 N.W.2d 738, 743 (Wis. Ct. App. 2002).

[141] *Id.* at 871. *See* 2-J Corporation v. Tice, 126 F.3d 539 (3d Cir. 1997) (applying Pennsylvania law); A.J. Decoster Co. v. Westinghouse Electric Corp., 634 A.2d 1330 (Md. 1994).

[142] 520 U.S. 875 (1997).

[143] *Id.* at 879. For other decisions attempting to determine what qualifies as 'other property' for purposes of the economic loss rule, see Travelers Indem. Co. v. Dammann & Co., Inc., 594 F.3d 238 (3d Cir. 2010) (applying New Jersey law); Albers v. Deere & Co., 599 F. Supp. 2d 1142 (D.N.D. 2008)

"other property" and the initial user's sale of the product to a subsequent user does not change these characterizations. The Court held that the initial user's added equipment constituted "other property" within the meaning of the *East River* doctrine, allowing the plaintiff to recover damages for its destruction.

§ 10.04 PUNITIVE DAMAGES

[A] Introduction

In August 2005, a jury of seven men and five women in Angleton, Texas, decided a product liability action brought against the pharmaceutical company Merck by a woman who alleged that her husband's death from a heart attack in 2001 was caused by taking the prescription painkiller Vioxx.[144] By a 10-2 vote, the minimum required under Texas law to find a defendant liable, the jury awarded the woman $450,000 in economic damages for her husband's lost income, $24.5 million for her mental anguish and loss of companionship, and $229 million in punitive damages.[145] A Texas judge later reduced the award to $26 million, with punitive damages capped at $1.7 million, the maximum permitted under a Texas statute. However, in 2008, a Texas appeals court reversed the judgment, holding that the woman failed to prove the necessary causation between Vioxx and her husband's death.[146] Although the woman ultimately received no damages, for supporters and critics of punitive damages, the size of the verdict was another example either of a jury sending a message to a large corporation that its reckless conduct will not be tolerated or of a jury that was out of control and harming business and the country with its verdict.

One reason for the controversy over the verdict in the Vioxx case is that, in all but five states,[147] plaintiffs are eligible to recover, in certain situation, punitive damages in addition to their compensatory damages.[148] Punitive damages, also referred to by courts as "exemplary damages,"[149] are intended to punish defendants as well as to deter them and others who might engage in the same type of conduct in the future.[150] Traditionally, punitive damages were a matter solely for

---

(applying North Dakota law); Dean v. Barrett Homes, Inc., 8 A.3d 766 (N.J. 2010); Miidas Greenhouses, LLC v. Global Horticulture, Inc., 244 P.3d 579 (Ariz. Ct. App. 2010); Indus. Risk Insurers v. Amer. Eng'g Testing, Inc., 769 N.W.2d 82 (Wis. Ct. App. 2009).

[144] At the time of the case, more than 4200 state and federal Vioxx-related lawsuits were pending in the United States.

[145] *Jury Calls Merck Liable in Death of Man on Vioxx*, THE NEW YORK TIMES, Aug. 20, 2005, p. 1.

[146] Merck & Co., Inc. v. Ernst, 296 S.W.3d 81 (Tex. App. 2008). The same day that the Texas appellate court reversed the award of damages in the *Ernst* case, a New Jersey appellate court reversed an award of $9 million in punitive damages against Merck in a case involving an anti-inflammatory drug. McDarby v. Merck & Co., 949 A.2d 223 (N.J. Super. Ct. App. Div. 2008).

[147] Five states (Louisiana, Michigan, Nebraska, New Hampshire, and Washington) prohibit punitive damages entirely or in products liability cases.

[148] For a discussion of whether compensatory damages are a prerequisite for punitive damages, see Cush-Crawford v. Adchem Corp., 271 F.3d 352 (2d Cir. 2001).

[149] *See* Pacific Mutual Life Insurance Co. v. Haslip, 499 U.S. 1, 7 (1991).

[150] Smith v. Wade, 461 U.S. 30, 54 (1983) ("Punitive damages are awarded in the jury's discretion 'to

the common law. In the past two decades, however, the Supreme Court and many state legislatures have placed constitutional and statutory limitations and guidelines on the award of punitive damages. As a result, three questions surround punitive damages in products liability cases: (1) what must a plaintiff prove in order to recover punitive damages? (2) what limitations, if any, are there on the amount of punitive damages a plaintiff can receive? and (3) what limitations does the Constitution place on the award of punitive damages? The first question is governed by state statutes and common law. In order to answer the second question, it is necessary to look at the legislation adopted in many states that places caps and other restrictions on the amount of punitive damage a plaintiff can receive. Finally, the Supreme Court has addressed the third question in a number of cases and has set out "guideposts" for the review of punitive damages awards to help lower courts determine what ratios of punitive to compensatory damages meet the requirements of the Due Process clause.[151]

[B]   Conduct and Standard of Proof Required for Punitive Damages

Although the states vary widely in the amount of punitive damages they permit a plaintiff to recover in a products liability action, there is general agreement on the type of conduct required of a defendant before punitive damages may be awarded and on the standard of proof required of that conduct.[152] Typical of the type of conduct required for punitive damages is the statement of the New Mexico Supreme Court that, since the purpose of punitive damages is to punish wrongdoing, the plaintiff must prove that the defendant's behavior rose to "a willful, wanton, malicious, reckless, oppressive, or fraudulent" level.[153] This standard also is used in products liability cases. The Connecticut products liability statute, for example, states that plaintiffs may be awarded punitive damages in products liability cases if "the harm suffered was the result of the product seller's reckless disregard for the safety of product users, consumers or others who were injured by the product."[154] Courts have interpreted this to mean that punitive damages require a showing of reckless disregard for the rights of others and

---

punish [the defendant] for his outrageous conduct and to deter him and others like him from similar conduct in the future.' RESTATEMENT (SECOND) OF TORTS, § 908(1) (1979). The focus is on the character of the tortfeasor's conduct — whether it is of the sort that calls for deterrence and punishment over and above that provided by compensatory awards."). For a brief history of punitive damages, see Justice David Souter's opinion of the Court in Exxon Shipping Co. v. Baker, 128 S. Ct. 2605 (2008). For an economic rationale for punitive damages, see Judge Richard Posner's opinion in Kemezy v. Peters, 79 F.3d 33 (7th Cir. 1996).

[151] *See* State Farm Mutual Automobile Ins. Co. v. Campbell, 538 U.S. 408 (2003); BMW of North America, Inc. v. Gore, 517 U.S. 559 (1996).

[152] According to the RESTATEMENT (SECOND) OF TORTS, § 908 (1979), "[p]unitive damages may be awarded for conduct that is outrageous, because of the defendant's evil motive or his reckless indifference to the rights of others."

[153] Clay v. Ferrellgas, Inc., 881 P.2d 11, 14 (N.M. 1994).

[154] CONN. GEN. STAT. § 52-240b.

intentional and wanton violations of those rights.[155] Similarly, the Kansas Supreme Court has stated that punitive damages are permissible in products liability cases "whenever the elements of fraud, malice, gross negligence, or oppression mingle in the controversy."[156]

Since punitive damages have a quasi-criminal nature, more than 35 states require the plaintiff to prove the defendant's conduct with a higher standard of "clear and convincing evidence."[157] This standard is contained in the Mississippi punitive damages statute, which also sets out the required conduct: "Punitive damages may not be awarded if the claimant does not prove by clear and convincing evidence that the defendant against whom punitive damages are sough acted with actual malice, gross negligence which evidence a willful, wanton, or reckless disregard for the safety of others, or committed actual fraud."[158] The "clear and convincing" standard is a compromise between "a preponderance of the evidence" usually required in civil cases and higher standard of "beyond a reasonable doubt" used in criminal law.

An example of a product liability case where the manufacturer's conduct resulted in the award of punitive damages is *Grimshaw v. Ford Motor Co.*[159] In *Grimshaw*, a driver rear-ended a stalled 1972 Ford Pinto, causing it to burst into flames. The plaintiff, a 13-year-old passenger in the Pinto, suffered severe and permanent disfiguring burns to his face and body. The plaintiff sued Ford Motor Company for negligence and strict liability, claiming that Ford was aware from crash tests that the Pinto contained a design defect that would cause the passenger area to catch fire in the event of a rear-end collision.[160] A jury awarded the plaintiff $2.5 million in compensatory damages and $125 million in punitive damages.[161] On Ford's motion for a new trial, the judge required the plaintiff to remit all but $3½ million of the punitive award as a condition for the denial of the motion.[162] However, Ford appealed, claiming that punitive damages were statutorily and constitutionally impermissible in products liability cases, and that no evidence supported the jury's finding of malice.[163]

Ford argued that the world "malice" as used in § 3294 of the California Civil Code[164] was intended to apply only to traditional tort claims, and not to products

---

[155] Ames v. Sears, Roebuck & Co., 514 A.2d 352 (Conn. App. Ct. 1986) (*quoting* Collens v. New Canaan Water Co., 234 A.2d 825 (Conn. 1967)).

[156] Tetuan v. A.H. Robins Co., 738 P.2d 1210, 1239 (Kan. 1987).

[157] For examples, *see* FLA. STAT. § 768.73; GA. CODE ANN. § 51-12-5.1; N.C. GEN. STAT. § 10-15(b); OKLA. STAT. ANN. tit. 23, § 9.1. Colorado requires that the proof be "beyond a reasonable doubt." COLO. REV. STAT. § 13-21-102.

[158] MISS. CODE ANN. § 11-1-65(4).

[159] 174 Cal. Rptr. 348 (Ct. App. 1981).

[160] *Id.* at 363.

[161] *Id.* at 358.

[162] *Id.*

[163] *Id.* at 380.

[164] "In an action for the breach of an obligation not arising from contract, where it is proven by clear and convincing evidence that the defendant has been guilty of oppression, fraud, or malice, the plaintiff,

liability actions.[165] However, the California appellate court rejected that argument, citing the state's long-standing allowance of punitive damages at common law, and defining "malice" as used in the California Civil Code as "conduct evincing 'a conscious disregard of the probability that the actor's conduct will result in injury to others.' "[166] Stating that the primary purpose of punitive damages is to punish "conduct evincing callous and conscious disregard of public safety by those who manufacture and market mass produced articles," and defending punitive damage awards as "the most effective remedy for consumer protection against defectively designed mass produced articles," the court refused to find any statutory impediment to the award of punitive damage.[167] The court concluded that, because Ford knew of the defect and could have remedied it at a small per-car cost, it had acted with the required malice.[168] Finding the trial judge's calculation of punitive damages was "fair and reasonable," the court upheld the $3.5 million punitive damage award.[169]

[C] Statutory Controls on Punitive Damage Awards

Once the plaintiff has shown that the defendant's conduct met the standard required for punitive damages, the next question is: What limitations, if any, are there on the amount of punitive damages that the plaintiff can receive? This is the most controversial issue concerning punitive damages. Twenty-five states place no legislative or common law cap on the amount of punitive damages a trier or fact may award.[170] However, as a result of tort reform efforts, 20 states place some statutory limitations on the amount of punitive damages a plaintiff can recover. These states take different approaches to how they limit punitive damages. Virginia simply imposes an absolute cap of $350,000 on punitive damages.[171] Connecticut[172] and Ohio[173] limit an award of punitive damages to a multiplier of twice the amount of compensatory damages. The most widely used method of imposing a cap on punitive damages is to use a multiplier of compensatory damages along with an absolute cap. The multipliers and absolute amounts vary among the states.[174] A variation of this is the Kansas approach, which limits punitive damages to the

---

in addition to the actual damages, may recover damages for the sake of example and by way of punishing the defendant." CAL. CIV. CODE § 3294(a).

[165] 174 Cal. Rptr. at 381.

[166] *Id. See* Simon v. San Paolo U.S. Holding Co., 113 P.3d 63 (Cal. 2005).

[167] 174 Cal. Rptr. at 383.

[168] *Id.* at 385.

[169] *Id.* at 391.

[170] These states include California, Illinois, Minnesota, Missouri, New York, and Pennsylvania.

[171] VA. CODE ANN. § 8.01-38.1.

[172] CONN. GEN. STAT. ANN. § 52-240b.

[173] OHIO REV. CODE ANN. § 2315.21(D)(2)(a).

[174] For example, in Indiana punitive damages are limited to three times the amount of compensatory damages or $50,000 (IND. CODE § 34-51-3-4); in North Carolina, the amount is the greater of three times the amount of compensatory damages or $250,000 (N.C. GEN. STAT. § 1D-25(b)); in New Jersey, it is greater of five times the amount of compensatory damages or $350,000 (N.J. STAT. ANN. § 2A:15-5.14); in Wisconsin punitive damages are limited $200,000 or twice the amount of compensatory damages (WIS. STAT. § 895.043).

lesser of a defendant's annual gross income based on the defendant's highest gross annual income for any one year over the five years before the act or $5 million.[175] The most complex formula for punitive damages in products liability cases was adopted by Mississippi in 2004.[176] Under the sliding scale used in the state's statute, punitive damages are limited to $20 million for a defendant with a net worth of more than $1 billion; $15 million for a defendant with a net worth between $750 million and $1 billion; $5 million for a defendant with a net worth of more than $500 million but not more than $750 million; $3.75 million for a defendant with a net worth of more than $100 million but not more than $500 million; $2.5 million for a defendant with a net worth of more than $50 million but not more than $100 million; and 2% of the defendant's net worth for a defendant with a net worth of $50 million or less.

Some states limit punitive damages by procedural methods rather than by caps. Illinois, for example, prohibits a plaintiff from requesting punitive damages in the complaint. Instead, after a plaintiff files the complaint, he or she must make a pretrial motion to amend the complaint to seek punitive damages.[177] The decision whether or not punitive damages are appropriate for the jury in the case is in the discretion of the trial judge.[178] Other states reverse the approach and let the jury decide whether punitive damages are appropriate in the case and then leave it to the judge to determine the amount.[179] In doing so, the Kansas Supreme Court has stated that the trial judge must base the award of punitive damages on "the actual damages sustained, the actual damage award, the circumstances of the case, the evidence presented, the relative positions of the plaintiff and the defendant, and the defendant's financial worth."[180]

Another procedural method designed to limit the amount of punitive damages is to bifurcate the trial, with the jury first determining the question of liability and whether punitive damages are appropriate, and a second proceedings to determine the amount of punitive damages.[181] Other states limit the amount of punitive damages that the plaintiff can recover by requiring that a certain percentage of the award be paid to the state or a designated beneficiary.[182] About half-a-dozen states have adopted what is referred to as the "FDA defense" to punitive damages.[183]

---

[175] Kan. Stat. Ann. §§ 60-3701 and 3702.

[176] Miss. Code Ann. § 11-1-65(3)(a).

[177] 735 Ill. Comp. Stat. 5/2-604.1.

[178] Schenker v. Chicago Title & Trust Co., 470 N.E.2d 1264 (Ill. App. Ct. 1984).

[179] See Connecticut (Conn. Gen. Stat. § 52-240b) and Kansas (Kan. Stat. Ann. § 60-3702(a)).

[180] Tetuan v. A.H. Robins Co., 738 P.2d 1210, 1239 (Kan. 1987).

[181] For examples, see Alaska (Alaska Stat. § 09.17.020(a)) and Ohio (Ohio Rev. Code Ann. § 2315.21(B)).

[182] Indiana law, for example, requires plaintiffs who receive punitive damage awards to deposit 75% of the award in a violent crime victim's compensation fund. Ind. Code § 34-51-3-6. Missouri requires that plaintiffs deposit 50% of punitive damage awards into a state tort victim's compensation fund. Mo. Rev. Stat. § 537.675(3). For other examples, see Alaska Stat. § 09.17.020(j); Ga. Code Ann. § 51-12-5.1(e)(2); and Iowa Code Ann. § 668A.1(2)(b).

[183] For examples, see Ariz. Rev. Stat. § 12-701(A)(1) and Colo. Rev. Stat. § 13-64-302.5(5)(a); Tenn. Code Ann. § 29-39-104(d).

Under these statutes, a pharmaceutical company is not liable for punitive damages if its product complies with FDA standards.

In addition to the statutory limitations placed on punitive damages, every state subjects a jury's award to review, first by the trial judge, and then on appeal. The trial judge may set aside a punitive damages award if it is excessive as a matter of law or is so grossly disproportionate as to raise the presumption that it was the product of passion or prejudice. An award of punitive damages also is subject to review on appeal. In deciding whether an award is excessive, the California court in *Grimshaw* stated that four factors should be weighed: (1) the degree of reprehensibility of the defendant's conduct; (2) the wealth of the defendant; (3) the amount of compensatory damages; and (4) an amount which would serve as a deterrent effect on like conduct by defendant an others.[184] These factors also are reflected in the Restatement (Second) of Torts which sets out three factors that a trier of fact can consider in making its calculation of punitive damages: (1) the character of the defendant's act; (2) the nature and extent of the harm; and (3) the defendant's wealth.[185]

[D]   The Constitutionality of Punitive Damages

Although punitive damages once were a matter solely for state legislatures and the courts, they now are a frequent source of constitutional litigation. The basis for much of this litigation is the Due Process clause of the Fourteenth Amendment, which prohibits states from depriving any person of "life, liberty, or property, without due process of law."[186] In the case of punitive damage awards, the Supreme Court has stated that "the Due Process Clause of the Fourteenth Amendment prohibits the imposition of grossly excessive or arbitrary punishments on a tortfeasor."[187] Since the mid-1980s, the Court has addressed the constitutionality of punitive damages on a number of occasions and has set out guidelines for awarding such damages. Although these decisions have established "guidelines" for resolving many of the questions about the award of punitive damages, one important issue — the permissible ratio of punitive damages to compensatory damages — remains unclear.

Until 1996, the Supreme Court deferred to state law when examining the constitutionality of punitive damage awards.[188] The Supreme Court made its first attempt to impose limits on punitive damages in *BMW of North America, Inc. v. Gore.*[189] In *Gore*, an automobile buyer purchased a new BMW that, as a result of

---

[184]   Grimshaw v. Ford Motor Co., 174 Cal. Rptr. 348, 388 (Ct. App. 1981).

[185]   RESTATEMENT (SECOND) OF TORTS, § 908(2) (1979). *See also* Franz v. Calaco Development Corp., 818 N.E.2d 357, 371 (Ill. App. Ct. 2004).

[186]   U.S. CONST. AMEND. XIV, § 1.

[187]   State Farm Mutual Automobile Insurance Co. v. Campbell, 538 U.S. 408, 415–16 (2003).

[188]   Among the early Supreme Court cases involving punitive damages are Honda Motor Corp. v. Oberg, 512 U.S. 415 (1994); TXO Production Corp. v. Alliance Resources Corp., 509 U.S. 443 (1993); Pacific Mutual Life Ins. Co. v. Haslip, 499 U.S. 1 (1991); Browning-Ferris Industries of Vermont, Inc. v. Kelco, 492 U.S. 257 (1989); Michael P. Allen, *The Supreme Court, Punitive Damages and State Sovereignty*, 13 GEO. MASON L. REV. 1 (2004).

[189]   517 U.S. 559 (1996).

BMW's policy of not disclosing damage under a certain percentage of the car value, had been painted to cover minor body damage during delivery. This reduced the value of the car by approximately 10%, and, for that, the Alabama jury awarded the buyer $4,000 in compensatory damages and $4 million dollars in punitive damages, a 1000 to 1 ratio, "based on a determination that [BMW's] nondisclosure policy constituted 'gross, oppressive or malicious' fraud."[190] The Alabama Supreme Court reduced the award to $2 million, an amount that still was 500 times the amount of the compensatory damages.[191] The Supreme Court granted certiorari to "illuminate 'the character of the standard that will identify unconstitutionally excessive awards' of punitive damages."[192] In its opinion, the Court set out three "guideposts" to help lower courts determine the constitutionality of punitive damages awards: (1) the degree of reprehensibility of the defendant's act; (2) the ratio of actual harm as demonstrated by the compensatory damages to the punitive damages; and (3) the sanctions imposed by the state legislature for similar misconduct.[193]

Applying the guideposts to the facts of *Gore*, the Court held that the punitive damage award was unconstitutional. First, BMW's conduct was not reprehensible. The harm to the buyer was purely economic and the Court found none of the "deliberate false statements, acts of affirmative misconduct, or concealment of evidence of improper motive" present in cases with Court sanction punitive damages awards.[194] Second, in light of the lack of reprehensibility, a punitive damages award of more than four hundred times the compensatory damages was not within a constitutionally acceptable range.[195] Finally, $2 million dollars was a significantly larger dollar amount than what was permitted by state statute to punish similar wrongdoing.[196]

The Supreme Court's second attempt to clarify when punitive damages awards are excessive under the Due Process clause was *State Farm Mutual Automobile Insurance Co. v. Campbell*.[197] In *Campbell*, a driver insured by State Farm was involved in an automobile accident that resulted in another driver's death and a third driver's permanent disability. Despite advice to the contrary, State Farm refused to settle the claim for the policy limits of $50,000, and, at trial, a jury returned a judgment against the plaintiff for $186,000. Although State Farm eventually agreed to pay the entire judgment, the plaintiff brought suit against the company "alleging bad faith, fraud, and intentional infliction of emotional distress."[198] The Utah appellate court reduced the trial jury's award of $2.6 million in compensatory damages and $145 million in punitive damages. The Utah

---

[190] *Id.* at 564–65.

[191] *Id.* at 567.

[192] *Id.* at 568.

[193] *Id.* at 575, 580, 583.

[194] *Id.* at 577, 579.

[195] *Id.* at 583.

[196] *Id.* at 584.

[197] 538 U.S. 408 (2003).

[198] *Id.* at 414.

Supreme Court analyzed the award under the three guideposts set out in *Gore* and reinstated the award.[199] The Supreme Court granted certiorari and held that Utah Supreme Court was in "error to reinstate the jury's $145 million punitive damages award."[200]

In examining the facts in *Campbell*, the Court reaffirmed and clarified the three *Gore* guideposts. First, courts must analyze the reprehensibility of an act by considering the following: (1) the nature of the harm; (2) whether the conduct "evinced an indifference to or a reckless disregard of the health or safety of others;" (3) the financial vulnerability of the plaintiff; (4) whether the act was an isolated incident or repeated occurrence; and (5) whether "the harm was the result of intentional malice, trickery, or deceit, or mere accident."[201] The Court concluded that, while State Farm's actions were not laudable, they were not so reprehensible that the state's interest in deterring similar conduct could not have been achieved by a more modest punitive damages award.[202]

In its discussion of the ratio guidepost, the Court declined to adopt bright-line rules on what constitutes a constitutional ratio of punitive to compensatory damages. Instead, the Court stated that "in practice, few awards exceeding a single-digit ratio between punitive and compensatory damages, to a significant degree, will satisfy due process."[203] However, as the Court stated in *Gore*, in cases of extremely reprehensible conduct, punitive damages of multiple-digit ratios can survive constitutional scrutiny, so long as the punitive damage award is "reasonable and proportionate to the amount of harm to the plaintiff and to the general damages recovered."[204] In *Campbell*, the ratio of punitive to compensatory damages was 145 to 1, which, when considered in light of the nature of the act, was constitutionally disproportionate.[205]

In analyzing the third *Gore* guidepost, statutory penalties for similar misconduct, the Court in *Campbell* cautioned against using "the civil process to assess criminal penalties that can be imposed only after the heightened protections of a criminal trial have been observed, including, of course, its higher standards of proof."[206] The possibility that the act of a tortfeasor might lead to criminal punishment does not automatically justify an award of punitive damages. Because Utah's statutory fine for fraud was $10,000, the punitive damage award of $145 million did not meet the test set out in the third *Gore* guidepost.

Shortly after it decided *Campbell*, the Supreme Court vacated and remanded four products liability cases for reconsideration of the awards of punitive damages. Although those cases provided little guidance as to how courts will apply *Gore* and

---

[199] *Id.* at 415.

[200] *Id.* at 418.

[201] *Id.* at 419.

[202] *Id.* at 420.

[203] *Id.* at 425.

[204] *Id.* at 425–26.

[205] *Id.* at 426–28.

[206] *Id.* at 428.

Campbell, the decisions on remand show an attempt by state courts to bring awards of punitive damages within the constitutional guidelines concerning ratios. In *Bocci v. Key Pharmaceuticals Inc.*,[207] the Oregon appellate court had to determine the appropriate award of punitive damages for the failure of a pharmaceutical company to provide the plaintiff with adequate information concerning the potential toxicity of a certain drug, resulting in permanent brain damage. The appellate court concluded on remand that, while a 45 to 1 ratio was "clearly in excess of the single-digit neighborhood that the Court has suggested lies at the outer edge of constitutionality," a 7 to 1 punitive damages award was constitutionally permissible.[208] Similarly, on remand in *Romo v. Ford Motor Co.*,[209] the California appellate court held that if the plaintiffs agreed to remit all of the punitive damages judgment except $23,723,287, approximately a 5 to 1 ratio, the punitive damages judgment would be modified and affirmed in that amount. However, if they did not agree to the remittitur, the punitive damages judgment would be reversed and the case would be remanded for a new trial on the amount of the punitive damages. In *Sand Hill Energy, Inc. v. Ford Motor Co.*,[210] a products liability suit against a truck manufacturer, the Kentucky appellate court initially reduced the trial court's $20 million damage award to $15 million in light of the relationship between the defendant's conduct and the plaintiff's injury.[211] On remand from the Supreme Court, the Kentucky Supreme Court found that the jury had considered the manufacturer's conduct on a nationwide scale in arriving at the punitive damages award. The court ordered a new trial on the amount of punitive damages since the jury instructions contained no limitation on extraterritorial punishment as required by *Campbell.*[212]

The fourth of the products liability cases remanded by the Supreme Court, *Philip Morris USA v. Williams*,[213] later returned for a second time. In *Williams*, the plaintiff brought suit against Philip Morris, alleging that the company fraudulently caused the death of her husband, who smoked Philip Morris cigarettes for over 40 years. An Oregon jury found that the company knowingly and falsely led him to believe that smoking was safe and awarded the plaintiff $821,000 in compensatory damages and $79.5 million in punitive damages. On remand from the Supreme Court, the Oregon appellate court held that the punitive damages award was "reasonable and proportionate to the wrong inflicted on decedent and the public of this state" and did not violate due process under the *Gore* guideposts.[214] In its second time before the Supreme Court, the Court reversed by a 5-4 vote. However, the Court did not consider the appropriateness of the punitive damage award, which was more than 96 times the amount of the compensatory damages. Thus, whether the guideline set out in *Gore* for the ratio of

---

[207] 76 P.3d 669 (Or. Ct. App. 2003).

[208] *Id.* at 675.

[209] 6 Cal. Rptr. 3d 793 (Ct. App. 2003).

[210] 83 S.W.3d 483 (2002).

[211] *Id.* at 496.

[212] Sand Hill Energy, Inc. v. Smith, 142 S.W.3d 153 (Ky. 2004).

[213] 549 U.S. 346 (2007).

[214] 92 P.3d 126, 146 (Or. Ct. App. 2004).

punitive damages to compensatory damages is firm or flexible remains unclear.

Instead of dealing with the amount of punitive damages, the Court in *Williams* held that the Due Process Clause forbids a state from using punitive damages to punish a defendant for injury inflicted on "strangers to the litigation,"[215] something that had been done by the lower courts in awarding punitive damages in *Gore* and *State Farm Mutual.* This is important in products liability cases since the Supreme Court, in effect, held that punitive damages cannot be used to punish manufacturers or sellers for harm their products cause to parties other than they injured party. However, the Court held that, in assessing the "defendant's reprehensibility," the jury may consider harm to third persons.[216]

The most recent of the Supreme Court's punitive damages decision is *Exxon Shipping Co. v. Baker*,[217] involving the question whether Exxon was liable for $2.5 billion in punitive damages in connection with the Exxon Valdezoil spill in Alaska in March 1989. Since the case was tried under general maritime law, the Court was acting like a common law court and was not interpreting the Due Process Clause or a federal statute. The five Justices in the majority on the issue of punitive damages held that the award to the victims of the spill should be reduced from $2.5 billion to $500 million. The Court reasoned that, although punitive damages were warranted, they could not exceed what Exxon already had paid to compensate the victims for their economic losses, which was about $500 million.[218] Justice Souter stated that a one-to-one ratio between punitive and compensatory damages was a "fair upper limit" in maritime cases that involved recklessness, compared to the higher liability for intentional conduct.[219] The Court adopted a 1:1 ratio for maritime cases since that is the ratio in many states and in analogous federal statutes. The majority looked to studies showing the median ratio of punitive to compensatory awards. Those studies reflect the judgments of juries and juries in thousands of cases as to what punitive awards were appropriate in circumstances from the least blameworthy conduct to malice and recklessness. The data put the median ration for the entire gamut at less than 1:1, meaning that the compensatory award exceeds the punitive award in most cases. Thus, awards at or below the median roughly express jurors' sense of reasonable penalties in cases like *Exxon* that have no exceptional blameworthiness.[220]

Exxon was neither a products liability case nor was it decided using the Due Process Clause. However, the 1:1 ratio that the Supreme Court adopted for general maritime cases may have a great persuasive effect not only on the Court in future cases but also on lower federal courts and on state courts in reviewing the award of punitive damages.[221]

---

[215] 549 U.S. at 353.

[216] *Id.* at 359.

[217] 128 S. Ct. 2605 (2008).

[218] *Id.* at 2634.

[219] *Id.* at 2633.

[220] *Id.* at 2624–26.

[221] *See* Raymond L. Mariani & Barbara A. Lukeman, *Constitutional Limits on Punitive Damages After* Exxon Shipping Co. v. Baker, THE BRIEF, (Vol. 39, No. 4, Summer 2010).

§ 10.05   PRE-JUDGMENT AND POST-JUDGMENT INTEREST

If a jury awards a plaintiff damages in a products liability case, the plaintiff may be entitled to recover pre-judgment and post-judgment interest on the award. Whether a plaintiff is able to recover interest on an award, as well as the amount of the interest, is governed by statutes that vary from state-to-state.

The controversy over awarding interest on damages awards centers on pre-judgment interest. The rationale behind pre-judgment interest is to ensure that plaintiffs are compensated fully for the loss of the use of the money due them as damages between the date their claim arose and the date of judgment.[222] When interest rates are high or where large sums of money are involved, plaintiffs often argue that defendants attempt to stall their cases in order to use the money for as long as possible. Defendants, however, counter that plaintiffs are the ones who delay in order to demonstrate additional pain and suffering, as well as complications from their injuries, and that an award of pre-judgment interest penalizes them and overcompensates plaintiffs. Thus, both supporters and opponents of pre-judgment interest cast their arguments in terms of preventing delays in litigation, and promoting efficiency and settlements, and fairness to the plaintiff or defendant.

Every state permits pre-judgment interest and most provide that it is applicable to all damages. Some states, however, limit pre-judgment interest on amounts that were liquidated or ascertainable at the time of the loss. The states also differ as to the starting point from which pre-judgment interest begins to accrue in breach of warranty and tort actions. Among these are the date of the injury,[223] the date the suit was filed,[224] or a stated number of days after a written demand is rejected,[225] or at the discretion of the court or jury.[226] Finally, the amount of pre-judgment interest varies from a specific amount (the most common method)[227] to a one using the Federal Reserve District discount rate,[228] the prime rate,[229] or the U.S. Treasury Bill rate.[230] In addition, more than a dozen states have made pre-judgment interest part of their tort reform packages in recent years. Most of this legislation deals with the amount of the pre-judgment interest rate and the date on which pre-judgment interest begins to accrue. While most states also do not permit plaintiffs to recover pre-judgment interest on punitive damages,[231] a few states have held that it is recoverable.[232]

---

[222] City of Milwaukee v. Cement Division, National Gypsum Co., 515 U.S. 189 (1995).

[223] See Haw. Rev. Stat. § 636-16; S.D. Codified Laws § 21-1-13.1.

[224] Okla. Stat. tit. 12, § 727.1.

[225] Mo. Rev. Stat. § 408.040(2).

[226] Va. Code Ann. § 8.01-382.

[227] See Mont. Code Ann. § 27-1-210(1).

[228] See Alaska Stat. § 09.30.070(a).

[229] See Ga. Code Ann. § 7-4-12 (primate rate plus 3%).

[230] See Iowa Code § 668.13; Neb. Rev. Stat. § 45-103.02.

[231] See Alaska Stat. § 09.30.070(c); Ind. Code § 34-51-4-3; Ohio Rev. Code Ann. § 2315.21(D)(3).

[232] Werremeyer v. K.C. Auto Salvage Co., 134 S.W.3d 633 (Mo. 2004).

Post-judgment interest is less controversial. Like pre-judgment interest, it is meant to prevent delay and to compensate a plaintiff for the lost use of money because of delay. However, the argument for post-judgment interest is stronger because the money on which the plaintiff seeks interest already has been awarded to the plaintiff by the court. Every state permits the award of post-judgment interest, either from the date of the verdict[233] or from the date of judgment.[234] The amount of post-judgment interest also is set by state statutes and varies greatly. As with pre-judgment interest, most statutes set the interest rate at a specific amount[235] or at a specific percentage above the Federal Reserve's discount rate.[236]

§ 10.06   JOINT AND SEVERAL LIABILITY

As products liability litigation becomes increasingly complex, many cases involve more than one defendant, that is, a component part manufacturer, the manufacturer of the finished product, the retailer of the product. Traditionally, a finding that multiple defendants were liable resulted in them being "jointly and severally liable," that is, each defendant was responsible for the entire amount of the damages suffered by the plaintiff, regardless of its actual responsibility for the damages. As a result, "the injured person may sue one or all of the tortfeasors to obtain a recovery for his injuries; the fact that one of the tortfeasors is impecunious or otherwise immune from suit does not relieve another tortfeasor of his liability for damage which he himself has proximately caused."[237]

Joint and several liability grew out of situations where the defendants acted in concert, concurrently, or successively to bring about the plaintiff's injuries.[238] Commentators and courts offered three principal rationales for holding each defendant liable potentially for the entire amount of the damages in these cases: (1) each of the defendants caused the plaintiff's injuries; (2) joint and several liability relieves the plaintiff of having to identify and to sue each person responsible for the injury in order to receive full compensation; and (3) if one (or more) of the defendants is unable to pay the damages, the remaining defendants should be responsible so that the innocent plaintiff receives the full amount awarded by the jury or judge.[239] However, critics of joint and several liability point to the possibility that a defendant who is only slightly responsible for the plaintiff's damages may be required to pay the entire amount because of the financial inability of other defendants whose percentage of the responsibility is much greater.[240] These critics

---

[233] *See* Ind. Code § 24-4.6-1-101; Tenn. Code Ann. § 47-14-122.

[234] *See* Cal. Civ. Proc. Code § 685.020(a); 735 Ill. Comp. Stat. 5/2-1303.

[235] *See* Mont. Code Ann. § 25-9-204, 205(1) (10% per annum).

[236] *See* Alaska Stat. § 09.30.070.

[237] Richards v. Owens-Illinois, Inc., 60 Cal. Rptr. 2d 103, 108 (1997) (*quoting* American Motorcycle Association v. Superior Court, 578 P.2d 899, 904 (Cal. 1978)).

[238] F. James, F. Harper & O. Gray, The Law of Torts, Vol. 2 § 10.1 (2d ed. 1986).

[239] *See* William L. Prosser, *Joint Torts and Several Liability*, 25 Cal. L. Rev. 413 (1936); John Henry Wigmore, *Joint-Tortfeasors and Severance of Damages; Making the Innocent Party Suffer Without Redress*, 17 Ill. L. Rev. 458 (1923); Woods v. Cole, 693 N.E.2d 333 (Ill. 1998).

[240] Stevenson v. Keene Corp., 603 A.2d 521 (N.J. Super. Ct. App. Div. 1992).

argue that, instead, liability should be apportioned among the defendants based upon their share of the liability for the damage. Critics also point to strict liability cases which are not based upon any showing of fault on the part of the defendant. Joint and several liability results in a defendant who is strictly liable being held responsible for other defendants who also are strictly liable or who actually are at fault.

As a result of these criticisms, almost 40 states have made some changes in their laws governing joint and several liability in recent years. The result is that the state laws governing joint and several liability and contribution among tortfeasors now are so state specific that it is impossible to make anything more than broad generalizations about them. Among the approaches adopted by the states there are four principal ones. First, a number of states have abolished joint liability, either entirely or selectively. In these states, defendants no longer are individually liable for the entire amount of the plaintiff's damages. Instead, a judgment must be entered against each defendant on the basis of several liability according to each defendant's relative percentage of fault.[241] However, if one of the potential defendants is immune from liability to the plaintiff, some states hold that the trier of fact must exclude it when determining the relative percentage of the total fault.[242] Second, other some states apply joint and several liability only if the defendant's fault is more than a specific percentage of the total fault. If the defendant's fault is below the required amount, it is severally liable.[243] Third, other states provide that, if one of the tortfeasors is insolvent, its share is reapportioned among the solvent defendants and the plaintiff in proportion to their respective percentage of the fault.[244] Finally, some states retain joint and several liability for economic damages but apply several liability for non-economic losses.[245]

---

[241] *See* Alaska Stat. § 09.17.080; Colo. Rev. Stat. § 13-21-111.5.

[242] Wash. Rev. Code § 4.22.070(1). *See also* Geurin v. Winston Industries, Inc., 316 F.3d 879 (9th Cir. 2002) (applying Washington law).

[243] *See* Tex. Civ. Prac. & Rem. Code § 33.013(b)–(c).

[244] *See* Or. Rev. Stat. § 31.610(3).

[245] *See* Cal. Civ. Code § 1431.2(a).

Chapter 11

RESEARCH AND PRACTICE IMPLICATIONS OF CHOICE OF THEORY

SYNOPSIS

§ 11.01 INTRODUCTION

§ 11.02 PRE-FILING QUESTIONS IN PRODUCTS LIABILITY LITIGATION

§ 11.03 THE MAJOR RESEARCH TASKS IN PRODUCTS LIABILITY LITIGATION

§ 11.04 RESEARCH TIME FRAMES

§ 11.05 CRITERIA FOR SELECTION OF TIME FRAMES

§ 11.01 INTRODUCTION

There are a series of real world considerations that consistently attend products liability litigation, requiring focused attention by counsel for either side of the particular case involved. All litigation, regardless of kind, is an exercise in attempting to prove a set of historical facts upon which legal responsibility may or may not be eventually imposed. It is the same in civil as in criminal law. The plaintiff or state proffers facts, disputed in part by the respondent, from a typically circumscribed point in the history of the defendant and/or the victim of a crime. Did the defendant run the stop sign and cause the collision with the plaintiff's vehicle that resulted in two deaths? Did defendant threaten a bank teller with harm to get money on a certain day? Did the defendant in a stalking prosecution engage in a historical pattern of behavior sufficient to meet the statutory requirements?

In most litigation in American courts, the past history of importance is usually quite limited in time, as the above examples illustrate. Some litigation such as anti-trust, sexual or age discrimination, or stock fraud, often involves a more extensive examination into a defendant's past business history. Even in the latter cases, however, the period of history that may be arguably relevant to the issues is generally not decades long. Products liability investigation and preparation, however, typically involve the investigation of decades of science, industry development, government regulatory activities and the research development, production and marketing of a products liability defendant.

Products liability litigation is grounded in the range of sophisticated policy considerations discussed in Part I of this book. It is, perhaps, more than any other area of tort practice, inseparable from the litigation process itself. Accordingly, it involves all of the intricacies of modern civil procedure, discovery practice, evidence theory and trial technique. Tort litigation, of which products liability litigation is a major component, essentially second-guesses the judgment of the defendant individual, doctor, hospital, company or other institution in taking or failing to take the specified actions set forth in each count of the complaint. Products litigation, centered as it is in the decisions of international companies heavily invested in science and global economics, necessarily requires extensive scientific and technical research, close examination of international manufacturing and marketing structures and an understanding of the document production process of the company involved. As a result, the pre-filing, filing, pre-trial investigation and discovery issues associated with twenty-first century products liability litigation involves an enormous investment of time and money on the part of plaintiff and defense counsel. This is a considerably more difficult undertaking than that typically encountered in more focused tort litigation such as negligence or even in the more scientifically sophisticated medical malpractice case.

Chapters 1–10 analyze the history of products liability and provide detailed discussions of the current theories used to channel any particular litigation. Each of the liability theories and their policy bases considered in Chapters 1 through 10 focus on disparate activities within the defendant corporation over some period of time in its manufacturing history. When chosen by a party to forward and channel a products liability claim, each of these theories, while broadly based and policy driven, are nonetheless inextricably centered in a searching examination by plaintiff and defense counsel of significant historical scientific and business-related materials. Depending on the product and the specific theory of liability used to focus the investigation, counsel can be involved in an investigative span of a quarter of a century or longer. While discovery requests for excessively extensive periods may be denied as unreasonable or irrelevant, courts will typically allow decades long discovery if the complexity or age of the product history warrants it.[1]

It is at the complaint stage that legal theory enters and serves as the major catalyst in the process of structuring the products litigation. The rules of civil practice necessitate the encapsualization of the basic facts and require the plaintiff to state how he wishes the court or jury to officially characterize the defendant's conduct, here, whether it is negligence, breach of warranty, strict liability or misrepresentation. The routine post-complaint processes of motion practice, discovery and pre-trial motions-in-limine are no different in products liability cases. This preliminary unofficial labeling of liability counts sets in motion the plethora of litigation-related rules which determine the manner and pace at which the problem is to be channeled through the process to eventual resolution. In turn, the conceptual defect mode(s) used to characterize the actual case facts — manufacturing defect, misrepresentation, failure to instruct, failure to warn or overall

---

[1] *See* In re John Crane Inc., 2003 Tex. App. LEXIS 9684 (Nov. 13, 2003). Here, the request, as written, required John Crane to produce documents related to acquisitions spanning 86 years of asbestos-related business. The court ruled that the burden imposed on John Crane was far out of proportion to any benefit to the plaintiff. In its discovery response, John Crane acknowledged that it did not contest responsibility for the sales of asbestos-containing materials of any of its predecessors; therefore, the court ruled, plaintiff's justification for seeking the documents was rendered moot.

design defect — also trigger a host of discovery rules that will determine the documentary center of the litigation.[2]

Experienced products litigators acknowledge that as a base line precondition to success, the plaintiff must answer three essential questions: (1) did the defect or defects alleged in the complaint cause the claimed death or injury? (2) was the defendant aware of the risk that allegedly materialized and caused the claimed damage? [Was it even a risk according to scientific and related statistical theory?] (3) what, if anything, did the defendant company do about the alleged risk of its products once it was aware of it?

The answer to each of these questions, in turn, involves the examination of a significant amount of historical data involving the following broad subjects: (1) scientific literature addressed to important aspects of the science underlying the suspect product [Cancer causing potential of the suspect pharmaceutical's basic ingredients or the findings of certain tests to determine the failure rate of metals at varying stress levels]; (2) the historical and contemporary corporate members of the industry of which the defendant is a member; (3) comparative analyses of the design or chemical formulation of competing products in America and internationally; (4) the warnings and instructions history of any such products; (5) government agency regulatory efforts as regards the suspect product category; and (6) the documentary history of the defendant's development, testing, production, marketing and post-marketing of the suspect product or similar product lines.

§ 11.02   PRE-FILING QUESTIONS IN PRODUCTS LIABILITY LITIGATION

As noted, the products liability theories discussed in Part I of this book each have their own, typically extensive, scientific, regulatory and company documentary references in the life of the defendant company. While the basic overriding corporate organizational processes, inter-industry, are generally the same, each corporation, with regard to each product, may nonetheless have its own body of state of the art materials and internal corporate standard operating procedures and product-focused documentation that will serve as the basis for hard fought discovery and trial.

Regardless of the particular products liability theory chosen to pursue the litigation, there are a series of initial questions that must be addressed in this type of case. Although a particular theory, such as a failure to warn or instruct, has its own very focused research goals for both sides to the dispute, there is a wide area of knowledge to be determined across theoretical lines. At the outset of every product liability litigation, the lawyer-researcher, whether plaintiff or defendant, is required to address a wide range of questions that must be satisfactorily answered through the course of pre-filing research and investigation. Defense counsel has the initial advantage of ready access to most of the materials only available to plaintiff counsel after hard fought discovery. Nonetheless the learning curve is the same for

---

[2] *See* Terrence F. Kiely, *The Art of the Neglected Obvious in Products Liability Cases: Some Thoughts on Llewellyn's The Common Law Tradition*, 25 DePaul L. Rev. 914, 921 (1975). *See generally* Terrence F. Kiely, Science and Litigation: Products Liability in Theory and Practice (CRC Press 2002).

individual trial counsel and consumes considerable time and effort.

Answering these questions will require many hours of study of sources normally unfamiliar to those other than experienced specialists in the products field. Even then, new products and industries will invariably raise a host of new questions. Whether a plaintiff or defense lawyer, counsel will require answers to the majority of the following questions:

Initial Questions in Products Liability Litigation

[1]   Is there an identifiable defect that was remediable prior to or subsequent to the original manufacture?

[2]   Is the problem essentially one of manufacture, packaging, instructions, warnings or design?

[3]   Is it a combination of several of them?

[4]   How is the product manufactured [engineered product, pharmaceutical, chemical]?

[5]   What is its physical makeup or chemical ingredients?

[6]   How do its design and materials composition compare to competing products in the same market?

[7]   What companies are involved in supplying materials or component parts?

[8]   What other companies are involved in the vertical chain of distribution of this product?

[9]   Is a foreign corporation involved? [Manufacturer, distributor, retailer?]

[10]   Has there been a sale of the manufacturer creating a successor liability problem?

[11]   How do the product's instructions and warnings compare to competing products given the apparent risks involved?

[12]   What is the price differential among similar products with enhanced safety features?

[13]   What share of the market does this product have?

[14]   What does the authoritative literature say about this arguable defect or range of defects?

[15]   Is the alleged defect well documented in authoritative sources?

[16]   Has the defendant company ignored clearly expressed and authoritative concerns about this alleged defect?

[17]   Do all competing products have the same basic problem to a greater, same or lesser degree?

[18]   What are the leading authoritative journals in this area?

[19]   Who are the recognized individual authorities?

[20] What are the in-house statistics regarding the potential for product failure and resultant projections regarding death or injury?

[21] What are the publicly available statistics regarding the potential for product failure and resultant projections regarding death or injury?

[22] Were there or are there government regulations in effect or proposed that have a direct bearing on, or can be used by analogy concerning the product under scrutiny?

[23] Have there been government imposed recalls or defect investigations in the past?

[24] Is there company documentation available in agency files that are accessible prior to discovery through a Freedom of Information Act request?

[25] Has there been a concerted effort by the industry and/or this defendant to alter or impede safety regulations?

[26] How do existing or proposed performance standards compare to thinking in the scientific community regarding the relevant performance feature?

[27] Is there a good argument for government agency preemption as a basis for dismissal of the litigation?

[28] How is the defendant manufacture organized over the period of the target product's life in the company?

[29] How long have they been involved in this business and this product line or similar products?

[30] Have they or do they manufacture, distribute or sell this product in foreign countries or nation communities such as the European Community?

[31] Are the products liability laws different in each of those countries or groupings?

[32] How does a products liability case proceed in such jurisdictions? Is there any provision for pre-trial discovery similar to those available in the United States?

[33] Are there international treaties that govern any aspect of this litigation that may affect the efforts of plaintiff and defense counsel?

[34] Has this defendant and product been involved in previous litigation?

These and a host of other questions face the products litigator at the beginning of each products case undertaking. It is the goal of this section of the book to address the practice aspects of each of the inquiries set out above. Once the litigation is joined and discovery begins, a host of additional questions will arise and also be addressed in the subsequent chapters.

§ 11.03 THE MAJOR RESEARCH TASKS IN PRODUCTS LIABILITY LITIGATION

The choices made from the theories of liability analyzed in Part I will substantially influence to what extent specific research and preparation factors come into play. Set out below is a detailed checklist of the major work product subjects and routine activities involved in representing a client in a products liability case.

Pre-Filing Product-Related Research Responsibilities

[1]   Lengthy time frames for conducting pre-filing research and discovery (typically 10–25 years or in some recent instances such as asbestos, as many as 50 years).

[2]   Extensive scientific and technical investigation of the authoritative sources regarding the type of product line and specific aspect of the product involved in the case.

[3]   Extensive investigation of the industry wherein the defendant does business and its organizational history in relation to the subject product or product line.

[4]   Comparative product analyses, to include domestic and foreign manufacture, distribution or sales.

[5]   Extensive investigation of past, present, and future regulatory activity affecting the subject product or product lines in the relevant industry.

[6]   Mastering the defendant company's document producing Standard Operating Procedures (SOPs) respecting the design, testing, production, marketing and post-marketing activities, including record retention policies for paper and digital records.

[7]   The intricacies of company document retention and destruction policies and their system for electronic storage of records.

[8]   Discovery planning and the issuance of interrogatories, document requests and depositions.

[9]   The ongoing issue of motions for discovery enforcement.

[10] The issuance of protective orders.

[11] The international/domestic business organizations issues increasingly involved in litigation with multi-national corporations.

[12] International treaties relative to service of process, damage caps, and foreign discovery [or the lack of it by national law].

[13] Language/translation issues.

§ 11.04 RESEARCH TIME FRAMES

The period of historical research that is relevant to any particular case will vary according to the reason it is being conducted. There are typically three such research periods in a products liability case:

[A] **Broad-based pre-filing investigative research** [How long has this product or chemical been used commercially? Has the relevant scientific community addressed any health related concerns? Has there been any effort by governmental units to regulate any aspect of the commerce for this ingredient or product? Have there been prior lawsuits regarding this product?]

[B] **Discovery research** [In what period in the documentary history of the defendant company may a plaintiff justifiably seek information by way of interrogatories, document requests, or depositions?]

[C] **Trial evidence** [What are the selected periods of defendant's design, testing, production, marketing and post-marketing product history that will need to be addressed in plaintiff's effort to prove the case?]

The central initial decision in the entire investigative and research aspects of the case is to approximate the chronological period or periods within which to seek out scientific, industry, regulatory and company information. This decision will eventually result in the historical period or time frame within which the plaintiff will ask the court for discovery and eventually the jury to assess the appropriateness of defendant corporation's conscious business decisions.

For solely *investigative purposes* counsel may choose any period considered of background importance for purposes of scientific, industry, regulator, and company research. However, the selection of a relevant and manageable time frame *for discovery* purposes requires considerable thought and will be the subject of heated pre-trial motions to expand or limit the period. The discovery time frame will, in turn, have great bearing on the historical period within which evidence will be accepted at trial. It must be emphasized here, that the typical time frame for products liability cases is 15–20 years, with periods as long as 50 years in certain settings such as asbestos litigation. Initial discovery skirmishes will eventually result in a court-imposed time period perceivably too long for defendant and too short for plaintiff.

The introduction of a drug or manufactured item into the marketplace is the result of more than a few years of investigation, testing and careful planning by the defendant company. Often a new product in a marketing sense — i.e., a new line of sports-utility vehicles — utilizes existing technology for the materials of the new product. In automotive design for example, manufacturers typically recycle existing axles, door locks, engines or other technological components. Retooling is expensive, time-consuming and usually unnecessary. Most engineered products are rarely made of whole cloth. It is characteristic that the broad outlines of new or improved products are manufactured by pre-existing technology both in the company and the industry worldwide. However, it is the case that new pharmaceuticals and products from the chemical industry often are made of new designs and ingredients.

The task for the products litigator is to determine the relevant historical antecedents of the case product in state-of-the-art literature, industry publications, government agency filings and the defendant company's internal files. As will be discussed in Chapters 16 through 19, the susceptibility of similar product data is always a very large bone of contention.[3] For example, knowledge of the limits of certain ball-joint technology that is used across defendant's pickup truck lines would seem to be fair game in a case based upon a catastrophic failure during the range of intended uses of the vehicle. Defense counsel are sensitive to this problem and are constantly cautioned to take preemptive, if questionable, steps to minimize or eliminate it. As recently noted in a products defense attorney publication:

> Products Liability actions are not easy cases to prepare, nor are they easy cases to try. More often than not, such cases involve complex industrial or consumer products, monumental amounts of documents, intricate theories of liability and defense, and horrific injuries. Defense counsel must make sense of a variety of complex issues and present a coherent, cohesive, and streamlined theory of defense to the jury. . . . [T]he defense attorney who is successful in preventing the introduction of "extraneous" issues to the jury will be far ahead of the game in terms of limiting the scope of the case and concentrating the jury's focus on the salient legal issues. One of the most successful ways of limiting the introduction of "extraneous" issues is to prevent the plaintiff's attorney from finding out about them during the course of discovery.[4]

The clear-cut demarcation identification of relevant discovery time frames routinely cannot be had until the conclusion of discovery depositions, often resulting in supplemental requests for documentation.[5]

It is plaintiff's responsibility to throw down the timing gauntlet by initiating an historical period in the life of the defendant company by indicating over what period of years her discovery requests are to extend. An example would be an interrogatory requesting the test numbers of all pickup truck ball-joint stress tests for the years 1990–2005. This 15-year period would initiate defense relevancy arguments objecting to the length of time over which the information is being requested. Interrogatories are the usual place for the time frame arguments to begin and such arguments resurface at all ensuing phases of discovery. Chapter 19, Protective Orders and Discovery Enforcement, will discuss this process in depth.

Consequently, a key purpose and goal of pre-filing investigation and research is to mark out the years in the past history of state-of-the-art, regulatory and company life that will arguably have discovery relevance, shedding light on the good judgment, or absence of it, of the conscious design choices engaged in by the defendant in getting the product into the hands of the targeted consumers. It is

---

[3] See Bradley C. Nahrstadt, *Narrowing the Scope of Discovery for Substantially Similar Products*, PRAC. LITIG., Nov. 2004, at 38.

[4] *Id.*

[5] The Catch-22 in the process is that counsel is unable to effectively engage in pre-filing research or discovery without some fairly firm idea of just what those time frames may be. *See* KIELY, SCIENCE AND LITIGATION, *supra* note 2, at 245.

important to note here, that the concept of *relevancy* in discovery is considerably broader than that utilized in determinations of the admissibility of trial evidence. This is a point that plaintiff's counsel often fail to emphasize and one that defense lawyers at times pass over in discovery enforcement debates.

The definition of relevance is provided by Rule 401 of the Federal Rules of Evidence. That provision defines relevant evidence as follows: "Relevant evidence' means evidence having any tendency to make the existence of a fact that is of consequence to the determination of the action more probable or less probable than it would be without the evidence." By referencing this broad standard and providing for the free discovery of data that may be reasonably calculated to lead to the discovery of such, the federal courts have mandated a liberal discovery scheme.

As noted by Justice Powell of the United States Supreme Court, writing for a unanimous court in *Oppenheimer Fund, Inc. v. Sanders*, 437 U.S. 340, 351 (1978):

> The key phrase in this definition — 'relevant to the subject matter involved in the pending action' — has been construed broadly to encompass any matter that bears on, or that reasonably could lead to other matter that could bear on, any issue that is or may be in the case. (citations omitted). . . . Consistently with the notice-pleading system established by the Rules, discovery is not limited to issues raised by the pleadings, for discovery itself is designed to help define and clarify the issues. (citation omitted). Nor is discovery limited to the merits of a case, for a variety of fact-oriented issues may arise during litigation that are not related to the merits.

A request for discovery should be considered relevant if there is any possibility that information sought may be relevant to the subject matter of the action. Discovery is not limited to formally admissible evidence because its primary purpose is to formulate, define and narrow issues to be tried, increase the chances for settlement, and give each party the opportunity to inform himself of the facts that may come out at trial.[6] As stated in the 1984 case of *Chubb Integrated-Systems Ltd. v. National Bank of Washington, et al.*[7]:

> Whether this information is found to be admissible at trial has little bearing on the issue of discoverability. Rule 26(b) makes a clear distinction between information that is relevant to the subject matter for pretrial discovery and the ultimate admissibility of that information at trial.[8]

Admissibility at trial is not the yardstick of permissible discovery.[9] The relevancy of the information sought also bears directly on the issue of whether discovery requests are burdensome. If the requested material is relevant, no matter the

---

[6] Detweiler Bros., Inc. v. John Graham & Co., 412 F. Supp. 416 (E.D. Wash. 1976); Duplan Corp. v. Deering Milliken, Inc., 397 F. Supp. 1146 (D.S.C. 1974); Carlson Companies, Inc. v. Sperry & Hutchinson Co., 374 F. Supp. 1080 (D. Minn. 1973); Sylgab Steel & Wire Corp. v. Imoco-Gateway Corp., 357 F. Supp. 659 (N.D. Ill. 1973).

[7] 103 F.R.D. 52 (D.D.C. 1984.).

[8] *Id.* at 59.

[9] *See* Roesberg v. Johns-Manville Corp., 85 F.R.D. 292 (E.D. Pa. 1980); Chubb Integrated Sys. v. National Bank of Washington, 103 F.R.D. 52 (D.D.C. 1984). *See also* FED. R. CIV. P. 26(b)(1) advisory committee's note, 1970 Amendment.

volume, it must be produced. The initial focal point to determine the actual scope of this broadly-interpreted concept is the plaintiff's complaint. As noted in the leading case of *Roesberg v. Johns-Manville Corp.*: "The detail in the complaint specifies the necessary relevance of the interrogatories. . . . The burden now falls upon GAF, the party resisting discovery, to clarify and explain its objections and to provide support therefor."[10] The allegations of the complaint serve to determine the broad subject matters involved in the case, and relevance is to be measured, not according to the specific issues raised by the pleadings, but rather, by reference to such subject matters.[11]

The distinction between the scope of relevancy for discovery and trial admissibility purposes is a substantial one. The fixing of time frames in discovery requests, in turn, has a significant bearing on the admissibility of evidence at trial. Fed. R. Civ. P. 26(b)(1) provides that materials subject to review in the discovery process are much broader, since the materials accessible in discovery are all materials that are relevant in an evidentiary sense plus those likely to lead to the discovery of relevant evidence. The latter concept allows for far reaching examination of materials in defendant's possession or control.[12] Nonetheless, this expansive view of discovery relevancy is tempered by the provision that discovery may be limited by the court if it determines that: (i) the discovery sought is unreasonably cumulative or duplicative, or is obtainable from some other source that is more convenient, less burdensome, or less expensive; (ii) the party seeking discovery has had ample opportunity by discovery in the action to obtain the information sought; or (iii) the burden or expense of the proposed discovery outweighs its likely benefit. . . ."[13]

Courts have recognized that while it is true that relevance in discovery is broader than that required for admissibility at trial, "the object of inquiry must have some evidentiary value before an order to compel disclosure of otherwise inadmissible material will issue."[14] Further, the information must be "reasonably calculated to lead to the discovery of admissible evidence."[15] Courts have also recognized that "the legal tenet that relevancy in the discovery context is broader than in the context of admissibility should not be misapplied so as to allow fishing expeditions in discovery."[16] Therefore, discovery methods will be limited by the Court if it determines that the discovery sought is unreasonably cumulative or duplicative.[17]

---

[10] 85 F.R.D. at 297.

[11] Smith v. F.T.C., 403 F. Supp. 1000 (D. Del.1975).

[12] *Id.* The discovery rules are accorded a broad and liberal treatment to affect their purpose of adequately informing litigants in civil trials. Herbert v. Lando, 441 U.S. 153 (1979). Nevertheless, discovery does have "ultimate and necessary boundaries," Oppenheimer Fund, Inc. v. Sanders, 437 U.S. 340, 351 (1978) (*quoting* Hickman v. Taylor, 329 U.S. 495, 507 (1947)), and "it is well established that the scope of discovery is within the sound discretion of the trial court." Coleman v. Am. Red Cross, 23 F.3d 1091, 1096 (6th Cir. 1994).

[13] Fed. R. Civ. P. 26(b)(2).

[14] Zenith Elec. Corp. v. Exzec, Inc., 1998 U.S. Dist. LEXIS 215, at *8 (N.D. Ill. Jan. 2, 1998) (*quoting* Piacenti v. Gen. Motors Corp., 173 F.R.D. 221, 223 (N.D. Ill. 1997)).

[15] *Id.*

[16] *Id.*

[17] Fed. R. Civ. P. 26(b)(2)(i). *See* Volvo Trucks North America, Inc. v. Crescent Ford Truck Sales, 2006

§ 11.05 CRITERIA FOR SELECTION OF TIME FRAMES

The choice of investigative, discovery, and evidentiary time frames, involves a complex mix of factors, especially plaintiff's choice of the available theoretical defect categories. Actual defect allegations involving communications between the public and the company, such as instructions and warnings run the gamut from the decision to publish those communications up to the date of the alleged injury. Time frames for those defect types can run for many years, depending upon how long the product has been on the market. Many popular pharmaceuticals such as Percodan or familiar household products such as Drano may serve as examples. Overall design defect cases involve time frames extending from the date the particular design was officially adopted up to the date of the alleged injury.

Accordingly, scientific, industry, governmental and internal corporate data is fair game for discovery and the subject of intense discovery motion practice. The typically voluminous state of the art materials are readily available to the litigators who are aware of how to locate them and how to absorb what they have to offer. The self-education of both plaintiff and defense counsel is an ever present fact of life in these cases no matter how much funding is available for expert witness assistance.

The preliminary study engaged in by products litigators will familiarize the lawyers with the location and extent of relevant primary source materials and introduce them to the terminology and general outlines of the relevant technology and industry involved. Because of their centrality to the entire products liability undertaking, the subject of investigative and trial admissibility time frames will be noted throughout the remainder of this book. Set out below is a capsule summary of the remaining chapters of Part II of this book.

Chapter 12. Researching the Products Case, addresses the identification of the theoretical defect mode [Manufacturing defect? Failure to instruct? Failure to Warn? Overall design defect? Misrepresentation?]; identification of the precise scientific defect [defectively designed ball joints in trucks resulting in loss of a wheel]; and the quantitative [significant adverse reaction or product failure reports] and qualitative extent of the scientific defect's harm [the injury pattern, while infrequent, is of a devastating nature] over the various research and investigative periods.

Chapter 13. The Expert Witness, discusses the early task of determining expert witness needs by category case-wide. This potentially involves experts in the relevant areas of science, government regulation, the profile of the entire industry, the history of the named defendant(s)' research and development, testing programs, production, marketing and/or advertising, and damages. The chapter also discusses considerations in choosing expert witnesses, and using expert witnesses for pretrial, discovery and trial purposes.

Chapter 14. Products Liability and Discovery, addresses the key topics of discovery relevancy versus trial relevancy, duties of full and ongoing disclosure, the

---

U.S. Dist. LEXIS 5811 (E.D. La. Feb. 14, 2006). Relevancy for discovery purposes is extremely broad. The information sought need not be admissible in court in order to be relevant. Rather, the relevancy burden is met if the party can show that the information sought "appears reasonably calculated to lead to the discovery of admissible evidence."

general discovery rules as related to products liability settings, relevancy in relation to case investigative time frames, relevancy as applied to the discovery of a company's historical materials as they relate to its industry relations, research and development testing, their interaction with regulatory agencies, their particular manufacturing processes. The chapter also addresses the general topic of destructive testing; categorizing case information needs over the desired historical period in the history of the company, the drafting of discovery documents, and the crucial new expansion and increasing complexity of electronic discovery.

Chapter 15. Drafting the Complaint and Discovery Focus, analyzes important aspects of the complaint drafting process, such as the judicial education function, the controlling relation between the product defect allegations and discovery and the subject of proximate cause.

Chapter 16. Interrogatories and Request to Admit Facts, will focus on the purpose of interrogatories in products liability cases, the introduction by plaintiff of preliminary discovery time frames, the categorization of interrogatories and their relationship to document requests, statutory limitation on the initial number of interrogatories, supplemental interrogatories, the organization and specificity of interrogatories, and an introduction to discovery objections and enforcement.

Chapter 17. Requests to Produce Documents, will discuss the purpose of document requests in product liability cases, the refinement of the discovery request period, the categorization of document requests, supplemental requests for documentation, the organization and specificity of document requests, objections to document requests and some thoughts on objections to requests and motions to enforce discovery.

Chapter 18. Discovery and Evidence Depositions, analyzes the scope of discovery and evidence depositions, the choice of deponents, the basis for objections in discovery or evidence depositions, and the trial use of discovery and evidence depositions.

Chapter 19. Protective Orders and Discovery Enforcement, provides discussions of trade secrets and other bases for the imposition of a protective order, trial relevancy versus discovery relevancy and the enforcement of discovery rights.

Chapter 12

RESEARCHING THE PRODUCTS CASE

SYNOPSIS

§ 12.01 INTRODUCTION

§ 12.02 THE RANGE OF WORK AREAS IN PRODUCTS LIABILITY LITIGATION

§ 12.03 DUAL ASPECTS OF RESEARCH DATA

§ 12.04 RESEARCH POINTS OF REFERENCE

§ 12.05 IDENTIFICATION OF THE THEORETICAL DEFECT TYPE

§ 12.06 IDENTIFYING THE PRODUCT'S INJURY-PRODUCING ASPECT

§ 12.07 THE EXTENT OF THE ALLEGED INJURIES TO CONSUMERS

§ 12.08 THE SERIOUSNESS OF THE ALLEGED INJURIES TO CONSUMERS

§ 12.09 STATE-OF-THE-ART COMMENTARY ON THE ALLEGED DEFECTS AND INJURIES

§ 12.10 GOVERNMENT REGULATION OF THE DEFENDANT'S INDUSTRY

§ 12.11 THE HISTORY OF THE INDUSTRY REACTION TO THE SCIENTIFIC PROBLEM

§ 12.12 STUDY OF DEFENDANT CORPORATION'S ORGANIZATION AND MANUFACTURING PROCESSES

§ 12.13 THE DEVELOPMENT OF THE CORPORATE DEFENDANT'S REACTION TO THE ALLEGED SCIENTIFIC DEFECT

§ 12.14 PRIOR LITIGATION, SETTLEMENTS, OR CASE FILINGS

§ 12.15 MATERIALS SUPPLIERS AND COMPONENT PART MANUFACTURERS INFORMATION SOURCE CATEGORIES

§ 12.16 LIBRARY COLLECTIONS

§ 12.17 GOVERNMENT DATABASES

§ 12.18 BOOKS AND PERIODICALS

§ 12.19 DIALOG INFORMATION SERVICES

§ 12.20 POPULAR PUBLICATIONS

§ 12.21 ACADEMIC AND PROFESSIONAL JOURNALS

§ 12.22 ACADEMIC AND PROFESSIONAL ANNUAL MEETINGS AND SPECIAL CONFERENCES

§ 12.23   RESEARCH IN PROGRESS AND GRANTS

§ 12.24   STATISTICAL PUBLICATIONS AND DATA BANKS

§ 12.25   MATERIALS, DESIGN, AND PERFORMANCE STANDARDS

§ 12.26   CONSUMER INTEREST GROUPS AND ASSOCIATED PUBLICATIONS

§ 12.27   PROFESSIONAL AND TRADE ASSOCIATIONS AND ORGANIZATIONS

§ 12.28   TRADE ASSOCIATIONS

§ 12.29   PATENTS

§ 12.30   COMPANY RESEARCH

§ 12.31   ANNUAL REPORTS

§ 12.32   DIRECTORY OF CORPORATE AFFILIATIONS

§ 12.33   THOMAS REGISTER OF AMERICAN MANUFACTURERS

§ 12.34   FOREIGN CORPORATIONS

§ 12.35   SUMMARY

§ 12.36   APPENDIX: PRODUCTS LIABILITY INTERNET RESEARCH SITES

§ 12.01   INTRODUCTION

There are four broad evidentiary clusters that serve as plaintiff counsel's focal points for the preparation of a product liability case:

1. Information potentially demonstrating corporate knowledge of product defects and feasible alternative designs.

2. Unacceptable management decisions in light of such knowledge.

3. Proof that one or more of the identified defects in fact caused the death or injury to the client.

4. Proof that one or more of the feasible alternative designs, warnings or instructions would have minimized or eliminated such death or injury.

Defense counsel must examine the same body of information to build a case for responsible, defect-free design, testing, manufacturing and marketing by its corporate client.

This undertaking involves the gathering and analysis of large amounts of data from without and within the defendant corporation. Much of this information is often difficult technical data. A substantial amount of the internal company documents received via discovery will reflect the internal processes of the corporation in all stages of manufacture from design to the inventory shelf. Plaintiff lawyers must compete with substantially superior investigative, expert witness and law firm staff typically available to the corporate defendant. Nonetheless, defense counsel faces the same daunting learning curve experienced by plaintiff. Both sides must face the considerable task of making sense of all of these documents to a series of motion judges, and most importantly, a trial judge and jury.

A very considerable amount of the *pre-filing* state-of-the-art literature required by counsel is available through public, often cost-free sources. The contemporary explosion of information sites on the Internet makes that research task less onerous every day. In addition to the broad availability of technical literature in engineering, pharmaceuticals and chemistry, substantial data sources on regulatory activity is available even without a Freedom of Information Act Request. Large amounts of preliminary industry corporate information are also accessible from a number of web-based sources.

The greatest amount of information reviewed by counsel will yield its primary value in respect to its *investigative importance*. What does this information tell me about this technology, industry or corporation that I did not know before? In what directions does it point for additional research? Hard choices must be made at the conclusion of research and discovery to convert the massive accumulation of data into a controllable as well as communicable case for jury consumption. The bulk of the information that counsel will marshal most likely will not be admissible at trial under the rules of evidence, but has great value in forwarding written discovery and evidence depositions. Accordingly, counsel must be able to determine the unique value that each item of information will have to both the investigation and formal legal requirements of the planned lawsuit. This dual perspective will be referenced throughout the remainder of this work.

§ 12.02 THE RANGE OF WORK AREAS IN PRODUCTS LIABILITY LITIGATION

A simple graphic can illustrate the basic nature of pre-filing and pre-trial products liability research:

PRETRIAL PRODUCT-RELATED RESEARCH

Products Liability Research-Related

Information Sources

EXTERNAL DATA	INTERNAL COMPANY DATA
[Pre-Filing Research]	[Discovery]
1. State-of-the-Art Literature	1. Design Documents
2. Industry Custom	2. Testing Documents
3. Regulatory Activity	3. Production Documents
4. Injury History	4. Marketing Documents
5. Litigation History	5. Post-Marketing Documents

BASIC RESEARCH ISSUES

1. What mechanical or chemical or pharmacological aspect of defendant's product actually caused the plaintiff's death or injury?
2. How did it do that?
3. Was the defendant aware of that injury-producing potential? When?
4. Could the defendant have done something to have eliminated or minimized that risk and still have aggressively competed in its chosen markets?
5. If it could have, why didn't it?

Set out below is a detailed checklist of the major work product subjects and routine activities involved in representing a client in a products liability case.

Pre-Filing Product-Related Research Responsibilities

[1]   Lengthy time frames for conducting pre-filing research and discovery (typically 10-25 years or in some recent instances such as asbestos, as many as 50 years).

[2]   Extensive scientific and technical investigation of the authoritative sources regarding the type of product line and specific aspect of the product involved in the case.

[3]   Extensive investigation of the industry wherein the defendant does business and its organizational history in relation to the subject product or product line.

[4]   Comparative product analyses, to include domestic and foreign manufacture, distribution or sales.

[5]   Extensive investigation of past, present and future regulatory activity affecting the subject product or product lines in the relevant industry.

[6]   Mastering the defendant company's document producing processes

(SOP's) as respects the design, testing, production, marketing and post-marketing activities, including record retention policies for paper and digital records.

[7]   The intricacies of company retention and destruction policies and their system for electronic storage of records, especially e-mails.

[8]   Discovery planning and the issuance of interrogatories, document requests and depositions.

[9]   The ongoing issue of motions for discovery enforcement.

[10]   The issuance of protective orders.

[11]   The international/domestic business organizations issues increasingly involved in litigation with multi-national corporations.

[12]   International treaties relative to service of process, damage caps, and foreign discovery [or the lack of it by national law].

[13]   Language/translation issues.

§ 12.03   DUAL ASPECTS OF RESEARCH DATA

It is important in every aspect of product research that counsel maintain a dual perspective toward each item of information gathered and analyzed. Those two considerations are the *investigative* and *legal* significance of each item of information gathered. The bulk of materials examined will have only investigative significance — i.e., what does this tell me about the development and injury-producing potential of the product? Where does it lead me in furthering the pre- and post-filing research effort? How does it help to interpret documents sought or received in the discovery stage of the case? How do case experts value this information?

In terms of *legal significance*, does this item of information aid, in whole or in part, to establish one or more of the essential elements of the complaint. Does it establish knowledge of risk or the lack of it? Does it go toward establishing a feasible alternative design? Does it show that any such alternative is a subsequent remedial measure and thus required to be excluded from evidence? Does it help establish proximate cause?

All research serves an investigative function, however slight. Some small portion of it will constitute proof necessary to get to a jury. A considerable task at the end of the research period is making the hard choice of documents to use at trial from the mountain of materials gathered through pretrial research and discovery.[1]

---

[1] This important issue is addressed and discussed in Chapter 17, Requests to Produce Documents, and Chapter19, Protective Orders and Discovery Enforcement.

§ 12.04 RESEARCH POINTS OF REFERENCE

The suspect product is normally one of a generic type of manufactured goods produced in an industry which draws on an existing body of technology and business practices. In the broad scientific divisions of product creation-engineering, pharmaceuticals and chemicals, products have been and will continue to be produced on a vast scale. The associated scientific, industry and manufacturing literature is substantial and varied, ranging from highly sophisticated journals to books, newsletters and symposia papers. Many specific product industries or particular product lines or precise technological issues such as pain killers, infant car seats, pesticides, auto rollover protection and the like are often subject to some form of government regulation. Each of these regulatory efforts will yield important documents of keen interest to plaintiff and defense counsel. In addition, with respect to the design feature under scrutiny, there may be an injury-producing history, which in turn may provide important data for study and later introduction in evidence.

Each of these areas for inquiry involves extensive amounts of literature, documentary submissions and corporate documents that must be located and reviewed. As noted above, the greatest part of the relevant data sought may be found in sources outside of the defendant corporation. The multi-year generation of internal corporate documentation addressing the design, testing, production and marketing of the product may only be reviewed following difficult and long-term discovery efforts.

§ 12.05 IDENTIFICATION OF THE THEORETICAL DEFECT TYPE

The initial task for both plaintiff or defense counsel is to settle on just what it is that was actually wrong with the suspect product in common sense terms. Was there some flaw in the product unit that caused the injury not present in other units sold by the defendant? Was the client injured by the product packaging and not the product itself? Is it a question of misleading instructions or inadequate or non-existent warnings? Is there something wrong with the basic design of the product in a particular respect? Prior to purchase, was the client misled by some material misrepresentation about the product that he relied upon to his detriment? Are more than one of these problems involved?[2]

Regardless of the broad classification of actual case product defects alleged in a count of a products complaint, there are only seven *theoretical categories* within which any particular litigation can be described:

- **Unit Defect** [One unit that was defective or flawed]

- **Packaging Defects** [The access to the product is allegedly dangerous, not the product itself]

---

[2] Typically a product liability complaint involves at least one of the defects in addition to a failure to warn. Product shortcomings are generally classified in legal parlance as being either manufacturing or design defects. *See* Chapter 15, Products Liability and Discovery.

- **Instructions Defects** [The instructions for use are inadequate or confusing resulting in potential injury to the user]

- **Warnings Defects** [The manufactured good, pharmaceutical or chemical has no warnings specific to the alleged risk of injury or contains misleading or insufficient warning]

- **Overall Design Defects** [Some feature, aspect, or component to all the products in the line of which the suspect product is a member, has a design flaw that effects all units of like manufacture]

- **Misrepresentation** [The consumer justifiably relied upon a false or misleading statement of fact about product's features made in advertising or other marketing literature]

- **Breach of Warranty** [Failure to meet actual or implied warranties as to performance and safety][3]

These theoretical, non-fact-specific defect types, determine the reach of pre-filing research, and in large part determine the limits of discovery and the acceptability of trial evidence. Each of these generic defect types has unique research requirements and the typical products litigation will often involve one or more of them alleged concurrently. The discussion to follow will focus on several basic pre-filing research points that will help to center and guide the entire research undertaking.

§ 12.06   IDENTIFYING THE PRODUCT'S INJURY-PRODUCING ASPECT

In products cases grounded in each type of defect category, it is obvious that any real injury was *caused* by some physical aspect of the product itself, although the legal responsibility may arise from the company's *facilitation of that event*, by its allegedly poor manufacturing methods, misleading instructions for use, faulty warnings, risky design choices, or fraudulent misrepresentation.[4] It is clear that the failure to warn about the potential dangers of the drug Vioxx cannot cause any physical injury to anyone, nor can a faulty design of an automobile part or a pharmaceutical or chemical composition cause cancer. The products liability policy discussed throughout Chapters 1 through 10 supplies the basic rationale for allowing this type of litigation. The law asks if the defendant company *facilitated* any such injury by encouraging the consumer's use in the face of any of the defect types discussed. The actual, physical or biological cause of the injury is not within the company's control, and is never the central issue in modern products liability litigation.[5] What *is always at issue* is the extent and manner of the defendant's *facilitation of* death or injury resulting from its associating the consumer with the

---

[3] *See* OWEN & PHILLIPS, PRODUCTS LIABILITY (2005).

[4] See discussion in Chapter 8, Problems of Proof: Defect and Causation.

[5] The *Parlodel* litigation may serve as an example, where defendant manufacturer argues that the chemical brocriptomine, a central component of its anti-lactation drug Parlodel was biologically incapable of causing brain aneurysms in young mothers. The central factual issue in the seminal *Daubert* case was whether the ingredients of the drug Bendectin could cause fetal malformations in the group of

product with established risks of injury flowing from defective designs or communications, via instructions and/or warnings.

Whenever someone is injured or killed through their interaction with a manufactured item, pharmaceutical or chemical, there arises the preliminary inference that some aspect of the product was flawed, individually or, more often, generically to all units of the product. Examples would be failed ball joints on several models of pickup trucks resulting in the loss of a wheel during travel; confusing instructions for use of paint removers resulting in asphyxiation; inadequate warnings as to heart problems resulting from the ingestion of painkillers for arthritis. Once counsel has estimated the precise technical cause of the injury-producing event, the general category or categories of defects within which the case falls, must be decided upon. Depending upon the particular theoretical defect type involved in the case, the actual biological, engineering or chemical aspects of the product will have varying degrees of importance to the litigation.[6]

§ 12.07 THE EXTENT OF THE ALLEGED INJURIES TO CONSUMERS

Once the underlying biological, structural or chemical contributors of the injury have been tentatively identified, it must be estimated how extensive the problem has been for consumers of the suspect or comparable products. Outside of the individual unit case, the real world extent of the problem can have a dramatic bearing on the success or failure of the lawsuit. When the legal focus is on a design, instructions or warnings aspect for an entire line of goods, a relatively insignificant injury history makes it difficult to prove that the product was in a "defective condition unreasonably dangerous." While the broader based design defect category of cases do balance numerous factors in the effort to judge the social acceptability of defendant's conscious design choices, the cold figures delineating the product's injury history are often the decisive point in the analysis. This is particularly so in drug cases.[7]

§ 12.08 THE SERIOUSNESS OF THE ALLEGED INJURIES TO CONSUMERS

An equally important area of research is the determination of just how serious any injuries are flowing from the alleged defects. The honored liability theorem of Judge Learned Hand balancing the foreseeability of harm against the seriousness

---

expectant mothers who ingested the drug. *See, e.g.*, 19 No. 7 Andrews Pharmaceutical Litig. Rep. 8.

Questioning the credibility of causal evidence offered by a woman who says her use of the lactation suppressant Parlodel led her to suffer a stroke, a federal judge in Greensboro, N.C. declared the data inadmissible and granted defendant Sandoz Pharmaceuticals Corp.'s motion for summary judgment. Dunn v. Sandoz Pharmaceuticals Corp., 275 F. Supp. 2d 672 (M.D.N.C. 2003).

[6] *See* JAMES A. HENDERSON, JR. & AARON D. TWERSKI, PRODUCTS LIABILITY: PROBLEMS AND PROCESS (5th ed. 2004); DAVID G. OWEN, PRODUCTS LIABILITY LAW HORNBOOK (2005).

[7] *See* TERRENCE F. KIELY, SCIENCE AND LITIGATION: PRODUCTS LIABILITY IN THEORY AND PRACTICE 237 (CRC Press 2002).

of the harm if it does occur, and the efforts required to minimize or eliminate it comes into play here.[8]

An injury profile of a severe magnitude can counterbalance a statistically low injury occurrence record. In instances where an actor can foresee statistically insignificant, but catastrophic injuries potentially materializing from his acts or omissions, the law has always required that the party best able to minimize or eliminate the risk take precautions not normally required of the reasonably prudent person.[9] The policy base of product liability law adds support to this famous modern legal maxim.

§ 12.09   STATE-OF-THE-ART COMMENTARY ON THE ALLEGED DEFECTS AND INJURIES

A primary pre-filing research task once the specific scientific defect has been tentatively identified and the range of the alleged injuries in terms of magnitude and severity preliminarily estimated, is to establish the level at which the relevant scientific authorities have even acknowledged that a problem actually exists. Equally important is the determination of the extant literature that addresses efforts to minimize or eliminate the risks allegedly associated with the suspect product. This research constitutes the foundation of what is referred to as the "state of the art" investigations, which focuses on historical developments and materials *outside* the life of the defendant company. This broad literature ranges from highly specialized engineering, pharmaceutical, chemical and medical journals, to industry trade association journals, newsletters and popular publications available in chain bookstores, such as recreational vehicle magazines. This latter type of publication exists in and around all consumer product areas and often provides highly relevant information such as alternative design products providing greater safety. Stabilizing bars for recreational vehicles to prevent unit sway and chain saw guards are examples.

Product litigators, with or without the initial advice of experts, must determine the identity and availability of the key books, journals, other publications, databases and websites considered authoritative in the field. These can be specific to a select topic such as the large number of text and journals devoted to discrete areas such as diabetes, heart, lung, kidney and anesthesia,[10] or prestigious journals more general in nature such as Lancet,[11] The New England Journal of Medicine[12] or The Journal of the American Medical Association (JAMA).[13]

It is important to realize that the authoritative sources that need to be consulted to resolve the defect-injury issue are rarely product, and on occasion, not even

---

[8] "Possibly it serves to bring this notion into relief to state it in algebraic terms: if the probability be called P; the injury, L; and the burden, B; liability depends upon whether B is less than L multiplied by P: i.e., whether $B < PL$." United States v. Carroll Towing Co., 159 F.2d 169, 173 (2d Cir. 1947).

[9] *Id.*

[10] See the extensive listing of medical journals provided free at http://www.freemed icaljournals.com/.

[11] http://www.thelancet.com/.

[12] http://content.nejm.org/.

[13] http://jama.ama-assn.org/.

industry specific. Available websites and databases are numerous and incredibly comprehensive.

§ 12.10   GOVERNMENT REGULATION OF THE DEFENDANT'S INDUSTRY

The majority of the nation's major industries are subject to some degree of government regulation through the activities of a number of federal agencies. They are a group that looms above most products cases in one degree or another, regulating the introduction of a product to the market, such as the Food and Drug Administration (FDA)[14] or mandate performance standards for existing technology, such as the National Highway Safety Administration (NHTSA)[15] for automobiles, the Environmental Protection Agency (EPA)[16] for industrial emissions or the Consumer Product Safety Commission (CPSC)[17] for consumer goods, such as bicycles or shower door glass. It is unusual in the present time to come across a manufactured good that is not subject, in some respect, to a proposed or existing federal agency regulation.

The issuance of a proposed performance standard by an agency is one of the most important investigative finds in the early stage of products liability research. Crash tests required by NHTSA to determine the resistance to fires resulting from rear end collisions or seat belt integrity in a relatively small and light weight vehicle such as the GEO may serve as an example.[18] These proposed regulations typically require some level of performance from the targeted products in an industry — i.e., zero fuel leakage following a 30-mile per hour rear end collision of the targeted vehicle into a flat laboratory barrier or actual vehicle at 30 miles an hour. (NHTSA) Strength tests for architectural glass used in shower doors (CPSC) are another early example. The proposed performance level may be a certain coefficient of friction on backyard pool slides to prevent injuries to small children (CPSC) or a specified level of mercury emissions from industrial stacks. (EPA)

These proposed regulations are important in several respects to product litigators focused on the same performance range:

(A)   The very issuance of the proposal assumes that the companies within the affected industry are not currently meeting the proposed performance level and the tentative belief of the agency that such level can and should be met.

(B)   The typical 90-day or longer period within which the industry can respond to the need and/or specifics of any proposal typically prompts the issuance of a large body of internal company documents directed towards all

---

[14]   http://www.fda.gov/.

[15]   http://www.nhtsa.gov/.

[16]   http://www.epa.gov/.

[17]   http://www.cpsc.gov/.

[18]   *See, e.g.*, Reports Accepted During October 2004 For FY 2003 Test . . . 33. 208. Occupant Crash Protection. Vehicle-19. TEST. 34. 209. NEO GEN CX3V9VM1203. . . . www.nhtsa.dot.gov/cars/testing/comply/monthly/2004/statrept.0412.doc-2005-02-09.

aspects of the ability, inability or lack of agreement that any such performance levels are necessary or economically or technologically feasible. Do we currently achieve the proposed performance level? If not, why not? Can we achieve it if eventually required by agency action finalizing the proposed rule? What design changes are needed to achieve this level of performance? What about the economic feasibility? Does the cost outweigh the benefits to the company? The documents issued in-house in these regulatory contacts are often some of the most telling in the discovery and trial stages of the case.

(C)   These documents are discoverable inasmuch as they typically address the very defect issue involved in the litigation. This is not to say they are easily discoverable, since company defendants will quite properly oppose any such submission on relevancy, privilege and other grounds.[19]

(D)   Defendants often take the position that if there was no existing agency performance standard then the court should rule as a matter of law that they complied with any and all government regulation and hence no defect can be found. Contemporary case law, however, is clear that agency performance standards are to be considered minimum standards only and do not eliminate a consumer's right to bring an action for injuries under negligence or strict liability arising out of design features which are the actual subject of a regulation.[20]

In cases where the industry members have complied with a mandated agency performance standard, such as windshield retention standards in auto collisions, or a set of mandated instructions or warnings in the pharmaceutical or chemical industry, it tends to shift the case analysis to the subject regulation as *the* "reasonable" standard. This argument has been found wanting many more times than not and is an understandable item in all contemporary state and federal products liability reform proposals.[21]

The difficulty here is that often the proposed performance standards are, indeed, merely minimal safety considerations that perhaps should have been designed to a higher level by the manufacturers themselves. The requirements that automobile windshields do not fly out or door locks not fail and allow doors to open in highway crash situations are two simple examples.[22]

---

[19] See Chapter 19, Protective Orders and Discovery Enforcement, for a detailed discussion of the objection to discovery and the accompanying motions to enforce discovery.

[20] This is a position of long standing. *See, e.g.*, Usery v. Tamiami Trail Tours, Inc., 531 F.2d 224 (5th Cir. 1976). *See also* Evidence as to Compliance or Noncompliance with Federal Safety Laws or Standards, 63B Am. Jur. 2d Products Liability § 2022 (2005).

[21] Corporations which have made a significant investment in time, manpower and money to comply with the standard, quite understandably argue that the standard is equivalent to the reasonable standard which should end the case, at least as respects the alleged defect that is addressed by the regulation.

[22] Federal Motor Vehicle Safety Standard 212 (FMVSS 212) provides requirements for retention of the windshield. FMVSS 219 provides requirements for intrusion into the windshield. *See* http://www.nhtsa.dot.gov/.

Industries are given the opportunity to comment on proposals and to provide issue opposing position papers and supporting documentation to the issuing agency. Unless classified as privileged by the agency, these historical materials are generally available to plaintiff counsel, even prior to filing suit, through a Freedom of Information Act request.[23]

§ 12.11   THE HISTORY OF THE INDUSTRY REACTION TO THE SCIENTIFIC PROBLEM

All products under scrutiny in these cases are typically designed, manufactured and marketed within an industry of like-minded manufacturing concerns. The aerospace industry, automobile industry, electronics industry, pharmaceutical industry and the chemical industry are the major players that provide the technical and managerial backdrop to the lion's share of all individual products litigation. There are common technologies and common concerns among these large groupings of companies in addition to keen competitive issues. Each industry has several industry-wide associations that keep track of the activities of state and federal regulators and legislatures that may affect their members. The cooperation in these industries is as keen as the competition.[24]

It is within this industry context that the idea of comparative product analysis has its research value. There is a considerable commonality of design in such industries as the automobile industry. It is of value to determine early the differences, if any, among the design under study in the case at hand and the same design feature in the competition. This will extend to the precise technology, such as the stability of automobile door locks and windows in highway crash settings to the instructions, warnings and other communicative aspects of the marketing of such products. This is especially the case for foreign manufacture and sale of the same product. International requirements for warnings and even basic design features can often veer sharply from United States domestic manufacture.

While conformity to industry custom is not legally equivalent to due care, the fact that all participants in an industry follow identical protocols for select design features, such as fuel system integrity[25] or seat belt or airbag technology, make it very difficult to maintain that an alternative design should have been adopted by an individual industry member. Often referred to as the "everybody was doing it" defense, it is nonetheless a very powerful argument. Initially, it requires the plaintiff to challenge the decisions of highly trained and respected scientists and

---

[23] *See* http://www.usdoj.gov/04foia/. Each federal agency is responsible for meeting its FOIA responsibilities for its own records. A list of principal FOIA contacts at federal agencies is available from this site. The Act has provisions allowing for confidentiality of certain classes of company data heretofore submitted to an agency during an investigation. *See* Janene Boyce, *Disclosure of Clinical Trial Data: Why Exemption 4 of the Freedom of Information Act Should Be Restored*, 2005 Duke L. & Tech. Rev. 3 (2005).

[24] See The Directory of Associations, a comprehensive source of information on professional, business, and trade associations, 501(c) non-profit organizations, chambers of commerce, and other charity and community institutions, at http://www.marketingsource.com/associations/.

[25] Fuel System Integrity refers to design features aimed at keeping the fuel inside the gas tank, thus minimizing fuel-fed fires in automobile collisions.

business executives. It also casts the plaintiff's proposed alternative in an isolated spot with a considerable uphill battle to convince a jury to buck an entire industry as well as the state and federal governments that had failed to require any higher performance or design standards.

Fortunately for plaintiffs, other manufacturers, as well as the named corporation, often manufacture similar lines of goods in different models of the base product line such as automobiles, space heaters and power saws, that make use of different levels of technology resulting in higher safety performance. It is easy to see $150, $350 and $500 space heaters and the variance in their design and on-board safety features such as automatic shut off and denser grill openings. In such instances, plaintiff is provided with an inhouse comparative product demonstration of a feasible alternative design.

The issue of a corporation's right to participate in various market levels with accompanying variances in safety, is a multifaceted one and is the subject of many policy debates. Nonetheless, a solid basis for establishing the feasibility of an alternate package, instruction, warning or design, is that either the defendant itself or others in the industry have actually incorporated it in a product line. This in turn, raises the appropriateness of the application of the evidence rule prohibiting the introduction of subsequent remedial measures.[26]

Comparative product analysis thus necessitates close familiarity with the industry of which the defendant is a part and detailed understanding of the technology of comparable or competing products. Not only does this research demonstrate the relevant industry's position as to the alleged scientific problem, but may reveal a concerted industry endeavor to hinder or eliminate an alleged safety-prone design methodology. Product industry research is an essential aspect of product liability research.

§ 12.12 STUDY OF DEFENDANT CORPORATION'S ORGANIZATION AND MANUFACTURING PROCESSES

In the typical scenario, where the defendant is a major corporation, plaintiff and defense counsel face the daunting task of following the operational string through the labyrinth of the company's document production and decision-making processes. While defense counsel has a distinct advantage in this often herculean effort, both counsel must nonetheless determine the key dates and the identity of the offices, departments, sections and major committees involved in the central design decisions that are the basis of the allegations in the complaint. In what years and

---

[26] FEDERAL RULE OF EVIDENCE 407. Subsequent Remedial Measures.

When, after an injury or harm allegedly caused by an event, measures are taken that, if taken previously, would have made the injury or harm less likely to occur, evidence of the subsequent measures is not admissible to prove negligence, culpable conduct, a defect in a product, a defect in a product's design, or a need for a warning or instruction. This rule does not require the exclusion of evidence of subsequent measures when offered for another purpose, such as proving ownership, control, or feasibility of precautionary measures, if controverted, or impeachment.

from what office, department, committee or individual was relevant documentation of a wide variety of types issued and accompanying decisions made?

A business phenomenon that can befuddle litigators seeking to locate and identify relevant offices, departments, sections, committees and committee personnel, is that as the world of science and marketing changes so do the nomenclature and function of the organizational structures of the corporations that adopt and make use of such changes. This means that a department or office playing an active role in one period of the development and marketing of a product may disappear in an ensuing period. It is important to understand that corporate defendants are under no obligation to educate plaintiff counsel about the changes to the company over the years. It is plaintiff's obligation to study the relevant markets, theories of corporate organizations and track changes in the targeted defendant.

As an example, the shifting emphasis in the automobile industry to compact and sub-compact cars in the late 1960s significantly changed the nomenclature of the corporate entities charged with the new ventures and manufacturing operational entities in the several competing companies. New departments such as Light Vehicle Development Offices began to replace traditional functional units, putting the outsider litigant at a distinct disadvantage in efforts to locate document generating units for discovery purposes. In cases where the investigative time frame is considerable, this provides defense counsel with potent opportunities to impede discovery based on the plaintiff's counsel's incorrect use of corporate nomenclature when requesting historical documents.[27]

§ 12.13 THE DEVELOPMENT OF THE CORPORATE DEFENDANT'S REACTION TO THE ALLEGED SCIENTIFIC DEFECT

The central issue in products liability litigation is whether the defendant ignored clear risks of injury to consumers in conscious design choices in the face of economically and technically feasible alternatives in their instructions, warnings, overall design or through flat out misrepresentation. The plaintiff in a products case must initially realize that the famous "smoking gun" rarely surfaces. Alleged corporate failings will occur, if at all, in the course of the company's ordinary business processes. It may appear at the end of a case that a defendant ignored clear warning signs in their pre-production clinical trials, or metal fatigue or crash tests that, in balance, should have been acted upon for the benefit of future consumers. Standard operating procedures (SOPs) more often tell the tale in products cases, not an outrageously irresponsible document stressing money over safety.[28]

---

[27] *See* Terrence F. Kiely, *The Paper Chase: Organization and Analysis of Corporate Documents in a Product Case*, 22 TRIAL 105 (1986).

[28] This is not to say that such documents do not periodically surface. This is especially the case with the modern phenomenon of e-mail. See Chapter 14, Drafting the Complaint and Discovery Focus, for a discussion of recent developments in electronic discovery.

The complete internal organization of modern corporations is considered, quite properly, as a trade or business secret or privileged information. Corporations understand that the more information a competitor has about their organizational structure and nomenclature, the closer they are to knowing what is being developed and planned for their domestic or foreign markets. This concern is in addition to concerns over discovery requests in products liability litigation. The detailed, routine internal processes of a corporation in planning, designing, testing and marketing a product are multifaceted, sometimes following routine, trackable stages, and sometimes not. Line responsibilities for decision-making often veer from standard operating procedures by the assignment of functional responsibility to one or more units for specific project purposes. Nothing nefarious about that, but it makes for discovery nightmares for plaintiff or defense lawyers trying to lay out a clear paper trail.[29]

Getting from point A to point Z is the result of assembling a road map from disparate pieces of a company's total document generation over the period of the case discovery time frame and whatever public documents, such as annual reports that are usually accessible. There are typically thousands of documents that may be arguably relevant to the investigation by counsel. In major actions such as the recent cigarette or Vioxx litigation there can be up to a million documents placed in Multi-district litigation document depositories. The harsh reality of the trial aspect of products liability litigation is that only a handful of such documents will be used at trial, following a rigorous document review and selection process.[30] The entire document discovery process is one of the most time-consuming and frustrating aspects of products liability case preparation.

§ 12.14   PRIOR LITIGATION, SETTLEMENTS, OR CASE FILINGS

An important initial research step is to determine the existence of appellate decisions, prior litigation verdicts, case settlements or current case filings. Lawyers for either side of the issue can provide tremendous assistance to the neophyte in narrowing research issues and identifying relevant information sources, key areas of the scientific literature, expert witnesses and the like. In addition to plaintiff and defense information sharing organizations, such as the plaintiff's American Trial Lawyers Association (ATLA)[31] and the Defense Research Institute (DRI)[32] directed to defense counsel, there are numerous services available on Lexis/Nexis and Westlaw and law libraries that track appeals, trials, verdicts, and settlements in products liability cases.[33] Both organizations, in addition to offering expert witness

---

[29] *See* Kiely, Science and Litigation, *supra*, note 7, at Chapter 7, Science and Business Documentation.

[30] See Chapter 17, Requests to Produce Documents, for a more detailed discussion of document rating and selection criteria.

[31] *See* http://www.atla.org/.

[32] *See* http://www.dri.org/.

[33] For example, Lexis provides the following services: Jury Verdicts and Settlements, Combined; What's It Worth? A Guide to Personal Injury Awards and Settlements; Mealey's Jury Verdicts and

databases and referrals to other lawyers sharing the same or similar interests, provide listings of verdicts, settlements and products liability filings.

§ 12.15   MATERIALS SUPPLIERS AND COMPONENT PART MANUFACTURERS INFORMATION SOURCE CATEGORIES

Determining who are the suppliers of materials and component parts to the defendant company is an important research obligation. Intermediary parties, in addition to being potential defendants, can be a fertile source of important documentary evidence, especially in instances where the materials or component parts are made to precise specifications by the defendant. Common practice is to name all material suppliers and component parts manufacturers. The considerable cost and annoyance to these entities is an unfortunate by product of the inability of plaintiffs to get needed information aside from discovery rights. In some instances the alleged defects do stem from failings on the part of one or more of these middle-men.[34]

§ 12.16   LIBRARY COLLECTIONS

A very valuable source of bibliographic information is available free of charge from a growing number of Internet accessible university library database networks such as OCLC. These systems allow the user to search through the collections of groups of university libraries on title, author, and in some instances, subject matter. These library networks are a tremendous source of bibliographic information. In increasing numbers, these systems are accessible, and free of charge to alumni or student clerks. Products litigators should determine what online alumni privileges are available from the various general and law libraries of firm members. These resources are expanding at a great rate and alumni should keep current as to what free research tools are available to them. A simple Yahoo or Google search will yield extensive listings of public and private libraries arranged by topic. It is relatively easy to locate specialized collections where needed information can be had.[35]

§ 12.17   GOVERNMENT DATABASES

There is an enormous amount of information available to the public at little or no cost, that is contained in United States government agency sponsored and maintained websites and database systems. At the present time there are numerous

---

Settlement Report; National Jury Verdict Review & Analysis; National Law Journal Annual Verdict and Settlement Review; Verdicts, Settlements and Tactics and Jury Verdicts by Jurisdiction.

[34] A Google or Yahoo search on "materials suppliers" returns literally thousands of company names and websites organized by product type or industry.

[35] For example, a very small portion of a Yahoo search on libraries yielded Public Libraries (5327); Academic Libraries (515); Business Libraries (26); Digital Libraries (84); Librarians (28); Professional Resources (140); Library and Information Science (332); National Libraries (48); Archives; Arts Libraries; Commercial Library Services; Conferences (10); Countries (26); Environmental Libraries; Government Documents and Health Libraries.

and varied websites offering information from every federal government agency. The Louisiana State University (LSU) Libraries maintain a Federal Agencies Directory,[36] divided by executive, legislative, judicial, independent and quasi-independent websites that currently references over 1100 sites, each offering information of great interest to products litigators.

Several of the government-sponsored databases of greatest importance to the products litigator, such as the Medline system, produced by the National Library of Medicine, and the National Technical Information Service, are easily accessible for cost-free bibliographic searches. The Medline collection currently numbers ten million bibliographic references in the areas of medicine, bio-medicine and health. It is accessible free of charge through the Internet at the National Institutes of Health's (NIH) National Library of Medicine website[37] which provides links to PubMed (biomedical journal information), Medline Plus (health and drug information) and the Household Products Database (health and safety information on household products). The Medline system is one of the most productive of the vast array of government information websites available free of charge to the public.

The FedWorld website, maintained by the United States Department of Commerce links to the massive National Technical Information Service database which is the largest central resource for government-funded scientific, technical, engineering, and business related information available today. Here you will find information on more than 600,000 information products covering over 350 subject areas from over 200 federal agencies. FedWorld also links to FirstGov, allowing search access to over 30 Million Government Web Pages covering Government R&D Reports and numerous science and technical sites.[38]

The Government Printing Office website[39] provides access to all publications of the Unites States government from all three branches of the federal government, including an extensive list of official federal resources available on GPO Access.[40]

CRISP (Computer Retrieval of Information on Scientific Projects) is a searchable database of federally funded biomedical research projects conducted at universities, hospitals, and other research institutions. The database, maintained by the Office of Extramural Research at the National Institutes of Health, includes projects funded by the National Institutes of Health (NIH), Substance Abuse and Mental Health Services (SAMHSA), Health Resources and Services Administration (HRSA), Food and Drug Administration (FDA), Centers for Disease Control and Prevention (CDCP), Agency for Health Care Research and Quality (AHRQ), and Office of Assistant Secretary of Health (OASH). Users, including the public, can use the CRISP interface to search for scientific concepts, emerging trends and

---

[36] http://www.lib.lsu.edu/gov/.

[37] http://www.nlm.nih.gov/.

[38] See SciTech Resources, http://www.loc.gov/rr/scitech/resources.html/, which provides easy access to key government science and technology web sites.

[39] http://www.gpo.gov/.

[40] The University of North Texas Libraries also maintains a website called the Government information Connection, which provides links to a wide variety of state, federal and foreign government agency information cites. See http://www.library.unt.edu/govinfo/default.htm.

techniques, or identify specific projects and/or investigators.[41]

§ 12.18 BOOKS AND PERIODICALS

Books, scientific and technical journals, consumer magazines and industry newsletters, are the primary sources of pre-trial non-corporate information in products cases. The great bulk of these publications are available in selected university or public library collections as well, in increasing numbers, on a free or minimal fee base on the Internet. There are very few, if any, scientific or other specialty journals that are not available to the litigator prior to trial. The Library of Congress is an excellent early source for information on medical, pharmaceutical, engineering or chemical books in print.[42] The very comprehensive Bowker Books In Print database is available in public and private libraries and is the most comprehensive book listing on the Internet and in print form.[43] The OCLC service, available in most public, university and private libraries provides access to books from the Americas, Europe and Asia.

All litigators, especially small firms, should have all partners and associates check the alumni library privileges of their respective universities and law schools. These are often substantial and can provide readily available and focused free research sources.

§ 12.19 DIALOG INFORMATION SERVICES

The Dialog Information Services System is the grandaddy of database collections and is still the premier system to use for serious scientific or technical research. Dialog is a massive collection of the online databases of thousands of information services, available through a common search language.[44] This massive collection of searchable databases covers virtually every world data source in the broad areas of business, intellectual property, science and technology, news and trade journals and all aspects of market research. Many of the hundreds of available databases are bibliographic in nature, but an increasing number are offered full-text.

Descriptive *Dialog Bluesheets* are written guides for the use of every database on the Dialog® service. They contain detailed instructions on search techniques for the special features of each database, including file description, subject coverage, date range, update frequency, sources of the data, and the origin of the information. On the Bluesheet you will also find a sample record that shows what you can expect to obtain when you perform a search in the database. A most important part of the Bluesheets is the Search Options section, where you see the field labels that you can use to focus or narrow your search, as well as examples of how to use them online.

---

[41] http://crisp.cit.nih.gov/.

[42] http://www.loc.gov/.

[43] *See* http://www.booksinprint.com/bip/.

[44] http://www.Dialog.com/.

Bluesheets on the Web are updated regularly and reflect the most current database information available.

The Dialog website[45] provides complete listings of all its bibliographic and full-text sources which may be downloaded for private research examination. There is virtually nothing in print in multiple languages that is not accessible via the Dialog system. In addition to bibliographic cites, Dialog provides an increasing number of full-text articles for download. Both Lexis and Westlaw provide gateways to this terrific resource.

§ 12.20 POPULAR PUBLICATIONS

Popular print publications such as monthly magazines or bi-annual editions address a great variety of subjects of interest and value to the products litigator at the early stage of pretrial investigation and research. Many of them are also currently available online on the Internet.[46] Extensive listings of trade association publications are easily located on the Internet, for download or tracking in library holdings or reprint services.[47] In the home products area alone there are hundreds of magazines covering an amazing variety of subjects that contain valuable investigative leads, from infant car seats, strollers, toys, flammable fabric clothing concerns, bicycle and other protective headwear, etc. There are also numerous publications devoted to recreational vehicles, camping equipment, firearms, pesticides, and the like. Many of these publications conduct annual reviews and comparisons of the product categories they cover, including comparative product specifications.

Consumer-oriented publications such as Consumer Reports, which have perspectives on a wide variety of products, usually provide comparative product reviews that are of special interest to product litigators. The Gale Group Magazine Database, available on Dialog and directly from Gale, provides current and retrospective news from more than 400 popular magazines on such subjects as consumer behavior, media trends, popular culture, political opinion, leisure activities, and contemporary lifestyles. Gale Group Magazine Database also contains large collections of entertainment reviews and ratings of books, films, theater, concerts, hotels, and restaurants. This database is ideal for searchers who need background material and a variety of perspectives to supplement any business search. Gale Group Magazine Database includes indexes and abstracts for 400 publications and the full text for more than 250 magazines.

These publications also typically carry a considerable number of advertisements for alternative technology that reflects on the feasibility of feasible alternative designs, and thereby may provide significant investigative leads. Advertisements for stabilizing bars to minimize recreational vehicles' rolling motion or products

---

[45] See http://www.Dialog.com. An additional several hundred databases are available on the DataStar System for commercial access via a Thomson/Dialog portal to more than three hundred databases in diverse areas including news, business, medicine, and healthcare. See www.datastarweb.com/.

[46] See the extensive subject listing at the NewsDirectory website located at http://newsdirectory.com/listmag.php.

[47] Id.

increasing power tool safety may serve as examples.

These publications invariably list the various trade associations involved in the industry's purposes, a quick reference for litigators. There are thousands of trade associations, big and small, which are a tremendous source of information and further investigative leads. Each trade association publishes a journal and often industry newsletters, easily located in many public and university libraries and on the Internet.[48] In some instances, such as the automobile, aerospace, pharmaceutical and chemical industries, the trade association serves as an investigator and depository of injury statistics and serves as an important force in the industry efforts to minimize or eliminate proposed government agency performance or design regulations.

Finally, these popular publications have new product announcements, trade show and upcoming conference dates and other details of potential value to products litigators. It is a good idea for counsel to subscribe to all of the popular publications addressing the product type and industry in litigation.

§ 12.21 ACADEMIC AND PROFESSIONAL JOURNALS

The peer-reviewed studies and articles published in academic and professional journals, such as *The Lancet* or the *New England Journal of Medicine*, constitute the heart of the state-of-the-art literature. It is the grist for the expert witness' mill in establishing and supporting the scientific reliability of expert opinion. They also establish the outlines of what was considered the state-of-the-art in design, research and manufacture during the relevant period of the defendant corporation's history at issue. The number, variety and variances in quality and academic or professional reputation of these publications are enormous. Since peer-reviewed studies[49] are one of the primary items on the Supreme Court's short list of factors to be used to assess the reliability of a science underlying an expert's opinion,[50] it is essential that products counsel identify the premier journals in the scientific field involved in the case.[51]

The Elsevier and Blackwell health and science publishers[52] maintain websites searchable by medical or other health related subjects and will return information about the journals considered key to their field. These websites are excellent and a great source for litigators' initial investigation into the body of authoritative state-of-the-art publications.

---

[48] *See, e.g.,* Newsletter Access, located at http://www.newsletteraccess.com/directory.php.

[49] The whole subject of peer-review and just what it is and is not from a scientific and ethical basis is a current concern world-wide as more information is emerging about ghost authors, financial entanglements and other serious ethical issues. *See* KIELY, SCIENCE AND LITIGATION, supra, note 7, at Chapter 3, Science and Peer Review, 77-131.

[50] See Chapter 13, The Expert Witness, for a discussion of the famous Daubert criteria for determining scientific reliability for purposes of allowing expert opinion testimony.

[51] Research librarians and expert witnesses can provide this list, although counsel should always be satisfied of its solidity based on their own inquiries.

[52] *See* http://journals.elsevierhealth.com/; http://www.blackwellpublishing.com/.

§ 12.22   ACADEMIC AND PROFESSIONAL ANNUAL MEETINGS AND SPECIAL CONFERENCES

A routine task for products litigators should be the location of schedules of academic and professional annual meetings and special conferences, both domestic and international, which address the scientific issues involved in the case. This is readily obtained on Dialog on the Internet through a Google search. Often these listings provide the titles of papers to be presented and the credentials of the participants. In addition to learning the nature of the concerns of the experts in the field, these papers are usually available for download in English shortly after their presentation. These conference source sites also typically go back two to three years, so the identity of recent conference papers can be readily assessed. These conference paper listings also provide early leads on the identity of potential expert witnesses or fodder for the deposition or cross-examination of an opposing expert.[53]

§ 12.23   RESEARCH IN PROGRESS AND GRANTS

A products liability case, depending upon its complexity, can often last for periods up to five years or more. During that period the world of science and technology proceeds apace. Ongoing research of interest or crucial to one or the other of the sides in the case may become finalized, published and available for study and use. While it is not possible to identify all research in progress, there are sources available to provide interested parties with basic information on a variety of ongoing scientific research. This has been accomplished by the publication of the identity of the recipients of government and private research fund grants. This information is available in both print and database form from commercial vendors such as Dialog and various free or low-cost Internet sites.[54]

The Federal Research In Progress (FEDRIP) website[55] provides access to information about ongoing federally funded projects in the fields of the physical sciences, engineering, and life sciences. The ongoing research announced in FEDRIP is an important component to the technology transfer process in the U.S. FEDRIP's uniqueness lies in its structure as a non bibliographic information source of research in progress. Project descriptions generally include: project title, keywords, start date, estimated completion date, principal investigator, performing and sponsoring organizations, summary, and progress report. Record content varies depending on the source agency.

---

[53] The AllConferences website, located at http://www.allconferences.com/, is a directory focusing on conferences, conventions, trade shows, exhibits, workshops, events and business meetings. Inside Conferences is produced by the British Library. The database contains details of all papers given at every congress, symposium, conference, exposition, workshop, and meeting received at the British Library Document Supply Centre (BLDSC) since October 1993. Each year over 16,000 proceedings are indexed, covering a wide range of subjects published as serials or monographs. Over 500,000 bibliographic citations for individual conference papers are added annually. Most records are in English, with many languages represented in the source documents. *See also* http://www.medical.theconferencewebsite.com/.

[54] *See* http://www.dialog.com.

[55] http://grc.ntis.gov/fedrip.htm.

Federal agencies that contribute to FEDRIP include the Department of Agriculture (AGRIC Subfile); Department of Energy (ENRGY Subfile); Department of Veterans Affairs (VA Subfile); Environmental Protection Agency (EPA Subfile); Federal Highway Administration (FHWA Subfile); National Institutes of Health (CRISP Subfile); NASA (NASA Subfile); National Science Foundation (NSF Subfile); U.S. Geological Survey (USGS Subfile); National Institute of Standards and Technology (NBS Subfile); Nuclear Regulatory Commission (NRC Subfile); and the Small Business Innovation Research (SBIR Subfile). A modest annual fee can provide access to this very important body of current information about research in progress in fields of great interest to products litigators.

Foundation and other non-governmental grants information can be accessed through Dialog in the Foundation Grants Index[56] and GRANTS files.

§ 12.24 STATISTICAL PUBLICATIONS AND DATA BANKS

Statistics comprise a very important component in the development, testing, production and marketing of a wide variety of products in every field. The very question of whether a risk of cancer or heart problems is associated with the use of a pharmaceutical requiring a warning is grounded in statistical theory and various statistical analytical models. The fact that a risk of cancer or heart attack or other medical anomaly may occur does not in itself mandate the issuance of a drug or chemical warning. The manufacturer has the right to base that decision on the statistical probabilities or percentages of occurrence and may not be required to warn for incidents below a set percentage.

The whole idea of the practical application of products liability theory is often grounded in some aspect of the statistical incident projections. All industries use one or more statistical models to estimate risks and their accompanying level of responsibilities. It is incumbent on products litigators to familiarize themselves with the statistical databases and system used by the government, national and international health research bodies, and the industry and company under scrutiny.

There are three basic aspects of statistical materials that counsel must separate out for study: the standards applied to the collection of the data used to generate the statistics, the statistical methodology applied to such data, and finally, the figures themselves.

The data bank may have been collected using criteria that do not allow for a complete or accurate analysis of the issues of importance to the case. This can seriously distort the reality behind the statistics. There are a bewildering number of statistical theories that may be applied to data. Counsel will need to become conversant with the range of statistical methodologies arguably available for use with such data so as to determine the possibility of results at variance with the actual figures under study. Finally, the results themselves must be checked against the actual method used to create them, to determine their accuracy within that methodology. The Internet is an excellent source for the identification of health statistics and projections. The federal government has a significant collection of

---

[56] http://fdncenter.org/.

readily accessible collections of statistics ranging from automobile fatalities to the carcinogenic risks from chemicals and other industrial artifacts.

The FedStats website[57] provides topic links from A to Z, statistical profiles of States, counties, cities, Congressional Districts, and Federal judicial districts, statistics by geography from U.S. agencies with international comparisons, a statistical reference shelf of published collections of statistics available online including the Statistical Abstract of the United States, a search feature going across agency websites, a listing of websites listed alphabetically with descriptions of the statistics they provide and links to their websites, contact information, and key statistics. It also provides an extensive listing of federal agencies by subject and selected agency online databases, such as the NIH National Cancer Institute's statistics[58] or the Fatal Accident Reporting System (FARS) data maintained by the National Highway Traffic Safety Administration [Statistics and Analysis].[59]

§ 12.25 MATERIALS, DESIGN, AND PERFORMANCE STANDARDS

Every product of whatever type is designed, tested and manufactured according to some set of standards, whether issued by international, national or industry standards setting bodies. The American National Standards Institute (ANSI)[60] or the American Society for Testing Materials (ASTM)[61] are examples of the more prestigious standards issuing organizations. The lion's share of manufactured products in America are produced with strict adherence to national standards for products, although not mandatory. There are published standards for a bewildering number of products ranging from laboratory test tubes to garden hose nozzles. It is important to be familiar with any relevant standards, the standards issuing entity, as well as the proposed standards constantly being issued by them. The current and proposed standards provide a ready frame of reference when establishing the reasonableness of a suspect design. Since these bodies are often funded by an industry, the committees are typically staffed by representatives of the companies engaged in the manufacture of products referenced by a set of standards.

The National Institute of Standards and Technology (NIST)[62] founded in 1901 is a non-regulatory federal agency within the U.S. Commerce Department's Technology Administration. NIST's mission is to develop and promote measurement, standards, and technology to enhance productivity, facilitate trade, and improve the quality of life. Computer databases maintained by the National Center for Standards and Certification Information (NCSCI) provides detailed information on over 270,000 government and private materials, design and performance standards.

---

[57] http://www.fedstats.gov/.

[58] http://www.nci.nih.gov/statistics/.

[59] http://www-nrd.nhtsa.dot.gov/.

[60] The American National Standards Institute (ANSI) is a private, non-profit organization (501(c)(3)) that administers and coordinates the U.S. voluntary standardization and conformity assessment system. *See* http://www.ansi.org/.

[61] http://www.astm.org/.

[62] http://www.nist.gov/.

Accessing and mastering these public and private standards is important in several key respects. Initially, they provide basic background information on the actual standards utilized or considered to be appropriate for the industries they address. Accordingly, these standards provide counsel with a means of assessing the extent to which he will be required to counter defense arguments based on conformity to industry custom at various stages over the preparation and trial of the case. Often, the testing methodology utilized by a target defendant closely follows the guidelines set forth in one of these standards. The publications of these bodies are also an entre to additional state-of-the-art materials that must eventually be identified, located and studied.

These bodies of standards are under continual review and thus counsel can determine the latest authoritative perspectives on the processes covered by them. Also, in cases involving new technology or products, these standards setting bodies will often promulgate preliminary proposed standards issuing from committees or sub-committees researching materials and performance testing issues relating to them. This provides counsel with a body of data highlighting the technological priorities set by these important industry organizations relative to the product or processes of concern to counsel.[63]

§ 12.26   CONSUMER INTEREST GROUPS AND ASSOCIATED PUBLICATIONS

The Consumer Product Safety Commission (CPSC) website[64] provides extensive and up-to-date listings of products recalls, safety news and the CPSC's work in the area of voluntary safety standards. The CPSC also provides many safety reports on various product groupings, including all-terrain vehicles, bicycles, child safety, children's furniture, clothing safety, crib safety and SIDS reduction, electrical safety, home heating equipment, household products safety, older consumers' safety, outdoor power equipment safety, playground, pool and Spa safety and a wide variety of recreational products. The CPSC is a powerful regulatory agency whose investigative files, generally available under FOIA requests as with most other agencies, often is a primary source of data in products cases involved with consumer goods. The Federal Trade Commission's Consumer Page is also a helpful resource.[65]

Large and influential consumer interest organizations also provide a wealth of information of interest to the product litigator. These groups range from substantial entities such as the Center for Auto Safety,[66] the Insurance Institute for Highway Safety,[67] and Public Citizen,[68] to federally funded government organizations such as

---

[63] See the extensive testing data supplied by Underwriters Laboratory at http://www.ul.com/.

[64] http://www.cpsc.gov/.

[65] See http://www.ftc.gov/ftc/consumer.htm.

[66] http://www.autosafety.org/.

[67] http://www.iihs.org/.

[68] http://www.citizen.org/. (Safer drugs advocacy.)

the Center for Disease Control[69] and the National Institutes of Health.[70] There are, in addition, thousands of smaller consumer interest groups addressing virtually every area of consumer concern, ranging from toddler clothing and toys, sports equipment, dietary supplements and the like.

Each year number of new websites appear providing general information, government contact sites and phone numbers, pamphlets and chat rooms. The larger organizations publish magazines available online and in public and university periodical collections. Consumers Union, publisher of Consumer Reports,[71] is an independent, nonprofit testing and information site that is a comprehensive source for unbiased advice about products and services, personal finance, health and nutrition, and other consumer concerns. Products litigators are able to check on international consumers organizations at the Consumers International site.[72] Listing of all state consumer agencies are also available that contain a wealth of information of interest to products litigators.[73]

§ 12.27   PROFESSIONAL AND TRADE ASSOCIATIONS AND ORGANIZATIONS

Identifying the professional organizations whose members have been historically involved in the study and development of the technology of interest to counsel is another important investigational goal. These organizations are a focal point for the professional activities of their members and generally publish one or more journals addressing current technological matters of interest to that membership and the industries that they serve. For example, one of the more important state-of-the-art data sources in automobile products litigation is the Journal of the Society of Automotive Engineers[74]. Professional organizations and related publications exist for virtually every area of technology of interest to the products litigator. In addition to the technical studies published by these organizations, they are also a primary research source for information relating to private performance and materials standards, addressing virtually every aspect of the product type under study. The membership of most organizations and association's technical committees and sub-committees is generally composed of industry representatives. This is an important focal point for detailed cross-referencing of state-of-the-art and company documents received in the course of discovery.

Two standard references, The Encyclopedia of Associations[75] (Detroit: Gale Research Co.) and the Yearbook of International Associations (Brussels: Union of International Associations) list national and international organizations by subject

---

[69] http://www.cdc.gov/.

[70] http://www.nih.gov/.

[71] http://www.consumerreports.org/main/home.jsp. See also their Consumer WebWatch page at http://www.consumerwebwatch.org/.

[72] http://www.consumersinternational.org/.

[73] http://www.ifg-inc.com/StateAgencies.html. (Excellent and extensive listing.)

[74] http://www.sae.org/servlets/index.

[75] http://www.infoplease.com/ipa/A0004878.htm.

matter and include in many instances their annual conferences, meetings and publications. A simple Google search on professional associations will bring up a number of comprehensive listings sites.

§ 12.28 TRADE ASSOCIATIONS

In addition to the more academically oriented professional associations noted above, each industry normally has one or more trade associations. Trade association publications address a variety of practical issues such as industry economics, government regulation, public relations and other more purely marketing concerns affecting its membership. There are a large number of such associations, ranging from very powerful bodies such as the Automotive Manufacturers Association or the Pharmaceutical Manufacturers[76] organizations that represent concentrated industries, to a variety of smaller bodies which serve the interests of broad-based multi-member industries such as the electronics industry.

Trade associations, like professional associations, generally publish journals, newsletters or other materials that can be of great value to the products litigator. The practical ramifications of technological innovations or government regulation are often the subject matter of these publications. They provide a ready source of historical information as well as current industry thinking on those important issues. They are also a repository of valuable investigative leads on contemporary state-of-the-art source materials referenced throughout them. A very important aspect of trade association activity is the gathering of statistical data on a wide variety of subjects of interest to the product litigator.

Collections of injury data and profiles related to industry product lines are often made by these bodies. This latter information can be of inestimable value not only as a source of investigative material but on the central issue of corporate knowledge of defect itself. In less concentrated industries, these statistical collections may be the primary basis upon which a particular company could determine the extent of any risk potential associated with its product. Even in highly concentrated industries, these trade associations often serve as repositories of data generated by its members, providing them with a clear assessment of the danger associated with a design parameter common to the total membership.

Additional data collections and statistics may exist on materials availability and costs. They often contain position papers addressed to government agencies on the industry's behalf arguing for the elimination or reduction in performance levels of proposed agency regulations. All of these materials are informative and in some instances, central to the successful completion of case preparation. In some instances, the volume or nature of trade association information gathering and dissemination may be such that they should be seriously considered as a named defendant.

A publication entitled Encyclopedia of Associations provides a comprehensive geographical listing of the nation's trade associations. The Dialog System also provides detailed listings of such materials as well as abstracts and, in some

---

[76] See http://www.phrma.org/.

instances, full text of the journals published by them. Commercial sites currently provide extensive fee-based searches for trade associations.[77]

§ 12.29 PATENTS

Patent research is highly complex and should be only attempted after counsel has a solid grounding in the technical and industry context of the technology under investigation. Patents provide a wealth of detailed technical information about a particular design as well as information on generically similar designs. An additional value of the patent research is to learn whether or not the target defendant actually holds the patent on what counsel feels are feasible alternative designs that were not implemented by it.

Patent research may be conducted in major public libraries as well as the Dialog commercial databases.[78] The Patent Office database contains complete abstracts of all patents issued since 1970. This is very time consuming and difficult research. Counsel is well advised to seek expert assistance in this effort.

§ 12.30 COMPANY RESEARCH

Conducting thorough pre-filing company research is important in several key respects. It is essential to the final determination of the pool of potential defendants and the eventual selection of named parties. This will require a search through the research sources to be discussed below to determine the existence of parent companies, subsidiaries and holding companies. It will also be necessary to determine the possible sale of one of the defendants in the pool to estimate whether or not a successor liability problem exists. The identity of all component parts and materials suppliers and participants in the vertical chain of distribution must also be determined before case planning and complaint drafting can be effectively begun.

Chapters 14 through 17 will analyze in detail how essential pre-filing company research is to the entire discovery process. It is important to note here that maximum results in accessing defendant's internal documentation cannot be achieved without it. To complete counsel's comparative product analyses, he must determine the existence of generically similar product lines within the target defendant as well as that of similar product lines manufactured by competitors. Defendant's market share and assets are crucial to the punitive damage count.

The source material to be discussed below will identify some of the basic company research sources available to the litigator prior to initiating discovery.

All companies, foreign and domestic, are required by the Securities and Exchange Commission to file registration statements, periodic reports, and other forms electronically through EDGAR.[79] This source is a good start to gather preliminary information about a company in products liability litigation. Commercial, but cost-effective commercial services are also readily available through Dialog

---

[77] *See, e.g.*, http://www.marketingsource.com/associations/.

[78] *See* http://www.uspto.

[79] http://www.sec.gov/edgar.shtml.

or comprehensive business information research websites such as D&B's Hoover's website.[80]

§ 12.31   ANNUAL REPORTS

Annual reports are an excellent, readily accessible source with which to determine the broad outlines of a corporation's business activity and its organizational structure. Annual reports, in some instances going back decades, are normally available for study at most large public and university libraries. They are also accessible through the Dialog System in its PTS ANNUAL REPORTS ABSTRACTS and the ICC British Company Annual Reports. While these abstracts are very useful, it is often important to give a close reading of the entire series of reports once a selection has been made. A very useful website is AnnualReports-.com, whose free service allows users to review an annual report in an easy and convenient manner.

Annual reports generally provide broad based information on corporate divisions, major offices, boards of directors, earnings and major purchases and divestments. They often list the names of top-level managers and central staff committees as well. The close examination of annual reports will provide a solid context for ensuing detailed investigation of the target defendant in the type of publications referenced below.

§ 12.32   DIRECTORY OF CORPORATE AFFILIATIONS

D&B, The Dunn and Bradstreet Directory of Corporate Affiliations "Who Owns Whom"[81] available on Dialog, is a worldwide company directory file that links a company to its corporate family, showing the size of the corporate structure, family hierarchy, and key information on the parent company, headquarters, branches, and subsidiaries worldwide. Corporate family structure information is provided in one easy-to-read online record.

It is also accessible through the Lexis/Nexis Information website,[82] where you can research corporate hierarchies ("who owns whom") to the seventh level — starting with as little information as a brand name. The D&B Directory of Corporate Affiliations™ database covers more than 180,000 of the most prominent parent companies, affiliates, subsidiaries, and divisions worldwide to help users to research corporate ownership. This directory of corporate affiliations covers companies listed on the major exchanges, the Fortune 1000 and a large selection of both privately owned and traded-over-the counter companies. The first section lists over 4000 parent companies, including high level managers, divisions, subsidiaries and affiliates. A second section cross-references over 45,000 divisions, subsidiaries and affiliates to their parent company set out in section one. Similar information and cross-referencing is provided for parent corporations located in foreign countries.

---

[80] http://www.hoovers.com/free/.

[81] http://library.dialog.com/bluesheets/html/bl0522.html.

[82] http://www.lexisnexis.com/dca/.

§ 12.33   THOMAS REGISTER OF AMERICAN MANUFACTURERS

The Thomas Register of American Manufacturers (NY: Thomas Pub. Co. Annual) is another valuable tool, especially with respect to initiating comparative product analyses. This seven-volume print set lists companies by the category of product that they manufacture. Volume Seven contains a brand name and product index. This is a readily available reference source, now available on the Internet, allowing for a quick introduction to the companies and products involved in the industry under investigation.[83]

§ 12.34   FOREIGN CORPORATIONS

It is becoming increasingly the case that the products litigator is faced with the problem of accessing information on a party defendant who is a foreign corporation. Several standard reference tools, periodically updated, can greatly assist in that task.

Jane's Major Companies of Europe[84] provides company listings by country and type of business as well as directors and subsidiaries. It is available in most public and university libraries. Moody's International Manual has listings for over 3000 foreign corporations which cover company history, subsidiaries, offices, directors and financial status.

The New York Public Library maintains a website providing information on directories of foreign manufacturers doing business in the United States.[85]

§ 12.35   SUMMARY

Pre-filing research must be tailored to the specific industry, product and design feature of concern to the litigator. The materials in this chapter are intended to point the product litigator in the right direction and highlight those areas and focal points within them that will serve as the most efficacious guidelines for this very time-consuming but vital aspect of case preparation. The subject of products liability research will be a continuing one throughout the remainder of this book.

---

[83] http://www.thomasnet.com/.

[84] (London: Macdonald and Jane's Publishers).

[85] Worldwide Business Directories (http://www.nypl.org/research/sibl/directories/namerica.htm). This is a guide to general business directories covering geographic areas around the world held by the Science, Industry and Business Library, located at 188 Madison Ave., at 34th St. in Manhattan. These lists include coverage of International Directories, North America, Europe, Asia and the Pacific, the Middle East, Latin America, the Caribbean, and Africa.

§ 12.36   APPENDIX: PRODUCTS LIABILITY INTERNET RESEARCH SITES

Each of the sites listed below, such as the Food and Drug Administration (FDA), National Institutes of Health (NIH) or the Center for Disease Control (CDC) sites, will provide many related links. For that reason we have not set out all of the related sites.

PHARMACEUTICAL INFORMATION

- **VIRTUAL LIBRARY PHARMACY**

  http://www.pharmacy.org/

- **PHARMWEB**

  http://www.pharmweb.net/

- **THE PHARMACEUTICAL RESEARCH AND MANUFACTURERS OF AMERICA [PHRMA]**

  http://www.phrma.org/

- **PHARMACEUTICAL ON-LINE**

  http://www.pharmaceuticalonline.com/content/homepage/default

ENGINEERING INFORMATION

- **GLOBALSPEC ENGINEERING SEARCH DATABASE**

  http://www.globalspec.com/ProductFinder/FindProducts?query=chemical%20manufactur

- **WWW VIRTUAL LIBRARY SEARCH PAGE**

  http://vlib.org/

- **YAHOO ENGINEERING CATEGORIES**

  http://dir.yahoo.com/Science/Engineering/

- **ELSEVIER ENGINEEERING DATABASES**

  http://www.ei.org/

- **EEVL TECHNICAL LITERAURE**

  http://www.eevl.ac.uk/lit_searching.html

CHEMICAL INFORMATION

- **CHEMICAL MANUFACTURERS VIRTUAL LIBRARY**

  http://www.globalspec.com/

- **CHEMICAL INDUSTRIES DIRECTORIES**

  http://www.liv.ac.uk/Chemistry/Links/chemcomps1.html

- **CHEMICAL PRODUCTS REGISTER**

  http://www.chemicalregister.com/

- **CHEMICAL SCIENCE AND TECHNOLOGY LABORATORY**

  http://www.cstl.nist.gov/

- **AMERICAN CHEMICAL SOCIETY**

  http://www.chemistry.org/portal/a/c/s/1/home.html

MEDICINE AND HEALTH INFORMATION

- **FOOD AND DRUG ADMINISTRATION (FDA)**

  http://www.fda.gov/

- **OCCUPATIONAL SAFETY AND HEALTH ADMINISTRATION (OSHA)**

  http://www.osha.gov/

- **NATIONAL CENTER FOR HEALTH PROMOTION AND DISEASE PREVENTION (VA)**

  http://www.nchpdp.med.va.gov/

- **NATIONAL CENTER FOR COMPLEMENTARY AND ALTERNATIVE MEDICINE (NCCAM)**

  http://nccam.nih.gov/

- **MEDLINE PLUS**

  http://medlineplus.gov/

- **YAHOO HEALTH & MEDICINE**

  http://dir.yahoo.com/Health/Medicine/

- **ARCHIVES OF INTERNAL MEDICINE**

  http://archinte.ama-assn.org/

- **NATIONAL HEART, BLOOD AND LUNG INSTITUTE**

  http://www.nhlbi.nih.gov/index.htm

- **WORLD HEALTH ORGANIZATION**

  http://www.who.int/en/

- **NATIONAL INSTITUTE OF ALLERGY AND INFECTIOUS DISEASES**

  http://www3.niaid.nih.gov/

- **AMERICAN MEDICAL ASSOCIATION**

  http://www.ama-assn.org/

- **ELSEVIER HEALTH JOURNALS**

  http://journals.elsevierhealth.com/

- **BLACKWELL MEDICAL JOURNALS**

  http://www.blackwellpublishing.com/

- **FREE ACCESS TO MEDICAL JOURNALS**

  http://www.freemedicaljournals.com/

CLINICAL TRIALS

- **CLINICAL TRIALS. GOV**

  http://www.clinicaltrials.gov/

- **CENTERWATCH CLINICAL TRIALS LISTING**

  http://www.centerwatch.com/

- **VERITAS MEDICINE**

  http://www.veritasmedicine.com/index.cfm

- **SOCIETY FOR CLINICAL TRIALS**

  http://www.sctweb.org/

- **MEDLINE PLUS — CLINICAL TRIALS**

  http://www.nlm.nih.gov/medlineplus/clinicaltrials.html

- **APPLIED CLINICAL TRIALS [EU]**

  http://www.actmagazine.com/appliedclinicaltrials/

- **NATIONAL CANCER INSTITUTE — CLINICAL TRIALS**

  http://www.cancer.gov/clinicaltrials

- **TRIALS CENTRAL [Must See]**

  http://www.trialscentral.org/

- **CURRENT CONTROLLED TRIALS**

  http://www.controlled-trials.com/

BIOMEDICAL INFORMATION

- **MEDWEB EMORY UNIVERSITY**

  http://www.medweb.emory.edu/MedWeb/

- **AMERICAN INSTITUTE FOR MEDICAL AND BIOLOGICAL ENGINEERING**

  http://www.aimbe.org/

- **BIOPHYSICAL SOCIETY**

  http://www.biophysics.org/

- **BIOMEDICAL ENGINEERING ONLINE**

  http://www.biomedical-engineering-online.com/

- **BIOMECHANICS WORLDWIDE**

  http://www.per.ualberta.ca/biomechanics/bwwframe.htm

- **INTERNATIONAL FEDERATION FOR MEDICAL AND BIOLOGI-CAL ENGINEERING**

  http://www.ifmbe.org/

- **WILEY INTERSCIENCE**

  http://www3.interscience.wiley.com/cgi-bin/home

- **WHITEHEAD INSTITUTE FOR BIOMEDICAL RESEARCH**

  http://www.wi.mit.edu/research/papers.html

- **INSTITUTE OF BIOMEDICAL SCIENCE**

  http://www.ibms.org/

- **KAROLINSKA INSTITUTET [EU]**

  http://www.mic.ki.se/Other.html

- **MEDSCAPE MEDICAL CONFERENCE LISTINGS**

  http://www.medscape.com/conferencedirectory/Default

- **FOUNDATION FOR BIOMEDICAL RESEARCH**

  http://www.fbresearch.org/

- **BIOMEDICAL ENGINEERING NETWORK**

  http://www.bmenet.org/BMEnet/

- **BIOMEDICAL ENGINEERING SOCIETY**

  http://www.bmes.org/

- **GENETESTS**

  http://www.geneclinics.org/

- **HUMAN GENOME PROJECT: MEDICINE AND THE NEW GENETICS**

  http://www.ornl.gov/sci/techresources/Human_Genome/medicine/medicine.shtml

- **CENTER FOR MEDICAL GENETICS**

  http://research.marshfieldclinic.org/genetics/Default.htm

- **AMERICAN BOARD OF MEDICAL GENETICS**

  http://www.abmg.org/

- **BIOMED CENTRAL**

  http://www.biomedcentral.com/

- **OFFICE OF SCIENTIFIC AND TECHNICAL INFORMATION**

  http://www.osti.gov/

- **NATIONAL TECHNICAL INFORMATION SERVICE**

  http://www.ntis.gov/

- **NATIONAL SCIENCE FOUNDATION**

  http://www.nsf.gov/

- **NATIONAL HUMAN GENOME RESEARCH INSTITUTE**

  http://www.genome.gov/

- **NATIONAL INSTITUTE OF BIOMEDICAL IMAGING AND BIOENGINEERING**

  http://www.nibib1.nih.gov/

FEDERAL GOVERNMENT SOURCES

- **FEDERAL MINE SAFETY AND HEALTH REVIEW COMMISSION**

  http://www.fmshrc.gov/

- **ENVIRONMENTAL PROTECTION AGENCY (EPA)**

  http://www.epa.gov/

NATIONAL INSTITUTES OF HEALTH (NIH)

http://www.nih.gov/

- **NATIONAL CENTER ON MINORITY HEALTH AND HEALTH DIS-PARITIES (NCMHD)**

  http://www.ncmhd.nih.gov/

- **NATIONAL EYE INSTITUTE**

  http://www.nei.nih.gov/

- **NATIONAL INSTITUTE OF DIABETES & DIGESTION & KIDNEY DISEASES**

  http://www.niddk.nih.gov/

- **UNITED STATES DEPARTMENT OF HEALTH AND HUMAN SERVICES**

  http://www.hhs.gov/

- **CENTER FOR BIOLOGICS EXAMINATION AND RESEARCH**

  http://www.fda.gov/cber/

- **OFFICE OF PUBLIC HEALTH AND SAFETY**

  http://www.osophs.dhhs.gov/ophs/

- **OFFICE OF THE SURGEON GENERAL**

  http://www.surgeongeneral.gov/

- **NATIONAL INSTITUTE OF DENTAL AND CRANIOFACIAL RESEARCH**

  http://www.nidcr.nih.gov/

- **AGENCY FOR HEALTH CARE RESEARCH AND QUALITY (AHRQ)**

  http://www.ahrq.gov/

- **AGENCY FOR TOXIC SUBSTANCES AND DISEASE REGISTRY (ATSDR)**

  http://www.atsdr.cdc.gov/atsdrhome.html

- **AIRFORCE AIR SAFETY CENTER**

  http://afsafety.af.mil/

- **NATIONAL LIBRARY OF MEDICINE**

  http://www.nlm.nih.gov/

- **OFFICE OF OCCUPATIONAL SAFETY AND HEALTH**

  http://www1.va.gov/vasafety/

- **OFFICE OF INSPECTOR GENERAL**

  http://www.oig.doi.gov/

- **UNITED STATES PATENT AND TRADEMARK OFFICE**

  http://www.uspto.gov/

- **GOVERNMENT ACCOUNTABILITY OFFICE — REPORTS**

  http://www.gpoaccess.gov/gaoreports/index.html

- **OFFICE OF NAVAL RESEARCH — SCIENCE AND TECHNOLOGY**

  http://www.onr.navy.mil/sci_tech/engineering/331_physical/default.asp

- **NATIONAL TRANSPORTATION SAFETY BOARD (NTSB)**

  http://www.ntsb.gov/

- **NATIONAL HIGHWAY TRAFFIC SAFETY ADMINISTRATION [NHTSA]**

  http://www.nhtsa.dot.gov/

- **SMITHSONIAN INSITUTION**

  http://www.si.edu/

- **LIBRARY OF CONGRESS**

  http://www.loc.gov/

- **NATIONAL CENTER FOR STATISTICS AND ANALYSIS [NHTSA/DOT]**

  http://www-nrd.nhtsa.dot.gov/departments/nrd-30/ncsa/

- **FATALITY ANALYSIS REPORTING SYSTEM (FARS)-WEB- BASED ENCYCLOPEDIA**

  http://www-fars.nhtsa.dot.gov/

- **NHTSA RESEARCH AND DEVELOPMENT**

  http://www-nrd.nhtsa.dot.gov/

- **NHTSA-OFFICE OF DEFECTS INVESTIGATION**

  http://www-odi.nhtsa.dot.gov/cars/problems/recalls/recallsearch.cfm

- **FHWA/NHTSA NATIONAL CRASH ANALYSIS CENTER (NCAC)**

  http://www.ncac.gwu.edu/

- **LSU LIBRARIES FEDERAL AGENCIES DIRECTORY**

  http://www.lib.lsu.edu/gov/fedgov.html

- **CONSUMER PRODUCTS SAFETY COMMISSION (CPSC)**

  http://www.cpsc.gov/

- **FEDWORLD GOVERNMENT INFORMATION**

  http://www.fedworld.gov/

- **FEDERAL FOOD SAFETY INFORMATION**

  http://www.foodsafety.gov/

- **FOOD SAFETY INFORMATION CENTER**

  http://www.nalusda.gov/foodsafety/

- **FOOD SAFETY AND INSPECTION SERVICE (FSIS)**

  http://www.fsis.usda.gov/

- **ANIMAL AND PLANT HEALTH INSPECTION SERVICES (APHIS)**

  http://www.aphis.usda.gov/

- **TOXICOLOGY DATA NETWORK (TOXNET)**

  http://toxnet.nlm.nih.gov/

- **COMPUTER RETRIEVAL OF INFORMATION ON SCIENTIFIC**

PROJECTS (CRISP)

http://crisp.cit.nih.gov/

- **UNIVERSITY OF NORTH TEXAS GOVERNMENT INFORMATION DATABASE**

  http://www.library.unt.edu/govinfo/subject/catsindx.html

- **FEDSTATS-FEDERAL STATISTICAL DATA**

  http://www.fedstats.gov/

- **CENTERS FOR DISEASE CONTROL AND PREVENTION (CDC)**

  http://www.cdc.gov/

- **NATIONAL CANCER**

  http://www.cancer.gov/

- **HEALTH RESOURCES AND SERVICES ADMINISTRATION**

  http://www.hrsa.gov/

- **NATIONAL CENTER FOR HEALTH STATISTICS (NCHS)**

  http://www.cdc.gov/nchs/

- **BUREAU OF LABOR STATISTICS**

  http://www.bls.gov/

- **U.S. GOVERNMENT PRINTING OFFICE**

  http://www.gpo.gov/

- **GPO ACCESS**

  http://www.gpoaccess.gov/index.html STANDARDS ORGANIZATIONS

- **AMERICAN NATIONAL STANDARDS INSTITUTE (ANSI)**

  http://www.ansi.org/

- **NATIONAL INSTITUTE OF STANDARDS AND TECHNOLOGY (NIST)**

  http://www.nist.gov/

- **AMERICAN NATIONAL STANDARDS INSTITUTE (ANSI)**

  http://www.ansi.org/

- **ASTM INTERNATIONAL-STANDARDS WORLDWIDE (ASTM)**

  http://www.astm.org/cgi-bin/SoftCart.exe/index.shtml?E+mystore

COMPANY INFORMATION

- **SEC FILINGS AND FORMS (EDGAR)**

  http://www.sec.gov/edgar.shtml

- **HOOVER'S COMPANY INFORMATION**

  http://www.hoovers.com/free/

- **DIALOG INFORMATION SYSTEM BLUE SHEETS**

  http://library.dialog.com/bluesheets/

- **ANNUAL REPORTS GALLERY**

  http://www.reportgallery.com/

- **D&B — WHO OWNS WHOM**

  http://library.dialog.com/bluesheets/html/bl0522.html

- **DIRECTORY OF CORPORATE AFFILIATIONS**

  http://www.lexisnexis.com/dca/

- **THOMASNET COMPANY INFORMATION**

  http://www.thomasnet.com/

Chapter 13

THE EXPERT WITNESS

SYNOPSIS

§ 13.01   EXPERT WITNESSES: PRE-TRIAL CONSIDERATIONS

   [A]   Analyzing Expert Witness Needs

      [1]   Determining Expert Witness Needs

      [2]   Categorizing Expert Witness Needs

   [B]   Choosing the Expert Witness

      [1]   Expert Witness Research Sites

      [2]   Expert Witness Clearing Houses

      [3]   ATLA Exchange and DRI

      [4]   Lexis and Westlaw Listings

   [C]   Organizational Factors

   [D]   Categories of Experts

§ 13.02   PLAINTIFF REQUIRED TO PRESENT EXPERT TESTIMONY

§ 13.03   THE LEGAL REQUIREMENTS OF EXPERT TESTIMONY

§ 13.04   EXPERT TESTIMONY NOT SUPPORTED BY RELIABLE SCIENCE

§ 13.05   TESTING ALTERNATIVES IN UNIT DEFECT CASES

§ 13.06   TESTING ALTERNATIVES IN DESIGN DEFECT CASES

§ 13.07   QUALIFICATIONS TO TESTIFY AT TRIAL

§ 13.08   SOURCES REASONABLY RELIED UPON BY EXPERTS IN THE FIELD

§ 13.01   EXPERT WITNESSES: PRE-TRIAL CONSIDERATIONS

There are a wide variety of factors that are involved in the area of the initial pretrial use of expert witnesses in products liability cases. Set out below is a brief discussion of the most important basic pretrial considerations with regard to expert witness.

[A]   Analyzing Expert Witness Needs

[1]   Determining Expert Witness Needs

The question of expert witness requirements should be analyzed from the dual perspectives of counsel's legal and investigative needs since the expert often has much to offer in the purely investigative aspects of case preparation. Such choices are often one of the most difficult due to counsel's initial unfamiliarity with the range of state of the art, regulatory and corporate issues involved in the case. Several categories of experts need not be utilized until counsel is ready to initiate discovery, while others need not be called upon to any significant degree until the case approaches trial. The ever present need to control expert witness costs requires close planning regarding the actual uses of the expert. The following sections will address several considerations that should enter into the decision to engage an expert or experts. It is also important to note that experts may not be easily substituted later in the case and case planning requires an early and solid relationship.

[2]   Categorizing Expert Witness Needs

The preliminary research on the broad state-of-the-art context of the case will point toward the specific technical areas generally involved in cases of the type under review. In any products case, state of the art, regulatory and corporate information are central concerns. The key legal and technical issues are those specifically related to defect, feasible alternative design and proximate causation. As preliminary legal, state of the art, regulatory, industry and company research advance, the general outlines of the specific research areas central to the case will emerge. In a case involving a disintegrating ball-joint on a pickup truck resulting in the loss of a wheel, where is the technical ball-joint theoretical literature to be located? Is the National Highway Traffic Safety Administration the primary regulatory agency? How do I access information about industry trade associations and the company itself?

Counsel for both sides may initially determine that the following categories of expertise may be required: general automotive design; ball joint system design and materials selection in particular; automobile crash testing methodology; metallurgy; accident reconstruction; National Highway Traffic Safety Administration regulatory processes; corporate documentation and decision-making processes; corporate accounting principles; and statistical analyses. Once the scope of expert witness categories has been estimated, counsel should then make a determination of what additional specialized expertise, if any, may be required by the particular facts of the case under investigation. Considerable attention must also be given to experts in the damages area, which will involve medical expertise and economists and often, statisticians on the issue of future damages.

[B]   Choosing the Expert Witness

[1]   Expert Witness Research Sites

The Internet provides an amazing number of websites devoted to the listing of expert witnesses in every area of possible interest to products liability litigators. Many are free of charge, others like that of fee-based listings[1] such as the service of the plaintiff's bar American Trial Lawyers Association (ATLA)[2] provide names of firms with past experience with the experts of interest. Sites such as Expert Law[3] break experts down by area such as automobile products cases.[4]

[2]   Expert Witness Clearing Houses

In addition to the numerous websites providing expert witness location and resumes, there are a number of expert witness corporations that provide extensive, multi-tiered expert services and the latest system support laboratories and equipment.[5]

[3]   ATLA Exchange and DRI

The ATLA Exchange is a legal research service available to ATLA plaintiff lawyers. The Exchange provides contacts with lawyers with previous experience in similar cases and those who are currently or have recently utilized the type of expert being sought. The Exchange also provides current information on product recalls and provides leads to procuring depositions, court documents, case abstracts, CLE materials, experts, Law Reporter Court Document sets, and a wealth of other information such as Injury Collections, Abstract Sets, and Ultimate Document Sets.

The Defense Research Institute[6] (The Voice of the Defense Bar) provides similar services to the defense bar, and as does ATLA, is affiliated with state and local support groups[7] for product liability defense counsel.

---

[1] *See, e.g.*, The Leading Global Source, http://www.LECG.com; JurisPro Expert Witnesses, http://www.JurisPro.com; Expert Pages, http://expertpages.com; Expert Witness Directory, http://ExpertWitness.com; Martindale-Hubbell's Directory, http://www.martindale.com/resources; http://www.matcoinc.com; http://www.lawyersandsettlements.com; http://www.romingerlegal.com; http://www.legal-database.com. There are many more listings on the Internet resulting from an "expert witnesses" Google search.

[2] http://www.atla.org/.

[3] http://www.expertlaw.com/experts/Products/.

[4] http://www.expertlaw.com/experts/Products/Automotive.html.

[5] A good example is Packer Engineering, http://www.packereng.com/index.cfm, providing sophisticated expert witness services in the areas of aerospace, automotive, bioengineering, building technology, chemical engineering, electrical engineering, electronics, engineering mechanics, explosions, fires, human factors, machinery, materials engineering, mechanical engineering, safety engineering, and structural engineering.

[6] http://www.dri.org. This is the major counterpart to ATLA, which serves the community of plaintiff personal injury litigators.

[7] *See also* The Federation of Defense and Corporate Council, http://www.thefederation.org; The

[4] Lexis and Westlaw Listings

The LexisNexis legal research system[8] provides extensive access to the leading expert witness listing sources. Their Combined Verdicts, Settlements and Expert Directories, Expert Witness Directories, include expert4law, LA County Bar Association Expert Witness Dir, ALM Experts New England Directory, JurisPro Expert Witness Directory, ALM Experts New Jersey Directory, ALM Experts Legal Expert Pages, ALM Experts New York Directory, Martindale-Hubbell(R) Law Directory — Experts & Services, ALM Experts Southeastern Directory, ALM Experts Mid-Atlantic Directory Source, ALM Experts Southwestern Directory and the ALM Experts Mid-Western Directory.

The Westlaw legal research system provides access to a full range of expert witness sources. Its database listings include (WLD-EXPERTS), Expert Witness Resumes (EXPTRESUME), Expert Witness Journal (EXP-WITJ), Profiler — Profiles of Expert Witnesses (PROFILER-EW), Datamonitor Expert View (DATAMEXPVIEW), ExpertNet (EXPNET), Expert Witnesses in Civil Trial (EXPWIT-CIV), and Expert Witness Checklists (EXPWITC).

[C] Organizational Factors

In addition to the interview with the prospective expert, counsel should definitely consult with attorneys who are currently using or have used the expert. Counsel should also be sure to consult attorneys with whom the expert has worked who are not on the expert's list of formal references. Such attorneys can provide invaluable insights into virtually every area of concern to the product litigator faced with the difficult task of engaging a particular expert witness. Of primary concern are whether he is a sole practitioner, the extent of his staff support, the nature and modernity of his specialized equipment, his preferred method of approach and his current workload and accessibility.

There has been a dramatic change in the nature of expert witness involvement in product liability cases over the past several decades resulting from the rapid development of expert witness service corporations of increasing size and complexity. This has resulted in the attendant displacement of the sole practitioner or several member firms as the primary players in the preparation and trial of the products case. Accordingly, an initial discussion of the advantages and disadvantages of the sole practitioner versus the expert witness service organization is in order. It should first be recalled that counsel may not have a choice due to his or her being the first to bring a suspect product type to litigation. In those areas, the fields of expertise may be such that the large expert witness organizations are simply unable or unwilling to supply or sub-contract with an individual possessed of sufficient background to meet counsel's broad requirements. Admittedly, this hypothetical situation is becoming a rare phenomenon, due to expert witness service organizations constantly expanding the range of experts working for them.

International Association of Defense Council, http://www.iadclaw.org; and The Federation of Defense & Corporate Counsel (FDCC), http://www.thefederation.org/professional development.

[8] http://www.lexisnexis.com.

A sole practitioner may be unacceptable due to a lack of technical facilities with which to compete with the most recent scientific methods for product and occurrence evaluation. The increasingly hierarchical nature of expert witness service corporations, with their highly refined areas of responsibility, wealth of scientific equipment, extensive support staffs and expanding areas of expertise, put great strain upon the sole practitioner in attempts to compete with the well financed and supported corporate defendant.[9]

There are definite advantages to using the sole practitioner if counsel is confident that he has the technological capability and experience to counter the expertise provided by a large expert witness service corporation. There is an opportunity to develop a personal relationship and shared commitment to the case and the client, important factors often sorely lacking when utilizing the services of an assigned employee of a large expert witness corporation. There is also the possibility of more flexible fee and payment modes.

[D] Categories of Experts

Expert testimony is the centerpiece of a products liability case. Automotive engineers, consumer products designers, pharmacologists, chemists and medical device designers are just a few of the type of experts typically involved in products litigation. Aside from the obvious technical expert witnesses, there are often a range of non-technical experts that are required to address complex issues resulting from the complexity of modern manufacturing processes. Such non-technical witnesses will include experts in management principles and corporate processes, regulatory agency procedures and policy, statisticians, corporate accountants and marketing and advertising experts.

Formal company systems for integrating safety in design, company protocols for cooperating with or fending off regulatory measures, the statistical models used to determine if a statistical risk is equivalent to a risk that must be considered in manufacture and marketing, internal corporate accounting factors that assign "costs" that may not be actually reflected in a showroom or market price, and drafts of advertising proposals and marketing campaign analyses may each require explanatory expertise at trial. For example, the Vioxx litigators will show keen interest in discussions had in the company about whether statistical data required the company to include or ignore any concerns over risk of heart attacks in their warnings insert or advertising. A complex series of corporate decision-making processes may require expertise to unravel it for a jury. In an SUV rollover case, discussions of the wording of brochures or the content of television advertising spots may require emphasis or explanation. Costs will affect the use of non-

---

[9] *See* TERRENCE F. KIELY, SCIENCE AND LITIGATION: PRODUCTS LIABILITY IN THEORY AND PRACTICE 268 (CRC Press 2002). Another potential drawback to the utilization of the sole practitioner is the problem of accessibility. In addition to the increasing technological inadequacies of the sole practitioner, there is the important factor of available time as a central consideration. The sole practitioner, especially in the fields relevant to engineered products, has little or no backup support and — if effective in their field — are generally constantly on the go, studying accident sites and product units across the country. Their unavailability in instances where time is of the essence can have harmful and at times long lasting negative effects on the prosecution of a products case. *Id.*

technical experts, but they should be considered as research progresses.

In addition to technical experts giving opinions, experts are often employed as narrative experts only, to explain the history and basics of the science involved in the case.

§ 13.02 PLAINTIFF REQUIRED TO PRESENT EXPERT TESTIMONY

In *Rosenberg v. Otis Elevator* Co.,[10] a 2004 New Jersey opinion, invitees brought an action against an elevator company, who both manufactured and maintained the subject elevator, and the building owner after they were injured when elevator in which they were riding dropped three floors. The Superior Court, Law Division, Ocean County, granted summary judgment in favor of the elevator company and the building owner. The Appellate Division reversed and remanded.

The appellate court ruled that the jurors did not require expert testimony to address the issue whether the elevator company and the building owner met their duty to invitees. The court held that judicial evaluation of the need for expert testimony in a products liability case should take account of the complexity of evidence related to the instrumentality involved in an accident, rather than simply focusing on whether the instrumentality is complex.

Likewise, in *Jones v. Toyota Motor Sales USA, Inc.*, 2004 U.S. App. LEXIS 5399 (3d Cir. Mar. 22, 2004), the court ruled that under Pennsylvania law, a tow tractor operator was required to produce expert evidence in order to support his products liability claim against the manufacturer under crashworthiness doctrine based on lack of operator restraints, despite the operator's contention that the concept of providing belt or restraint to bilateral open-sided machine was not beyond comprehension of ordinary lay persons, where the issue required consideration of engineering, medical, and bio-mechanical analysis that was not within know-how of ordinary layperson.

§ 13.03 THE LEGAL REQUIREMENTS OF EXPERT TESTIMONY

Although forensic scientists in criminal cases are required to conduct a variety of science-based tests and report and interpret their findings,[11] this has not been the practice in civil law products liability cases. For one thing, the scientific testimony in those cases typically references some generic design, instructions or warnings issues that was pre-existent to the occurrence giving rise to the case. In addition, the purposes in doing any such case-science would be distinctly different from that supporting scientific inquiry in a criminal case. The issue of whether the drug Parlodel can cause brain aneurysm in a products liability lawsuit, is quite different from the forensic issue of whether blood, semen, hair or fiber expert testimony may be used to link a defendant to a crime scene in a rape-homicide prosecution.

---

[10] 841 A.2d 99 (N.J. Super. App. Div. 2004).

[11] *See* TERRENCE F. KIELY, FORENSIC EVIDENCE: SCIENCE AND THE CRIMINAL LAW (CRC Press, 2d ed. 2006).

Experts in products liability cases, including those engaged by defendant companies, do not typically conduct actual scientific work for the case proper, but rather base their opinions on previously published scientific material. Nobel Prize winner Stanley Miller referred to articles or opinions based on other articles as merely *paper science*,[12] as opposed to hard fought work in research laboratories. It is quite likely that expert testimony by way of *paper science* is what will continue to be the basis of the expert witnesses' contribution to the products liability process. Indeed, in some cases, such as the questioning of the adequacy of 1960s titanium alloy foundry techniques central to the Iowa DC-10 crash filings and discovery, any other requirement may very well be both technological and economic impossibilities. Where the questioned science or engineering practice or allegedly inadequate instructions or warnings are susceptible to some actual investigation by the expert what, if anything should be required other than the expert's bare opinion?[13]

The controlling evidence rule governing the admissibility of expert testimony in products liability litigation is Federal Rule of Evidence 702 (or its equivalents under state law[14]) which provides:

> If scientific, technical, or other specialized knowledge will assist the trier of fact to understand the evidence or to determine a fact in issue, a witness qualified as an expert by knowledge, skill, experience, training, or education, may testify thereto in the form of an opinion or otherwise, if (1) the testimony is based upon sufficient facts or data, (2) the testimony is the product of reliable principles and methods, and (3) the witness has applied the principles and methods reliably to the facts of the case.[15]

---

[12] See KIELY, *supra* note 9, at 55. See also *ATLA's Litigating Tort Cases*, A. Russell Smith, Chapter 14, Discovery Strategy and Privileges (2004), for a good recent summary of the various *Daubert* related issues; Robert C. Morgan & Ashe P. Puri, *Expert Witnesses and Daubert Motions*, 5 SEDONA CONF. J. 15 (2004); Douglas Hanna & Paul R. Ferreira, EXPERT WITNESS OVERVIEW A COMMON SENSE APPROACH, 229-AUG. N.J. LAW 11 (2004).

[13] Recently, efforts have been made to ostracize errant experts from their respective professional organizations. *See* Terry Carter, M.D., WITH A MISSION: A PHYSICIAN BATTLES AGAINST COLLEAGUES HE CONSIDERS ROGUE EXPERT WITNESSES, 90-AUG. A.B.A.J. 41 (2004).

[14] *See generally* PAUL C. GIANNELLI, UNDERSTANDING EVIDENCE (2d ed. LexisNexis 2006), Chapter 24 Expert Testimony: FRE 702, 704, 706. This is an excellent general treatise on modern evidence law.

[15] It is the position of both state and federal courts that plaintiffs must present some expert testimony as a minimal requirement to prove a product design defect. *See, e.g.*, Burgad v. Jack L. Marcus, Inc., 345 F. Supp. 2d 1036 (D.N.D. 2004) (In light of the absence of any expert testimony as to whether vendor of sports bra breached any standard of care in its design and manufacture of the bra, whether the bra was defective, unsafe, or unreasonably dangerous, or whether there was any causal connection between any design defect and plaintiff's injuries, vendor of sports bra was not liable in negligence, under North Dakota law, to purchaser allegedly burned while wearing the garment. As a general rule, a plaintiff is required to prove a product defect through an expert witness.); Jones v. Toyota Motor Sales USA, Inc., 2004 U.S. App. LEXIS 5399 (3d Cir. Mar. 22, 2004) (Under Pennsylvania law, tow tractor operator was required to produce expert evidence in order to support his products liability claim against manufacturer under crashworthiness doctrine based on lack of operator restraints, despite operator's contention that concept of providing belt or restraint to bilateral open-sided machine was not beyond comprehension of ordinary lay persons, where issue required consideration of engineering, medical, and biomechanical analysis that was not within know-how of ordinary layperson.). *But see* Rosenberg v. Otis Elevator Co., 841 A.2d 99 (N.J. Super. App. Div. 2004) (Invitees brought action against elevator company, who both manufactured and maintained elevator, and building owner after they were injured when elevator in

The famous *Daubert* case and its progeny, centered in Rule 702, have been discussed in detail in Chapter 8, Problems of Proof: Defect and Causation.[16] It is the purpose of the ensuing discussion to examine the very practical issue of recent court pronouncements on the actual presentation of expert opinions and feasible alternative design testimony.

§ 13.04 EXPERT TESTIMONY NOT SUPPORTED BY RELIABLE SCIENCE

In *Goodyear Tire & Rubber Co. v. Rios*,[17] a widow brought a products liability action against a tire manufacturer alleging that the tire contained a manufacturing defect and failure to warn defect. The 229th Judicial District Court, Duval County, Alex W. Gabert, J., entered judgment on jury verdict in favor of plaintiff and against manufacturer in the amount of $40 million. The appellate court reversed, holding that plaintiff's tire expert's testimony regarding cause of tire failure was not reliable evidence of whether a manufacturing defect existed. The expert's opinion was based only on visual and tactile testing of tire, and no evidence indicated that other experts used same methodology to determine that a manufacturing defect existed, as opposed to a defect caused by the use and abuse of tire over time. Additionally, the expert did not refer to any article or publication that specifically supported his approach.

The plaintiffs offered the testimony of two experts to establish the existence of a manufacturing defect, Robert Ochs and John Crate. Goodyear asserted that the testimony of these experts provided no evidence of a manufacturing defect because the experts were either unqualified or their opinions were not reliable. The court ruled that to be reliable, the expert's testimony must be grounded in scientific method and procedure such that it amounts to more than subjective belief or unsupported speculation. The Texas Supreme Court had enumerated a list of *Daubert-type* factors to determine the reliability of expert testimony, including: (1) the extent to which the theory has or can be tested; (2) the extent to which the technique relies upon subjective interpretation of the expert; (3) whether the theory has been subjected to peer review and publication; (4) the technique's potential rate of error; (5) whether the underlying theory or technique has been generally accepted as valid by the relevant scientific community; and (6) the nonjudicial uses that have been made of the theory or technique.[18]

---

which they were riding dropped three floors. Judicial evaluation of the need for expert testimony in a products liability case should take account of the complexity of evidence related to instrumentality involved in an accident, rather than simply focusing on whether the instrumentality is complex.).

[16] See *Seeley v. Hamilton Beach/Proctor-Silex, Inc.*, 349 F. Supp. 2d 381 (N.D.N.Y. 2004), where homeowners sued a toaster manufacturer for negligence, strict products liability, and breach of warranties, seeking to recover damages for which they were not compensated by their insurer due to fire that allegedly resulted from toaster malfunction. The manufacturer moved to preclude testimony of the homeowners' proposed expert witness. The case, in the process of denying the defendant's motion, provides a very detailed discussion of the *Daubert* and *Kumho Tire* cases in the context of engineering expertise. See also *Cooper Tire & Rubber Co. v. Mendez*, 155 S.W.3d 382 (Tex. App. 2004) for an even more extensive discussion of the basic *Frye*, *Daubert*, and *Kumho Tire* requirements.

[17] 143 S.W.3d 107 (Tex. App. 2004).

[18] See E.I. du Pont de Nemours & Co. v. Robinson, 923 S.W.2d 549, 557 (Tex. 1995). However, in

On appeal, the manufacturer defendant contended that the expert's opinions were not reliable because none of the *Robinson/Daubert* factors were satisfied, and that Ochs offered nothing to establish the reliability of "his naked opinion." Ochs's opinion was based on demonstrable facts, which he observed either by touch or visually. He stated that tire manufacturers use certain failure analysis techniques and principles to adjust warranty claims, including (1) examination of the tire's exposed surfaces to determine the tire's condition, (2) whether those conditions included abuse, and (3) an examination of exposed surfaces to identify the surface's characteristics so that the characteristics can be related back to mechanisms such as abrasion or polishing. He testified there were a number of generally accepted explanations for the type of separation that occurred in this tire, including (1) the circumstances under which the tire was used, (2) the operation of the tire in an over-deflected state due to either underinflating the tire for a given load or using proper inflation but applying an excessive load, (3) impact or trauma that causes a local fracture or failure of components in the belt that expands into a greater separation, (4) any of these conditions coupled with a manufacturing or design defect, (5) a design or manufacturing defect alone, or (6) operating the tire at an excessively high speed. He said his opinion was based on his experience, training, and background, as well as documents describing surface conditions and relating these conditions to materials used in construction of the tire.[19]

Despite the tire's age and condition, Ochs concluded that the tread separation resulted from a manufacturing defect. He testified the tire separated because of a lack of adhesion between the brass cable and the rubber over the cable, which he explained as follows. Poor adhesion allows the brass plating on the cable to separate from the rubber, which results in the cable ceasing to be part of the tire's structure. The cable separates, resulting in cracking and polishing of the cables. Exposed cable wires, the color of steel instead of brass, indicates polishing, i.e., that the brass has been rubbed away and this was the beginning of the separation. The separation continues through the spread of the tire, resulting in enough of an area opening up so that the tread and upper belt, through centrifugal force, begin to lift away from the lower belt and carcass of the tire. Ochs admitted he had never seen the specifications for this tire, he conducted no tests on the tire other than visual and tactile, and he was not relying on any of the documents in a "museum" that contains various information about tire failures.[20]

Goodyear asserted that Ochs's purely visual and tactile test was unreliable because his technique was entirely subjective. The court disagreed, observing that the issue was "not the reasonableness *in general* of a tire expert's use of a visual and tactile inspection to determine what caused the tire's tread to separate from its steel-belted carcass."[21] Instead, the court stated, "it [is] the reasonableness of using such an approach, along with [the expert's] particular method of analyzing the data

---

Gammill v. Jack Williams Chev., Inc., 972 S.W.2d 713, 726 (Tex. 1998), the court held that the *Robinson* factors do not always apply to expert testimony because they do not always fit. "Experience alone may provide a sufficient basis for an expert's testimony in some cases, but it cannot do so in every case."

[19] *Rios*, 143 S.W.3d at 113–14.

[20] *Id.* at 114.

[21] *Id.* (*quoting* Kumho Tire Co. v. Carmichael, 526 U.S. 137, 153–54 (1999)).

thereby obtained, to draw a conclusion regarding *the particular matter to which the expert testimony was directly relevant.*"[22] Here, the court noted, as in that matter concerned the likelihood that a defect in the tire caused its tread to separate from its carcass. Also here, the relevant issue was whether the expert could reliably determine the cause of this tire's separation.

The court found that the analysis employed by the Court applied here. Ochs attempted to rule out other possible causes for the tread separation. However, the issue concerns Ochs's use of visual/tactile inspection to conclude that a manufacturing defect was present without any evidence in the record indicating that other experts in the industry use Ochs's methodology (the existence of steel wires with little to no coverage of rubber) to determine that a manufacturing defect exists, as opposed to a defect caused by the use and abuse of the tire over time. Ochs did not refer to any article or publication that specifically supported his approach. For these reasons, his testimony was not reliable and, therefore, amounted to no evidence of a manufacturing defect.[23] Goodyear argued that plaintiff expert John Crate was not qualified to render an opinion because he had no experience with tires outside the litigation setting. He also had no experience, education, or training in tire design, manufacture, or forensic analysis of tire treads.

Crate was a research scientist at the Georgia Institute of Technology in Atlanta, Georgia. He had a bachelor's degree in chemistry and a master's degree in polymer science and engineering. He received his master's degree in 2000. In the summer of 1991 before he began work at the Institute, he worked as an analytical chemist, which he did for about ten years, analyzing the failure of polymeric products and rubber. Although Crate's background included research generally into the adhesion properties of various materials, the court noted, none of his experience was specific to tires. He had no background in tires, and did not consider himself an expert on them. He admitted that the vast amount of his experience in failure analysis has been related to products other than tires. He had tested a tire only once, to determine the presence of foreign substances. None of the texts upon which he relied to give his opinion in this case were specific to tires. Instead, the court observed, the focus of the texts were adhesion, failure, and fracture surfaces generated on various surfaces.[24]

He had never done any studies to determine the effects of aging, puncture holes, torn or damaged beads, patched tires, and overloaded tires. Although his background may have enabled Crate to discuss adhesion failures generally, he was not qualified to opine on the specifics of the actual subject matter for which he was called to testify: whether the Rios's tire failed because of an adhesion defect present at the time of manufacture. Accordingly, the court held that Crate was not qualified as an expert in the field of tire failure analysis; therefore, his testimony amounts to legally insufficient evidence of a manufacturing defect.[25]

---

[22] *Kumho Tire*, 526 U.S. at 154.

[23] *Rios*, 143 S.W.3d at 115.

[24] *Id.*

[25] *Id.*

§ 13.05 TESTING ALTERNATIVES IN UNIT DEFECT CASES

Short of requiring expert witnesses to unrealistically replicate high-tech laboratories to test their opinions, just what can post-*Daubert* trial courts require the testifying expert to do other than closely review the state-of-the- art literature and come up with a supportable opinion? This issue is the latest twist in the progression of the *Daubert* principles through the *Joiner* and *Kumho Tire* progression.[26]

This requirement in design defect cases must be distinguished from cases alleging a unit defect case, where the defect allegation refers only to the specific unit used by the plaintiff. An example would be a skateboard with a defective wheel attaching apparatus not typical of the product line. The distinction was discussed in the recent decision of *The Hartford Insurance Company v. Broan-Nutone LLC*,[27] a subrogation action arising from a fire originating in an apartment stove. The court addressed the issue of requiring experts who proffer an alternative design in a design defect case to present evidence that it was tested. The court observed that given the importance of testing alternative designs when alleging a design defect, plaintiffs have failed to provide sufficient evidence to support a claim under that theory. However, the court noted, plaintiffs' response to the motion for summary judgment indicated that they were actually alleging a manufacturing defect, not a design defect. Therefore, the importance of testing an alternative design did not apply, since Hartford and State Farm alleged there was a failure specific to the product that gave rise to the alleged injury — an electrical malfunction in the range hood due to improper wiring by defendant. The experts' opinions finding the origin of the fire to be the range hood and the cause of the fire to be an electrical malfunction in the hood, certainly supported plaintiffs' allegations. The lack of testing by Agosti and Anderson did not render their opinions inadmissible.

In design defect cases, where some aspect of the manufacture and sale of the product is singled out but is common to all product units, current judicial rulings are expecting something more than a bare opinion from an expert that a feasible alternative design was available to the manufacturer. A recent trend, originating in the Seventh Circuit Court of Appeals, is requiring that the expert, before he will be allowed to proffer an opinion on a safer alternative design, present evidence that any such alternative was *actually tested* by the expert. Courts have not been specific about just what any *testing* might consist of. Obviously it would be impossible to require an expert to maintain a state-of-the-art research and design facility or to engage in independent drug or chemical research in order to proffer an opinion about safer alternative warnings. In failure to warn or instruct cases, is submission to standards setting groups, or existing federal or state regulatory agencies for approval a realistic requirement? On the other hand, simple justice would seem to require that costly corporate research and development efforts of product manufacturers not be adequately challenged on the basis of a bare opinion by an expert.

---

[26] *See* Chapter 8, Problems of Proof: Defect and Causation.

[27] 2004 U.S. Dist. LEXIS 6765 (N.D.Ill. 2004).

This issue does not arise in manufacturing defect cases, where the existence of an alternative design does not arise.[28]

§ 13.06   TESTING ALTERNATIVES IN DESIGN DEFECT CASES

This very practical *post-Daubert* question was recently addressed in the 2005 federal district court opinion in the case *Phillips v. The Raymond Corporation*,[29] where, following the removal of a worker's products liability action against a forklift manufacturer, the parties moved to strike the opposing party's experts. The federal district court ruled that a mechanical engineer's testimony regarding an alternate rear door design for a doorless stand-up forklift was inadmissible, but that a biomechanical engineer's testimony was admissible for the limited purpose of determining how a worker sustained his leg injuries. The latter opinion, however, was not admissible to determine what the mechanism of worker's injury would have been if the forklift was equipped with mechanical engineer's alternative design feature. The action arose out of an accident in which one Phillips was involved while working on a forklift manufactured by Raymond.[30]

Phillips and Raymond sought to introduce the testimony of two experts each. Each party moved to strike the opposing party's experts.

Phillips was employed at the Jewel Food Stores warehouse in Melrose Park, Illinois and was operating a stand-up forklift in connection with his normal work duties. He was driving a Model 31i forklift manufactured by Raymond, which was a stand-up, rear-entry forklift. The forklift had a door-less opening in the back of the forklift through which the driver of the forklift would pass when entering or leaving the machine. Phillips claims that during his shift, while traveling in reverse, he unknowingly struck a "wood chip" with a wheel of the forklift. Given the small size of the forklift's wheels, the wood chip became pinned between the wheel and the floor, jamming the wheel's ability to revolve. Consequently, Phillips alleged, the forklift stopped suddenly, and he was ejected from the forklift onto the floor through the uncovered opening in the back of the forklift. Phillips landed in the path of the forklift. Although the forklift has a "dead-man pedal," which must be depressed for the forklift to be able to move (rendering it impossible, at least theoretically, to have a pilotless, runaway forklift), the forklift's momentum carried it over the lower portion of Phillips's right leg. As a result of this trauma, doctors had to amputate Phillips's leg below the knee.

---

[28] *See also* Allstate Ins. Co. v. Maytag Corp., 1999 U.S. Dist. LEXIS 5083 (N.D. Ill. Mar. 29, 1999) (*quoting* Cummins v. Lyle Industries, 93 F.3d 362, 369 (7th Cir.1996)) ("[T]esting is not an absolute prerequisite to the admissibility of expert testimony.") The Seventh Circuit has emphasized that a court's inquiry into the reliability of an expert's opinion should be flexible and that the factors of reliability listed in *Daubert* should not be viewed as an exhaustive list. *See* Bourelle v. Crown Equipment Corp., 220 F.3d 532, 536 (7th Cir. 2000); United States v. Vitek Supply Corp., 144 F.3d 476, 485 (7th Cir.1998).

[29] 364 F. Supp. 2d 730 (N.D. Ill. 2005).

[30] Counts One and Three asserted that Raymond was strictly liable for Phillips's injury, while Counts Two and Four asserted that Raymond was negligent in its maintenance and sale of the forklift. Raymond successfully petitioned to remove the case from the Circuit Court of Cook County in April 1999.

Phillips alleged that the forklift was unreasonably dangerous because there was a satisfactory alternate design, specifically a latching-rear door, which would have safeguarded Phillips from the foreseeable event of being thrown from the open operator's compartment when the forklift stopped suddenly and forcefully.

Phillips retained and offered John Sevart ("Sevart") and Dr. Y King Liu ("Liu") as experts. Sevart was a mechanical engineer who, among other things, has designed and tested rear entry forklifts, in particular, a latching-rear door that he maintains should have been present on the Raymond 31i forklift. Dr. Liu was a biomechanical engineer whose purpose was to testify about the "mechanism" or physics behind Phillips's injury and what the mechanics (or lack thereof) would have been had the forklift had a rear door.

Raymond's motion to strike any testimony alleged that Liu was unqualified to offer opinions relevant to a stand-up forklift and that both Sevart and Liu could offer nothing more than their subjective beliefs as to the cause of this accident, and propose the addition of John Sevart's allegedly safer alternative design, which each speculates would have prevented the accident.[31]

Raymond retained Edward Caulfield ("Caulfield"), a mechanical engineer, and Dr. Catherine Ford Corrigan ("Corrigan"), a biomechanical engineer, to support its contentions that the latching-rear door was not a viable or beneficial alternative design.

The court noted that governed the admission of expert testimony:

> If scientific, technical, or other specialized knowledge will assist the trier of fact to understand the evidence or to determine a fact in issue, a witness qualified as an expert by knowledge, skill, experience, training, or education, may testify thereto in the form of an opinion or otherwise if (1) the testimony is based upon sufficient facts or data, (2) the testimony is the product of reliable principles and methods, and (3) the witness has applied the principles and methods reliably to the facts of the case.

The court observed that an expert must possess sufficient specialized expertise to render his opinion on the topic reliable, as required by *Daubert*.[32] Of specific importance, the court found that an expert's competence in the general field at issue must extend to his specific testimony on the matter before the court.[33] Once a court determines that an individual is qualified to be considered an expert, the *Raymond* court continued, it must apply a two-step analysis to determine whether the expert's opinion is admissible. First, a district court must ascertain whether the expert's testimony is reliable, and second, the court must determine whether the evidence assists the trier of fact in understanding the evidence or determining a fact in

---

[31] Raymond's motion was substantially based on the Seventh Circuit's decision in *Dhillon v. Crown Controls Corp.*, 269 F.3d 865, 867–70 (7th Cir. 2001), which affirmed the exclusion of Sevart's testimony in a similar case.

[32] *See also* United States v. Allen, 390 F.3d 944, 949 (7th Cir. 2004) (discussing Rule 702).

[33] *See* Ty, Inc. v. Pub. Int'l., Ltd., 2004 U.S. Dist. LEXIS 20942 (N.D. Ill., Oct. 19, 2004); *accord* Carroll v. Otis Elevator Co., 896 F.2d 210, 212 (7th Cir. 1990).

issue.[34] The question of admissibility, the court noted, asks whether "there is simply too great an analytical gap between the data and the opinion proffered."[35]

In order for the opinion to be considered scientific, and thus admissible, the court set out the familiar famous criteria to determine the question set forth in the 1993 U.S. Supreme Court opinion in *Daubert v. Merrell Dow Pharmaceuticals.*[36] The testimony must:

> (1) be based upon sufficient facts or data; (2) be the product of reliable principles and methods; and (3) come from a witness who has applied the principles and methods reliably to the facts of the case. Factors that may illuminate the analysis include: (1) whether the theory or technique can be and has been verified by the scientific method through testing; (2) whether the theory or technique has been subject to peer review and publication, (3) the known or potential rate of error of the technique, and (4) whether the theory or technique has been generally accepted by the relevant scientific community. These factors are merely guides, however, and do not serve as a series of prerequisites; their applicability depends on the particular facts and circumstances of each case. Nonetheless, a court must focus on the principles and methodology, not on the substance generated by the methodology — the latter is the province of the jury.[37]

The court observed that a subset of *Daubert*-type expert cases concern alternate designs, where a party claims that a manufacturer should be liable because a safer, alternate design existed at the time of the accident than the one employed by the defendant's product. Alternative design cases, the court noted, often require potential experts to take into account certain factors, including the degree to which the alternative design is compatible with existing systems; the relative efficiency of the two designs; the short- and long-term maintenance costs associated with the alternative design; the ability of the purchaser to service and to maintain the alternative designs; the relative cost of installing the two designs; and the effect, if any, that the alternative design would have on the price of the machine.[38] Many of these alternative considerations, the *Raymond* court observed, are product- and manufacturer-specific and cannot be reliably determined without testing.[39]

The court began by examining expert Sevart's methodology. Sevart's expertise and methodology were extensively questioned in the Seventh Circuit, namely in *Dhillon v. Crown Controls Corp.*[40] In *Dhillon*, the court noted, the Seventh Circuit affirmed the trial court's exclusion of Sevart in a strict liability and negligence action, arising out of injuries sustained in a forklift accident, similar to this case.

---

[34] *See, e.g.*, Riach v. Manhattan Design Studio, 2001 U.S. Dist. LEXIS 15480, at *9 (N.D. Ill. Sept. 24, 2001) *(quoting Daubert*, 509 U.S. at 590); *see also* Walker v. Soo Line R.R. Co., 208 F.3d 581, 587 (7th Cir. 2000).

[35] General Elec. v. Joiner, 522 U.S. 136, 146 (1997).

[36] 509 U.S. 579 (1993).

[37] *Raymond* at *3. *See also Daubert*, 509 U.S. at 590–91.

[38] *See* Cummins v. Lyle Indus., 93 F.3d 362, 369 (7th Cir. 1996).

[39] *See* Dhillon v. Crown Controls Corp., 269 F.3d 865, 870 (7th Cir. 2001).

[40] 269 F.3d 865 (7th Cir. 2001).

Sevart's proffered testimony and methodology were almost identical to his methodology and testimony in the *Phillips* case. His testimony was to the effect that the defendant's forklift was improperly designed because it did not come with a latching-rear door.[41]

The Phillips court found efforts by plaintiff to overcome Sevart's problems in *Dhillon* unavailing.[42] The court noted two unsuccessful attempts. The court found that the existence of a single patent application was not helpful to Phillips, as it was not indicative of any meaningful acceptance within a relevant scientific or design community. The Crown forklift with a rear door presented as a working alternative design the court observed, was for freezers only and not for general warehouse use. None of the trade magazines offered by Phillips discussed *latching-rear* doors, nor did they indicate that the rear doors are standard or non-optional features.[43] The manual presented, which was an *operator's manual* and not any design analysis, had no apparent relevance as related to forklift design. None of the materials presented, individually or collectively, would suggest that the sensible course was to depart from the path set forth in *Dhillon*.

As to the reliability of Sevart's methodology in concluding that Raymond's design was defective, the court noted several factors against acceptance by the court:

> Notwithstanding Sevart's rejection by the Seventh Circuit in *Dhillon*, Sevart performed no new tests for the instant case, instead relying on the tests previously criticized because they were done after Sevart reached his conclusions about the rear-door forklift. In addition, Phillips's briefs only discussed the conclusions of the tests, not their underlying methodology. Furthermore, Phillips's discussion of the egress time for a latching-rear door is misplaced, as escape is only one small, tangential issue. (D.E. 95 at 9-10.) To the extent it is relevant to Phillips's briefing, it may be that in this

---

[41] The *Phillips* court observed that in the *Dhillon* case, the Seventh Circuit was troubled by Sevart's utter lack of testing and professional rigor, *Dhillon*, 269 F.3d at 869–70, the fact that the tests he did were performed on a different type of forklift *after* Sevart formed his conclusions, *id.* at 870, and that Sevart did not perform any of the *Cummins* analysis for alternate design cases, *id.* at 870-71. Furthermore, Sevart did not favorably subject his methodology to any peer review and publication, nor could Sevart establish that his design had been accepted for general application by any manufacturer, regulatory body, or standards organization. *Id.*

[42] Phillips unsuccessfully attempts to overcome *Dhillon's* damaging pronouncements. To attempt to refute Sevart's prior lack of general acceptance (his proposed design appears to have been overwhelming rejected by virtually everyone), Phillips cites to several publications and entities that purportedly support Sevart's assertion that latching-rear doors are generally accepted as necessary. He cites to the Swedish Board of Occupational Safety and Health, an unnamed patent applicant, a 1989 edition of a forklift operator's manual, trade magazines, ten (unnamed) forklift manufacturers who "provide a rear post or rear door at [sic] standard equipment," an uncited report from 1977, and the fact that Crown, another forklift manufacturer, makes a forklift with a rear door. (D.E. 95 at 5–6.) Finally, Phillips maintains that the American National Standards Institute's ("ANSI") overwhelming rejection of Sevart's proposed design is based on bias and fear, since the chairman of the committee "is a Raymond employee and 28 of the 31 members are employees of . . . entities who have a vested financial interests in resisting mandatory improvements for forklifts." *Id.* at 5.

[43] As for the "ten forklift manufacturers," alleged to have adopted Sevart's general design idea, the court found that claim *imprecise and unhelpful*, because they include forklifts with a "rear post," which was not at issue, and it was unclear how many, if any, of the ten manufacturers offered rear doors as opposed to rear posts. *Raymond Corporation* at *4.

one regard the latching-rear door does not make the forklift more dangerous, but that does not mean that a forklift without a latching- rear door is inherently unsafe or less safe overall than a forklift with a latching door.[44]

Simply put, the court concluded that Sevart had not persuaded it that any of the *Daubert* factors were met:

> There is no apparent peer review or publication of Sevart's methods. Sevart's "analysis" amounts to little more than a series of foregone and conclusory assertions that are not supported by serious documentation, peer review, or acceptable testing. Furthermore, Sevart's method did not include any testing to indicate whether his design would be feasible, and he never created or tested a prototype or other tangible demonstration of his design. Sevart's testing also appears to treat a rear door and a rear guard or post as interchangeable without any substantiation or justification. Additionally, Sevart did not conduct any new tests after the Seventh Circuit's decision in *Dhillon,* and in *Dhillon* the Court concluded that all his previous tests had occurred after he had already made up his mind about a rear door forklift design. It is difficult to understand how Sevart could seek to testify under such circumstances. Sevart also did not abide by the steps he himself believed a design engineer should take before reaching an opinion concerning a marketable and safe design.[45]

Moreover, the court continued, Sevart's methodology and design had not been generally accepted, and in fact, had been overwhelmingly and resoundingly rejected by the only design community discussed and he had not established that any other manufacturer offered his design as a standard feature.[46]

§ 13.07   QUALIFICATIONS TO TESTIFY AT TRIAL

The decision in the case of *Phillips v. The Raymond Corporation*,[47] also addressed the important issue of an expert's qualifications to give a particular opinion, while otherwise acceptable as an expert in the general area of science or technology involved. The court next turned to the proffered testimony of the biomedical engineer Dr. Y King Liu. Dr. Liu was retained to address two points: (1) the mechanism of injury to Phillips as a result of the accident as it occurred and (2) what the extent and mechanism, if any, of Phillips's injury would have been had the forklift had a latching-rear door of the type promoted and endorsed by Sevart. After reviewing the relevant information, the Court concluded that Dr. Liu could testify concerning the first issue, but he could not do so regarding the second, as it was derivative of the excluded Sevart testimony.

Raymond argued that although Liu was an experienced biomechanical engineer, he was not qualified to give testimony in this forklift design case because his

---

[44] *Raymond Corporation* at *6.

[45] *Id.* at *8.

[46] *See* Cummins v. Lyle Indus., 93 F.3d 362, 369 (7th Cir. 1996).

[47] 364 F. Supp. 2d 730 (N.D. Ill. 2005).

expertise did not "fit" the facts of the present case. The court rejected this argument, finding that Dr. Liu was, in fact, perfectly qualified. He was a professor of biomechanical engineering, was the founder and president of the University of Northern California, and had testified at over 100 depositions or trials:

> While Liu may not have thorough experience with injuries resulting from forklifts, his knowledge and experience as a biomechanical engineer is enough for him to testify on the mechanics of the injury in this case. Liu need not be an expert in the specific machine involved with an injury if, taking the circumstances of the injury as true, he uses an appropriate methodology to discuss the extent and manner of the injury.[48]

Having determined that Liu was a qualified expert, the Court focused on whether his specific testimony was reliable. Raymond argued that Liu's testing was improperly "designed for the courtroom" since it discussed what the likely injuries would be when a body was ejected from a forklift, as opposed to replicating the facts of the case to determine whether a person would actually be ejected. The court held that Liu did not address whether Phillips reasonably could fall out of a forklift as he contends, but rather what would happen to a person if he were ejected from the forklift. Raymond was free to argue at trial that the jury should not put much weight in Liu's study since its results do not adequately shed light on the instant case before the trier of fact.

Raymond next argued that Liu's testimony was unreliable because it had not been the subject of any peer review or publication. This absence, however, was not determinative on the facts of this case. The court noted that the particular tests performed by Liu were specialized to the facts of this case as alleged by Phillips and thus were not worthy of industry-wide analysis or peer review. Without a further explanation of the connection between lack of publication and reliability *in this case*, the court could not determine the extent to which this factor had on the reliability of the methodologies used by Liu.

However, the court noted, it appeared that the potential rate of error of Liu's calculations were unknown, which weighed against admissibility:

> Apparently, for Liu to be able to determine the rate of error for his tests (thus helping to make them scientifically valid), he would have had to engage in a "retrospective analysis." Liu did not conduct such a "retrospective analysis." Thus, Liu cannot provide a potential rate of error. This cuts against admissibility.[49]

An additional factor undercutting the admissibility of Lilly's testimony was the *Daubert* factor that the science upon which the opinion was based was generally accepted in the scientific community. Phillips argued that Liu's testing met all the standards of the Society of Automotive Engineers (SAE) and the International Organization for Standardization (ISO), asserting that "the testing performed by Dr. Liu has been accepted in the industry as the gold standard in evaluating the biomechanical forces on the human body in crashes. (Appendix A1)." The court

---

[48] *Raymond Corporation* at *8.

[49] *Raymond Corporation* at *9.

observed that nonetheless, Dr. Liu provided nothing more than his own opinion as to the acceptability of his own tests. It would have been helpful, the court observed, if Phillips had demonstrated what the SAE or ISO standards were, noting that unsubstantiated testimony, such as presented here, did not ensure that the experts' opinion had a reliable basis in knowledge and experience of his discipline.[50]

Nevertheless, the *Phillips* court, emphasizing that district courts were not hidebound to the *Daubert* factors, concluded that Dr. Liu's tests were very basic, using straightforward (albeit somewhat intuitive) procedures to arrive at a general conclusion, regardless of whether they are actually "the gold standard." While concluding that Phillips should have better supported his allegation that Liu's methods were in accordance with the "gold standard of the industry," given the simplicity of the issue to be addressed and the tests Liu conducted, the court found Liu passed the *Daubert* standard for the limited purpose of determining, in his opinion, how Phillips sustained his leg injuries.[51]

Since Liu's tests were sufficiently reliable, albeit barely, the Court turned to the second admissibility prong: determining whether the testimony can help the trier of fact to understand the evidence. The Court concluded that the trier of fact may or may not agree with his view of how Phillips injured his leg, but that it would be up to the trier of fact to assess, in light of the flaws Raymond believes it has identified, what significance to place on Dr. Liu's testimony.

In contrast, the Court did not find Liu's testimony relevant with regards to his second charge: determining what the mechanism of Phillips's injury would have been if the forklift was equipped with Sevart's latching-rear door. The court held that since the ultimate issue and all germane tests were premised on and relied on Sevart's findings and proposals, which had been found to be inherently unreliable and inadmissible, it would be affirmatively unhelpful for Liu to offer testimony discussing tests on an essentially nonexistent alternative design. Therefore, Raymond's motion to strike Liu's testimony was granted with regard to any statements he might make concerning hypothetical injuries (or lack thereof) relating to Sevart's testimony and design. Raymond's motion was denied as to Liu's explanation of the mechanism of Phillips's actual injury in the case with the Raymond forklift.

Phillips then moved to exclude Raymond Corporation expert witnesses Dr. Catherine Ford Corrigan and Dr. Edward Caulfield.

Raymond sought to introduce the testimony of Dr. Catherine Ford Corrigan, a biomechanical engineer, to evaluate, from a biomechanical perspective, the nature of Phillips's injuries, the mechanism of his injury and the occupant kinematics to reconstruct the accident. She would also analyze the biomechanical issues surrounding the existence of a rear door for the Raymond 31i-DR45, the type of forklift involved in Phillips's accident. On the first basic qualifications issue, background, and specialized training and experience, Dr. Corrigan passed with flying colors:

---

[50] *See* Deimer v. Cincinnati Sub-Zero Prods., Inc., 58 F.3d 341, 345 (7th Cir. 1995). *See also* Chapman v. Maytag Corp., 297 F.3d 682, 688 (7th Cir. 2002).

[51] *Raymond Corporation* at *9.

Corrigan's qualifications entitled her to testify about the two aforementioned areas. Corrigan had a Ph.D. in medical engineering, after participating in a combined doctoral program at Harvard and the Massachusetts Institute of Technology ("MIT"), and she also obtained a masters degree in mechanical engineering from MIT. She is currently the Principal Engineer in the Biomechanics Practice at Exponent Failure Analysis Associates, where she specializes in human tolerance, occupant kinematics, bone and fracture mechanics, and rigid body mechanics. She also serves as a visiting Lecturer at Princeton University. In addition to being member of various biomechanical societies, Corrigan is a reviewer for the Journal of Biomechanics. She has also published multiple articles concerning bone mechanics and the mechanism of injuries.[52]

Given this extensive experience, the court concluded, Corrigan was qualified, overall, to testify about Phillips's injury and related biomechanical issues.

As far as the acceptability of her particular opinions in the instant case, the court then turned to the reliability of the scientific methodology used to support her opinions. The court noted that Corrigan reviewed roughly twenty-nine categories of documents that were sent to her, including accident statements, the reports of Sevart and Liu, diagrams of the accident site, other experts' inspection and testing notes, various regulations, photos and testing data from Dr. Liu's testing, and Phillips's medical records and radiographs. The court found that Dr. Corrigan was qualified to analyze these documents given both her education and her extensive training in radiological anatomy. She had also, through her associates, inspected and took measurements of two exemplar Model 31i forklifts, using this information to study the geometry of the Raymond forklift and how it interacted with injury mechanisms. Furthermore, the court observed, Dr. Corrigan reviewed a considerable amount of medical literature. On the issue of the alternative design of a rear door, the court observed, Dr Corrigan used computer simulations and historical testing of stand-up rear entry forklifts regarding alternative designs. Finally, the court concluded, she had applied all this information to this case using her experience, training, knowledge, and understanding of principles of human tolerance, biomechanics and physics in order to reach her conclusions.[53]

Phillips objected on the basis that, as opposed to adopting any specific, scientifically valid, biomechanical method, Corrigan relied on mere "background and experience" and impermissible factors, thus rendering Corrigan's opinion nothing more than *ipse dixit*. The Court respectfully disagreed:

> First, the process of analyzing assembled data while using experience to interpret the data is not illicit; an expert need not actively conduct his or her own tests to have a valid methodology. Thus, Corrigan's review of others' human testing was a valid methodology that legitimately led to her conclusion that the operator, under the same or similar circumstances

---

[52] *Id.* at *10.

[53] *Id.* at *11.

described by Phillips, could not have been forcibly ejected from the forklift.[54]

Second, Phillips maintains that Corrigan failed to engage in an objective analysis by improperly reaching opinions on witnesses' credibility, namely by concluding that the version of events Phillips alleges did not and could not have happened. However, it was not improper for Corrigan to have subjected Phillips's version of the facts to a rigorous analysis. Coming to her conclusion, Corrigan relied on objective analysis, test results, and medical records. As a result, she came to a conclusion at odds with Phillips's testimony and theory of the case. This version may or may not be accepted by the jury, and Phillips is certainly free to attempt to undermine Dr. Corrigan by cross-examining her. But Phillips's objection to Corrigan was not well taken. Finally, Phillips questioned the accuracy of Corrigan's conclusions. However, the miscalculations and inaccuracies Phillips contends he has identified go to the weight of the evidence and not its admissibility. They are not a basis to exclude Corrigan.[55]

Phillips next sought to exclude Dr. Edward Caulfield, President and Chief Technical Officer of Packer Engineering, Inc., retained to investigate Phillips's accident and to assist with relevant technical issues. Specifically, Caulfield reviewed the background file, conducted multiple inspections and analyses of the accident site, and conducted multiple tests of forklifts and human tolerance. He concluded that the design and manufacture of the Raymond forklift did not cause the accident.[56]

As far as basic qualifications to give any opinion, Dr. Caulfield was found to be more than qualified to testify as an expert. He had a Ph.D. in Theoretical and Applied Mechanics from the University of Illinois and served as an assistant professor in the Department of Mechanical Engineering at the University of Illinois. He had twenty-five years of industrial experience, had published multiple articles, and had served and been qualified as an expert many times.[57]

Most relevant to the instant motion the court determined were three general categories of tests Caulfield conducted: (1) five tests and an informal survey in 1987 whose purpose was to "quantify and measure" the injury levels "if a person were to go off a dock in a forklift and stayed with the machine during the off the dock event and not step off"; (2) a 2000 test essentially identical to the one Caulfield conducted in 1987; and (3) a test in 2003 designed to replicate Phillips's accident scenario to "determine whether relative displacement of the operator . . . occurred as a result of collisions" with wooden objects on the floor.

Phillips argued that Caulfield's survey was unreliable and inadmissible, arguing the survey did not pass *Daubert* scrutiny. However, the court noted, Phillips's

---

[54] *Id.* The court cited *Clark v. Takata Corp.*, 192 F.3d 750, 758 (7th Cir.1999) (holding that either "hands-on testing" or "review of experimental, statistical, or other scientific data generated by others in the field" may suffice as a reasonable methodology upon which to base an opinion).

[55] *Raymond Corporation* at *12.

[56] *Id.*.

[57] *Id.* at *13.

invocation of *Daubert* was misplaced, in that Raymond did not submit the survey, nor did Caulfield conduct the survey, to demonstrate any statistical significance. Rather, the court noted, its purpose was simply as generic background information, one piece of information that helped Caulfield form his opinions with regard to the 1987 testing as a whole. Raymond also had not claimed, and would not attempt, to offer the survey as a statistically conclusive sample.[58]

As far as the tests utilized by Caulfield, the court found that they were in fact relevant. That the 1987 and 2000 tests concerned step off or off-the-dock accident while the instant case did not, was not material. When taking into account an alternative design, such as a latching-rear door, the district court noted, the Seventh Circuit required that the parties should be cognizant of the entire impact of the new design,[59] Off-the-dock accidents appear to be a foreseeable occurrence in the industry, and thus should factor into any consideration of the net benefit of a new design. In sum, the court concluded:

> Caulfield's methods and results were discernible, clear, and rooted in real science. Put differently, they were empirically testable and "intellectually rigorous."[60] As such, they were unlikely to give the jury a misguided impression, especially since Phillips could question vigorously Caulfield's results as he saw fit, and Raymond will almost certainly try to bolster Caulfield's testimony by demonstrating how the figures are allegedly calculated correctly. This was all a matter of the weight of the testimony, not its admissibility. Consequently, Phillips's motion to strike Caulfield's testimony was denied.[61]

In *Clark v. Safety-Kleen Corp.*,[62] a 2004 New Jersey Supreme Court decision, an auto mechanic brought a defective design and inadequate warning products liability action against the manufacturer of a carburetor cleaner after he used the cleaner and developed an infection in a cut on his finger, which subsequently led to loss of substantial function in the finger. The Supreme Court held that a research chemist was sufficiently qualified to give expert testimony regarding basic toxicological effects that cresylic acid, which was contained in cleaner, had on human skin; that the research chemist's opinion testimony, in which the chemist testified how cresylic acid got into mechanic's skin, was admissible; and that a research chemist's testimony, that hospitals do not typically have access to apparatuses to determine

---

[58] Phillips also argued that the 1987 and 2000 tests were unreliable, claiming that Caulfield failed to consider certain facts (such as human reaction time), relied heavily on the allegedly infirm survey, did not subscribe to an acceptable methodology, and that the tests did not sufficiently fit the facts of the case. The court noted that Phillips provided no factual support for his assertion that the survey played a commanding role in the 1987 test or that that the entire test was somehow meaningfully tainted so as to render Caulfield's testimony inadmissible. Furthermore, Phillips's quarrels with Caulfield's inclusion or rejection of certain factors or calculations (such as grip strength), implicated his conclusions and were thus properly left for exploration through cross-examination. *Id.* at *13.

[59] Cummins v. Lyle Indus., 93 F.3d 362, 369 (7th Cir. 1996).

[60] *Citing Kumho Tire*, 526 U.S. at 139, 152 (1999).

[61] *Raymond Corporation* at *14.

[62] 845 A.2d 587 (N.J. 2004).

natural or chemical composition of an irritant that gets into an open wound, was also admissible.

The question in the case centered on the admissibility of testimony from non-physicians regarding medical causation in a products liability action. The New Jersey Supreme Court ruled that the admissibility of testimony from non-physicians regarding medical causation in a products liability action will depend on the facts and on the non-physician's qualifications. As in any case involving the admissibility of such testimony, the preliminary requirements are that she must be sufficiently qualified by education, knowledge, training, and experience in the specific field of science, and she must possess a demonstrated professional capability to assess the scientific significance of the underlying data and information, to apply the scientific methodology, and to explain the bases for the opinion reached.[63]

Here the court found that a proffered research chemist was sufficiently qualified to give expert testimony regarding basic toxicological effects that cresylic acid, which was contained in carburetor cleaner used by auto mechanic, had on human skin. The chemist testified that he had engaged in research relating to various chemicals and worked with cresylic acid and observed the damage that it could do to human tissue. The chemist testified to the scientific materials that he consulted in preparation for the case and stated that they were the types of data an expert in his field would rely on in formulating an opinion.[64]

A similar result was had in *Smalls v. Pittsburgh-Corning Corp.*,[65] a Pennsylvania decision, where a former employee who in course of employment prior to retirement handled valve-packing products containing asbestos, filed a personal injury lawsuit against defendant/former employer, claiming asbestos-related injuries. The court found that the expert was a board-certified as pulmonary specialist and could testify about relationship between breathing asbestos and development of asbestos-related disease. The court also allowed the testimony by the expert that "Each and every breath of asbestos fibers is [a] significant and substantial contributing factor to the asbestos related disease that Mr. Smalls has."[66]

---

[63] *See* Fed. R. Evid. 702.

[64] *See also* Cottrell, Inc. v. Williams, 596 S.E.2d 789 (Ga. Ct. App. 2004). (Engineer whose education, training and experience had familiarized him with the flammability rating of glass cleaner kept by driver in his truck cab properly was permitted to testify as expert and to offer an opinion about that flammability rating in a products liability action brought by truck driver, who alleged that a fire in his truck cab was triggered by wire hanger coming in contact with exposed switch that auto equipment manufacturer had installed in cab.)

[65] 843 A.2d 410 (Pa. Super. Ct. 2004).

[66] See also *Bitler v. A.O. Smith Corp*, 391 F.3d 1114 (10th Cir. 2004), where the victim of a propane gas water heater explosion brought products liability action in state court against water heater manufacturer and installer of heater and propane piping. The Tenth Circuit upheld a verdict against the manufacturer, finding that a fire investigator's proffered testimony, namely, that the water heater was source of the explosion, was based on sufficiently reliable methodology, and that an accident investigator's proffered testimony that gas leak was caused by copper sulfide contamination on water heater's safety valve seat was also reliable. The court also found that evidence of prior accidents involving unscreened safety valves was admissible, notwithstanding fact that the safety valve involved in the instant explosion contained a mesh screen.

In *Nemir v. Mitsubishi Motors Corp*, 381 F.3d 540 (6th Cir. 2004), a driver who was injured in an automobile accident brought a products liability suit against automobile manufacturers, alleging that the seatbelt was defectively designed and that dashboard seatbelt light failed to warn him that seatbelt was only partially latched. The Sixth Circuit Court of Appeals held that a protective order prohibiting driver's counsel from unilaterally contacting any of manufacturer's complaining consumers was not warranted; that the District Court's failure to rule on driver's motion for sanctions against manufacturer for obstructing discovery required remand, that the testimony of the driver's automotive safety engineer was admissible, and that the driver was erroneously prevented from introducing relevant impeachment evidence.

The plaintiff's automotive safety engineer's testimony about his testing of seat belt latching mechanism was relevant, and therefore admissible. The engineer's method of testing mechanism, i.e., purposeful manipulation of buckle at varying speeds and angles, was appropriate for his conclusion that defective mechanism caused driver's injuries.

The court also found that the plaintiff was entitled to call court-appointed expert to testify in the case. The expert's testimony would have corroborated plaintiff's automotive safety engineer's testimony that the defective seat belt latching mechanism caused the driver's injuries, and that even infrequent partial latching of mechanism could constitute a serious defect would have bolstered weight afforded to engineer's research, which found partial engagement in two out of 20 attempts.

The driver was erroneously prevented from introducing relevant impeachment evidence when, as the driver attempted to impeach manufacturer's expert by confronting him with excerpt from a book co-authored by another expert retained by manufacturer the court instructed him to save such questioning for authoring expert's upcoming testimony, and then precluded such questioning on ground that it was outside scope of authoring expert's direct testimony, where excerpt was offered to impeach earlier-testifying expert, not to have him comment on authoring expert's upcoming testimony.[67]

§ 13.08   SOURCES REASONABLY RELIED UPON BY EXPERTS IN THE FIELD

In the 2004 South Dakota opinion in *First Premier Bank v. Kolcraft Enterprises, Inc.*,[68] an infant's guardian ad litem brought claims against manufacturer of a playpen for defective and unreasonably dangerous design and failure to warn, resulting in the infant's severe burns from fire. Also challenged was the product's use of foam pads which were not fire retardant. The trial court entered judgment on the jury's verdict for manufacturer.

The South Dakota Supreme Court ruled that a playpen manufacturer's expert could base his opinion in the underlying products liability action, that dropping of cigarette or knocking off of cigarette ash when the infant was placed in playpen was

---

[67] *See* Fed. R. Evid. 706. *See also* Cottrell, Inc. v. Williams, 596 S.E.2d 789 (Ga. Ct. App. 2004).

[68] 686 N.W.2d 430 (S.D. 2004).

most likely cause of the fire, on the fact that infant's parents smoked, regardless of whether their smoking habits were admissible as evidence or were instead inadmissible hearsay. The fact that residents of the dwelling smoked was evidence of a type an expert could reasonably rely upon to form an opinion regarding the cause of a fire.

The fact that the fire inspector had ruled out cigarette butts as an ignition source for fire in playpen, because he could not find any cigarette butts in children's bedroom after the fire and because burn characteristics for playpen were inconsistent with cigarette ignition, did not preclude playpen manufacturer's expert from forming opinion, that the dropping of a cigarette or knocking off of cigarette ash when infant was placed in playpen was the most likely cause of the fire. The court found that the manufacturer's expert was not required to begin and end his analysis with the fire inspector's premise, but was instead free to use his expertise to reach his own conclusion.

Peggy and Ken Boone, the infant's parents, were both smoking in the home on the day of the fire. Defendant Kolcraft established to the court's satisfaction that improper disposal of cigarettes was "a way of life in the Boone household." Photographs showed extensive smoking, overflowing ashtrays, and the improper disposal of cigarettes on windowsills and on floors. Terry Flakus, the Fire Inspector for Sioux Falls, however, ruled out cigarettes altogether as an ignition source because he could not find any cigarette butts in the children's bedroom after the fire, and the burn characteristics were inconsistent with a cigarette ignition. Based on that conclusion, plaintiff argued that no reliable foundation existed from which Kolcraft's expert, Robert Wargin, could state that careless cigarette smoking could have been the cause of the fire. Defense expert Wargin studied the burn patterns and other evidence and concluded that the point of origin for the fire was not the Playard, defendant's product, but some item within the playpen. Based on this conclusion, he could not rule out cigarette smoking as a cause of the fire. He found that the fire originated inside the playpen.[69]

In examining the Playard, he concluded that the playpen pad and fiberboard bottom showed that the fire was from the top down and not from under the playpen. Major fuel material for the fire consisted of pillows, a quilted comforter, a blanket, and clothing draped over the playpen. He believed that the urethane foam inside the playpen pad was not responsible for the spread of the fire. Less than thirty percent of both the pad and fiberboard bottom were consumed in the ten-minute fire. Finally, he deduced, through "process of elimination, the dropping of a cigarette or knocking off of cigarette ash when Daniel was placed in the Playard is the most likely cause of the fire." In sum, the court concluded, Wargin declined to begin and end his analysis on Inspector Flakus's premise that cigarette smoking was not the cause. The court found that Wargin was free to do so, and Kolcraft was free to present his opinion because there were sufficient facts to support it.

Plaintiff next contended that Wargin's testimony did not suffice to prove proximate cause. The court first noted that plaintiff, not Kolcraft, had the burden of proving proximate cause and that Wargin's testimony was offered to refute

---

[69] *Id.* at 445.

plaintiff's claim that the Playard was the source of the fire. Plaintiff raised the question of whether under an analysis, Wargin could have properly based his opinion on evidence of smoking in the Boone apartment?[70] The court noted that the question was whether a *plaintiff's* expert could testify when the methodology used was not generally accepted in the relevant scientific community, reasoning that proposed testimony must be supported by appropriate validation — i.e., "good grounds," based on what is known.[71] The focus, the *Daubert* court ruled, must be solely on principles and methodology, not on the conclusions that they generate. The present court noted that the *Daubert* court stated that vigorous cross-examination, presentation of contrary evidence, and careful instruction on the burden of proof are the traditional and appropriate means of attacking shaky but admissible evidence and that those conventional devices, rather than wholesale exclusion under an uncompromising "general acceptance" test, were the appropriate safeguards where the basis of scientific testimony meets the standard of Rule 702.[72]

The South Dakota court found that Wargin's testimony fit squarely within the Supreme Court's "traditional and appropriate means" of assailing plaintiff's expert testimony:

> Plaintiff would seemingly have us declare that one expert's opinion is invulnerable. Plaintiff argues that because other experts did not draw a definitive conclusion about the origin of the fire, one defense expert must be precluded from testifying on other causes of the fire. By his own testimony, Inspector Flakus must have initially considered the possibility of a cigarette causing the fire. He conducted a layer search of the burned area. During this search he attempted to locate possible causes. He stated that he did not find a cigarette butt; therefore, he believed careless cigarette disposal did not start the fire. Wargin did not stop with that hypothesis. He did not have the benefit of searching the area immediately after the fire. However, this does not mean that he had to accept all of Inspector Flakus's conclusions based on that search. He was free to use his expertise to reach his own conclusions. To Wargin, the absence of a cigarette butt only proved that a cigarette butt was not found.[73]

Federal Rule of Evidence 703 provides:

> The facts or data in the particular case upon which an expert bases an opinion or inference may be those perceived by or made known to him at or before the hearing. If of a type reasonably relied upon by experts in the particular field in forming opinions or inferences upon the subject, the facts or data need not be admissible in evidence.[74] Here, the court ruled, the statute allowed Wargin to base his opinion on the fact that the Boones smoked, whether their smoking habits were admissible as evidence or were inadmissible hearsay. The only qualification was that the fact must be

---

[70] Daubert v. Merrell Dow Pharmaceuticals, Inc., 509 U.S. 579 (1993).

[71] *Id.* at 590.

[72] *Id.*

[73] *First Premier Bank*, 686 N.W.2d at 445.

[74] *Id.* at 447.

reasonably relied upon by other experts in the field. Surely, the *Kolcraft* court found, the fact that the residents of the apartment smoked was a reasonable basis from which to infer that smoking *may* have caused a fire. This inference was no less reasonable than an inference drawn by fire inspector Flakus that smoking *could not* have caused the fire because there was no evidence of smoking in a particular room despite evidence of smoking everywhere else in the apartment.[75]

---

[75] *Id.*

Chapter 14

DRAFTING THE COMPLAINT AND DISCOVERY FOCUS

SYNOPSIS

§ 14.01 INTRODUCTION

§ 14.02 STANDARD ALLEGATIONS IN THE PRODUCTS CASE

§ 14.03 SAMPLE COMPLAINT: PRESSURIZED BEVERAGE CANISTER

§ 14.04 DISTRIBUTIVE CHAIN

§ 14.05 ABSENCE OF ALTERATION OR MODIFICATION

§ 14.06 DEFENDANT'S DUTY OR OBLIGATION

§ 14.07 INTENDED USE

§ 14.08 INJURY-PRODUCING EVENT

§ 14.09 BREACH OF DUTY OR OBLIGATION: SETTING OUT THE DEFECT MODES

§ 14.10 PROXIMATE CAUSE

§ 14.11 PUNITIVE DAMAGES

§ 14.12 SAMPLE COMPLAINT: STANDUP FORKLIFT TRUCK

§ 14.01 INTRODUCTION

It is not the purpose of this chapter to analyze the development and nuances of strict liability theory. That broad subject is comprehensively addressed in Chapters 1 through 10 in this book. This chapter will, instead, focus on the practical questions faced by plaintiff counsel in initiating a product liability lawsuit. A selection of Sample Complaints will illustrate the transition from products liability theory analysis to products liability litigation. In particular, it will stress the ongoing effect that decisions made in the initial filings have on each ensuing step in case preparation, especially on the discovery process. It is essential to realize that the acts or omissions of any named corporate defendant alleged as warranting negligence or strict liability findings, are to be proven, if at all, somewhere in a massive body of corporate documentation. This documentation will be accessible in relevant portions, during the discovery process, depending on the artfulness with which the complaint counts are drafted. There is a close relationship between the specific factual allegations of the complaint and the potential discovery of their documentary counterparts in corporate archives.

§ 14.02   STANDARD ALLEGATIONS IN THE PRODUCTS CASE

It is important that counsel realize the importance of the complaint in the pre-trial process. A clearly drafted, technically correct complaint is one of the major keys to successful discovery, motions in limine and trial practice. During the entire pre-trial period and the course of the trial itself, this document will serve as the court's primary basis for deciding a wide variety of crucial issues.

The propriety of plaintiff's interrogatories, requests to admit fact, requests for documentation and defendant's motions in limine, are all resolved by reference to the language of the plaintiff's complaint. The same holds true for all proffers of evidence made by counsel during the trial of the case. Counsel can rest assured that corporate defense lawyers will go through the complaint with a fine-toothed comb searching for weaknesses with which to frustrate discovery or otherwise dampen plaintiff's efforts.

It is appropriate here to analyze the stock allegations that are present in any product liability case involving any product under any available theory of design liability. The following allegations may be tailored to counsel's specific product, company, and occurrence facts:

(1)   The defendant manufacturer was in the business of designing, producing, and marketing product lines of the type involved on, prior to and subsequent to the occurrence date, and in fact designed, produced, and marketed the product unit at issue.

(2)   The intermediary (distributor/wholesaler/retailer) was in the business of distributing, wholesaling, or retailing product lines of the type involved on, prior to and subsequent to the occurrence date, and in fact distributed, wholesaled or retailed the product unit at issue.

(3)   The plaintiff purchased the unit at the bottom of the vertical chain or came in contact with the unit by way of someone who did purchase it.

(4)   The product unit was, when received by the purchaser and at the time of the occurrence, in substantially the same condition as when it left the hands of the manufacturer.

(5)   The defendant manufacturer, distributor, wholesaler, or retailer had a duty to use due care in the design, manufacture, and marketing of such product so as not to expose purchasers or foreseeable users to an unreasonable risk of harm, and that such duty ran to the plaintiff as purchaser and/or foreseeable user.

(6)   The defendant manufacturer, distributor, wholesaler, or retailer had an obligation to refrain from placing in the stream of commerce products which were in a defective condition unreasonably dangerous to purchasers and/or foreseeable users of such products and that such obligation was owed to plaintiff as purchaser and/or foreseeable user.

(7)   The defendant breached the duty of care owed to plaintiff in one or all of the specified respects or placed in the stream of commerce the suspect

product that was in a defective condition unreasonably dangerous in one or all of the specified respects.

(8)   A statement that at all relevant times the plaintiff was using the product for its intended purpose.

(9)   A brief description of the injury-producing event and injury and an allegation that such injury was a direct and proximate result of the aforementioned breaches of defendant's duty of care or corporate obligation.

(10)   Ad damnum clause of statement of jurisdictional amount, as appropriate.

These allegations, with the important exception of item 7, are standard in products cases and need little other than minor factual adjustments to meet the needs of a particular case. The factual allegations of those sub-paragraphs constituting item 7, however, are the heart of plaintiff's case. Each serves as a separate basis for recovery. They are determinative of the extent of the discovery and the admissibility of the defect evidence that plaintiff offers at the trial.

§ 14.03   SAMPLE COMPLAINT: PRESSURIZED BEVERAGE CANISTER

The sections to follow will analyze the drafting of a hypothetical four-count product liability complaint directed against four manufacturers resulting from the explosion of a pressurized beverage container that resulted in the loss of an eye by an employee of a soft drink distributor.

In this factual scenario, plaintiff John Denton, an employee of the Benton Brothers Beverage Company, was leaning over a pallet of empty containers in the process of releasing the remaining pressure and removing the beverage identification labels, prior to the containers' sterilization and reuse down the line. As he was doing this, one of the containers nozzle fittings exploded next to his head, resulting in the loss of Denton's eye.

The first defendant is The Fremantle Tire & Rubber Company, the primary manufacturer of the complete pressurized beverage container. The second defendant is the Polymer Plastic Corporation, the manufacturer of the plastic cap or closure that struck plaintiff's eye as a result of the explosion. The third defendant is the Apex Grinding Company, manufacturer of the pressure release or relief mechanism for incorporation into the stainless steel beverage canister involved herein. Finally, the fourth defendant is the Premier Plastic Corporation, manufacturer of a plastic material known as BasicPro V56-77 that was incorporated into the plastic cap or closure on the pressurized stainless steel beverage canister involved in the *Denton* case.

The complaint here contains two counts against each defendant: negligence and strict liability. The complaint example is reduced here for ease of illustration and example. Products liability complaints typically plead multiple counts grounded in the products theories discussed in detail in Part I of this book. Sample paragraphs will be given to cover each of the standard allegations in such complaints set out below. Extended treatment will be given to the allegations of product defect and their centrality in the hard-fought discovery process.

§ 14.04 DISTRIBUTIVE CHAIN

The allegations necessary to adequately identify the defendants' participation in the vertical chain of distribution are simply stated by examining selections from the Sample Complaint of *Denton v. The Freemantle Tire and Rubber Company et al.*:

- On and prior to January 29, 2001, defendant, **THE FREMANTLE TIRE & RUBBER COMPANY**, designed, manufactured, maintained, assembled, distributed and sold a pressurized stainless steel beverage canister, which was offered for sale to the public, a unit of which is the pressurized stainless steel beverage canister involved in this case.

- On and prior to January 29, 2001, defendant, **POLYMER PLASTIC COMPANY**, located in Cuyahoga Falls, Ohio, designed, manufactured, maintained, assembled, distributed and sold plastic caps or closures for installation in pressurized stainless steel beverage canisters, an individual unit of which caps or closures was installed in the pressurized stainless steel beverage canister involved in this case.

- On and prior to January 29, 2001, defendant, **APEX GRINDING COMPANY**, located in Mogadore, Ohio, designed, manufactured, maintained, assembled, distributed and sold a pressure release or relief mechanism for incorporation into stainless steel beverage canisters, an individual unit of which mechanism was installed in the pressurized stainless steel beverage canister involved in this case.

- On and prior to January 29, 2001, defendant, **PREMIER PLASTIC CORPORATION**, designed, manufactured, maintained, assembled, distributed and sold a plastic material known as BasicPro V56-77, for incorporation into the plastic cap or closure on pressurized stainless steel beverage canisters, which plastic was incorporated into the plastic cap or closure on the pressurized stainless steel beverage canister involved in this case.

§ 14.05 ABSENCE OF ALTERATION OR MODIFICATION

In order to meet the requirement of Section 402A of the Restatement of Torts (2d) and (3d) that the product at the time of the injury was in substantially the same condition as when it left the hands of the "seller," an optional pleading might state:

- That no changes or alterations were made to said canister or any of its component parts prior to its purchase by plaintiff's employer or John Denton or anyone on their behalf prior to or on the date of January 29, 2001, and that said pressurized canister was in substantially the same condition on such date as when it and its component parts left the hands of the Defendant Freemantle Tire and Rubber Company.

§ 14.06   DEFENDANT'S DUTY OR OBLIGATION

A statement of defendant's responsibility to foreseeable consumers, users and bystanders is essential in a negligence count and appropriate in a count based on strict liability.

[NEGLIGENCE]

- The defendants THE FREMANTLE TIRE & RUBBER COMPANY, POLYMER PLASTIC COMPANY, APEX GRINDING COMPANY, and PREMIER PLASTIC CORPORATION, and each of them owned a duty of due care in the design, testing, manufacture and marketing of the aforesaid pressurized beverage canister involved in this cases or any of its component parts such as the plastic caps or closures, pressure release or relief mechanisms, for installation in pressurized stainless steel beverage canisters, or a plastic material known as BasicPro V56-77, used in any component part, to avoid unreasonable risk of death or injury to purchasers or foreseeable users of such pressurized beverage canisters. Said duty was owed to plaintiff John Denton as a foreseeable purchaser or user of said canister.

[FAILURE TO WARN]

- The defendants THE FREMANTLE TIRE & RUBBER COMPANY, POLYMER PLASTIC COMPANY, APEX GRINDING COMPANY, and PREMIER PLASTIC CORPORATION, and each of them breached a duty of due care to plaintiff John Denton in that said canister was not reasonably safe in that defendants, and each of them, failed to provide adequate warnings of the dangers involved in the handling of said canister, including, but not limited to the over pressurization of the canister and the resultant shattering or exploding of the plastic closure or cap or other portions of said canister.

[STRICT LIABILITY VERSION]

- The defendants THE FREMANTLE TIRE & RUBBER COMPANY, POLYMER PLASTIC COMPANY, APEX GRINDING COMPANY, and PREMIER PLASTIC CORPORATION, and each of them, at all relevant times mentioned herein, had an obligation to refrain from placing in the stream of commerce products which were in a defective condition unreasonably dangerous to foreseeable purchasers and users of their products, and to instruct and warn such users as to any such conditions. This obligation extended to the design, testing, manufacture and marketing of the aforesaid pressurized beverage canister involved in this cases or any of its component parts such as the plastic caps or closures, pressure release or relief mechanisms, for installation in pressurized stainless steel beverage canisters, or a plastic material known as BasicPro V56-77, used in any component part, to avoid risk of death or injury to purchasers or foreseeable users of such pressurized beverage canisters. Said duty was owed to plaintiff John Denton as a foreseeable purchaser or user of said canister.

[FAILURE TO WARN]

- The defendants THE FREMANTLE TIRE & RUBBER COMPANY, POLYMER PLASTIC COMPANY, APEX GRINDING COMPANY, and PREMIER PLASTIC CORPORATION, and each of them breached an obligation to plaintiff John Denton in that said canister was not reasonably safe for its intended use in that defendants, and each of them, failed to provide adequate warnings of the dangers involved in the handling of said canister, including, but not limited to the over pressurization of the canister and the resultant shattering or exploding of the plastic closure or cap or other portions of said canister.

§ 14.07   INTENDED USE

A statement that the product was being used for its intended purpose is required under both negligence and strict liability theories:

- That at all relevant times herein, plaintiff John Denton was using said pressurized beverage canister for the purposes for which it was intended by defendants.

§ 14.08   INJURY-PRODUCING EVENT

A brief statement of the injury-producing event is required. These paragraphs should contain sufficient information to sketch the outlines of the occurrence without binding plaintiff to fine points of detail that could be problematic as judicial admissions later in the case.

- Plaintiff John Denton, while an employee of the Benton Brothers Beverage Company, was leaning over a pallet of empty pressurized beverage containers in the process of releasing the remaining pressure and removing the beverage identification labels, prior to the containers sterilization and reuse down the line. As he was doing this one of the nozzle fittings exploded next to his head, resulting in the loss of Denton's eye. The container was manufactured in whole or part by the defendants THE FREMANTLE TIRE & RUBBER COMPANY, POLYMER PLASTIC COMPANY, APEX GRINDING COMPANY, and PREMIER PLASTIC CORPORATION, and each of them.

§ 14.09   BREACH OF DUTY OR OBLIGATION: SETTING OUT THE DEFECT MODES

These sub-paragraphs inform both the court and defense counsel what it is that plaintiff deems is wrong with the suspect product and how that defect caused plaintiff's injury. As such, these allegations must be carefully drawn to reach a balance between the absence of any true description of product failings and a too-detailed description of them that may later limit plaintiff's full discovery efforts and evidentiary submissions at trial.

The allegations must set forth the basic defect modes involved in the case in clear terms. Allegations cannot be restricted to broad general allegations that the product was not "properly designed," was not "safe," was "defective," was not "adequately tested," or that defendant "failed to issue proper warnings or instructions." Allegations such as these are of little assistance to a court in attempting to determine the precise extent of plaintiff's right to examine internal corporate documents or whether to grant comprehensive defense motions in limine.

[FREEMANTLE TIRE AND RUBBER COMPANY]

- On and before January 29, 2001, and at the time the aforesaid canister left the control of defendant, THE FREMANTLE TIRE & RUBBER COMPANY, the canister was in a defective condition unreasonably dangerous in one or all of the following respects:

  a. Said canister was not reasonably safe in design due to the substantial risk that the plastic closure or cap on said canister would shatter or explode;

  b. Said canister was not reasonably safe in design due to inadequate pressure release or relief mechanisms to prevent the shattering or exploding of the plastic closure or cap or other portions of said canister;

  c. Said canister was not reasonably safe in design due to inadequate mechanisms to prevent the over pressurization of said canister, thereby creating the risk of the shattering or exploding of the plastic closure or cap or other portions of said canister;

  d. Said canister was not reasonably safe in that defendant, failed to provide adequate warnings of the dangers involved in the handling of said canister, including, but not limited to the over pressurization of the canister or the shattering or exploding of the plastic closure or cap or other portions of said canister.

[POLYMER PLASTIC COMPANY]

- On and before January 29, 2001, and at the time the aforesaid canister left the control of defendant, POLYMER PLASTIC COMPANY, the plastic cap or closure manufactured by defendant was in a defective condition unreasonably dangerous in one or all of the following respects:

  a. Said plastic cap or closure was not reasonably safe in design due to the substantial risk that it would shatter or explode after being installed for purposes of capping or closing the pressurized stainless steel beverage canister involved in this case;

  b. Said plastic cap or closure was not reasonably safe in design due to inadequate materials strength to withstand the over pressurization of said canister, thereby creating the risk of the shattering or exploding of the plastic cap or closure;

    c.   Said plastic cap or closure was not reasonably safe in that defendant, failed to provide adequate warnings of the dangers involved in the handling of said canister, including, but not limited to the over pressurization of such canister or the shattering or exploding of the plastic cap or closure or other portions of said canister.

[APEX GRINDING COMPANY]

- On and before January 29, 2001, and at the time the aforesaid canister left the control of defendant, APEX GRINDING, the aforesaid pressure release or relief mechanism was in a defective condition unreasonably dangerous in one or all of the following respects:

    a.   Said pressure release or relief mechanism was not reasonably safe in design due to inadequate pressure relief mechanisms to prevent the shattering or exploding of the plastic closure or cap or other portions of said pressure release mechanism;

    b.   Said pressure release or relief mechanism was not reasonably safe in design due to inadequate mechanisms to prevent the over pressurization of said canister, thereby creating the risk of the shattering or exploding of the plastic closure or cap or other portions of said canister;

    c.   Said pressure release or relief mechanism was not reasonably safe in that defendant, failed to provide adequate warnings of the dangers involved in the handling of said pressure release or relief mechanism, including, but not limited to over pressurization of such canister or the shattering or exploding of the plastic closure or cap or other portions of said canister.

[POLYMER PLASTIC CORPORATION]

- On and before January 29, 2001, and at the time the aforesaid BasicPro V56-77 plastic left the control of defendant, the aforesaid BasicPro V56-77 plastic was in a defective condition unreasonably dangerous in one or all of the following respects:

    a.   Said BasicPro V56-77 plastic was not reasonably safe in design, when incorporated into caps or closures for pressurized beverage canisters, due to defendant's failure to provide adequate materials strength to prevent the shattering or exploding of the plastic cap or closure on pressurized beverage canister of the type involved in this case;

    b.   Said BasicPro V56-77 plastic was not reasonably safe in that defendant, failed to provide adequate warnings of the dangers involved in the utilization of said plastic for the manufacture of pressurized beverage canister caps or closures, including, but not limited to the over pressurization of such canister or the shattering or exploding of the plastic cap or closure.

§ 14.10 PROXIMATE CAUSE

The proximate cause allegation, linking the breach of duty or obligation to the occurrence facts, ties together all of the preceding allegations of the complaint.

- As a proximate result of one or all of the aforesaid conditions, plaintiff, JOHN DENTON, suffered and in the future will continue to suffer injuries of a personal and pecuniary nature.

§ 14.11 PUNITIVE DAMAGES

The punitive damage count is grounded in the callous and reckless manner in which defendant disregarded known risks to consumers. It is tied to the particular corporate failings alleged in the formal negligence and strict liability counts that precede it. The essential ingredients of a punitive damage count are a substantial risk of knowledge of serious risk and utter indifference to consumer safety in light of such risk. It is also grounded in improper motives, such as financial gain, in failing to instruct, warn or properly design. A growing number of states have statutes controlling the allowance of a punitive damages count in a products liability case.

[PUNITIVE DAMAGES]

1. That plaintiff realleges, reaffirms, and incorporates by reference herein, each and every allegation contained in Counts I-IV of this complaint.

2. That at all times mentioned herein, defendants THE FREMANTLE TIRE & RUBBER COMPANY, POLYMER PLASTIC COMPANY, APEX GRINDING COMPANY, and PREMIER PLASTIC CORPORATION, and each of them, knew of the defective and dangerous conditions of the pressurized beverage container and its component parts and other defects as aforesaid. Defendants and each of them, were aware of their duties and obligations to consumers to provide safe products to them and/or warn such consumers of all known dangerous and defective conditions of said product.

3. Despite the defendants' knowledge of the dangerous and defective conditions inherent in the Freemantle pressurized beverage container, defendants and each of them callously, recklessly, willfully and wantonly failed to take appropriate steps to remedy the defects in said container or to warn plaintiff of said dangers. Plaintiff alleges that the failure of the defendants, and each of them, to remedy said defects and/or failure to warn consumers was solely the result of their desires for financial gain.

4. Plaintiff alleges that defendants, and each of them, mass produced their respective products and that defendants and each of them, knew of the numerous defective and dangerous conditions in said canisters. Despite their knowledge of said defects, and despite the extremely high risk of injury to user of such canisters, defendants, and each of them, callously, recklessly, willfully and wantonly disregarded the state-of-the-art literature regarding safer designs, adequate testing, safer materials selection and safer construction methods.

5.   It is further alleged that the aforesaid callous, reckless, willful and wanton acts and omissions by defendants, and each of them, were the proximate cause of the injuries to plaintiff John Denton as stated.

6.   Plaintiff therefore asks for exemplary and punitive damages in an amount sufficient so that an example will be made of these defendants, and each of them, in order to promote safety and to provide an incentive for defendants and others so situated to engage in safer design, testing, production and marketing practices.

§ 14.12   SAMPLE COMPLAINT: STANDUP FORKLIFT TRUCK

The next scenario involves a worker seriously injured while operating a forklift truck at his place of employment. The forklift allegedly failed to properly brake and the absence of a rear guard rail resulted in his leg being smashed against a post in the factory.

Count I (Strict Liability)

Plaintiff, JOHN HUSSEY, complaining of defendant, THE STOCKLIFT CORPORATION, a foreign corporation, (hereinafter referred to as STOCKLIFT), states:

1.   On and prior to August 1, 2002, defendant, THE STOCKLIFT CORPORATION, (hereinafter referred to as STOCKLIFT), designed, manufactured, maintained, assembled, distributed and sold a certain product commonly known as a Stocklift Pacer Model 60 standup forklift, which was offered for sale to the public.

2.   On and prior to August 1, 2002, defendant, STOCKLIFT placed the aforesaid forklift into the stream of commerce.

3.   On August 1, 2002, plaintiff, JOHN HUSSEY, was operating said forklift on the premises of Matoon Distribution Company located at 5000 Proviso Drive, in the City of Matoon Park, County of Cook, State of Illinois.

4.   On August 1, 2002, while the plaintiff, JOHN HUSSEY, was operating said forklift in the course of his duties for the Matoon Distribution Company, said forklift failed to stop its forward motion, resulting in the crushing of plaintiff's leg between the forklift and a concrete pillar.

5.   On and before August 1, 2002, and at the time the aforesaid forklift left the control of defendant, STOCKLIFT, the forklift was in a defective condition unreasonably dangerous in one or all of the following respects:

   a.   Said forklift was not reasonably safe in design due to the substantial risk that the acceleration and braking systems in said forklift could malfunction;

   b.   Said forklift was not reasonably safe in that defendant, STOCKLIFT, provided inadequate braking mechanisms which failed to stop said fork lift when the braking mechanism was engaged;

c.   Said forklift was not reasonably safe in that defendant, STOCKLIFT, failed to provide an expanded deck or other extension to the operator's platform to prevent the operator from being crushed in the event of collision with or intrusion by stationery objects.

d.   Said forklift was not reasonably safe in that defendant, STOCKLIFT, failed to provide a metal or other sufficiently strong gate across the back of the operator's platform to prevent the operator from being crushed in the event of collision with or intrusion by stationery objects.

e.   Said forklift was not reasonably safe in that defendant, STOCKLIFT, failed to provide adequate width or depth for the operator's platform to allow the operator to adequately operate said forklift in emergency situations.

f.   Said forklift was not reasonably safe in that defendant, STOCKLIFT, failed to provide adequate posts or other protective features around the operator's platform to prevent the operator from being crushed in the event of collision with or intrusion by stationary objects.

g.   Said forklift was not reasonably safe in that defendant, STOCKLIFT, failed to provide adequate warnings of the dangers involved in the operation of said forklift.

6.   As a proximate result of one or all of the aforesaid conditions, plaintiff, JOHN HUSSEY, suffered and in the future will continue to suffer injuries of a personal and pecuniary nature.

WHEREFORE, plaintiff, JOHN HUSSEY, asks judgment against the defendant, THE STOCKLIFT CORPORATION, a foreign corporation, in a sum in excess of FIFTEEN THOUSAND DOLLARS ($15,000.00).

Count II

(Negligence)

Plaintiff, JOHN HUSSEY, complaining of defendant, THE STOCKLIFT COR-PORATION, a foreign corporation, (hereinafter, referred to as STOCKLIFT), states:

1.   On and prior to August 1, 2002, defendant, STOCKLIFT, designed, manufactured, maintained, assembled, distributed and sold a certain product commonly known as a Stocklift Pacer model 60 standup forklift, which was offered for sale to the public.

2.   On and prior to August 1, 2002, defendant, STOCKLIFT, placed the aforesaid forklift into the stream of commerce.

3.   On August 1, 2002, plaintiff, JOHN HUSSEY, was operating said forklift on the premises of Matoon Distribution Company located at 5000 Proviso Drive, in the City of Matoon Park, County of Cook, State of Illinois.

4. On August 1, 2002, while the plaintiff, JOHN HUSSEY, was operating said forklift in the course of his duties for the Matoon Distribution Company, said forklift failed to stop its forward motion, resulting in the crushing of plaintiff's leg between the forklift and a concrete pillar.

5. On and before August 1, 2002, defendant, STOCKLIFT, had a duty to exercise due care in the design, testing, production and marketing of the Stocklift Pacer Model 60 forklift truck, which duty extended to plaintiff JOHN HUSSEY a foreseeable user of said forklift.

6. That on and before August 1, 2002, defendant, STOCKLIFT, through its duly authorized agents and employees, breached the duty of care owed to plaintiff JOHN HUSSEY and was negligent in one or all of the following respects:

    a. Said forklift was not reasonably safe in design due to the substantial risk that the acceleration and braking systems in said forklift could malfunction;

    b. Said forklift was not reasonably safe in that defendant, STOCKLIFT, provided inadequate braking mechanisms which failed to stop said forklift when the braking mechanism was engaged;

    c. Said forklift was not reasonably safe in that defendant, STOCKLIFT, failed to provide an expanded deck or other extension to the operator's platform to prevent the operator from being crushed in the event of collision with or intrusion by stationery objects;

    d. Said forklift was not reasonably safe in that defendant, STOCKLIFT, failed to provide a metal or other sufficiently strong gate across the back of the operator's platform to prevent the operator from being crushed in the event of collision with or intrusion by stationery objects;

    e. Said forklift was not reasonably safe in that defendant, STOCKLIFT, failed to provide adequate width or depth for the operator's platform to allow the operator to adequately operate said forklift in emergency situations;

    f. Said forklift was not reasonably safe in that defendant, STOCKLIFT, failed to provide adequate posts or other protective features around the operator's platform to prevent the operator from being crushed in the event of collision with or intrusion by stationery objects;

    g. Said forklift was not reasonably safe in that defendant, STOCKLIFT, failed to provide adequate warnings of the dangers involved in the operation of said forklift.

7. As a proximate result of one or all of the foregoing negligent acts or omissions, plaintiff, JOHN HUSSEY, suffered and will continue to suffer injuries of a personal and pecuniary nature.

WHEREFORE, plaintiff, JOHN HUSSEY, asks judgment against defendant, THE STOCKLIFT CORPORATION, a foreign corporation, in a sum of money in excess of FIFTEEN THOUSAND DOLLARS ($15,000.00).

Chapter 15

PRODUCTS LIABILITY AND DISCOVERY

SYNOPSIS

§ 15.01   INTRODUCTION
§ 15.02   THE PURPOSES AND REACH OF DISCOVERY
   [A]   Illinois Supreme Court Rule 201. General Discovery Provisions
   [B]   FRCP 26 General Provisions Governing Discovery; Duty of
       Disclosure
§ 15.03   THE DISCOVERY TOOLS
§ 15.04   INTERROGATORIES
§ 15.05   REQUESTS TO PRODUCE DOCUMENTS
§ 15.06   REQUESTS TO ADMIT FACTS OR THE GENUINENESS OF
       DOCUMENTS
§ 15.07   DEPOSITIONS
§ 15.08   RELEVANCY IN THE DISCOVERY PROCESS
§ 15.09   SETTING THE DISCOVERY TIME FRAME
§ 15.10   DEFECT CATEGORY AND TIME FRAMES
§ 15.11   TIME FRAMES IN UNIT DEFECT CASES
§ 15.12   TIME FRAMES IN DESIGN DEFECT CASES
§ 15.13   TIME FRAMES IN FAILURE TO INSTRUCT OR WARN CASES
§ 15.14   TIME FRAMES IN MISREPRESENTATION CASES
§ 15.15   ORGANIZATION AND DRAFTING OF DISCOVERY REQUESTS
§ 15.16   INADVERTENT DISCLOSURE IN DISCOVERY
§ 15.17   ELECTRONIC DISCOVERY
§ 15.18   SUMMARY

§ 15.01   INTRODUCTION

The discovery process is one of the most challenging stages in products liability litigation. The plaintiff must access large amounts of information from within the defendant company's files in order to prove her case. Complaints grounded in allegations of defectively designed packaging or products as well as those centered in failure to instruct or warn and misrepresentation, require the review of thousands of documents generated over periods ranging from 10 to 50 years. The discovery effort requires detailed planning and careful drafting of discovery requests.[1] In every products liability litigation there is a great disparity between the very limited information that may be provided by the plaintiff in discovery and that of the corporate defendant. Corporate defendants always possess considerable amounts of information in the form of corporate documents generated over years of corporate life pursuant to standard operating procedures.

Chapters 16 through 18[2] will discuss the products liability-focused aspects of interrogatories, requests to admit facts, requests for production of documents and depositions. It is the purpose of the present chapter to provide an overview of the civil discovery processes in state and federal courts, which is essential to garner a competent understanding of products liability theory and practice. Discovery requests are quite properly vigorously opposed by defense counsel and contested discovery motions are a common feature of these cases. Chapter 19, Protective Orders, Discovery Enforcement, and Motions-in-Limine will discuss the discovery enforcement aspect of products litigation in detail.

Discovery planning is central to the successful prosecution of any litigation. It is essential in product liability cases. The innate difficulty of tracking the stages in the progress of a product over a multi-year time frame and the significant amount of documentation attendant to such, require a concentrated discovery effort.

The standard and most utilized discovery tools are interrogatories, requests to admit fact or the genuineness of documents, the request for the production of documents, and discovery and evidence depositions. The Federal Rules of Civil Procedure govern discovery in federal courts.[3] While many states follow the Federal Rules regarding discovery, a number of states are following somewhat different approaches to discovery. In Illinois, for example, Illinois Supreme Court Rule 201 provides the general guidelines for discovery. Many states require a case

---

[1] For an introductory overview of federal and state products liability discovery planning, see JAMES A. LOWE & MARK L. WAKEFIELD, AMERICAN LAW OF PRODUCTS LIABILITY, PART 16. PRACTICE, CHAPTER 66. PLAINTIFF'S PRETRIAL PRACTICE: PREPARING A DISCOVERY PLAN; INTERROGATORIES. *See also* AMERICAN LAW REPORTS, INDEX TO ANNOTATIONS: DISCOVERY: PRODUCTS LIABILITY, covering ALR2d, ALR3d, ALR4th, ALR5th, ALR6th, ALR Fed., and ALR Fed.2d (2005).

[2] *See infra*, Chapter 16, Interrogatories and Requests to Admit Fact; Chapter 17, Requests to Produce Documents; and Chapter 18, Discovery and Evidence Depositions.

[3] The Federal Rules governing discovery include:

    Rule 26 — General Provisions Governing Discovery; Duty of Disclosure

    Rule 27 — Depositions Before Action or Pending Appeal

    Rule 28 — Persons Before Whom Depositions May be Taken

    Rule 30 — Depositions Upon Oral Examination

    Rule 31 — Depositions Upon Written Questions

    Rule 32 — Use of Depositions in Court Proceedings

    Rule 33 — Interrogatories to Parties

    Rule 34 — Production of Documents and Things and Entry Upon Land for Inspection and Other Purposes

    Rule 35 — Physical and Mental Examinations of Persons

    Rule 36 — Requests for Admission

    Rule 37 — Failure to Make Disclosure or Cooperate in Discovery: Sanctions

management conference at the onset of a case as a means of policing the flow and problems involved.[4] The same requirement exists under the Federal Rules of Civil Procedure.[5]

The federal system requires opposing counsel to submit a variety of important information even without a formal request by opposing counsel.[6] The federal rules,

---

[4] The Illinois provision may serve as a typical example:

Illinois Supreme Court Rule 218. Pretrial Procedure.

(a) Initial Case Management Conference. Except as provided by local circuit court rule, which on petition of the chief judge of the circuit has been approved by the Supreme Court, the court shall hold a case management conference within 35 days after the parties are at issue and in no event more than 182 days following the filing of the complaint. At the conference counsel familiar with the case and authorized to act shall appear and the following shall be considered:

    (1) the nature, issues, and complexity of the case;

    (2) the simplification of the issues;

    (3) amendments to the pleadings;

    (4) the possibility of obtaining admissions of fact and of documents which will avoid unnecessary proof;

    (5) limitations on discovery including:

        (i) the number and duration of depositions which can be taken;

        (ii) the area of expertise and the number of opinion witnesses who can be called; and

        (iii) deadlines for the disclosure of opinion witnesses and the completion of written discovery and depositions;

    (6) the possibility of settlement and scheduling of a settlement conference;

    (7) the advisability of alternative dispute resolution;

    (8) the date on which the case should be ready for trial;

    (9) the advisability of holding subsequent case management conferences; and

    (10) any other matters which may aid in the disposition of the action.

[5] Federal Rule 26. General Provisions Governing Discovery; Duty of Disclosure.

(f) Meeting of Parties; Planning for Discovery.

Except in actions exempted by local rule or when otherwise ordered, the parties shall, as soon as practicable and in any event at least 14 days before a scheduling conference is held or a scheduling order is due under Rule 16(b), meet to discuss the nature and basis of their claims and defenses and the possibilities for a prompt settlement or resolution of the case, to make or arrange for the disclosures required by subdivision (a)(1), and to develop a proposed discovery plan. The plan shall indicate the parties' views and proposals concerning:

    (1) what changes should be made in the timing, form, or requirement for disclosures under subdivision (a) or local rule, including a statement as to when disclosures under subdivision (a)(1) were made or will be made;

    (2) the subjects on which discovery may be needed, when discovery should be completed, and whether discovery should be conducted in phases or be limited to or focused upon particular issues;

    (3) what changes should be made to limitations on discovery imposed under these rules or by local rule, and what other limitations should be imposed; and

    (4) any other orders that should be entered by the court under subdivision (c) or under Rule 16(b) and (c).

[6] Federal Rule 26. General Provisions Governing Discovery; Duty of Disclosure.

(a) Required Disclosures; Methods to Discover Additional Matter.

    (1) Initial Disclosures. Except to the extent otherwise stipulated or directed by order or local rule, a party shall, without awaiting a discovery request, provide to other parties:

        (A) the name and, if known, the address and telephone number of each individual likely to have discoverable information relevant to disputed facts alleged with particularity in the pleadings, identifying the subjects of the information;

        (B) a copy of, or a description by category and location of, all documents, data compilations, and tangible things in the possession, custody, or control of the party

as all state discovery schemes, require the responding party to seasonably update discovery previously answered, a requirement rarely, if ever, complied with by the parties, especially products litigators.[7] It is the intention of discovery provisions that the parties themselves provide full disclosure, more a fond wish rather than current routine practice.[8]

It is important to note at the outset that without adequate pre-filing research and analysis,[9] the only party involved in the case who has detailed knowledge of the nature and extent of the manufacturing information is the corporate defendant. The greatest amount of time and frustration encountered by plaintiff's counsel in preparing these cases occurs in the discovery process. It is important to note that in general terms counsel has only one opportunity to conduct discovery. While plaintiff counsel has the right to supplemental discovery after study of the materials received pursuant to the original issuance of discovery requests, she does not have the prerogative of starting over if the original discovery requests were inadequately analyzed and poorly written. In addition to showing an example of superficial preparation, it can get discovery off on a wrong track that cannot be easily corrected.

---

that are relevant to disputed facts alleged with particularity in the pleadings;

(C)   a computation of any category of damages claimed by the disclosing party, making available for inspection and copying as under Rule 34 the documents or other evidentiary material, not privileged or protected from disclosure, on which such computation is based, including materials bearing on the nature and extent of injuries suffered; and

(D)   for inspection and copying as under Rule 34 any insurance agreement under which any person carrying on an insurance business may be liable to satisfy part or all of a judgment which may be entered in the action or to indemnify or reimburse for payments made to satisfy the judgment.

Unless otherwise stipulated or directed by the court, these disclosures shall be made at or within 10 days after the meeting of the parties under subdivision (f). A party shall make its initial disclosures based on the information then reasonably available to it and is not excused from making its disclosures because it has not fully completed its investigation of the case or because it challenges the sufficiency of another party's disclosures or because another party has not made its disclosures.

[7] A party is under a duty seasonably to amend a prior response to an interrogatory, request for production, or request for admission if the party learns that the response is in some material respect incomplete or incorrect and if the additional or corrective information has not otherwise been made known to the other parties during the discovery process or in writing.

[8] Illinois Supreme Court Rule 201. General Discovery Provisions:

(1) Full Disclosure Required. Except as provided in these rules, a party may obtain by discovery full disclosure regarding any matter relevant to the subject matter involved in the pending action, whether it relates to the claim or defense of the party seeking disclosure or of any other party, including the existence, description, nature, custody, condition, and location of any documents or tangible things, and the identity and location of persons having knowledge of relevant facts. The word "documents," as used in these rules, includes, but is not limited to, papers, photographs, films, recordings, memoranda, books, records, accounts, communications and all retrievable information in computer storage.

[9] See Chapter 12, Researching the Products Case.

§ 15.02   THE PURPOSES AND REACH OF DISCOVERY

PRETRIAL PRODUCT-RELATED RESEARCH

BASIC RESEARCH ISSUES

1. What mechanical or chemical or pharmacological aspect of defendant's product actually caused the plaintiff's death or injury?

2. How did it do that?

3. Was the defendant aware of that injury-producing potential? When?

4. Could the defendant have done something to have eliminated or minimized that risk and still have aggressively competed in its chosen markets?

5. If it could have, why didn't it?

PRODUCTS LIABILITY RESEARCH-RELATED
INFORMATION SOURCES

EXTERNAL DATA	INTERNAL COMPANY DATA
[Pre-Filing Research]	[Discovery Tools]
1. State-of-the-Art Literature	1. Design
2. Industry Custom	2. Testing
3. Regulatory Activity	3. Production
4. Injury History	4. Marketing
5. Litigation History	5. Post-Marketing

Set out below are selections from the general discovery rules of the United States Courts and a state court, Illinois, as illustrative of the statutory measures that will channel and control the extensive effort undertaken in products liability pretrial discovery.

[A]   Illinois Supreme Court Rule 201. General Discovery Provisions

(1) Full Disclosure Required. Except as provided in these rules, a party may obtain by discovery full disclosure regarding any matter relevant to the subject matter involved in the pending action, whether it relates to the claim or defense of the party seeking disclosure or of any other party, including the existence, description, nature, custody, condition, and location of any documents or tangible things, and the identity and location of persons having knowledge of relevant facts. The word "documents," as used in these rules, includes, but is not limited to, papers, photographs, films, recordings, memoranda, books, records, accounts, communications, and all retrievable information in computer storage.

(2) Privilege and Work Product. All matters that are privileged against disclosure on the trial, including privileged communications between a party or his agent and the attorney for the party, are privileged against disclosure through any discovery procedure. Material prepared by or for a party in preparation for trial is subject to discovery only if it does not contain or disclose the theories, mental impressions, or litigation plans of the party's attorney. The court may apportion the cost involved in originally securing the discoverable material, including when

appropriate a reasonable attorney's fee, in such manner as is just.

[B]   FRCP 26. General Provisions Governing Discovery; Duty of Disclosure

(b) Discovery Scope and Limits. Unless otherwise limited by order of the court in accordance with these rules, the scope of discovery is as follows:

(1)   In General. Parties may obtain discovery regarding any matter, not privileged, which is relevant to the subject matter involved in the pending action, whether it relates to the claim or defense of the party seeking discovery or to the claim or defense of any other party, including the existence, description, nature, custody, condition and location of any books, documents, or other tangible things and the identity and location of persons having knowledge of any discoverable matter. The information sought need not be admissible at the trial if the information sought appears reasonably calculated to lead to the discovery of admissible evidence.

(2)   Limitations. By order or by local rule, the court may alter the limits in these rules on the number of depositions and interrogatories and may also limit the length of depositions under Rule 30 and the number of requests under Rule 36. The frequency or extent of use of the discovery methods otherwise permitted under these rules and by any local rule shall be limited by the court if it determines that:

   (i)   the discovery sought is unreasonably cumulative or duplicative, or is obtainable from some other source that is more convenient, less burdensome, or less expensive;

   (ii)   the party seeking discovery has had ample opportunity by discovery in the action to obtain the information sought; or

   (iii) the burden or expense of the proposed discovery outweighs its likely benefit, taking into account the needs of the case, the amount in controversy, the parties' resources, the importance of the issues at stake in the litigation, and the importance of the proposed discovery in resolving the issues. The court may act upon its own initiative after reasonable notice or pursuant to a motion under subdivision (c).

§ 15.03   THE DISCOVERY TOOLS

The discovery tools set out below are essentially the same whether issuing from Congress or a state legislature. The basic discovery tools include written interrogatories, requests for the production of documents and depositions. The sections to follow will provide selections from the relevant rules and proceed to discuss each of them in the context of products liability litigation. It bears reminding that the choice of legal theory from among the body of products law discussed in Chapters 1–10 will control how discovery plays out in any litigation.

§ 15.04   INTERROGATORIES

FRCP Rule 33 — Interrogatories to Parties

(a)   In General.

    (1)   *Number.* Unless otherwise stipulated or ordered by the court, a party may serve on any other party no more than 25 written interrogatories, including all discrete subparts. Leave to serve additional interrogatories may be granted to the extent consistent with Rule 26(b)(2).

    (2)   *Scope.* An interrogatory may relate to any matter that may be inquired into under Rule 26(b). An interrogatory is not objectionable merely because it asks for an opinion or contention that relates to fact or the application of law to fact, but the court may order that the interrogatory need not be answered until designated discovery is complete, or until a pretrial conference or some other time.

(b)   Answers and Objections.

    (1)   *Responding Party.* The interrogatories must be answered:

        (A)   by the party to whom they are directed; or

        (B)   if that party is a public or private corporation, a partnership, an association, or a governmental agency, by any officer or agent, who must furnish the information available to the party.

    (2)   *Time to Respond.* The responding party must serve its answers and any objections within 30 days after being served with the interrogatories. A shorter or longer time may be stipulated to under Rule 29 or be ordered by the court.

    (3)   *Answering Each Interrogatory.* Each interrogatory must, to the extent it is not objected to, be answered separately and fully in writing under oath.

    (4)   *Objections.* The grounds for objecting to an interrogatory must be stated with specificity. Any ground not stated in a timely objection is waived unless the court, for good cause, excuses the failure.

    (5)   *Signature.* The person who makes the answers must sign them, and the attorney who objects must sign any objections.

(c)   Use. An answer to an interrogatory may be used to the extent allowed by the Federal Rules of Evidence.

(d)   Option to Produce Business Records. If the answer to an interrogatory may be determined by examining, auditing, compiling, abstracting, or summarizing a party's business records (including electronically stored information), and if the burden of deriving or ascertaining the answer will be substantially the same for either party, the responding party may answer by:

(1)   specifying the records that must be reviewed, in sufficient detail to enable the interrogating party to locate and identify them as readily as the responding party could; and

(2)   giving the interrogating party a reasonable opportunity to examine and audit the records and to make copies, compilations, abstracts, or summaries.

§ 15.05   REQUESTS TO PRODUCE DOCUMENTS

FRCP Rule 34 — Producing Documents, Electronically Stored Information, and Tangible Things, or Entering onto Land, for Inspection and Other Purposes

(a)   In General. A party may serve on any other party a request within the scope of Rule 26(b):

   (1)   to produce and permit the requesting party or its representative to inspect, copy, test, or sample the following items in the responding party's possession, custody, or control:

      (A)   any designated documents or electronically stored information — including writings, drawings, graphs, charts, photographs, sound recordings, images, and other data or data compilations — stored in any medium from which information can be obtained either directly or, if necessary, after translation by the responding party into a reasonably usable form; or

      (B)   any designated tangible things; or

   (2)   to permit entry onto designated land or other property possessed or controlled by the responding party, so that the requesting party may inspect, measure, survey, photograph, test, or sample the property or any designated object or operation on it.

(b)   Procedure.

   (1)   Contents of the Request. The request:

      (A)   must describe with reasonable particularity each item or category of items to be inspected;

      (B)   must specify a reasonable time, place, and manner for the inspection and for performing the related acts; and

      (C)   may specify the form or forms in which electronically stored information is to be produced.

   (2)   Responses and Objections.

      (A)   Time to Respond. The party to whom the request is directed must respond in writing within 30 days after being served. A shorter or longer time may be stipulated to under Rule 29 or be ordered by the court.

(B) Responding to Each Item. For each item or category, the response must either state that inspection and related activities will be permitted as requested or state an objection to the request, including the reasons.

(C) Objections. An objection to part of a request must specify the part and permit inspection of the rest.

(D) Responding to a Request for Production of Electronically Stored Information. The response may state an objection to a requested form for producing electronically stored information. If the responding party objects to a requested form — or if no form was specified in the request — the party must state the form or forms it intends to use.

(E) Producing the Documents or Electronically Stored Information. Unless otherwise stipulated or ordered by the court, these procedures apply to producing documents or electronically stored information:

(i) A party must produce documents as they are kept in the usual course of business or must organize and label them to correspond to the categories in the request;

(ii) If a request does not specify a form for producing electronically stored information, a party must produce it in a form or forms in which it is ordinarily maintained or in a reasonably usable form or forms; and

(iii) A party need not produce the same electronically stored information in more than one form.

(c) Nonparties. As provided in Rule 45, a nonparty may be compelled to produce documents and tangible things or to permit an inspection.

§ 15.06   REQUESTS TO ADMIT FACTS OR THE GENUINENESS OF DOCUMENTS

FRCP Rule 36 — Requests for Admission

(a) Scope and Procedure.

(1) Scope. A party may serve on any other party a written request to admit, for purposes of the pending action only, the truth of any matters within the scope of Rule 26(b)(1) relating to:

(A) facts, the application of law to fact, or opinions about either; and

(B) the genuineness of any described documents.

(2) Form; Copy of a Document. Each matter must be separately stated. A request to admit the genuineness of a document must be accom-

panied by a copy of the document unless it is, or has been, otherwise furnished or made available for inspection and copying.

(3)   Time to Respond; Effect of Not Responding. A matter is admitted unless, within 30 days after being served, the party to whom the request is directed serves on the requesting party a written answer or objection addressed to the matter and signed by the party or its attorney. A shorter or longer time for responding may be stipulated to under Rule 29 or be ordered by the court.

(4)   Answer. If a matter is not admitted, the answer must specifically deny it or state in detail why the answering party cannot truthfully admit or deny it. A denial must fairly respond to the substance of the matter; and when good faith requires that a party qualify an answer or deny only a part of a matter, the answer must specify the part admitted and qualify or deny the rest. The answering party may assert lack of knowledge or information as a reason for failing to admit or deny only if the party states that it has made reasonable inquiry and that the information it knows or can readily obtain is insufficient to enable it to admit or deny.

(5)   Objections. The grounds for objecting to a request must be stated. A party must not object solely on the ground that the request presents a genuine issue for trial.

(6)   Motion Regarding the Sufficiency of an Answer or Objection. The requesting party may move to determine the sufficiency of an answer or objection. Unless the court finds an objection justified, it must order that an answer be served. On finding that an answer does not comply with this rule, the court may order either that the matter is admitted or that an amended answer be served. The court may defer its final decision until a pretrial conference or a specified time before trial. Rule 37(a)(5) applies to an award of expenses.

(b)   Effect of an Admission; Withdrawing or Amending It. A matter admitted under this rule is conclusively established unless the court, on motion, permits the admission to be withdrawn or amended. Subject to Rule 16(e), the court may permit withdrawal or amendment if it would promote the presentation of the merits of the action and if the court is not persuaded that it would prejudice the requesting party in maintaining or defending the action on the merits. An admission under this rule is not an admission for any other purpose and cannot be used against the party in any other proceeding.

§ 15.07   DEPOSITIONS

FRCP Rule 30 — Depositions Upon Oral Examination

(a)   When a Deposition May Be Taken.

(1) Without Leave. A party may, by oral questions, depose any person, including a party, without leave of court except as provided in Rule 30(a)(2). The deponent's attendance may be compelled by subpoena under Rule 45.

(2) With Leave. A party must obtain leave of court, and the court must grant leave to the extent consistent with Rule 26(b)(2):

    (A) if the parties have not stipulated to the deposition and:

        (i) the deposition would result in more than 10 depositions being taken under this rule or Rule 31 by the plaintiffs, or by the defendants, or by the third-party defendants;

        (ii) the deponent has already been deposed in the case; or

        (iii) the party seeks to take the deposition before the time specified in Rule 26(d), unless the party certifies in the notice, with supporting facts, that the deponent is expected to leave the United States and be unavailable for examination in this country after that time; or

    (B) if the deponent is confined in prison.

(b) Notice of the Deposition; Other Formal Requirements.

(1) Notice in General. A party who wants to depose a person by oral questions must give reasonable written notice to every other party. The notice must state the time and place of the deposition and, if known, the deponent's name and address. If the name is unknown, the notice must provide a general description sufficient to identify the person or the particular class or group to which the person belongs.

(2) Producing Documents. If a subpoena duces tecum is to be served on the deponent, the materials designated for production, as set out in the subpoena, must be listed in the notice or in an attachment. The notice to a party deponent may be accompanied by a request under Rule 34 to produce documents and tangible things at the deposition.

(3) Method of Recording.

    (A) Method Stated in the Notice. The party who notices the deposition must state in the notice the method for recording the testimony. Unless the court orders otherwise, testimony may be recorded by audio, audiovisual, or stenographic means. The noticing party bears the recording costs. Any party may arrange to transcribe a deposition.

    (B) Additional Method. With prior notice to the deponent and other parties, any party may designate another method for recording the testimony in addition to that specified in the original notice. That party bears the expense of the additional record or transcript unless the court orders otherwise.

(4) By Remote Means. The parties may stipulate — or the court may on motion order — that a deposition be taken by telephone or other remote means. For the purpose of this rule and Rules 28(a), 37(a)(2), and 37(b)(1), the deposition takes place where the deponent answers the questions.

(5) Officer's Duties.

(A) Before the Deposition. Unless the parties stipulate otherwise, a deposition must be conducted before an officer appointed or designated under Rule 28. The officer must begin the deposition with an on-the-record statement that includes:

(i)   the officer's name and business address;

(ii) the date, time, and place of the deposition;

(iii) the deponent's name;

(iv) the officer's administration of the oath or affirmation to the deponent; and

(v)   the identity of all persons present.

(B) Conducting the Deposition; Avoiding Distortion. If the deposition is recorded nonstenographically, the officer must repeat the items in Rule 30(b)(5)(A)(i)–(iii) at the beginning of each unit of the recording medium. The deponent's and attorneys' appearance or demeanor must not be distorted through recording techniques.

(C) After the Deposition. At the end of a deposition, the officer must state on the record that the deposition is complete and must set out any stipulations made by the attorneys about custody of the transcript or recording and of the exhibits, or about any other pertinent matters.

(6) Notice or Subpoena Directed to an Organization. In its notice or subpoena, a party may name as the deponent a public or private corporation, a partnership, an association, a governmental agency, or other entity and must describe with reasonable particularity the matters for examination. The named organization must then designate one or more officers, directors, or managing agents, or designate other persons who consent to testify on its behalf; and it may set out the matters on which each person designated will testify. A subpoena must advise a nonparty organization of its duty to make this designation. The persons designated must testify about information known or reasonably available to the organization. This paragraph (6) does not preclude a deposition by any other procedure allowed by these rules.

(c) Examination and Cross-Examination; Record of the Examination; Objections; Written Questions.

(1)   Examination and Cross-Examination. The examination and cross-examination of a deponent proceed as they would at trial under the Federal Rules of Evidence, except Rules 103 and 615. After putting the deponent under oath or affirmation, the officer must record the testimony by the method designated under Rule 30(b)(3)(A). The testimony must be recorded by the officer personally or by a person acting in the presence and under the direction of the officer.

(2)   Objections. An objection at the time of the examination — whether to evidence, to a party's conduct, to the officer's qualifications, to the manner of taking the deposition, or to any other aspect of the deposition — must be noted on the record, but the examination still proceeds; the testimony is taken subject to any objection. An objection must be stated concisely in a nonargumentative and nonsuggestive manner. A person may instruct a deponent not to answer only when necessary to preserve a privilege, to enforce a limitation ordered by the court, or to present a motion under Rule 30(d)(3).

(3)   Participating Through Written Questions. Instead of participating in the oral examination, a party may serve written questions in a sealed envelope on the party noticing the deposition, who must deliver them to the officer. The officer must ask the deponent those questions and record the answers verbatim.

(d)   Duration; Sanction; Motion to Terminate or Limit.

(1)   Duration. Unless otherwise stipulated or ordered by the court, a deposition is limited to 1 day of 7 hours. The court must allow additional time consistent with Rule 26(b)(2) if needed to fairly examine the deponent or if the deponent, another person, or any other circumstance impedes or delays the examination.

(2)   Sanction. The court may impose an appropriate sanction — including the reasonable expenses and attorney's fees incurred by any party — on a person who impedes, delays, or frustrates the fair examination of the deponent.

(3)   Motion to Terminate or Limit.

(A)   Grounds. At any time during a deposition, the deponent or a party may move to terminate or limit it on the ground that it is being conducted in bad faith or in a manner that unreasonably annoys, embarrasses, or oppresses the deponent or party. The motion may be filed in the court where the action is pending or the deposition is being taken. If the objecting deponent or party so demands, the deposition must be suspended for the time necessary to obtain an order.

(B)   Order. The court may order that the deposition be terminated or may limit its scope and manner as provided in Rule 26(c). If terminated, the deposition may be resumed only by order of the court where the action is pending.

(C) Award of Expenses. Rule 37(a)(5) applies to the award of expenses.

(e) Review by the Witness; Changes.

(1) Review; Statement of Changes. On request by the deponent or a party before the deposition is completed, the deponent must be allowed 30 days after being notified by the officer that the transcript or recording is available in which:

(A) to review the transcript or recording; and

(B) if there are changes in form or substance, to sign a statement listing the changes and the reasons for making them.

(2) Changes Indicated in the Officer's Certificate. The officer must note in the certificate prescribed by Rule 30(f)(1) whether a review was requested and, if so, must attach any changes the deponent makes during the 30-day period.

(f) Certification and Delivery; Exhibits; Copies of the Transcript or Recording; Filing.

(1) Certification and Delivery. The officer must certify in writing that the witness was duly sworn and that the deposition accurately records the witness's testimony. The certificate must accompany the record of the deposition. Unless the court orders otherwise, the officer must seal the deposition in an envelope or package bearing the title of the action and marked "Deposition of [witness's name]" and must promptly send it to the attorney who arranged for the transcript or recording. The attorney must store it under conditions that will protect it against loss, destruction, tampering, or deterioration.

(2) Documents and Tangible Things.

(A) Originals and Copies. Documents and tangible things produced for inspection during a deposition must, on a party's request, be marked for identification and attached to the deposition. Any party may inspect and copy them. But if the person who produced them wants to keep the originals, the person may:

(i) offer copies to be marked, attached to the deposition, and then used as originals — after giving all parties a fair opportunity to verify the copies by comparing them with the originals; or

(ii) give all parties a fair opportunity to inspect and copy the originals after they are marked — in which event the originals may be used as if attached to the deposition.

(B) Order Regarding the Originals. Any party may move for an order that the originals be attached to the deposition pending final disposition of the case.

(3) Copies of the Transcript or Recording. Unless otherwise stipulated or ordered by the court, the officer must retain the stenographic notes of a deposition taken stenographically or a copy of the recording of a deposition taken by another method. When paid reasonable charges, the officer must furnish a copy of the transcript or recording to any party or the deponent.

(4) Notice of Filing. A party who files the deposition must promptly notify all other parties of the filing.

(g) Failure to Attend a Deposition or Serve a Subpoena; Expenses. A party who, expecting a deposition to be taken, attends in person or by an attorney may recover reasonable expenses for attending, including attorney's fees, if the noticing party failed to:

(1) attend and proceed with the deposition; or

(2) serve a subpoena on a nonparty deponent, who consequently did not attend.

§ 15.08 RELEVANCY IN THE DISCOVERY PROCESS

In addition to similar discovery tools, the state and federal discovery schemes share a common philosophy of discovery as to what materials are discoverable and the ongoing duties and obligations of the litigants during this crucial stage. The central idea in both systems is the concept of relevancy.

The legal standard used to determine the information available to the parties in the course of discovery is stated in Federal Rule of Civil Procedure 26(b)(1):

. . . Parties may obtain discovery regarding any nonprivileged matter that is relevant to any party's claim or defense — including the existence, description, nature, custody, condition, and location of any documents or other tangible things and the identity and location of persons who know of any discoverable matter. For good cause, the court may order discovery of any matter relevant to the subject matter involved in the action. Relevant information need not be admissible at the trial if the discovery appears reasonably calculated to lead to the discovery of admissible evidence.[10]

The definition of relevance is provided by Federal Rule of Evidence 401, which defines relevant evidence as information having any tendency to make the existence of a fact that is of consequence to the action more probable or less probable than it would be without it.[11] Hence, by providing for the discovery of data that may *be reasonably calculated to lead to* formally admissible evidence both federal and state courts have fashioned a very liberal discovery format.

---

[10] FED. R. CIV. P. 26(b)(1).

[11] FED. R. EVID. 401.

As noted by Justice Powell of the United States Supreme Court, writing in 1978 for a unanimous court in *Oppenheimer Fund, Inc. v. Sanders*:[12]

> . . . The key phrase in this definition — "relevant to the subject matter involved in the pending action" — has been construed broadly to encompass any matter that bears on, or that reasonably could lead to other matter that could bear on, any issue that is or may be in the case.[13] Consistently with the notice-pleading system established by the Rules, discovery is not limited to issues raised by the pleadings, for discovery itself is designed to help define and clarify the issues. Nor is discovery limited to the merits of a case, for a variety of fact-oriented issues may arise during litigation that are not related to the merits.[14]

A request for discovery should be considered relevant if there is "any possibility" that information sought may be relevant to the subject matter of the action. The primary focal point to determine the actual scope of discovery relevancy is the plaintiff's complaint. As noted in the leading case of *Roesberg v. Johns-Manville Corp*:[15]

> . . . The detail in the complaint specifies the necessary relevance of the interrogatories. . . . The burden now falls upon GAF, the party resisting discovery, to clarify and explain its objections and to provide support therefor. . . .[16]

The allegations of each count in the complaint determine the broad subject matters involved in the case. However, relevance is to be measured, not strictly according to the specific fact issues raised by the pleadings, but by reference to the broader logical parameters of those facts.[17]

Arguments over the application of this liberal interpretation of relevancy in the discovery process are at the center of most pre-trial motions seeking to limit plaintiff's requests, whether in time or subject matter or both.[18] More recent cases, while emphasizing that discovery does indeed have limits,[19] tend to follow the open

---

[12] 437 U.S. 340 (1978).

[13] *Id.* (*citing* Hickman v. Taylor, 329 U.S. 495, 501 (1947)).

[14] *Hickman*, 329 U.S. at 500–01.

[15] 85 F.R.D. 292, 296–97 (E.D. Pa. 1980).

[16] *Id.* at 297.

[17] Smith v. F.T.C., 403 F. Supp. 1000 (D. Del. 1975).

[18] *See* Chapter 19, Protective Orders, Discovery Enforcement, and Motions-In-Limine.

[19] *See* Rule 26. General Provisions Governing Discovery; Duty of Disclosure:

(1) In General. Parties may obtain discovery regarding any matter, not privileged, which is relevant to the subject matter involved in the pending action, whether it relates to the claim or defense of the party seeking discovery or to the claim or defense of any other party, including the existence, description, nature, custody, condition and location of any books, documents, or other tangible things and the identity and location of persons having knowledge of any discoverable matter. The information sought need not be admissible at the trial if the information sought appears reasonably calculated to lead to the discovery of admissible evidence.

(2) Limitations. By order or by local rule, the court may alter the limits in these rules on the

interpretation of Justice Powell.[20]

In re Kevin Silva v. Basin Western Inc.,[21] involved a trial court order compelling the production of information regarding insurance reserves and settlement authority in a personal injury claim. The question of whether insurance reserves and settlement authority fell within the scope of discovery was a question of first impression in Colorado requiring the court to explore the nature of insurance reserves and settlement authority to determine whether such information was reasonably calculated to lead to admissible evidence in a personal injury action and thus discoverable.

The court noted that this question was to be resolved by reference to Colorado Rules of Civil Procedure 26(B)(1), which provided that:

> [P]arties may obtain discovery regarding any matter, not privileged, which is relevant to the subject matter involved in the pending action, whether it relates to the claim or defense of the party seeking discovery or to the claim or defense of any other party, including the existence, description, nature, custody, condition and location of any books, documents, or other tangible things, and the identity and location of persons having knowledge of any discoverable matter. The information sought need not be admissible at trial if the information sought appears reasonably calculated to lead to admissible evidence.[22]

The court emphasized that relevancy for purposes of discovery was not the same as relevancy for admissibility of evidence at trial.[23] Section 26(b)(1) permitted parties to obtain "discovery regarding any unprivileged, relevant matter that 'relates to the claim or defense of the party seeking discovery or to the claim or defense of any other party' if it is 'reasonably calculated to lead to the discovery of admissible evidence.'" Further, it is not a proper ground for objection that the information

---

number of depositions and interrogatories and may also limit the length of depositions under Rule 30 and the number of requests under Rule 36. The frequency or extent of use of the discovery methods otherwise permitted under these rules and by any local rule shall be limited by the court if it determines that:

(i)   the discovery sought is unreasonably cumulative or duplicative, or is obtainable from some other source that is more convenient, less burdensome, or less expensive;

(ii)   the party seeking discovery has had ample opportunity by discovery in the action to obtain the information sought; or

(iii)   the burden or expense of the proposed discovery outweighs its likely benefit, taking into account the needs of the case, the amount in controversy, the parties' resources, the importance of the issues at stake in the litigation, and the importance of the proposed discovery in resolving the issues. The court may act upon its own initiative after reasonable notice or pursuant to a motion under subdivision (c).

[20] *See, e.g.*, J.W. v. B.B., 700 N.W.2d 277 (Wis. Ct. App. 2005); In re Estate of Mechanic, 2005 N.J. Super. Unpub. LEXIS 807 (Mar. 24, 2005); Kirk v. Ford Motor Co., 116 P.3d 27 (Idaho 2005); In re TIG Ins. Co., 361 Ill. App. 3d 1095 (2005); City of King City v. Community Bank of Central California, 2005 Cal. LEXIS 13081 (Nov. 16, 2005). Virtually all cases addressing this point cite and/or quote the language of Justice Powell in the *Oppenheimer* case.

[21]   47 P.3d 1184 (Colo. 2002).

[22]   Colo. R. Civ. P. 26(B)(1).

[23]   *See* Williams v. Dist. Court, 866 P.2d 908, 911 (Colo. 1993); Kerwin v. Dist. Court, 649 P.2d 1086, 1088 (Colo. 1982).

sought will be inadmissible at trial if the information appears reasonably calculated to lead to the discovery of admissible evidence. The court observed that while the law generally favored discovery, the scope of discovery was not limitless. The need for discovery must be balanced by weighing a party's right to privacy and protection from harassment against the other party's right to discover information that is relevant. Thus, the information sought through discovery must be relevant to the subject matter of the action and reasonably calculated to lead to the discovery of admissible evidence.[24]

§ 15.09   SETTING THE DISCOVERY TIME FRAME

The period of time within which discovery is to be conducted is not an issue until plaintiff files his first set of interrogatories. Until that time, pre-filing research is strictly a matter of personal choice based on plaintiff's preliminary investigative goals. During formal discovery, however, plaintiff must indicate the years over which documentation is to be forthcoming from the defendant corporation.

Initial defense objections to plaintiff's discovery requests are typically centered in the excessive number of years over which information is requested. The primary theoretical basis for objection lies in the alleged irrelevancy of requested materials generated by defendant in years preceding and following the model year or date of manufacture of the product unit involved in the case. Extensive time frame requests also prompt objections based on the burdensome nature of lengthy multi-year interrogatories and requests for documents.

The problem from the perspective of products liability defense lawyers was simply put in an article by a defense attorney:

> More often than not, plaintiffs' attorneys serve defense counsel with interrogatories or requests for production of documents which request volumes of information regarding not only the product at issue, but other products that have also been manufactured by the defendant. . . . When faced with such expansive discovery requests, defense counsel must take a restrictive, conservative approach to providing information to plaintiff's counsel regarding products other than the product at issue in that particular case. The reasons for serious, aggressive attempts by defense counsel to limit the amount and type of information supplied about the manufacture of other products should be obvious. . . . Most importantly, improper introduction of damaging evidence concerning other products manufactured by the defendant can make the difference between a plaintiff's verdict and a defense verdict, an award of punitive damages as opposed to only compensatory damages, or a moderate compensatory damage award and an excessive compensatory damage award.[25]

This standard response to time frame and subjects of initial discovery filed by plaintiffs sets the stage for the intense motion practice involving discovery

---

[24] *Silva*, 47 P.3d at 1188 n.5.

[25] Bradley C. Nahrstadt, *Narrowing the Scope of Discovery for Substantially Similar Products*, 15 No. 6 PRAC. LITIG. 37, 38 (2004).

enforcement, protective orders and motions-in-limine. These periods are often unavoidably extensive due to the nature of the suspect product or technology at issue. For example, in asbestos cases, a time frame going back as far as 40 years may be necessary to responsibly prepare the litigation. In other cases such as those involving Firestone tires and SUV rollovers, where the basic design has remained constant, counsel may legitimately argue for a time frame that begins a decade or more earlier when the product was originally developed and widely used in similar product lines. The manufacturer's experience with a component item such as ball joints on an entire line of pickup trucks is fair game in a case questioning the design of a ball-joint system.[26]

A common objection in the course of products liability cases is that the plaintiff's requests are unduly broad in both chronology and subject matter, resulting in irrelevant and burdensome requests. This issue was addressed in the case of *State ex rel. Ford Motor Co. v. Nixon.*[27]

Roy Dietiker, a former employee of Ford, filed a worker's compensation suit against Ford and a products liability suit against multiple other defendants for allegedly having been exposed to defective products containing asbestos while working for Ford that resulted in him contracting lung cancer. These two lawsuits were ongoing at the time of Dietiker's death from the cancer, and discovery in these suits had been obtained from Ford. After Dietiker's death, his relatives filed a wrongful death action against Ford, and discovery requests were served in this third lawsuit. Plaintiffs sought information and documents regarding every product containing asbestos that was ever manufactured, sold or distributed by Ford in its 102-year history without limitation as to locality or as to the specific products to which Dietiker was allegedly exposed. Ford did not comply with the discovery requests in this action, and the trial court issued an order to compel production.

Ford claimed that the discovery requests in the wrongful death action were overbroad and unduly burdensome because there were no geographical, time or subject matter restrictions in the discovery requests. Ford also argued that discovery should be limited to the products-related claims, because the court lacks jurisdiction over the employment-related claims. Finally, Ford asserted that the discovery requests were duplicative because counsel was the same in all of these cases and had already received many of the requested materials.

The court held that discovery without temporal, geographic or subject matter limitation was overbroad. It also noted that discovery already obtained by counsel from other ongoing cases between the same parties provided a means to lessen the burden of duplicate discovery requests on Ford.[28]

Here, the trial court abused its discretion when ordering Ford to comply with all of Dietiker's discovery requests. Adhering to Rule 56, the trial court was ordered to vacate its order to compel and limit discovery to the reasonable parameters of the petition allowing discovery of relevant and temporal subject matter that has not

---

[26] *See Durango Ball Joint Woes Persist* [CBS News], http://www.cbsnews.com/stories/ 2004/03/03/ eveningnews/main603833.shtml.

[27] 160 S.W.3d 379 (Mo. 2005).

[28] *Id.* at 381.

already been discovered. The trial court was ordered to establish a factual record of individual challenges to discovery materials and issue protective orders when required.

§ 15.10   DEFECT CATEGORY AND TIME FRAMES

The primary consideration on the question of determining the beginning and end points for investigative research and discovery is the generic type or types of defect involved in the case. Each defect type has a fairly clear period of history associated with it that bears directly on the issue of relevancy in both a discovery and evidentiary sense.

During pre-filing research counsel for both sides should follow whatever historical leads may be found with respect to the science, technology, industry, regulation and the company under investigation. Becoming acquainted with the general areas where any such data may be found is one of the most important goals for the products litigator. It will provide a feel for the scientific, governmental and business context of the litigation and facilitate identification of the range of relevant issues that may be involved. Once accomplished, counsel may then be able to isolate those points in time in the life of the defendant corporation when state-of-the-art material and internal company documents addressing central technological and manufacturing issues were likely generated.

Another important discovery goal is the education of the judges who will be involved in resolving key pretrial complaint process and discovery in the litigation. Whether a contested motion judge or trial judge, the reality is that they are normally totally unfamiliar with the scientific, industry, regulatory or company aspects of the nascent litigation. Hence, judicial education is a primary goal for both plaintiff and defense counsel.

§ 15.11   TIME FRAMES IN UNIT DEFECT CASES

The unit defect case involves the most restrictive time frame, which usually runs from the date that plaintiff purchased a unit of the product to the date of the injury. This is the only category of defect where strict liability truly exists. Here, the product unit that injured the client contains an identifiable flaw. Due to this flaw or defect, the unit is dangerously different from the other units in the same line manufactured by the defendant. In most instances the flaw can be identified with some precision and the product unit isolated from the general line of similar goods manufactured by the defendant.[29]

In this category of defect, true strict liability principles control the information flow in the trial. In these settings, the basic public policy underpinnings of strict liability have full force and effect. The time, effort and money spent by defendant to prevent mismanufactured units from reaching the inventory shelf, the inherent merits of its design or its relative position when examined in reference to the state

---

[29] TERRENCE F. KIELY, SCIENCE AND LITIGATION: PRODUCTS LIABILITY IN THEORY AND PRACTICE 342 (CRC PRESS 2002).

of the art, are all irrelevant to the analysis.[30]

Plaintiff needs to prove the flaw or defect in the unit, absence of alterations or modifications, use within the anticipated range of intended uses of the product and proximate causation. The legal focus is the single offending product unit. The defendant's production of the defective unit provides the frame of reference that reflects the defective nature of this unit. The relevant time frame in the unit manufacturing defect case is the period of time from the date that the suspect product was manufactured and left the hands of the manufacturer, up to the date of the date of the injury producing event.

This does not mean that lawyers for the plaintiff are relieved of an obligation to engage in product research relative to the basic design, materials composition and production of the product. That data is needed to determine if the case product unit is truly a defective unit. The extensive time frame over which technical research must be conducted in the typical design category case is not present here. The right or wrong of defendant's conscious design choices prior to marketing the product have no bearing on the overriding issue of the integrity of the offending product unit.[31]

§ 15.12   TIME FRAMES IN DESIGN DEFECT CASES

In products liability cases centered in the *design* categories (Packaging, Overall Design, Instructions, and Warnings) the inception of the time frame is typically the point when the earliest references in the authoritative literature to the technology or design feature involved in the case are found. The time frame begins at that period and arguably ends at the point in company history when the specifications for the suspect design were frozen and production authorized. As we have seen that can be and often is a decades long period of scientific, industry, regulatory and corporate history. Warnings related to the use of the pain killer Percodan, for example, can go back to the early 1950s. A significant amount of science has come and gone over such a period that would reflect on the manufacturer's knowledge of potentially dangerous side-effects. The same can be said for potential problems associated with attention deficit drugs such as Ritalin[32] or a wide range of current anti-depression medications.[33]

There are three important focal considerations in estimating investigative, discovery and trial time frames in cases centered within one of the design defect categories:

1. The model year of the product unit or the year of the introduction of a drug or chemical with their respective sets of instructions and warnings.

---

[30] *Id.*

[31] *See, e.g.*, O'Brien v. Muskin Corp., 463 A.2d 298 (N.J. 1983).

[32] FDA Probing ADHD Drug Side Effects. Ritalin, Concerta Possibly Linked to Psychiatric Problems, http://www.msnbc.msn.com/id/8403762.

[33] See the FDA letter requiring increased warnings of suicide for sellers of antidepressants, http://www.fda.gov/cder/drug/antidepressants/SSRIlabelChange.htm.

2.   Whether the suspect design, component instructions or warnings have been utilized in earlier years or in earlier model year offerings of the same or comparable product lines in the United States or foreign markets.

3.   The period of time over which the technology or instruction or warning in the case has been addressed in the state of the art literature and/or been adopted or utilized in the industry within which defendant does business.

These three areas provide a wide but manageable set of boundaries for pretrial research of the type discussed in Chapter 12, Researching the Products Case. While the model year of the suspect unit may be an arguably terminal date in the manufactured product design case, it is by no means determinative of the inception of the relevant time frame. In instances of a technology basic to an industry, such as the design of automobile door locks or gas tanks, of which the offending unit is a result, the relevant historical time frame can be extensive. Accordingly, relevant state of the art materials and internal company records often antedate the model year of the suspect unit by several years.

In the design defect counts, plaintiff is necessarily challenging the propriety of defendant's conscious design choices for the entire line of goods of which the offending unit is a member. The company, being considered an expert, is deemed to have constructive knowledge of the findings of all authoritative literature in its fields of research and development.[34] Plaintiffs can also argue for the discovery of documents addressing *subsequent* technological developments to the extent they indicate the existence of a feasible alternative design prior to the point in time when the specifications of the suspect design were fixed for production purposes.[35]

§ 15.13   TIME FRAMES IN FAILURE TO INSTRUCT OR WARN CASES

Cases centered in allegations of failure to properly instruct in the safe use of a manufactured article or in allegations of failure to warn of risks and side-effects in prescription drug settings, constitute a large part of the products liability litigation in American state and federal courts. In these cases, the time frame for investigative and discovery research typically runs from the initial development of the item to the date of the injury-producing event. This is because the legal focus is on the absence or inadequacy of the instruction or warning accompanying the product, and thus the heart of the case lies in defendant's knowledge of danger. Prior to release of the product into the stream of commerce, any such knowledge would be had from study of the relevant scientific literature and any knowledge gained from studying commercial uses of the design feature allegedly raising the risk. The end point of the time frame is the date of the injury-producing event. The defendant manufacturer's obligation to adequately warn or instruct is an ongoing one over the course

---

[34]   Lindsay v. Ortho Pharmaceutical Corp., 637 F.2d 87 (2d Cir. 1980).

[35]   *See* D.L. v. Huebner, 329 N.W.2d 890 (Wis. 1983); Schelbauer v. Butler Mfg. Co., 673 P.2d 743 (Cal. 1984). Additionally, some courts hold that the traditional ban against the admissibility of subsequent remedial measures has no applicability to strict liability cases. Sanderson v. Steve Snyder Enterprises, 196 Conn. 134 (1985); Holmes v. Sahara Coal Company, 475 N.E.2d 1383 (Ill. App. Ct. 1985); Caprara v. Chrysler Corporation, 417 N.E.2d 545 (N.Y. 1981).

of the product's market life. Such duty does not depend upon any internal corporate guidelines as to finalization of product specifications for production purposes.

In these cases, the legal and factual focus is on the defendant's opportunities for determining product risks and acting responsibly in light of them. The concern over the adequacy of warnings about heart attacks for users of Merck Corporation's Vioxx pain killer is an excellent example of this point. All scientific information, whether internal or external to the defendant company that demonstrates the possibility of gaining knowledge is subject to discovery and admissible at trial. This would include all testing and related documentation on the basic design feature at issue in the case generated after the release of the suspect unit for sale. In cases of products such as basic automotive features such as axles or prescription drugs that experience little or no change after their initial production, amount of discoverable post-production data can be substantial.[36]

§ 15.14   TIME FRAMES IN MISREPRESENTATION CASES

In the 402B or misrepresentation case,[37] the start of the relevant discovery time frame, as with all design cases, begins with the first inklings in the literature relative to the design feature under scrutiny. Since the risks involved stem from some design flaw typically lies at the heart of the defendant's misstatement, it logically determines the starting point for analysis.

In determining the end point of the time frame in misrepresentation cases, the same considerations as pertain to instruction and warning cases apply. In all three instances, the focus is on the form and nature of communications that were made to the consumer in marketing literature as opposed to technological considerations proper. In the misrepresentation case, however, the time frame is generally considered to be terminated at the date of purchase, inasmuch as the central legal focal point is justifiable reliance on a misstated inducement to buy. Accordingly, the terminal point of the time frame can be substantially shorter than in counts grounded in failure to instruct or warn.

§ 15.15   ORGANIZATION AND DRAFTING OF DISCOVERY REQUESTS

Interrogatories and requests to produce documents seek information from internal documents in the possession of the defendant. Interrogatories seek very specific answers to questions tailored to elicit the organizational structure of the defendant, the names and titles of committee members, the names of groups, offices, department and sections, wherein the decisions of interest to plaintiff were processed and finalized. Requests for the Production of Documents address the

---

[36] *See* Robert B. Patterson, *Products Liability: The Manufacturer's Continuing Duty to Improve His Product or Warn of Defects After Sale*, 62 ILL. B.J. 92 (1973); LaBelle v. McCauley Indus. Corp., 649 F.2d 46 (1st Cir. 1981).

[37] See Chapter 3, Misrepresentation, for a detailed analysis of this category of products liability litigation.

same corpus of corporate documentation and should be planned with a consistent organizational method and terminology.

There are a series of corporate activities that may serve as the organizational focal points bases for the actual drafting of discovery requests, whether interrogatories or document requests:

1.　The case time frames.

2.　The routine corporate phases over the case time frame(s) from the idea stage to the inventory shelf and the document types typically generated in any one of such phases. Design, Testing, Production, Marketing and Post-Marketing are typical stages over the course of product development and manufacture.

3.　The identifiable activities occurring within any one phase in that overall process. The early Design phase will generate documents that tend to cross lines since designers, technicians, financial personnel, labor supervisors and marketing staff all add input to the design details and prospects for government regulatory problems, competition and the like.

4.　The types of documents likely generated at any one point in time as a result of such activities. The Testing period of a product will obviously generate documents distinctly different from those concerned with the overall marketing and distributorship planning.

5.　The offices, departments, sections, committees and key personnel involved in those document generating functions.

Initially planning requests around those broad aspects of the manufacture of a product will provide a structured approach to discovery that lends itself to consistent responses to the inevitable objections to any broad-based discovery requests. Concentrating on routine document generating processes over designated time periods and grounding requests in the document types logically associated with the defect modes involved in the case, provides organizational clarity. This clarity substantially minimizes the defendant's opportunities to divert the court's attention from the underlying documentary reality of the case. Discovery requests obtained from form books not only make for a very poor impression, but are simply inadequate. Closely considered customized requests are the most effective devices for achieving success in these cases.[38]

§ 15.16　INADVERTENT DISCLOSURE IN DISCOVERY

The issues involved in instances of inadvertent production of privileged documents in discovery are not new. Complex litigation involving the increased use of photocopy machines, facsimile transmission, electronic mail, and other technologies have resulted in a significant increase in these cases, in which parties contend that their privileged information has inadvertently been disclosed to opponents. The courts vary as to whether they will find a waiver in such circumstances, whether

---

[38] *See* KIELY, *supra* note 29, at 347–48.

they will remedy the situation, and, if a waiver is to be found, the scope of such waiver.

The problem of inadvertent discovery has come to the fore in very recent days due to the fact that electronically stored information has become the dominant form of discovery in the litigation process. Two recent annotations address the important issues involved and the range of judicial solutions under federal and state law.[39]

A survey conducted by the ABA Digital Evidence Project, a working group of the Section of Science and Technology Law, reported that 12% of respondents found that privileged information was inadvertently produced during the gathering and subsequent production of electronic evidence.[40]

§ 15.17   ELECTRONIC DISCOVERY

As noted by author Jason Krause in an *ABA Journal* article:

> It's mainly a matter of volume. The discovery phase of a trial can involve millions of pages of documents from e-mail, word processing, instant messaging, handheld devices or even deleted data that has been recovered and restored.
>
> The chair of the ABA's Digital Evidence Project, attorney George Paul of Phoenix, notes that the handling of privileged documents is one of the most controversial aspects of proposed new civil procedure rules. Proposed rule 26(b)5(B) includes a clawback provision that would apply to any type of document involved in discovery.
>
> Under the proposed rule, if one side were to claim a document is privileged after producing it to opposing counsel, the side that received the document would have to return, sequester or destroy the document and retrieve any copies that it distributed, pending a court ruling on the document's admissibility.
>
> Privileged documents, including inadvertently produced documents, are now handled according to different rules and standards in each jurisdic-

---

[39] *See* Annotation, *Waiver of Evidentiary Privilege by Inadvertent Waiver of Evidentiary Privilege by Inadvertent Disclosure — Federal Law,* 159 A.L.R. Fed. 153 (For several years, courts and commentators have debated vigorously whether and to what extent an inadvertent release of privileged information should be construed as a waiver of evidentiary privilege under federal law.); Annotation, *Waiver of Evidentiary Privilege by Inadvertent Disclosure — State Law,* 51 A.L.R. 5th 603; Paul R. Rice, Attorney-Client Privilege in the United States, Second Edition [Database updated April 2005], Chapter 9, § 9:70 Waiver, F. Exceptions to Waiver by Voluntary Disclosure. *See also* Anita Ramasastry, *The Proposed Federal E-Discovery Rules: While Trying to Add Clarity, the Rules Still Leave Uncertainty,* http://writ.news. findlaw.com/ramasastry/20040915.html.

By far, the greatest number of judicial discussions of inadvertent discovery are had in criminal cases involving issues of plain view search claims by the state or federal government. This is a quite distinct problem from the topic when centered in discovery in complex civil cases.

[40] *See* Jason Krause, *Porous Privilege: Lawyers Struggle to Keep Work Product, Legal Advice Secret in Electronic Discovery,* 91-Aug. A.B.A. J. 61 (2005).

tion.[41]

In today's current litigation climate the greatest number of important documents in large-scale products liability cases are to be found in electronically generated emails, word processed documents, or spreadsheets.[42] The electronic archiving of corporate information is nothing new to litigators seeking corporate records. The most significant aspect of the current obsession with electronic discovery is really centered in e-mails, including those that were deleted but are still accessible by software and hard drive examinations.[43] The new catch phrase *data forensics* has been coined to describe the processes involved in the crucial mining of electronic data on a wide variety of corporate computer-related equipment.[44]

There is a growing body of books,[45] practice literature,[46] and websites[47] devoted to this relatively new and complex litigation phenomenon. All of them seek to address the problem of attempting, let alone adequately completing electronic discovery. The problem is especially acute in product liability cases involving a product with international sales over a multi-year time frame.[48] The recent

---

[41] *Id.* at 62.

[42] *See* LPT Virtual Roundtable: A Goldmine of Electronic Discovery Expertise: A Conversation Among Veterans of Electronic Discovery Battles, http://www.abanet.org/lpm/lpt/articles/ftr07041.html. (Interesting and wide-ranging discussion by seasoned lawyers in the fields of complex litigation and electronic discovery.)

[43] *See* Carole Longendyke, *SEEK AND FIND: Data Forensics Brings CSI to Your Office*, 24 No. 4 LEGAL MGMT. 20 (2005) (Data forensics in your office may not hold the same allure as the forensic sciences that deal with blood evidence, fingerprints, DNA and fiber analysis, but your trace data are relevant and useful in investigations. Administrators need to be aware of what their systems capture and store — and how that information can be used.).

[44] Data forensics is the collection, preservation, analysis and presentation of evidence found on electronic devices. In contrast to traditional crime scene investigation that involves the collection of fingerprints, blood, fibers, etc., at the scene of the crime, the "crime scene" in the data forensic investigation is typically a computer or other electronic device. *Id.* at 20.

[45] *See* PAUL R. RICE, ELECTRONIC EVIDENCE: LAW AND PRACTICE (ABA 2005); MICHELE C.S. LANGE & KRISTIN NIMSGER, ELECTRONIC EVIDENCE AND DISCOVERY: WHAT EVERY LAWYER SHOULD KNOW (ABA 2004); MICHAEL R. ARKFELD, ELECTRONIC DISCOVERY AND EVIDENCE (Ring-bound) (Law Partner Publishing 2003).

[46] *See* Monique C.M. Leahy, J.D., *Recovery and Reconstruction of Electronic Mail as Evidence*, 41 AM. JUR. 3D 1 (POF) (American Jurisprudence Proof of Facts) [Database updated June 2005]; Symposium on Proposed Change to FRCP Federal Rule of Civil Procedure; Ken Withers, *Two Tiers and a Safe Harbor: Federal Rulemakers Grapple with E-Discovery*, 51-SEP. FED. L. 29 (2004); Patrick R. Grady, *Discovery of Computer Stored Documents and Computer Based Litigation Support Systems: Why Give Up More Than Necessary*, 14 J. MARSHALL COMPUTER & INFO. L. 523, 539 (1996); Richard L. Marcus, *Confronting the Future: Coping with Discovery of Electronic Material*, 64 LAW & CONTEMP. PROBS. 253, 253 (2001); LANGE & NIMSGER, *supra* note 45, at 30–40; Kenneth J. Withers, *Computer Based Discovery in Federal Civil Litigation*, 2000 FED. CTS. L. REV. 2 (2000).

[47] See the excellent and extensive collection of e-discovery materials collected by Kenneth J. Withers, *Annotated Case Law and Further Reading on Electronic Discovery* [Updated Mar. 10, 2004], http://www.kenwithers.com. (This website is maintained by Ken Withers of the Federal Judicial Center, but is unofficial. It contains articles on electronic discovery, sets of PowerPoint slides and text from judicial education and bar association seminars on electronic discovery, and additional resources.) *See also* Kroll-Ontrack, http://www.krollontrack.com/LawLibrary/ (commercial e-discovery company).

[48] *See* Kenneth J. Withers, *Computer Based Discovery in Federal Civil Litigation*, 2000 FED. CTS. L. REV. 2 (2000). This is an excellent guide to navigating the initial conferences in cases heavily invested in various forms of electronic discovery. *See also* Lorie J. Marco & Katie M. Connoly, *Electronic Records:*

cigarette and Vioxx cases will serve as good examples. There are and will be several million paper and electronic sources subject to identification, retrieval and analysis over the course of those litigations.

In addition to the categories of documents traditionally associated with various types of manufactured products such as engineered goods, chemicals or pharmaceuticals, counsel must also be concerned with the identification of the defendant's computer systems, e-mail programs, digital archives and a host of other minutiae not typically associated with an already burdensome discovery workload. It is clear that a respondent's limitation of discovery to hard copies will no longer suffice.[49] Areas which would be the subject of interrogatories and document requests would include the names and current company position if any of all personnel with authority for the use of computers or management of data systems, identification of all computers currently in use and those no longer in use but accessible; all software systems such as networks, databases, spreadsheets, graphics, word processors, e-mail programs, tape and digital archival systems and programs, telecommunications and internet software and systems and all data storage and retrieval capabilities for current and warehoused hardware and software.[50]

The costs of retrieval of data from retired hard drives and older archival programs, let alone current documents and e-mails can be staggering. The recent cigarette and Vioxx litigations may serve as example of cases where literally millions of documents are potentially involved. This reality has resulted in a number of recent articles examining the topic of cost-shifting and cost-sharing in such cases.[51] A series of decisions known as the *Zubulake* cases, addresses a wide range of cost-shifting issues, and are considered authoritative references on the subject.[52]

What to Look and Ask for (With Glossary), 15 No. 2 PRAC. LITIG. 39 (2004).

[49] *See* Zubulake v. UBS Warburg, 217 F.R.D. 309 (S.D.N.Y. 2003) (despite defendant's offer of 100 pages of hard copy e-mails, further electronic production was required).

[50] Kroll Ontrack provides a comprehensive set of Sample Interrogatories for use in the federal district courts. *See* Kroll OnTrack, Sample Interrogatories, http://www.krollontrack.com/practicaltools/interrogatory_mailer.pdf. The complete starter set, free of charge, includes Rule 16(c) Pretrial Conference Agenda for Computer-Based Discovery, Sample Preservation letter — to client, Sample Preservation letter — to opponent or third party, Sample Fed. R. Civ. P. 30(b)(6) Deposition Notice, Sample E-Discovery Interrogatories and a Sample Motion to Compel Electronic Discovery.

[51] *See, e.g.*, Mohammad Iqbal, *The New Paradigms of E-Discovery and Cost-Shifting. Determining Who Pays for Electronic Discovery*, 72 DEF. COUNS. J. 283 (2005). This is an excellent, comprehensive article setting out all of the issues involved in the move towards cost allocations in electronic discovery, with a very useful arrangement and summary of the key cases. *See also* Michele C.S. Lange, *Who Should Pay for Electronic Discovery?*, 48-Feb. B.B.J. 14 (2005); Shira A. Scheindlin & Jeffery Rabkin, *Electronic Discovery in Federal Civil Litigation: Is Rule 34 up to the Task?* 41 B.C. L. REV. 327, 368. (2000); Virginia Llewellyn, *Electronic Discovery Best Practices*, 10 RICH. J.L. & TECH. 51. (2004). *See also* Toshiba America Electronic Components v. The Superior Court of Santa Clara County, 124 Cal. App. 4th 762, 21 Cal. Rptr. 3d 532 (2004) (The court concluded that proper cases may require the demanding party to pay retrieval expenses. The determination of a proper case is a factual matter best left to the discretion of the trial court.).

[52] There are five *Zubulake* decisions, two dealing with cost-shifting, two with sanctions, and one unrelated to e-discovery.
- Zubulake I, May 13, 2003: Zubulake v. UBS Warburg, 217 F.R.D. 309 (S.D.N.Y. 2003) (stating legal standards for determining cost-shifting for producing emails stored on backup tapes);
- Zubulake II, May 13, 2003: Zubulake v. UBS Warburg, 230 F.R.D. 290 (S.D.N.Y. 2003) (denying

In *Zubulake IV*,[53] the court noted a distinction between accessible electronic evidence, such as evidence on hard drives, servers, optical disks, magnetic tapes, or removable media, and inaccessible electronic evidence, such as evidence on a backup tape or erased, fragmented, or damaged data. As to accessible evidence, the court said the cost of production should presumptively remain with the responding party, just as with conventional paper discovery. The court treated inaccessible evidence differently. It held that costs of production could be apportioned depending on the following seven factors, in order of importance:

(1) the extent to which the request is specifically tailored to discover relevant information;

(2) the availability of such information from other sources;

(3) the total cost of production compared to the amount in controversy;

(4) the total cost of production compared to the resources available to each party;

(5) the relative ability of each party to control costs and its incentive to do so;

(6) the importance of the issue at stake in the litigation; and

(7) the relative benefits to the parties of obtaining the information.[54]

The *Zublake* and other cases have utilized the idea of sampling to avoid undue expense and delay to estimate whether producing a larger volume of electronic evidence is worth the cost, and, if so, which party should pay for the effort. In sampling settings the requesting party highlights a small selection of electronic data for the producing party to restore and submit for inspection, typically from difficult to access sources such as backup tapes and discontinued archival systems, where restoration and production costs are routinely high. The court will then evaluate the sample and craft an appropriate production and cost-allocation order, based on whatever multi-factor test the court considers appropriate.[55]

A steady stream of very thoughtful articles and conference materials are becoming available online. They range from comprehensive, related articles, in

---

release of deposition transcript to securities regulators);

• Zubulake III, July 24, 2003: Zubulake v. UBS Warburg, 216 F.R.D. 280 (S.D.N.Y. 2003) (allocating backup tape restoration costs between parties);

• Zubulake IV, Oct. 22, 2003: Zubulake v. UBS Warburg, 220 F.R.D. 212 (S.D.N.Y. 2003) (ordering sanctions against UBS for violating its duty to preserve evidence); and

• Zubulake V, July 20, 2004: Zubulake v. UBS Warburg, 229 F.R.D. 422 (S.D.N.Y. 2004) (imposing sanctions). *See* Iqbal, *supra* note 51.

[53] Zubulake v. UBS Warburg, 217 F.R.D. 309 (S.D.N.Y. 2003).

[54] *Id. See also* David K. Isom, *Electronic Discovery Primer for Judges*, 2005 FED. CTS. L. REV. 1 (Feb. 2005) (excellent and comprehensive).

[55] Jonathan M. Redgrave Erica J. Bachmann, *Cost-Shifting in Electronic Discovery*, 50-DEC. FED. L. 31 (2003). A good recent summary of the key issues and suggested guidelines for action can be found in *The Sedona Principles: Best Practices Recommendations & Principles for Addressing Electronic Document Production* (Mar. 2003), http://www.thesedonaconference.org/publicationshtml. *See* http://www.thesedonaconference.org/wgs for more information on the Sedona Conference and its working groups.

Trial Magazine[56] to the recent publication of the Sedona Conference[57] Principles for Electronic Document Production.[58] The latter are receiving increased attention in the growing literature addressed to the pressing problems in products liability and other areas of complex litigation.

---

[56] *See Electronic Evidence*, TRIAL, Oct. 2005. *See also:*

Gathering digital data

Richard J. Arsenault & John Randall Whaley

(In the digital age, it's not enough to know what documents or information to ask for in discovery. You also need to know what kind of computer system the defendant is using to store those documents, how the system works, and how to frame your requests. A clear, specific preservation letter and detailed requests for production will ensure that you get exactly what you need.)

A practical guide to e-mail discovery

Craig Ball

(Do you know the difference between IMAP and POP? Or whether it matters if the opposing party uses Gmail or Hotmail? With e-mail replacing communication that used to happen over the phone, in person, or by letter, these digital missives are an essential target of discovery.)

Electronic evidence in everyday cases

William S. Friedlander & Mark A. Buchanan

(Digital evidence can play a role in almost any type of lawsuit. A search through electronic records might reveal a deceitful spouse in a matrimonial case. And an employment case might turn up a "smoking gun" showing an intent to retaliate.)

Make the most of e-data experts

Keith L. Altman

(When it comes to electronic data, two heads are definitely better than one. Match your subject-matter expert with a hands-on technical expert who can search the defendant's database, find hidden information, or run specialized queries.)

Can this photo be trusted?

Edward J. Imwinkelried

(Digital cameras produce pictures that are easy to work with; computer technology can change the colors, sharpnesss, or other elements of a photo. But this ease of alteration also means that photos produced as evidence may not be what they seem. Here's how to recognize when your opponent's digital photos may be misleading, and how to use your own digital images to best effect.)

Ethics in the era of electronic evidence

Christopher D. Wall

(Electronic records are fairly new to litigation, so you may not have had a chance to brush up on the ethics involved in this type of discovery. What do the federal rules and bar codes of conduct say about your e-discovery obligations? And how can you make sure that you — and your opponent — are fulfilling your duties? High-tech tools like online document repositories can help.)

[57] The Sedona Conference exists to allow leading jurists, lawyers, experts, academics and others, at the cutting edge of issues in the area of antitrust law, complex litigation, and intellectual property rights, to come together — in conferences and mini-think tanks (Working Groups) — and engage in true dialogue, not debate, all in an effort to move the law forward in a reasoned and just way. The documents currently available from the Sedona Conference may be acccessed at http://www.thesedonaconference.org/.

[58] *See, e.g.*, https://thesedonaconference.org/publication/The%20Sedona%20Principles (last visited on February 12, 2013).

§ 15.18 SUMMARY

Chapters 16 through 18 will address the subject of discovery in greater detail by analyzing the theory and practice for interrogatories, requests for admission of fact, requests for documentation and depositions. Chapter 19 will discuss objections to discovery, protective orders and motions-in-limine.

Chapter 16

INTERROGATORIES AND REQUESTS TO ADMIT FACTS

SYNOPSIS

§ 16.01   INTRODUCTION

§ 16.02   INTERROGATORIES: STATUTORY DEFINITIONS — FEDERAL

§ 16.03   INTERROGATORIES: STATUTORY DEFINITIONS — STATE

§ 16.04   INTERROGATORIES: LIMITATIONS ON NUMBER

§ 16.05   ORGANIZING AND DRAFTING THE INTERROGATORIES

§ 16.06   SAMPLE INTERROGATORIES

§ 16.07   SAMPLE INTERROGATORIES: FOURWHEEL CORPORATION

§ 16.08   PLAINTIFF'S FIRST SET OF INTERROGATORIES TO DEFENDANT ROLLBAR CORPORATION

§ 16.09   SAMPLE INTERROGATORIES: PRESSURIZED STAINLESS STEEL BEVERAGE CANISTER

§ 16.10   SAMPLE INTERROGATORIES: STANDUP FORKLIFT TRUCK

§ 16.11   OBSERVATIONS ON SAMPLE INTERROGATORIES

§ 16.12   REQUESTS TO ADMIT FACT OR THE GENUINENESS OF DOCUMENTS

§ 16.01   INTRODUCTION

This chapter focuses on the general structure and style of interrogatories in products liability cases. Examples of interrogatories in an automobile rollover case, an exploding pressurized stainless steel beverage container and a defectively designed stand-up forklift case are provided to illustrate the points made.

§ 16.02   INTERROGATORIES: STATUTORY DEFINITIONS — FEDERAL

The Federal Rules of Civil Procedure provide for the issuance and management of interrogatories in Rule 33:

Rule 33. Interrogatories to Parties

(a) In General.

(1) *Number.* Unless otherwise stipulated or ordered by the court, a party may serve on any other party no more than 25 written interrogatories, including all discrete subparts. Leave to serve additional interrogatories may be granted to the extent consistent with Rule 26(b)(2).

(2) *Scope.* An interrogatory may relate to any matter that may be inquired into under Rule 26(b). An interrogatory is not objectionable merely because it asks for an opinion or contention that relates to fact or the application of law to fact, but the court may order that the interrogatory need not be answered until designated discovery is complete, or until a pretrial conference or some other time.

(b) Answers and Objections.

(1) *Responding Party.* The interrogatories must be answered:

(A) by the party to whom they are directed; or

(B) if that party is a public or private corporation, a partnership, an association, or a governmental agency, by any officer or agent, who must furnish the information available to the party.

(2) *Time to Respond.* The responding party must serve its answers and any objections within 30 days after being served with the interrogatories. A shorter or longer time may be stipulated to under Rule 29 or be ordered by the court.

(3) *Answering Each Interrogatory.* Each interrogatory must, to the extent it is not objected to, be answered separately and fully in writing under oath.

(4) *Objections.* The grounds for objecting to an interrogatory must be stated with specificity. Any ground not stated in a timely objection is waived unless the court, for good cause, excuses the failure.

(5) *Signature.* The person who makes the answers must sign them, and the attorney who objects must sign any objections.

(c) Use. An answer to an interrogatory may be used to the extent allowed by the Federal Rules of Evidence.

(d) Option to Produce Business Records. If the answer to an interrogatory may be determined by examining, auditing, compiling, abstracting, or summarizing a party's business records (including electronically stored information), and if the burden of deriving or ascertaining the answer will be substantially the same for either party, the responding party may answer by:

(1) specifying the records that must be reviewed, in sufficient detail to enable the interrogating party to locate and identify them as readily as the responding party could; and

(2) giving the interrogating party a reasonable opportunity to examine and audit the records and to make copies, compilations, abstracts, or summaries.

§ 16.03   INTERROGATORIES: STATUTORY DEFINITIONS — STATE

State law provides a similar scheme for the issuance and parameters of the interrogatories discovery tool. Illinois Supreme Court Rule 213 may serve as an example:

Rule 213. Written Interrogatories to Parties

(a)   **Directing Interrogatories.** A party may direct written interrogatories to any other party. A copy of the interrogatories shall be served on all other parties entitled to notice.

(b)   **Duty of Attorney.** It is the duty of an attorney directing interrogatories to restrict them to the subject matter of the particular case, to avoid undue detail, and to avoid the imposition of any unnecessary burden or expense on the answering party.

(c)   **Number of Interrogatories.** Except as provided in subparagraph (j), a party shall not serve more than 30 interrogatories, including sub-parts, on any other party except upon agreement of the parties or leave of court granted upon a showing of good cause. A motion for leave of court to serve more than 30 interrogatories must be in writing and shall set forth the proposed interrogatories and the reasons establishing good cause for their use.

(d)   **Answers and Objections.** Within 28 days after service of the interrogatories upon the party to whom they are directed, the party shall serve a sworn answer or an objection to each interrogatory, with proof of service upon all other parties entitled to notice. Any objection to an answer or to the refusal to answer an interrogatory shall be heard by the court upon prompt notice and motion of the party propounding the interrogatory. The answering party shall set forth in full each interrogatory being answered immediately preceding the answer. Sworn answers to interrogatories directed to a public or private corporation, or a partnership or association shall be made by an officer, partner, or agent, who shall furnish such information as is available to the party.

(e)   **Option to Produce Documents.** When the answer to an interrogatory may be obtained from documents in the possession or control of the party on whom the interrogatory was served, it shall be a sufficient answer to the interrogatory to produce those documents responsive to the interrogatory. When a party elects to answer an interrogatory by the production of documents, that production shall comply with the requirements of Rule 214.

(f)   **Identity and Testimony of Witnesses.** Upon written interrogatory, a party must furnish the identities and addresses of witnesses who will testify at trial and must provide the following information:

(1)   *Lay Witnesses.* A "lay witness" is a person giving only fact or lay opinion testimony. For each lay witness, the party must identify the

subjects on which the witness will testify. An answer is sufficient if it gives reasonable notice of the testimony, taking into account the limitations on the party's knowledge of the facts known by and opinions held by the witness.

(2) *Independent Expert Witnesses.* An "independent expert witness" is a person giving expert testimony who is not the party, the party's current employee, or the party's retained expert. For each independent expert witness, the party must identify the subjects on which the witness will testify and the opinions the party expects to elicit. An answer is sufficient if it gives reasonable notice of the testimony, taking into account the limitations on the party's knowledge of the facts known by and opinions held by the witness.

(3) *Controlled Expert Witnesses.* A "controlled expert witness" is a person giving expert testimony who is the party, the party's current employee, or the party's retained expert. For each controlled expert witness, the party must identify: (i) the subject matter on which the witness will testify; (ii) the conclusions and opinions of the witness and the bases therefor; (iii) the qualifications of the witness; and (iv) any reports prepared by the witness about the case.

(g) **Limitation on Testimony and Freedom to Cross-Examine.** The information disclosed in answer to a Rule 213(f) interrogatory, or at *in a discovery* deposition, limits the testimony that can be given by a witness on direct examination *at trial.* Information expressed disclosed in a discovery deposition need not be later specifically identified in a Rule 213(f) answer, but, upon objection at trial, the burden is on the proponent of the witness to prove the information was provided in a Rule 213(f) answer or in the *discovery* deposition. *Except upon a showing of good cause, information in an evidence deposition not previously disclosed in a Rule 213(f) interrogatory answer or in a discovery deposition shall not be admissible upon objection at trial.*

Without making disclosure under this rule, however, a crossexamining party can elicit information, including opinions, from the witness. This freedom to cross-examine is subject to a restriction that applies in actions that involve multiple parties and multiple representation. In such actions, the cross-examining party may not elicit undisclosed information, including opinions, from the witness on an issue on which its position is aligned with that of the party doing the direct examination.

(h) **Use of Answers to Interrogatories.** Answers to interrogatories may be used in evidence to the same extent as a discovery deposition.

(i) **Duty to Supplement.** A party has a duty to seasonably supplement or amend any prior answer or response whenever new or additional information subsequently becomes known to that party.

(j) **The Supreme Court, by administrative order, may approve standard forms of interrogatories for different classes of cases.**

(k) **Liberal Construction.** This rule is to be liberally construed to do substantial justice between or among the parties.

§ 16.04   INTERROGATORIES: LIMITATIONS ON NUMBER

A continuing problem in organizing and drafting interrogatories are limitations placed on the number of interrogatories allowed in the first wave of discovery and whether sub-parts in a question will count against the total allowed. This issue is of considerable importance given the very large, essentially disparate areas of inquiry that are legitimate investigative targets and a general initial limit of 30 questions, including all "sub-parts. The limitation on the number of initial interrogatories was an attempt to force litigators to think about their information needs and to organize their discovery along reasonable lines. All too often in the past parties seeking answers to interrogatories would issue shotgun requests running into a hundred or more poorly considered and repetitious inquiries.[1] While such limitations may cause hardship in cases involving significant time frames, they are nonetheless becoming standard in state discovery statutes and motion practice. This is not a new development,[2] but continues to draw attention as products liability cases increase in complexity.[3] Some jurisdictions make no mention of specific numerical limits, instead allowing the courts to monitor any excesses.[4]

A recent decision addressing the issue of interrogatory sub-parts and the limitation of the number of interrogatories is the 2002 Colorado case of *Leaffer v. Zarlengo*,[5] holding that only discrete subparts of *non-pattern* interrogatories, and not those logically or factually subsumed within and necessarily related to the primary question, need be counted toward the interrogatory limit.[6] In *Leaffer*, a patient and her spouse brought a medical malpractice and wrongful death action against physician and others, contending that patient received inadequate care during her pregnancy. The Colorado Supreme Court held that on a matter of first impression, only discrete subparts of non-pattern interrogatories counted toward the interrogatory limit, holding that the legal question of how subparts to interrogatories should be counted was issue of significant importance and presented matter of first impression.

---

[1] *See* Cohn, *Federal Discovery: A Survey of Local Rules and Practices in View of Proposed Changes to the Federal Rules*, 63 MINN. L. REV. 253 (1979). It is the intent of such rules to force lawyers to carefully consider the categories of information they are seeking and organize their written requests accordingly.

[2] *See* R. HAYDOCK & D. HERR, DISCOVERY PRACTICE 288–96 (Boston: Little, Brown & Co. 1982).

[3] *See* Ronald J. Berke & Andrew L. Berke, *ATLA's Litigating Tort Cases*, Chapter 16. Interrogatories (Database updated July 2004).

The practitioner must review local rules to determine the number of interrogatories allowed. Counsel must determine whether the number of interrogatories includes sub-parts, and whether, if multiple parties are represented by a single law firm, that firm is bound by the restriction.

[4] BERKE & BERKE (citing Pennsylvania Rules of Civil Procedure, Rule 4005(c) ("The number of interrogatories or of sets of interrogatories to be served may be limited as justice requires to protect the party from unreasonable annoyance, embarrassment, oppression, burden, or expense.").

[5] 44 P.3d 1072 (Colo. 2002).

[6] *See also* In re SWEPI L.P., 103 S.W.3d 578 (Tex. App. 2003).

During the discovery stage of the litigation, Petitioners served 16 non-pattern interrogatories, among other discovery demands, to Respondents. Respondents argued that each subpart of each interrogatory should be considered a separate question. Since the Case Management Order limited the number of non-pattern interrogatories to *twenty*, Respondents separated the interrogatories into sixty separate questions, renumbered them, and advised Petitioners to choose twenty of the sixty for Respondents to answer. For example, Plaintiffs' Interrogatory No. 11 asked: " 'Describe your medical training specific to the conditions of cardiomyopathy, pre-eclampsia, and high-risk pregnancies (particularly involving twin pregnancies and *advanced maternal age).'* Respondents treated this interrogatory as three separate interrogatories directed to their training for each of the conditions in question."

Petitioners filed a motion to compel responses to their first set of written discovery with the trial court, arguing that pursuant to only "discrete" subparts should be counted separately. Petitioners argued that discrete subparts are those that are not "logically or factually subsumed within and necessarily related to the primary question." Therefore, Petitioners contended, none of their interrogatories contained discrete subparts; rather, any subparts focused on issues that were logically and factually related to the primary question and therefore should not be counted separately.

The court addressed the policy bases for an initial interrogatory limitation:

> We, like the federal courts that have interpreted, recognize the importance of determining how subparts should be counted. On one hand, the extensive use of subparts could defeat the numerical limit imposed by the Case Management Order unless each subpart counts as a separate question; however, if each subpart counts as a separate interrogatory, then a party's fact-gathering ability might be unduly stymied or requests for an increase in the numerical limit might become automatic.[7]

The order provided in relevant part: "Any party may serve upon any other party written interrogatories, not exceeding the number, *including all discrete subparts*, set forth in the Case Management Order, to be answered by the party served." "Any pattern interrogatory and its subparts shall be counted as one interrogatory. *Any subpart* to a non-pattern interrogatory shall be considered as a separate interrogatory."

The interrogatories at issue were *non-pattern* interrogatories. The court noted that the "any subpart" language conflicted with the "all discrete subparts" language. While subsection (e) stated that "any subpart" of a non-pattern interrogatory shall be considered a separate interrogatory, subsection (a) included "all discrete subparts." The court observed that to count each subpart — irrespective of whether it is a discrete subpart — toward the interrogatory limit would lead to the absurd result of unreasonably frustrating legitimate discovery.

---

[7] *Leaffer*, 44 P.3d at 1076 (*citing* Nyfield v. Virgin Islands Tel. Corp. 200 F.R.D. 246, 247 (D.V.I. 2001)); Williams v. Bd. of County Comm'rs of the Unified Gov't of Wyandotte County, 192 F.R.D. 698, 701 (D. Kan. 2000); Safeco v. Rawstron, 181 F.R.D. 441, 443 (C.D. Cal. 1998).

Examples from the case provided illustrations of this problem. Petitioners' Interrogatory No. 12 asked Respondents to "[d]escribe the occasions on which [they] have diagnosed and/or treated individuals with cardiomyopathy, including [Respondents'] role in those cases and the circumstances and outcomes of those diagnoses and/or treatments." Respondents divided this request for a description into three questions: (1) the description; (2) Respondents' role in the cases; and (3) the circumstances or outcome of the diagnoses and/or treatments. If this interrogatory had asked for no more than a description, it would have been impossible for Respondents to split it into separate questions; however, because Petitioners followed their request for a description with requests that the description contain particular information, Respondents split it into multiple inquiries.

In addition, Petitioners' Interrogatory No. 19 asked Respondents to "[d]escribe any complaints, lawsuits, grievances, license suspension revocation proceedings, reprimands, or denials of certification instituted against [them], including the name of the complainant, the nature of the complaint, and its resolution." Respondents split this request for a description into four interrogatories: (1) the description; (2) the identity of the complainant; (3) the nature of the complaint; and (4) the resolution of the complaint. The court observed that the identity of the complainant and nature and resolution of the complaint were integral parts of the description itself.[8]

> As these examples make clear, to parse out each of the requests for specific details of a particular event and require that they count as separate interrogatories would penalize a litigant for requesting information that the opposing party would already reasonably be expected to provide. Indeed, to do so would force parties to create general — perhaps even vague — open-ended interrogatories, leading to absurd results and frustrating the legitimate purpose of using interrogatories to ascertain specific facts. We emphasize that "[l]egitimate discovery efforts should not have to depend upon linguistic acrobatics."[9]

Therefore, given the application of the principles of statutory construction, the court found that the only reasonable construction of subsection (e) was that its reference to "[a]ny subpart" meant "any discrete subpart."

In fact, the court observed, federal courts interpreting local rules that do not contain the "discrete subparts" language — and thus do not have the same conflict as — still have refused to necessarily count each subpart toward the interrogatory limit; instead, they have counted a subpart as part of a single question if a direct relationship exists between the specific information called for in the interrogatory.[10]

---

[8] *Leaffer*, 44 P.3d at 1079–80.

[9] *Id.* (*citing* Ginn v. Gemini Inc., 137 F.R.D. 320, 322 (D. Nev. 1991)).

[10] *See* Clark v. Burlington N. R.R., 112 F.R.D. 117, 118 (N.D. Miss. 1986) (interpreting local rule providing that "each subpart of a question shall be counted as a question," reasoning that the local rule was not "intended to frustrate legitimate discovery efforts," and concluding that "an interrogatory is to be counted as but a single question . . . even though it may call for an answer containing several separate bits of information, if there is a direct relationship between the various bits of information called for"). *See also Ginn*, 137 F.R.D. at 320, 322 (interpreting local rule limiting number of interrogatories to 40 "including subparts" and holding that "subparts are to be counted as part of but one interrogatory for

This appears to be the general 11 position of the authorities who have addressed this important discovery issue.[11]

§ 16.05   ORGANIZING AND DRAFTING THE INTERROGATORIES

Interrogatories in products liability cases serve as an organizational prototype for the entire discovery stage of the case. They should be structured along the chronology and phases of the development of the suspect product. There are typically five such stages:

(1) **Product Design** [Concept, market, costing, facilities and labor needs, comparative product analysis, regulatory reviews, material, initial designs, alternative designs, component parts, international requirements]

(2) **Product Testing** [Testing parameters, test facilities, test requests, test goals, testing for regulatory compliance, alternative design testing, comparative product testing, drafts of test reports]

(3) **Product Production** [Final product specifications, production runs, design changes]

(4) **Product Marketing** [Marketing goals, market test studies, advertising campaigns and documentation]

(5) **Product Post-Marketing** [Adverse reaction or defect complaint reports, regulatory activity, new design, testing and marketing documentation]

Each interrogatory should be closely reviewed to estimate any opportunity that defense counsel may have to refuse to answer on the grounds of relevancy, vagueness, or undue hardship. The basic drafting style and focus try to limit objections to a relevancy or privilege objection. Any objections potentially based on an alleged lack of clarity in the question should be immediately eliminated during the drafting process.

§ 16.06   SAMPLE INTERROGATORIES

At this point we will examine two sets of products liability interrogatories to serve as examples of organizational and drafting considerations unique to this type of complex litigation. The first set involves a products case brought as a result of severe injuries resulting from the rollover of a jeep-type vehicle on a superhighway.

---

the purposes of [the local rule] if they are logically or factually subsumed within and necessarily related to the primary question").

[11] While discrete subparts are counted separately, subparts that are related to the primary question are not. *See* 7 James Wm. Moore, Moore's Federal Practice § 33.30[2] (3d ed. 1997) ("The better view is that subparts may be counted as part of one interrogatory if they are logically and necessarily related to the primary question. This approach is most consistent with the intent of the discovery rules to provide information, not hide information, within reasonable limits."); 8A Charles Alan Wright, Arthur R. Miller, & Richard L. Marcus, Federal Practice and Procedure § 2168.1, at 261 (2d ed. 1994) ("[A]n interrogatory containing subparts directed at eliciting details concerning the common theme should be considered a single question, although the breadth of the area inquired about may be disputable.")

The interrogatories are directed to the manufacturer of the rollover vehicle, Fourwheel Corporation and Rollbar Incorporated, manufacturer of a rollbar that was allegedly defective resulting in its collapse during the rollover. We will address the drafting of interrogatories in those cases that focus on various aspects of the product development and manufacturing process for the vehicle.

This set will be followed in turn by an examination of interrogatories in two other products cases. The first of these involves an exploding commercial pressurized stainless steel beverage container and the second looks at a case of an allegedly defectively designed standup fork lift.

§ 16.07   SAMPLE INTERROGATORIES: FOURWHEEL CORPORATION

In this example, John Consumer was driving a Jeep CJ-5 type vehicle manufactured by the defendant Fourwheel Corporation. When executing a sharp turn to avoid a sudden obstruction on the highway, the vehicle rolled over several times, during which the rollbar failed, striking plaintiff on the head. He was also hit by the collapse of the windshield frame and ejected from the vehicle due to the allegedly defective occupant restraint system. Fourwheel is a wholly owned subsidiary of the Outdoors Motor Company.

The Plaintiff John Q. Consumer, Pursuant to Rule 33 of the Federal Rules of Civil Procedure, requests that the Defendant Fourwheel Corporation answer each of the following interrogatories fully, in writing, under oath, within thirty-three (33) days of service hereof, which interrogatories shall be deemed continuing so as to require prompt supplemental answers if the Defendant obtains or recalls further information relative thereto between the time the answers are submitted to Plaintiff and the time of trial. The answers to these interrogatories should include the knowledge and beliefs of the Defendant.

INSTRUCTIONS AND DEFINITIONS

I. "Identify" when used in reference to a person (whether individual, corporation, or other entity), means to state his or its full name, present address and present telephone number if known, and in the case of an individual, his present or last known position and business affiliation.

II. "Identify" when used in reference to a document, means to state the date and author, addressee or intended recipient, type of document, or some other means of identifying it, and its present or last known location or custodian. If such document was, but no longer is, in your possession or subject to your control, state what disposition was made of it.

III. "Document" as used herein, includes but is not limited to, all abstracts, agreements, all physical forms of correspondence, including FAX transmissions, analyses, applications, books, certificates, charter charts, computer print-outs, computer read-outs, computer tapes, contracts, diaries, PDA recorded data, drafts, drawings, estimates, films, forms, graphs, journals, letters, licenses, manuals, maps, meeting reports, memoranda, memoranda of all conversations including telephone calls, notes, orders, opinions, permits, photographs, photo-maps, plans, press releases, recordings, reports, resolutions, sketches, summaries, tapes, telegrams, texts, time records, transcripts, videotapes, writings and work papers, and any copies not identical to the original, regardless whether the documents are an original or a copy and all e-mails, whether ever sent or received or intended to be sent or received, or deleted but not destroyed or otherwise erased from any PDA, laptop, desktop or computer work station.

IV. "Person or persons" means all entities, and without limiting the generality of the foregoing, includes natural persons, joint owners, associations, companies, partnerships, joint ventures, corporations, trusts and estates.

V. The answers to these INTERROGATORIES are to include any such information requested for products sold in the United States and in member nations of the European Community (EC), Asia, Africa, Mexico and Central and South America.

VI. The time period covered by these interrogatories is from 1993 to 2004.

INTERROGATORY NO. 1:

State the names of the Fourwheel Corporation (hereinafter referred to as FWC) Divisions, Groups, or Offices having any responsibility for either the design, testing, production or marketing of the Fourwheel Models line of utility motor vehicles and the names of the offices, departments, sections or other functional employee groupings within such Divisions, Groups or Offices, for the years 1993 to 2004, as well as the names, title and current company position, if any, of the individual employees managing such group, office, department or section for each of the designated years.

INTERROGATORY NO. 2:

State the names of the FWC committee or committees having any responsibility for the review of and/or the making of corporate decisions regarding any aspect of the design, testing, production or marketing of the Fourwheel model line of utility motor vehicles for the years 1993–2004, as well as the names, title, and current company position, if any, of the members of such committee or committees for each of the designated years.

INTERROGATORY NO. 3:

State with particularity, the corporate relationship between Outdoors Motors Corporation and Fourwheel Corporation and Rollbar, Inc., relative to Outdoors Motors Corporation's (hereinafter referred to as OMC) ownership interest in Fourwheel Corporation and Rollbar, Inc.

INTERROGATORY NO. 4:

State whether any OMC offices, departments, sections, committees or any other applicable OMC organizational entity, or individual OMC employees have, for the years 1993–2004, either participated in or exercised supervisory authority in any respect, over Fourwheel Corporation policy or decisions in regard to either the design, testing, production or marketing of the Fourwheel line of utility motor vehicles, including, but not limited to the rollbars installed in such vehicles.

INTERROGATORY NO. 5:

If the answer to Interrogatory No. 4 is in the affirmative, state:

1. The name of the office, department, section, committee, or other applicable OMC organizational entity either participating in or exercising supervisory capacity as stated, as well as the nature or subject matter of the same for each of the designated years.

2. The names, titles and current company position, if any, of the individual members of such offices, departments, sections, committees or other applicable OMC organizational entity for each of the designated years.

INTERROGATORY NO. 6:

State whether any FWC offices, departments, sections, committees or any other applicable FWC organizational entity, or individual FWC employees have, for the years 1993–2004, either participated in or exercised supervisory authority in any respect, over Rollbar, Inc. policy or decisions in regard to either the design, testing, production or marketing of the Rollbar, Inc. rollbars installed in Fourwheel Corporation's Fourwheel line of motor vehicles.

INTERROGATORY NO. 7:

If the answer to Interrogatory No. 6 is in the affirmative, state:

1. The name of the office, department, section, committee, or other applicable FWC organizational entity either participating in or exercising supervisory capacity as stated, as well as the nature or subject matter of the same for each of the designated years.

2. The names, titles and current company position, if any, of the individual members of such offices, departments, sections, committees or other applicable FWC organizational entity for each of the designated years.

INTERROGATORY NO. 8:

State the name of the office, department, section, committee or other applicable FWC organizational entity having any responsibility for liaison with Fourwheel Corporation regarding the relationship of the Fourwheel Corporation with the National Highway Traffic Safety Administration relative to Federal Motor Vehicle Safety Standards, defect investigations, recalls or other matters involving the Fourwheel line of motor vehicles, for each of the years 1993–2004. State as well, the names, title and current company position, if any, of the individual members of such offices, departments, sections, committees or other applicable FWC organizational entity for each of the designated years.

INTERROGATORY NO. 9:

State the name of the individual or individuals employed by FWC, whether Operating Officers on the Central Staff level, Product Development or Manufacturing Group Vice-President or other applicable FWC organizational title, having primary responsibility for liaison between FWC and the National Highway Traffic Safety Administration, Federal Trade Commission or other federal regulatory agencies having jurisdiction over any aspect of the design, testing, production or marketing of the Fourwheel line of motor vehicles for the years 1993–2004.

INTERROGATORY NO.10:

State for the years 1993–2004, whether FWC has made either formal or informal responses to complaints filed with the National Highway Traffic Safety Administration or its predecessor the National Highway Traffic Safety Board or the Federal Trade Commission, alleging safety related problems with the Fourwheel line of utility motor vehicles or its advertising or promotional literature. If the answer to this interrogatory is in the affirmative, state the name of the individual or group filing such petition or complaint, the date or dates of the same and a brief description of all FWC submissions in response to such petitions or complaints.

INTERROGATORY NO. 11:

State for the years 1993–2004, whether any FWC offices, departments, sections, committees or other applicable FWC organizational entity generated engineering or styling design layouts, specifications, blueprints, models, mathematical analyses, or other renderings of original, intermediate, alternative or final designs of the Fourwheel line of utility motor vehicles, including, but not limited to designs relative to rollbar materials specification, rollbar configuration, rollbar placement and attaching apparatus; windshield framing configuration and attaching apparatus; vehicle center of gravity and track width; and occupant restraint systems

INTERROGATORY NO. 12:

State whether tests were conducted on the Fourwheel line of utility vehicles, whether on a test track or in a laboratory, to determine in whole or in part, the following:

1.   Rollbar strength.

2.   Rollover potential.

3.   Windshield framing stability.

4.   Adequacy of occupant restraint systems.

INTERROGATORY NO. 13

If the answer to Interrogatory No. 12 is in the affirmative, state:

1.   The test number.

2.   The test title.

3.   The requesting office, department, section, committee or individual.

4.   The name of the testing organization.

5.   The make and model of the vehicle tested.

6.   The purpose of the test.

7.   The test conditions and vehicle configuration.

8.   The date and the current location of every such test.

INTERROGATORY NO. 14:

State whether, for the years 1993–2004, tests were conducted by FWC or anyone on their behalf, whether conducted on a test track or in a laboratory, to determine the feasibility of alternate designs other than those eventually incorporated in the production models of the Fourwheel line of utility vehicles.

INTERROGATORY NO. 15:

If the answer to Interrogatory No. 14 is in the affirmative, state:

1.   The test number.

2.   The test title.

3.   The requesting office, department, section, committee or individual.

4.   The name of the testing organization.

5.   The make and model of the vehicle tested.

6.   The purpose of the test.

7.   The test conditions and vehicle configuration.

8.   The date and the current location of every such test.

INTERROGATORY NO. 16:

State whether FWC has ever recommended to the Fourwheel Corporation, changes in the design, materials or attaching apparatus of the rollbars installed in the Fourwheel line of utility vehicles for the years 1993–2004. If the answer is in the affirmative, state the name of FWC offices, departments, sections, committees or individuals making such recommendations, as well as the action, if any, taken by Fourwheel Corporation in response to such recommendations for each of the designated years.

INTERROGATORY NO. 17:

Identify by reference to standard operating procedures number or other applicable FWC organizational designation, the record retention and record destruction policies of FWC, relative to the retention or destruction of records of all types, including but not limited to financial memoranda, engineering memoranda, test reports and customer, retailer or service representative complaints regarding the safety or performance of the Fourwheel line of utility vehicles.

INTERROGATORY NO. 18:

State whether FWC has received any notification or complaints relative to the safety of the Fourwheel line of utility vehicles, from any source, with respect to rollover problems, rollbar failure, occupant restraint systems or windshield framing materials, design and attaching apparatus. If the answer is in the affirmative, state the following for each of the years 1993–2004:

1. The total number of such complaints by reference to the above categories.

2. The name and address of the individual, group or company making such complaint.

3. The FWC office, department, section, committee or individuals processing such complaints.

INTERROGATORY NO. 19:

Identify for the years 1993–2004, all lawsuits, both pending and closed, by case title, jurisdiction, docket number, date of filing and name and address of all plaintiff's counsel, in which FWC was named as a defendant against allegations alleging a negligently or defectively designed Fourwheel utility vehicle, relative to rollover problems; rollbar failure; windshield framing, materials selection or attaching apparatus problems; occupant restraint systems problems; or failure to warn and/or instruct consumers with respect to any or all of such problems.

INTERROGATORY NO. 20:

For each lawsuit referred to in Interrogatory No. 19, state:

1. The model and model year of the vehicle and a brief statement of the alleged defects in said vehicle.

2. The name and address of the owner of such vehicle.

3. A brief description of the factual circumstances giving rise to the lawsuit.

4.   A brief description of the damage alleged to such vehicle.

INTERROGATORY NO. 21:

State the name of the manufacturer of the rollbar installed in the Fourwheel model 2 utility vehicle involved in the instant action, as well as the names of all manufacturers who have manufactured rollbars for the Fourwheel line of utility vehicles for each of the years 1993–2004.

INTERROGATORY NO. 22:

State whether FWC, Fourwheel Corporation or Rollbar, Inc., or any person acting on its behalf has inspected the Fourwheel model 2 utility vehicle involved in the instant action, with respect to the mechanical and/or physical condition of said vehicle, If the answer is in the affirmative, state the dates and location of any such inspection, the identity of the person or organization making such inspection, and whether any written reports and/or photographs were generated as a result of such inspection.

INTERROGATORY NO. 23:

State the name and current address of each person known to FWC who was present or claims to have been present at the scene of the accident giving rise to this lawsuit, as well as the names and current addresses of any other persons known to FWC who claim to have knowledge or information regarding this occurrence.

INTERROGATORY NO. 24:

Does FWC have in its possession any statements of witnesses to this occurrence or photographs of the scene or vehicles involved? If so, state the name and current address of the individuals issuing such statements and the number and subject matter of any photographs.

INTERROGATORY NO. 25:

If FWC was covered by any policy of liability insurance effective on the date of the occurrence giving rise to this action, state the effective dates, policy number, company or companies issuing such policy or policies and the maximum coverage of any such policy for each individual and each occurrence.

§ 16.08   PLAINTIFF'S FIRST SET OF INTERROGATORIES TO DEFENDANT ROLLBAR CORPORATION

Rollbar Corporation

[Manufacturer of the rollbar installed in the jeep-type vehicle in suit.]

The Plaintiff John Q. Consumer, Pursuant to Rule 33 of the Federal Rules of Civil Procedure, requests that the Defendant Rollbar, Inc. answer each of the following interrogatories fully, in writing, under oath, within thirty-three (33) days of service hereof, which interrogatories shall be deemed continuing so as to require prompt supplemental answers if the Defendant obtains or recalls further information relative thereto between the time the answers are submitted to Plaintiff and the time of trial. The answers to these interrogatories should include the knowledge and beliefs of the Defendant.

[Definitions as above]

INTERROGATORY NO. 1:

State the names of the Rollbar, Inc. Corporation (hereinafter referred to as RBI) Divisions, Groups, or Offices having any responsibility for either the design, testing, production or marketing of the Fourwheel Models line of utility motor vehicles and the names of the offices, departments, sections or other functional employee groupings within such Divisions, Groups or Offices, for the years 1993 to 2004, as well as the names, title and current company position, if any, of the individual employees managing such group, office, department or section for each of the designated years.

INTERROGATORY NO. 2:

State the names of the RBI committee or committees having any responsibility for the review of and/or the making of corporate decisions regarding any aspect of the design, testing, production or marketing of the Fourwheel Models line of utility motor vehicles for the years 1993–2004, as well as the names, title, and current company position, if any, of the members of such committee or committees for each of the designated years.

INTERROGATORY NO. 3:

State with particularity, the corporate relationship between Outdoors Motors Corporation and Fourwheel Corporation and Rollbar, Inc., relative to Outdoors Motors Corporation's ownership interest in Rollbar, Inc.

INTERROGATORY NO. 4:

State whether any Outdoors Motors Corporation offices, departments, sections, committees or any other applicable organizational entity of either, or individual employees of either have, for the years 1993–2004, either participated in or exercised supervisory authority in any respect, over Rollbar, Inc. policy or decisions in regard to either the design, testing, production or marketing of the Fourwheel line of utility motor vehicles, including, but not limited to the rollbars installed in such vehicles.

INTERROGATORY NO. 5:

If the answer to Interrogatory No. 4 is in the affirmative, state:

    1.   The name of the office, department, section, committee, or other applicable organizational entity of the aforesaid corporation either

participating in or exercising supervisory capacity as stated, as well as the nature or subject matter of the same for each of the designated years.

2.   The names, titles and current company position, if any, of the individual members of such offices, departments, sections, committees or other applicable Outdoors Motors Corporation organizational entity for each of the designated years.

INTERROGATORY NO. 6:

State whether any Fourwheel Corporation offices, departments, sections, committees or any other applicable Fourwheel Corporation organizational entity, or individual Fourwheel Corporation employees have, for the years 1993–2004, either participated in or exercised supervisory authority in any respect, over Rollbar, Inc. policy or decisions in regard to either the design, testing, production or marketing of the Rollbar, Inc. rollbars installed in the Fourwheel line of utility motor vehicles.

INTERROGATORY NO. 7:

If the answer to Interrogatory No. 6 is in the affirmative, state:

1.   The name of the office, department, section, committee, or other applicable Fourwheel Corporation organizational entity either participating in or exercising supervisory capacity as stated, as well as the nature or subject matter of the same for each of the designated years.

2.   The names, titles and current company position, if any, of the individual members of such offices, departments, sections, committees or other applicable Fourwheel Corporation organizational entity for each of the designated years.

INTERROGATORY NO. 8:

State the name of the office, department, section, committee or other applicable Rollbar, Inc. organizational entity having any responsibility for liaison for Rollbar, Inc. regarding the relationship of Rollbar, Inc. with the National Highway Traffic Safety Administration relative to Federal Motor Vehicle Safety Standards, defect investigations, recalls or other matters involving the Fourwheel line of motor vehicles, for each of the years 1993–2004. State as well, the names, title and current company position, if any, of the individual members of such offices, departments, sections, committees or other applicable Rollbar, Inc. organizational entity for each of the designated years.

INTERROGATORY NO. 9:

State the name of the individual or individuals employed by Rollbar, Inc., whether Operating Officers on the Central Staff level, Product Development or Manufacturing Group Vice-President or other applicable Rollbar,

Inc. organizational title, having primary responsibility for liaison between Rollbar, Inc. and the National Highway Traffic Safety Administration, Federal Trade Commission or other federal regulatory agencies having jurisdiction over any aspect of the design, testing, production or marketing of the Fourwheel line of motor vehicles for the years 1993–2004.

INTERROGATORY NO. 10:

State for the years 1993–2004, whether Rollbar, Inc. has made either formal or informal responses to complaints filed with the National Highway Traffic Safety Administration or its predecessor the National Highway Traffic Safety Board or the Federal Trade Commission, alleging safety related problems with the Fourwheel line of utility motor vehicles or its advertising or promotional literature. If the answer to this interrogatory is in the affirmative, state the name of the individual or group filing such petition or complaint, the date or dates of the same and a brief description of all Rollbar, Inc. submissions in response to such petitions or complaints.

INTERROGATORY NO. 11:

State for the years 1993–2004, whether any Rollbar, Inc. offices, departments, sections, committees or other applicable Rollbar, Inc. organizational entity generated engineering or styling design layouts, specifications, blueprints, models, mathematical analyses, or other renderings of original, intermediate, alternative or final designs of the Fourwheel line of utility motor vehicles, including, but not limited to designs relative to rollbar materials specification, rollbar configuration, rollbar placement and attaching apparatus; windshield framing configuration and attaching apparatus; vehicle center of gravity and track width; and occupant restraint systems.

INTERROGATORY NO. 12:

State whether tests were conducted on the Fourwheel line of utility vehicles, whether on a test track or in a laboratory, to determine in whole or in part, the following:

1.   Rollbar strength.

2.   Rollover potential.

3.   Windshield framing stability.

4.   Adequacy of occupant restraint systems.

INTERROGATORY NO. 13:

If the answer to Interrogatory No. 12 is in the affirmative, state:

1.   The test number.

2.   The test title.

3.   The requesting office, department, section, committee or individual.

4.   The name of the testing organization.

5.   The make and model of the vehicle tested.

6.   The purpose of the test.

7.   The test conditions and vehicle configuration.

8.   The date and the current location of every such test.

INTERROGATORY NO. 14:

State whether, for the years 1993–2004, tests were conducted by Rollbar, Inc. or anyone on their behalf, whether conducted on a test track or in a laboratory, to determine the feasibility of alternate designs other than those eventually incorporated in the production models of the Fourwheel line of utility vehicles.

INTERROGATORY NO. 15:

If the answer to Interrogatory No. 14 is in the affirmative, state:

1.   The test number.

2.   The test title.

3.   The requesting office, department, section, committee or individual.

4.   The name of the testing organization.

5.   The make and model of the vehicle tested.

6.   The purpose of the test.

7.   The test conditions and vehicle configuration.

8.   The date and the current location of every such test.

INTERROGATORY NO. 16:

State whether Outdoors Motors Corporation or Fourwheel Corporation have ever recommended to Rollbar, Inc., changes in the design, materials or attaching apparatus of the rollbars installed in the Fourwheel line of utility vehicles for the years 1993–2004. If the answer is in the affirmative, state the name of the Outdoors Motors or Fourwheel offices, departments, sections, committees or individuals making such recommendations, as well as the action, if any, taken by Rollbar, Inc. in response to such recommendations for each of the designated years.

INTERROGATORY NO. 17:

Identify by reference to standard operating procedures number or other applicable Rollbar, Inc. organizational designation, the record retention and record destruction policies of Rollbar, Inc., relative to the retention or destruction of records of all types, including but not limited to financial memoranda, engineering memoranda, test reports and customer, retailer or service representative complaints regarding the safety or performance of the Fourwheel line of utility vehicles.

INTERROGATORY NO. 18:

State whether Rollbar, Inc. has received any notification or complaints relative to the safety of the Fourwheel line of utility vehicles, from any source, with respect to rollover problems, rollbar failure, occupant restraint systems or windshield framing materials, design and attaching apparatus. If the answer is in the affirmative, state the following for each of the years 1993–2004:

1. The total number of such complaints by reference to the above categories.

2. The name and address of the individual, group or company making such complaint.

3. The Rollbar, Inc. office, department, section, committee or individuals processing such complaints.

INTERROGATORY NO. 19:

Identify for the years 1993–2004, all lawsuits, both pending and closed, by case title, jurisdiction, docket number, date of filing and name and address of all plaintiff's counsel, in which Rollbar, Inc. was named as a defendant against allegations alleging a negligently or defectively designed Fourwheel utility vehicle, relative to rollover problems; rollbar failure; windshield framing, materials selection or attaching apparatus problems; occupant restraint systems problems; or failure to warn and/or instruct consumers with respect to any or all of such problems.

INTERROGATORY NO. 20:

For each lawsuit referred to in Interrogatory No.19, state:

1. The model and model year of the vehicle and a brief statement of the alleged defects in said vehicle.

2. The name and address of the owner of such vehicle.

3. A brief description of the factual circumstances giving rise to the lawsuit.

4. A brief description of the damage alleged to such vehicle.

INTERROGATORY NO. 21:

State the name of the manufacturer of the rollbar installed in the Fourwheel model 2 utility vehicle involved in the instant action, as well as the names of all manufacturers who have manufactured rollbars for the Fourwheel line of utility vehicles for each of the years 1993–2004.

INTERROGATORY NO. 22:

State whether Rollbar, Inc., or any persons acting on its behalf has inspected the Fourwheel model 2 utility vehicle involved in the instant action, with respect to the mechanical and/or physical condition of said vehicle, If the answer is in the affirmative, state the dates and location of any such inspection, the identity of the person or organization making such inspection, and whether any written reports and/or photographs were generated as a result of such inspection.

INTERROGATORY NO. 23:

State the name and current address of each person known to Rollbar, Inc. who was present or claims to have been present at the scene of the accident giving rise to this lawsuit, as well as the names and current addresses of any other persons known to Rollbar, Inc. who claims to have knowledge or information regarding this occurrence.

INTERROGATORY NO. 24:

Does Rollbar, Inc. have in its possession any statements of witnesses to this occurrence or photographs of the scene or vehicles involved? If so, state the name and current address of the individuals issuing such statements and the number and subject matter of any photographs.

INTERROGATORY NO. 25:

If Rollbar, Inc. was covered by any policy of liability insurance effective on the date of the occurrence giving rise to this action, state the effective dates, policy number, company or companies issuing such policy or policies and the maximum coverage of any such policy for each individual and each occurrence.

§ 16.09   SAMPLE INTERROGATORIES: PRESSURIZED STAINLESS STEEL BEVERAGE CANISTER

This set of interrogatories seeks information about the manufacture of a returned pressurized stainless steel beverage canister that exploded while being prepared for sterilization by a worker who was attempting to release the remaining pressure in the tank. Fremantle manufactured the tank. The second defendant is the Polymer Plastic Corporation, the manufacturer of the plastic cap or closure that struck plaintiff's eye as a result of the explosion. The third defendant is the Apex Grinding Company, manufacturer of the pressure release or relief mechanism for incorporation into the stainless steel beverage canister involved herein. Finally, the fourth defendant is the Premier Plastic Corporation, manufacturer of a plastic material known as BasicPro V56-77, that was incorporated into the plastic cap or closure on the pressurized stainless steel beverage canister involved in the Denton case. The sample set will be restricted to selected inquiries to the manufacturer Fremantle, although full sets would also be issued to the other noted defendants.

[See this complaint in § 14.03 *et seq., supra.*]

Denton v. Fremantle Tire and Rubber Company

INTERROGATORY NO. 1:

Please summarize, and identify by reference to standard operating procedures number or other applicable organizational designation, the record retention and record destruction policies, of the defendant THE FREMANTLE TIRE AND RUBBER COMPANY, relative to the retention or destruction of records of all types, including financial memoranda; sales data; test requests, test reports, test summaries, synopses and evaluations; warning decals, labels and labeling or warning or instructional related memoranda and drafts; operating instructions; consumer inquiries; warranty service of particular units; quality control documents; computer archive copies of data; communications with suppliers and distributors of stainless steel pressurized beverage canisters.

INTERROGATORY NO. 2:

Please list for the years 1975 to the present, the office or department and individual or individuals and the company position and current company position, if any, of those who had or currently have as their duties or part of their duties the accumulation and/or summarizing of internal reports, analyses, studies, tests, reviews or working papers in any form, generated by individual engineers, technicians, scientists or others, whether or not in your employ, respecting the issue of the design of or warnings respecting the normal use and handling of pressurized stainless steel beverage canisters.

INTERROGATORY NO. 3:

State, for the years 1975–1987, the names of THE FREMANTLE TIRE AND RUBBER COMPANY committee or committees having any responsibility for the review of and/or the making of corporate decisions regarding any aspect of the design, testing, production, sale or marketing of the pressurized stainless steel beverage canisters of the type involved in this lawsuit, as well as the names, title, and current company position, if any, of the members of such committee or committees for each of the designated years.

INTERROGATORY NO. 4:

Please list, for the years that you have manufactured and/or distributed the pressurized stainless steel beverage canisters of the type involved in this lawsuit, the date, title, author and journal for all published article(s) and all other published information, regardless of the date of publication, and whether or not the author is in your employ, regarding the uses, safety, and potential or actual health hazards associated with the handling of said canisters, on which you relied in the formulation of your design, labeling, warning and instructional policy as regards the manufacture, distribution and/or sale of such canisters.

INTERROGATORY NO. 5:

Please identify for the years 1975 to date, and provide current addresses, for all companies involved in the manufacture of components, assemblies, and sub-assemblies incorporated in the pressurized stainless steel beverage canisters of the type involved in this lawsuit, and briefly describe the component, assembly, or sub-assembly for each company so listed.

INTERROGATORY NO. 6:

Please state whether THE FREMANTLE TIRE AND RUBBER COMPANY is a member of any trade association that addresses the manufacture and/or sale of pressurized stainless steel beverage canisters or canister caps or closures, of the type involved in this lawsuit. If the answer is in the affirmative, state whether any of the officers of the defendant has or are currently serving as officers of directors of any such trade association and indicate the position held and the years in which such person has served in that capacity.

INTERROGATORY NO. 7:

For each year from 1975 to date, please state the number of units of the pressurized stainless steel beverage canisters of the type involved in this lawsuit, sold and/or distributed within the United States by the FREMANTLE TIRE AND RUBBER COMPANY, in which the canister cap or closure was made of plastic and those in which the canister cap was made of steel or other metal materials. Please list separately by cap material for each of the designated years.

INTERROGATORY NO. 8: [TESTING]

Please state whether any tests, experiments or other exercises have been performed on pressurized stainless steel beverage canisters of the type involved in this lawsuit, by or at the direction of THE FREMANTLE TIRE AND RUBBER COMPANY, to determine in whole or in part, the adequacy of pressure release or relief mechanisms, the adequacy and strength of plastic or metal caps or closures, or the feasibility of alternative pressure release or relief mechanisms or cap or closure designs other than those eventually manufactured and sold by the defendant.

If the answer to the foregoing is in the affirmative, for each test identify:

    a.   the company, person, office, or department conducting the test;

    b.   the person requesting the test and the date of the test;

    c.   the model or other identifying name of the canister being tested;

    d.   the purpose for which the test was conducted; and

e. the title or other identifying name for all documents relating to any such test.

Interrogatories of this type [TESTING] are directed to several important blocks of data.

Initially, they solicit information on the core testing program respecting the suspect product unit in the context of the defect modes identified as having causal relevance to the case. Secondly, they focus on the offices, departments, sections, committees and individuals involved in that process over the case time frame. Finally, such questions lend themselves to focused argument respecting their scope in ensuing debates over defendant's obligation to respond. A question formulated along these lines should leave little doubt as to the nature of the information that it seeks and should eliminate needless argument over the essential technical context of the case towards which it is directed.

INTERROGATORY NO. 9:

For each year from 1975 through the present, please identify each model of pressurized canisters which incorporate pressure release or relief mechanisms or plastic or metal caps or closures of the type involved in this lawsuit, manufactured and/or distributed by THE FREMANTLE TIRE AND RUBBER COMPANY and the number of units of each such model distributed and/or sold for each of the designated years.

INTERROGATORY NO. 10:

Please state whether THE FREMANTLE TIRE AND RUBBER COMPANY is a party to any lawsuits, pending or closed, involving the design, manufacture, sale, or distribution of pressurized beverage canisters wherein the plaintiff was allegedly injured while handling or otherwise utilizing any such canister.

If the answer in the affirmative, state:

a. the full caption of the case;

b. the court or jurisdiction in which the case has been filed;

c. the docket number of the case;

d. the date the case was filed;

e. the model of canister involved;

f. the name and address of the opposing party's counsel; and

g. the disposition, if any, of the claims.

INTERROGATORY NO. 11:

State whether THE FREMANTLE TIRE AND RUBBER COMPANY has received any notification or complaints relative to the safety of pressurized beverage canisters of the type involved in this lawsuit, from any source, with respect to explosions of such canisters, including but not limited to the explosion or other failure, under pressure, of the plastic or metal cap or closure on such canisters. If the answer to the foregoing is in the affirmative, state:

    a.   The total number of such complaints by reference to the above categories.

    b.   The name and address of the individual, group or company making such complaint.

    c.   The FREMANTLE TIRE AND RUBBER office, department, section, committee or individuals processing such complaints.

INTERROGATORY NO. 12:

Has THE FREMANTLE TIRE AND RUBBER COMPANY ever offered as optional equipment for the pressurized beverage canisters of the type involved in this case with respect to pressure release or relief mechanisms or cap or closure mechanisms?

If the answer to the foregoing is in the affirmative, state separately, each of such options, the name, part number, catalog number, price and function of all items of optional equipment or features of the types specified, for each of the years 1975 to the present.

INTERROGATORY NO. 13:

Are FREMANTLE TIRE AND RUBBER COMPANY pressurized beverage containers of the type involved in this lawsuit sold in foreign countries? If the answer is in the affirmative, identify each of such countries and the years within which any such sales were made, including the present time.

INTERROGATORY NO. 14:

Identify all voluntary standards, or standards mandated by any agency of the United States government, by issuing body and standards number, that were or are followed in the design, testing, production and marketing of the type of pressurized beverage canisters involved in this lawsuit, including, but not limited to standards prepared and/or issued by the American Society of Mechanical Engineers (ASME) and/or the American National Standards Institute (ANSI).

Information relative to the defendant's relationship with federal regulatory agencies is also a primary subject for discovery. Interrogatories addressing this issue should also be concentrated along the lines of corporate organization rather than being directed towards detailed information.

§ 16.10   SAMPLE INTERROGATORIES: STANDUP FORKLIFT TRUCK

[See this complaint in § 14.12, *supra*.]

INSTRUCTIONS AND DEFINITIONS (as before)

INTERROGATORY NO. 1:

Please state the full name, title, residence address, business address and telephone number of the person completing these interrogatories.

INTERROGATORY NO. 2:

Please identify, for the years 1995 to present, the offices, departments, person or persons, having primary responsibility for communications with the Occupational Safety and Health Administration of the United States government, respecting any aspect of the design, labeling, marketing, distribution, or sale of the STOCKLIFT Pacer Model 60 standup forklift truck manufactured and/or distributed by you.

INTERROGATORY NO. 3:

Please summarize, and identify by reference to standard operating procedures number or other applicable organizational designation, the record retention and record destruction policies, of the STOCKLIFT CORPORATION, relative to the retention or destruction of records of all types, including financial memoranda; sales data; test requests; test reports; test summaries; synopses and evaluations; warning decals; labels and labeling or warning or instructional related memoranda and drafts; operating instructions; consumer inquiries; warranty service of particular units; quality control documents; computer archive copies of data; communications with suppliers and distributors of STOCKLIFT products; and communications to and from the Occupational Safety and Health Administration of the United States government and the Industrial Truck Association (ITA).

INTERROGATORY NO. 4:

Please list for the years 1995 to the present, the office or department and individual or individuals and the company position and current company position, if any, of those who had or currently have as their duties or part of their duties:

    a.   The accumulation and/or summarizing of internal reports, analyses, studies, tests, reviews or working papers in any form, generated by individual engineers, technicians, scientists or others, in your employ, respecting the issue of operator safety or safety design for standup forklift trucks.

    b.   The accumulation and/or summarizing of scientific reports, analyses, studies, tests, reviews or working papers in any form, generated by individual engineers, technicians, scientists or others, not in your employ, respecting the issue of operator safety or safety design for standup forklift trucks.

c. The accumulation and/or summarizing of scientific reports, analyses, studies, tests, reviews or working papers in any form, generated by individual engineers, technicians, scientists or others, not in your employ, respecting injuries to the operators of standup forklift trucks.

d. The preparation and the review and evaluation of the preparation of all labels, labeling, operating instructions, warnings, graphs, diagrams, drawings, illustrations or advertising or promotional material used by the STOCKLIFT Corporation in connection with the distribution and sale of the STOCKLIFT CORPORATION's line of standup forklift trucks.

e. The preparation and the review and evaluation of all standard operating procedures or other memoranda that establish, describe or otherwise address the processes respecting the literature reviews noted in sub-sections (a) through (c).

INTERROGATORY NO. 5:

State the names of the STOCKLIFT CORPORATION committee or committees having any responsibility for the review of and/or the making of corporate decisions regarding any aspect of the design, testing, production, sale or marketing of the STOCKLIFT Pacer Model 60 standup forklift truck for the years 1995–2005, as well as the names, title, and current company position, if any, of the members of such committee or committees for each of the designated years.

INTERROGATORY NO. 6:

Please list, for the years that you have manufactured and/or distributed the STOCKLIFT Pacer Model 60 standup forklift truck, the date, title, author and journal for all published article(s) and all other published information, regardless of the date of publication, whether or not the author is in your employ, regarding the uses, safety, and potential or actual health hazards associated with the operation of standup forklift trucks, on which you relied in the formulation of your labeling, warning and instructional policy as regards the distribution and/or sale of the STOCKLIFT Pacer Model 60 standup forklift trucks.

INTERROGATORY NO. 7:

Please identify all companies involved in the manufacture of components, assemblies, and subassemblies incorporated in the STOCKLIFT Pacer Model 60 standup forklift trucks, and briefly describe the component, assembly, or subassembly for each company so listed.

INTERROGATORY NO. 8:

Please state whether the STOCKLIFT CORPORATION is a member of the Industrial Truck Association. If the answer is in the affirmative, state whether any of the officers of the STOCKLIFT CORPORATION have or are currently serving as officers of directors of the Industrial Truck Association and indicate the position held and the years in which such person has served in that capacity.

INTERROGATORY NO. 9:

State for the years 1995 to the present whether the STOCKLIFT CORPORATION sells standup forklift trucks to any branch of the United States military. If the answer is in the affirmative, state:

a. the branch or branches of the United States military where such units are or have been sold.

b. whether any such standup forklift trucks are built to specification of such military branch or branches.

c. the model of standup forklift truck so sold.

INTERROGATORY NO. 10:

Please state whether any copyrightable material is used in the manufacture, distribution or sale of the STOCKLIFT Pacer Model 60 standup forklift truck, including, but not limited to any and all warnings, labeling, package inserts, graphs and instructional material.

If the answer to the above is in the affirmative, then

a. state the type of work in which a copyright is claimed;

b. identify the author;

c. state the date of creation;

d. state whether the work was registered with the Copyright Office;

e. and, if the work is registered, state the Certificate of Registration number.

INTERROGATORY NO. 11:

Please state whether a patent has been claimed or is being sought in any process, machine, manufacture, composition of matter, or new, original ornamental design incorporated in or used in the design, manufacture, or operation of the STOCKLIFT Pacer Model 60 standup forklift truck.

If the answer is in the affirmative, state:

a. The short title of the invention;

b. The full name and mailing address of the inventor;

c. The government issuing the patent;

    d.   The registration and file number of the patent or patent application; and

    e.   The full name and mailing address of any assignee of the patent.

INTERROGATORY NO. 12:

For each year from 1995 through the present, please state the number of units of the STOCKLIFT Pacer Model 60 standup forklift truck sold and/or distributed within the United States by the STOCKLIFT CORPORATION.

INTERROGATORY NO. 13:

Please state whether any tests, experiments or other exercises have been performed by or at the direction of the STOCKLIFT CORPORATION to determine the extent to which the STOCKLIFT CORPORATION line of standup forklift trucks compare in maneuverability, stability, durability or general functioning compare to standup forklift trucks manufactured by others.

If the answer to the foregoing is in the affirmative, for each test identify:

    a.   the company, person, office, or department conducting the test;

    b.   the person requesting the test and the date of the test;

    c.   the model or the prototype of the standup forklift truck being tested;

    d.   the purpose for which the test was conducted; and

    e.   all documents relating to the test.

INTERROGATORY NO. 14:

Please state whether any tests, experiments or other exercises have been performed by or at the direction of the STOCKLIFT CORPORATION to determine the risk of injury to operators of standup forklift trucks resulting from tip overs, intrusion of objects into the operator's platform, the collision of the forklift into stationery objects or the failure of any of the methods employed in decreasing or stopping the forward or backward motion of the unit.

If the answer to the foregoing is in the affirmative, for each test identify:

a.   the company, person, office, or department conducting the test;

b.   the person requesting the test and the date of the test;

c.   the model or the prototype of the standup forklift truck being tested;

d.   the purpose for which the test was conducted; and

e.   all documents relating to the test.

INTERROGATORY NO. 15:

Please state whether the STOCKLIFT CORPORATION has reviewed and/or had any knowledge of any tests performed by persons other than the STOCKLIFT CORPORATION to determine the risk of injury to operators of standup forklift trucks resulting from tip overs, intrusion of objects into the operator's platform, the collision of the forklift into stationery objects or the failure of any of the methods employed in decreasing or stopping the forward or backward motion of the unit.

If the answer to the foregoing is in the affirmative, for each test identify:

a.   the company, person, office, or department conducting the test;

b.   the person requesting the test and the date of the test;

c.   the model or the prototype of the standup forklift truck being tested;

d.   the purpose for which the test was conducted; and

e.   all documents relating to the test.

INTERROGATORY NO. 16:

For each year from 1995 through the present, please identify each model of standup forklift truck other than the STOCKLIFT Pacer Model 60 standup forklift truck manufactured and/or distributed by the STOCKLIFT CORPORATION and the number of units of each such model distributed and/or sold.

INTERROGATORY NO. 17:

Please state whether the STOCKLIFT CORPORATION is a party to any lawsuits, pending or closed, involving the design, manufacture, sale, or distribution of the STOCKLIFT Pacer Model 60 standup forklift truck wherein the plaintiff was an operator of a Pacer Model 60, allegedly injured while operating such a forklift.

If the answer in the affirmative, state:

a.   the full caption of the case;

b.   the court or jurisdiction in which the case has been filed;

c.   the docket number of the case;

d.   the date the case was filed;

e.   the nature of the cause of action;

f.   the name and address of the opposing party's counsel; and

g.   the disposition, if any, of the claims.

INTERROGATORY NO. 18:

For each lawsuit referred to in Interrogatory NO. 17, state:

   a.   The model and model year of the forklift truck and a brief statement of the alleged defects in said forklift truck.

   b.   The name and address of the owner of such forklift truck.

   c.   A brief description of the factual circumstances giving rise to the lawsuit.

   d.   A brief description of the damage alleged to have been caused by said defect.

INTERROGATORY NO. 19:

Please state the method for determining the identification of the manufacturing plant of a particular unit of the STOCKLIFT Pacer Model 60 standup forklift truck.

INTERROGATORY NO. 20:

Please state, for the years 1995–2001, whether any tests, experiments, design drawings, proposals, renderings or other work was conducted by you, or anyone on your behalf, to determine the feasibility of alternate designs with respect to designs, other than those actually incorporated in the STOCKLIFT Pacer Model 60 standup forklift truck manufactured, distributed and/or sold by you, with respect to the following:

   a.   an expanded deck or other extension to the operator's platform to prevent the operator from being crushed in the event of collision with or intrusion by stationery objects.

   b.   a metal or other sufficiently strong gate across the back of the operator's platform to prevent the operator from being crushed in the event of collision with or intrusion by stationery objects.

   c.   increased width or depth for the operator's platform to allow the operator to more safely or efficiently operate said forklift in emergency situations.

   d.   posts or other protective features around the operator's platform to prevent the operator from being crushed in the event of collision with or intrusion by stationery objects.

   e.   warnings respecting the dangers involved in the operation of said forklift.

INTERROGATORY NO. 21:

If the answer to Interrogatory No. 20 is in the affirmative, state:

   a.   The document title and date.

   b.   The test date and test number.

c.   The requesting office, department, section, committee or individual.

d.   The name of the testing organization.

e.   The make and model of the prototype or standup forklift tested.

f.   The purpose of the test.

g.   Whether a prototype system was built.

h.   The date and the current location of every such test.

INTERROGATORY NO. 22:

State whether the STOCKLIFT CORPORATION has received any notification or complaints relative to the safety of the STOCKLIFT Pacer Model 60 standup forklift truck, from any source, with respect to tip overs, intrusion of objects into the operator's platform, the collision of the forklift into stationery objects or the failure of any of the methods employed in decreasing or stopping the forward or backward motion of the unit. If the answer is in the affirmative, state the following for each of the years from 1995–2001:

a.   The total number of such complaints by reference to the above categories.

b.   The name and address of the individual, group or company making such complaint.

c.   The STOCKLIFT CORPORATION office, department, section, committee or individuals processing such complaints.

INTERROGATORY NO. 23:

State the gross profits generated by the STOCKLIFT CORPORATION resulting from its manufacture, distribution and/or sale of the STOCKLIFT Pacer Model 60 standup forklift truck for each of the years from 1995–2001.

INTERROGATORY NO. 24:

State whether the STOCKLIFT CORPORATION maintains a policy of liability insurance. If the answer is in the affirmative state the name of any and all liability insurance carriers, the policy number or numbers and the limits of any such policies as to each individual and occurrence.

INTERROGATORY NO. 25:

State the names and addresses and telephone numbers of all witnesses known to you who claim to have witnessed the events giving rise to this lawsuit. Also please state whether you have in your possession statements of any such persons, identifying each by witness name.

INTERROGATORY NO. 26:

Describe the name, part number, catalog number, price and function of all items of optional equipment or features available to purchasers of the STOCKLIFT Pacer Model 60 standup forklift truck, for the years 1995 to the present.

INTERROGATORY NO. 27:

Has the STOCKLIFT CORPORATION ever offered as optional equipment for the STOCKLIFT Pacer Model 60 standup forklift truck any of the following or similar equipment or features:

    a.   an expanded deck or other extension to the operator's platform.

    b.   a metal or other sufficiently strong gate across the back of the operator's platform.

    c.   increased width or depth for the operator's platform.

    d.   posts, pillars or other protective features around the operator's platform.

    e.   warnings respecting the dangers involved in the operation of said forklift.

INTERROGATORY NO. 28:

If the answer to the foregoing interrogatory is in the affirmative, state separately, each of such options, the name, part number, catalog number, price and function of all items of optional equipment or features of the types, for the years 1995 to the present.

INTERROGATORY NO. 29:

Are STOCKLIFT Pacer Model 60 standup forklift trucks sold in foreign countries? If the answer is in the affirmative, identify each of such countries and the years within which any such sales were made, including the present time.

INTERROGATORY NO. 30:

Identify all voluntary standards, by issuing body and standards number, that are followed in the design, testing, production and marketing of STOCKLIFT CORPORATION standup forklift trucks, including, but not limited to standards prepared and/or issued by the American Society of Mechanical Engineers (ASME) and/or the American National Standards Institute (ANSI) relative to standup forklift operations and operator safety.

§ 16.11   OBSERVATIONS ON SAMPLE INTERROGATORIES

The above selections of products liability interrogatories may serve as examples of a structured approach to drafting focusing primarily on the identification of the document-generating processes of the corporation and the organizational and individual participants in relevant decision-making processes. Rather than seeking specific facts more appropriately and efficiently obtained through document requests and depositions, interrogatories should aim towards determining the identity of company committee work productive of relevant documents generated within the case time frame. Basic corporate organization consisting of groups, offices, departments, sections and committees allow for a consistent service of interrogatories across product lines. The answers to interrogatories in the products case can often serve as a road map through the details of potentially thousands of pages of material accessed through document requests.

§ 16.12   REQUESTS TO ADMIT FACT OR THE GENUINENESS OF DOCUMENTS

Requests to admit facts under Fed. R. Civ. P. Rule 36 or a state equivalent are not generally considered a major discovery tool in products liability cases.[12] For one thing there are simply too many important factual issues that are nuanced and need

---

[12]   FRCP Rule 36 — Requests for Admission

    (a)   Request for Admission. A party may serve upon any other party a written request for the admission, for purposes of the pending action only, of the truth of any matters within the scope of Rule 26(b)(1) set forth in the request that relate to statements or opinions of fact or of the application of law to fact, including the genuineness of any documents described in the request. Copies of documents shall be served with the request unless they have been or are otherwise furnished or made available for inspection and copying. Without leave of court or written stipulation, requests for admission may not be served before the time specified in Rule 26(d).

    Each matter of which an admission is requested shall be separately set forth. The matter is admitted unless, within 30 days after service of the request, or within such shorter or longer time as the court may allow or as the parties may agree to in writing, subject to Rule 29, the party to whom the request is directed serves upon the party requesting the admission a written answer or objection addressed to the matter, signed by the party or by the party's attorney. If objection is made, the reasons therefore shall be stated. The answer shall specifically deny the matter or set forth in detail the reasons why the answering party cannot truthfully admit or deny the matter. A denial shall fairly meet the substance of the requested admission, and when good faith requires that a party qualify an answer or deny only a part of the matter of which an admission is requested, the party shall specify so much of it as is true and qualify or deny the remainder. An answering party may not give lack of information or knowledge as a reason for failure to admit or deny unless the party states that the party has made reasonable inquiry and that the information known or readily obtainable by the party is insufficient to enable the party to admit or deny. A party who considers that a matter of which an admission has been requested presents a genuine issue for trial may not, on that ground alone, object to the request; the party may, subject to the provisions of Rule 37(c), deny the matter or set forth reasons why the party cannot admit or deny it.

    The party who has requested the admissions may move to determine the sufficiency of the answers or objections. Unless the court determines that an objection is justified, it shall order that an answer be served. If the court determines that an answer does not comply with the requirements of this rule, it may order either that the matter is admitted or that an amended answer be served. The court may, in lieu of these orders, determine that final disposition of the request be made at a pre-trial conference or at a designated time prior to trial. The provisions of Rule 37(a)(4) apply to

careful development over the course of discovery. Any use of this discovery device is sure to result in time consuming motion practice due to defense objections. They are the least utilized of available discovery devices.[13] The opportunities are great for opposing counsel to supply equivocal answers or to allege inability to admit or deny. Most importantly, any such facts that do stand admitted are generally not subject to proof at trial. This can result in gaps in the dynamic presentation of the case that must be filled by the reading of the dry admission responses themselves.[14]

---

the award of expenses incurred in relation to the motion.

   (b)   Effect of Admission. Any matter admitted under this rule is conclusively established unless the court on motion permits withdrawal or amendment of the admission. Subject to the provision of Rule 16 governing amendment of a pretrial order, the court may permit withdrawal or amendment when the presentation of the merits of the action will be subserved thereby and the party who obtained the admission fails to satisfy the court that withdrawal or amendment will prejudice that party in maintaining the action or defense on the merits. Any admission made by a party under this rule is for the purpose of the pending action only and is not an admission for any other purpose nor may it be used against the party in any other proceeding

Illinois Supreme Court Rule 216. Admission of Fact or of Genuineness of Documents

   (a)   Request for Admission of Fact. A party may serve on any other party a written request for the admission by the latter of the truth of any specified relevant fact set forth in the request.

   (b)   Request for Admission of Genuineness of Document. A party may serve on any other party a written request for admission of the genuineness of any relevant documents described in the request. Copies of the documents shall be served with the request unless copies have already been furnished.

   (c)   Admission in the Absence of Denial. Each of the matters of fact and the genuineness of each document of which admission is requested is admitted unless, within 28 days after service thereof, the party to whom the request is directed serves upon the party requesting the admission either (1) a sworn statement denying specifically the matters of which admission is requested or setting forth in detail the reasons why he cannot truthfully admit or deny those matters or (2) written objections on the ground that some or all of the requested admissions are privileged or irrelevant or that the request is otherwise improper in whole or in part. If written objections to a part of the request are made, the remainder of the request shall be answered within the period designated in the request. A denial shall fairly meet the substance of the requested admission. If good faith requires that a party deny only a part, or requires qualification, of a matter of which an admission is requested, he shall specify so much of it as is true and deny only the remainder. Any objection to a request or to an answer shall be heard by the court upon prompt notice and motion of the party making the request.

   (d)   Public Records. If any public records are to be used as evidence, the party intending to use them may prepare a copy of them insofar as they are to be used, and may seasonably present the copy to the adverse party by notice in writing, and the copy shall thereupon be admissible in evidence as admitted facts in the case if otherwise admissible, except insofar as its inaccuracy is pointed out under oath by the adverse party in an affidavit filed and served within 14 days after service of the notice.

   (e)   Effect of Admission. Any admission made by a party pursuant to request under this rule is for the purpose of the pending action and any action commenced pursuant to the authority of section 13-217 of the Code of Civil Procedure (ILL. REV. STAT. 1983, ch. 110, par. 13-217) only. It does not constitute an admission by him for any other purpose and may not be used against him in any other proceeding.

[13] See R. HAYDOCK & HERR, supra note 2, at 375.

[14] See TERRENCE F. KIELY, SCIENCE AND LITIGATION: PRODUCTS LIABILITY IN THEORY AND PRACTICE 355–56 (CRC Press 2002).

Chapter 17

REQUESTS TO PRODUCE DOCUMENTS

SYNOPSIS

§ 17.01 INTRODUCTION

§ 17.02 THE DISCOVERY RULES — DOCUMENT PRODUCTION

§ 17.03 PLANNING DOCUMENT REQUESTS

§ 17.04 THE GENERATION OF CORPORATE DOCUMENTS

§ 17.05 STAGES OF DOCUMENT GENERATION

§ 17.06 SAMPLE: AUTOMOBILE MANUFACTURING PROCESSES

    [A] OVERALL PRODUCT PLANNING

    [B] PRODUCT DESIGN TESTING

    [C] PRODUCT PRODUCTION RUNS

    [D] PRODUCT MARKETING

    [E] PRODUCT POST-MARKETING

§ 17.07 OVERLAP IN DOCUMENT GENERATION

§ 17.08 DRAFTING REQUESTS FOR DOCUMENTS

§ 17.09 SAMPLE REQUEST FOR DOCUMENTS: PRESSURIZED STAINLESS STEEL BEVERAGE CANISTERS

§ 17.10 SAMPLE REQUEST FOR DOCUMENTS: JEEP-TYPE VEHICLE ROLLOVER

§ 17.11 SAMPLE REQUEST FOR DOCUMENTS: STAND-ALONE FORKLIFT TRUCK

§ 17.12 SUPPLEMENTAL DISCOVERY

§ 17.13 SUMMARY

§ 17.01 INTRODUCTION

The central pretrial goal of the plaintiff's lawyer in a products liability case is obtaining of internal working documents created and distributed by the defendant company over the course of the selected time frame. A Request for the Production of Documents, available in the federal and all state discovery schemes, provides the vehicle for this considerable discovery obligation. These requests will generally be rigorously opposed by defense counsel. The intricacies of that effort will be discussed in detail in Chapter 19, Protective Orders and Discovery Enforcement.

Discovery planning is central to the successful prosecution of any litigation. It is especially important in product liability cases. The inherent complexity of tracing the development of a product over a multi-year time frame and the large amount of corporate documentation attendant to such a process mandate an intensive discovery effort. Careful planning and thorough pre-filing research are required to counter defense tactics designed to delay and frustrate discovery.

Discovery is viewed today as liberal in nature. It is believed by the courts to be the most effective way to streamline the search for the truth and to allow counsel to bring the full range of his professional skills to the analysis of the facts underlying the claim. Liberal discovery, however, cannot operate in a factual vacuum. Without adequate pre-filing research and analysis, the only party involved in the case who has detailed knowledge of the nature and extent of those facts is the corporate defendant. This gives the trial court little choice but to lean towards corporate counsel's perspective as to the appropriateness of discovery requests. The greatest amount of time and frustration encountered by plaintiff's counsel in preparing these cases occurs in the discovery process. Adequate discovery is the key to a successful settlement or verdict.

It is important to recall that counsel has only one opportunity to conduct discovery. Plaintiff has the right to supplemental discovery after study of the materials received pursuant to the original issuance of discovery requests. However, he does not have the prerogative of starting fresh if the original discovery was insufficiently thought out and drafted. Getting started on the wrong foot can be fatal to the successful prosecution of these cases. It is essential that the discovery phase of product liability litigation receive close attention before any discovery requests are issued to defendant.

The material to follow will concentrate on effective strategies for both the planning and drafting of document discovery requests. Chapter 19 will address the complexities of motion practice attendant to the discovery phase of product liability litigation. Federal Rule 34 sets the conditions for such requests.

§ 17.02 THE DISCOVERY RULES — DOCUMENT PRODUCTION

FRCP 34. Producing Documents, Electronically Stored Information, and Tangible Things, or Entering onto Land, for Inspection and Other Purposes

(a) In General. A party may serve on any other party a request within the scope of Rule 26(b):

(1) to produce and permit the requesting party or its representative to inspect, copy, test, or sample the following items in the responding party's possession, custody, or control:

(A) any designated documents or electronically stored information — including writings, drawings, graphs, charts, photographs, sound recordings, images, and other data or data compilations — stored in any medium from which information can be obtained either directly or, if necessary, after translation by the responding party into a reasonably usable form; or

(B)   any designated tangible things; or

(2)   to permit entry onto designated land or other property possessed or controlled by the responding party, so that the requesting party may inspect, measure, survey, photograph, test, or sample the property or any designated object or operation on it.

(b)   Procedure.

(1)   Contents of the Request. The request:

(A)   must describe with reasonable particularity each item or category of items to be inspected;

(B)   must specify a reasonable time, place, and manner for the inspection and for performing the related acts; and

(C)   may specify the form or forms in which electronically stored information is to be produced.

(2)   Responses and Objections.

(A)   Time to Respond. The party to whom the request is directed must respond in writing within 30 days after being served. A shorter or longer time may be stipulated to under Rule 29 or be ordered by the court.

(B)   Responding to Each Item. For each item or category, the response must either state that inspection and related activities will be permitted as requested or state an objection to the request, including the reasons.

(C)   Objections. An objection to part of a request must specify the part and permit inspection of the rest.

(D)   Responding to a Request for Production of Electronically Stored Information. The response may state an objection to a requested form for producing electronically stored information. If the responding party objects to a requested form — or if no form was specified in the request — the party must state the form or forms it intends to use.

(E)   Producing the Documents or Electronically Stored Information. Unless otherwise stipulated or ordered by the court, these procedures apply to producing documents or electronically stored information:

(i)   A party must produce documents as they are kept in the usual course of business or must organize and label them to correspond to the categories in the request;

(ii)   If a request does not specify a form for producing electronically stored information, a party must produce it in a form or forms in which it is ordinarily maintained or in a reasonably usable form or forms; and

   (iii)   A party need not produce the same electronically stored information in more than one form.

(c)   Nonparties. As provided in Rule 45, a nonparty may be compelled to produce documents and tangible things or to permit an inspection.

A typical state provision is Illinois Supreme Court Rule 214:

Illinois Supreme Court Rule 214. Discovery of Documents, Objects, and Tangible Things — Inspection of Real Estate provides a typical state version of the Request for the Production of Documents.

Any party may by written request direct any other party to produce for inspection, copying, reproduction photographing, testing or sampling specified documents, objects or tangible things, or to permit access to real estate for the purpose of making surface or subsurface inspections or surveys or photographs, or tests or taking samples, or to disclose information calculated to lead to the discovery of the whereabouts of any of these items, whenever the nature, contents, or condition of such documents, objects, tangible things, or real estate is relevant to the subject matter of the action. The request shall specify a reasonable time, which shall not be less than 28 days except by agreement or by order of court, and the place and manner of making the inspection and performing the related acts. One copy of the request shall be served on all other parties entitled to notice. A party served with the written request shall (1) produce the requested documents as they are kept in the usual course of business or organized and labeled to correspond with the categories in the request, and all retrievable information in computer storage in printed form or (2) serve upon the party so requesting written objections on the ground that the request is improper in whole or in part. If written objections to a part of the request are made, the remainder of the request shall be complied with. Any objection to the request or the refusal to respond shall be heard by the court upon prompt notice and motion of the party submitting the request. If the party claims that the item is not in his or her possession or control or that he or she does not have information calculated to lead to the discovery of its whereabouts, the party may be ordered to submit to examination in open court or by deposition regarding such claim. The party producing documents shall furnish an affidavit stating whether the production is complete in accordance with the request.

A party has a duty to seasonably supplement any prior response to the extent of documents, objects or tangible things which subsequently come into that party's possession or control or become known to that party. This rule does not preclude an independent action against a person not a party for production of documents and things and permission to enter upon real estate.

§ 17.03   PLANNING DOCUMENT REQUESTS

There are several important considerations that the product litigator must address with respect to the planning of or responding to, requests for documents. The cases for plaintiff and defendant typically stand or fall on the timing and content of internal documents received in the course of discovery. There are several initial tasks for counsel for both sides:

1.   Identifying the category of company documents that are routinely contained in corporate archives at the ensuing stages of product development, testing, production, marketing and postmarketing.

2.   Determining of whether those categories of documents over the case time frame would or would not meet the discovery relevancy standard for disclosure.

3.   Assessing initial objections to the requests as filed.

4.   Estimating how to oppose or enforce discovery rights with respect to such documents.

5.   How to organize and analyze them once the appropriate body of documents has been set.

6.   How to rate the investigative or legal significance of any one document with an eye towards including it in the documentary component of defendant's or plaintiff's case-in-chief.

Corporate defendants have no legal obligation to voluntarily identify, organize and package all arguably "relevant" documentation in the course of document discovery. It is incumbent upon plaintiff counsel to assess what documents may be available, over what periods of the case time frame they may have been generated and to clearly identify them by type in succinct requests for documentation. It is also requesting counsel's burden to understand it once received and to read the materials closely for purposes of drafting supplementary requests for documents.

It is of central importance at this point in the discussion to address the topic of the types of documents routinely generated at the design, testing, production, marketing and post-marketing stages of manufacture. These are generally quite similar in related industries such as automobiles or pharmaceuticals.

§ 17.04   THE GENERATION OF CORPORATE DOCUMENTS

All commercial products are planned, tested, produced and marketed with a corporate structure that is quite comparable to other companies in the same or related industries. While there are many hypothetical ways in which any company in an industry could be organized, the reality is that they tend to follow only several classic organizational formats that have been standard for years. Radical shifts in development ideas do not typically change the manner in which things are done. The interest for products litigators here is that there is a consistency in when and how documents are generated and that a fairly similar set of steps followed. Each of these steps or stages will generate corporate documents that tend to be of like kind. The latter point is brought home by the factor of Standard Operating Procedures (SOPs) that guide the form and generic content of corporate documents. Assuming it wanted to, it would be cumbersome for a corporation to try to eliminate sensitive documents that were generated pursuant to standard operating procedures that mandate set forms of document content and distribution along well established systems of corporate communication. These organizational facts of life are of great importance in thinking about and drafting the document discovery stage of the product liability undertaking.

§ 17.05 STAGES OF DOCUMENT GENERATION

An essential pre-trial investigative task is the identification of the categories of documentation consistently generated at the various phases or sub-phase of the totality of the product development, manufacturing and marketing effort. It is also essential to get a rough sense of the system and manner in which that documentation is disseminated throughout the organization, especially today, via electronic communication protocols.

While litigation and corporate experts may vary in choice of labels, the major stages along the product development and manufacturing continuum in large corporations, are principally five: (1) Design, (2) Testing (3) Production, (4) Marketing and (5) Post-Marketing. These broad categories can be further sub-divided for document discovery purposes by a further division of the routine activities that are the primary focus of corporate energies at that point in the overall manufacture of the product.

Documents supporting or weakening the positions of plaintiff or defense counsel are going to be found in one or more of these product development and manufacture stages. Recent release of clinical trial stage documents in the VIOXX cases serve as a contemporary example. In a typical products liability case involving a multi-national corporation defense and plaintiff counsel must be prepared to organize and review many thousands of such documents in the search for those useful or dispositive at trial.

§ 17.06 SAMPLE: AUTOMOBILE MANUFACTURING PROCESSES

A rough breakdown of corporate activities in the development of a new automobile or upgraded model can serve as an example of factors useful in the planning and drafting of document requests in a products liability case. This breakdown is intended to give an idea of the stages products go through and the topics typically encountered that will generate corporate documents that must be sought in the document production phase of the litigation. As was seen in Chapter 16, interrogatories are designed to facilitate this step by eliciting detailed organization data and nomenclature that will greatly support the document production in the case.

The basic stages in any such overall product planning would routinely include the following subjects and resulting documentation.

[A] OVERALL PRODUCT PLANNING

[1]   Market Feasibility Reviews

[2]   Technical Feasibility Reviews

[3]   Financial Feasibility Reviews

[4]   Tooling Reviews

[5]   Regulatory Reviews

[6]   Detailed Component Reviews

[7]   Prototype Testing

[8]   Final Project Approvals

[B] PRODUCT DESIGN TESTING

[1]   Regulatory Certification Testing

[2]   Prospective Regulatory Testing

[3]   Alternative Design Testing

[4]   Detailed Component Testing

[5]   Production Validation Testing

[C] PRODUCT PRODUCTION RUNS

[1]   Finalization of Specifications Manuals

[2]   Production Runs Documentation

[3]   Quality Control Reviews

[D] PRODUCT MARKETING

[1]   Instructions and Warnings Drafting

[2]   Marketing Campaigns (Domestic and International)

[3]   Advertising Campaigns and Media Presentations

[4]   Product Complaint Processing and Reviews

[E] PRODUCT POST-MARKETING

[1]   Post-Production Design Changes

[2]   Advanced Marketing Planning

[3]   Prospective Government Regulatory Activity[1]

---

[1] For an excellent and detailed analysis of key topics in pharmaceutical products cases, see DOUGLAS DANNER & LARRY L. VARN, PATTERN DISCOVERY: PRODUCTS LIABILITY (3d ed. 2003), Chapter 32, Injuries from

[4]   Post-Production Injury Reports

§ 17.07   OVERLAP IN DOCUMENT GENERATION

Each of the above-noted production and manufacturing steps has a separate function from the others in the long process of getting the product to market. As noted, each such phase has within it identifiable, progressive steps each of which, in turn, will normally generate routine types of documents written with predictable document formats. It is important to realize that there is a continuing overlap among the various phases and sub-phases of the product development and manufacturing process. This is so even though each separate phase is primarily involved with a specific task, such as testing, of the total product development and manufacturing cycle. The best that can be done is to isolate within the case time frame the chronological segments *primarily involved* with design, testing, production, marketing and post-marketing. The facts of corporate life are that there will be ongoing generation of documents relating to each of those activities across chronological lines.

Product development work in particular, cannot progress in isolation from future production, marketing and regulatory concerns of the central production and manufacturing project. Accordingly, while each particular stage has specific tasks to complete, each must be considered in its own effect on the total organizational effort. Decisions on a particular design aspect of a specific model line are routinely made with an eye to other planned corporate activities that may be affected. This reality is further complicated by the fact that broad decisions, especially with respect to regulatory policy, are made across model or product category lines.

§ 17.08   DRAFTING REQUESTS FOR DOCUMENTS

As the interrogatories and requests for documentation both target the same generic category of information, they should attempt to follow the same organizational pattern and be grounded in the same areas of interest. Like interrogatories, document requests are directed towards large blocks of data composed of a variety of standard document types routinely generated in predictable stages over the case time frames. Requests pursuant to Rule 34 (FED. R. CIV. P. 34) or a state equivalent, are necessarily best made by reference to generic document types in the initial requests. Once the first wave of documents have been received and studied, supplemental requests for documents will be quite detailed and specific. The initial

---

Drug Products: D. Interrogatories. Areas highlighted by the authors include the following:
    [A]   Similar Products
    [B]   Trade Names
    [C]   Tests and Inspections
    [D]   F.D.A.
    [E]   Recalls
    [F]   Consulting Opinions
    [G]   Advertising
    [H]   Warnings
    [I]   Instructions or Manuals
    [J]   Trade Associations

set however should be drafted around the defect allegations made in the complaint and corporate organizational or operational processes and mechanisms.

What follows in this chapter are three examples of products liability requests for documents. These are provided to serve as examples of a structured approach to this vital stage in the discovery process. The products and defects vary considerably, but the basic approach remains the same.

§ 17.09 SAMPLE REQUEST FOR DOCUMENTS: PRESSURIZED STAINLESS STEEL BEVERAGE CANISTERS

[Complaint set out in § 14.03, *supra*.]

Plaintiff John Denton requests the above named defendant, THE FRE-MANTLE TIRE AND RUBBER COMPANY, to produce and permit plaintiff and his representatives to inspect and copy all documents in the possession, custody or control of the defendant, their subsidiaries, agents or attorneys, which are relevant to the claims and defenses asserted by the parties in this matter or appear reasonably calculated to lead to the discovery of relevant information, which documents are specified more particularly to include the following:

INSTRUCTIONS AND DEFINITIONS

I. "Identify" when used in reference to a person (whether individual, corporation, or other entity), means to state his or its full name, present address and present telephone number if known, and in the case of an individual, his present or last known position and business affiliation.

II. "Identify" when used in reference to a document, means to state the date and author, addressee or intended recipient, type of document, or some other means of identifying it, and its present or last known location or custodian. If such document was, but no longer is, in your possession or subject to your control, state what disposition was made of it.

III. "Document" as used herein, includes but is not limited to, all abstracts, agreements, all physical forms of correspondence, including FAX transmissions, analyses, applications, books, certificates, charter charts, computer print-outs, computer read-outs, computer tapes, contracts, diaries, PDA recorded data, drafts, drawings, estimates, films, forms, graphs, journals, letters, licenses, manuals, maps, meeting reports, memoranda, memoranda of all conversations including telephone calls, notes, orders, opinions, permits, photographs, photo-maps, plans, press releases, recordings, reports, resolutions, sketches, summaries, tapes, telegrams, texts, time records, transcripts, video tapes, writings and work papers, and any copies not identical to the original, regardless whether the documents are an original or a copy and all e-mails, whether ever sent or received or intended to be sent or received, or deleted but not destroyed or otherwise erased from any PDA, laptop, desktop or computer work station.

IV. "Person or persons" means all entities, and without limiting the generality of the foregoing, includes natural persons, joint owners, associations, companies, partnerships, joint ventures, corporations, trusts and estates.

V. The documents to be produced pursuant to this DOCUMENT REQUEST are to include any such information requested for products sold in the United States and in member nations of the European Community (EC), Asia, Africa, Mexico and Central and South America.

VI. The time period covered by these interrogatories is from 1990 to 2005.

DOCUMENTS TO BE PRODUCED

REQUEST NO. 1:

Corporate organization charts or other applicable listings of THE FREMANTLE TIRE AND RUBBER COMPANY for the years 1990 to 2005, including, but not limited to any and all Divisions, Groups, Offices, Departments, Sections, Committees or any other FREMANTLE TIRE AND RUBBER COMPANY functional employee group designations, for those employees having any responsibility for either the design, testing, production or marketing of the pressurized beverage canisters of the type involved in this lawsuit.

REQUEST NO. 2:

The names, company position or title and current company position, if any, of the Vice Presidents or managers of the above-noted THE FREMANTLE TIRE AND RUBBER COMPANY organizational entities and the members of the designated committees for each of the years 1990 to 2005.

REQUEST NO. 3:

Any and all documents, memoranda, summaries, synopses, graphs, computer printouts or other data recordations in any form, either generated or reviewed by THE FREMANTLE TIRE AND RUBBER COMPANY entities referred to above, relative to any aspect of the design, testing, production or marketing of the pressurized beverage canisters of the type involved in this lawsuit, including, but not limited to financial and engineering documents addressing pressure release or relief mechanisms and/or plastic or metal caps or closures for such canisters.

REQUEST NO. 4:

Any and all memoranda, reports, summaries, synopses, engineering or styling design layouts, specifications, blueprints, models, mathematical analyses, or other renderings as respects the original, intermediate, alternative or final designs of the pressurized beverage canisters of the type involved in this lawsuits including, but not limited to designs relative to pressure release or relief mechanisms and/or plastic or metal caps or closures for such canisters.

REQUEST NO. 5:

Any and all final or intermediate test reports, test requests, test summaries, test synopses or test evaluations in any form, in your possession, and whether or not actually conducted by you, of tests that were conducted on pressurized beverage canisters of the type involved in this lawsuit, or any component parts thereof, including, but not limited to any such documents that address in whole or in part, pressure release or relief mechanisms and/or plastic or metal caps or closures for such canisters.

REQUEST NO. 6:

Any and all documents respecting the record retention and record destruction policies, of THE FREMANTLE TIRE AND RUBBER COMPANY, relative to the retention or destruction of records of all types, including financial memoranda; sales data; test requests, reports, summaries, synopses and evaluations; labels and labeling related memoranda and drafts; operating instructions; consumer inquiries; warranty service of particular units; quality control documents; computer archive copies of data; communications with suppliers and distributors of products; and communications to and from the Occupational Safety and Health Administration (OSHA) of the United States government.

REQUEST NO. 7:

Any and all complaints or notices of claimed injury, in any form, and all accident reports resulting from the use or handling of pressurized beverage canisters of the type involved in this lawsuits, which injury arose out of the use or handling of any such canisters.

REQUEST NO. 8:

Any and all labels, decals, operating instructions, warnings, graphs, diagrams, advertising or promotional material, letters or other communications used by THE FREMANTLE TIRE AND RUBBER COMPANY in connection with the distribution and sale of pressurized beverage canisters of the type involved in this lawsuit, including, but not limited to correspondence with respect to the utilization of plastic or metal caps or closures incorporated in such canisters.

REQUEST NO. 9:

Any and all standard operating procedures or other memoranda that establish, describe or otherwise address the processes in THE FREMANTLE TIRE AND RUBBER COMPANY respecting the accumulation, listing, reviewing, summarizing or synopsizing, of scientific, professional, engineering or industry trade association literature addressing the design, testing, manufacture, distribution and/or sale of pressurized beverage canisters or other pressurized canisters in which liquids are stored.

REQUEST NO. 10:

Any and all correspondence between THE FREMANTLE TIRE AND RUBBER COMPANY and the Occupational Safety and Health Administration (OSHA) of the United States government, discussing safety issues as related to the use or handling of the type of pressurized beverage canisters involved in this lawsuit.

REQUEST NO. 11:

Any and all correspondence, reports, or memoranda of any type, exchanged between THE FREMANTLE TIRE AND RUBBER COMPANY and any trade association with respect to the subjects of pressure release or relief mechanisms and/or plastic or metal caps or closures on pressurized beverage canisters, including, but not limited to any such exchanges with the Can Manufacturers Institute, the Closure Manufacturers Association, the Industrial Metal Containers Section of the Material Handling Institute, the Beverage Machinery Manufacturers Association, and the Carbonated Beverage Institute.

REQUEST NO. 12:

Any and all documents, notes, sketches or photographs resulting from any inspection of the pressurized beverage canisters of the type involved in this lawsuit involved in the instant action, with respect to the mechanical and/or physical condition of such canister.

REQUEST NO. 13:

Any statements in any form of witnesses to this occurrence or photographs of the scene or the pressurized beverage canister involved in the occurrence giving rise to this lawsuit.

REQUEST NO. 14:

Any and all catalogs, sales brochures and other marketing literature describing, illustrating or otherwise referencing all optional equipment available for purchasers of THE FREMANTLE TIRE AND RUBBER COMPANY lines of pressurized beverage canisters, including, but not limited to pressure release or relief mechanisms and/or plastic or metal closures for such canisters.

§ 17.10   SAMPLE REQUEST FOR DOCUMENTS: JEEP-TYPE VEHICLE ROLLOVER

The plaintiff John Q. Consumer, pursuant to Rule 34 of the Federal Rules of Civil Procedure, requests that the defendant Fourwheel Corporation, produce and permit plaintiff John Q. Consumer and his representatives to inspect and copy all documents in the possession, custody or control of the defendant, their subsidiaries, agents or attorneys, which are relevant to the claims and defenses asserted by the parties in this matter or appear reasonably calculated to lead to the discovery of relevant information, which documents are specified more particularly to include the following:

INSTRUCTIONS AND DEFINITIONS (as before)

REQUEST NO. 1:

Corporate organization charts or other applicable listings of FWC for the years 1990–2005, including, but not limited to any and all Divisions, Groups, Offices, Departments, Sections, Committees or any other FWC functional employee group designation, for those employees having any responsibility, either independently or in conjunction with offices of the Main Motors Corporation, or Rollbar, Inc., for either the design, testing, production or marketing of the Fourwheel Corporation line of utility motor vehicles.

REQUEST NO. 2:

The names, company position or title and current company position, if any, of the Vice Presidents or managers of the above-noted FWC entities and committees for each of the years 1990-2005.

REQUEST NO. 3:

Any and all documents, memoranda, summaries, synopses, graphs, computer printouts or other data recordations in any form, either generated or reviewed by the FWC entities referred to above, relative to any aspect of the design, testing, production or marketing of the Fourwheel line of utility vehicles, for the years 1990-2005, including, but not limited to financial and engineering documents addressing center of gravity and track width design and testing; rollbar materials selection, design and testing; windshield materials selection, design and testing; and occupant restraint systems.

REQUEST NO. 4:

FWC Annual Report to stockholders for the years 1990-2005.

REQUEST NO. 5:

FWC 10K and 8K filings with the Securities and Exchange Commission for the years 1990-2005.

REQUEST NO. 6:

Any and all documents, memoranda, summaries, synopses, graphs, computer printouts or other data recordations in any form, either generated or reviewed by the FWC entities referred to above, relative to any aspect of the design, testing, production or marketing of the Fourwheel line of utility vehicles for use by the United States military, for the years 1990-2005, including, but not limited to financial and engineering documents addressing center of gravity and track width design and testing; rollbar materials selection, design and testing; windshield materials selection, design and testing; and occupant restraint systems.

REQUEST NO. 7:

FWC corporate organization charts or other applicable listings indicating the name of the office, department, section, committee or other applicable FWC organizational entity having any responsibility for liaison with Fourwheel Corporation regarding the relationship of the Fourwheel Corporation with the National Highway Traffic Safety Administration relative to Federal Motor Vehicle Safety Standards, defect investigations, recalls or other matters involving the Fourwheel line of motor vehicles, for each of the years 1990-2005. Provide as well, documents setting forth the names, title and current company position, if any, of the individual members of such offices, departments, sections, committees or other applicable FWC organizational entity for each of the designated years.

REQUEST NO. 8:

FWC corporate organization charts or other applicable listings indicating the name of the office, department, section, committee or other applicable FWC organizational entity and the name of the individual or individuals employed by FWC, having primary responsibility for liaison between FWC and the National Highway Traffic Safety Administration, Federal Trade Commission or other federal regulatory agencies having jurisdiction over any aspect of the design, testing, production or marketing of the Fourwheel line of motor vehicles for the years 1990-2005.

REQUEST NO. 9:

Any and all submissions, correspondence or other submissions, or any other formal or informal responses to complaints filed with the National Highway Traffic Safety Administration or its predecessor the National Highway Traffic Safety Board or the Federal Trade Commission, or the United States military relative to safety related allegations with respect to the Fourwheel line of utility motor vehicles or its advertising or promotional literature.

REQUEST NO. 10:

Any and all engineering or styling design layouts, specifications, blueprints, models, mathematical analyses, or other renderings of original, intermediate, alternative or final designs of the Fourwheel line of utility motor vehicles, including, but not limited to designs relative to rollbar materials specification, rollbar configuration, rollbar placement and attaching apparatus; windshield framing configuration and attaching apparatus;

vehicle center of gravity and track width; and occupant restraint systems.

REQUEST NO. 11:

Any and all final or intermediate test reports, test requests, test summaries or test synopses in any form, of tests that were conducted on the Fourwheel line of utility vehicles, whether on a test track or in a laboratory, to determine in whole or in part, the following:

1. Rollbar strength.

2. Rollover potential.

3. Windshield framing stability.

4. Adequacy of occupant restraint systems.

REQUEST NO. 12:

Any and all documents respecting the record retention and record destruction policies of FWC, relative to the retention or destruction of records of all types, including but not limited to financial memoranda, engineering memoranda, test reports and customer, retailer or service representative complaints regarding the safety or performance of the Fourwheel line of utility vehicles.

REQUEST NO. 13:

Any and all complaints in any form relative to the safety of the Fourwheel line of utility vehicles, from any source, with respect to rollover problems, rollbar failure, occupant restraint systems or windshield framing materials, design and attaching apparatus.

REQUEST NO. 14:

Any and all documents, notes, sketches or photographs resulting from any inspection of the Fourwheel model 2 utility vehicle involved in the instant action, with respect to the mechanical and/or physical condition of such vehicle.

REQUEST NO. 15:

Any statements in any form of witnesses to this occurrence or photographs of the scene or vehicles involved.

§ 17.11   SAMPLE REQUEST FOR DOCUMENTS: STAND-ALONE FORKLIFT TRUCK

[Complaint set forth in § 14.12, *supra*.]

Plaintiff John Hussey requests the above named defendant, The STOCKLIFT Corporation, pursuant to Illinois Supreme Court Rules 201 and 214, to produce and permit plaintiff and his representatives to inspect and copy all documents in the possession, custody or control of the defendant, their subsidiaries, agents or attorneys, which are relevant to the claims and defenses asserted by the parties in this matter or appear reasonably calculated to lead to the discovery of relevant information, which documents are specified more particularly to include the following:

INSTRUCTIONS AND DEFINITIONS (as before)

REQUEST NO. 1:

Corporate organization charts or other applicable listings of The STOCKLIFT CORPORATION for the years 1990 to 2005, including, but not limited to any and all Divisions, Groups, Offices, Departments, Sections, Committees or any other STOCKLIFT CORPORATION functional employee group designations, for those employees having any responsibility for either the design, testing, production or marketing of the STOCKLIFT Pacer Model 60 standup forklift truck.

REQUEST NO. 2:

The names, company position or title and current company position, if any, of the Vice Presidents or managers of the above-noted The STOCKLIFT Corporation organizational entities and the members of the designated committees for each of the years 1990 to 2005.

REQUEST NO. 3:

Any and all documents, memoranda, summaries, synopses, graphs, computer printouts or other data recordations in any form, either generated or reviewed by The STOCKLIFT CORPORATION entities referred to above, relative to any aspect of the design, testing, production or marketing of the STOCKLIFT Pacer Model 60 forklift trucks, including, but not limited to financial and engineering documents addressing:

a. an expanded deck or other extension to the operator's platform to prevent the operator from being crushed in the event of collision with or intrusion by stationery objects.

b. a metal or other sufficiently strong gate across the back of the operator's platform to prevent the operator from being crushed in the event of collision with or intrusion by stationery objects.

c. increased width or depth for the operator's platform to allow the operator to more safely or efficiently operate said forklift in emergency situations.

d. posts or other protective features around the operator's platform to prevent the operator from being crushed in the event of collision with or intrusion by stationery objects.

e. warnings respecting the dangers involved in the operation of said forklift.

f.　the deadman pedal location and function.

g.　the directional speed control handle.

h.　optional equipment.

i.　accident statistics.

REQUEST NO. 4:

The STOCKLIFT Corporation corporate organization charts or other applicable listings indicating the name of the office, department, section, committee or other applicable The STOCKLIFT Corporation organizational entity and the name of the individual or individuals employed by The STOCKLIFT Corporation, having primary responsibility for liaison between The STOCKLIFT Corporation mv and the Occupational Safety and Health Administration (OSHA) of the United States government or other federal regulatory agencies having jurisdiction over any aspect of the design, testing, production or marketing of the STOCKLIFT Pacer Model 60 standup forklift trucks.

REQUEST NO. 5:

Any and all memoranda, reports, summaries, synopses, engineering or styling design layouts, specifications, blueprints, models, mathematical analyses, or other renderings as respects the original, intermediate, alternative or final designs of the STOCKLIFT Pacer Model 60 standup forklift trucks including, but not limited to designs relative to:

a.　the width, depth and height of the operator's platform.

b.　the deadman pedal.

c.　the directional/speed control.

d.　posts or other protective features around the operator's platform.

e.　warnings, decals, brochures and any educational materials respecting the dangers involved in the operation of said forklift.

REQUEST NO. 6:

Any and all final or intermediate test reports, test requests, test summaries, test synopses or test evaluations in any form, in your possession, and whether or not actually conducted by you, of tests that were conducted on STOCKLIFT standup forklift trucks, including, but not limited to Pacer Model 60 forklift trucks, that addressed in whole or in part, the risk of injury to operators of standup forklift trucks resulting from tip overs, intrusion of objects into the operator's platform, the collision of the forklift into stationery objects or the failure of any of the methods employed in decreasing or stopping the forward or backward motion of the unit.

REQUEST NO. 7:

Any and all final or intermediate test reports, test requests, test summaries, test synopses or test evaluations in any form, in your possession, and whether or not actually conducted by you, of tests that were conducted on STOCKLIFT standup forklift trucks, including, but not limited to Pacer Model 60 forklift trucks, to determine the extent to which The STOCKLIFT CORPORATION line of standup forklift trucks compare in maneuverability, stability, durability or general functioning compare to standup forklift trucks manufactured by others.

REQUEST NO. 8:

Any and all documents respecting the record retention and record destruction policies, of The STOCKLIFT CORPORATION, relative to the retention or destruction of records of all types, including financial memoranda; sales data; test requests, reports, summaries, synopses and evaluations; labels and labeling related memoranda and drafts; operating instructions; consumer inquiries; warranty service of particular units; quality control documents; computer archive copies of data; communications with suppliers and distributors of products; and communications to and from the Occupational Safety and Health Administration of the United States government.

REQUEST NO. 9:

Any and all complaints or notices of claimed injury, in any form, and all accident reports resulting from the operation of a STOCKLIFT standup forklift truck, including, but not limited to the STOCKLIFT Pacer Model 60 standup forklift trucks, which injury arose out of the operation of any such forklift truck.

REQUEST NO. 10:

Any and all labels, decals, operating instructions, warnings, graphs, diagrams, advertising or promotional material used by The STOCKLIFT Corporation in connection with the distribution and sale of STOCKLIFT standup forklift trucks, including, but not limited to the STOCKLIFT Pacer Model 60 standup forklift truck

REQUEST NO. 11:

Any and all standard operating procedures or other memoranda that establish, describe or otherwise address the processes in The STOCKLIFT Corporation respecting the accumulation, listing, reviewing, summarizing or synopsizing, of scientific, professional, engineering or industry trade association literature addressing the design, testing, manufacture, distribution and/or sale of standup forklift trucks.

REQUEST NO. 12:

Any and all correspondence between The STOCKLIFT CORPORA-
TION and the Occupational Safety and Health Administration (OSHA) of
the United States government, respecting operator safety in the operation
of standup forklift trucks, including, but not limited to:

a. an expanded deck or other extension to the operator's platform to
prevent the operator from being crushed in the event of collision
with or intrusion by stationery objects.

b. a metal or other sufficiently strong gate across the back of the
operator's platform to prevent the operator from being crushed in
the event of collision with or intrusion by stationery objects.

c. increased width or depth for the operator's platform to allow the
operator to more safely or efficiently operate said forklift in
emergency situations.

d. posts or other protective features around the operator's platform to
prevent the operator from being crushed in the event of collision
with or intrusion by stationery objects.

e. warnings respecting the dangers involved in the operation of
standup forklift trucks.

f. the deadman pedal location and function.

g. the directional speed control handle.

h. optional equipment.

i. accident statistics.

j. recommended standards prepared for the American Society of
Mechanical Engineers (ASME) and/or the American National Standards Institute (ANSI) relative to standup forklift operations and
operator safety.

REQUEST NO. 13:

Any and all correspondence between The STOCKLIFT CORPORA-
TION and the Industrial Truck Association (ITA) respecting operator
safety in the operation of standup forklift trucks, including, but not limited
to:

a. an expanded deck or other extension to the operator's platform to
prevent the operator from being crushed in the event of collision
with or intrusion by stationery objects.

b. a metal or other sufficiently strong gate across the back of the
operator's platform to prevent the operator from being crushed in
the event of collision with or intrusion by stationery objects.

c. increased width or depth for the operator's platform to allow the
operator to more safely or efficiently operate said forklift in

emergency situations.

d.   posts or other protective features around the operator's platform to prevent the operator from being crushed in the event of collision with or intrusion by stationery objects.

e.   warnings respecting the dangers involved in the operation of standup forklift trucks.

f.   the deadman pedal location and function.

g.   the directional speed control handle.

h.   optional equipment.

i.   accident statistics.

j.   recommended standards prepared for the American Society of Mechanical Engineers (ASME) and/or the American National Standards Institute (ANSI) relative to standup forklift operations and operator safety.

REQUEST NO. 14:

Any and all documents, notes, sketches or photographs resulting from any inspection of the STOCKLIFT Pacer Model 60 standup forklift truck involved in the instant action, with respect to the mechanical and/or physical condition of such truck.

REQUEST NO. 15:

Any statements in any form of witnesses to this occurrence or photographs of the scene or STOCKLIFT Pacer Model 60 standup forklift truck involved in the occurrence giving rise to this lawsuit.

REQUEST NO. 16:

Any and all catalogs, sales brochures and other marketing literature describing, illustrating or otherwise referencing all optional equipment available for purchasers of The STOCKLIFT CORPORATION lines of standup forklift trucks, including, but not limited to the STOCKLIFT Pacer Model 60 standup forklift truck.

REQUEST NO. 17:

Any and all correspondence between The STOCKLIFT CORPORATION and the Department of Defense or any branch of the United States military respecting operator safety in the operation of standup forklift trucks, including, but not limited to:

a.   an expanded deck or other extension to the operator's platform to prevent the operator from being crushed in the event of collision with or intrusion by stationery objects.

b. a metal or other sufficiently strong gate across the back of the operator's platform to prevent the operator from being crushed in the event of collision with or intrusion by stationery objects.

c. increased width or depth for the operator's platform to allow the operator to more safely or efficiently operate said forklift in emergency situations.

d. posts or other protective features around the operator's platform to prevent the operator from being crushed in the event of collision with or intrusion by stationery objects.

e. warnings respecting the dangers involved in the operation of standup forklift trucks.

f. the deadman pedal location and function.

g. the directional speed control handle.

h. optional equipment.

i. accident statistics.

j. recommended standards prepared for the American Society of Mechanical Engineers (ASME) and/or the American National Standards Institute (ANSI) relative to standup forklift operations and operator safety.

§ 17.12 SUPPLEMENTAL DISCOVERY

Federal Rule of Civil Procedure 26(e) and comparable state provisions impose a continuing duty to supplement any incomplete discovery responses and correct any inaccuracies.[2] Counsel should insist on these requirements.

However, it is unwise to do so in lieu of comprehensive supplemental interrogatories and requests for documentation. It must be recalled that the right to supplemental discovery does not mean that counsel can start over fresh if defendant's submissions show serious flaws in plaintiff's original discovery plan.[3]

During the course of counsel's close examination of documents obtained in the initial round of discovery, many questions will appear that could not have reasonably been anticipated prior to having had the chance to organize and closely read the documents. This initial review will normally reveal the existence of large amounts of additional documentation referenced therein that counsel will need to fill the

---

[2] *See* HAYDOCK, HERR & STEMPEL'S FUNDAMENTALS OF PRETRIAL LITIGATION (American Casebook Series®, 5th ed. 2001), Part Three, Discovery Practice: Depositions, Interrogatories, Requests for Production and Physical Examinations, Requests for Admissions, Enforcing Discovery Rights. *See also* ANATOMY OF A PERSONAL INJURY LAWSUIT: CREATIVE DISCOVERY (ATLA PRESS); FULL DISCLOSURE: COMBATING STONEWALLING AND OTHER DISCOVERY ABUSES (ATLA PRESS); SCOTT BALDWIN, FRANCIS H. HARE, JR. & FRANCIS E. MCGOVERN, PREPARATION OF A PRODUCT LIABILITY CASE (Aspen Publishers) [Latest Supplemented Date: Apr. 4, 2005]; DANNER & VARN, *supra* note 1.

[3] *See* TERRENCE F. KIELY, SCIENCE AND LITIGATION: PRODUCTS LIABILITY IN THEORY AND PRACTICE 361–62 (CRC Press 2002).

documentary gaps that will be encountered in the initial document analysis. Rule 26(e) allows for supplemental discovery and counsel should take full advantage of it.

§ 17.13 SUMMARY

Chapter 19, Protective Orders, Discovery Enforcement and Motions-In-Limine will return to the major themes of products liability discovery in the context of defense motions for comprehensive protective orders, based upon trade secrets and other objections to publication. It will also address in detail motion practice centered in discovery enforcement and requests for discovery sanctions. Requests for motions-in-limine seeking to bar certain evidence such as that considered to be subsequent remedial measures will also be discussed.

Chapter 18

DISCOVERY AND EVIDENCE DEPOSITIONS

SYNOPSIS

§ 18.01 INTRODUCTION

§ 18.02 THE DEPOSITION RULES

§ 18.03 RELEVANCY AND DEPOSITIONS

§ 18.04 OBJECTIONS IN DEPOSITIONS

§ 18.05 DEPOSITION PLANNING

§ 18.06 DOCUMENT ORGANIZATION AND DEPOSITION PREPARATION

§ 18.07 DEPOSING DEFENSE EXPERTS

§ 18.01 INTRODUCTION

Discovery depositions provide the opportunity for the requesting party to ask the corporate defendant's key personnel a series of very detailed inquiries about the design, testing, production, marketing and post-marketing phases of the product development cycle involving the product under scrutiny. Sophisticated pre-filing scientific, regulatory, industry and company research sets the stage for the type of intensive discovery discussed in the preceding chapters. That effort, in turn, supplies the groundwork for discovery or evidence depositions, which serve several central purposes in the pretrial process. Gaps in the chronology of events reflected in the answers to interrogatories and requests for documents may be filled. The names and function of all relevant committees and the details about personnel involved in generating important documents may be ascertained. The defendant's interpretation of key documents can be determined, as well as the fine points of defendant's defense. The depositions of expert witnesses can provide clear knowledge of the expert's positions and the bases for them from his or her experience and the relevant scientific literature.

There is a very large and growing body of deposition guides to practice available from respected trial lawyer organizations such as the National Institute for Trial Advocacy (NITA),[1] the Defense Research Institute (DRI) and the Association of

---

[1] An excellent overview and guide to the taking of depositions is provided in the National Institute for Trial Advocacy publication entitled THE EFFECTIVE DEPOSITION: TECHNIQUES AND STRATEGIES THAT WORK (NITA Practical Guide Series 2001), written by David M. Malone and Peter T. Hoffman. This volume, also available on Amazon, addresses key components of successful deposition practice: Purposes of Taking Depositions; Advantages and Disadvantages of Depositions; Planning and Scheduling Deposi-

Trial Lawyers of America (ATLA). State bar journals and specialty journals aimed at the trial lawyers are filled with deposition advice from planning to execution.[2] There are also numerous purely commercial offerings by a variety of providers in the burgeoning area of skills literature, audio-tapes and DVDs.[3] Each of the 50 state bar associations and the federal bar[4] also provide a steady stream of continuing legal education courses and specialty deposition training programs.[5]

---

tions; Preparing to Take the Deposition; Questioning Techniques; Style, Organization, and Other Matters; Using Documents; Preparing the Witness to be Deposed; Defending the Deposition; Depositions for Use at Trial; Videotape Depositions; Overview of the Expert Deposition.

See also Stuart M. Israel, *Twelve Deposition Principles, Mechanics, Strategies, and Practices*, PRAC. LITIG. (May 2004), at 31. (This excellent article addresses 12 basic deposition principles, mechanics, strategies, and practices, including who may be deposed, when, where, and how to get them there, limitations on the number and duration of depositions, the relationship between depositions and "paper" discovery, "Rambo" litigation tactics, and "other nuts, bolts, and screws that hold the deposition process together.")

[2] There are a number of excellent contemporary articles discussing deposition practice aimed at both neophyte and veteran. They are well worth consulting. *See, e.g., Effective Depositions in Employment and Other Cases*, PRAC. LITIG. (July 2005), at 35. (There are no secrets to a good deposition, just a lot of preparation.); David S. Wachen, *Preparing Fact Witnesses for Deposition*, PRAC. LITIG. (July 2005), at 7 (With the exception of the "pros" who have been through depositions on many occasions, the typical fact witness is likely to be both curious and a little apprehensive about the deposition process. So your preparation must put the witness at ease to the extent possible. You can do this by explaining the process, who will be there, how it will happen, and what the basic rules are. Nearly all witnesses will find considerable comfort in this kind of preparation. And with the confidence that it inspires, they will be effective witnesses who will know what to say — and what not to say.) *Id.* at 11; Paul Horowitz, *Deposition Tips Your Parents Taught You*, N.Y.S. B.J. 18 (Mar./Apr. 2005) (An amusing but informative article on the basic principles of communication we were supposed to absorb as children.); Association of Trial Lawyers of America (ATLA), ATLA Winter 2003 Convention Reference Materials, Advocacy Track: *Discovery Can Make Your Case — How to Do It Right, Planning and Executing Depositions* (Numerous pointed articles on all aspects of pretrial discovery applicable to products liability litigation, with a focus on planning.); Association of Trial Lawyers of America (ATLA), Feb. 2001 ATLA Winter Convention Reference Materials, Advocacy Track: *Getting Full Disclosure — Discovery and Depositions, Practical Aspects of Planning and Executing Depositions*; Charles H. Samel, *The Five People You Meet Preparing for Your Deposition*, 31 No. 4 LITIG. 35 (2005) (Interesting article on preparing company executives for deposition.); Stephen M. Terrell, *Preparing Your Client for a Video Deposition*, 48-DEC. RES GESTAE 26 (2004); Nina Ivanichvili, *A Lawyer's Guide to Cross-Cultural Depositions*, 28-OCT. CHAMPION 38 (2004) (Interesting and useful discussion regarding the deposition of foreign nationals, an increasing factor in products liability cases involving multi-national corporations.).

[3] See, for example, the website of the National Institute of Trial Lawyers (NITA), http://www.nita.org/, for a listing of locations for deposition planning and skills seminars and materials available for purchase. The American Trial Lawyers Association website and print publications provide a large amount of information about effective deposition planning and practice in the form of seminars, current and past, audio and video tapes and DVD, as well as print and digital copies of depositions actually conducted in a wide variety of product liability cases. *See* http://www.atla.org/. The Defense Law Research Site also offers a wealth of information on the effective planning and execution of depositions in products liability cases of all types at http://www.dri.org.

[4] See the listings of discovery related continuing legal education programs at http://www.fedbar.org/cle.html.

[5] A simple Google search on *state bar deposition* will yield hundreds of listings for deposition training and reading and viewing materials. The same result will be had when searching for interrogatories and document discovery.

§ 18.02 THE DEPOSITION RULES

The utilization of discovery and evidence depositions, as with most discovery rules, is comparable in federal and state court practice.[6] Depositions in federal courts are controlled by Federal Rules of Civil Procedure Rule 30, which provides in part:

FRCP Rule 30 — Depositions Upon Oral Examination

(a)　When a Deposition May Be Taken.

(1)　Without Leave. A party may, by oral questions, depose any person, including a party, without leave of court except as provided in Rule 30(a)(2). The deponent's attendance may be compelled by subpoena under Rule 45.

(2)　With Leave. A party must obtain leave of court, and the court must grant leave to the extent consistent with Rule 26(b)(2):

(A)　if the parties have not stipulated to the deposition and:

(i)　the deposition would result in more than 10 depositions being taken under this rule or Rule 31 by the plaintiffs, or by the defendants, or by the third-party defendants;

(ii)　the deponent has already been deposed in the case; or

(iii)　the party seeks to take the deposition before the time specified in Rule 26(d), unless the party certifies in the notice, with supporting facts, that the deponent is expected to leave the United States and be unavailable for examination in this country after that time; or

(B)　if the deponent is confined in prison.

(b)　Notice of the Deposition; Other Formal Requirements.

(1)　Notice in General. A party who wants to depose a person by oral questions must give reasonable written notice to every other party. The notice must state the time and place of the deposition and, if known, the deponent's name and address. If the name is unknown, the notice must provide a general description sufficient to identify the person or the particular

---

[6] For depositions taken in foreign countries, see generally George Blum, 26B C.J.S. Depositions § 26, Corpus Juris Secundum (Database updated June 2005):

Depositions may be taken in foreign countries only before persons authorized to take depositions, examine witnesses, or administer oaths therein . . . Under some statutes depositions are authorized to be taken in other jurisdictions before persons empowered to take depositions, examine witnesses, or administer oaths therein. Such depositions can be taken only by officials of the kind or class designated. In some jurisdictions, an American consul or vice consul residing in a foreign country and duly accredited there is authorized to take depositions in such country. . . . The rule that when assistance is asked of an officer of another state or country in matter of taking testimony, affidavits, or administering oaths for use in local forum, if it is performed, it is done by virtue of local and not foreign authority, applies to authority which may be extended by federal government.

class or group to which the person belongs.

(2)   Producing Documents. If a subpoena duces tecum is to be served on the deponent, the materials designated for production, as set out in the subpoena, must be listed in the notice or in an attachment. The notice to a party deponent may be accompanied by a request under Rule 34 to produce documents and tangible things at the deposition.

(3)   Method of Recording.

    (A)   Method Stated in the Notice. The party who notices the deposition must state in the notice the method for recording the testimony. Unless the court orders otherwise, testimony may be recorded by audio, audiovisual, or stenographic means. The noticing party bears the recording costs. Any party may arrange to transcribe a deposition.

    (B)   Additional Method. With prior notice to the deponent and other parties, any party may designate another method for recording the testimony in addition to that specified in the original notice. That party bears the expense of the additional record or transcript unless the court orders otherwise.

(4)   By Remote Means. The parties may stipulate — or the court may on motion order — that a deposition be taken by telephone or other remote means. For the purpose of this rule and Rules 28(a), 37(a)(2), and 37(b)(1), the deposition takes place where the deponent answers the questions.

(5)   Officer's Duties.

    (A)   Before the Deposition. Unless the parties stipulate otherwise, a deposition must be conducted before an officer appointed or designated under Rule 28. The officer must begin the deposition with an on-the-record statement that includes:

        (i)   the officer's name and business address;

        (ii)   the date, time, and place of the deposition;

        (iii)   the deponent's name;

        (iv)   the officer's administration of the oath or affirmation to the deponent; and

        (v)   the identity of all persons present.

    (B)   Conducting the Deposition; Avoiding Distortion. If the deposition is recorded nonstenographically, the officer must repeat the items in Rule 30(b)(5)(A)(i)–(iii) at the beginning of each unit of the recording medium. The deponent's and attorneys' appearance or demeanor must not be distorted through recording techniques.

(C)   After the Deposition. At the end of a deposition, the officer must state on the record that the deposition is complete and must set out any stipulations made by the attorneys about custody of the transcript or recording and of the exhibits, or about any other pertinent matters.

(6)   Notice or Subpoena Directed to an Organization. In its notice or subpoena, a party may name as the deponent a public or private corporation, a partnership, an association, a governmental agency, or other entity and must describe with reasonable particularity the matters for examination. The named organization must then designate one or more officers, directors, or managing agents, or designate other persons who consent to testify on its behalf; and it may set out the matters on which each person designated will testify. A subpoena must advise a nonparty organization of its duty to make this designation. The persons designated must testify about information known or reasonably available to the organization. This paragraph (6) does not preclude a deposition by any other procedure allowed by these rules.

(c)   Examination and Cross-Examination; Record of the Examination; Objections; Written Questions.

(1)   Examination and Cross-Examination. The examination and cross-examination of a deponent proceed as they would at trial under the Federal Rules of Evidence, except Rules 103 and 615. After putting the deponent under oath or affirmation, the officer must record the testimony by the method designated under Rule 30(b)(3)(A). The testimony must be recorded by the officer personally or by a person acting in the presence and under the direction of the officer.

(2)   Objections. An objection at the time of the examination — whether to evidence, to a party's conduct, to the officer's qualifications, to the manner of taking the deposition, or to any other aspect of the deposition — must be noted on the record, but the examination still proceeds; the testimony is taken subject to any objection. An objection must be stated concisely in a nonargumentative and nonsuggestive manner. A person may instruct a deponent not to answer only when necessary to preserve a privilege, to enforce a limitation ordered by the court, or to present a motion under Rule 30(d)(3).

(3)   Participating Through Written Questions. Instead of participating in the oral examination, a party may serve written questions in a sealed envelope on the party noticing the

deposition, who must deliver them to the officer. The officer must ask the deponent those questions and record the answers verbatim.

(d)   Duration; Sanction; Motion to Terminate or Limit.

   (1)   Duration. Unless otherwise stipulated or ordered by the court, a deposition is limited to 1 day of 7 hours. The court must allow additional time consistent with Rule 26(b)(2) if needed to fairly examine the deponent or if the deponent, another person, or any other circumstance impedes or delays the examination.

   (2)   Sanction. The court may impose an appropriate sanction — including the reasonable expenses and attorney's fees incurred by any party — on a person who impedes, delays, or frustrates the fair examination of the deponent.

   (3)   Motion to Terminate or Limit.

      (A)   Grounds. At any time during a deposition, the deponent or a party may move to terminate or limit it on the ground that it is being conducted in bad faith or in a manner that unreasonably annoys, embarrasses, or oppresses the deponent or party. The motion may be filed in the court where the action is pending or the deposition is being taken. If the objecting deponent or party so demands, the deposition must be suspended for the time necessary to obtain an order.

      (B)   Order. The court may order that the deposition be terminated or may limit its scope and manner as provided in Rule 26(c). If terminated, the deposition may be resumed only by order of the court where the action is pending.

      (C)   Award of Expenses. Rule 37(a)(5) applies to the award of expenses.

(e)   Review by the Witness; Changes.

   (1)   Review; Statement of Changes. On request by the deponent or a party before the deposition is completed, the deponent must be allowed 30 days after being notified by the officer that the transcript or recording is available in which:

      (A)   to review the transcript or recording; and

      (B)   if there are changes in form or substance, to sign a statement listing the changes and the reasons for making them.

   (2)   Changes Indicated in the Officer's Certificate. The officer must note in the certificate prescribed by Rule 30(f)(1) whether a review was requested and, if so, must attach any changes the

deponent makes during the 30-day period.

(f) Certification and Delivery; Exhibits; Copies of the Transcript or Recording; Filing.

(1) Certification and Delivery. The officer must certify in writing that the witness was duly sworn and that the deposition accurately records the witness's testimony. The certificate must accompany the record of the deposition. Unless the court orders otherwise, the officer must seal the deposition in an envelope or package bearing the title of the action and marked "Deposition of [witness's name]" and must promptly send it to the attorney who arranged for the transcript or recording. The attorney must store it under conditions that will protect it against loss, destruction, tampering, or deterioration.

(2) Documents and Tangible Things.

(A) Originals and Copies. Documents and tangible things produced for inspection during a deposition must, on a party's request, be marked for identification and attached to the deposition. Any party may inspect and copy them. But if the person who produced them wants to keep the originals, the person may:

(i) offer copies to be marked, attached to the deposition, and then used as originals — after giving all parties a fair opportunity to verify the copies by comparing them with the originals; or

(ii) give all parties a fair opportunity to inspect and copy the originals after they are marked — in which event the originals may be used as if attached to the deposition.

(B) Order Regarding the Originals. Any party may move for an order that the originals be attached to the deposition pending final disposition of the case.

(3) Copies of the Transcript or Recording. Unless otherwise stipulated or ordered by the court, the officer must retain the stenographic notes of a deposition taken stenographically or a copy of the recording of a deposition taken by another method. When paid reasonable charges, the officer must furnish a copy of the transcript or recording to any party or the deponent.

(4) Notice of Filing. A party who files the deposition must promptly notify all other parties of the filing.

(g) Failure to Attend a Deposition or Serve a Subpoena; Expenses. A party who, expecting a deposition to be taken, attends in person or by an attorney may recover reasonable expenses for attending, including attorney's fees, if the noticing party failed to:

(1)   attend and proceed with the deposition; or

(2)   serve a subpoena on a nonparty deponent, who consequently did not attend.

State court discovery schemes by and large have adopted the broad principles of the Federal Rules of Civil Procedure, which allow discovery depositions in some settings to be used as evidence at trial.[7]

§ 18.03   RELEVANCY AND DEPOSITIONS

Relevancy controls the flow of questions and answers in depositions as it does all of the discovery devices. It is important to remember that the term has an expansive meaning in discovery, including discovery depositions.[8] This principal was recently stressed in a state court context in the 2005 Illinois decision in *Tomczak v. Ingalls Memorial Hospital*,[9] where the defendant hospital contended that the circuit court abused its discretion by ordering compliance with the discovery request because the information sought was not so material or relevant as to justify the burden of securing its disclosure. The Circuit Court granted an administrators' motion to compel information related to emergency room records of nonparty patients. The hospital refused, and on its own motion, was held in contempt and fined $50 for refusal to comply. The appellate court rejected the hospital's argument based on relevancy:

> Supreme Court Rule 201(b)(1) allows a party to "obtain by discovery full disclosure regarding any matter relevant to the subject matter involved in the pending action." (Citations omitted.) The circuit court is afforded great latitude in determining the scope of pretrial discovery, as the concept of

---

[7] Illinois is the only jurisdiction in the United States that promotes separate discovery and evidence depositions:

> While many of the state discovery rules — and civil procedural rules in general — have moved toward the model of the federal rules, Illinois has stridently held onto its two-step deposition strategy. It is time to relinquish the notion that the two-step requirement serves a legitimate purpose.
>
> In Illinois, unless specified otherwise, a deposition is by default limited to discovery. If both discovery and evidence depositions are desired of the same witness they must be taken separately, unless the parties stipulate otherwise or the court orders otherwise upon notice and motion. This rule establishes a clear delineation between discovery depositions and evidence depositions in Illinois.

See Mark E. McNabola, *It's Time to Move Beyond Separate Discovery and Evidence Depositions in Illinois*, ILL. B.J., July 2004, at 344.

[8] *See* In re StarFlite Management Group, Inc., 162 S.W.3d 409 (Tex. App. 2005). (Although the scope of discovery is broad, requests must show a reasonable expectation of obtaining information that will aid the dispute's resolution; therefore, discovery requests must be reasonably tailored to include only relevant matters.); Stewart v. Colonial Western Agency, Inc., 87 Cal. App. 4th 1006, 105 Cal. Rptr. 2d 115 (2001) (Admissibility is not the test and information unless privileged, is discoverable if it might reasonably lead to admissible evidence. . . . These rules are applied liberally in favor of discovery, and (contrary to popular belief), fishing expeditions are permissible in some cases.). *See also* David Young, *A New Theory of Relativity: The Triumph of the Irrelevant at Depositions*, 36 UWLA L. REV. 56 (2005) (Discussing the wide range of opinion on the idea of "relevancy" in a discovery deposition context as opposed to a trial.).

[9] 834 N.E.2d 549 (Ill. App. Ct. 2005).

relevance for discovery purposes encompasses not only what is admissible at trial, but also that which may lead to the discovery of admissible evidence. (Citations omitted.) We will reverse a circuit court's ruling on a motion to compel discovery only where the appellant "affirmatively and clearly" shows an abuse of discretion.[10]

Here, the information requested contained neither the nonparty patients' names, nor a history of their prior or present medical conditions, treatments, or diagnoses. As such, the court concluded that the nonparty patients' identities could not be determined from the information the court ordered Ingalls to disclose. Accordingly, the court ruled that the nonparty patients' triage times, treatment times, and triage acuity designations fall outside the category of "protected health information." Moreover, the court continued, even if they were to assume arguendo that the information sought was "protected health information," they would still find that it was discoverable in the absence of a qualified protective order.[11]

Attempts by a party to stay discovery pending a motion to dismiss the complaint typically fall on deaf ears. This important issue was recently addressed in the 2005 case of *Evitts v. DaimlerChrysler Motors Corp.*,[12] where automobile owners brought a putative class action suit against automobile manufacturer and extended service contract provider alleging breach of warranty and violation of consumer protection statutes based on allegedly defective rear window defroster. The court stressed the function of discovery in helping the plaintiff to refine or even establish his theory of liability during the discovery process:

Plaintiffs contended that the circuit court abused its discretion by staying discovery pending its ruling on DCMC's motion to dismiss. They argued that the court's refusal to reopen discovery in effect required them to prove their case at the pleading stage and violated Supreme Court Rule 201(a). Defendants responded that the circuit court was correct to circumscribe discovery because plaintiffs' discovery requests were overly broad and were submitted with the intent of supporting wide-ranging class action litigation, when plaintiffs' complaints were insufficient to allege their own individual claims.

The court supported plaintiff's position, stating:

Parties may obtain discovery by full disclosure regarding any relevant matter, even where the discovery relates to the claims of the parties seeking disclosure. (Citations omitted.) A circuit court has wide latitude in ruling on discovery motions, and we will not disturb such a ruling unless it constitutes a manifest abuse of discretion. A court abuses its discretion only

---

[10] *Id.* at 556 (*citing* Dufour v. Mobil Oil Corp., 703 N.E.2d 448 (1998)).

[11] A proper reading of Regulation 164.512(e)(1) shows that a qualified protective order must only be secured when a disclosure is being made in "response to a subpoena, discovery request, or other lawful process, that is not accompanied by an order of a court." 45 C.F.R. § 164.512(e)(1)(ii) (2002). Here, Ingalls was ordered by the circuit court to comply with the plaintiffs' discovery request and produce the specified information. *Ingalls*, 834 N.E.2d at 556.

[12] 834 N.E.2d 942 (Ill. App. Ct. 2005).

where its ruling is arbitrary, fanciful, or unreasonable, or where no reasonable person would adopt the court's view.[13]

. . . A circuit court may properly stay or quash a discovery request when it has sufficient information upon which to rule on a motion to dismiss. However, a court should not refuse a discovery request and grant a motion to dismiss where it reasonably appears discovery might assist the nonmoving party.[14]

The question of the bounds of relevancy in a discovery deposition was recently analyzed in the 2005 Florida case of *Sterling Casino Lines, L.P. v. Plowman-Render*.[15] There it was held that the trial court abused its discretion in admitting irrelevant evidence which impugned the character of one of Sterling's chief witnesses, the emergency medical technician who treated Plowman-Render. The questions Plowman-Render's counsel asked Gardner in his deposition concerning his alcohol-induced coma, suicide attempt, stays in a mental facility and the reason for his termination from employment with Sterling may have been appropriate in a discovery context. The court stressed that the concept of "relevancy" was broader in discovery than at trial and a party may be permitted to discover relevant evidence that would be inadmissible at trial so long as it may lead to the discovery of admissible evidence.

However, the court stated, these questions were irrelevant to the issues at trial and served simply to portray Gardner in an unfavorable light. Plowman-Render did not establish Gardner's memory had been impaired by the coma or any other medical condition. Likewise, Plowman-Render did not show any reason for delving into the specific reason for Gardner's termination from Sterling. Gardner was attempting to protect his privacy at his deposition but his refusal to answer some questions may have seemed evasive to the jury.

The credibility of witnesses was clearly crucial in this case. Plowman-Render's friends apparently did not see the incident and Dean has been diagnosed with Alzheimer's and did not testify. Thus the case came down to Plowman-Render's version of events or Gardner's and Jones' version, which were in direct conflict. These questions impugned Gardner's character and may have destroyed his effectiveness as a witness. In these circumstances, the court concluded, Sterling was entitled to a new trial.

Similarly, in *J.W. v. B.B.*,[16] the court held that information concerning a physician's sexual orientation was not discoverable concerning a job applicants' claim that the physician failed to obtain informed consent before conducting digital-rectal exams on applicants while performing pre-employment medical examinations. The court ruled that the physician's motive or intent in conducting exams was not relevant to the dispositive inquiry of whether the applicants were

---

[13] *Id.* (*citing* Mutlu v. State Farm Fire & Casualty Co., 785 N.E.2d 951 (Ill. App. Ct. 2003)).

[14] *Id.* (*citing* Adkins Energy, LLC. v. Delta-T Corp., 806 N.E.2d 1273 (Ill. App. Ct. 2004)). The court also observed, however, that discovery is not necessary where a cause of action has not been stated.

[15] 902 So. 2d 938 (Fla. Dist. Ct. App. 2005).

[16] 700 N.W.2d 277 (Wis. Ct. App. 2005).

provided with information that a reasonable patient would want to know before consenting to such a procedure.

§ 18.04   OBJECTIONS IN DEPOSITIONS

FRCP 30(c)(2) provides that [a]n objection at the time of the examination — whether to evidence, to a party's conduct, to the officer's qualifications, to the manner of taking the deposition, or to any other aspect of the deposition — must be noted on the record, but the examination still proceeds; the testimony is taken subject to any objection. An objection must be stated concisely in a nonargumentative and nonsuggestive manner. A person may instruct a deponent not to answer only when necessary to preserve a privilege, to enforce a limitation ordered by the court, or to present a motion under Rule 30(d)(3).

Rules 30(d)(2) and (3) address the abuse of the deposition process, unfortunately not a rare occasion in contemporary practice:

(2) Sanction. The court may impose an appropriate sanction — including the reasonable expenses and attorney's fees incurred by any party — on a person who impedes, delays, or frustrates the fair examination of the deponent.

(3) Motion to Terminate or Limit.

(A)   Grounds. At any time during a deposition, the deponent or a party may move to terminate or limit it on the ground that it is being conducted in bad faith or in a manner that unreasonably annoys, embarrasses, or oppresses the deponent or party. The motion may be filed in the court where the action is pending or the deposition is being taken. If the objecting deponent or party so demands, the deposition must be suspended for the time necessary to obtain an order.

(B)   Order. The court may order that the deposition be terminated or may limit its scope and manner as provided in Rule 26(c). If terminated, the deposition may be resumed only by order of the court where the action is pending.

Facing a flurry of objections made during the course of a deposition is a very common problem in products liability cases, regardless of whether the deponent is an expert, corporate officer or other employee. There seems to be a lack of agreement as to just what is or is not objectionable, whether the question must be answered nonetheless over objection, whether the deposition may be terminated and resumed, and a host of civility related issues. As recently noted by trial attorney David Paul Horowitz:

> There is a fair amount of disagreement over what constitutes a proper objection under particular circumstances, and what effect interposing an objection has on the witness's obligation to answer the question. There is also disagreement about what types of behavior and demeanor are appropriate for attorneys questioning and defending depositions, and what conduct on the part of the witness may be objectionable.

Counsel may seek to have sanctions imposed for the failure of a party or witness to appear at the deposition, and may raise objections to the form or substance of questions posed. Objections may also be raised regarding the qualifications of the person officiating, the competency of a witness or the behavior of adverse counsel.

A court will not rule on the propriety of a particular question in advance of a deposition. Instead, the question must be posed, objection taken, and then the court may rule on the question.[17]

There are differing views on this subject. While inappropriate deposition conduct may offend civility principles and be regulated, overarching discovery rules, seeking court intervention is not always desirable. As noted by Stewart Israel in his recent article, *Twelve Deposition Principles, Mechanics, Strategies, and Practices*, it may cause delay and a host of other unwanted results:

> It can be time-consuming and expensive. And often it is difficult to communicate the obstructive impact of the other side's behavior to someone who wasn't there, i.e., the judge. Worse, seeking court intervention often is ineffective because many judges are unable or unwilling to devote the time, effort and attention necessary to understanding discovery motions. Some are too busy. Some find discovery disputes beneath them. Some are lazy or impatient with details. Too many react to discovery motions with the a-plague-on-both-your-houses attitude or by automatically blaming the victim. Most litigators spend most of their litigating time occupied with discovery, so judges ought to spend their valuable time addressing and deciding discovery disputes, but it's a fact of life that many judges just do not like discovery disputes. So, even if you're in the right, bringing a motion to compel or for a protective order may produce judicial antipathy or worse. As noted, when you go to court on a discovery motion, you risk application of the Law of Unintended Consequences, which may result in judicial micromanagement, burdensome discovery limitations, undesirable discovery extension and expansion, merits prejudgment ("premature adjudication"), and sanctions for having the temerity to file a motion that is denied.[18]

In the last half century or more, trial lawyers' development of the discovery deposition as a central information gathering and trial support vehicle has improved dramatically. Despite occasional calls by defense-oriented authors to ensure "mum's the word,"[19] discovery in general and depositions in particular have advanced

---

[17] *See* David Paul Horowitz, *Objections and Objectionable Conduct at Depositions*, 77-Jan. N.Y.S. B.J. 20 (2005).

[18] Israel, *supra* note 1, at 42.

[19] *See* Nahrstadt, *Narrowing the Scope of Discovery for Substantially Similar Products*, 15 No. 6 Prac. Litig. 37, 38 (2004) (Products liability actions are not easy cases to prepare, nor are they easy cases to try. More often than not, such cases involve complex industrial or consumer products, monumental amounts of documents, intricate theories of liability and defense, and horrific injuries. Defense counsel must make sense of a variety of complex issues and present a coherent, cohesive, and streamlined theory of defense to the jury. Obviously, the defense attorney who is successful in preventing the introduction of "extraneous" issues to the jury will be far ahead of the game in terms of limiting the scope of the case

towards full disclosure of relevant information. Unfortunately, some lawyers for both sides have developed quarrelsome and contentious tactics in the course of defending depositions that can seriously impede the flow of information from a witness. Courts and bar associations have made important efforts to eliminate or at least severely reduce this behavior.[20]

In *Mora v. Saint Vincent's Catholic Medical Center of New York*,[21] the defendant, in a medical malpractice case, sought to compel the plaintiff to appear for a continued deposition and to postpone the depositions of the defendants pending the completion of the plaintiff's continued deposition. During the course of the deposition counsel for Dr. Hsu attempted to ask the plaintiff the following questions, each of which plaintiff's counsel directed her not to answer: (1) whether the plaintiff was taking any medications at the time of the deposition, (2) whether the plaintiff was on disability (i.e., Social Security Disability Insurance), and if so, when she began receiving benefits and the nature of the disability, (3) whether the plaintiff had ever filed for bankruptcy, (4) whether the plaintiff had ever been diagnosed with a psychological disorder, (5) whether the plaintiff had ever experienced palpitations, and (6) whether the plaintiff had undergone surgery prior to the surgery giving rise to this action.[22]

The court ruled that the proper procedure during the course of an examination before trial was to permit the witness to answer all questions posed, subject to objections, unless a question was clearly violative of the witness's constitutional rights or of some privilege recognized in law, or was palpably irrelevant. The reason for this maxim, the court stated, was simple: only objections to form and the technical aspects of the deposition are waived if not timely raised at the deposition.[23]

The court noted that the goal of discovery schemes was to attempt to create an environment conducive to open, expansive disclosure during the taking of a deposition. Unfortunately, the court observed, this environment was *routinely polluted* by the conduct of attorneys at depositions. Judicially unsupervised depositions had become breeding grounds for a myriad of unprofessional and dilatory conduct.[24] So profound and widespread was this behavior that a series of recent law review articles have been dedicated to highlighting its existence, and proposed regulations have been suggested to stymie its proliferation.[25]

---

and concentrating the jury's focus on the salient legal issues. One of the most successful ways of limiting the introduction of "extraneous" issues is to prevent the plaintiff's attorney from finding out about them during the course of discovery.). *Id.*

[20] *See* Valerie A. Yarashus, *Don't Let Your Opponent Disrupt Depositions*, TRIAL, Nov. 2004, at 56. These authors cite what they feel are the most common forms of obstruction used during depositions are:
- [ ] conferences to frame a witness's answer or to interrupt the proceedings
- [ ] speaking objections and interjections to suggest answers or disrupt the flow of information
- [ ] errata sheets to change a witness's testimony. *Id.*

[21] 800 N.Y.S.2d 298 (Sup. Ct. 2005).

[22] *Id.* at 300.

[23] *Id.* (*citing* 1 PAYNE & ZALAYET, MODERN NEW YORK DISCOVERY § 8.55, at 136–38 (2d ed. 2004)).

[24] *Mora*, 800 N.Y.S.2d at 301.

[25] *Id. See* Horowitz, *Objections and Objectionable Conduct at Depositions*, 77-JAN. N.Y.S. B.J. 20

The deposition-related conduct in the case at bar highlighted one of the "abuses" the Advisory Committee was seeking to address, namely the practice of attorneys directing witnesses not to answer questions. Initially, plaintiff's counsel did not assert that any of the blocked questions implicated the plaintiff's constitutional rights or a privilege recognized in law. Rather, counsel essentially asserted that the blocked questions were palpably irrelevant.[26]

§ 18.05 DEPOSITION PLANNING

A primary purpose in deposing corporate staff is to fill in those gaps in the total products design, testing, production, marketing and post-marketing information already garnered by the parties. The products liability plaintiff has much to fill. Literally millions of pieces of paper are churned out over the course of a products initiation and subsequent life in the market. As noted in Chapter 17, Requests to Produce Documents, only a very small percentage of that mountain of paper is of interest to plaintiff or defense counsel, let alone relevant from a trial standpoint. What is supplied by the company in discovery is necessarily only a small, very disjointed portion of what is present in defendant's files. The phenomenon of email and ensuing electronic discovery only swells the total. Depositions in these cases require considerable preparation in the form of document organization, analysis and cross-referencing.

There are several basic goals that should be focal points for planning the depositions of corporate personnel and expert witnesses. In the broadest sense, counsel need to answer and flesh out the following points over the Course of the depositions taken:

- Remaining questions about the defendant's decision-making processes as relates to the suspect product or line of product.

- Identifying the corporation's state of the art defense strategies.

- Getting the details of the defendant's response to proposed governmental regulations.

- Discovering the details of defendant's foreign operations and marketing.

- Discovering the corporate defendant's and its experts' position on the importance of individual or a related series of documents, such as testing or clinical trials.

(2005); Cary, *Rambo Depositions: Controlling an Ethical Cancer in Civil Litigation*, 25 HOFSTRA L. REV. 561 (1996); 2005 Report of Advisory Comm. on Civil Practice, at 90–94 (regulations aimed at curbing the practice of "speaking objections" and delineating when an attorney can direct a witness not to answer a question).

[26] Here, plaintiff's counsel improperly directed plaintiff not to answer defense counsel's questions as to whether plaintiff was taking any medications at the time of the deposition, whether plaintiff was receiving disability benefits, and whether plaintiff had ever filed for personal bankruptcy. Plaintiff's counsel also improperly blocked questions relating to plaintiff's general health and prior surgeries. Those questions were relevant on the issue of damages. In addition, plaintiff was directed to answer questions regarding her mental health history unless she withdrew any claims for emotional or psychological damages.

- Identifying the defense strategy with respect to the defendant's design, testing, production, marketing and post-marketing processes as relates to the suspect product or line of product.

- Identifying the corporation's interpretation of key documents of all types.

- Identifying the corporation's proximate cause defenses.[27]

- Preparing the depositions of corporate staff and defense experts around these broad areas will go a long way towards the resolution of most of the gaps in knowledge encountered over the course of case investigation and early discovery.

§ 18.06   DOCUMENT ORGANIZATION AND DEPOSITION PREPARATION

Depositions in the products liability case are centered on issues raised by the information received in discovery. This is especially so with documents addressing the chronological stages of the production and marketing of the product. A close review and organization of such materials is essential, both for further information and determining issues and related documentation for use at trial. There are a series of organizational and analytical focal points that need to be addressed prior to initiating case depositions:

DOCUMENT GENERATING PROCESSES AND BASIC CONTENT

- Grading the Importance of Corporate Documents

- Indexing by Nature or Type of Document

- Routine Informational Content of Documents

- Identifying Document Points of Interest/Fields

- Indexing of All Corporate Documents by Date and Subject Matters

- Indexing of All Documentary Materials: State-of-the-Art and Internal Processes

- Preparing a Glossary of Terms

- Isolating Selected Activity over the Case Time Frame

---

[27] *See* Terrence F. Kiely, Science and Litigation: Products Liability in Theory and Practice 362–63 (CRC Press 2002). *See also* Mark J. Evans, *Make the Most of Company-Employee Depositions*, Trial, Nov. 2003, at 36:

> A corporate representative will usually have experience testifying, which makes it more likely that his or her deposition will be best used for discovery purposes. It is a good idea to take these depositions as early as possible so you have time to conduct additional discovery to follow up on any answers that require more investigation. The other group comprises company employees who are not corporate representatives. Their depositions serve an entirely different purpose. They should be conducted with the jury, not discovery, in mind. They will typically involve a narrow area of inquiry, focusing on the employee's involvement in and knowledge of events directly related to the alleged defect. They may involve knowledge of testing that showed the product was susceptible to failure, or alternative designs considered by the manufacturer. *Id.* at 37.

- Gaps in the Generation of Documentation

INTERNAL ORGANIZATION AND STANDARD OPERATING PROCEDURES

- Requesting Offices and Department

- Requesting Individuals

- Distribution Lists

- Committees and Committee Meetings

- Key Tests or Clinical Trials

- Government Regulation

- Consumer Complaints

- Law Suits or Recalls

MATCHING THE DOCUMENTS TO LEGAL THEORY OF LIABILITY

- Knowledge of Defect

- Knowledge of Alternative Design

- Legal Theories and Relevancy

- Proximate Cause

Depositions of corporate staff[28] should only follow the organization and analysis of answers to interrogatories and the documents received after the resolution of requests for documentation.[29] The examination and organization of such materials must be accompanied by the preparation of a readily accessible database system allowing for both the rapid retrieval and cross-referencing of names, dates, topics, meetings and other key points across the design, testing, production and marketing of the product at issue. Microsoft Access and Filemaker are the two more popular database programs used by small to medium size firms. Both are inexpensive yet powerful additions to any firm's technological arsenal, with a number of easy to read guides.[30] Making the best use of available technology, such as the now common

---

[28] In products cases, the most helpful depositions are often given by company employees. Don't make the mistake of using these witnesses only as fonts of discovery information. Instead, keep your eye on the ultimate goal — jury persuasion — and keep your cross-examination skills sharp. Evans, *supra* note 27, at 39.

[29] *Id.*

[30] **Filemaker:** *See* GEOFF COFFEY & SUSAN PROSSER: FILEMAKER PRO 8: THE MISSING MANUAL (O'Reilly MEDIA 2005); STEVEN A. SCHWARTZ & DENNIS R. COHEN: FILEMAKER PRO 7: BIBLE (Wiley 2004); STEVE SCHWARTZ, CREATING A DATABASE IN FILEMAKER PRO 8: VISUAL QUICKPROJECT GUIDE (Visual Quickproject Series) (Peachpit Press 2005).

Microsoft Access: MICROSOFT OFFICE ACCESS 2003 STEP BY STEP: ONLINE TRAINING SOLUTIONS (Online Training Solutions, Inc. 2003); JOHN L. VIESCAS & JOHN VIESCAS: MICROSOFT OFFICE ACCESS 2003 INSIDE OUT (Microsoft Press; Bk&CD-Rom edition (Aug. 27, 2003)); CARY N. PRAGUE, MICHAEL R. IRWIN & JENNIFER REARDON: ACCESS 2003 BIBLE (Wiley; Bk&CD-Rom edition (Oct. 3, 2003)).

videotaping of depositions, can often yield dramatic results.[31]

Federal Rule of Civil Procedure 30(b)(6) allows a party to request that a corporation designate one or more individuals to be deposed on subject matters specified in the deposition notice. The purpose of the rule is to allow for depositions on these matters when counsel is unable to adequately identify knowledgeable individuals at the time when the deposition is requested.[32] The organization and analysis of corporate documentation will identify key personnel who were actively involved in the product development and manufacturing processes of primary concern to counsel. These are the employees who typically have the most to offer. While these persons will be well prepared by defense lawyers, they are not professional witnesses. Counsel is much more likely to gain important testimony from them than from employees whose job description includes testifying at depositions.[33]

§ 18.07 DEPOSING DEFENSE EXPERTS

The deposition of the defense expert is one of the most important in the entire series of depositions that will be undertaken. They not only have significant amount of information and experience but will most likely be a major defense witness at trial.[34] While estimating the technical testimonial competence of any deponent is an important goal of deposition practice, it is especially important in products liability cases. The bulk of the testimony in these depositions will revolve around the state-of-the-art and proximate cause defenses. These technical expert witnesses typically have little to offer as to the details of company's document generating and decision- making processes. Their primary goal is to establish that the defendant's

---

[31] You should find a videographer who has experience working with sophisticated document cameras and presenters. This technology allows you to display the deposition document on a screen at trial while you question the witness about it. *See* Evans, *supra* note 27, at 36; Stephen M. Terrell, *Preparing Your Client for a Video Deposition*, 48-Dec. RESG 26 (Res Gestae 2004); Andre M. Lagomarsino, *Strategic Use of Video Depositions*, 11-June NEV. L. 8 (2003).

[32] While this and comparable state provisions have great utility in a wide variety of settings, they should as a matter of practice, be used as a last resort in product liability litigation. Most major corporations have engineers and other scientists whose sole function is to work with the legal staff in defending these cases. A primary part of their employment is to represent the corporation in 30(b)(6) depositions. While these individuals are totally familiar with all of the documentation involved in the case, they are also skilled at leading inexperienced counsel astray or providing little or no valuable information during the course of a deposition.

[33] A primary purpose of these depositions is establishing the precise chain of command for varying activities over the case time frames. It is important to track decision-making to the highest levels possible. Corporate line charts tell only part of the story. Specialized reporting formats are often at the heart of the development of new product lines. These would not normally appear on standard organization charts and are often utilized for the resolution of short term corporate goals. It is also common business practice for managers to establish various "activities," "task forces" or other functional groupings to carry out important work. Counsel must specifically identify any such organizational processes and the personnel involved to adequately assess the exact nature and extent of corporate knowledge. *See* KIELY, *supra* note 27, at 365.

[34] Members of defendant's technical and managerial staff deposed by plaintiff may not, and routinely are not called to testify. Chief among the reasons for relying on experts is the inhouse staff's inexperience as witnesses.

packaging, instructions, warnings or overall design reflected the state of the art when examined in light of either the authoritative literature in the field or the customary practice of the industry. The other key aspect of the defense expert is to establish that the feature of defendant's product involved in the case was not the proximate cause of plaintiff's death or injury.

The deposition of the defendant's technical experts will reveal in detail the substance of the defendant's state-of-the-art, documentary and proximate cause strategies. Expert witnesses for both sides are the center of attraction in these cases, and the success of the case often stands or falls on the quality of what they say and how they say it. The manner in which the expert communicates, or as the case may be, fails to communicate important information, is often of equal value to the substance of their testimony. There is a wealth of practice-oriented literature addressing every aspect of this crucial stage of products liability discovery.[35]

---

[35] *See, e.g.*, Nahrstadt, *supra* note 19, at 38; George Brent Mickum IV & Luther L. Hajek, *Guise, Contrivance, or Artful Dodging?: The Discovery Rules Governing Testifying Employee Experts*, 24 Rev. Litig. 301 (Spring 2005); 1 Douglas Danner & Larry L. Varn, Expert Witness Checklists § 1:64 (3d ed.), Chapter 1, General Use of the Expert Witness, VII. Pretrial Discovery of the Expert Witness (Database updated June 2005); 2 ATLA's Litigating Tort Cases § 18:56, Roxanne Barton Conlin & Gregory S. Cusimano, Editors-in-Chief, Chapter 18, Depositions by Linda Miller Atkinson, § 18:56. Deposing the opposing expert — Benefits of deposing the opposing expert (Database updated July 2005); Paul Lisnek & Michael Kaufman, Depositions: Procedure, Strategy & Technique, Part III, The Defending Party's Perspective, Chapter 15, The Deposition of an Expert Witness (Database updated Sept. 2005); Marilyn J. Holifield, *Deposing Expert Witnesses in Products Liability Cases*, 12 No. 2 Prac. Litig. 31 (2001); Richard D. Hailey, *Know the Science Before Deposing Medical Experts*, Trial, Dec. 2000, at 95.

In addition to the number of sources available through the American Trial Lawyers Association (ATLA), the Defense Research Institute (DRI) provides a number of excellent articles and papers on deposing expert witnesses from the defense position. *See* http://www.atla.org and http://www.dri.org/.

Chapter 19

PROTECTIVE ORDERS AND DISCOVERY ENFORCEMENT

SYNOPSIS

§ 19.01 INTRODUCTION

§ 19.02 PROTECTIVE ORDERS: THE RULES

§ 19.03 PROTECTIVE ORDERS IN PRODUCTS LITIGATION

§ 19.04 REQUIREMENT OF SPECIFIC SUPPORTIVE FACTS

§ 19.05 INFORMATION SHARING

§ 19.06 PROTECTION AGAINST FRAUD

§ 19.07 ANNOYANCE, EMBARRASSMENT, OPPRESSION

§ 19.08 TRADE SECRETS AND CONFIDENTIAL COMMERCIAL INFORMATION

§ 19.09 FACTUAL COMPONENTS OF THE ARGUMENT IN OPPOSITION

§ 19.10 MEETING THE ARGUMENTS FOR EACH DOCUMENT

§ 19.11 DISCOVERY ENFORCEMENT

§ 19.12 SAMPLE DISCOVERY ENFORCEMENT MEMORANDUM — STAINLESS STEEL PRESSURIZED BEVERAGE CANISTER LITIGATION

§ 19.13 THE DENTON v. FREMANTLE DISCOVERY ENFORCEMENT SUPPORT MEMORANDUM

§ 19.14 CONCLUSION

§ 19.01 INTRODUCTION

This chapter will address two crucial areas in the entire products liability litigation undertaking: Seeking or opposing protective orders and enforcing or opposing requests for discovery. In many ways, the success or failure of these two efforts can be dispositive in these cases. The first topic to be discussed is protective orders.

A major issue that plaintiff's counsel will encounter is defense motions for a comprehensive protective order. The entry of a protective order can significantly impede counsel's efforts to achieve a detailed understanding of defendant's document-generating and decision-making processes. This is because one of the major goals of such orders is to deprive plaintiff's counsel of the opportunity to consult with more experienced lawyers. This consultation may take the form of document tutorials and/or the exchange of information. Corporate concern over the sharing of information supplied in discovery with other lawyers, often a reason for increased filings against them, is a major factor in the routine requests for protective orders. The motion for a protective order has been usually deemed a disfavored motion, with the clear burden on the moving party to show some plainly important basis for the order.[1]

The question of the issuance or extent of protective orders seeking nondisclosure of material obtained in public trials has been of great concern for the long tenure of product liability litigation. The right of the public to documents issuing from public trial discovery processes and the countervailing interests of a wide variety of interested parties, including the government and industry is still very much in contention. The latest effort to resolve these complex matters is being produced by the highly thought of Sedona Conference in the Sedona Guidelines: Best Practices Addressing Protective Orders, Confidentiality & Public Access in Civil Cases (April 2005 Public Comment Version).[2] The Sedona Conference® Working Group Addressing Protective Orders, Confidentiality and Public Access (POPA) was established to foster *some clarity and uniformity to practices involving protective orders in civil litigation, and determinations affecting public access to documents filed or referred to in court.*[3]

§ 19.02   PROTECTIVE ORDERS: THE RULES

Protective orders in U.S. Courts are governed by Federal Rule 26(c) General Provisions Governing Discovery which provides:

(c)

> (1) *In General.* A party or any person from whom discovery is sought may move for a protective order in the court where the action is pending — or as an alternative on matters relating to a deposition, in the court for the district where the deposition will be taken. The motion must include a certification that the movant has in good faith

---

[1] *See, e.g.,* United States v. Purdome, 30 F.R.D. 338, 341 (W.D. Mo. 1962); Glick v. McKesson and Robbins, Inc., 10 F.R.D. 477 (W.D. Mo. 1950); Blankenship v. Hearst Corp., 519 F.2d 418 (9th Cir. 1975); U.S. v. International Business Machines Corp., 66 F.R.D. 186, 189 (S.D.N.Y. 1974); Davis v. Romney, 55 F.R.D. 337 (D.C. Pa. 1972); Hunter v. International Systems and Controls Corp., 51 F.R.D. 251 (W.D. Mo. 1970).

[2] 6 SEDONA CONF. J. 183 (Fall 2005). The important papers and conference produced by the Sedona Conference may be accessed online at http://www.thesedonaconference.org/.

[3] *Id.* Preliminary working assumptions are: Chapter 2. Discovery: **Principle 1.** There is no presumed right of the public to participate in the discovery process or to have access to the fruits of discovery that are not submitted to the court; **Principle 2.** A litigant has the right to disclose the fruits of discovery to non-parties, absent an agreement between the parties or an order based on a showing of good cause; **Principle 3.** A broad protective order entered under Fed. R. Civ. P 26(c) to facilitate the exchange of discovery materials does not substitute for the individualized judicial determination necessary for sealing such material, if filed with the court on a non-discovery matter; **Principle 4.** On a proper showing, non-parties should be permitted to intervene to challenge a protective order that limits disclosure of otherwise discoverable information.

conferred or attempted to confer with other affected parties in an effort to resolve the dispute without court action. The court may, for good cause, issue an order to protect a party or person from annoyance, embarrassment, oppression, or undue burden or expense, including one or more of the following:

(A) forbidding the disclosure or discovery;

(B) specifying terms, including time and place, for the disclosure or discovery;

(C) prescribing a discovery method other than the one selected by the party seeking discovery;

(D) forbidding inquiry into certain matters, or limiting the scope of disclosure or discovery to certain matters;

(E) designating the persons who may be present while the discovery is conducted;

(F) requiring that a deposition be sealed and opened only on court order;

(G) requiring that a trade secret or other confidential research, development, or commercial information not be revealed or be revealed only in a specified way; and

(H) requiring that the parties simultaneously file specified documents or information in sealed envelopes, to be opened as the court directs.

(2) *Ordering Discovery.* If a motion for a protective order is wholly or partly denied, the court may, on just terms, order that any party or person provide or permit discovery.[4]

State discovery schemes provide similar provisions. Illinois Supreme Court Rule 201(c)(1), General Discovery Provisions provides:

Protective Orders. The court may at any time on its own initiative, or on motion of any party or witness, make a protective order as justice requires, denying, limiting, conditioning, or regulating discovery to prevent unreasonable annoyance, expense, embarrassment, disadvantage, or oppression.[5]

§ 19.03   PROTECTIVE ORDERS IN PRODUCTS LITIGATION

The type of comprehensive protective orders often sought by corporate defense counsel read as follows:

1. All documents and materials which are produced and exhibited by the defendant in this action shall remain in the possession of the defendant's counsel.

---

[4] FED. R. CIV. P. 26(c) — General Provisions Governing Discovery.

[5] Illinois Supreme Court Rule 201(c)(1). General Discovery Provisions.

2. Any and all copies of said documents and materials made by or at the incidence of the plaintiff or his attorneys, shall remain in the physical custody, possession and control of the plaintiff's attorneys, and each such item which is not admitted into evidence at trial shall be returned to the defendant's counsel at the termination of this litigation. Moreover, each such item which is admitted into evidence shall be returned to the defendant's counsel at the termination of this litigation.

3. All experts retained by the plaintiff and by the plaintiff's counsel are prohibited from making any copy of any item produced in this action by the defendant. The plaintiff, his counsel, and all experts retained by the plaintiff or by the plaintiff's counsel are prohibited from, in any fashion, distributing or disseminating any documents or materials or copies thereof produced in this action by the defendant.

4. Any and all notes, whether handwritten, typed or recorded in any form, and any copies or reproductions thereof, which are made by or at the instance of the plaintiff, his attorneys, or any experts retained by the plaintiff or by his attorneys from any documents and materials which are produced and exhibited by the defendant in this action or copies thereof shall be turned over to defendant's counsel at the termination of this litigation.

5. The plaintiff, his counsel, and all experts retained by the plaintiff or by the plaintiff's counsel are prohibited from, in any fashion, distributing or disseminating any notes, whether handwritten, typed, recorded, or reproduced in any form made from any documents and materials which are produced and exhibited by the defendant in this action, or copies thereof.

6. Any contents of any documents or materials produced in this action by the defendant which deals with or concerns any matters other than the fuel storage and delivery systems may be excised and obliterated by the defendant prior to the production of said documents and materials.

The entry of an order along the above lines can seriously detract from counsel's efforts to maximize his knowledge of corporate documents and processes.

§ 19.04   REQUIREMENT OF SPECIFIC SUPPORTIVE FACTS

As with all objections to discovery requests, the moving party here must allege specific facts in support of the motion for a protective order. A bare repetition of the statutory grounds for such orders is inadequate. The party seeking the order must demonstrate *good cause* for its issuance. A showing of good cause requires facts demonstrating that disclosure of the information "will work a clearly defined and very serious injury."[6]

---

[6] United States v. International Business Machines Inc., 67 F.R.D.40, 46 (S.D.N.Y. 1975); Reliance Insurance Co. v. Barrons, 428 F. Supp. 200, 203 (S.D.N.Y. 1977); In re Halkin, 598 F.2d 176, 186, 191 (D.C. Cir. 1979).

§ 19.05 INFORMATION SHARING

It is an arduous task for a single plaintiff to complete discovery in a complex products liability case such as a Vioxx litigation when faced with a corporate opponent who has significantly greater resources and support staff. This is a products liability reality that has not escaped the attention of the nation's state and federal courts. In the leading case of *Williams v. Johnson & Johnson*, 50 F.R.D. 31, 33 (S.D.N.Y. 1970), the Court observed:

> In this situation (where numerous similar suits had been filed) it is at least theoretically advantageous for plaintiffs in the various suits to share the fruits of discovery. They thus reduce the time and money which must be expended to prepare for trial and are probably able to provide more effective, speedy, and efficient representation to their clients. . . . On its face, such collaboration comes squarely within the aims laid out in the first and fundamental rule of the Federal Rules of Civil Procedure. . . . Thus there is no merit to the all-encompassing contention that the fruits of discovery in one case are to be used in the case only.

In rejecting defendant's bald claim that plaintiff's counsel would encourage litigation against it and otherwise seek to harass defendant, the Court stated:

> It is difficult to draw a clear line between the legitimate educative activities of any attorney and the drumming up of business from those who might otherwise settle their disputes without the entanglements of litigation. . . . It is impossible to draw that line sharply and distinctly when virtually no facts are presented to the Court. The only specific allegations defendants make in this respect is that plaintiff's attorneys may sell or may have sold the fruits of discovery in this case with other materials and information to attorneys engaged in similar cases. Without more, the charging of fees between attorneys collaborating in similar cases and the collaboration itself both seem reasonable on their face. . . .[7]

In *Johnson Foils v. Huyck Corp.*, 61 F.R.D. 405, 410 (1973), the court echoed the ruling in Williams:

> . . . unless it can be shown that the discovering party is exploiting the instant litigation solely to assist in other litigation before a foreign forum, federal courts do allow full use of the information in other forums. . . . Indeed, there must be some evidence of bad faith in the institution of the suit on the part of the discovering party before a Court will act to limit the discovery process.

Defense arguments alleging the iniquity of information sharing are increasingly rejected by state and federal courts. In the recent case of *Earl v. Gulf & Western Manufacturing Company*, 366 N.W.2d 160 (Wis. Ct. App. 1985), the Court of Appeals of Wisconsin, in denying defendant's motion for a protective order stated:

> The only reason advanced by Gulf & Western for the protective order is its fears that the Earls might pass the information along to other plaintiffs

---

[7] *Williams*, 50 F.R.D. at 33.

involved in litigation against Gulf & Western. This does not rise to the level of "good cause" for a protective order. Gulf & Western has not shown that it has a legitimate interest in denying parties to other lawsuits access to the information. If the information is irrelevant to the issues raised in those cases, it will not be admissible against Gulf & Western; if it is relevant, the other plaintiffs can discover it from Gulf & Western in any event, and their obtaining it from the Earls will save Gulf & Western the trouble and expense of producing the same information several times over. Gulf & Western argues that there is no reason why the Earls should be allowed to disseminate the information "at will" because doing so will not help their case. Gulf & Western misunderstands its burden on a motion for a protective order. The presumption is that no order is necessary; the movant must show a positive reason (i.e., "good cause") for the entry of an order. It is insufficient merely to argue that no reason exists not to issue an order.[8]

The growth of plaintiff information sharing organizations is increasingly seen by courts as a positive factor in achieving the goal of efficient dispute resolution. Corporations view information sharing among plaintiff's attorneys as a serious problem, aimed at fomenting litigation. The recent Vioxx and cigarette litigations may serve as examples. The American Trial Lawyers Association (ATLA) fosters a large number of support groups for purposes of mutual education and exchange of motions, briefs, interrogatories, depositions and corporate documents received in discovery.[9] The Defense Research Institute and other defense oriented groups provide similar services.

In *Patterson v. Ford Motor Company*, 85 F.R.D. 152 (D.C. Tex. 1980), defendant sought the entry of a protective order on the basis that plaintiff's counsel were members of both state and national trial lawyers associations which engaged in information sharing among its members. In denying Ford's motion, the Court stated:

> For good cause shown, this Court will make any order which justice requires to protect Ford from annoyance, embarrassment, oppression, or undue burden or expense. Rule 26(C), F.R.C.P. To show good cause, Ford asserts that counsel for Plaintiff are members of the Texas Trial Lawyers Association and the American Trial Lawyers Association, which collect and distribute information with regard to manufacturers. Such collaboration among plaintiff's attorneys would come squarely within the aims of the Federal Rules of Civil Procedure — to secure the just, speedy, and inexpensive determination of every action.[10]

---

[8] *Earl*, 366 N.W.2d at 165.

[9] ATLA Litigation Groups in 2005, covers a wide variety of products such as Baycol, Benzene/Leukemia, Climbers and Other Diet Products: Fen-Phen, Electrical Accidents, Embolization Devices (Cyanoacrylate), Ephedra, Firearms and Ammunition, Heart Devices, Herbicides & Pesticides (including Agent Orange, Dioxin & PCB's), Hormone Therapy, Laparoscopy, Lead Paint, Orthopedic Implant Devices, Selective Serotonin Reuptake Inhibitors (Antidepressants including Paxil, Zoloft and Prozac), Sexual Dyfunction Drugs, Stand-up Forklifts, Vioxx/Bextra (includes all Cox-2 Inhibitor Arthritis Drugs such as Celebrex), and Zyprexa.

[10] 85 F.R.D. 152.

§ 19.06 PROTECTION AGAINST FRAUD

An additional reason often stated by the nation's courts in refusing to accept the alleged impropriety of information sharing as a basis for the issuance of broad-based protective orders is the prevention of fraud in the discovery process.[11] The possibility of a corporate defendant falsifying responses to discovery requests by an individual claimant who has no access to other sources of information is, although apparently rare, nonetheless very real.

In the case of *Rozier v. Ford Motor Company*, 573 F.2d 1332 (5th Cir. 1978), defendant falsified its answer to one of plaintiff's interrogatories regarding the existence of a certain document. After a verdict for defendant, the subject document came to light and plaintiff was granted a new trial. In condemning such action, the U.S. Court of Appeals for the Fifth Circuit stated:

> Through its misconduct in this case, Ford completely sabotaged the federal trial machinery, precluding the 'fair contest' which the Federal Rules of Civil Procedure are intended to secure. Instead of serving as a vehicle for ascertainment of the truth, the trial in this case accomplished little more than the adjudication of a hypothetical fact situation imposed by Ford's selective disclosure of information. The policy protecting the finality of judgments is not so broad as to require protection of judgments obtained in this manner. . . .[12]

In a similar context, in the case of *Buehler v. Whalen*, 374 N.E.2d 460 (Ill. 1978), the defendant company falsified answers to plaintiff's interrogations and otherwise failed to honestly honor requests for documents. As noted by the Illinois Supreme Court, only information sharing revealed the fraud:

---

[11] Alleged fraud in the discovery process is addressed in FED. R. CIV. P. RULE 60, Relief from Judgment or Order:

> (b) Mistakes; Inadvertence; Excusable Neglect; Newly Discovered Evidence; Fraud, Etc. On motion and upon such terms as are just, the court may relieve a party or a party's legal representative from a final judgment, order, or proceeding for the following reasons: (1) mistake, inadvertence, surprise, or excusable neglect; (2) newly discovered evidence which by due diligence could not have been discovered in time to move for a new trial under Rule 59(b); (3) fraud (whether heretofore denominated intrinsic or extrinsic), misrepresentation, or other misconduct of an adverse party; (4) the judgment is void; (5) the judgment has been satisfied, released, or discharged, or a prior judgment upon which it is based has been reversed or otherwise vacated, or it is no longer equitable that the judgment should have prospective application; or (6) any other reason justifying relief from the operation of the judgment. The motion shall be made within a reasonable time, and for reasons (1), (2), and (3) not more than one year after the judgment, order, or proceeding was entered or taken. A motion under this subdivision (b) does not affect the finality of a judgment or suspend its operation. This rule does not limit the power of a court to entertain an independent action to relieve a party from a judgment, order, or proceeding, or to grant relief to a defendant not actually personally notified as provided in Title 28, U.S.C., § 1655, or to set aside a judgment for fraud upon the court. Writs of coram nobis, coram vobis, audita querela, and bills of review and bills in the nature of a bill of review, are abolished, and the procedure for obtaining any relief from a judgment shall be by motion as prescribed in these rules or by an independent action.

[12] *Rozier*, 573 F.2d 1332 at 1346. *See also* Hesling v. CSX Transp., Inc., 396 F.3d 632 (5th Cir. 2005) (*Rozier* distinguished); Cummings v. General Motors Corp., 365 F.3d 944 (10th Cir. 2004) (*Rozier* distinguished).

This was vital information which was withheld by defendant Ford Motor Corporation. Whalen's attorney had obtained this Ford record from some litigation other than the instant one-a sad commentary on the effectiveness of the discovery here.[13]

§ 19.07   ANNOYANCE, EMBARRASSMENT, OPPRESSION

Corporations often seek protective orders on the basis that they will suffer significant *annoyance, embarrassment and oppression* if their documents are not protected from dissemination to other lawyers or the television and print media.[14] The discovery rules require that defense counsel point out with specificity each document or portion thereof which would lead to those results. Due to the obvious risk of illustrating the strength of plaintiff's case in doing so, such arguments are rarely forthcoming. The formal showing of annoyance, embarrassment and oppression should be insisted upon for each document so specified. Corporations seldom are specific with supporting reasons, since the greatest number of defense motions for protective orders based in these claims are actually grounded in fear of information sharing. They are also used as the basis for orders alleging that the documentation sought is commercially sensitive, a claim with much more legitimacy.

§ 19.08   TRADE SECRETS AND CONFIDENTIAL COMMERCIAL INFORMATION

In most products liability cases, defendants cannot support trade secret as the basis for a protective order with any degree of credibility. The factors of aggressive advertising and marketing and the obvious physical and public dissemination of the product would tend to militate against any legitimate trade secret basis for a protective order. The traditional test for determining whether information qualifies as a trade secret is threefold:

1.   Is the matter sought to be protected a trade secret or other confidential research, development or commercial information entitled to protection?

---

[13]   Buehler v. Whalen, 374 N.E.2d at 467. *See also* Delvecchio v. General Motors Corp., 255 Ill. App. 3d 189 (1993); Thomas M. Fleming, J.D., Annotation, *Propriety and Extent of State Court Protective Order Restricting Party's Right to Disclose Discovered Information to Others Engaged in Similar Litigation,* 83 A.L.R.4th 987 (1991). (This annotation collects and analyzes those civil cases in which the courts have considered the propriety or extent of a protective order, issued or sought in a state court action, which expressly or allegedly restricts a party's freedom to disclose or disseminate information obtained through discovery in that action to others who are engaged, or who may in the future be engaged, in similar litigation.)

[14]   Federal Rule 26 — General Provisions Governing Discovery:

(c) Protective Orders. Upon motion by a party or by the person from whom discovery is sought, accompanied by a certification that the movant has in good faith conferred or attempted to confer with other affected parties in an effort to resolve the dispute without court action, and for good cause shown, the court in which the action is pending or alternatively, on matters relating to a deposition, the court in the district where the deposition is to be taken may make any order which justice requires to protect a party or person *from annoyance, embarrassment, oppression, or undue burden or expense.*

2. Would disclosure cause a cognizable harm sufficient to warrant a protective order?

3. Has the party seeking protection shown good cause for invoking the court's protection?[15]

The question of competitive disadvantage resulting from the disclosure of discovery materials is considered to fall within the annoyance, embarrassment and oppression factors of Rule 26(c). The party seeking the order on this basis has a heavy burden to establish a sufficient basis for its entry.[16]

In the leading case of *Parsons v. General Motors Corp.*, 85 F.R.D. 724 (N.D. Ga.1980), the court gave an extensive discussion of the type of factual pleading that must accompany any claim of protection on the basis of confidential commercial information.

In *Parsons*, plaintiff claimed injury as a result of burns suffered from a ruptured fuel tank on an Oldsmobile automobile. Plaintiff sought discovery of information from General Motors relative to fuel system design and certain crash tests results. General Motors objected to the discovery and moved for a protective order based upon the confidentiality of the information. In denying its motion, the court stated:

> GM admits that this material is not a "trade secret" but argues that it constitutes "confidential research, development or commercial information," within the meaning of the Rule 26(c)(7). Fed. R. Civ. P. 26 (c)(7). GM has asked the Court to enter a protective order which would prohibit plaintiff and her attorneys from reproducing the crash test results or fuel system design information and from disclosing the material to any third party without the Court's permission. . . . Restrictions of discovery are allowed for "good cause" when disclosure of "a trade secret or other confidential research development or commercial information" is involved. Fed.R. Civ. P. 26(c) (7).
>
> The Court interprets "good cause" in the context of Rule 26(c) (7) to mean that the parties seeking the protective order must demonstrate that the material sought to be protected in confidential and that disclosure will create a competitive disadvantage for the party. The Court finds that the two Affidavits filed by GM do not establish that the information in question is confidential.
>
> One affidavit states that disclosure of crash test results and design information within GM is limited to the technical and engineering staffs of respective divisions. The affidavit does not reveal how many persons

---

[15] The term "trade secret" itself has a variety of state and federal court definitions, as noted in 26 CHARLES ALAN WRIGHT, ARTHUR R. MILLER & EDWARD H. COOPER, FEDERAL PRACTICE & PROCEDURE § 5644 (WRIGHT & MILLER Treatise) (2005 Pocket Part, Chapter 6, Privileges). (An inspection of judicial definitions of "trade secret" reveals great variety in the understanding of this crucial phrase. . . . These definitions have been criticized on many grounds but perhaps the most telling for purposes of the privilege is the assertion that they are devised ad hoc to meet the needs of a particular case and the criticism that most of them are "open-ended and fact intensive." It is little wonder that Wigmore wrote that he used the phrase "trade secret" to describe the privilege only "for lack of a better term.")

[16] Zenith Radio Corp. v. Matsushita Elec. Co., 529 F. Supp. 866 (E.D. Pa. 1981).

worked on their staffs, or how the secrecy of the reports is maintained. The second affidavit states that "initial distribution" of reports of crash tests is limited to "only a few employees." Circulation to others is permitted although reproduction of the reports of crash tests is controlled. The second affidavit mentions no specific controls on fuel system design information. Some of the information plaintiff seeks is ten years old; GM does not show that the information is still confidential after ten years. Moreover, GM admits that some of the information which plaintiff seeks must be disclosed to the government.

GM has not attempted to show what specific information is already part of the public record and what information remains confidentially held at GM. GM has not made a particularized showing that the information sought is confidential as required by Fed. R. Civ. P. 26(c)(7) for entry of a protective order. Moreover, GM's allegations of competitive harm are vague and conclusory when specific examples are necessary.[17]

§ 19.09   FACTUAL COMPONENTS OF THE ARGUMENT IN OPPOSITION

In *United States v. International Business Machines, Inc.*, 67 F.R.D. 40 (S.D.N.Y 1975), Chief Judge Edelstein of the Southern District of New York set forth the key facts that should be considered to determine if commercial information warrants the protection of a protective order on the basis of confidential commercial information:

1.   The extent to which such information is known outside the business.

2.   The extent to which such information is known to those in the business.

3.   Measures taken to guard the secrecy of the information.

4.   The value of the information to the business and its competitors.[18] The ultimate test, however, was whether disclosure would work a "clearly defined and very serious injury."[19]

In drafting the memorandum in opposition to the protective order, the argument will thus focus on the general availability of the technical processes that defendant manufacturer seeks to protect. Plaintiff's memorandum should demonstrate the commercial availability of the technology underlying the documents. The manufacturer's chances of success on the basis of *confidential commercial information*, decreases in direct proportion to the time that has passed since the introduction of the technology underlying the documents into the marketplace.

---

[17]   *Parsons*, 85 F.R.D. at 725–26. On this topic, see also *Federal Court Discovery in the 80's — Making the Rules Work*, 95 F.R.D. 245, 295 (1982); AMERICAN LAW OF PRODUCTS LIABILITY, § 53:67, Particular grounds for issuing protective orders — Trade Secrets (2005); Discovery Proceedings in Federal Court, § 20:13, Protective orders specifically authorized; Preclusion of disclosure discovery — Limitation on disclosure of confidential business information (2004).

[18]   67 F.R.D. 40, 46 (S.D.N.Y. 1975).

[19]   *Id.*

Counsel must educate the court as to the nature of the technology and research underlying defendant's motion. The expert witness affidavit can be used to great advantage here, setting out what is or is not "out there" with respect to the technology, pharmacology, or chemical formulation sought to be protected from disclosure. Here, however, that tutorial is directed to the technology and manufacturing processes themselves, rather than the arguable relevancy of underlying documentation to the legal and factual issues in the litigation.[20]

§ 19.10 MEETING THE ARGUMENTS FOR EACH DOCUMENT

Counsel should insist that defendant establish the basis of protection for each document covered by the motion. The burden is on the corporation to demonstrate both the degree and manner in which each would reveal the processes deemed *commercially sensitive*. Defense arguments directed to general document types are inadequate to warrant protection for the specific processes reflected in any one individual document.

Expert witness affidavits can provide significant support for plaintiff's position that the technology or commercial information reflected in the disputed documents are not *commercially sensitive*. For each area of technology for which protection is sought counsel should consult with his expert to estimate the validity of defendant's claim.

§ 19.11 DISCOVERY ENFORCEMENT

The central problem faced by plaintiff counsel in products liability litigation is the enforcement of their discovery requests. These matters are generally resolved after a long period of squabbling and one or more motions by plaintiff for sanctions for failure to comply with discovery. It is important to note that a defendant manufacturer is under no obligation to answer poorly drafted, vague or clearly irrelevant interrogatories or requests to produce documents. There is, of course a wide margin of differences of opinion on just what is or is not *relevant* to the cases. Poorly prepared or inexperienced plaintiff counsel often make a variety of "any and all, anywhere, whenever" type of requests that are clearly without the ken of even the most liberal interpretation of wide-ranging discovery. Having said that, it is clear that products defense counsel have their own "irrelevant, burdensome, oppressive, work product, attorney-client" shotgun response to discovery that is equally improper.

An often-encountered defense counsel position regarding discovery compliance was recently set forth in a recent article in the *Practical Litigator*:[21]

---

[20] *See* TERRENCE F. KIELY, SCIENCE AND LITIGATION: PRODUCTS LIABILITY IN THEORY AND PRACTICE 412 (CRC Press 2002).

[21] Nahrstadt, *Narrowing the Scope of Discovery for Substantially Similar Products*, 15 No. 6 PRAC. LIT. 37, 38 (2004) (This is a brief, well-written summary of the issues from a defense attorney standpoint.).

THE PROBLEM

Every defense attorney who has ever handled a products liability action is all too familiar with the unbelievably broad discovery requests propounded by plaintiffs' attorneys. More often than not, plaintiffs' attorneys serve defense counsel with interrogatories or requests for production of documents which request volumes of information regarding not only the product at issue, but other products that have also been manufactured by the defendant. These interrogatories and requests for production of documents often request information regarding the design, manufacture, production, distribution, and sale of any product the defendant has ever manufactured which is remotely similar (or in some cases not even remotely similar) to the product which the plaintiff claims caused his or her injury. When faced with such expansive discovery requests, defense counsel must take a restrictive, conservative approach to providing information to plaintiff's counsel regarding products other than the product at issue in that particular case.[22]

Plaintiff counsel counter that at the discovery stage, similar product lines that incorporate technology of the very type at issue in the case are clearly fair game. This position has always found significant support in United States courts. Justice Powell of the United States Supreme Court, writing in 1978 for a unanimous court in Oppenheimer Fund, Inc. v. Sanders stated:[23]

The key phrase in this definition — "relevant to the subject matter involved in the pending action" — has been construed broadly to encompass any matter that bears on, or that reasonably could lead to other matter that could bear on, any issue that is or may be in the case.[24] Consistently with the notice-pleading system established by the Rules, discovery is not limited to issues raised by the pleadings, for discovery itself is designed to help define and clarify the issues. Nor is discovery limited to the merits of a case, for a variety of fact-oriented issues may arise during litigation that are not related to the merits.[25]

Numerous cases have held that a request for discovery should be considered relevant if there is "any possibility" that the information sought may be relevant to the subject matter of the action. The primary focal point to determine the actual scope of discovery relevancy is the plaintiff's complaint. As noted in the leading cases of *Roesberg v. Johns-Manville Corp.*[26]:

The detail in the complaint specifies the necessary relevance of the interrogatories . . . The burden now falls upon GAF, the party resisting

---

[22] *Id.* at 38. The author goes on to say that aggressive attempts to limit the amount and type of information supplied about the manufacture of other products or product lines is required because such evidence can confuse the jury and may lead it to wrongly conclude that the product at issue is defective.

[23] 437 U.S. 340 (1978).

[24] *See* Hickman v. Taylor, 329 U.S. 495, 501 (1947).

[25] *Id.* at 500–01.

[26] 85 F.R.D. 292, 296–97 (E.D. Pa. 1980).

discovery to clarify and explain its objections and to provide support therefor.[27]

The allegations of each count in the complaint determine the broad subject matters involved in the case. However, relevance is to be measured, not strictly according to the specific fact issues raised by the pleadings, but by reference to the broader logical parameters of those facts.[28]

A routine response of products defendants is to answer or produce materials that could not credibly be objected to and to then refuse to answer interrogatories or produce the bulk of the requested documents. The phrase "defendant refuses to answer plaintiff interrogatories 3-30 [or document request 1-15] on the basis that the information sought is not relevant or not reasonably calculated to lead to the discovery of such information" is a familiar one in state and federal courtrooms across America.[29] This response sets the stage for each side's opportunity to attempt to draw the relevancy and time frame lines that will govern the remainder of discovery and the broad outlines of the trial itself.

§ 19.12   SAMPLE DISCOVERY ENFORCEMENT MEMORANDUM — STAINLESS STEEL PRESSURIZED BEVERAGE CANISTER LITIGATION[30]

Set out below is a sample memorandum in support of a plaintiff motion to strike the answer of the Defendant Fremantle Tire and Rubber Company for failure to answer plaintiff's interrogatories. This Sample Memorandum illustrates the manner in which the various liability and discovery theories discussed in this book may come together in an aggressive litigation in a hypothetical products liability case. Plaintiff's position was chosen as the most illustrative setting out this memorandum here, continues the effort of this book to supply real life examples of the application of the products liability theories set out in Chapters 2–10.[31]

---

[27] *Id.* at 297.

[28] Smith v. F.T.C., 403 F. Supp. 1000 (D. Del. 1975).

[29] As noted by Nahrstadt:

Obviously, the defense attorney who is successful in preventing the introduction of "extraneous" issues to the jury will be far ahead of the game in terms of limiting the scope of the case and concentrating the jury's focus on the salient legal issues. One of the most successful ways of limiting the introduction of "extraneous" issues is to prevent the plaintiff's attorney from finding out about them during the course of discovery.

Nahrstadt, *supra* note 21, at 38.

[30] John Denton v. The Fremantle Tire & Rubber Company, Polymer Plastic Company, Apex Grinding Company, and the Premier Plastic Corporation — Complaint set forth and examined in Chapter 14, Drafting the Complaint and Discovery Focus.

[31] The full *Denton v. Fremantle* complaint is set out in Chapter 14, Drafting the Complaint and Discovery Focus §§ 14.03–14.12. The *Denton* Interrogatories are set out in Chapter 16, Interrogatories and Request to Admit Facts, § 16.09 Sample Interrogatories: Pressurized Stainless Steel Beverage Canister. The *Denton* Requests for Documents are provided in Chapter 17, Requests to Produce Documents, § 17.09 Sample Request for Documents: Pressurized Stainless Steel Beverage Canisters.

§ 19.13   THE DENTON v. FREMANTLE DISCOVERY ENFORCEMENT SUPPORT MEMORANDUM

MEMORANDUM IN SUPPORT OF PLAINTIFF'S MOTION TO STRIKE DEFENDANT'S ANSWER FOR FAILURE TO ANSWER INTERROGATORIES

I

INTRODUCTION

This is a products liability case brought by Plaintiff John Denton against the manufacturers of a pressurized stainless steel commercial soft-drink beverage canister. The gist of plaintiff's complaint alleges that the defendant manufactured this container in a manner that caused it to be in an unreasonably dangerous condition when used by workers, such as Plaintiff, in the commercial soft-drink beverage industry. Specifically, Plaintiff alleges four basic problems with respect to the canister that is the subject of this action:

1. The canister was not reasonably safe in design due to the foreseeable risk that a canister lid or cap constructed of plastic materials would shatter or explode during the course of foreseeable routine handling by workers in the commercial soft-drink vending industry.

2. The canister was not reasonably safe in design due to inadequate pressure relief mechanisms to prevent the shattering or exploding of the plastic lid or cap or other portions of the canister during the course of routine foreseeable handling by workers in the commercial soft-drink vending industry.

3. The canister was not reasonably safe in design due to inadequate mechanisms to prevent the over pressurization of the canister, thereby creating the risk of the shattering or exploding of the plastic lid or cap or other portions of the canister during the course of foreseeable routine handling by workers in the commercial soft-drink vending industry.

4. The canister was not reasonably safe in that defendant failed to provide adequate warnings of the dangers involved in the handling of the canister, including, but not limited to the shattering or exploding of the plastic lid or cap or other portions of said canister during the course of foreseeable routine handling by workers in the commercial soft-drink vending industry.

The complaint contains three counts, sounding in strict liability, negligence and punitive damages. The defendant is the Fremantle Tire and Rubber Company.

In January of 2001, the Plaintiff John Denton was in the process of preparing a pallet of returned canisters for recycling at his place of employment, Joyce Beverages, when the plastic cap on one of the canisters exploded, causing permanent injury to his left eye and face.

Plaintiff has served both a First and Second Set of Interrogatories and Requests for the Production of Documents on Defendant. Defendant has filed responses to both sets of discovery requests, which, with minor exceptions, constitute a total refusal to respond to Plaintiff's focused and reasonable requests for information.

The Interrogatories and Requests for the Production of Documents directed to defendant Fremantle Tire and Rubber Company seek information relative to the design, testing, production and marketing of pressurized beverage syrup containers of the type involved in this lawsuit. Plaintiff's requests are focused on matters that are clearly either relevant to these proceedings or reasonably calculated to lead to the discovery of such relevant data.

The requests seek information from each defendant for a time frame ranging from 1975 to the present. The years-long manufacture of the suspect canisters by defendant and the complex nature of the scientific facts surrounding this case, require extensive interrogatories that might not be required in a simpler factual setting. The Defendant manufacturer has either refused to answer Plaintiff's Interrogatories or supplied "answers" that merely object to each individual question without supporting reasons. (See Section V.)

Plaintiffs must now come before this Court and seek an order compelling Defendant to fully and adequately supply answers to Plaintiff's legitimate, relevant and essential requests for information. It should be noted, that Plaintiff has fully responded to all discovery requests submitted by this defendant. In some instances Plaintiffs have answered supplemental interrogatories and document requests.

The defendant has based its refusal to answer these interrogatories on the following reasons:

- The interrogatories are too lengthy;

- They cover too long a period of time;

- It would take considerable man hours to locate the requested information;

- It would cost too much money to conduct the required search;

- The requested information is not kept in a central file where it could be readily accessed;

- The questions themselves are:

    (a.)   Not relevant or likely to lead to the discovery of relevant information;

    (b.)   Overly broad;

    (c.)   Vague;

    (d.)   Unreasonably burdensome;

    (e.)   Incapable of reasonable response.

These motions in opposition typically go well beyond what might be expected from a company legitimately attempting to protect its private papers from outside scrutiny. There has been a conscious decision by the defendant to totally ignore principles of discovery obvious to the novice attorney practicing in the federal courts. For that reason, Plaintiff is requesting costs and attorneys fees necessitated by the hours of unnecessary work needed to bring this motion and prepare this memorandum.

Defendant is no stranger to product liability litigation and the discovery rules of the federal courts. They have been through the process of responding to discovery in cases involving their other product lines to a sufficient degree that their expressed perplexity at the nature of the information sought by Plaintiff truly rings hollow. That same experience makes their studied ignoring of familiar case law interpretations of the Federal Rules and the language of the Rules themselves, totally unacceptable.

It should be noted that defendant does not question the propriety of the information *categories* addressed in the interrogatories themselves. It is important in a case of this complexity to address the general issue of just what categories of information are routinely and necessarily subject to discovery in a products liability case grounded in allegations of defective design, failure to warn and punitive damages.

II

DISCOVERABLE TYPES OF INFORMATION

Defendant Fremantle cannot take the position that it is not required to supply *any* information to plaintiffs in this case. All parties agree that certain categories of information are discoverable from this manufacturer over *some* past period of time in their manufacturing and marketing history with respect to the stainless steel pressurized beverage canister at issue in this case. The period of defendant's manufacturing history within which appropriate information is discoverable, is really separate from the question of the appropriate categories of information that are discoverable in the first instance. Accordingly, Plaintiff will address the question of information categories first.

In any products liability design or failure to warn case, the overriding fact question is the extent of the manufacturer's knowledge of the alleged risks associated with the normal use of the product. That central question can only be answered in part by examining the authoritative literature in the relevant fields of engineering. The study of such sources will identify the extent, if any, to which the alleged risks have been identified by knowledgeable scientists and alternative design principles noted. The only other major source of information on the question of feasible alternative designs and a manufacturer defendant's knowledge of the alleged risks is their own internal corporate documents.

Such documents reflect the extent of their experience with the suspect product, through the course of their formulating, testing, producing and marketing of it. The first stage of efficient discovery in products liability cases thus revolves, initially, around the issue of what categories of information contained in the defendant manufacturer's archives are arguably subject to discovery.

Regardless of the type of product being manufactured and whether or not it is a new offering or a subsequent model in a pre-existing line of goods, there are routine stages or steps that are followed in the manufacturing company to move the product from the idea stage to the inventory shelf.

Each broad stage in this multi-year process is further broken down into more focused sets of activity that consistently generate routine types and forms of documentation such as test reports and test analyses. These materials, in turn, are generally channeled along fairly fixed lines of distribution within the company for purposes of review by management. Accordingly, the principal initial goal in the discovery process in this litigation, is the identification of the categories of documentary information arguably generated by this defendant as a result of the various activities involved in the development, testing, manufacturing and marketing of the subject pressurized stainless steel beverage canister manufactured by them. Equally important is identifying the manner in which that documentation was disseminated throughout the company.

Requiring defendant to respond to structured, detailed and specific interrogatories seeking such information, will go a long way in eliminating costly and time consuming discovery motion practice in this litigation. It clearly meets the stated goals of Federal discovery practice, by facilitating efficient and effective discovery and trial planning.

While courts and litigators may differ in terminology, Plaintiff submits that the major stages along the product development and manufacturing continuum in large corporations, such as the defendant, are basically four in number:

1. Product Design or Drug Formulation

2. Product Testing

3. Product Manufacturing

4. Product Marketing

Defendant certainly would not dispute the fact that some information is accessible by Plaintiffs in this case during each of the above basic manufacturing stages, for some historical period of time. Due to the very nature of corporations, whatever information there may be that Plaintiff is entitled to, will be contained in company documents. These materials will have been generated by company technical and managerial staff as a result of specific activities occurring within the above-noted basic manufacturing stages.

These broad categories can be further sub-divided for discovery planning purposes by a functional breakdown of the activities that have traditionally been a primary focus of corporate energies in the course of product development and manufacture. Such activities would undoubtedly include some form of the following:

DESIGN:

- Overall Product Planning

- Marketing Feasibility Studies

- Technical, Pharmacological or Chemical Feasibility Studies

- Financial Feasibility Studies

- Federal or State Regulatory Reviews

- Detailed Component or Laboratory Studies
- Project Approval Discussions

TESTING:

- Prototype Testing, Animal Testing or Clinical Trials
- Testing Required by Regulatory Agencies
- Alternative Design Testing
- Drafting of Instructions and Warnings

PRODUCTION:

- Finalization of Product Specifications
- Actual Production Runs
- Quality Control Activities

MARKETING:

- Marketing Plans and Arrangements
- Advertising and promotional literature, films or documents
- Customer Complaint Processing

In addition to these basic information categories, plaintiffs in products liability cases are clearly entitled to access a certain amount of information respecting the organizational structure of the defendant company. This information is essential to identify the origination and flow of materials through the various offices, departments, sections and committees within the large scale manufacturing corporation. In this latter regard, Plaintiff submits that some information in the following categories is accessible by them in this case:

CORPORATE ORGANIZATION

- Overall Organization Charts
- Central Staff Organization Charts
- Listings of Groups, Offices, Departments and Sections and Managing
- Personnel
- Committee Structures and Membership
- Functional Employee Groupings

OPERATIONAL DOCUMENTATION

- Standard Operating Procedures
- Record Retention Policies
- Electronic creation, destruction and storage methods and history

- Complaint Processing Procedures

Plaintiff submits that selected information in the above-noted information categories is discoverable in this case, to the degree that such reflects on defendant's knowledge of risks, if any, associated with the design of the stainless steel pressurized beverage canister that is the subject of this case and was manufactured by them. Plaintiffs' Second Set of Interrogatories and Requests for Documents seek to access information in each of these obviously relevant categories, in a well organized, focused and clear manner.

Defendant has repeatedly stressed that the development, testing, production and marketing of a product such as the subject canister, is a very complex process, involving many people, over a substantial period of time. Plaintiff does not quarrel with that assertion. However, that reality results in the generation of a large body of corporate documentation. Often, that information is difficult and costly to locate. Defendant, however, cannot use the complexity inherent in modern industrial manufacture as a basis for refusing to supply any information.

Plaintiff clearly understands that it is not defendant's burden to try and figure out what information Plaintiff is seeking. What is required from Plaintiff is a reasonable, comprehensive, focused, precise and well organized set of information requests. Plaintiff has provided just that in the Interrogatories and Document Requests heretofore filed in this case.

The complexity of defendant Fremantle's business and the extensive corporate and engineering information involved in analyzing the possible risks associated with the use of the type of pressurized beverage canister involved in this case requires extensive discovery. Those same factors require that each question contain several sub-parts in order to provide defendant with the necessary degree of specificity for each information category addressed. The degree of specificity of Plaintiff's Interrogatories and Document Requests are intended to facilitate their record search.

Set out below is a categorization of the Plaintiff's Interrogatories:[32]

INTERROGATORIES 1–3: Corporate organization

INTERROGATORY 4: Engineering literature reviewed

INTERROGATORY 5: Component parts and manufacturers

INTERROGATORY 6: Trade Association activities

INTERROGATORY 7: Sales data

INTERROGATORY 8: Testing activities

INTERROGATORY 9: Comparable product lines

INTERROGATORY 10: Other lawsuits

INTERROGATORY 11: Injury history and complaints

INTERROGATORY 12: Profits information

---

[32] See full set in Chapter 16, Interrogatories and Requests to Admit Facts, § 16.11.

INTERROGATORY 13: Optional safety equipment

INTERROGATORY 14: Foreign sales data

INTERROGATORY 15: Manufacturing standards

III

TIME FRAME FOR DISCOVERY

Once court and counsel agree on the subject areas to which focused discovery requests may be directed, it must be determined over what historical period of time in the corporation's history any such information may be accessed. Defendant cannot seriously take the position that no period within their company histories is applicable. The Court must resolve this central discovery issue.

Plaintiffs have requested that defendant provide information in the above-noted information categories for a period from 1975 to date. This period is reasonable and was chosen for the following reasons:

1. Defendant has manufactured the type of canister involved in this case for at least that period of time. During that period, the overall design of the canister and its component parts has not changed, thereby allowing a constant factor against which to assess the appropriateness of defendant's response to the engineering literature and their own experience with the product.

2. The engineering literature addressing the relevant technologies stretches over a period of close to 25 years.

3. Plaintiff's complaint includes a punitive damage count against this defendant and such counts have traditionally been grounded in a defendant's long-term knowledge of a substantial risk to foreseeable users such as John Denton.

The appropriate time frame for discovery will vary with each case. Manufacturers in products liability cases must often search for information over lengthy periods in order to fully respond to discovery requests. This is especially the case in drug products litigation, where the chemical formulation of the drug has normally not been changed for decades. That reality, however, has never been considered by federal courts to be an adequate reason for not supplying any information.

Plaintiff's have, without objection, fully and seasonably answered the discovery requests submitted by defendant. Plaintiffs in a products liability action simply have much less information to provide in discovery than would a defendant manufacturer. The relevancy of information and the appropriate time over which it must be forthcoming are directly related to the information a party actually has and its relation to the allegations of the complaint. In the instant case, the period within which Plaintiff is seeking focused, specific information, is reasonable and well within the parameters of the scope of discovery in this litigation.

In the leading case of *Roesberg v. Johns-Manville Corp.*, 85 F.R.D. 292 (E.D. Pa. 1980), the court, in rejecting defendant's argument that a 55-year time frame specified in plaintiff's interrogatories was burdensome, stated:

> "In Interrogatory Number Three plaintiff seeks to discover asbestos products which GAF manufactured, processed, compounded, converted, sold, supplied or distributed since 1925. GAF's primary objection to this interrogatory is the broad time frame included by plaintiff, whose employment spanned the years 1942 to 1979. However, plaintiff alleges conspiracies antedating plaintiff's employment history and intended to disguise and distort information which would have suggested to plaintiff the unreasonably dangerous and ultrahazardous nature of working with asbestos.

Accordingly, plaintiff's selected time frame is not wholly unreasonable or irrelevant. Such a request for discovery should be considered relevant."

In the instant action, a 30-year time frame, especially given the inclusion by Plaintiff of a punitive damage count is reasonable and does not, by its terms, create any undue burden on this defendant.

IV

RELEVANCY IN THE DISCOVERY PROCESS

In the interests of fair trial, eliminating surprise and achieving justice, relevancy, construed liberally, creates a broad vista for discovery. *Oppenheimer Fund, Inc. v. Sanders*, 437 U.S. 340, 351, 98 S. Ct. 2380, 57 L.Ed.2d 253 (1978), *Schlagenhauf v. Holder*, 379 U.S. 104, 121, 85 S. Ct. 234, 13 L. Ed. 2d 152 (1964), *Hickman v. Taylor*, 329 U.S. 495, 507, 67 S. Ct. 385, 91 L. Ed. 451 (1947), *United States v. Purdome*, 30 F.R.D. 338, 340 (W.D. Mo. 1962), *Stonybrook Tenants Association, Inc. v. Alpert*, 29 F.R.D. 165, 168

(D. Conn.1961). It makes the trial "less a game of blind man's bluff and more a fair contest with the basic issues and facts disclosed to the fullest practicable extent." *United States v. Procter & Gamble Co.*, 356 U.S. 677, 682, 78 S. Ct. 983, 2 L. Ed. 2d 1077 (1958); *McClain v. Mack Trucks, Inc.*, 85 F.R.D. 53, 57 (E.D. Pa. 1979).

The facts and circumstances of each case determine and limit relevance of interrogatories. *Shang v. Hotel Waldorf Astoria Corp.*, 77 F.R.D. 468, 469 (S.D.N.Y.1978), *Hoffman v. Wilson Line, Inc.*, 7 F.R.D. 73, 74 (E.D. Pa. 1946).The standard to be used to determine the factual information available to the parties in the course of discovery under the Federal discovery rules is as follows:

> . . . Parties may obtain discovery regarding any matter, not privileged, which is relevant to the subject matter involved in the pending action, whether it relates to the claim or defense of any party, including the existence, description, nature, custody, condition and location of any books, documents, or other tangible things and the identity and location of persons having knowledge of any discoverable matter. It is not ground for objection that the information sought will be inadmissible at the trial if the information sought appears reasonably calculated to lead to the discovery of admissible evidence.

F.R.C.P 26(b)(1).

The definition of relevance is provided by Rule 401 of the Federal Rules of Evidence. That provision defines relevant evidence as follows: " 'Relevant evidence' means evidence having any tendency to make the existence of a fact that is of consequence to the determination of the action more probable or less probable than it would be without the evidence." By referencing this broad standard and providing for the free discovery of data that may be reasonably calculated to lead to the discovery of such, the Federal courts have mandated a liberal discovery scheme.

As noted by Justice Powell of the United States Supreme Court, writing for a unanimous court:

> . . . The key phrase in this definition — "relevant to the subject matter involved in the pending action" — has been construed broadly to encompass any matter that bears on, or that reasonably could lead to other matter that could bear on, any issue that is or may be in the case. (citations omitted). . . . Consistently with the notice-pleading system established by the Rules, discovery is not limited to issues raised by the pleadings, for discovery itself is designed to help define and clarify the issues. (citation omitted.) Nor is discovery limited to the merits of a case, for a variety of fact- oriented issues may arise during litigation that are not related to the merits.

Oppenheimer Fund, Inc. v. Sanders, 437 U.S. 340, 351(1978).

A request for discovery should be considered relevant if there is any possibility that information sought may be relevant to the subject matter of the action. Discovery is not limited to formally admissible evidence because its primary purpose is to formulate, define and narrow issues to be tried, increase the chances for settlement, and give each party the opportunity to inform himself of the facts that may come out at trial. *Detweiler Bros., Inc. v. John Graham & Co.*, 412 F. Supp. 416 (D.C. Wash. 1976); *Duplan Corp. v. Deering Milliken Inc.*, 397 F. Supp. 1146 (D.S.C. 1974); *Carlson Companies Inc. v. Sperry & Hutchinson Co.*, 374 F. Supp. 1080 (D. Minn. 1973); *Sylgab Steel & Wire Corp. v. Imoco-Gateway Corp.*, 357 F. Supp. 659 (N.D. Ill. 1973).

As stated in the 1984 case of *Chubb Integrated Systems v. National Bank of Washington et al:*

> . . . Whether this information is found to be admissible at trial has little bearing on the issue of discoverability. Rule 26(b) makes a clear distinction between information that is relevant to the subject matter for pretrial discovery and the ultimate admissibility of that information at trial.

Admissibility at trial is not the yardstick of permissible discovery." 103 F.R.D 52 (1984). FED. R. CIV. P. 26 (b)(1), advisory committee note, 1970 Amendment. The relevancy of the information sought bears directly on the issue of whether discovery requests are burdensome. If the requested material is relevant, no matter the volume, it must be produced. The initial focal point to determine the actual scope of this broadly interpreted concept is the plaintiff's complaint. As noted in *Roesberg v. Johns-Manville Corp., supra:*

. . . The detail in the complaint specifies the necessary relevance of the interrogatories . . . The burden now falls upon GAF, the party resisting discovery, to clarify and explain its objections and to provide support therefor.

The allegations of the complaint serve to determine the broad subject matters involved in the case, and relevance is to be measured, not according to the specific issues raised by the pleadings, but rather, by reference to such subject matters. *Smith v. F.T.C.*, 403 F. Supp. 1000 (D. Del. 1975).

In the instant case, defendant Fremantle does not question the appropriateness of the categories of information sought by Plaintiff. That is because the subject categories for which information is sought are those involved in any product liability case i.e., the design, testing, production and marketing of the suspect product.

V

SPECIFICITY IN OBJECTION

Defendant raises four recurring and totally unsupported objections as the basis for its refusal to provide anything close to adequate information to Plaintiff:

(1.)   The information sought is not relevant nor likely to lead to the discovery of relevant evidence;

(2.)   The interrogatories are overbroad;

(3.)   The interrogatories are oppressive or burdensome;

(4.)   The interrogatories are vague; In no instance does Fremantle specify in what respect any particular inquiry falls into any one or more of the above categories.

The initial failing of Fremantle's argument is that their various allegations are totally unsupported by affidavits that address the substance of the questions. Equally fatal, is the defendant's failure to provide the Court and Plaintiff with detailed objections to each question and sub-part to which objection may be had. Federal case law is clear that such unsupported "shotgun" responses constitute no answer.

The Federal Rules of Civil Procedure provide that if the party receiving interrogatories or document requests objects to any inquiry contained therein, the reasons for such objection shall be stated. FRCP Rule 33(a). The Federal trial courts have been uniform in holding that the objections must point to specific facts supporting the objection, and that a simple reiteration of "irrelevant," "oppressive," "burdensome" or "privilege" constitutes no answer. *Pressley v. Boehlke*, 33 F.R.D. 316 (W.D.N.C. 1963); *Josephs v. Harris Corp*, 677 F.2d 985 (3d Cir. 1982); *Goodman v. Wagner*, 553 F. Supp. 255 (E.D. Pa. 1982).

In *Chubb Integrated Systems v. National Bank of Washington et al.*, decided in 1984, the court soundly rejected factually unsupported objections to interrogatories:

An objection must show specifically how an interrogatory is overly broad, burdensome or oppressive, by submitting affidavits or offering evidence which reveals the nature of the burden. Plaintiff's objections do not reveal the nature of its burden. Without more, this Court cannot conclude that Chubb will be unduly burdened by the interrogatories. Accordingly, we reject this argument.

Chubb Integrated Systems Limited v. National Bank of Washington et al., 103 F.R.D 52 (1984). *See generally* 4A J. MOORE & J. LUCAS, MOORE'S FEDERAL PRACTICE § 33.27 (2d ed. 1983).

In the leading case of *Roesberg v. Johns-Manville Corp.*, 85 F.R.D.292, 296–97 (E.D. Pa. 1980), the court stated:

> Finally, GAF objects generally to this interrogatory as "overly broad, burdensome, oppressive, and irrelevant," a complaint which GAF echoes with virtually every other interrogatory. To voice a successful objection to an interrogatory, GAF cannot simply intone this familiar litany. Rather, GAF must show specifically how, despite the broad and liberal construction afforded the federal discovery rules, each interrogatory is not relevant or how each question is overly broad, burdensome, or oppressive, (citations omitted) by submitting affidavits or offering evidence revealing the nature of the burden. (Citations omitted). The court is not required to "sift each interrogatory to determine the usefulness of the answer sought." (citations omitted). . . .

See also Trabon Engineering Corp. v. Easton Manufacturing Co., 37 F.R.D. 51, 54 (N.D. Ohio 1964); *Stanley Works v. Haeger Potteries, Inc.*, 35 F.R.D. 551, 555 (N.D. Ill. 1964); *Klausen v. Sidney Printing & Publishing Co.*, 271 F. Supp. 783, 784 (D. Kan. 1967).

In the case of *In re Folding Carton Antitrust Litigation*, 83 F.R.D. 260, 264 (N.D. Ill. 1979), the court, as in *Roesberg, supra*, condemned the practice engaged in by the manufacturing defendant in the instant case, of rubber stamping each legitimate discovery request with an unsupported litany of objections:

> Objections to interrogatories must be specific and supported by a detailed explanation why the interrogatories are improper. General objections may result in waiver of the objections. . . . Plaintiff's catch-all objection named every conceivable ground including that the interrogatories are duplicative, not relevant to the subject matter of the litigation, oppressive, and overly vague. Plaintiff's response was so broad as to be meaningless. . . .

See also United States v. 58.16 Acres of Land, 66 F.R.D. 570, 572 (E.D. Ill. 1975); *Chubb Integrated Systems Limited v. National Bank of Washington et al.*, 103 F.R.D 52 (1984).

Defendant's objections to Plaintiff's legitimate and specific discovery requests in the instant case are a mirror image of the responses found totally lacking in the cases cited above. By responding with unsupported "shotgun" objections to or otherwise simply refusing to answer the Plaintiff's interrogatories and document requests, Defendant "intone(s) the litany of stock objections" condemned in

Roesberg, supra. This is totally inadequate to replace the factually supported objections to each question submitted, as is clearly required by federal case law.

Plaintiff understands that it is much easier for attorneys to dash off one and one-half page "affidavits" without having to bother examining the materials in their client's possession that may contain the requested information. Plaintiff also recognizes that it is much easier to address an entire set of interrogatories or document requests without having the bother of objecting to each request submitted. However, that approach is totally unsupported in repeated federal case law addressing the responsibilities of parties objecting to interrogatories or document requests.

Objections to each interrogatory and document request must be complete, explicit and responsive. If a party cannot furnish details, he must say so under oath, and say why and set forth the efforts used to obtain the information. *Milner v. National School of Health Technology*, 73 F.R.D. 628 (E.D. Pa. 1977). This basic requirement of federal discovery practice was reiterated in the case of *Chubb Integrated Systems v. National Bank of Washington*, where the court stated:

> "Defendant must show specifically how, despite the broad and liberal construction afforded the federal discovery rules, each interrogatory is not relevant or how each question is overly broad, burdensome or oppressive, by submitting affidavits or offering evidence revealing the nature of the burden." (Emphasis added). 103 F.R.D. 52, *60 (D.D.C. 1984)

VI

OVERBROAD, BURDENSOME AND OPPRESSIVE INTERROGATORIES

The allegedly burdensome and oppressive nature of Plaintiff's interrogatories and document requests are a standard component of the litany of the totally unsupported objections raised by defendant to them. Defendants' unsupported reiteration of the stock objections of "burdensome," "vague" and "oppressive," does not constitute a proper objection. *Sherman Park Community Ass'n v. Wauwatosa Realty Co.*, 486 F. Supp. 838 (E.D. Wis. 1980). *See also Swain v. General Motors Corp.*, 81 F.R.D. 698 (W.D. Pa. 1979) (scope of discovery in products cases).

The clear burden is on this defendant to indicate with specificity exactly in what respect each Interrogatory or document request is overbroad. Having failed to do so to any degree, defendant's allegation that such requests are overbroad fails to rise to the level of a proper answer. (See Authorities cited above.)

Rule 33 of the Federal Rules of Civil Procedure requires a corporation to furnish such information as is available from the corporation itself or from sources under its control after an examination of the requested materials. *Brunswick Corp. v. Suzuki Motor Co*, 96 F.R.D. 684 (E.D. Wis. 1983).

The number and detailed nature of the interrogatories and document requests at issue here, per se, are simply not a sufficient reason for disallowing them unless they are "egregiously burdensome or oppressive." *Wirtz v. Capitol Air Service, Inc.*, 42 F.R.D. 641 (D. Kan. 1967). Nor is the fact that answering them will require these companies to expend considerable time, effort and expense or may even interfere with their company business. *Wirtz, supra. See also In re Folding Carton Antitrust Litigation*, 83 F.R.D. 260 (N.D. Ill. 1979); *Krantz v. United States*, 56 F.R.D. 555 (W.D. Va. 1972). The bare allegation of oppressiveness is patently insufficient to warrant refusal to answer. *Josephs v. Harris Corp.*, 677 F.2d 985 (3d Cir. 1982); *Goodman v. Wagner*, 553 F. Supp. 255 (E.D. Pa. 1982).

Defendant's assertion that certain of Plaintiff's requests do not comport with its record keeping or organizational practices, is likewise, prima facie, an inadequate response. If corporations do not classify data in the manner requested, the defendant must seek the required answers by whatever reasonable means are available to it, whether by personal observation, recollection or otherwise. *Equal Employment Opportunity Commission v. Hickey-Mitchell Co.*, 372 F. Supp. 1117 (E.D. Mo. 1973).

In the case of *Altech Industries v. Al Tech Specialty Steel*, 528 F. Supp. 521, 523–24 (D. Del. 1981), the defendant's objection was nearly identical to the posture taken here that records are hard to find and that compliance would unduly burden and oppress defendant. In rejecting any such general objection as insufficient, the court applied the uniform requirement of a specific demonstration of burden for each interrogatory submitted:

> A second objection of the defendant is that it would be unduly burdensome for it to respond more fully than it has to interrogatory 4 of the first and third sets. In objecting to augmenting its answer . . . defendant alleges that to do so would be burdensome in that "plaintiff seeks information concerning possible meetings involving hundreds of present and former employees of GATX and the company maintains no separate records as to any such meetings involving such persons." Similarly, defendant's objection to augmenting the answers which it has supplied to interrogatory 4 . . . is that this too would be burdensome since plaintiff "seeks information concerning possible communications or conversations involving hundreds of present and former employees of GATX and the company maintains no separate records as to any such communications or conversations involving such persons." The defendant has provided no evidence to support its objection of burdensomeness. Consequently, no validity can be attributed to it.

Similarly, in the case of *F.D.I.C. v. Mercantile Nat. Bank of Chicago*, 84 F.R.D. 345, 348 (N.D. Ill. 1979), Judge Marovitz, in the face of a similar objection, stated:

> Concerning Mercantile's argument that compliance with plaintiff's interrogatories will be unduly burdensome, the Court begins with the proposition that the fact that a party will be put to some trouble and expense in the process of answering interrogatories is not alone a sufficient ground for objection. . . . An objection to a set of interrogatories on the ground that compliance would be unduly burdensome will only be sustained if the objecting party establishes that the burden upon him outweighs the benefit the information would provide to the party submitting the interrogatories.

See also Pollock v. Deere and Co., 282 N.W.2d 735 (Iowa 1979); *Roberts v. DeKalb Agr. Ass'n, Inc.*, 259 Iowa 131, 143 N.W.2d 338 (1966).

As with each of their objections, defendant Fremantle has failed to even minimally meet its burden of specifying a factual basis for their refusal to answer.

Defendant suggests that such detailed questions are more appropriate for deposition than written interrogatories. The permissible number and detail of interrogatories are directly related to the complexity of the case in which they are submitted. Plaintiff has asked the defendant to supply a listing of relevant documents or the documents themselves. This practice, in a case involving many more questions and sub-parts than involved here, was recently found fair and adequate under modern, liberal discovery rules.

In the recent case of *Compagnie Francaise D'Assurance Pour Le Commerce Exterieur and Constructions Navales Et Industrielles De La Mediterranee v. Phillips Petroleum Co.*, the court ruled:

> Defendant objects to several interrogatories on the ground that they purportedly ask for evidentiary detail more appropriately elicited at depositions. However, information obtained by interrogatories . . . may effect judicial economy and economic savings to the parties. Plaintiffs will know whom they have to depose; unnecessary depositions may be avoided; information which might not be obtained from the corporate defendants; important conversations, communications and documents will be highlighted; delay may be avoided; and the issues for trial may be narrowed. For these reasons, the Court believes plaintiffs' interrogatories may effect judicial economy. As a result, we find defendant's objection to be without merit.

105 F.R.D. 16, 43 (1984). *See also In re Shopping Carts Antitrust Litigation*, 95 F.R.D. 299, 1982-1 Trade Cas. p 64, 561, at 73, 74 (S.D.N.Y. 1982).

Federal Rule of Civil Procedure 33(d), provides:

> Option to Produce Business Records. If the answer to an interrogatory may be determined by examining, auditing, compiling, abstracting, or summarizing a party's business records (including electronically stored information), and if the burden of deriving or ascertaining the answer will be substantially the same for either party, the responding party may answer by:
>
> (1) specifying the records that must be reviewed, in sufficient detail to enable the interrogating party to locate and identify them as readily as the responding party could; and
>
> (2) giving the interrogating party a reasonable opportunity to examine and audit the records and to make copies, compilations, abstracts, or summaries.

This rule permits a party to answer detailed interrogatories by providing business records where the answers can be found. A specification supplied by the responding party should be in sufficient detail to permit the interrogating party to locate and to identify, as readily as can the party served, the records from which the answer may be ascertained. The idea behind the rule is that when the burden of deriving information from documents is equal between the parties, the interrogating party should bear the burden of compiling the information. *Saddler v. Musicland Pickwick Int'l, Inc.*, 31 Fed. R. Serv. 2d (Callaghan) 760, 761–62 (E.D. Tex. 1980); *Webb v. Westinghouse Elec. Corp.*, 81 F.R.D. 431, 435–36 (E.D. Pa. 1978); *Mid-America Facilities, Inc. v. Argonaut Co.*, 78 F.R.D. 497, 498 (E.D. Wis. 1978).One party's familiarity with the documents does not necessarily create a disparity in the ease of discovery that would preclude resort to Rule 33(c). *Sandler*, 31 Fed. R. Serv. 2d at 761.

However, Rule 33(c) is not an available alternative if an interrogatory can be responded to more readily and conveniently by written answer. *See Dai- flon, Inc. v. Allied Chemical Corp.*, 534 F.2d 221, 226 (10th Cir.), *cert. denied*, 429 U.S. 886, 97 S. Ct. 239, 50 L. Ed. 2d 168 (1976); *Atlanta Fixture & Sales Co. v. Bituminous Fire & Marine Ins. Co.*, 51 F.R.D. 311, 312 (N.D. Ga. 1970).

VII

VAGUE INTERROGATORIES

In addition to the above noted, factually unsupported objections to Plaintiffs' First and Second Set of Interrogatories and Requests for Documents, defendant also alleges that they are so vague as to be incapable of a reasonable answer. The court's examination of those interrogatories will demonstrate that each question is precise and clearly drawn. If any interrogatory is unclear, it is defendant's burden to specifically identify the questionable language in each interrogatory and answer the rest. The problem raised by Fremantle does not reside in any lack of specificity or clarity in Plaintiff's Interrogatories. Defendants would simply prefer not to answer them. In any event, the burden is squarely on the defendant to state in detail in what respect each interrogatory is unclear. In the event of uncertainty, the defendant must give each questioned term its common sense meaning. There is no option to simply refuse to answer.

As stated in *Compagnie Francaise D'Assurance Pour Le Commerce Exterieur et Constructions Navales et Industrielles De La Mediterranee v. Phillips Petroleum Company, supra*:

> Defendant argues that the ambiguity of the interrogatories precludes it from responding. The Court directs defendant, in answering the interrogatories, to attribute to any terms which it thinks are ambiguous their common, everyday meaning.

105 F.R.D. 16. *See also Roesberg*, 85 F.R.D. at 298.

VIII

CONCLUSION

Roesberg v. Johns-Manville Corp., 85 F.R.D. 292 (E.D. Pa. 1980) is considered the leading case delineating the broad scope of modern discovery.

The *Roesberg* case was centered in defendant's objections to answering a set of interrogatories in an asbestos products liability case.

Those interrogatories are attached as an appendix to the decision and are supplied here for the Court's examination. As the court will see, they are substantially longer and more complex than the two sets of interrogatories involved in this case.

The *Roesberg* holding was cited in virtually every decision noted in this brief as containing the most lucid discussion of the problem of the scope of modern federal discovery. The *Roesberg* court concluded its lengthy opinion with the following observations, which have compelling relevancy to this motion:

> In light of plaintiff's panoply of allegations his interrogatories have been tailored carefully to establish both the nature and extent of GAF's knowledge of the interrelationship between handling asbestos products and asbestos related diseases and what GAF did in connection therewith. Clearly this information relates to any duty GAF may have had to refrain from manufacturing or distributing unreasonably dangerous or ultrahazardous goods and whether GAF breached that duty. In a nutshell these interrogatories aim at establishing notice and causation. The exactitude of discovery, the lawyer's tool for fact finding, properly lies somewhere between the acuity of the surgeon's scalpel and the carpenter's hammer. Ideally, the lawyer probes for facts with the precision and delicacy of a cardiologist incising the aorta to receive a by-pass vehicle. Realistically, the lawyer's fact finding search shares a closer propinquity with the carpenter's trade and pounds much more bluntly. Balancing the one party's need for discovery against the other party's burden in producing it requires honing the need as narrowly as possible to prevent unreasonable burden. (Citations omitted). In the case at bar plaintiff has attained this desideratum artfully.

Roesberg, 85 F.R.D. at 304.

Based on the above arguments, points and authorities, Plaintiffs' request that this Court order the defendant Fremantle Tire and Rubber Company to fully answer Plaintiff's Interrogatories and Requests for Documents, within a reasonable time as determined by the Court.

§ 19.14 CONCLUSION

Pre-trial motion practice requires a significant amount of counsel's time and energy in products liability litigation. It is the most frustrating aspect of the preparation of these cases. The key to achieving success in product liability litigation is thorough pre-filing research. That research provides the basis for aggressive discovery and addressing motions for protective orders and typically contentious discovery enforcement motion practice.

TABLE OF CASES

[References are to pages]

58.16 Acres of Land; United States v.. 554

A

A.J. Decoster Co. v. Westinghouse Electric Corp.. 321

Aardema v. U.S. Dairy Systems, Inc.. 317

Aaron v. Hampton Motors, Inc.. 66

Abadie v. Metro. Life Ins. Co.. 285

Abbasi v. Paraskevoulakos. 246

Abbatiello v. Monsanto Co.. 312

Achin v. Begg Tire Center. 253

Ackermann v. Wyeth Pharmaceuticals. . . .208; 210

Acosta v. Glenfed Development Corp.. 119

Adames v. Sheahan 258

Adamo v. Brown & Williamson Tobacco Co.. . . 123; 142

Adams v. Buffalo Forge Co. 11

Adams v. G.D. Seale Co.,. 62

Adams v. Perry Furniture Co.. 187

Adams v. U.S.A.,. 307

Adeyinka v. Yankee Fiber Control, Inc..88; 178; 180

Adkins v. Ford Motor Co.. 73

Adkins Energy, LLC. v. Delta-T Corp.. 522

Adsit Company, Inc. v. Gustin 42

Aetna Life and Casualty Co. v. Imet Mason Contractors 229

AG v. Merck Sharp & Dohme Corp.. 288

"Agent Orange" Prod. Liab. Litig., In re 277

AgGrow Oils LLC v. National Union Fire Ins. Co. of Pittsburgh. .48

Agrofollajes, S.A. v. E.I. Du Pont De Nemours & Co.. . . . . .123; 132

Ahlstrom v. Minneapolis, St. Paul & Sault Ste. Marie RR. 308

Ahrens v. Ford Motor Co.. 186

Aig Aviation Insurance v. Avco Corp.. 70

Air Crash Disaster, In re. 221

Albers v. Deere & Co.. 321

Ali, U.S. ex rel. v. Daniel, Mann, Johnson & Mendenhall 275

Allemand v. Discovery Homes, Inc.. 307

Allen v. G.D. Searle & Co.. 214

Allen v. Minnstar, Inc.. 146

Allen; United States v.. 397

Allenberg v. Bentley Hedges Travel Service, Inc.. 103

Allgood v. R. J. Reynolds Tobacco Co.. 67

Alliance Mortgage Co. v. Rothwell. 66

Allison v. McGhan Medical Corp.. 230

Allison v. Stalter. 308

Alloway v. General Marine Industries, L.P.. .318; 320

Allstate Ins. Co. v. Hamilton Beach/Proctor Silex, Inc.. . . . . .218, 219; 228

Allstate Ins. Co. v. Maytag Corp.. 396

Allstate Insurance Co. v. Daimler Chrysler. 49

Almazan v. CTB, Inc.. 265

Altech Industries v. Al Tech Specialty Steel . . . 556

Altria Group, Inc. v. Good. 293

Alvarez v. American Isuzu Motors. 34; 38; 58

Alvis v. Ribar. 270

Amatulli v. Delhi Construction Corp.. 266

Ambassador Steel Co. v. Ewald Steel Co.. 42

Amdal v. F. W. Woolworth Co.. 168

American Fire and Casualty Co. v. Ford Motor Co.. 319

American Motorcycle Association v. Superior Court 333

American Paper Recycling Corp. v. IHC Corp.. .106

American Safety Equipment Corp. v. Winkler.71; 75

Ames v. Sears, Roebuck & Co.. 324

Anderson v. Bungee International Manufacturing Corp.,. 31

Anderson v. Dreis & Krump Mfg. Corp. . . . 253, 254

Anderson v. Farmers Hybrid Cos.. 113

Anderson v. M.W. Kellogg Co.. 122

Anderson v. Owens-Corning Fiberglas Corp.. . . .183

Anderson v. Piccadilly Cafeteria, Inc.. 172

Anderson v. Sears, Roebuck & Co.. 304

Anderson v. Smith. 95

Anderson v. Tyler 168

Anderson v. Weslo, Inc. 135; 145; 194

Andren v. White-Rodgers Company. 262

Andrews v. Harley Davidson, Inc.. 267

Apperson v. E.I. Du Pont De Nemours & Co.. . . 118

Appleby v. Miller 116

Arbino v. Johnson & Johnson 314, 315

Armentrout v. FMC Corp.. . . . . .148; 186

Armstrong v. Cione 109

Arnold Graphics Indus. v. Independent Agent Center 105, 106

Arriaga v. CitiCapital Commercial Corp.. 103

Asbestos Litig., In re 85

Asbestos Litigation: Thomas Milstead, In re . . . 184

Asbestos Products Liability Litigation, In re . . . 242

Atkins v. American Motors Corp.. 22

Atlanta Fixture & Sales Co. v. Bituminous Fire & Marine Ins. Co. 558
Atlanta Oculoplastic Surgery, P.C. v. Nestlehutt . 314
Attorney General v. Merck Sharp & Dohme Corp. .288
Austin v. Mitsubishi Elecs. Am. 148
Autzen v. John C. Taylor Lumber Sales, Inc. . . . 32
Avandia Marketing Sales Practices and Products Liability Litigation, In re 182; 211
Avner v. Longridge Estates 118
Ayala v. Joy Manufacturing Co. 49
Ayala v. V. & O. Press Co. 108
Ayers v. Jackson Township. 311, 312
Ayers v. Johnson & Johnson Baby Products Co. . 251
Azzarello v. Black Bros. Co., Inc. 91; 131

B

Bailey v. McDonnell Douglas Corp. 276; 278
Bailey v. V & O Press. 286
Balistreri v. Richard E. Jacobs Group, Inc. 223
Balke v. Central Missouri Elec. Coop. 115
Ball v. Joy Technologies, Inc. 309
Ballou v. Trahan. 35
Banks v. ICI Americas, Inc. 123; 140, 141; 148
Banner v. Hoffmann-La Roche Inc. 194
Banner Welders, Inc. v. Knighton 265, 266
Bannister v. Noble. 309
Barb v. Wallace 43
Barker v. Lull Engineering Co. . 123; 139; 147, 148; 158
Barnard v. Kellogg 3
Barnes v. Kerr Corp. 195
Barnett v. Royal Cup, Inc., ... 46
Barrett v. Harris 253
Barrow v. Bristol-Myers Squibb Co. 62
Barry v. Don Hall Laboratories 285
Barry v. Quality Steel Prods., Inc. 261
Barwick v. Celotex Corp. 282
Bass v. Cincinnati, Inc. 221
Bass v. General Motors Corp. 162
Bates v. Dow Agrosciences L.L.C. . . .290; 291; 293
Bates v. Richland Sales Corp. 188; 266
Bauerline v. Equity Residential Properties Management Corp. 153
Baughn v. Eli Lilly & Co. 306
Baughn v. Honda Motor Co. 75
Baxley v. Fischer. 285
Baxter v. Ford Motor Co. 27, 28; 71, 72

Baxter v. Ford Motor Co. 28
Bay Breeze Condominium Association, Inc. v. Norco Windows, Inc. 321
Bayliner Marine Corp. v. Crow. 31
Beagle v. Vasold 308
Beale v. Biomet, Inc. 208, 209
Beard v. Johnson & Johnson, Inc. 123; 142
Beattie v. Beattie. 100
Behrens v. W. S. Bills & Sons, Inc. 317
Bell v. Bayerische Motoren Werke Aktiengesellschaft. 142
Bell v. Industrial Vangas, Inc. 274
Bell v. Precision Airmotive Corp. 21
Bell v. T.R. Miller Mill Co., Inc. 161
Belleville v. Rockford Mfg. Group, Inc. 252
Bentzlin v. Hughes Aircraft Co. 278
Bergeron v. Pac. Food, Inc. 195
Bergquist v. MacKay Engines, Inc. 42
Berkebile v. Brandtly Helicopter Corp., ... 88
Bernal v. Daewoo Motor America, Inc. 154
Bernard v. Kee Mfg. Co. 106
Bernick v. Jurden 33
Berrier v. Simplicity Mfg., Inc. 85; 145
Berry v. G.D. Searle & Co. 50
Beshada v. Johns-Manville Products Corp. 261
Betehia v. Cape Cod Corp. 171
Beyer v. Aquarium Supply Co. (Div. of Hartz Mountain Corp.) 113
Beyette v. Ortho Pharmaceuticals Corp., . 29, 30; 214
Bidar v. Amfac, Inc. 243
Bielskis v. Louisville Ladder, Inc. 233
Bigbee v. Pacific Tel. & Tel. 93
Bigelow v. Agway, Inc. 33
Billman v. Crown-Trygg Corp. 120
Bilotta v. Kelley Co. 125
Birdsong v. Apple, Inc. 37
Birmingham v. Fodor's Travel Publications, Inc. . .117
Bisphenol-A (BPA) Polycarbonate Plastic Products Liability Litigation, In re. 65
Bitler v. A.O. Smith Corp. 233; 236; 238; 406
Blaha v. Stuard. 113
Blanchard v. Eli Lilly & Co. 230
Blankenship v. Hearst Corp. 532
Blue v. Environmental Engineering, Inc. . . .86; 152; 180; 186
BMW of North America, Inc. v. Gore. . . .323; 327
Bocci v. Key Pharms., Inc. 330
Boddie v. Litton Unit Handling Systems . . 112; 120

Boelens v. Redman Homes, Inc. 58, 59

Bogosian v. Mercedes-Benz of North America, Inc. 162

Boles v. Sun Ergoline, Inc. 263

Bombardi v. Pochel's Appliance & TV Co.. . . .221

Booth v. Black & Decker, Inc. 220

Borel v. Fibreboard Paper Products Corp.. . .162; 183

Borg-Warner Corp. v. Flores. 242

Bostick v. Flex Equip. Co., Inc.. 261

Boud v. SDNCO, Inc.. . . . . .31; 51

Boudreau v. Baughman. 122; 124

Bouher v. Aramark Services, Inc.. . . . . . 148; 187

Bourelle v. Crown Equipment Corp. 396

Bourke v. Ford Motor Co.. 153

Bourne v. Marty Gilman, Inc.. . . . . 122; 132

Bowen v. Cochran 263

Bowen v. Niagara Mohawk Power Corp. . . . 115, 116

Bowling v. Heil Co.. 261

Boyd v. Lincoln Elec. Co.. 184

Boyd v. Travelers Ins. Co.. 228

Boyle v. United Technologies Corp.. . . . .107; 276

Bragdon v. Perkins-Campbell Co.. 6

Bragg v. Hi-Ranger, Inc.. 289

Brandt v. Boston Scientific Corp.. . . . . . .36; 114

Brandt v. The Weather Channel. 117

Branham v. Ford Motor Co..85; 125; 127; 132; 145; 148; 162; 166; 221

Bray v. Marathon Corp.. . . . . .95; 314

Brazzell v. United States. 212

Bredberg v. Pepsico 163; 168

Breidenstein v. Ludlow Corp.. 108

Brejcha v. Wilson Machery, Inc.. 108

Brennaman v. R.M.I. Co.. 178

Brenner v. American Cyanamid Co.. 246

Brewer v. Harley-Davidson, Inc.. 151

Brinson v. Raytheon Co.. 277

Bristol-Myers Co. v. Gonzales. 211

Brooks v. Medtronic, Inc.. 209

Broussard v. St. Edward Mercy Med. Cntr.. . . .314

Brown v. Crown Equipment Co.. . . . .23; 150; 233

Brown v. Glaxo, Inc.. 210

Brown v. Nebiker 169

Brown v. The Raymond Corp.. 150

Brown v. Sears, Roebuck & Co.. 134

Brown v. Stone Manufacturing Co.. . . . . 227; 244

Brown v. Superior Court (Abbott Laboratories) . 185

Brown Forman Corp. v. Brunc 187

Browning-Ferris Industries of Vermont, Inc. v. Kelco 327

Broyles v. Kasper Machine Co.. . . . . . . 200; 249

Bruesewitz v. Wyeth LLC. 294

Brunswick Corp. v. Suzuki Motor Co. 555

Bruzga v. PMR Architects. 109

Bryant v. Giacomini, S.P.A.. 200

Bryant v. Tri-County Electric Membership Corp..116

Buck v. Ford Motor Co.. 233

Buckley v. Bell. 250

Budding v. SSM Healthcare System. 109

Buehler v. Whalen 136; 537, 538

Bugosh v. I.U. North America, Inc.,. 84

Bukowski v. CooperVision Inc.. 210

Bullard v. Barnes. 316

Bunch v. Hoffinger Industries, Inc.. 188

Burgad v. Jack L. Marcus, Inc.. 391

Burke v. Illinois Power Co.. 140

Burke v. Spartanics, Ltd.. 186

Burleson v. RSR Group Fla., Inc.. 270

Burley v. Kytec Innovative Sports Equip., Inc. . 230; 249

Burnett v. Covell 98

Burns v. Jaquays Mining Corp.. 311

Burt v. Makita USA, Inc. 126; 145

Busch v. Graphic Color Corporation 292

Butler v. City of Peru 115

C

Caboni v. General Motors Corp.. 28

Cafazzo v. Central Medical Health Services, Inc. 109

Caiazzo v. Volkswagenwerk A. G.. . . . . .128; 130

Caine v. Tech Air of CT, Inc.. 107

Caley v. Manicke. 308

Calhoun v. Yamaha Motor Corp., U.S.A.. . . 236; 240

Calles v. Scripto-Tokai Corp.. . . .132; 134; 141, 142; 151

Calumet Country Club v. Roberts Environmental Control Corp.. 120

Calumet Iron & Steel Co. v. Martin. 270

Campbell Soup Co. v. Dusek 168

Campo v. Scofield 151

Campos v. Firestone Tire & Rubber Co.. 189

Caprara v. Chrysler Corporation. 446

Caputzal v. Lindsay Co.. 249

Carlin v. Superior Court 210

Carlson Companies, Inc. v. Sperry & Hutchinson Co.. . . . . .343; 552

Carmichael v. Samyang Tire, Inc.. 234

Carollo v. Al Warren Oil Co.. 108

Carpenter v. Victoria's Secret Stores, LLC. 22

[References are to pages]

Carrel v. National Cord & Braid Corp. 193

Carroll v. Otis Elevator Co. 397

Carroll Towing Co.; United States v. . .85; 131; 140; 355

Carter v. Yardley & Co. 11

Carter Lincoln-Mercury, Inc. v. Emar Group, Inc. .92

Casa Clara Condominium Ass'n, Inc v. Charley Toppino & Sons, Inc. 317

Casey v. Pactiv Corp. 197

Caskey v. Merrick Constr. Co. 307

Casrell v. Altec Indus., Inc. 22

Castrignano v. E.R. Squibb & Sons, Inc. 185

Castro v. QVC Network. 37

Cataldo v. Lazy Days R.V. Center, Inc. 104

Caterpillar, Inc. v. Shears 186

Caterpillar Tractor Co. v. Beck. . .88; 124; 127; 147

Cedars-Sinai Medical Center v. Superior Court. .229

Chairez v. James Hamilton Constr. Co. 268

Chambley v. Apple Restaurants, Inc. 309

Chandler v. Gene Messer Ford, Inc. 74

Chandler v. Moreland Chemical Co. 163

Chapman v. Maytag Corp. 402

Chapman v. Upstate RV & Marine 56

Chauncey v. Peco, Inc. 264

Chauvin v. Sisters of Mercy Health System . . . 114

Chavez v. Glock, Inc. .124; 127; 132; 136; 183; 239; 252; 258

Chevron Chemical Co., Ex parte 21; 190

Chicago, City of v. American Cyanamid Co. 2

Chilton v. Homestead 260

Choate v. Champion Home Builders Co. 294

Chronister v. Bryco Arms 269

Chrysler Corp. v. Batten. 282

Chubb Integrated Sys. v. National Bank of Washington. 343; 552; 554, 555

Cigna Insurance Co. v. OY Saunatec, Ltd. . . 38, 39; 200; 268

Ciocca v. BJ's Wholesale Club, Inc. 263

Cipollone v. Liggett Group, Inc. 62; 290; 292

City of (see name of city). . . . .

Clark v. Burlington N. R.R. 461

Clark v. Leisure Vehicles, Inc. 243

Clark v. Safety-Kleen Corp. 405

Clark v. Takata Corp. 404

Clay v. Ferrellgas, Inc. 323

Cleveland v. Square-D Co. 27

Clime v. Dewey Beach Enters. 170

Cline v. Prowler Indus. Of Md., Inc. 86

Clinton v. Brown & Williamson Holdings, Inc. . . 62

CNH America, Inc. v. Roebuck 265

Coca-Cola Bottling Co. of Plainview v. White. . 173

Coello v. Tug Manufacturing Corp. 275

Cole v. Lantis Corp. 130

Coleman v. Am. Red Cross 344

Coll v. Sherry. 247

Collens v. New Canaan Water Co. 324

Collins v. Eli Lilly Co. 245, 246

Collins v. Hyster Co. 202

Collins v. Li. 249, 250

Collins v. Uniroyal, Inc. 28; 55

Collins v. Wayne Corp. 74

Colon v. BIC USA, Inc. 125; 145

Colville v. Pharmacia & Upjohn Co. 210

Commonwealth v. (see name of defendant). . . . . .

Compagnie Francaise d'Assurance Pour le Commerce Exterieur v. Phillips Petroleum Co. 557, 558

Compaq Computer Corp. v. Lapray 32; 50

Complex Int'l Co. v. Taylor. 48

Comstock v. General Motors Corp. 201

Condiff v. R.D. Werner Co., Inc. 223

Condos v. Musculoskeletal Transplant Foundation. 114; 289

Conley v. Boyle Drug Co. 245

Conley v. Lift-All Company, Inc. 193

Conn v. Fales Division of Mathewson Corp. 107

Connelly v. Uniroyal, Inc. 99

Continental Insurance Co. v. Herman 228

Controltek, Inc. v. Kwikee Enterprises, Inc. 44

The Conveyor Company v. Sunsource Technology Serv. Inc., ...68

Coogle v. Jahangard 113

Coons v. A.F. Chapman Corp. . .35; 85, 86; 178; 218; 244

Cooper v. Old Williamsburg Candle Corp. 199

Cooper v. Zimmer Holdings, Inc. 84

Cooper Tire & Rubber Co. v. Mendez 392

Cooperative Power Association v. Westinghouse Elec. Corp. 320

Coordinated Latex Glove Litigation, In re. .159, 160

Coplin, Meyer ex rel. v. Fluor Corp. 311

Corbin v. Camden Coca-Cola Bottling Co. 163

Corcoran v. Sears, Roebuck and Co. 158

Corral v. Rollins Protective Services Co. 29

Cottam v. CVS Pharmacy 195

Cotton v. Buckeye Gas Products Co. 193

Cottrell, Inc. v. Williams 406, 407

Coughtry v. Globe Woolen Co. 7

Country Mut. Ins. Co. v. Sunbeam Prods. 264

Counts v. MK-Ferguson Co. 107

County of (see name of county). . . . .

[References are to pages]

Cover v. Cohen. 201

Cox v. McDonnell-Douglas Corp.. 281

Crandell v. Larkin and Jones Appliance Co. . . . 104

Creazzo v. Medtronic, Inc.. 158

Crickenberger v. Hyundai Motor Amer. 87

Criscuolo v. Mauro Motors, Inc. 37

Crocker v. Winthrop Laboratories, Div. of Sterling Drug, Inc.. . . . . .73; 210

Cronin v. J.B.E. Olson Corp.. . . . . . . .85; 88, 89

Croskey v. BMW of North Amer., Inc.. 221

Cross v. Ainsworth Seed Co. 120

Crothers v. Cohen 29

Crump v. MacNaught P.T.Y. Ltd. 221

Crutchfield v. Marine Power Engine Co.. 105

Cryolife, Inc. v. Superior Court of Santa Cruz County. 114

Cullison v. Hilti, Inc.. 153

Culver v. Slater Boat Co. 305

Cummings v. General Motors Corp.. 537

Cummings v. HPG Int'l, Inc. 64; 68, 69

Cummins v. Lyle Industries. . . .396; 398; 400; 405

Cunningham v. C. R. Pease House Furnishing Co.. . . . . .69; 71

Cunningham v. MacNeal Memorial Hosp. 114

Cunningham v. Mitsubishi Motors Corp.. . .132; 137, 138

Curl v. Volkswagen of Amer., Inc. 57

Curry v. Meijer, Inc.. 86

Curtain v. Somerset. 6

Cush-Crawford v. Adchem Corp. 322

D

D.D. v. Idant Labs. 114, 115

D.L. v. Huebner 446

DaimlerChrysler Corp. v. Hillhouse. 195

Daniel v. Ben E. Keith Co. 199

Daniel v. Coleman Company Inc.. 182

Daniel v. Ind. Mills & Mfg.. 219

Daniell v. Ford Motor Co. 40

Daniels v. Bucyrus-Erie Corp.. 191

Darling v. Central Vermont Public Service Corp..116

Darryl v. Ford Motor Co.. 96

Dart v. Wiebe Manufacturing, Inc.. . . .125; 134; 148

Daubert v. Merrell Dow Pharms..232; 235–237; 398; 409

David v. Hett 23

Davidson v. Montgomery Ward 6

Davis v. Ford Motor Co.. 229

Davis v. Komatsu America Industries, Corp.. . . . 102

Davis v. Pak-Mor Mfg. Co.. 265

Davis v. Romney. 532

Davis v. Toshiba Machine Co., America 282

Davis v. Wells Aluminum Southeast, Inc.. 118

Davis v. Wyeth Laboratories. 212

Davis Industries Sales, Inc. v. Workman Construction Co.. 56

Dawson v. Chrysler Corp.. 122

Dayton v. Peck, Stow & Wilcox Co.. 105

Dean v. Barrett Homes, Inc.. 321

DeBattista v. Argonaut-Southwest Ins. Co.. 114

Debus v. Grand Union Stores 308

Deimer v. Cincinnati Sub-Zero Prods., Inc.. 402

Del Mar Beach Club Owners Assn. v. Imperial Contracting Co.. 119

Delaney v. Deere & Co.. . . . . 131; 176

Delph v. Jenkins 309

Delta Marine, Inc. v. Whaley. 37

DeLuryea v. Winthrop Laboratories. 211

Delvecchio v. General Motors Corp.. 538

Dennis v. Jones. 260

Denny v. Ford Motor Co.. . . . . 26; 125; 127; 141

Densberger v. United Technologies Corp.. .200; 279

Denton v. Northeast Illinois Regional Commuter Railroad Corp.. 228

Depositors Insurance Co. v. Wal-Mart Stores, Inc.. . . . . .35; 222, 223

Derienzo v. Trek Bicycle Corp.. 230

Detweiler Bros., Inc. v. John Graham & Co.. . .343; 552

Devlin v. Smith. 7

DeWitt v. Eveready Battery Co.. . . . . . .38; 161

Dhillon v. Crown Controls Corp.. 397–399

Dickerson v. Mountain View Equipment. . . .34, 35

Dickie v. Farmers Union Oil Co.. 282

Dicosolo v. Janssen Pharmaceuticals, Inc.. 88

Dierks v. Mitsubishi Motors Corp.. 158

Dillon v. Evanston Hosp.. 248

Dillon v. Legg 313

Dobbin v. Pacific Coast Coal Co.. 63

Dobrovolny v. Ford Motor Co.. 319

Docken v. Ciba-Geigy. 109

Doe v. Miles, Inc.. 42

Doe v. Miles Laboratories, Inc.. 114

Doe v. Solvay Pharmacies, Inc.,. 164

Doerner v. Swisher International, Inc.. 316

Donahue v. Phillips Petroleum Co.. 193

Donald v. City National Bank. 35

[References are to pages]

Donaldson v. Central Illinois Public Service Corp.. 243

Donegal Mutual Ins. v. White Consolidated Indus.. . . . . .147; 158; 238

Donovan v. Philip Morris USA, Inc.. .242; 311, 312

Doupnik v. General Motors Corp.. 161

Dow Agrosciences, LLC v. Bates 290

Downie v. Abex Corp.. 31

Downing v. Hyland Pharmacy. 207

Doyle v. The Pillsbury Co.. . . . . .168; 173

Drayton v. Jiffee Chemical Corp.. 227

Driscoll v. Standard Hardware 43

Dube v. Pittsburgh Corning 96

Dufour v. Mobil Oil Corp.. 521

Dugan by Dugan v. Sears, Roebuck & Co.. . . .253

Duncan v. U.S.. 260

Duncavage v. Allen 120

Dunham v. Vaughan & Bushnell Manufacturing Co.. 100

Dunn v. Nexgrill Indus.. 233

Dunn v. Sandoz Pharmaceuticals Corp.,. 353

Dunn v. Wixom Brothers 289

Duplan Corp. v. Deering Milliken, Inc.. . . . 343; 552

Dyke v. St. Francis Hospital. 274

E

E.I. du Pont de Nemours & Co. v. Robinson. . .392

E.J. Stewart, Inc. v. Aitken Products 249

E.R. Squibb & Sons, Inc. v. Cox 199

Eagle-Picher Industries, Inc. v. Balbos 194

Earl v. Gulf & Western Manufacturing Company. 535, 536

East River S.S. Corp. v. Transamerica Delaval, Inc.. . . . . .89; 319–321

Easter v. Aventis Pasteur, Inc.. 243

Eastman v. Stanley Works. 263

Eastwood v. Horse Harbor Found., Inc.. 319

Eberts v. Kawasaki Motors Corp., U.S.A.. 202

Edic v. Century Products Co.. 220

Edwards v. Basel Pharmaceuticals. 212; 214

EEOC v. Hickey-Mitchell Co.. 556

Ehlis v. Shire Richwood, Inc.. . . . . 207; 212

Eisert v. Greenberg Roofing & Sheet Metal Co.. 316

Elgin Airport Inn, Inc. v. Commonwealth Edison Co.. 115

Ellington v. Coca Cola Bottling Co., Inc.. 309

Ellingwood v. Stevens. 309

Elliot v. Sears, Roebuck Co., Inc.,. 268

Elliott v. Kraft Foods North America, Inc.. . . . 168

Ellis v. C.R. Bard, Inc.. 208

Ellsworth v. Sherne Lingerie, Inc.. . . . . . .263; 269

Elmore v. American Motors Corp.. 95

Elmore v. Owens-Illinois, Inc.. 183

Elmore v. Rockwell Automation. 277

Emery v. Federated Foods, Inc.. 188

Emory v. McDonnell Douglas Corp.. 278

Employers Mutual Casualty Co. v. Collins & Aikman Floor Coverings, Inc.. . . . . 32; 38

Engel v. Corrigan Company-Mechanical Contractors, Inc.,. 108

Engel v. Workers' Compensation Appeals Board. 274

Engelhardt v. Rogers Group, Inc.. 111

English v. General Electric Co.. 294

English v. Suzuki Motor Co., Ltd.. 73

Enpro Systems, Ltd. v. Namasco Corp.. 32

Enrich v. Windmere Corp.. 126

Escola v. Coca Cola Bottling Co.. .13, 14; 85; 87; 90, 91; 158; 163; 168; 222

Espeaignnette v. Gene Tierney Co.. 139

Estate of (see name of party) . . . .

Ettinger v. Triangle-Pacific Corp.. 111

Evitts v. DaimlerChrysler Motors Corp.. 521

Ex parte (see name of relator). . . . .

ex. rel. Johnson & Johnson Corp. V. Karl 207

Ex rel. (see name of relator). . . . .

Exxon Pipeline v. Zwahr. 238

Exxon Shipping Co. v. Baker 322; 331

ExxonMobil Oil Corp. v. Amex Const. Co., Inc.,. 76

F

F.D.I.C. v. Mercantile Nat. Bank of Chicago,. . .556

Fabian v. Fulmer Helmets, Inc.. 81

Falstaff Brewing Corp. v. Williams 163

Farnham v. Bombardier, Inc.. 122

Faught v. Washam. 308

Federal Insurance Company v. The Village of Westmont. 57

Feldman v. Lederle Laboratories. . . .126; 176; 183

Ferdon v. Wisconsin Patients Compensation Fund. 314

Ferguson v. Lieff, Cabraser, Heimann & Bernstein 249

Fickle v. State of Nebraska. 305, 306

Fidelity Federal Savings & Loan Association v. De la Cuesta. .294

Fields v. State 200

Fields v. Wyeth, Inc.. 245

Figgie International, Inc., Snorke-Economy Div. v. Tognocchi. 187

Figueroa v. Boston Scientific Corp.. 55

[References are to pages]

Filler v. Rayex Corp. 41
Fireman's Fund Ins. Co. v. Canon U.S.A., Inc.. .238
Firestone Tire and Rubber Co. v. Cannon 49
First National Bank & Trust Co. v. American
    Eurocopter Corp. 193
First National Bank in Albuquerque v. Nor-Am
    Agricultural Products, Inc.. 195
First National Bank of Louisville v. Brooks
    Farms. 67
First Premier Bank v. Kolcraft Enters. (In re
    Boone). 407; 409
First Springfield Bank & Trust v. Galman 255
Fish v. Amsted Indus., Inc. 106
Fisher v. APP Pharmaceuticals, LLC. 68
Fisher v. Professional Compounding Centers of
    America, Inc.. 194
Fitzgerald Marine Sales v. Le Unes. 166
Flax v. Daimlerchrysler Corp.. 176
Fleck v. Titan Tire Corp. 38
Fleet and Semple v. Hollenkemp. 4
Fletcher v. Dorchester Mutual Insurance Co.. . .228,
                                                229
Flight International v. Allied Signal. 230
Flock v. Scripto-Tokai Corp.. 202
Flowers v. Lea Power Partners 302
Flowers v. Viking Yacht Co.. 321
Fluor Corp. v. Jeppesen & Co. 117
Folding Carton Antitrust Litigation, In re . .554; 556
Foley v. Dayton Bank & Trust 35
Force v. Ford Motor Co.. . . . . .136, 137
Ford v. Polaris Indus., Inc.. 262
Ford Motor Co. v. Gonzalez. 158; 219
Ford Motor Co. v. Ledesma . . . 158; 220; 233; 242
Ford Motor Co. v. Mayes. 55
Ford Motor Co. v. Pool 166
Ford Motor Co. v. Zahn 162; 167
Ford Motor Co. Speed Control Deactivation Switch
    Prods. Liab. Litig., In re 318
Ford Motor Co., State ex rel. v. Nixon 443
Ford Motor Co. V. Reese. 200; 202
Fox v. Ethicon Endo-Surgery, Inc.. 281
Francioni v. Gibsonia Truck Corp. 99, 100
Franklin Grove Corp. v. Drexel 319
Franz v. Calaco Development Corp.. 327
Freas v. Prater Construction Corp.. 250
Freeman v. Hoffman-La Roche, Inc. . 21; 32; 62; 76;
                                          127; 158
Frey v. Montgomery Ward & Co.. 251
Friedland Family Enterprises v. Amoroso 99
Friedman v. C & S Car Service. 305
Friedman v. Merck & Co., Inc.. 68–70

Friends for All Children Inc. v. Lockheed Aircraft
    Corp.. 249
Frontier Ins. Co. v. Blaty 302
Frye v. United States. 231
Fuchsgruber v. Custom Accessories, Inc.. . . .91; 99
Fullreide v. Midstates Beverage Co. 34

G

Gable v. Boles. 54
Galena & Chicago Union Ry. v. Jacobs. 270
Galindo v. Precision American Corp.. 104
Galloway v. Big G. Express, Inc.. 239
Gammill v. Jack Williams Chev., Inc.. 392
Gamradt v. Federal Laboratories, Inc.. 92
Garavalia v. Heat Controller, Inc.. 57
Garcia v. Coe Mfg. Co. 106
Garcia v. Wyeth-Ayerst Labs. 287
Garlinger v. Hardee's Foodsystems, Inc. 237
Garlock, Inc. v. Gallagher 183
Garrett v. I.R. Witzer Co.. 86
Garside v. Osco Drug, Inc. 215
Garst v. General Motors Corp.. 126
Gaskin v. Sharp Elecs. Corp. 265
Gasque v. Mooers Motor Car, Inc. 57
Gateway Foam Insulators, Inc. v. Jokerst Paving &
    Contracting, Inc. 317
Gaudio v. Ford Motor Co.. 267
Gaumer v. Rossville Truck and Tractor Co., Inc. . 22,
                                                 23
Gay v. O. F. Mossberg & Sons, Inc. 250
Gaylord v. Lawler Mobile Homes, Inc.. 54
GE v. Joiner. 233, 234; 239; 398
Geboy v. TRL Inc.. 108
Geier v. American Honda Motor Co.. . . . . 21; 296
Genaust v. Illinois Power Co.. 116
General Motors, Camacho v. Honda Motor Co.. 138,
                                                139
General Motors Corp. v. Hebert. 315
General Motors Corp. v. Saint 261, 262
General Motors Corp. v. Sanchez. 272
Genereux v. American Beryllia Corp. . 192, 193; 280
Gentile v. MacGregor Mfg. Co.. 104
Gerber v. Hoffmann-La Roche Inc.. 194
Germann v. F.L. Smithe Machine Co.. 177
Gerrity v. R.J. Reynolds Tobacco Co. 23; 49
Getz v. Boeing Co.. 277
Geurin v. Winston Industries, Inc.. 334
Giant Food Inc. v. Satterfield 308
Gibbs v. E.I. DuPont De Nemours & Co.. 249
Gibbs v. Republic Tobacco, L.P.. 188

Giddings & Lewis, Inc. Vv. Industrial Risk Insurers 70; 76; 319
Gideon v. Johns-Manville Sales Corp. 310
Giehl v. Terex Utilities 89
Giglio v. Connecticut Light & Power Co.. 136
Gill v. Bluebird Body Co.. 56
Gillham v. Admiral Corp.. . . . . .65; 67
Gindy Manufacturing Corp. v. Cardinale Trucking Corp. 54
Ginn v. Gemini Inc. 461
Giuffrida v. Panasonic Industrial Co.. 99
Giuliani v. Guiler. 316
Gladden v. Cadillac Motor Car Division. . . .52; 55
Glasstech, Inc. v. Chi. Blower Corp.. 43
Glenn v. Overhead Door Corp. 148
Glick v. McKesson and Robbins, Inc.. 532
Glittenberg v. Doughboy Recreational Industries . 183
Glover v. BIC Corp.. 161
GMC v. Burry 313
Gnirk v. Ford Motor Co.. 313
Goad v. Celotex Corp.. 282
Goff v. Harold Ives Trucking Co., Inc. 228
Golden v. Den-Mat Corp.. 23; 29; 34; 36, 37; 39; 50
Goldsmith v. Olon Andrews, Inc.. 98
Goldstein v. G. D. Searle & Co. 49
Gonzales v. Caterpillar Tractor Co.. 89
Goodbar v. Whitehead Brothers 192
Goodby v. Vetpharm 312
Goodlander Mill Co. v. Standard Oil Co. 6
Goodman v. PPG Industries, Inc.. 29
Goodman v. Wagner 553; 556
Goodman v. Wenco Foods, Inc.. 170
Goodner v. Hyundai Motor Co. 123; 130
Goodwin v. Country Club of Peoria. 168
Goodyear Tire & Rubber Co. v. Rios 392–394
Gordon v. Goldman Bros., Inc. 242
Gorran v. Atkins Nutritionals, Inc.. 116
Gorton v. American Cyanamid Co. 123
Goudy v. Yamaha Motor Corp. 77
Gould v. Motel 6 Operating L.P. 223
Gourdine v. Crews. 267
Govich v. North American Systems, Inc.. 95
Grady v. American Optical Corp.. 178
Graff v. Robert M. Swendra Agency, Inc.. 306
Gramling, Godoy ex rel. v. E.I. Du Pont de Nemours & Co. 158
Grams v. Milk Prods., Inc.. 319
Gray v. Badger Mining Corp. 179; 192, 193
Great Lakes Reinsurance v. City of Fort Pierce . 195

Greaves v. Eli Lilly & Co.. 207
Green v. Allendale Planting Co 264
Green v. Alpharma, Inc.. 238
Green v. Kubota Tractor Corp. 154
Green v. Smith & Nephew AHP, Inc.. . . . 148; 253
Greene v. A.P. Products, Ltd. 188
Greene v. B.F. Goodrich Avionics Systems. . . .219
Greenman v. Yuba Power Products, Inc.. .17; 87–89; 99; 160
Gregory v. Cincinnati, Inc 201; 203
Griffin v. Allis-Chalmers Corp. Product Liability Trust. 118
Griggs v. Combe, Inc.. 191
Grills v. Philip Morris USA, Inc.. 64
Grimshaw v. Ford Motor Co.. . . . . .289; 324; 327
Gross v. Stryker 294
Grundberg v. Upjohn Co. 123; 185
Guardian Construction Co. v. Tetra Tech Richardson, Inc.. 318
Guarino v. Mine Safety Appliance Co.. 95
Gudmundson v. Del Ozone 102
Guevara v. Dorsey Laboratories. 191
Guilbeau v. W. W. Henry Co.. 191
Guinn v. AstraZeneca Pharmaceuticals LP 233
Gurski v. Wyeth-Ayerst Div. of Am. Home Prods. Corp.. 213
Guy v. Crown Equipment 236
Guzman v. MRM.Elgin 106

H

H&H Laundry v. TheLaundryList.Com. 52
Haag v. Bongers 131
Haase v. Badger Mining Corp. 92; 118
Haddix v. Playtex Family Products Corp.. 137
Haddock v. Arnspiger 222
Hagan v. Coca-Cola Bottling Co. 168; 310
Haimberg v. R & M Aviation, Inc.. 70
Halbrook v. Honda Motor Co. 93
Halkin, In re .534
Hall v. Ashland Oil. 193
Hall v. Elkins Sinn, Inc.. 212
Hall v. Gillins 316
Hall v. Porter Paints Store. 266
Halliday v. Sturm, Ruger & Co.. 127
Halliday v. Sturm, Ruger & Co.. . . . . . .131; 148
Halphen v. Johns-Manville Sales Corp.. 183
Haltiwanger v. Unisys Corp.. . . . . .276; 278
Hamon v. Digliani. 72

[References are to pages]

Hanberry v. Hearst Corp. 69

Hancock v. The Chattanooga Hamilton County Hosp. Auth.. 307

Hanks v. Cotler. 307

Hanlan v. Chandler. 202

Hansen v. Baxter Healthcare Corp. . . 133; 137; 144; 210

Hansen v. Mountain Fuel Supply Co.. 311

Hanson-Suminski v. Rohrman Midwest Motors, Inc.. .64; 77

Hanus v. Texas Utilities Co.. 115

Harber v. Altec Industries, Inc.. . . . . . . 90, 91; 104

Harned v. E-Z Finance Co.. 309

Harrell Motors, Inc. v. Flanery 230

Harris v. Bardwell 219

Harris v. Karri-On Campers, Inc.. 186

Harrison v. Bill Cairns Pontiac of Marlow Heights, Inc.. 222

Harris-Teeter, Inc. v. Burroughs. 170

Harsh v. Petroll & Hac.. 286

Harte v. Stuttgart Autohaus, Inc.. 28

Hartford Ins. Co. v. Broan-Nutone, LLC 395

Hatch v. Trail King Indus., Inc.. 20

Haugen v. Minnesota Mining & Mfg. Co. 263

Hauter v. Zogarts 74

Hawkins v. Leslie's Pool Mart, Inc.. 163

Haynes v. American Motors Corp.. 74

Haynes v. National R.R. Passenger Corp., ... 109

Hazen v. Municipality of Anchorage 228

Hazine v. Montgomery Elevator Co.. 282

Heatherly v. Alexander. 252

Heaton v. Ford Motor Co.. . . . . 134, 135; 221

Hedgepeth v. Whitman Walker Clinic. 312

Hedges v. U.S.. 47

Helene Curtis Industries, Inc. v. Pruitt 250

Helfend v. Southern California Rapid Transit Dist.. 306

Heller v. Cadral Corp.. 119

Helpin v. Trs. of the Univ. of Pa.. 305

Henningsen v. Bloomfield Motors, Inc. . . 16; 44, 45

Henrie v. Northrop Gruman Corp.. 126

Henry v. General Motors Corp.,. 196

Herber v. Johns-Manville Corp.. . . . . . . 247, 248

Herbert v. Lando. 344

Herceg v. Hustler Magazine 116

Hernandez v. Nissan Motor Corp.. 222

Hernandez v. Schering Corp.. 208

Hernandez v. Tokai Corp.. 269

Hesling v. CSX Transp., Inc.. 537

Hickey v. Otis Elevator Co.. 241

Hickman v. Taylor. 344; 440; 542; 551

Hickman v. William Wrigley, Jr. Co. 168

Hicks, Estate of v. Dana Companies 289

Hiigel v. General Motors Corp.. 177

Hilbrenner v. Kawasaki Motors Corp.. 73

Hill v. Searle Laboratories 185; 206; 214, 215

Hill v. Wilmington Chemical Corp.. 193

Hilliard v. Lummus Co., Inc.. 120

Hillrichs v. Avco Corp.. 126

Hillsborough County v. Automated Med. Labs.. .296

Hiner v. Deere and Co., Inc.. . . . . .266; 284

Hines v. Conrail 243

Hininger v. Case Corp.. 35

Hirsch v. General Motors Corp.. 227–229

Hisrich v. Volvo Cars of N. Am., Inc.. . . . 135; 139

Hittle v. Scripto-Tokai Corp.. 73

Hochberg v. O'Donnell's Restaurant, Inc.. 170

Hodges v. Johnson 34, 35

Hoffman v. Houghton Chemical Corp.. 192

Hoffman v. Paper Converting Machine Co. . . 29; 39

Hoffman v. Wilson Line, Inc.. 551

Holder v. Keller Industries, Inc.. 164

Holland v. TD Ameritrade, Inc.. 111

Hollenbeck v. Selectone Corp.. 249

Hollister v. Dayton-Hudson Corp.. . . . . . .38; 181

Holmes v. Amerex Rent-A-Car 228

Holmes v. Sahara Coal Company 446

Honda Motor Corp. v. Oberg 327

Honda of America Manufacturing, Inc. v. Norman. 145

Hood v. Ryobi America Corp.. . . . . .198; 254

Hopkins v. Chip-In-Saw, Inc.. 92

Horn v. Fadal Machining Ctrs., LLC 268

Horst v. Deere & Co.. . . . . .96; 123; 131, 132; 134

Horstmyer v. Black & Decker, (U.S.), Inc.. . . . 203

Horton v. American Tobacco Co.. 186

House v. Armour of Am.. 193

House v. Armour of America, Inc.. 186

Housman v. C. A. Dawson & Co.. 118

Howard v. Omni Hotels Management. 137; 289

Howes v. Hansen 96

Hubbard v. Chicago Housing Authority. 120

Hubbard v. General Motors Corp.. 49

Huddell v. Levin. 130

Huey v. United Parcel Service Inc.,. 233

Huff v. Elmhurst-Chicago Stone Co.. 194

Huff v. White Motor Corp.. 123

Hughes v. Magic Chef, Inc.. 267

Hughes v. The Tobacco Institute, Inc.. . . . . 28; 32

Humphreys v. General Motors Corp. 218
Hunnings v. Texaco, Inc.. 194
Hunter v. International Systems and Controls Corp.. 532
Hurley v. Frontier Ford Motors, Inc.. 66
Hurley v. Lederle Laboratories. 212, 213
Hurt v. Coyne Cylinder Co. 253
Huset v. J. I. Case Threshing Machine Co.. 6–8
Husky Industries v. Black. 124
Hutchings v. Childress. 306, 307
Hutto v. McNeil-PPC, Inc.. . . . . .22; 250; 259; 316
Hymowitz v. Eli Lilly & Co. 245
Hyundai Motor America, Inc. v. Goodin. 47
Hyundai Motor Co. v. Rodriguez. 37
Hyundai Motors America, Inc. v. Goodin 48

I

Ileto v. Glock, Inc.. 258
Immergluck v. Ridgeview House, Inc. 119
In re Estate of (see name of party) . . . .
In re (see name of party) . . . .
Inc. v. Allied Chemical Corp. 558
Incollingo v. Ewing 211
Indian Brand Farms, Inc. v. Novartis Crop Protection Inc.. . . . . .63; 125; 140
Indus. Risk Insurers v. Amer. Eng'g Testing, Inc. 321
Industrial Risk Insurers v. Creole Production Serv. Inc. 109
International Business Machines Corp.; U.S. v.. .532
International Business Machines Inc.; United States v.. . . . . .534; 540
International Petroleum Services, Inc. v. S & N Well Service, Inc. 41
Irrer v. Milacron, Inc. 193
Islam v. Modern Tour, Inc.. 265

J

J Corporation v. Tice. 321
J.H.O.C. v. Volvo Trucks, N.Amer.. 260
J.S. v. R.T.H.. 93
J.W. v. B.B.. . . . . .441; 522
Jablonski v. Ford Motor Co..125, 126; 150; 202, 203
Jackson v. General Motors Corp.. 137
Jackson v. Nestle-Beich, Inc.. . . . . .169, 170
Jacob E. Decker & Sons v. Capps. 3; 16
Jacobs v. Dista Prods. Co.. . . . . .208; 211
Jacobs v. E.I. du Pont de Nemours & Co.. . . . 194

Jacobson v. Benson Motors, Inc.. 74
Jahn v. Hyundai Motor Co.. 130
James v. Meow Media, Inc.. 117
James River Equipment Co. v. Beadle County Equipment, Inc.. . . . . 30; 51
Jamieson v. Woodward & Lothrop 186
Jaramillo v. Weyerhaeuser Co.. 108
Jeffers v. Wal-Mart Stores, Inc.. 163
Jefferson v. Lead Paint Industries. 246
Jenkins v. Amchem Prods. Inc. 134
Jenkins v. General Motors Corp. 161
Jenkins v. International Paper Co.. 145
Jenkins v. T & N PLC. 118
Jennings v. BIC Corp.. 139
Jimenez v. Daimler Chrysler Corp.. 68
Jimenez v. Sears Roebuck & Co. . . . 260; 268; 270
Jimenez v. Superior Court. 102
JKT Co., Inc. v. Hardwick 46
Jodoin v. Toyota Motor Corp.. 238
Johansson v. Central Garden & Pet Co.. 45
John Crane Inc., In re 336
John's Heating Service v. Lamb. 281
Johnson v. American National Red Cross. 310
Johnson v. American Standard, Inc.. . . . . .179; 193
Johnson v. Clark Equipment Co. 264
Johnson v. Colt Industries Operating Corp.. . . .197
Johnson v. Ford Motor Co.. 221
Johnson v. Harley-Davidson Motor Company Group, Inc.. . . . . .190; 198
Johnson v. Medtronic, Inc.. 269
Johnson v. Michelin Tire Corp.. 164
Johnson v. Niagara Machine & Tool Co.. 265
Johnson v. Zimmer, Inc.. 179
Johnson Foils v. Huyck Corp.. 535
Johnson Insulation; Commonwealth v.. 20
Joiner v. General Electric Co.. 234
Jones v. Amazing Products, Inc.. . . . .125; 158; 196
Jones v. A Best Products Co. 108
Jones v. City of L.A.. 309
Jones v. Davenport 29; 52
Jones v. Hogan. 308
Jones v. Hutchinson Manufacturing, Inc.. 289
Jones v. J. B. Lippincott. 116
Jones v. John Crane, Inc.. 137
Jones v. Toyota Motor Sales USA, Inc.. . . .390, 391
Jones v. White Motor Corp.. 124
Jones & Laughlin Steel Corp. v. Pfeifer 305
Jordan v. Carlisle Construction Co.. 52

Jordan v. Sunnyslope Appliance Propane & Plumbing Supplies Co............104
Joseph v. Bohn Ford, Inc............220
Josephs v. Harris Corp............553; 556
Josue v. Isuzu Motors America, Inc............188
Juliano v. Toyota Motor Sales, U.S.A., Inc.....178
June v. Union Carbide Corp............218
Junk v. Terminix Int'l Co............236
Jurado v. Western Gear Works............267

K

Kaempfe v. Lehn & Fink Products. Corp.....191
Kallio v. Ford Motor Co............145
Kambylis v. Ford Motor Co............227; 229
Kaneko v. Hilo Coast Processing............112; 118
Kaplan v. C Lazy U Ranch............113
Kately v. Wilkinson............314
Kates Millinery, Ltd. v. Benay-Albee Corp.....31
Katz v. Swift & Co............253
Kaylor v. Iseman Mobile Homes............111
Kearney & Trecker Corp. v. Master Engraving Co............54, 55
Keaton v. A.B.C. Drug Co............48
Keeler v. Richards Manufacturing Co., Inc..161; 219
Keeling v. Esurance Insurance Co............77
Kelleher v. Marvin Lumber and Cedar Co...30; 33; 57; 280, 281; 318
Keller v. A.O. Smith Harvestore Products, Inc....62
Keller v. Clark Equipment Co............106
Keller v. Inland Metals All Weather Conditioning, Inc............56
Kelly v. Fleetwood Enters............59
Kelso v. Bayer Corp............198
Kemezy v. Peters............322
Kemp v. Medtronic, Inc............85
Kemp v. Medtronic............292
Kemp v. Miller............99
Kendall v. Bausch & Lomb, Inc............202
Kennedy v. Cumberland Engineering Co.....282
Kerr v. Corning Glass Works............164
Kerstetter v. Pacific Scientific Co....276; 278, 279
Kerwin v. Dist. Court............441
Khan v. Shiley Inc............310
King City, City of v. Community Bank of Central California............441
Kinlaw v. Long Manufacturing N.C., Inc.....29
Kinser v. Gehl Co............122
Kinsey v. Louisville Ladder, Inc............265
Kinsman Transit Co., Petition of............250

Kirby v. B. I. Incorporated............73, 74
Kirk v. Ford Motor Co............441
Kirk v. Hanes Corp............92; 125; 151
Kirk v. Michael Reese Hospital & Medical Center............207; 209
Kirkland v. Emhart Glass S.A............180; 218
Kirkland v. General Motors Corp............131
Kirkland v. New York City Housing Authority..229
Kirkland v. Sam's East, Inc............307
Klages v. General Ordinance Equipment Co.,...73
Klausen v. Sidney Printing & Publishing Co.....554
Kleen v. Homak Mfg. Co............255
Klein v. Sears Roebuck & Co............40; 70
Klen v. Asahi Pool, Inc............189
Kneibel v. RRM Enterprises,............173
Knitz v. Minster Machine Co............148
Koehn v. R.D. Werner Co............221
Koellmer v. Chrysler Motors, Inc............53
Kohler Co. v. Marcotte............102
Koken v. Black & Veatch Construction, Inc.....179, 180; 186
Kokins v. Teleflex, Inc............148
Kolarik v. Cory International Corp............30; 171
Korando v. Uniroyal Goodrich Tire Co............130
Koruba v. American Honda Motor Co., Inc.....196
Koss Construction v. Caterpillar............24; 320
Kotecki v. Cyclops Welding Corp............275
Krajewski v. Enderes Tool Co............263
Krantz v. United States............556
Kremers v. Cocoa-Cola Co.,............78
Kriegler v. Eichler Homes, Inc............118
Kroger Co. v. Beck............310
Krummel v. Bombardier Corp............180
Kuelling v. Roderick Lean Mfg. Co............8
Kuhn v. Sandoz Pharmaceuticals, Corp.,.....243
Kumho Tire Co. v. Carmichael..234; 236, 237; 393, 394; 405
Kuras v. International Harvester Co............253
Kurns v. R.R. Friction Prods. Corp............295
Kutzler v. AMF Harley-Davidson............122; 151

L

L.G. v. United States............305
La. Public Service Com. v. FCC............291
Laaperi v. Sears, Roebuck & Co............188
LaBelle v. McCauley Indus. Corp............447
Lacy v. G.D. Searle & Co............214
Ladd by Ladd v. Honda Motor Co............74; 76

[References are to pages]

Lafayette Insurance Company v. CMA Dishmachines 229

Laing v. Volkswagen of Amer., Inc. 57

Lambertson v. Cincinnati Corp. 275

Lamkin v. Towner 93; 140; 147

Landree v. University Medical Products, USA, Inc. 38

Lang v. Federated Dep't Stores, Inc. 224

Langford v. Chrysler Motors Corp. 162

Lariviere v. Dayton Safety Ladder Co. . . .38; 40; 50

Larkin v. Pfizer, Inc. 207

Larsen v. General Motors Corp. 123; 128; 164

Larsen v. Pacesetter Sys., Inc. 38

Latham v. Wal-Mart Stores, Inc. 113

Lawhon v. L.B.J. Institutional Supply, Inc. 281

Lawson v. Mitsubishi Sales of America, Inc. .85; 222

Lawson v. U.S. 305, 306

Layne Atlantic Co. v. Koppers Co., Inc. 44

Lead Paint Litigation, In re. 2

Leaffer v. Zarlengo 459–461

Lear Siegler, Inc. v. Perez 243; 249

Learjet Corp. v. Spenlinhauer. 66

LeBlanc v. Louisiana Coca-Cola Bottling Co. . . 168

Lebourdais v. Vitrified Wheel Co. 6

Lebron v. Gottlieb Mem'l. Hosp. 314

Lee v. Crookston Coca-Cola Bottling Co. . .158; 164

Lee v. Mylan 48; 68

Leichtamer v. American Motors Co. 124; 129

Leland Industries, Inc. v. Suntek Industries, Inc.. .52

Lennon v. Wyeth-Ayerst Laboratories, Inc. 215

Leong v. Sears Roebuck and Co 91

Levine v. Wyeth, Inc. 66

Levondosky v. Marina Assoc. 100

Lewis v. Ariens Co. 202

Lewis v. CITGO Petroleum Corp. 309

Lewis v. Coffing Hoist Division, Duff-Norton Co., Inc. 289

Lewis v. Handel's Homemade Ice Cream & Yogurt. 169

Lewis v. Mobil Oil Corp. 57

Lewis v. Sea Ray Boats, Inc. 176; 195

Lewis & Lambert Metal Contractors, Inc. v. Jackson 74

Liberty Lincoln-Mercury, Inc. v. Ford Motor Co. . 31

Liberty Mut. Fire Ins. Co. v. Sharp Electronics Corp. 220

Lightolier v. Hoon 200

Lillebo v. Zimmer, Inc. 306

Limone v. U.S. 307

Lincoln Gen. Ins. Co. v. Detroit Diesel Corp. . . . 318

Linden v. Cascade Stone Co., Inc. 109

Lindquist v. Ayerst Laboratories, Inc. 162

Lindsay v. McDonnell Douglas Aircraft Corp. . . . 219

Lindsay v. Ortho Pharmaceutical Corp. 446

Liriano v. Hobart Corp. 178; 188

Lish v. Compton. 35

Little v. Liquid Air Corp. 263

Livingston v. Marie Callenders, Inc. 191

Lloyd v. General Motors Corp., . . . 64; 68; 70; 318

Long v. United States Brass Corp. 99

Lonon v. Pep Boys, Manny, Moe & Jack. 264

Loop v. Litchfield. 6

Lorenz v. Celotex Corp. 285

Lorillard Tobacco Co. v. Reilly 291

Losee v. Clute. .6

Lou v. Otis Elevator Co. 99

Louisiana Citizens Property Ins. Co. v. General Electric Co. .85

Lovick v. Wil-Rich. 201, 202

Low v. Power Tool Specialist, Inc. 267

Lowrie v. City of Evanston. 112; 119

Lozano v. Lozano 218

Lucas v. Bio-Lab, Inc. 163

Lueter v. California 229

Lugo v. LJN Toys 183

Lukowski v. Vecta Educational Corp. 108

Lumbermen's Underwriting Alliance v. Blount Int'l., Inc. 319

Lunsford v. Saberhagen Holdings, Inc. 96

Lutz v. Nat'l Crane Corp. 263

Lutz Farms v. Asgrow Seed Co. 33

Lyall v. Leslie's Poolmart 163

M

MacDonald v. Ortho Pharmaceuticals, ...210; 214

Mace v. Ford Motor Co. 228

MacKenzie v. Chrysler Corporation 57

MacPherson v. Buick Motor Co. . 9, 10; 44; 84; 157; 164

Madison v. American Home Products Corp. 109

Maggard v. Pemberton. 307

Magnuson v. Kelsey-Hayes Co. 161

Makripodis by Makripodis v. Merrell-Dow Pharmaceuticals. 109

Malawy v. Richards Manufacturing Co. 39

Maldonado v. Creative Woodworking Concepts, Inc. 37

[References are to pages]

Malen v. MTD Products, Inc., . . 104; 125; 127; 129; 145; 242; 272

Malicki v. Koci. 113, 114

Maness v. Boston Scientific. 23

Mangrum v. Pigue. 84

Manley v. Doe. 38

Mansour v. Leviton Mfg. Co. 313

Mansur v. Ford Motor Co. 137; 148

Marcus v. Specific Pharmaceuticals. 208

Marsh Wood Products Co. v. Babcock & Wilcox Co. .11

Marshall v. H. K. Ferguson Co. 273

Martin v. Abbott Laboratories. 245

Martin v. Burger King. 163

Martin v. Herzog. 285

Martin v. Medtronic, Inc. 292

Martinez v. Triad Controls, Inc. 131

Marvin Lumber and Cedar Co. v. PPG Industries, Inc. . . . . : 63

Maryland v. Louisiana. 290

Mason v. SmithKline Beecham Corp. 298

Massey-Ferguson, Inc. v. Laird. 33

Masters v. Hesston Corp. 233; 289

Matlock v. Greyhound Lines, Inc. 302

Matos v. Nextran, Inc. 42; 49

Matter of (see name of party). . . . .

Matthews v. Remington Arms Co. 22

Mattuck v. DaimlerChrysler Corp. 57

Mauro v. Raymark Industries, Inc. 247; 311

Mavilia v. Stoeger Industries 188

Maybank v. S. S. Kresge Co. 48; 50

Mayberry v. Volkswagen of Am., Inc. 56

Mazetti v. Armour & Co. 15; 44

McAlpine v. Rhone-Poulenc Ag Co. 88

McCafferty v. Centerior Serv. Co. 310

McCarthy v. Olin Corp. 127

McCarty v. Pheasant Run, Inc. 85

McClain v. Mack Trucks, Inc. 551

McCombs v. Southern Regional Medical Center . 114

McConnell v. Cosco, Inc. 180

McCormick v. Caterpillar Tractor Co. 274

McCorvey v. Baxter Healthcare Corp. 235

McCown v. International Harvester Co. 260

McCoy v. American Suzuki Motor Corp. 95

McCoy v. Whirlpool Corp. 244

McDaniel v. French Oil Mill Machine Co. 254

McDarby v. Merck & Co. 322

McDonald v. Mazda Motors of America. 55

McDougald v. Garber 307

McEwen v. Ortho Pharmaceutical Corp. 210

McGee v. AC & S, Inc. 304

McGregor v. The Scotts Co., LLC 163

McGuire v. Stein's Gift & Garden Center 223

McIntosh v. Melroe Co. 282

McKee v. Cutter Laboratories, Inc. 114; 289

McKenzie v. SK Hand Tool Corp. 221

McKisson v. Sales Affiliates, Inc. 100

McKnight v. Johnson Controls, Inc. 237

McLaughlin v. Michelin Tire Corp. . .26; 28; 30; 38; 40; 126

McLeod v. Linde Air Products Co. 11

McManus v. Fleetwood Enterprises, Inc. 32

Mechanic, In re Estate of 441

Medina v. Air-Mite Devices, Inc. 255

Medina v. Louisville Ladder, Inc. 199

Medtronic, Inc., Sprint Fidelis Leads Products Liability Litigation, In re 294

Mekertichian v. Mercedes-Benz U.S.A. 47

Mele v. Howmedica, Inc. 136

Menz v. New Holland N.A., Inc. 200; 230

Mercedes-Benz of North America, Inc. v. Dickenson 51

Mercer v. Pittway Corp. 162; 201; 221

Mercer v. Uniroyal, Inc. 274

Merck & Co., Inc. v. Ernst 322

Merck & Co. Inc. v. Garza. 180; 243

Merrill v. Navegar, Inc. 86

Merrill, Estate of v. Jerrick 317

Messer v. Amway Corp. 24; 126; 162

Methyl Tertiary Butyl Ether ("MTBE") Products Liability Litigation, In re. 2; 218; 241

MetLife Auto & Home v. Joe Basil Chevrolet, Inc. 229

Metronic, Inc. v. Lohr 123; 160; 292

Metro-North Commuter Railroad v. Buckley. . .249; 310, 311

Metropolitan Property & Casualty Ins. Co. v. Deere & Co. .220

Metzgar v. Playskool Inc. 127; 140; 188

Mexicali Rose v. Superior Court. 169; 172

Meyers v. Southern Builders, Inc. 308

Micallef v. Miehle Co. 126; 151

Michael v. Warner/Chilcott 198

Mickle v. Blackmon 128

Mid-America Facilities, Inc. v. Argonaut Co. . . .558

Midgley v. S. S. Kresge Co. 177

Miidas Greenhouses, LLC v. Global Horticulture, Inc. 321

Mikolajczyk v. Ford Motor Co. 22; 148; 150

Miles v. Desa Heating LLC. 22

[References are to pages]

Miles v. S. C. Johnson & Son, Inc. 137; 281
Miller v. Bernard. 238; 250
Miller v. Pacific Trawlers, Inc. 305
Miller v. Pfizer Inc. 66; 76; 233
Miller v. Todd 129
Milner v. National School of Health Technology.555
Milwaukee, City of v. Cement Division, National
    Gypsum Co.. 332
Milwaukee, City of v. NL Indus.. 2
Mitchell v. Collagen Corp.. 292
Mitchell v. Fridays. 170
Mitchell v. Gencorp, Inc. 236
Mitchell v. Gonzales. 218
Mitchell v. Lone Star Ammunition, Inc.. 278
Mitchell v. Volkswagenwerk, A.G. 130
Mitsch v. GMC 53; 59
Mix v. Ingersoll Candy Co. 169
Mixon v. Chrysler Corp.. 164
Mocek v. Alfa Leisure, Inc.. 34
Modelski v. Navistar Int'l Transp. Corp. 203
Modesto Redevelopment Agency, City of v. Superior
    Court. 2
Mohammad v. Toyota Motor Sales, U.S.A., Inc. . 88;
    160; 223; 230
Moning v. Alfono 95
Monroe v. Savannah Elec. & Power Co. 116
Montez v. Ford Motor Co.. 159
Montgomery Rubber and Gasket Co., Inc. v. Belmont
    Machinery Co., Inc. 63
Moore v. Anesthesia Services, P.A.. 85
Moore v. Coachmen Industries, Inc. 55
Moore v. Ford Motor Co.. . . . . . . 176; 179, 180
Moore v. Harley-Davidson Motor Co.. 231
Moore v. Mack Trucks, Inc. 30; 51; 55
Moore v. Miss. Valley Gas Co. 244
Moore v. Vanderloo 183
Moorman v. National Tank Co. 70; 318
Mora v. Saint Vincent's Catholic Med. Ctr.. . . .525
Morales v. American Honda Motor Co.. 252
Morales v. E.D. Etnyre & Co.. 202
Moran v. Raymond Corp. 264
Morrell v. Precise Engineering, Inc.. 126
Morris v. Chrysler Corp.. 161
Morris v. Osmose Wood Preserving. 318
Morson v. Superior Court 137; 160
Moss v. Batesville Casket Co. 42
Moss v. Polyco, Inc. 96; 99
Motley v. Fluid Power of Memphis, Inc. . . 219; 222
Motus v. Pfizer Inc. 212
Moyer v. United Dominion Indus. Inc. . . . 131; 237

Mozee v. Kuplen 35
Mulcahy v. Eli Lilly & Co.. 244
Mulhern v. Outboard Marine Corp. 100
Mullaney v. Hilton Hotels Corp.. . .95; 99; 125; 127;
    131, 132
Murphy v. Steeplechase Amusement Co. 262
Murthy v. Abbott Labs.. . . . . .207; 212; 215; 287
Musser v. Vilsmeier Auction Co. 108
Mutlu v. State Farm Fire & Casualty Co.. 522
Mydlach v. DaimlerChrysler Corp.. . . . . . .28; 57
Myers v. Putzmeister, Inc.. 105
Myrlak v. Port Authority of N.Y. and N.J. . 158; 164;
    223

N

Nally v. Charbonneau 262
Napier v. Atlantic C. L. R. Co. 295
National Bank of Bloomington v. Westinghouse
    Electric Corp.. 92
National Oil Co. v. Rankin. 3
Nationwide Agribusiness Ins. Co. v. SMA Elevator
    Const. Inc.,. 99; 180
Nelson v. Nelson Hardware, Inc. 104
Nemir v. Mitsubishi Motors Corp.. . . . . .238; 407
Neri v. R. J. Reynolds Tobacco Co. Inc.. . . .65, 66
Nesselrode v. Executive Beechcraft, Inc.. 87
Neumann v. Gloria Marshall Figure Salon 262
Neurontin Marketing, Sales Practices and Products
    Liability Litigation, In re. 66
Neville Construction Co. v. Cook Paint & Varnish
    Co. 29
New Texas Auto Auction Services, L.P. v. Gomez de
    Hernandez. 108
New York Asbestos Litigation, Matter of. 308
Newell Rubbermaid, Inc. v. The Raymond
    Corp.. . . . . .132; 137; 140; 148; 150; 235; 238
Newman v. Motorola, Inc.. 123
Newman v. Utility Trailer & Equipment Co.. . . .252
Newmark v. Gimbel's Inc.. . . . . .41; 109
Newton v. Roche Laboratories, Inc.. 243
Newton v. Standard Candy Co. 166
Niccum v. Hydra Tool Corp.. 107
Nicklaus v. Hughes Tool Co. 162
Niemann v. McDonnell Douglas Corp.. 278
Niemela v. Imperial Mfg. Co.. . . . . .23; 286
Niemiera v. Schneider 213
Nissen Corp. v. Miller. 106
Nobility Homes of Texas, Inc. v. Shivers 45
Norcold, Inc. v. Gateway Supply Co.. 43
Norplant Products Liability Litigation, In re . . .215

Norris v. Baxter Healthcare Corp. 238; 243, 244

Northern Power & Engineering Corp. v. Caterpillar
Tractor Co. 318

Norwood v. Raytheon Co. 311

Nunnally v. R.J. Reynolds Tobacco Co.. 140

Nutting v. Northern Energy 223

Nye v. Bayer Cropscience, Inc. 207

Nyfield v. Virgin Islands Tel. Corp. 460

O

O'Brien v. Muskin Corp. 124; 158; 445

O'Dell v. De Jean's Packing Co. 169

O'Flynn v. Owens-Corning Fiberglas 183

O'Neil v. Crane Co. 88; 123; 184; 190

O'Neil v. Electrolux Home Prod., Inc., ...196

O.S. Stapley Co. v. Miller. 90; 268

Oak Point Associates v. Southern States Screening,
Inc. 30

Oaklawn Jockey Club v. Pickens-Bond
Construction. 275

Obendorf v. Hug Spray Co., Inc. 85

Oberg v. Advanced Transformer Company, Inc., . 177

Ocampo v. Paper Converting Mach. Co. . . . 271; 275

Oceanside at Pine Point Condominium Owners
Association v. Peachtree Doors, Inc.. 318

Oden v. Chemung County Industrial Development
Agency 306

Odgers v. Ortho Pharmaceutical Corp. 214

Oestreicher v. Alienware Corp. 64

Ogeltree v. Navistar International Transportation
Corp.. . . . . .123; 152

Oja v. Howmedica, Inc. 292

Oliver v. Oshkosh Truck Corp. 278

Olson v. Hansen 262

Olson v. Prosoco, Inc. 179

Oman v. Johns-Manville Corp.. . . . . . . .194, 195

1836 Callowhill St. v. Johnson Controls, Inc.. . .162

Ontai v. Straub Clinic & Hospital, Inc. 147; 176

Oppenheimer Fund, Inc. v. Sanders . .343, 344; 440;
542; 551, 552

Oregon (Mason v. Mt. St. Joseph, Inc. 261

Osorio v. One World Technologies 123; 141

Otte v. Dayton Power & Light Co. 115

P

Pabon v. Hackensack Auto Sales, Inc. 69

Pace v. McClow 219

Pacific Mutual Life Insurance Co. v. Haslip.322; 327

Pack v. Damon 47; 51

Padilla v. Black & Decker Corp.. . . . . . .201, 202

Padilla v. Hunter Douglas Window Coverings,. . .101

Palmer v. A.H. Robins Co. 48

Palmer v. Avco Distrib. Corp.. . . . . .97; 252

Palmer v. Nan King Restaurant, Inc. 309

Palmer v. Volkswagen of America, Inc.. 315

Pannu v. Land Rover North America 139; 147

Papp v. Rocky Mountain Oil & Minerals. 119

Pappas v. Pella Corp.. . . . . .73; 77

Paracelsus Healthcare Corp. v. Philips Electronics
North America, ...110

Parish v. Health & Fitness, Inc.. . . . . . .123; 147

Parker v. Mobil Oil Corp.. 231

Parker v. Wellman 311

Parker Tractor & Implement Co. v. Johnson. . . .57

Parris v. M.A. Bruder & Sons, Inc.. 260

Parrot v. DaimlerChrysler Corp. 57

Parsons v. Ford Motor Co.. 218

Parsons v. General Motors Corp. 539, 540

Pasquale v. Speed Prods. Eng'g. 312

Patch v. Hillerich & Bradsby & Co. 95; 180

Patters Enters. v. Johnson 264

Patterson v. Ford Motor Co.. 536

Patton v. Hutchinson Wil-Rich Manufacturing
Co. 200, 201; 203

Paul v. Rodgers Bottling Co. 168

Paul Harris Furniture Co. v. Morse. 15

Pavlik v. Lane Ltd./Tobacco Exporters
International, ...196

Payton v. Abbott Laboratories 310

Paz v. Brush Engineered Materials, Inc.. 311

Pearsall v. Emhart Industries, Inc.. 312

Peck v. Bridgeport Machines. 127; 148

Peck v. Ford Motor Co. 250

Pelman v. McDonald's Corp.. . . . . .78; 80

Peltz v. Sears, Roebuck and Co.. 317

Pennsylvania (Pa. Dept. Of Gen. Servs. v. U.S.
Mineral Prods. Co.,. 261; 317

People ex rel. (see name of relator). . . . .

Perez v. Fidelity Container Corp. 112

Perez v. Sunbelt Rentals, Inc. 265

Perez v. VAS S.p.A. 268

Perez v. Wyeth 215

Perez-Trujillo v. Volvo Car Corp. 219

Perfection Paint & Color Co. v. Konduris 100

Perkins v. F.I.E. Corp. 188

Perlmutter v. United States Gypsum Co. 179

Perrotti v. Gonicberg. 312

Perry v. Heavenly Valley. 274

Peterson v. Lou Bachrodt Chevrolet Co. 103

Peterson v. North American Plant. 31

[References are to pages]

Peterson v. Superior Court. 87; 109
Petition of (see name of party) . . . .
Phelps v. Sherwood Med. Indus. 208
Philadelphia, City of v. Beretta U.S.A. Corp. 2
Philadelphia Electric Co. v. Hercules, Inc. 105
Philip Morris USA v. Williams 330
Phillips v. Cricket Lighters 37; 91
Phillips v. Kimwood Mach. Co.. . . . . . . .89; 183
Phillips v. Raymond Corp.. . . . . .396; 400
Phillips v. Town of West Springfield 170
Phipps v. General Motors Corp. 49
Piacenti v. Gen. Motors Corp.. 344
Pierson v. Sharp Memorial Hosp. 109; 112
Pilcher v. Suttle Equip. Co.. 43
Pillars v. R. J. Reynolds Tobacco Co.. 168
Pineda v. Ford Motor Co.. 239
Pinney v. Nokia, Inc.. . . . . .123; 295
Piper v. Bear Medical Systems, Inc.. 254
Pipitone v. Biomatrix, Inc.. 237
Pitler v. Michael Reese Hosp.. 73
Pitts v. Northern Telecom, Inc.. 27
Plaza v. Fisher Development, Inc.. 119
PLIVA, Inc. v. Mensing 298
Polk v. Ford Motor Company 129
Pollock v. Deere and Co. 556
Pool v. Ford Motor Co. 166
Poplar v. Bourjois, Inc. 253
Port Auth. v. Arcadian Corp.. 252
Port Authority of New York and New Jersey v.
    Arcadian Corp.. . . . . .251, 252; 255
Porteous v. St. Ann's Cafe & Deli. 170
Porter v. United Steel & Wire Co.. 260
Potter v. Chicago Pneumatic Tool Co. . 87; 132; 146;
                       149; 152–154; 266
Pottle v. Up-Right, Inc. 198
Pouncey v. Ford Motor Co. 164; 219
Prempro Products Liability Litigation,, In re . . 211;
                               281
Prentis v. Yale Manufacturing Co.. . . . . . .123, 124
Presidio Enterprises, Inc. v. Warner Bros. Distributing
    Corp.. 64
Pressley v. Boehlke 553
Price v. Blaine Kern Artista, Inc. 254
Price v. Wilson Sporting Goods Co.. 161
Primiano v. Cook. 233
Prince v. B.F. Ascher Co., Inc. 268
Pritchett v. Cottrell, Inc.. . . . . 122; 132
Procter & Gamble Co.; United States v. 551
Proctor v. Davis 210

Progressive Insurance Co. v. General Motors
    Corp.. 318
Propulsid Products Liability Litigation, In re. . .247
Providence & Worcester Railroad Co. v. Sargent &
    Greenleaf, Inc.. 52
Purdome; United States v. 532; 551
Purina Mills, Inc. v. Odell. 27
Pustejovsky v. Pliva, Inc. 211

Q

Queen City Terminals, Inc. v. General American
    Transportation Corp.. 91

R

Rader v. Teva Parental Medications, Inc.. 285
Ragin v. Porter Hayden Co.. 95
Rahmig v. Mosley Manufacturing Co. 268
Rainer v. Union Carbide Corp. 274
Ralston v. Smith & Nephew Richards, Inc.. 210
Ramirez v. Plough, Inc.. 198
Randy Knitwear, Inc. v. American Cyanamid Co.. 72
Ranger Conveying & Supply Co. v. Davis 101
Ransome v. Wisconsin Electric Power Co.. 115
Ratkovich v. SmithKline and French Lab.. 49
Rawson v. Conover. 30; 54
Ray v. Alad Corp. 106, 107
Ray v. Ford Motor Co.. 260
Ray by Holman v. BIC Corp.. 150
Realmuto v. Straub Motors, Inc.. 26
Redland Soccer Club v. Department of the
    Army 249
Reed v. Carlyle & Martin, Inc. 260
Reed v. Chrysler Corp.. 128
Reed v. City of Chicago. 46
Reed v. Landstar Ligon, Inc.. 85
Reed & Barton Corp. v. Maas 12
Reichhold Chemical, Inc. v. Haas. 45
Reilly v. D'Errico 229
Reiss v. Komatsu Amer. Corp.. . . . . .99; 110; 179
Reliance Insurance Co. v. Barrons. 534
Reservoir Manor Corp. v. Lumbermens Mutual
    Casualty Co.. 66
Restatement (Third) of Torts. Brown v. Crown Equip.
    Corp.. 202
Resteiner v. Sturm, Ruger & Co. 188
Reyes v. Wyeth Laboratories. 209; 212
Reynolds v. Strauss Veal, Inc.. 241
Rezulin Products Liability Litigation, In re 62

[References are to pages]

Rheem Manufacturing Co. v. Phelps Heating Air, . 45
Rhode Island, State of v. Lead Indus. Ass'n. Inc . . 2
Rhodes v. McDonald 57
Riach v. Manhattan Design Studio 398
Ribera-Emerling v. M. Fortunoff of Westbury Corp., ... 100
Rice v. Santa Fe Elevator Corp. 290; 294
Richards v. Owens-Illinois, Inc. 333
Richardson v. Holland 188
Richardson v. Volkswagenwerk, A.G. 128
Richter v. Limax International, Inc. 178, 179
Rickey v. Chicago Transit Authority 312
Riddell, Inc. v. Schutt Sports, Inc. 81
Ridgway v. Ford Motor Co. 166
Riegel v. Medtronic, Inc. 294
Rife v. Hitachi Constr. Mach. Co. 88
Riley v. Becton Dickinson Vascular Access, Inc. . 141
Riley v. De'Longhi Corp. 220
Riley v. Keenan 307
Rimbert v. Eli Lilly and Co. 207
Rink v. Cheminova, Inc. 237, 238
Riordan v. Int'l Armament Corp. 188
Rios v. Niagara Machine & Tool Works 254
Rite Aid Corp. v. Levy-Gray 30; 33; 36; 207
Ritter v. Custom Chemicides, Inc. 76
Ritter v. Narragansett Elec. Co. 148
Rivera v. Philip Morris, Inc. 180; 315
Rivera v. Philip Morris, Inc. 200
Rivers v. Great Dane Trailers, Inc. 250
Rizzuto v. Davidson Ladders, Inc. 228
Robert F. Bullock, Inc. v. Thorpe 100
Roberts v. DeKalb Agr. Ass'n, Inc. 556
Roberts v. Performance Site Management, Inc. . .179
Robinson v. McNeil Consumer Healthcare 199
Robinson v. S.D. Brandtjen & Kluge, Inc. . 166; 186
Robinson Helicopter Co., Inc. v. Dana Construction 67
Rodarte v. Philip Morris, Inc. 29, 30
Rodriguez v. Lockheed Martin Corp. 276
Roesberg v. Johns-Manville Corp. . . .343; 440; 542; 550; 552; 554, 555; 558, 559
Rogers v. Ingersoll-Rand Co. 180
Rogers v. Toni Home Permanent Co. 72
Roginsky v. Richardson-Merrell, Inc. 66
Rohde v. Smiths Medical. 207; 210
Rojas v. Lindsay Mfg. Co. 148
Romero v. Mervyn's. 57
Romo v. Ford Motor Co. 330
Roney v. Gencorp. 179; 192
Rosa v. City of Seaside 183

Rosales v. Verson Allsteel Press Co. 274
Rosenberg v. Otis Elevator Co. 390, 391
Rossell v. Volkswagen of America 92; 253
Rostocki v. Southwest Florida Blood Bank, Inc. . 114
Rotshteyn v. Klos Const., Inc., ... 107
Routzahn v. Garrison. 264
Royal Business Machines, Inc. v. Litton Business Systems, Inc. 30, 31
Royer v. Catholic Medical Center. 109
Rozier v. Ford Motor Company. 537
Rudeck v. Wright. 242
Rudloff v. Wendy's Restaurant of Rochester . . . 171
Ruminer v. General Motors Corp. 88; 222
Russell v. Wilson 54
Russo v. NCS Pearson, Inc. 116
Rutherford v. Owens-Illinois, Inc. 242
Ryan v. Amer. Honda Motor Corp. 57

S

Sabloff v. Yamaha Motor Co., Ltd. 99
Sabloff v. Yamaha Motor Co. 99
Saddler v. Musicland Pickwick Int'l, Inc., ... 558
Safeco v. Rawstron. 460
Salinas v. Amteck of Kentucky, Inc. 177, 178
Saller v. Crown Cork & Seal Co. 123; 139
Salmon v. Libby, McNeil & Libby. 4
Salmon v. Parke, Davis, & Co. 210
Salmon Rivers Sportsman Camps Inc. v. Cessna Aircraft Co. 51
Sam Shainberg Co. of Jackson v. Barlow 99
Samsel v. Wheeler Transportation Services. . . .314
Samson v. The Greenville Hosp. Sys. 114
Samson v. Riesing. 36
San Antonio v. Warwick Club Ginger Ale Co. . . .51
Sand Hill Energy, Inc. v. Ford Motor Co. 330
Sand Hill Energy, Inc. v. Smith 330
Sandage v. Bankhead Enterprises, Inc. 151
Sanders v. Lull International, Inc. 252; 267
Sanderson v. Steve Snyder Enterprises 446
Santa Clara, County of v. Atlantic Richfield Co. . . 2
Santiago v. Sherwin Williams Co. 246
Santoro v. Donnelly 178
Sapp v. Ford Motor Corp. 318
Saratoga Fishing Co. v. J. M. Martinac & Co. . .321
Sauder Custom Fabrication, Inc. v. Boyd. 187
Savage Arms, Inc. v. Western Auto Supply Co. . 105
Savina v. Sterling Drug, Inc. 23
Scanlon v. General Motors Corp. 222
Schafer v. JLC Food Systems, Inc. . . .170, 171; 173

[References are to pages]

Schedin v. Ortho-McNeil-Janssen Pharmaceuticals, Inc. 182

Schelbauer v. Butler Mfg. Co. 446

Schenker v. Chicago Title & Trust Co. 326

Schipper v. Levitt & Sons, Inc. 118

Schlagenhauf v. Holder 551

Schmaltz v. Nissen 53; 55

Schmid v. Milwaukee Elec. Tool Corp. 229

Schmidt v. Boardman Co. 106; 313

Schreiner v. Fruit. 306

Schroeder v. Barth, Inc. 56

Schultz v. Ford Motor Co. 155

Schump v. Firestone Tire and Rubber Co. 274

Schuster; United States v. 211

Scittarelli v. The Providence Gas Co. 162

Scoggin v. Listerhill Employees Credit Union. . . .30

Scordino v. Hopeman Brothers, Inc. 191

Scott v. American Brands Tobacco Co., Inc. 67

Scott v. Black & Decker, Inc. 182

Scott v. Dorel Juvenile Group, Inc. 29

Scott v. Garfield 306

Scovil v. Chilcoat 31

Sease v. Taylor's Pets, Inc. 113

Seattle-First National Bank v. Tabert . . 88; 122; 132

Seegers Grain Co. v. United States Steel Corp. . .186

Seeley v. Hamilton Beach/Proctor-Silex, Inc. . . .392

Seely v. White Motor Co. 318; 320

Seibel v. Symons Corp. 176

Semenetz v. Sherling & Walden, Inc. 105, 106

Sepulveda-Esquivel v. Central Machine Works. .124

Service Corp. .218

Sessa v. Riegle. 43

Sexias Woods, ... 3

Shackil v. Lederle Laboratories 245

Shaffer v. AMF Inc. 151; 188

Shang v. Hotel Waldorf Astoria Corp. 551

Shatz v. Ford Motor Co. 221

Sheehan v. Anthony Pools 261

Sheehan v. The North Amer. Marketing Corp. . . .263

Sheffield v. Owens-Corning Fiberglass Corp. . . .244

Sherman Park Community Ass'n v. Wauwatosa Realty Co. 555

Shinholster, Estate of v. Annapolis Hospital . . . 305

Shoenberger v. Mcewen 4

Shopping Carts Antitrust Litigation, In re. 557

Shoshone Coca-Cola Bottling Co. v. Dolinski . . 173

Show v. Ford Motor Co. 150; 230

Shramek v. General Motors Corp. 222

Shreve v. Sears, Roebuck & Co. 123

The Shutter Shop, Inc v. Amersham Corp. . . .29; 64

Siciliano v. Capitol City Shows, Inc. 109; 316

Siemen v. Alden. 35; 44

Sigler v. Amer. Honda Motor Co. . . .134; 150; 233; 239

Silva v. Basin Western, Inc. 441, 442

Simmons v. Christus Schumpert Med. Cntr. . . . 307

Simmons v. Hoegh Lines 306

Simon v. San Paolo U.S. Holding Co. 325

Simonetta v. Viad Corp. 179, 180; 182

Sims v. General Motors Corp. 86

Sindell v. Abbott Laboratories 245

Singleton v. Manitowoc Co., Inc. 122

Skalski v. Elliot Equipment Co. 55

Slaughter's Administrator v. Gerson 3

Slepski v. Williams Ford, Inc. 136

Slisze v. Stanley-Bostitch 125

Small v. Lorillard Tobacco Co. Inc. 67

Smalls v. Pittsburgh-Corning Corp. 406

Smallwood v. Ncsoft Corp. 63

Smith v. Anheuser-Busch, Inc. 32

Smith v. Brown & Williamson Tobacco Corp. . .122; 200

Smith v. Bryco Arms. 152

Smith v. Eli Lilly & Co. 245

Smith v. F.T.C. 344; 440; 543; 553

Smith v. GMC 244

Smith v. Home Light & Power Co. 115, 116

Smith v. Ingersoll-Rand Co. 268

Smith v. Louisville Ladder Co. 197

Smith v. Mitlof 46

Smith v. Peerless Glass Co. 11

Smith v. Pfizer, Inc. 42; 44; 48; 64; 207; 253

Smith v. Robertshaw Controls Co. 50

Smith v. Smith, 18 Mass. 259

Smith v. Stewart. 35; 42

Smith v. Wade 322

Smoot v. Mazda Motors of America, Inc. 223

Smothers v. Gresham Transfer, Inc. 274

Snell v. G.D. Searle & Co. 49

Sobolik v. Briggs & Stratton Power Products Group. Inc. 263

Sohngen v. Home Depot USA, Inc. 267

Sollami v. Eaton 88; 183; 187, 188

Solo v. Trus Joist MacMillan 125

Sorrells v. M.Y.B. Hospitality Ventures 260

Soto v. Nabisco, Inc. 274

Soufflas v. Zimmer, Inc. 70

Soule v. General Motors Corp. 135; 137–139

Southern Bakeries, Inc. v. Knipp 310

Southwest Bell Telephone Co. v. FDP Corp. 27

Spaulding v. Lesco International Corp. 187
Speakers of Sport, Inc. v. ProServ, Inc.. 64
Speller v. Sears, Roebuck & Co. 224
Sperry-New Holland v. Prestage. 140; 152
Spitzer, People ex rel. v. Sturm, Ruger & Co., Inc.. .2
Spring Motors Distributors, Inc. v. Ford Motor
  Co.. 47
Spruill v. Boyle-Midway, Inc.. 197
Sprung v. MTR Ravensburg, Inc.. 91
St. Joseph Hospital v. Corbetta Constr. Co.. . . . 65
St. Jude Med., Inc. Silzone Heart Valves Products
  Liability Litigation, In re. 247
St. Louis v. Rockwell Graphic Systems. 120
St. Mary's Hospital, Inc. v. Brinson. 228
Stackhouse v. Logangate Property Mgt., ... 317
Stadtherr v. Elite Logistics, Inc. 24
Stahl v. Novartis Pharmaceuticals Corp. 210
Stahlecker v. Ford Motor Co.. 86
Stang v. Hertz Corp.. 32
Stanley Works v. Haeger Potteries, Inc.. 554
Stanton v. Astra Pharmaceutical Products, Inc.. . .211
Stanton v. Carlson Sales, Inc.. 104
StarFlite Management Group, Inc., In re 520
State ex rel. (see name of relator). . . . .
State Farm Fire & Casualty Co. v. Chrysler
  Corp.. 164
State Farm Mutual Automobile Ins. Co. v.
  Campbell. 323; 327, 328
State of (see name of state). . . . .
Statler v. George A. Ray Manufacturing Co.. . . . 7
Staymates v. ITT Holub Industries 264
Stayton v. Clariant Corp.. 274
Stazenski v. Tennant Co.. 253
Stegall v. Catawba Oil Co.. 211
Stegemoller v. ACandS, Inc.. 96
Stephens v. G.D. Searle & Co.. 213–215
Stephenson v. Greenberg 41
Sterling Casino Lines, L.P. v. Plowman-Render . 522
Sterling Drug, Inc. v. Cornish. 208
Stevens v. Cessna Aircraft Co.. 190
Stevens v. Parke, Davis & Co. 210
Stevenson v. Keene Corp.. 333
Stewart v. Colonial Western Agency, Inc.. 520
Stoebner Holdings, Inc. v. Automobili Lamborghini
  S.P.A.. 59
Stonehocker v. General Motors Corp.. 130
Stones v. Sears, Roebuck & Co.. . . . . . 26; 40; 42
Stoney v. Franklin. 47
Stonybrook Tenants Association, Inc. v. Alpert. .551
Stout v. Borg-Warner Corp.. 278

Strasser v. Transtech Mobile Fleet Service, Inc. . 183
Straub v. Fisher and Paykel Health Care 314
Stringer v. NFL. 182, 183
Stringer v. Packaging Corporation of America . . 229
Stringham v. United Parcel Service, Inc.. 305
Stupak v. Hoffman-La Roche, Inc.. . . . . .178; 183
Sturm, Ruger & Co. v. Bloyd 181
Sugawara v. Pepsico, Inc.. 78
Sullivan v. Combustion Engineering 310
Sullivan v. Young Brothers & Co., Inc. 49
Sumnicht v. Toyota Motor Sales, U.S.A., Inc. . . 123
Suter v. San Angelo Foundry & Machine Co. . . 137
Sutowski v. Eli Lilly & Co.. 245
Sutton v. St. Jude Medical S.C., Inc.. 247–249
Suvada v. White Motor Co.. 11
Swain v. General Motors Corp.. 555
Swayze v. McNeil Laboratories, Inc.. 211
SWEPI L.P., In re 459
Swift v. State Farm Mut. Auto. Ins. Co. 309
Swix v. Daisy Manufacturing Co.. . . . . . .152; 189
Sylgab Steel & Wire Corp. v. Imoco-Gateway
  Corp.. . . . . .343; 552
Syrie v. Knoll International 125
Szajna v. General Motors Corp.. 47

T

Tabieros v. Clark Equip. Co.. . . . . .131; 203
Tabor v. Metal Ware Corp.. . . . . . .105, 106; 177
Tacke v. Vermeer Manufacturing Co.. 186
Tague v. Autobarn Motors, Ltd.. 59
Tamraz v. Lincoln Electric Co.. 233
Tanksley v. ProSoft Automation, Inc.. 266
Tate v. Boeing Helicopters. 278
Tatum v. Schering Corp.. 211
Taylor v. American Chemical Council, ...64
Taylor v. Elliott Turbomachinery Co., Inc. . 101; 177
Taylor v. Monsanto Co. 179; 190
Taylor v. Smithkline Beecham Corp.. 287
Taylor AG Industries v. Pure-Gro 292
Tellez-Cordova v. Campbell Hausfeld/Scott Fetzger
  Co.. .178; 267
Tenaglia v. Procter & Gamble, Inc.. 163
Tennessee Carolina Transportation, Inc. v. Strick
  Corp.. 52
Terhune v. A.H. Robins Co.. 214
Tetuan v. A.H. Robins Co.. . . . . . .214; 324; 326
Tex Enterprises, Inc. v. Brockway Standard, Inc., .45;
                                                  47
Texsun Feed Yards, Inc. v. Ralston Purina Co.. . .177

Thibault v. Sears, Roebuck & Co.. 124

Thom v. Bristol-Myers Squibb Co.. . . . . 210; 212

Thomas v. Bombardier-Rotax Motorenfabrik. . . .46

Thomas v. Kaiser Agricultural Chemicals. 264

Thomas v. Mallett 246

Thomas v. Winchester. 4; 7

Thompson v. Brown & Williamson Tobacco Corp.. . . . . .270; 307

Thompson v. Sunbeam Products, Inc. . 141; 158; 176

Thongchoom v. Graco Children's Products, Inc. . 182

Thorndike v. DaimlerChrysler Corp. 101

Threats v. General Motors Corp. 96; 269

Tidemann v. Nadler Golf Car Sales, Inc. 272

Tietsworth v. Harley-Davidson 67

TIG Ins. Co., In re 441

Timber Tech Engineered Building Products v. The Home Insurance Co. 229

Timmons v. Ford Motor Co.. 250

Timms v. Verson Allsteel Press Co.. 306

Timpte Industries, Inc. v. Gish. 141

Tiner v. General Motors Corp.. 241

Tober v. Graco Children's Products 265

Todd v. Societe BIC, S.A.. . . . . 133; 135

Tokio Marine & Fire Ins. Co., Ltd. v. Grove Manufacturing Co.. 140

Tomczak v. Ingalls Mem. Hosp.. . . . . . .520, 521

Tomczuk v. Cheshire 49

Tomer v. American Home Prods. Corp.. 210

Tompkins v. R. J. Reynolds Tobacco Co. 67

Torkie-Tork v. Wyeth 63

Torres v. Goodyear Tire & Rubber Co.. 99

Torres-Rios v. LPS Laboratories, Inc., ... 198

Torrington Co. v. Stutzman 278

Torsiello v. Whitehall Laboratories, Division of Home Products Corp. 198

Toshiba America Electronic Components v. The Superior Court of Santa Clara County. 451

Touchet Valley Grain Growers, Inc. v. Opp & Seibold General Construction, Inc.. 29

Town of (see name of town). . . . .

Township of (see name of township) . . . .

Toyota Motor Corp., Burton v. Danel Medical, Inc.,. 75

Toyota Motor Corp., In re 62; 64

Trabon Engineering Corp. v. Easton Manufacturing Co.. 554

Tracy v. General Motors Corp.,. 229

Transue v. Aesthetech Corp.. 160

Travelers Indem. Co. v. Dammann & Co., Inc.. . .321

Trenholm v. Ratcliff. 64

Trevino v. General Dynamics Corp.. 276

Trevino v. Ortega. 229

Truck Insurance Exchange v. MagneTek, Inc. . . 235

Trull v. Volkswagen of America, Inc.. . .86; 126; 130

TRW Vehicle Safety Sys., Inc. v. Moore 125

Tucker v. Paxson Mach. Co.. 105

Tufano Motorcar, Inc. v. Equipment and Resources International, Ltd. 50

Tuosto v. Philip Morris USA, Inc.. 63

Tweedy v. Wright Ford Sales, Inc.. . . . . .218; 220

Two Old Hippies, LLC v. Catch the Bus, LLC . . 77

TXO Production Corp. v. Alliance Resources Corp.. 327

Ty, Inc. v. Publ'ns Int'l, Ltd. 397

Tyler v. Natchitoches Coca-Cola Bottling Co. . . 168

U

U.S. v. (see name of defendant). . . . .

U.S. Automatic Sprinkler Co. v. Reliable Automatic Sprinkler Co.. 106

U-Haul Int'l., Inc. v. Waldrip 304; 307

Union Carbide Corp. v. Kavanaugh. 194

Union Pump Co. v. Allbritton 241; 255

The Union Supply Co. v. Pust. 88; 127

United States v. (see name of defendant). . . . . .

Unrein v. Timesavers, Inc.. 180

Usery v. Tamiami Trail Tours, Inc. 357

USX Corp. v. Salinas 161

V

Valente v. Sofamor 63

Van Bracklin v. Fonda 3; 34

Van Doren v. Coe Press Equip. Corp. . 141; 144; 274

Van Duzer v. Shoshone Coca Cola Bottling Co. . 163

Van Wyk v. Norden Laboratories 161

Vandermark v. Ford Motor Co.. . . . . .19; 99

Vanlandingham v. Gartman 308

Varano v. Jabar. 183

Veil v. Vitek, Inc.. 177

Vela v. Yamaha Motor Corp.. 188

Veloso v. Western Bedding Supply Co.. 229

Venturelli v. Cincinnati, Inc. 39

Vermett v. Fred Christen & Sons Co.. 107

Vickery v. Waste Management of Georgia, Inc. . 282

Vietnam Association for Victims of Agent Orange/Dioxin v. Dow Chemical Co. (In re "Agent Orange" Products Litigation). 309

Village Builders 96, L.P. v. U.S.Laboratories, Inc.. 106

Village of (see name of village). . . . .

[References are to pages]

Vince v. Broome. 36

Vincer v. Esther Williams All-Aluminum Swimming Pool Co.. . . . . .132; 134

Vintage Homes, Inc. v. Coldiron 50

Vitanza v. Upjohn Co.. . . . . 208; 212

Vitek Supply Corp.; United States v. 396

Vitiello v. Captain Bill's Restaurant. 170

Vlases v. Montgomery Ward & Co, Inc.. 26

Vogler v. Blackmore. 316

Volunteers of Amer. Colorado Branch v. Gardenswartz. 306

Volvo Trucks North America, Inc. v. Crescent Ford Truck Sales. 344

Vondra v. Chevron, U.S.A.. . . . . . . .88; 179; 194

Voss v. Black & Decker Manufacturing Co.. . . .140; 145

W

Wade v. Terex-Telelect, Inc.. . . . . . 153; 286; 289

Waering v. BASF Corp.. 163

Wagatsuma v. Patch 127

Wagner v. Hesston Corp.. 145

Wagner v. Union Pacific R.R.. 305

Walker v. Clark Equipment 313

Walker v. Soo Line R.R. Co. 398

Wallace v. Owens-Illinois, Inc. 253

Wallis v. Townsend Vision, Inc.. . . . . . .267; 272

Wal-Mart Stores, Inc. v. Wheeler. 48

Walters v. Seventeen Magazine. 69

Walton v. Avco Corp.. . . . . .177; 200

Wankier v. Crown Equipment Corp.. 145

Ward v. Morehead City Sea Food Co.. . . . . .3; 15

Watts v. Lester E. Cox Med. Ctrs.. 314

Way v. Boy Scouts of America 117

Way v. Tampa Coca Cola Bottling Co.. 309

Weakley v. Burnham Corp.. 21

Web Press Services Corp. v. New London Motors, Inc.. 30

Webb v. Westinghouse Elec. Corp. 558

Webster v. Blue Ship Tea Room. 168, 169

Weisgram v. Marley Co.. 235

Weiss v. Chrysler Motors Corp.. 162

Welch Sand & Gravel, Inc. v. O & K Trojan, Inc.. 267

Welge v. Planters Lifesavers Co.. . . .163, 164; 224

Weng v. Allison 30

Wernimont v. International Harvester Corp..218; 222

Werremeyer v. K.C. Auto Salvage Co. 332

West v. Broderick & Bascom Rope Co.. 162

West v. Jayne 57

Westberry v. Gislaved Gummi AB 243

Westbrook v. General Tire & Rubber Co.. 308

Westinghouse Electric Corp. v. Nutt. 126

Westlye v. Look Sports, Inc.. 75

Weyerhaeuser Co. v. Thermogas Co.. 99

Whelchel v. Briggs & Stratton Corp.. . . . . 109; 186

White v. ABCO Engineering Corp.. 195

White v. Cooper Tools, Inc.. 227

White v. Ford Motor Co.. 250

White v. Jubitz Corp.. 306

White v. R. J. Reynolds Tobacco Co.. . . . . . 31; 66

White v. Smithkline Beecham Corp.. 288

Whitehead v. St. Joe Lead Co.. 250

Whitehead v. Toyota Motor Corp.. . . . . . .261; 270

Whiteley v. Philip Morris Inc.. 65–67

Whitley v. Cubberly 210

Whitmer v. Schneble. 113

Whitted v. General Motors Corp.. 128

Whittle v. Timesavers, Inc.. 35

Wiedeman v. Keller. 4

Wieland v. C. A. Swanson & Sons 173

Wilkinson v. Bayshore Lumber Co.. 118

Willett v. Baxter International, Inc.. 208

Williams v. American Medical Systems. 223

Williams v. Bd. of County Comm'rs of the Unified Gov't of Wyandotte County 460

Williams v. Bennett 22; 123; 141

Williams v. Brown Manufacturing Co.. 260

Williams v. Dist. Court 441

Williams v. Johnson & Johnson 535

Williams v. Philip Morris, Inc. 330

Williams v. Smart Chevrolet Co.. . . . . . . 221; 224

Williamson v. Mazda Motor of Am., Inc.. 297

Willis v. Floyd Brace Co.. . . . . 164; 219

Willis Mining, Inc. v. Noggle.. 36

Wilson v. Dryvit Systems, Inc.. 68

Wilson v. Midway Games, Inc.. 117

Wilson v. Piper Aircraft Corp.. 148

Wilson v. Stilwill. 239

Winnett v. Winnett. 97; 251

Winter v. G. P. Putnam's Sons. 73; 116

Winters v. Fru-Con Inc.. . . . . 107, 108

Wirth v. Mayrath Industries, Inc.. 116

Wirtz v. Capitol Air Service, Inc.. 555

Wise v. CNH America, LLC.. 107

Wolfe v. Ford Motor Co.. 182

Wolfe v. McNeil-PPC, Inc.. 75

Wood v. Advance Rumely Thresher Co.. 44

Wood v. Old Trapper Taxi. 158

[References are to pages]

Wood v. Phillips Petroleum, ...192

Wood v. Public Service Company of New Hampshire. 116

Woodell v. Proctor Gamble Manufacturing Co.. .285

Woodill v. Parke Davis & Co.. . . . . . . .183, 184

Woods v. Cole 333

Woods v. Maytag Co.. 63

Woods v. R. J. Reynolds Tobacco Co.. . .63, 64; 68

Workman v. AB Electrolux Corp.. 229

Worrell v. Elliott & Frantz. 23; 108

Worrell v. Sachs 113

Worsham v. A.H. Robins Co.. 219

Worsley v. Corcelli. 308

Wright v. Brooke Group, Ltd.. . . . . .22; 125; 159

Wright v. Carter Prods. 210

Wright v. St. Mary's Medical Center of Evansville, Inc.. 241

Wyeth v. Levine 297

Wyrulec Co. v. Schutt 115

X

Xavier v. Philip Morris USA Inc.. . . . . . .242; 249

Y

Yamaha Motor Co., Ltd. v. Thornton 161

Yarrow v. Sterling Drug 211

Yetter v. Rajeski 130

Yielding v. Chrysler Motor Co.. 222

Yong v. Marriott Corp.. 170

Young v. Key Pharmaceuticals, ...185

Yount v. Deibert 250

Yun Tung Chow v. Reckitt & Colman, Inc.. . . .187

Z

Zabner v. Howard Johnson's, Inc.. 170

Zamora v. Mobil Corp.. 100

Zavala v. Burlington Northern Santa Fe Corp.. .145; 158; 176

Zeigler v. Fisher-Price, Inc.. 309

Zenith Elecs. Corp. v. ExZEC, Inc.. 344

Zenith Radio Corp. v. Matsushita Elec. Co. . . . 539

Zerby v. Warren 260

Zubulake v. UBS Warburg 451, 452

INDEX

[References are to sections.]

A

ADMIT FACTS, REQUESTS TO
Generally . . . 16.11
Discovery 15.06

ADVERTISEMENTS
Deceptive trade practices statutes . . . 3.06[C]
Direct-to-consumer advertising . . . 7.06[E][4]
Innocent misrepresentation . . . 3.04[D]

ALLERGIC REACTIONS
Warnings to persons with . . . 7.03[B]

**AMERICAN TRIAL LAWYERS ASSOCIATION
(ATLA) EXCHANGE**
Expert witnesses . . . 13.01[B][3]

ANIMALS
Product, as . . . 4.05[B]

ASSUMPTION OF RISK
Defenses . . . 9.02[C]

ATLA EXCHANGE (See AMERICAN TRIAL
LAWYERS ASSOCIATION (ATLA) EX-
CHANGE)

B

BLOOD
Product, as . . . 4.05[C]

BOOKS AND PERIODICALS
Research tasks . . . 12.18

BREACH OF WARRANTY
Generally . . . 2.08

BURDEN OF PROOF
Design defects . . . 5.03[C][4]

BYSTANDERS
Generally . . . 4.03[C]; 7.03[A]; 10.02[C][3]

C

CAUSE-IN-FACT (See PROBLEMS OF PROOF,
subhead: Cause-in-fact)

CAVEAT EMPTOR
Generally . . . 1.02[A]

**CHOICE OF THEORY, RESEARCH AND
PRACTICE IMPLICATIONS OF**
Generally . . . 11.01
Major research tasks . . . 11.03
Pre-filing questions . . . 11.02
Time frames
    Criteria for selection of . . . 11.05
    Research . . . 11.04

COMPARATIVE FAULT
Generally . . . 9.02[F]

COMPENSATORY DAMAGES (See DAMAGES,
subhead: Compensatory damages)

COMPLAINT AND DISCOVERY FOCUS
Generally . . . 14.01
Alteration or modification, absence of . . . 14.05
Breach of duty or obligation . . . 14.09
Defendant's duty or obligation . . . 14.06
Distributive chain . . . 14.04
Injury-producing event . . . 14.08
Intended use . . . 14.07
Products case, standard allegations in . . . 14.02
Proximate cause . . . 14.10
Punitive damages . . . 14.11
Sample complaint . . . 14.03; 14.12

COMPONENT PART MANUFACTURERS
Special category of seller . . . 4.04[B][1]

CONDUCT-BASED DEFENSES
Generally . . . 9.02[A]
Assumption of risk . . . 9.02[C]
Comparative fault . . . 9.02[F]
Contributory negligence . . . 9.02[B]
Product
    Alteration of . . . 9.02[D]
    Misuse of . . . 9.02[E]

CONSORTIUM, LOSS OF
Damages for . . . 10.02[A][4]

CONSUMER EXPECTATION TEST
Design defects (See DESIGN DEFECTS)
Manufacturing defects (See MANUFACTURING
    DEFECTS)

CONTRACEPTIVES
Learned intermediary doctrine . . . 7.06[E][2]

CONTRIBUTORY NEGLIGENCE
Defense . . . 9.02[B]

CORPORATIONS
Directory of corporate affiliations . . . 12.32
Foreign corporations . . . 12.34
Generation of corporate documents . . . 17.04
Reaction of corporate defendant to alleged scientific
    defect, development of . . . 12.13
Successor corporations as special category of seller
    . . . 4.04[B][3]

CRASHWORTHINESS DOCTRINE
Generally . . . 5.02[C]

D

DAMAGES
Generally . . . 10.01
Breach of warranty 2.08

[References are to sections.]

DAMAGES—Cont.
Compensatory damages
  Generally . . . 10.02
  Emotional distress, damages for (See subhead: Emotional distress, damages for)
  Noneconomic damages, limitations on . . . 10.02[D]
  Pain and suffering, damages for . . . 10.02[B]
  Personal injury, damages for (See subhead: Personal injury, damages for)
  Property, damage to . . . 10.02[F]
  Survival actions . . . 10.02[E]
  Wrongful death actions . . . 10.02[E]
Economic loss doctrine . . . 10.03
Emotional distress, damages for
  Bystanders . . . 10.02[C][3]
  Impact rule . . . 10.02[C][1]
  Medical monitoring . . . 10.02[C][2]
Fraudulent misrepresentation . . . 3.02[F]
Innocent misrepresentation . . . 3.04[F]
Joint liability . . . 10.06
Negligent misrepresentation . . . 3.03[B]
Personal injury, damages for
  Collateral source rule . . . 10.02[A][3]
  Consortium, loss of . . . 10.02[A][4]
  General damages . . . 10.02[A][1]
  Present cash value . . . 10.02[A][2]
  Special damages . . . 10.02[A][1]
Post-judgment interest . . . 10.05
Pre-judgment interest . . . 10.05
Punitive damages (See PUNITIVE DAMAGES)
Several liability . . . 10.06

DANGERS
Open and obvious dangers . . . 5.04

DAUBERT TEST (See EXPERT WITNESSES, subhead: *Daubert* test)

DECEPTIVE TRADE PRACTICES STATUTES (See MISREPRESENTATION, subhead: Deceptive trade practices statutes)

DEFECTS
Design defects (See DESIGN DEFECTS)
Manufacturing defects (See MANUFACTURING DEFECTS)
Warning defects (See WARNING DEFECTS)

DEFENDANTS
Complaint and discovery focus . . . 14.06
Government regulation of defendant's industry . . . 12.10
Organization and manufacturing processes of defendant corporation, study of . . . 12.12
Plaintiff's first set of interrogatories to defendant . . . 16.08
Potential defendants (See NEGLIGENCE, subhead: Potential defendants)
Reaction of corporate defendant to alleged scientific defect, development of . . . 12.13

DEFENSES
Generally . . . 9.01

DEFENSES—Cont.
Conduct-based defenses (See CONDUCT-BASED DEFENSES)
Government standards
  Generally . . . 9.05; 9.05[A]
  Pharmaceutical industry and . . . 9.05[B]
Industry standards . . . 9.05; 9.05[C]
Preemption
  Generally . . . 9.06[A]
  Conflict preemption . . . 9.06[D]
  Express preemption . . . 9.06[B]
  Field preemption . . . 9.06[C]
Status-based defenses (See STATUS-BASED DEFENSES)
Times-based defenses (See TIMES-BASED DEFENSES)

DEPOSITIONS
Generally . . . 18.01
Defense experts . . . 18.07
Discovery . . . 15.07
Document organization . . . 18.05
Objections in . . . 18.03
Planning . . . 18.04
Preparation . . . 18.06
Relevancy . . . 18.02
Rules . . . 18.01

DESIGN DEFECTS
Characteristics of . . . 5.02[A]
Consumer expectations test
  Food and drink cases . . . 6.05[B]
  Manufacturing defects . . . 6.04[A]
Crashworthiness doctrine . . . 5.02[C]
Determining design defect, tests for
  Generally . . . 5.03[A]
  Alternative tests . . . 5.03[D]
  Consumer expectation test
    Generally . . . 5.03[B][1]
    Ordinary consumer (See subhead: Ordinary consumer)
  Risk-utility analysis (See subhead: Risk-utility analysis)
Manufacturing defects . . . 6.01[B]
Negligent design . . . 5.02[B][1], [B][2]
Open and obvious dangers . . . 5.04
Ordinary consumer
  Generally . . . 5.03[B][2]
  Application of test . . . 5.03[B][4]
  Product, expectation of . . . 5.03[B][3]
Product defects . . . 5.01; 5.02[B]
Risk-utility analysis
  Generally . . . 5.03[C][1]
  Burden of proof . . . 5.03[C][4]
  Manufacturing defect cases . . . 6.04[B]
  Reasonable alternative design . . . 5.03[C][3]
State-of-the-art . . . 5.05
Strict liability . . . 5.02[B][1], [B][3]
Warn, failure to . . . 7.01[D]

DIALOG INFORMATION SERVICES
Generally . . . 12.19

[References are to sections.]

DISCOVERY
Generally . . . 15.01; 15.18
Admit facts, requests to . . . 15.06; 16.11
Defect category . . . 15.10
Depositions (See DEPOSITIONS)
Electronic discovery . . . 15.17
Enforcement
    Generally . . . 19.11; 19.14
    Denton versus Fremantle support memoran-
      dum . . . 19.13
    Sample memorandum . . . 19.12
Genuineness of documents . . . 15.06; 16.11
Inadvertent disclosure . . . 15.16
Interrogatories . . . 15.04
Organization and drafting of requests . . . 15.15
Produce documents, requests to . . . 15.05
Purposes and reach of
    Generally . . . 15.02
    Duty of disclosure . . . 15.02[B]
    General discovery provisions . . . 15.02[A]
    General provisions governing discovery
      . . . 15.02[B]
Relevancy . . . 15.08
Time frame
    Generally . . . 15.10
    Design defect cases . . . 15.12
    Failure to instruct or warn cases . . . 15.13
    Misrepresentation cases . . . 15.14
    Setting of . . . 15.09
    Unit defect cases . . . 15.11
Tools . . . 15.03

DISTRIBUTOR STATUTES
Generally . . . 4.04[D]

DOCUMENTS, REQUESTS TO PRODUCE (See
PRODUCE DOCUMENTS, REQUESTS TO)

E

ECONOMIC LOSS DOCTRINE
Generally . . . 10.03

ELECTRICITY
Product, as . . . 4.05[D]

ELECTRONIC DISCOVERY
Generally . . . 15.17

EMOTIONAL DISTRESS, DAMAGES FOR (See
DAMAGES, subhead: Emotional distress, damages for)

EVIDENCE DEPOSITIONS (See DEPOSITIONS)

EXPERT WITNESSES
Generally . . . 8.03[A]
American Trial Lawyers Association exchange
    . . . 13.01[B][3]
Daubert test
    Generally . . . 8.03[B][2]
    Opinion testimony and . . . 8.03[B][3]
    Scope of . . . 8.03[B][4]
Defense research institute (DIR) . . . 13.01[B][3]

EXPERT WITNESSES—Cont.
Expert testimony
    Legal requirements of . . . 13.03
    Plaintiff required to present . . . 13.02
    Reliable science, not supported by . . . 13.04
Gatekeeper, district court judge as
    Generally . . . 8.03[B][5]
    Relevance . . . 8.03[B][5][b]
    Reliability . . . 8.03[B][5][a]
Lexis and Westlaw listings . . . 13.01[B][4]
Permissible scope of . . . 8.03[D]
Pre-trial considerations
    Generally . . . 13.01
    Analyzing expert witness needs
      Categorizing . . . 13.01[A][2]
      Determining . . . 13.01[A][1]
    Categories of . . . 13.01[D]
    Choice of
      American Trial Lawyers Association ex-
        change . . . 13.01[B][3]
      Clearing houses . . . 13.01[B][2]
      Defense research institute (DIR)
        . . . 13.01[B][3]
      Lexis and Westlaw listings
        . . . 13.01[B][4]
      Research sites . . . 13.01[B][1]
    Organizational factors . . . 13.01[C]
Qualifications
    Generally . . . 8.03[C]
    Testify, to . . . 13.07
Research sites . . . 13.01[B][1]
Sources reasonably relied upon by . . . 13.08
Testimony, standards for admissibility of
    Daubert test (See subhead: *Daubert* test)
    District court decision, review of
      . . . 8.03[B][6]
    Frye Test . . . 8.03[B][1]
    Gatekeeper, district court judge as (See sub-
      head: Gatekeeper, district court judge as)
Testing alternatives
    Design defect cases . . . 13.06
    Unit defect cases . . . 13.05

EXPRESS WARRANTIES (See WARRANTIES,
subhead: Express warranties)

F

FOOD AND DRINK CASES (See MANUFAC-
TURING DEFECTS, subhead: Food and drink
cases)

FOOD INDUSTRY
Deceptive trade practices statutes . . . 3.06[B]

FOREIGN CORPORATIONS
Research tasks . . . 12.34

FOREIGN-NATURAL TEST
Food and drink cases . . . 6.05[A]

FORESEEABILITY
Proximate cause . . . 8.05[B]

[References are to sections.]

FRAUDULENT MISREPRESENTATION
Generally . . . 3.02[A]
Damages . . . 3.02[F]
False statement of material fact . . . 3.02[B]
Intent to induce reliance on misrepresentation
. . . 3.02[D]
Justifiable reliance . . . 3.02[E]
Scienter . . . 3.02[C]

FRYE TEST
Generally . . . 8.03[B][1]

G

GENUINENESS OF DOCUMENTS
Generally . . . 15.06; 16.11

GOVERNMENT CONTRACTOR DEFENSE
(See STATUS-BASED DEFENSES, subhead:
Government contractor defense)

GOVERNMENT DATABASES
Research tasks . . . 12.17

H

HISTORY OF PRODUCTS LIABILITY LAW
Generally . . . 1.01
Choice of theories . . . 1.06
Influence of contract law
Generally . . . 1.02
Caveat Emptor . . . 1.02[A]
Privity rule (See subhead: Privity rule)
Negligence
Rise of
Generally . . . 1.03
Adoption of . . . 1.03[B]
Fall of privity . . . 1.03[A]
Res Ipsa Loquitur . . . 1.03[C]
Strict liability, to (See STRICT LIABILITY)
Privity rule
Generally . . . 1.02[B]
Exceptions to . . . 1.02[C]
Fall of privity . . . 1.03[A]; 1.04[B]
Restatements . . . 1.05

HUMAN TISSUE
Product, as . . . 4.05[C]

HYBRID TEST
Food and drink cases . . . 6.05[C]

I

IMMUNIZATIONS
Mass immunizations, duty to warn of risks with
. . . 7.06[E][1]

INADVERTENT DISCLOSURE
Discovery . . . 15.16

INFORMATION
Product, as . . . 4.05[E]

INJURY-PRODUCING EVENT
Complaint . . . 14.08
Identification of . . . 12.06

INNOCENT MISREPRESENTATION
Advertising . . . 3.04[D]
Damages . . . 3.04[F]
Engaged in business of selling chattels . . . 3.04[B]
Justifiable reliance . . . 3.04[E]
Material fact concerning character or quality of
chattel . . . 3.04[C]
Restatement (second) of torts, Section 402b
. . . 3.04[A]

INTERROGATORIES
Generally . . . 16.01
Drafting of . . . 16.05
Fourwheel corporation . . . 16.07
Limitations on number . . . 16.04
Observations on . . . 16.11
Organization of . . . 16.05
Plaintiff's first set of interrogatories to defendant
. . . 16.08
Pressurized stainless steel beverage canister
. . . 16.09
Sample
Generally . . . 16.06
Fourwheel corporation . . . 16.07
Observations on . . . 16.11
Pressurized stainless steel beverage canister
. . . 16.09
Standup forklift truck . . . 16.10
Statutory definition
Federal . . . 16.02
State . . . 16.03

J

JOINT LIABILITY
Damages . . . 10.06

L

LEARNED INTERMEDIARY DOCTRINE (See
WARNING DEFECTS, subhead: Learned intermediary doctrine)

LEXISNEXIS LEGAL LISTINGS
Generally . . . 13.01[B][4]

LIBRARY COLLECTIONS
Research tasks . . . 12.16

M

MAGNUSON-MOSS ACT
Generally . . . 2.09

MANUFACTURING DEFECTS
Consumer expectation test . . . 6.04[A]; 6.05[B]
Design defects . . . 6.01[B]
Deviation from design . . . 6.01[A]
Diversity of
Inspection, testing and . . . 6.02[B]

[References are to sections.]

MANUFACTURING DEFECTS—Cont.
Diversity of—Cont.
    Labeling and packaging . . . 6.02[C]
    Packaging, labeling and . . . 6.02[C]
    Testing and inspection . . . 6.02[B]
    Types of . . . 6.02[A]
Food and drink cases
    Generally . . . 6.05
    Consumer expectation test . . . 6.05[B]
    Defect, proof of . . . 6.05[D]
    Foreign-natural test . . . 6.05[A]
    Hybrid test . . . 6.05[C]
Foreign-natural test . . . 6.05[A]
Hybrid test . . . 6.05[C]
Inspection, testing and . . . 6.02[B]
Labeling and packaging . . . 6.02[C]
Negligent manufacture . . . 6.03; 6.03[A]
Packaging, labeling and . . . 6.02[C]
Risk-utility analysis, rejection of . . . 6.04[B]
Strict liability manufacture . . . 6.03; 6.03[B]
Testing and inspection . . . 6.02[B]

MISREPRESENTATION
Generally . . . 3.01
Damages
    Fraudulent misrepresentation . . . 3.02[F]
    Innocent misrepresentation . . . 3.04[F]
    Negligent misrepresentation . . . 3.03[B]
Deceptive trade practices statutes
    Generally . . . 3.06[A]
    Food industry . . . 3.06[B]
    Helmets and deceptive advertising
        . . . 3.06[C]
Discovery time frame . . . 15.14
Fraudulent misrepresentation (See FRAUDULENT
    MISREPRESENTATION)
Innocent misrepresentation (See INNOCENT MIS-
    REPRESENTATION)
Negligent misrepresentation
    Damages . . . 3.03[B]
    Elements of action . . . 3.03[A]
Restatement (third) of torts, products liability
    . . . 3.05
Strict liability misrepresentation (See INNOCENT
    MISREPRESENTATION)

N

NEGLIGENCE
Generally . . . 4.01; 4.02[A]
Contributory negligence . . . 9.02[B]
Manufacturing defects . . . 6.03; 6.03[A]
Misrepresentation
    Damages . . . 3.03[B]
    Elements of action . . . 3.03[A]
Potential defendants
    Distributor statutes . . . 4.04[D]
    Persons engaged in business of selling
        . . . 4.04[A]
    Persons not covered by . . . 4.04[C]
    Special categories of sellers (See subhead:
        Sellers, special categories of)

NEGLIGENCE—Cont.
Potential plaintiffs
    Generally . . . 4.03
    Bystanders . . . 4.03[C]
    Duty issue in . . . 4.03[A]
    Unintended users and uses of products
        . . . 4.03[D]
Product
    Generally . . . 4.05[A]
    Animals . . . 4.05[B]
    Blood . . . 4.05[C]
    Electricity . . . 4.05[D]
    Human tissue . . . 4.05[C]
    Information . . . 4.05[E]
    Raw materials . . . 4.05[F]
    Real estate . . . 4.05[G]
Sellers, special categories of
    Generally . . . 4.04[B]
    Component part manufacturers . . . 4.04[B][1]
    Successor corporations . . . 4.04[B][3]
    Used products, sellers of . . . 4.04[B][2]
Warning defects . . . 7.01[C]

O

OBJECTIONS
Depositions . . . 18.03

ORDERS, PROTECTIVE (See PROTECTIVE
    ORDERS)

ORDINARY CONSUMER (See DESIGN DE-
    FECTS, subhead: Ordinary consumer)

P

PAIN AND SUFFERING
Damages for . . . 10.02[B]

**PARTICULAR PURPOSE, FITNESS FOR IM-
    PLIED WARRANTY OF**
Generally . . . 2.04[A], [B]
Reliance . . . 2.04[C]

PATENTS
Research tasks . . . 12.29

PERIODICALS, BOOKS AND
Research tasks . . . 12.18

PLAINTIFFS
Interrogatories to defendant, plaintiff's first set of
    . . . 16.08

PREEMPTION (See DEFENSES, subhead: Pre-
    emption)

PRIVITY RULE (See HISTORY OF PRODUCTS
    LIABILITY LAW, subhead: Privity rule)

PROBLEMS OF PROOF
Generally . . . 8.01
Cause-in-fact
    Generally . . . 8.04[A]
    But for test . . . 8.04[B]

PROBLEMS OF PROOF—Cont.

Cause-in-fact—Cont.

    Future injury, exposure to risk of . . . 8.04[D]

    Manufacturer, establishing the identity of
      . . . 8.04[C]

    Substantial factor test . . . 8.04[B]

Defect, proof of

    Circumstantial evidence . . . 8.02[A]

    Direct evidence . . . 8.02[A]

    Evidence, spoliation of . . . 8.02[C][2]

    Product defect, inference of . . . 8.02[B]

    Product testing . . . 8.02[C][1]

    Res Ipsa Loquitur . . . 8.02[B]

    Spoliation of evidence . . . 8.02[C][2]

Evidence, spoliation of . . . 8.02[C][2]

Expert witnesses (See EXPERT WITNESSES)

Proximate cause (See PROXIMATE CAUSE)

Spoliation of evidence . . . 8.02[C][2]

PRODUCE DOCUMENTS, REQUESTS TO

Generally . . . 15.05; 17.01; 17.13

Automobile manufacturing processes, sample

    Generally . . . 17.06

    Design testing, product . . . 17.06[B]

    Overall product planning . . . 17.06[A]

    Post-marketing, product . . . 17.06[E]

    Product marketing . . . 17.06[D]

    Product production runs . . . 17.06[C]

Corporate documents, generation of . . . 17.04

Discovery rules . . . 17.02

Document generation

    Overlap . . . 17.07

    Stages of . . . 17.05

Drafting requests for documents . . . 17.08

Planning document requests . . . 17.03

Sample request for documents

    Jeep-type vehicle rollover . . . 17.10

    Pressurized stainless steel beverage canisters
      . . . 17.09

    Stand-alone forklift truck . . . 17.11

Supplemental discovery . . . 17.12

PROTECTIVE ORDERS

Generally . . . 19.01; 19.14

Annoyance, embarrassment and oppression
    . . . 19.07

Confidential commercial information . . . 19.08

Each document, meeting arguments for . . . 19.10

Fraud, protection against . . . 19.06

Information sharing . . . 19.05

Opposition, factual components of argument in
    . . . 19.09

Products litigation . . . 19.03

Rules . . . 19.02

Specific supportive facts, requirement of . . . 19.04

Trade secrets . . . 19.08

PROXIMATE CAUSE

Generally . . . 8.05[A]

Complaint and discovery focus . . . 14.10

Condition versus cause . . . 8.05[D]

Foreseeability . . . 8.05[B]

Natural and probable consequences . . . 8.05[C]

PUNITIVE DAMAGES

Generally . . . 10.04[A]

Complaint and discovery focus . . . 14.11

Conduct required for . . . 10.04[B]

Constitutionality of . . . 10.04[D]

Standard of proof required for . . . 10.04[B]

Statutory controls on awards of . . . 10.04[C]

Q

QUALIFICATIONS

Expert witnesses . . . 8.03[C]; 13.07

R

RAW MATERIALS

Product, as . . . 4.05[F]

REAL ESTATE

Product, as . . . 4.05[G]

RECALLS

Judicially mandated product recalls . . . 7.05[B][1]

Legislative product recalls . . . 7.05[B][2]

RELEVANCY

Depositions . . . 18.02

Discovery process . . . 15.08

Expert witnesses . . . 8.03[B][5][b]

REQUESTS TO PRODUCE DOCUMENTS (See
    PRODUCE DOCUMENTS, REQUESTS TO)

RESEARCH TASKS

Generally . . . 12.01; 12.35

Academic and professional journals . . . 12.21

Alleged injuries to consumers

    Extent of . . . 12.07

    Seriousness of . . . 12.08

Annual meetings and special conferences, academic
    and professional . . . 12.22

Annual reports . . . 12.31

Books and periodicals . . . 12.18

Company research . . . 12.30

Consumer interest groups and associated publica-
    tions . . . 12.26

Data banks . . . 12.24

Defendant's industry, government regulation of
    . . . 12.10

Dialog information services . . . 12.19

Directory of corporate affiliations . . . 12.32

Dual aspects of research data . . . 12.03

Foreign corporations . . . 12.34

Government databases . . . 12.17

Grants . . . 12.23

Industry reaction to scientific problem, history of
    . . . 12.11

Injury-producing aspect of product, identification of
    . . . 12.06

Internet research sites . . . 12.36

Library collections . . . 12.16

Manufacturers of component parts, information of
    . . . 12.15

[References are to sections.]

RESEARCH TASKS—Cont.

Organization and manufacturing processes of defendant corporation, study of . . . 12.12

Patents . . . 12.29

Points of reference . . . 12.04

Popular publications . . . 12.20

Prior litigation, settlements, or case filings . . . 12.14

Professional and trade associations and organizations . . . 12.27

Reaction of corporate defendant to alleged scientific defect, development of . . . 12.13

Research in progress . . . 12.23

Standards . . . 12.25

State-of-the-art commentary on alleged defects and injuries . . . 12.09

Statistical publications . . . 12.24

Suppliers of materials . . . 12.15

Theoretical defect type, identification of . . . 12.05

Thomas register of American manufacturers . . . 12.33

Trade associations . . . 12.28

Work areas, range of . . . 12.02

RES IPSA LOQUITUR

Generally . . . 1.03[C]

Defect, proof of . . . 8.02[B]

RISK-UTILITY ANALYSIS (See DESIGN DEFECTS, subhead: Risk-utility analysis)

S

SEVERAL LIABILITY

Damages . . . 10.06

STATUS-BASED DEFENSES

Employees, employer liability to . . . 9.03[A][1]

Employer immunity, liability to
    Employees . . . 9.03[A][1]
    Third parties . . . 9.03[A][2]

Government contractor defense
    Expansion of defense . . . 9.03[B][3]
    Framework for defense . . . 9.03[B][1]
    Three prongs of defense . . . 9.03[B][2]

Third parties, employer liability to . . . 9.03[A][2]

STATUTE OF LIMITATIONS

Defenses . . . 9.04[A]

STATUTE OF REPOSE

Defenses . . . 9.04[B]

STRICT LIABILITY (See also NEGLIGENCE)

Generally . . . 1.04; 4.01; 4.02[B]

Citadel of privity, fall of . . . 1.04[B]

Design defects . . . 5.02[B][1], [B][3]

Manufacturing defects . . . 6.03; 6.03[B]

Misrepresentation (See INNOCENT MISREPRESENTATION)

Policy justifications . . . 4.02[C]

Potential defendants
    Distributor statutes . . . 4.04[D]
    Persons engaged in business of selling . . . 4.04[A]

STRICT LIABILITY (See also NEGLIGENCE)—Cont.

Potential defendants—Cont.
    Persons not covered by . . . 4.04[C]

Potential plaintiffs
    Generally . . . 4.03
    Bystanders . . . 4.03[C]
    Unintended users and uses of products . . . 4.03[D]

Product
    Generally . . . 4.05[A]
    Animals . . . 4.05[B]
    Blood . . . 4.05[C]
    Electricity . . . 4.05[D]
    Human tissue . . . 4.05[C]
    Information . . . 4.05[E]
    Raw materials . . . 4.05[F]
    Real estate . . . 4.05[G]

Sellers, special categories of
    Generally . . . 4.04[B]
    Component part manufacturers . . . 4.04[B][1]
    Successor corporations . . . 4.04[B][3]
    Used products, sellers of . . . 4.04[B][2]

Theory behind . . . 1.04[A]

Triumph of strict liability in tort . . . 1.04[C]

User or consumer requirement . . . 4.03[B]

Warning defects . . . 7.01[C]

SUBSTANTIAL FACTOR TEST

Generally . . . 8.04[B]

SUCCESSOR CORPORATIONS

Special category of seller . . . 4.04[B][3]

SURVIVAL ACTIONS

Damages . . . 10.02[E]

T

THEORIES IN PRODUCTS LIABILITY CASES

Choice of . . . 1.06

THIRD PARTIES

Employer liability to . . . 9.03[A][2]

THOMAS REGISTER OF AMERICAN MANUFACTURERS

Research tasks . . . 12.33

TIMES-BASED DEFENSES

Statute
    Limitations, of . . . 9.04[A]
    Repose, of . . . 9.04[B]

Useful shelf-life . . . 9.04[C]

TRADE SECRETS

Protective orders . . . 19.08

U

UNINTENDED USERS AND USES OF PRODUCTS

Generally . . . 4.03[D]

[References are to sections.]

USED PRODUCTS, SELLERS OF
Special category of seller . . . 4.04[B][2]

USEFUL SHELF-LIFE
Generally . . . 9.04[C]

W

WARNING DEFECTS
Adequacy of warning
    Content of warning . . . 7.04[C]
    Criteria for determining scope and
       . . . 7.04[A]
    Form of warning . . . 7.04[B]
    Learned intermediary doctrine . . . 7.06[C]
Characteristics of
    Negligence . . . 7.01[C]
    Persons having duty to warn . . . 7.01[B]
    Strict liability . . . 7.01[C]
    Warnings and instructions . . . 7.01[A]
Contraceptive devices . . . 7.06[E][2]
Design defects and failure to warn . . . 7.01[D]
Direct-to-consumer advertising . . . 7.06[E][4]
Food and Drug Administration mandate
    . . . 7.06[E][3]
Judicially mandated product recalls . . . 7.05[B][1]
Learned intermediary doctrine
    Adequacy of warning . . . 7.06[C]
    Causation . . . 7.06[D]
    Exceptions to
        Generally . . . 7.06[E]
        Contraceptive devices . . . 7.06[E][2]
        Direct-to-consumer advertising
           . . . 7.06[E][4]
        FDA mandate . . . 7.06[E][3]
        Mass immunization . . . 7.06[E][1]
        Oral contraceptives . . . 7.06[E][2]
    Origin and scope of . . . 7.06[A]
    Physicians, when warning must given to
        . . . 7.06[B]
Legislative product recalls . . . 7.05[B][2]
Mass immunization . . . 7.06[E][1]
Negligence . . . 7.01[C]
Open and obvious dangers . . . 7.02[C]
Oral contraceptives . . . 7.06[E][2]
Persons who must warned
    Allergic reactions, persons with . . . 7.03[B]
    Bulk supplier . . . 7.03[C]
    Bystanders . . . 7.03[A]
    Consumers . . . 7.03[A]
    Sophisticated supplier doctrine . . . 7.03[C]
    Users
        Generally . . . 7.03[A]
        Sophisticated user . . . 7.03[C]
Post-sale duty to warn . . . 7.05[A]
Recalls
    Judicially mandated product recalls
       . . . 7.05[B][1]
    Legislative product recalls . . . 7.05[B][2]
Strict liability . . . 7.01[C]
Unavoidably unsafe products . . . 7.02[B]

WARNING DEFECTS—Cont.
When warning must given
    Generally . . . 7.02[A]
    Open and obvious dangers . . . 7.02[C]
    Unavoidably unsafe products . . . 7.02[B]

WARRANTIES
Breach of warranty, damages for . . . 2.08
Disclaimers and limitations of
    Generally . . . 2.07[A], [A][4]
    Exclusion or modification of (See subhead:
       Exclusion or modification of)
Exclusion or modification of
    "As is" disclaimers . . . 2.07[A][4]
    Express warranties . . . 2.07[A][1]
    Fitness for particular purpose, implied warran-
       ties of . . . 2.07[A][3]
    Merchantability, implied warranties of
       . . . 2.07[A][2]
Express warranties
    Generally . . . 2.02[A]
    Basis of bargain . . . 2.02[C]
    Exclusion or modification of . . . 2.07[A][1]
    Statement of fact v. opinion . . . 2.02[B]
Horizontal privity . . . 2.05[B]
Implied warranty
    Merchantability, of (See subhead: Merchant-
       ability)
    Particular purpose, fitness for (See subhead:
       Particular purpose, fitness for)
Limitations of . . . 2.07[B]
Magnuson-Moss Act . . . 2.09
Merchantability
    Generally . . . 2.03[A], [C]
    Exclusion or modification of . . . 2.07[A][2]
    Seller as merchant of goods . . . 2.03[B]
    Unforeseeable use of goods . . . 2.03[D]
Notice
    Generally . . . 2.06[A]
    Adequate notice . . . 2.06[C]
    Buyer and seller . . . 2.06[B]
    Reasonable time . . . 2.06[D]
    Seller, buyer and . . . 2.06[B]
Particular purpose, fitness for
    Generally . . . 2.04[A], [B]
    Exclusion or modification of . . . 2.07[A][3]
    Reliance . . . 2.04[C]
Role of . . . 2.01
Scope of
    Generally . . . 2.05[A]
    Horizontal privity . . . 2.05[B]
    Vertical privity . . . 2.05[C]
Vertical privity . . . 2.05[C]

WESTLAW LISTINGS
Generally . . . 13.01[B][4]

WITNESSES, EXPERT (See EXPERT WIT-
NESSES)

WRONGFUL DEATH ACTIONS
Damages . . . 10.02[E]